Camping Caravanning
Britain 2006

Originally compiled by
Frederick Tingey

Published by
Butford Technical Publishing Ltd.
Hall Farm, Birlingham, Pershore, Worcs. WR10 3AB

Editor: Stephen Morris
Assistant Editor: Natalia Żak

First published 2006

Copyright © 2006 Butford Technical Publishing Ltd.

British Library Cataloguing in Publication Data
A catalogue record for this book is available from the British Library

ISBN 0-9552474-0-3

Printed in Great Britain

Contents

Introduction

This guide lists campsites in Britain open to all. It groups all campsites of an acceptable standard accommodating six or more tents or caravans into sixteen regions based on local authority boundaries. This division seems logical enough since most campers and caravanners first choose the region they want to visit and second the campsite at which they propose to stay. With the aim of making both choices easier, each region has an introduction indicating in broad terms the areas best for camping and caravanning within it.

The guide attempts to cater as much for the adventure camper as for the family caravanner. The regional introductions indicate scenic drives as well as long-distance footpaths and the information on each campsite includes its telephone number for those who need or prefer to book their pitch in advance, though not all sites accept bookings.

The symbols used to describe the facilities at campsites are those which, for most of us, are immediately recognisable, thereby avoiding the need for the reader to refer constantly to a key when comparing the amenities of one site with another.

Where the information has been supplied to us we give details of campsite charges. Charges marked with an asterisk are the prices for last year and may have been increased for the current season. Publication of campsite charges is in no way binding on the site operator concerned and there is nothing to prevent him increasing his prices halfway through the season.

The AA's pennant scheme makes a valuable contribution to the raising of site standards in Britain. We have played our part by eliminating from the guide any sites not equipped with flush lavatories and showers – although a few sites without showers are included because there is no alternative anywhere near.

The aim of this guide is to make camping and caravanning in Britain easier and so more enjoyable. We should therefore be grateful to any readers willing to help us make it so by sending us details of any corrections or additions to the information on campsites or of any not already listed that they would like to see included in the guide.

Tourist Information Centre

Place name in
alphabetical order
within the region

Sights of tourist interest in place
named or within a few miles

Grid reference on
map at start of
regional section

Early closing and
market days

Recommended restaurant or
pub serving food in or near
place named

BRIDGWATER, Somerset   **Map C4**
EC Thurs MD Wed, Sat SEE Town Hall (tapestry, portraits), Admiral Blake House, Sedgemoor
Battlefield 4m E
🅘 High St ✆ (01278) 427652
✗ Admirals Table, Bristol Rd ✆ (01278) 685671 Open Mon-Sat 12-9.30, Sun 12-9
Fairways International Touring Park, Bath Road, Bawdrip TA7 8PP ✆ (01278) 685569
  Prop: Fairways Partnership OS map 182/348403 3½m NE of Bridgwater off A39 (Glastonbury) on
right of B3141 (Woolavington) Open Mar 1-Nov 15 200 pitches 6 acres level grass 🔋 ▣ ▣ ∅ ✿
∅ ⊜ ⤴ ⌂ ♿ games room, rallies welcome, off licence nearby £6.00-£14.50 (all cards)
fairwaysint@btinternet.com www.fairways.btinternet.co.uk

Ordnance Survey
Landranger map
number and grid
reference giving exact
location of site (see
facing page)

Dates open and total
number of pitches
including any occupied
permanently by
caravans or mobile
homes, referred to in
this guide as 'statics'

Distance and direction of
site from centre of place
under which it is listed, the
place name in brackets
following the road number
indicating which route to
take. *See note below*

Site proprietor

Symbols for amenities on
site (see key on facing page)
with additional facilities in
words at end. All sites in this
guide have flush lavatories
and, except where marked,
showers. Symbols for these
amenities are therefore
omitted from site entries

E-mail address and website

Place name that the site is listed under is omitted to
avoid repetition. Sites are listed under the nearest
place likely to be shown on the average map

Note - Directions
To give detailed directions for finding a site would either mean a more expensive guide or
fewer sites. In any case most are now signposted form the nearest numbered road. Taking the
place under which a site is listed as the starting point, as this guide does, enables you to
pinpoint it on a suitable map. That way you can approach it from wherever you happen to be.
There is no need to go to the place concerned

How to use this book

This guide groups campsites into regions, then lists them alphabetically under key towns likely to be shown on the average map. The name of the campsite, its address and telephone number is followed by the Ordnance Survey grid reference. As metric scale 1:50 000 maps covering the whole of Britain have now been introduced, these are the ones that have been used.

Pinpointing a site on a OS map is easy enough. The first number or numbers before the oblique stroke refer to the relevant map in this series, the six numbers that follow being the grid reference. In this, the first three figures give the east-west location of the place referred to, the second the north-south, the first two figures in each case relating to the number of the kilometre square shown at the edge of the map, the third figure to tenths of the square. For example, the grid reference for church of Llanbedrog in North Wales is 123/329315, that is, map number 123, east-west square 32 and north-south square 31, the third figure representing tenths of the square. (The maps at the beginning of each regional section show each of the key towns in the region and the major roads leading to them.)

The OS grid reference in each entry is followed by the distance and direction of the campsite from the *centre* of the key town under which it appears. Then comes the inclusive opening dates and the permitted number of tents or caravans or both the campsite can accept, including any there semi-permanently.

Prices supplied by the site operator are for two people with car and tent or caravan per night. Awnings are invariably charged extra, as are mains electric hook-ups.

While every care was taken to ensure that the information in this guide was accurate at the time of going to press neither the author nor the publisher can accept any liability for errors or omissions.

KEY TO SYMBOLS

🛒	shop	⌀	gas supplies	🖳	winter storage for caravans
✕	restaurant	⊕	chemical disposal point	ⓟ	parking obligatory
⚲	bar	∅	payphone	❀	no dogs
🍴	takeaway food	▧	swimming pool	🚐	caravan hire
➤	off licence	⊛	games area	🏠	bungalow hire
▣	laundrette	🖒	children's playground	♿	facilities for disabled
🔌	mains electric hook-ups	🖵	TV	◖	shaded

Additional facilities are given in words at end.

Except where marked, all sites in this guide have flush lavatories and showers. Symbols for these amenities have therefore been omitted from site entries.

At the end of the guide there is an index of all sites listed in the guide, followed by an index of towns.

Key to regions

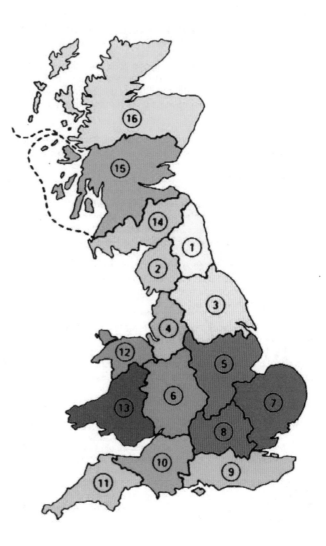

1 Northumbria
Northumberland
Durham

2 Cumbria

3 Northeast
North Yorkshire
South Yorkshire
West Yorkshire

4 Northwest
Lancashire
Greater Manchester
Merseyside
Cheshire

5 **East Midlands**
Derbyshire
Nottinghamshire
Lincolnshire
Leicestershire
Northamptonshire

6 Central England
Shropshire
Staffordshire
West Midlands
Herefordshire
Worcestershire
Warwickshire
Gloucestershire

7 **East Anglia**
Cambridgeshire
Norfolk
Suffolk
Essex

8 **London and Home
Counties**
Berkshire
Oxfordshire
Buckinghamshire
Bedfords hire
Hertfordshire
Greater London

9 Southern England
Hampshire
Surrey
Kent
East Sussex
West Sussex
Isle of Wight

10 Southwest
Wiltshire
Dorset
Somerset

11 West Country
Cornwall
Devon

12 North Wales
Isle of Anglesey
Conwy
Gwynedd
Shires of Flint, Denbigh
and Wrexham

13 **South and Central Wales**
Carmarthenshire
Pembrokeshire
Powys
Ceredigion
Monmouthshire
Vale of Glamorgan

14 South Scotland
Dumfries and Galloway
Borders

15 Central Scotland
N, S and E Ayrshire
N and S Lanarkshire
Stirling
Argyll and Bute
Fife
Perth and Kinross
Angus

16 North Scotland
Aberdeenshire
Highland
Moray
Western Isles

Bounded on the north and south by the Scottish and Yorkshire borders and on the east and west by the North Sea and the Pennines, Northumbria is made up of Northumberland, Durham and a number of relatively new unitary authorities.

North of Newcastle is a wildly beautiful coastline of rolling dunes and springy turf punctuated by fishing harbours and modest resorts, and guarded by impressive castles like massive Warkworth near the mouth of the Coquet, fortress home of the fighting Percys. Beyond, on the Great North Road and the threshold of Scotland is Berwick, its old quarter on the north bank of the Tweed contained within the massive ramparts. Offshore is Holy Island, dominated by its castle and melancholy priory ruins, and the Farne Islands, with their colonies of grey seals. Holy Island is linked to the mainland by a mile-long causeway uncovered at low tide, and there are boats to the Farnes from Seahouses.

Inland, from the natural barrier of the Pennine Fells in the south to the rolling Cheviots in the north, is wild and remote country laced by the dales or valleys of Wear, Coquet, Tees and Tyne and bisected by Hadrian's Wall, northernmost frontier of the Roman Empire, begun by order of Emperor Hadrian in AD 122, which formed a continuous frontier across England from Wallsend to Bowness on Solway until abandoned in 383. A convenient centre for exploring the wall and the national park to the north of it is Hexham, near the important Roman sites of Housesteads and Corbridge. Linking Heddon on the Wall and Greenhead is the old military road B6318, which runs on or beside the wall at many points.

Main features of the national park are the Border Forest around Kielder, the beautiful river valleys and the Pennine Way, a route for walkers which passes through Once Brewed, Bellingham and Byrness to cross the Scottish border. Another ancient road which can be followed by walkers is the Devil's Causeway north of Hexham. Otterburn, famed for its

tweed and as the site of the battle in 1388 between the Percys of England and the Douglases of Scotland, is well placed as a touring centre.

One of the newest sights in the region is Kielder Reservoir, the largest man-made lake in Europe, with plenty of scope for recreation.

Other sights include the fortresses of Alnwick, Bamburgh, Staindrop, Dunstanburgh and Raby, the churches of Escomb, Bywell and Hexham, the great cathedral of Durham and the ancient priory of Finchale. Three important museums are the Beamish near Stanley in Durham, the Grace Darling at Bamburgh and the Trailside Centre at Kielder.

Campsites, not numerous in Northumbria, exist in the national park, along the Northumbrian coast and at each of the main tourist centres.

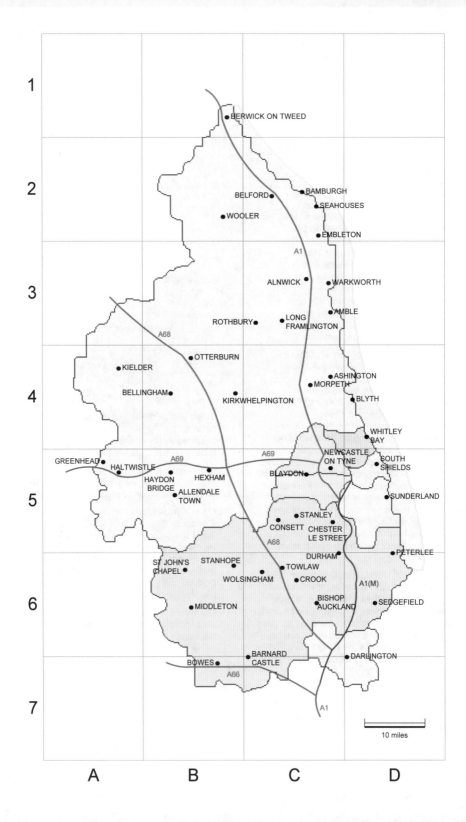

ALNWICK, Northumberland — Map C3

EC Wed MD Sat SEE castle, church of SS Mary and Michael, Bondgate Tower, Alnwick Fair (last Sun Jun) ⓘ The Shambles, Northumberland Hall ☎(01665) 510665
✖ White Swan, Bondgate Within ☎(01665) 602109

Cherry Tree Farm, Edlingham NE66 2BL ☎(01665) 574635 OS map 81/115090 5m W of Alnwick on B6341 (Rothbury) Open Apr-Sept 20 pitches 1 acre, gentle slope *No showers*

ALWINTON–see Rothbury

ASHINGTON, Northumberland — Map C4

EC Wed MD Fri, Sat SEE Wansbeck riverside park, Bothal castle and church
✖ Queen's Head 6m W at Morpeth ☎(01670) 512083

Wansbeck Riverside Park NE68 8TX ☎(01670) 812323 OS map 81/257863 ½m SW of Ashington off A106 (Bedlington) Open all year 75 pitches (enclosed) 5½ acres, part level, hard standings 🛒🖥🚿🅿⊕↩🚿🏠🚾🛈 fishing

BAMBURGH, Northumberland — Map C2

EC Wed SEE Bamburgh Castle, Grace Darling museum ✖ Lord Crewe Arms ☎(01668) 214243

Bradford Kaims Caravan Park NE70 7JT ☎(01668) 213432 Fax (01668) 213891 OS map 75/165315 2m W of Bamburgh on B1341 (Lucker) Open Mar 16-Nov 15 350 pitches (270 static) 40 acres 🛒⚡🖥🚿⊕⊘🚿↩🚿 sauna/solarium £12.00-£15.00 (Delta/Mastercard/Visa/Switch) *lwrib@tiscali.co.uk www.bradford-leisure.co.uk*

Glororum Caravan Park, Glororum NE69 7AW ☎(01668) 214457 Fax (01668) 214622 OS map 75/166334 1½m SW of Bamburgh on B1341 (Adderstone) Open Apr-Oct 100 pitches (150 static) 20 acres level grass, sheltered 🛒⚡🖥🚿🅿⊕⊘🚿↩ £15.00-£17.00 *info@glororum-caravanpark.co.uk www.glororum-caravanpark.co.uk*

BARNARD CASTLE, Co. Durham — Map C7

EC Thur MD Wed SEE ruined castle, Bowes museum, market cross
ⓘ Flatts Rd ☎(01833) 690909
✖ Moorcock Inn, Hill Top, Eggleston ☎(01833) 650395 Open May-Sep 11.30-9, Oct-Apr 11.30-2/6-9

Bendholm Farm Caravan Park, Egglestone DL12 0AX ☎(01833) 650457 *Prop: J & K Daly* OS map 92/990246 6m NW of Barnard Castle off B6278 (Stanhope) Open Mar-Oct 99 pitches (65 static) 5 acres level grass and hard standing, sheltered 🛒🖥🚿🅿⊕🚿🚾 £8.00-£12.00 hook-up £2

West Roods Working Farm, Boldron DL12 9SW ☎(01833) 690116 OS map 92/032139 2m SW of Barnard Castle off A66 (Scotch Corner-Brough) Open May-Oct 6 pitches Level and sloping grass, hard standings 🚿⊕↩

Winston Caravan Park, Winston on Tees DL2 3RH ☎(01325) 730228 OS map 92/140168 5½m E of Barnard Castle on A67 (Darlington) Open Mar-Oct 21 pitches (11 static) 2 acres level grass and hard standing, sheltered 🖥🚿🅿⊕🚾 river bathing *m.willetts@ic24.net www.touristnetuk.com/ne/winston*

BEADNELL–see Seahouses

BELFORD, Northumberland — Map C2

EC Thurs SEE St Mary's church ✖ Blue Bell, Market Place ☎(01668) 213543

Blue Bell Farm, West Street NE70 7QS ☎(01668) 213362 OS map 75/107339 ¼m W of Belford on B6349 (Wooler) Open Mar-Oct 75 pitches (45 static) 5 acres mainly level ✖♿⚡🖥🚿🅿⊕ 🚿🏠♿

Budle Bay Camp, Waren Mill NE70 7EE ☎(01668) 214598 OS map 75/146341 2m E of Belford on B1342 (Bamburgh) Open Mar-Oct 250 pitches 6 acres mainly level grass, hard standings, sheltered 🛒✖♿🖥🚿🅿⊕🚿↩🚿

Waren Caravan Park, Waren Mill NE70 7EE ☎(01668) 214366 Fax (01668) 214224 OS map 75/155343 2m E of Belford on B1342 (Bamburgh) Open Apr-Oct 480 pitches (286 static)–booking advisable 100 acres level grass and hard standings, sheltered 🛒✖♿⚡🖥🚿🅿⊕🚿🚾⊕↩🚿🚾♿ (Mastercard/Visa/Switch/Delta) *waren@meadowhead.co.uk www.meadowhead.co.uk*

For other sites near Belford see also Bamburgh   *See listing under Morpeth*

Forget-Me-Not is a family run Holiday Park set in the beautiful Northumbrian countryside on the edge of the Northumberland National Park.

Haggerston Castle
Caravan Park

**5-Star facilities,
fabulous location**

Haggerston Castle is truly a five-
star delight. Boasting it's very own
Golf Course & Boating lake,
Haggerston Castle is one of our
finest & most well appointed Parks.

✆ (01289) 381333

BELLINGHAM, Northumberland   Map B4
EC Tues, Sat SEE Kielder forest (largest in Europe), Kielder reservoir (largest in Britain) 15m NW
🛈 Main St ✆ (01434) 2220616
✗ Cheviot ✆ (01660) 220216

Brown Rigg Camping Caravan Park NE48 2JY ✆ (01434) 220175 OS map 80/835826 ½m S of
Bellingham on B6320 (Hexham) Open Easter-Oct 80 pitches 5 acres level grass and hard
standings, sheltered 🛍🖥🔌🗑⊕∅↩ fishing permits, indoor play area, craft shop, tea room
£8.00-£14.50 (Delta/Mastercard/Switch/Visa) ross@brcaravanpark.fsbusiness.co.uk
www.northumberlandcaravanparks.com
For other sites near Bellingham see Kielder

BERWICK ON TWEED, Northumberland   Map B1
EC Thur MD Wed, Fri, Sat *Small and ancient seaport of great charm at mouth of river Tweed* SEE
ramparts, castle remains, Jacobean bridge, Trinity church
🛈 106 Marygate ✆ (01289) 330733
✗ Queen's Head, Sandgate ✆ (01289) 307852

Haggerston Castle Caravan Park, Beal TD15 2PA ✆ (01289) 381333 OS map 75/042435 6m SE
of Berwick on Tweed on A1 (Alnwick) Open all year 1,255 pitches (1100 static) Level grass,
sheltered 🛍✗♀↩⊁🖥🔌⊕∅🗔⊕↩⊡🅿🗄& boating, tennis, putting green, 9 hole par 3
golf course, bike hire, live entertainment £12.00-£64.00* (Mastercard/Visa)
www.haggerstoncastle-park.co.uk

Marshall Meadows Farm, A1 Road TD15 1UT ✆ (01289) 330735 OS map 75/982567 2½m N of
Berwick on Tweed off A1 (Dunbar) Open Apr-Oct 95 pitches (55 static) Level grass, sheltered
🖥🔌⊕∅

Ord House Country Park, East Ord TD15 2NS *Well equipped site in pleasant surroundings*
✆ (01289) 305288 Fax (01289) 330832 OS map 75/981516 1½m SW of Berwick on Tweed off
bypass and East Ord road Open all year 280 pitches (206 static) Level grass and hard standing,
sheltered 🛍✗♀🖥🔌⊕∅⊕↩🗄& family room, crazy golf £6.00-£17.40*
(Mastercard/Visa/Delta/Switch) enquiries@ordhouse.co.uk www.ordhouse.co.uk

BISHOP AUCKLAND, Co. Durham   Map C6
EC Wed MD Sat SEE 12c church, Roman hypocaust at Vinovium (Binchester)
🛈 Town Hall, Market Pl ✆ (01388) 602610
✗ Queen's Head, Market Pl ✆ (01388) 603477

Witton Castle, Witton le Wear DL14 0DE ✆ (01388) 488230 OS map 92/154304 4m NW of Bishop
Auckland on A68 (West Auckland-Tow Law) Open Mar-Oct 502 pitches (313 static) Level/sloping
grass, sheltered 🛍✗♀↩⊁🖥🔌⊕∅🗔⊕↩⊡🔆 paddling pool, flyfishing £8.50-£12.00
www.wittoncastle.com

KEY TO SYMBOLS

🛍	shop	∅	gas supplies	🔆	winter storage for caravans
✗	restaurant	⊕	chemical disposal point	🅿	parking obligatory
♀	bar	∅	payphone	⊗	no dogs
↩	takeaway food	🗔	swimming pool	🗄	caravan hire
⊁	off licence	⊕	games area	🏠	bungalow hire
🖥	laundrette	↩	children's playground	&	facilities for disabled
🔌	mains electric hook-ups	⊡	TV	⊈	shaded

BLAYDON, Gateshead   Map C5
EC Wed SEE Derwent Walk country park, Gibside chapel at Rowlands Gill 2m S
✗ Black Bull, Bridge St ☎(0191) 414 2846

Derwent Park Camping, Rowland's Gill NE39 1LG ☎(01207) 543383 OS map 88/168586 3½m S
of Blaydon on A694 (Consett) near junction with B6314 beside river Derwent Open Apr-Sept 72
pitches (25 static) 4 acres level grass and hard standings, sheltered 🔲🅿️📶✅⊘🅶⤙🎮♿
(Mastercard/Visa/Eurocard)

CASTLESIDE–see Consett

CONSETT, Co. Durham   Map C5
EC Wed MD Fri, Sat SEE moors, Roman baths at Ebchester 2m N
✗ Bellamys near bus station ☎(01207) 503654

Allensford Park Camping Site, Allensford, Castleside DH8 9BA *Secluded riverside location in
Derwent valley* ☎(01207) 505572 OS map 88/082504 2½m SW of Consett off A68 (Tow Law-
Hexham) Open Mar-Oct 80 pitches (50 static) Level grass, sheltered 🚿🔲🅿️📶✅⤙
www.snootyfoxresorts.co.uk

Byreside Caravan Site, Hamsterley NE17 7RT ☎(01207) 560280 OS map 88/124562 3m NE of
Consett off B6310 (Rowlands Gill) at Medomsley Open all year 26 pitches–booking advisable 2
acres part level, grass and hard standing 🚿🅿️📶✅⊘

Manor Park Caravan Site, Broadmeadows, Castleside DH8 9HD ☎(01207) 501000/503706 OS
map 88/104461 3½m S of Consett off A68 (Tow Law) via Castleside Open Apr-Oct 40 pitches
(10 static) Part level grass, sheltered 🔲🅿️📶✅⊘🅶🎮🏠♿

COTHERSTONE–see Barnard Castle

CRASTER–see Embleton

DARLINGTON   Map D7
EC Wed MD Mon, Thurs, Sat SEE North Road rail museum, St Cuthbert's church
✗ Cricketers, Parkgate ☎(01325) 384444

Newbus Grange, Neasham DL2 1PE ☎(01325) 720973 OS map 93/320097 5m SE of Darlington
off A167 (Northallerton) Open Mar-Dec 150 pitches (130 static) Level grass 🔲🖵🅶

DURHAM, Co. Durham   Map C6
EC. Wed MD Sat SEE Cathedral, Norman castle, Gulbenkian Museum of Oriental Art
🎫 Gala Theatre ☎(0191) 384 3720
✗ Three Tuns, New Elvet ☎(01385) 64326

Finchale Abbey (Priory) Caravan Park, Finchale Priory DH1 5SH ☎0191-386 6528 OS map
88/295468 4m N of Durham off A167 (Chester le Street) and Newton Hall/Brasside road, beside
river Wear Open all year 180 pitches (100 static)–adv booking 6 acres level grass and hard
standing, sheltered 🚿(café) ⤙🏕🔲🅿️📶✅⊘🅶⤙🖵🎮🏠♿🔧 fishing £13.00-£15.00 (most
cards) *godricawatson@hotmail.com www.finchaleabbey.co.uk*

EMBLETON, Northumberland   Map C2
EC Wed SEE castle, old church, vicarage with pele tower
✗ Craster 2m S at Craster ☎(01665) 576230/576233

Proctors Stead, Craster NE66 3TF ☎(01665) 576613 OS map 75/248202 1½m S of Embleton on
Craster road Open Mar-Oct 60 pitches 3 acres level grass and hard standings, sheltered
🚿🔲🅿️📶✅⊘🎮🖵

GREENHEAD, Northumberland   Map A5
SEE Roman Wall, Featherstone Castle
✗ Holmhead, Hadrian's Wall ☎(01697) 247402

Roam-n-Rest Caravan Park, Raylton House CA6 7HA ☎(01697) 747213 OS map 86/656654 ¼m
W of Greenhead on right of A69 (Brampton) Open Mar-Oct 20 pitches (5 static) 1 acre level
grass, sheltered 🅿️📶✅⤙

Seldom Seen Caravan Park

A family run country park. Private fishing on the river South Tyne. Licensed Club. Peaceful walks. Two miles from historian's Wall World Heritage Site.
☎ (01434) 320571

CHARGES

Charges quoted are the minimum and maximum for two people with car and caravan or tent. They are given only as a guide and should be checked with the owner of any site at which you plan to stay.
Charges markded * are the prices for last year. Otherwise, the prices are those quoted for the current season.
Remember to ask whether hot water or use of the pool (if any) is extra and make sure that VAT is included.

HALTWHISTLE, Northumberland   **Map A5**
EC Wed MD Thurs SEE Hadrian's Wall, Featherstone Castle, 13c parish church of Holy Cross, South Tyne valley S, Blenkinsopp Hall gardens 1m W
🚆 Railway St ☎ (01434) 322002
✗ Milecastle Inn, Military Rd ☎ (01434) 321372

Seldom Seen Caravan Park NE49 0NE ☎ (01434) 320571 Prop: W & JE Dale OS map 86/87/718638 1m E of Haltwhistle off A69 (Hexham) Open Mar-Jan 70 pitches (50 static) Level grass, sheltered ♀🏕🅿◪⊕ club room, fishing £12.50 seldomseen.cp@btinternet.com www.seldomseencaravanpark.co.uk

Yont the Cleugh, Coanwood NE49 0QN ☎ (01434) 320274 OS map 87/685585 4½m S of Haltwhistle off Alston road Open Mar-Jan 107 pitches (77 static) 9 acres level grass and hard standings, sheltered ♀⊸🅿🏕⊘⊕𝟅✓🕮 www.yontthecleugh.co.uk

HAYDON BRIDGE, Northumberland   **Map B5**
EC Wed SEE 18c bridge, old church, Langley Castle SW
✗ Anchor ☎ (01434) 684427

Poplars Riverside Park, Eastland Ends NE47 6BY ☎ (01434) 684427 OS map 87/836642 ¼m W of Haydon Bridge on A69 (Carlisle-Newcastle) Open Mar-Oct 43 pitches (30 static) 2½ acres level grass, sheltered 🅿🏕⊘⊕∅✓🕮 fishing

HEXHAM, Northumberland   **Map B5**
EC Thurs MD Tues, Fri SEE Housesteads Roman Camp, abbey church
🚗 Wentworth Car Park ☎ (01434) 652220
✗ Miners Arms, Main St, Acomb ☎ (01434) 603909

Barrasford Park NE48 4BE ☎ (01434) 681210 OS map 87/935738 5½m N of Hexham off A68 (Corbridge-Carter Bar) Open Apr-Oct 150 pitches (120 static)–no adv bkg 60 acres woodland, hard standings, grass sloping, sheltered 🔋♀🅿🏕⊘⊕∅🕮

Causey Hill Caravan Park, Causey Hill NE46 2JN ☎ (01434) 602834 Fax (01434) 602834 OS map 87/925627 1¼m SW of Hexham on B6306 or B6305 (Alston) Open Mar-Oct–must book public holidays 145 pitches Level/sloping grass and hard standing 🔋🅿🏕🅿⊕⊘✓🕮 £8.00-£13.00* causeyhillcp@aol.com

Fallowfield Dene, Acomb NE46 4RP ☎ (01434) 603553 Prop: PH Straker OS map 87/938678 2m NW of Hexham off A69 (Carlisle) on A6079 (Wall) in Acomb village Open Apr-Oct 160 pitches (100 seasonal) 17 acres mainly level, grass and hardstanding 🔋🅿🏕🏕⊕🕮⅊ £9.50-£14.50 (Switch/Visa/Mastercard) den@fallowfielddene.co.uk

Hexham Racecourse, High Yarridge NE46 2JP ☎ (01434) 606847 Prop: Hexham Steeplechase Company OS map 87/918623 1½m S of Hexham off B6035 (Alston) Open May-Sept 50 pitches Grass, part level, open 🅿🏕🏕⊕∅⊕✓⊡ £9.00-£12.00

KIELDER, Northumberland　　　　　　　　　　　　　　　　　　　　　　**Map A4**
✘ Riverside Hall 15m SE at Bellingham　✆(01660) 220254

Kielder Forest Camp Site NE48 1EP　✆(01434) 250291　OS map 80/628938　¼m N of Kielder centre near Forestry Commission visitor centre　Open Apr-Sept　70 pitches　10 acres level grass and hard standings, sheltered　💪🏹🗄️🔲🔗🔆🔵🔄👣♿　access to forest walks and cycle routes (Mastercard/Visa/Switch)

KIRKWHELPINGTON, Northumberland　　　　　　　　　　　　　　　　　　**Map B4**
SEE Bartholomew's church, river bridge
✘ The Hadrian 6m SW at Wall　✆(01434) 681232

Raechester Farm NE19 2RH　✆(01830) 540345　OS map 81/979871　2m NW of Kirkwhelpington on right of A696 (Carter Bar)　Open Easter-Sept　15 pitches　½ acre mainly level grass and hard standing　✘(snack) ⚲

LONGFRAMLINGTON, Northumberland　　　　　　　　　　　　　　　　　　**Map C3**
SEE Coquet valley and Swarland forest walk NE
✘ Granby on A697　✆(01665) 570228

Percy Wood Caravan Park, Chesterhill, Swarland NE65 9JW　*Peaceful site in mixed woodland 2m from A1*　✆(01670) 787649　OS map 81/159040　2m NE of Longframlington at Swarland adj golf course–signposted　Open Mar-Jan　210 pitches (150 static)　Level grass and hard standings, sheltered　💪🗄️🔲🔗🔆🔵🔄👣🔳　full service pitches, tennis courts (Mastercard/Visa/Switch/Delta)

MIDDLETON IN TEESDALE, Co Durham　　　　　　　　　　　　　　　　　**Map B6**
EC Wed MD alt Tues　SEE church, old clock tower,　High Force waterfall 5m NW
🅸 10 Market Place　✆(01833) 641001　✘ Teesdale, Market Pl　✆(01833) 640264

Cote House Caravan Park, Cote House Farm DL12 0PN　✆(01833) 640515　*Prop: TP & PA Mitcalfe*　OS map 91/951233　1m S of Middleton in Teesdale near Mickleton off B6277 (Barnard Castle) by Grassholme reservoir　Open Mar-Oct　102 pitches (82 static)　Level grass, sheltered by woodland　🔗👣🔳　fishing　£4.00 hook-up £1.50

Daleview Caravan Park DL12 0NG　✆(01833) 640233　OS map 92/948248　½ W of Middleton in Teesdale on Brough Road　Open Mar-Oct　80 pitches (64 static)　4½ acres level grass and hard standing, sheltered　💪✘(snack) ⚲🗄️🔗🔳

MORPETH, Northumberland　　　　　　　　　　　　　　　　　　　　　　**Map C4**
EC Thurs MD Wed　SEE courthouse, parish church, clock tower
🅸 The Chantry, Bridge St　✆(01670) 511323
✘ Queens Head, Bridge Street　✆(01670) 512083

Forget-me-Not Holiday Park, Longhorsley NE65 8QY　✆(01670) 788364 Fax (01670) 788715　OS map 81/126946　7m NW of Morpeth off A697 (Wooler)　Open Mar-Oct　60 pitches　Hard standings and grass　✘⚲🗄️🔲🔗🔆🔵🔄👣🔳♿　£10.50-£17.00* (Delta/Mastercard/Switch/Visa)　*info@forget-me-notholiday.park.co.uk www.forget-me-notholiday.park.co.uk*

OTTERBURN, Northumberland　　　　　　　　　　　　　　　　　　　　**Map B4**
SEE Otterburn Tower, Battle of Otterburn Memorial, Pennine Way
✘ Percy Arms, Main St　✆(01830) 520261

Border Forest Caravan Park, Cottonshope, Burnfoot NE19 1TF　✆(01830) 520259　*Prop: AM Flanagan*　OS map 80/780014　8m NW of Otterburn on A68 (Carter Bar)　Open Mar-Oct　45 pitches　3 acres level grass　🔲🔗🔆🔵🔳　£9.50-£12.00 (Visa/Amex/Mastercard)　*borderforest@btinternet.com www.borderforestcaravanpark.com*

ROTHBURY, Northumberland　　　　　　　　　　　　　　　　　　　　**Map C3**
EC Wed　SEE Cragside Gardens, Callaby Castle, Brinkburn Priory
🅸 Nat Park Info Centre, Church St　✆(01669) 620887
✘ Granby 3m E at Longframlington　✆(01665) 570228

Clennell Hall Riverside Holiday Park, Alwinton NE65 7BG　✆(01669) 650341 Fax (01669) 650341　OS map 80/928072　10m NW of Rothbury off B6341 (Alwinton)　Open Mar-Oct　70 pitches　13 acres level grass　🗄️🔗👣🔳♿　sep pitches　£12.00-£15.00　*enquiries@clennellhall.co.uk www.clennellhall.co.uk*

Coquetdale Caravan Park, Whitton NE65 7RU　✆(01669) 620549 Fax (01669) 620559　OS map 81/056008　½m SW of Rothbury on Newtown road　Open Easter-Oct　200 pitches (160 static)　Level grass, sheltered　💪🗄️🔲🔗🔆🔵🔄👣　fishing, swimming near　£8.00-£14.00*　*enquiries@coquetdalecaravanpark.co.uk www.coquetdalecaravanpark.co.uk*

ROWLAND'S GILL–see Blaydon

ST JOHN'S CHAPEL, Co. Durham　　　　　　　　　　　　　　　　　　**Map B6**
✘ Golden Lion, Market Pl　✆(01388) 537231

Briton Hall, Westgate in Weardale DL13 1LN　OS map 81/905380　1m E of St John's Chapel on A689 (Stanhope)　Open Mar-Oct　50 pitches　💪🔗　fishing, bathing

Clennell Hall Riverside Holiday Park   Alwinton, Rothbury, Northumberland, NE65 7BG   **t/f: 01669 650 341**

See listing under Rothbury

SEAHOUSES, Northumberland   **Map C2**
EC Wed SEE fishing port, marine life centre, fishing museum
🅔 Seafield Rd ☎ (01665) 720884
✖ Olde Shop, Main St ☎ (01665) 720200

Beadnell Links, The Harbour, Beadnell NE67 5BN ☎ (01665) 720526 Fax (01665) 720526 OS
  map 75/233287 2m S of Seahouses off B1340 (Alnwick) Open Apr-Oct 167 pitches (150
  static)–no tents 10 acres level grass   🔲🔳🔷🔶🔵🟡 £14.50-£17.00* (Delta/Mastercard/Switch/Visa)
  b.links@talk21.com www.caravanningnorthumberland.com

Seafield Park, Seafield Road NE68 7SP ☎ (01665) 720628 Fax (01665) 720088 OS map
  75/207322 In centre of Seahouses on Bamburgh road Open Mar-Dec 230 pitches (207 static)
  Level grass and hard standings, sheltered ✖🔲🔳🔷🔶🔵🟡🔻🔹🔷🔳🔶 £15.00-£28.00 (all cards)
  info@seafieldpark.co.uk www.seafieldpark.co.uk

Swinhoe Links, Beadnell NE67 5BW ☎ (01665) 720589 OS map 75/230285 1½m S of Seahouses
  on B1340 (Beadnell) Open Apr-Oct 163 pitches (140 static) 24 acres level grass 🔲🔳🔷🔶🔵🟡
  🔵🔹🏠

STANHOPE, Co. Durham   **Map B6**
*Attractive old market and quarrying town, main centre for walks on moors flanking Weardale SEE
18c castle, lime trees, St Thomas church*
🅔 Durham Dales Centre, Castle Gdns ☎ (01388) 527650
✖ Teesdale 12m S at Middleton in Teesdale ☎ (01833) 640264

Stanhope Caravan Park, Melton House DL13 2PF ☎ (01388) 528398 OS map 92/992392 ¼m S
  of Stanhope off A689 (Wolsingham) Open Mar-Oct 70 pitches 🔲🔳🔷

STANLEY, Co. Durham   **Map C5**
EC Wed MD Thurs SEE Beamish Open Air Museum (industrial archaeology) 1m N
✖ Blue Boar Tavern, Front St (off A693) ☎ (01207) 231167

Bobby Shafto Caravan Park, Beamish DH9 0RY *Tranquil site in wooded setting* ☎ (0191) 370
  1776 OS map 88/232545 2m E of Stanley off A693 (Chester le Street) and Beamish museum
  road Open Mar-Oct 75 pitches (40 static) 8 acres, level, sheltered grass and hard standing
  🔻🔲🔳🔷🔶🔵🟡🔹🔳 £11.50-£14.50* (most cards)

Harperley Country Park, Tanfield Lea DH9 8TB ☎ (01207) 234011 OS map 88/171535 1m NW of
  Stanley off A693 (Leadgate) Open Apr-Oct 25 pitches (hard standings) ✖🔲🔷 hotel facilities

WOLSINGHAM, Co. Durham   **Map C6**
EC Wed SEE Killhope Wheel lead mine 2m W
✖ Queen's Head 10m SE at Bishop Auckland ☎ (01388) 603477

Bradley Mill Caravan Park DL13 3JH ☎ (01388) 527285 OS map 92/107360 2m E of Wolsingham
  on A689 (Crook) Open Apr-Oct–booking preferable 100 pitches (80 static) Level grass and hard
  standing, sheltered 🔲🔳🔷🔶🔵🟡🔹🔳 *www.bradleyburn.co.uk*

The Eilands, Frosterley, Landieu Weardale DL13 2SJ ☎ (01388) 527230 OS map 92/040368 1½m
  W of Wolsingham off A689 (Stanhope) at Frosterley, by river Wear Open Mar-Oct 100 pitches–no
  tents 15 acres level/sloping grass, sheltered 🔻🔲🔳🔷🔹🔳

WOOLER, Northumberland   **Map B2**
EC Thurs MD Mon, Wed, Sat SEE Ancient British Camps
🅔 Bus Station Car Park ☎ (01668) 282123
✖ Ryecroft, Ryecroft Way ☎ (01668) 281233

Riverside Caravan Park NE71 6QG ☎ (01668) 281447 OS map 75/997278 ¼m SE of Wooler off
  A697 (Newcastle) Open Easter-Oct 400 pitches (333 static) Level grass, sheltered
  🔻✖🔳🔹🔲🔳🔷🔶🔵🟡🔻🔳🔹🔳 riding stables, trout fishing, family club with entertainment

Cumbria replaces the old counties of Cumberland, Westmorland and that part of 'Lancashire across the sands' which juts out into Morecambe Bay. Bounded on the north and south by the estuaries of the Kent and Esk and on the east and west by the Pennines and the Irish Sea, the region is centred on the Cumbrian Mountains which reach their highest point in the 3200ft Scafell Pikes north of Eskdale. The lakes fan out from Scafell like the spokes of a wheel, forming the essential element in a beautiful landscape noted less for its benevolent climate than for its spectacular variations of colour and contour, and the crowds that swamp the more accessible resorts in season. Yet May and June are usually the sunniest and driest months.

Best known of the lakes are Derwentwater (the acknowledged 'queen'), Windermere, Ullswater, Buttermere, Coniston, Thirlmere, Rydal and Bassenthwaite; but the undisputed hub of the lakes is Keswick, its limestone buildings typical of Cumbrian architecture.

Main gateways to the region are Kendal and Penrith. A miniature railway runs from Eskdale to Ravenglass, near the coast, and ferries operate on the larger lakes, some linking up with bus services, but public transport generally is poor. For walkers at least distances are short, since most of Cumbria is contained within a fifteen mile radius of Scafell. Main roads are feasible for most vehicles, but many secondary roads are narrow and gradients on both major and minor roads can be as steep as one in three. Some passes like Honister, Hardknott, Wrynose and Newlands are particularly dangerous and many others are unfit for anything on wheels.

Coastal resorts include Grange over Sands and, farther north, smaller and quieter Silloth, Seascale and St Bees. The most remote parts of Cumbria are the contrasting peninsulas of Furness and Cartmel, newly won from Lancashire. Where a railway now crosses Morecombe Bay to link them with the mainland travellers once had to make the dangerous journey on foot at low tide. Both areas are rewarding for the amateur archaeologist – among recent finds are flint

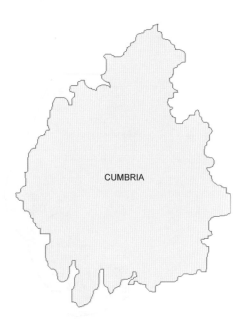

CUMBRIA

tools, stone circles and Iron Age camps.

Cumbria is best appreciated in its quiet valleys, like lovely Eskdale, where Beckfoot is a popular centre for climbing Scafell. Other centres for walkers and climbers are Ambleside for the Langdale Pikes and Keswick for the 3000ft Skiddaw Peak. There are many rewarding discoveries to be made in the Eden Valley (for which Appleby is the obvious centre) as there are in the remote country adjoining the Scottish border.

This is not a region rich in historic buildings. The Roman fort on Hardknott and the bath-house at Ravenglass are noteworthy, as are the castles of Carlisle, Cockermouth, Wetherall and Muncaster and the country houses of Levens Hall and Abbots Hall. There are Wordsworth museums at Grasmere and Cockermouth.

Most campsites in the lakes are simply equipped and in quiet situations. The widest choice is around Carlisle, at Penrith and Silloth, but all the major centres – and other places on the coast – have several sites.

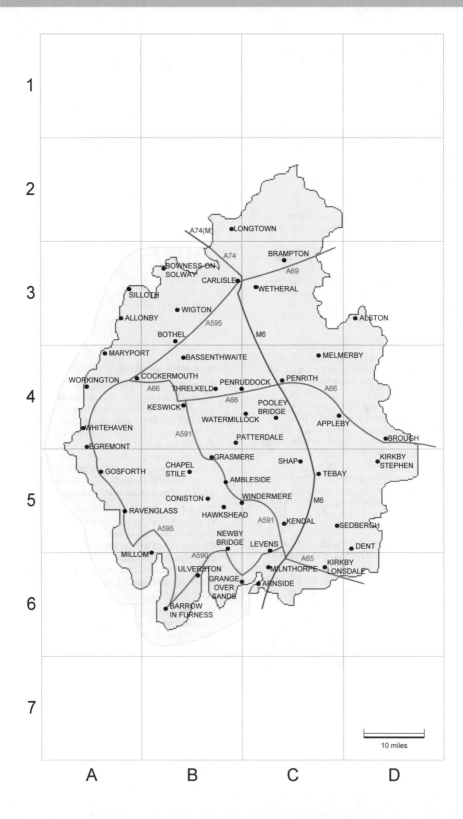

A   B   C   D

ALLONBY, Cumbria   **Map A3**
SEE extensive sands of Allonby Bay
✗ Waverley 5m S at Maryport ☎ (01900) 812115

Blue Dial Caravan Park CA15 6PB ☎ (01900) 881277 OS map 85/075407 1m S of Allonby on
B5300 (Maryport) Open Apr-Oct 150 pitches 🔲🏕🏕🏕🏕🏕🏕🏕🏕

Manor House Caravan Park, Edderside Road CA15 6RA ☎ (01900) 881236 OS map 85/092450
1m NE of Allonby off B5300 (Silloth) on Edderside road Open Mar-Oct 180 pitches (160 static)
Level grass and hard standing 🏕✗🏕🏕🏕🏕🏕🏕🏕🏕🏕🏕🏕 fitness room & sauna (all
cards)

Mealo House Farm CA15 6PB ☎ (01900) 881210 OS map 85/079416 ½m S of Allonby near junct
of B5300 (Maryport) and Hayton road Open Apr-Oct 140 pitches (120 static) Level grass
🔲🏕🏕🏕🏕🏕🏕 (Mastercard/Visa)

Spring Lea Caravan Park CA15 6QF ☎ (01900) 881331 Prop: John Williamson OS map
85/086433 On B5300 (Maryport-Silloth) in Allonby near beach Open Apr-Oct 131 pitches (96
static) 5 acres level grass and hard standings ✗🏕🏕🏕🏕🏕🏕🏕(indoor) 🏕🏕 sauna, games
room £11.00-£15.00 (Mastercard/Visa/Switch) mail@springlea.co.uk www.springlea.co.uk

ALSTON, Cumbria   **Map D3**
EC Tues MD Sat SEE market cross, church, Pennine Way, Gilderdale Forest SW
✗ Victoria, Front Street ☎ (01498) 381269

Horse and Wagon Caravan Park, Nentsbury CA9 3LH ☎ (01434) 382805 OS map 87/764452 3m
E of Alston on A689 (Durham) Open Mar-Oct 36 pitches (26 static) 3 acres, mainly level grass,
sheltered 🔲🏕🏕🏕🏕🏕🏕

AMBLESIDE, Cumbria   **Map B5**
EC Thurs MD Wed SEE lake Windermere, House on the Bridge, Stock Ghyll Force, White Craggs
rock garden 1m W
🎫 Old Courthouse, Church St ☎ (01539) 432582 ✗ Queens, Market Pl ☎ (01539) 432206

Skelwith Fold Caravan Park, Skelwith Fold LA22 0HX In grounds of former manor near lakeside
☎ (01539) 432277 Fax (01539) 434344 OS map 90/355029 1¼m SW of Ambleside off B5286
(Hawkshead) Open Mar-Nov 15 450 pitches (300 static) Level, sheltered hard standing
🏕🏕🔲🏕🏕🏕🏕🏕🏕🏕(15) 🏕 £12.50-£15.00* (Mastercard/Visa/Switch/Solo/Delta)
info@skelwith.com www.skelwith.com
For other sites near Ambleside see Coniston, Hawkshead and Windermere

APPLEBY, Cumbria   **Map C4**
EC Thurs MD Sat SEE St Lawrence church, High Cross, 16c Moot Hall, castle, Eden Valley
🎫 Moot Hall, Boroughgate ☎ (017683) 51177
✗ Masons Arms, Long Marton ☎ (017683) 61395

Low Moor, Kirkby Thore CA10 1XG ☎ (017683) 61231 OS map 91/626260 4½m NW of Appleby
on A66 (Penrith) Open Apr-Oct 37 pitches (25 static) 2 acres, level/gentle slope, grass and hard
standings 🏕🏕🏕🏕🏕 £7.00

Silver Band Caravan Park, Silver Band, Knock CA16 6DL ☎ (017683) 61218 Prop: PW Green OS
map 91/675276 5m N of Appleby off A66 (Penrith) at Kirkby Thore on Knock road at Silverband
Open Mar-Oct (weekends Nov-Feb)—must book 12 pitches ½ acre, sloping grass, part shaded
🏕🏕🏕🏕🏕🏕 garage services, post office £8.00-£10.00 (inc. elect)

Three Greyhounds, Great Asby CA16 6EX ☎ (017683) 51428 OS map 91/682132 2m S of
Appleby off B6260 (Tebay) on Great Asby road Open Mar-Oct 18 pitches 3 acres mainly level
grass 🏕🏕🏕🏕🏕

Wild Rose Caravan and Camping Park, Ormside CA16 6EJ Top level facilities meticulously
maintained ☎ (017683) 51077 Prop: DA Stephenson OS map 91/697165 2m SSE of Appleby off
B6260 (Orton) Open all year 440 pitches (200 static) 40 acres; caravans, hard standing and
grass; tents, level, slightly sloping grass and hard standings 🏕✗🏕🏕🔲🏕🏕🏕🏕🏕(heated)
🏕🏕🏕🏕 fishing, farm produce, cycle hire, indoor toddlers' playroom, mini-golf, safety-surfaced
outdoor playpark, teenage games room £11.00-£25.00 (inc hot water and heated pool)
(Mastercard/Visa) reception@wildrose.co.uk www.wildrose.co.uk

ASPATRIA–see Cockermouth

AYSIDE–see Newby Bridge

✗ RESTAURANTS
The restaurants recommended in this guide are of three kinds – pubs, independent restaurants
and those forming part of hotels and motels. They all serve lunch and dinner – at a reasonable
price – say under £10 a head. We shall be glad to have your comments on any you use this season
and if you think they are not up to standard, please let us have your suggestions for alternatives.

Welcome to Wild Rose Park

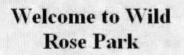

Ormside, Appleby-in-Westmorland
Cumbria CA16 6EJ
Telephone: Appleby (017683) 51077
Fax: (017683) 52551
E-mail: reception@wildrose.co.uk

KEY TO SYMBOLS

ᕦ	shop	⊕	games area
✗	restaurant	↩	playground
⚲	bar	⬚	TV
⟋	takeaway food	▣	winter storage
⚒	off licence	℗	parking oblig.
▣	laundrette	⊘	no dogs
⚡	elec hook-ups	⌑	caravan hire
⬭	gas supplies	⌂	bungalow hire
⊕	chem. disposal	♿	disabled facs.
∅	payphone	♧	shaded
⊡	swimming pool		

SITE DIRECTIONS

The distance and direction of a campsite is given from the centre of the town under which it appears.

See listing under Appleby

BARROW IN FURNESS, Cumbria   **Map B6**
EC Thurs MD Wed, Fri, Sat SEE ruins of Furness Abbey, Walney Island nature reserves, Biggar village
🛈 Civic Hall, Duke St ☎ (01229) 870156
✗ Victoria Park, Victoria Rd ☎ (01229) 821159

Longlands Caravan Park, Kirkby in Furness LA17 7XZ ☎ (01229) 889342 OS map 96/239836 8m N of Barrow in Furness off A595 (Whitehaven) Open Mar-Oct 130 pitches ⬭ ↩

South End Caravan Site, Walney Island LA14 3YQ *Site near sea and nature reserves* ☎ (01229) 472823/471556 OS map 96/208633 3½m S of Barrow in Furness on unclass road, via Biggar Open Mar-Oct 150 pitches (100 static) Sloping grass ᕦ ⚲ ▣ ⬭ ⚡ ∅ ⊕ ∅ ⊡ (indoor heated) ⊕ ↩ ⬚ lic club, bowling green £12.00-£20.00 (Mastercard/Visa) www.walney-island-caravan-park.co.uk

---

BASSENTHWAITE, Cumbria   **Map B4**
SEE old church at lakeside
✗ Pheasant Inn ☎ (01768) 776234

Trafford Caravan Park, Low Wood CA12 4QH ☎ (01768) 776298 OS map 90/228316 1m W of Bassenthwaite on A591 (Bothel-Keswick) Open Mar-Oct 80 pitches (50 static) Level grass and hard standing ᕦ ⬭ ⚡ ⊕ ∅ farm produce

North Lakes Caravan Park, Bewaldeth CA13 9SY ☎ (01768) 776510 OS map 89/207354 2m NW of Bassenthwaite on A591 (Bothel-Keswick) at Bewaldeth Open Mar-Nov 145 pitches (50 static) 30 acres, level grass and hard standings ᕦ ⚲ ▣ ⬭ ⚡ ∅ ⊕ ⊕ ↩ ⌑

Robin Hood Caravan Park CA12 4RJ ☎ (01768) 776334 OS map 89/207354 ½m N of Bassenthwaite off Caldbeck road Open Mar-Nov 35 pitches (20 static) grass and hard standing level/sloping, sheltered 2 acres, part level ⊕ ⊕ ⌑ fishing, pony trekking

---

BOTHEL, Cumbria   **Map B3**
✗ The Greyhound Inn ☎ (016973) 20601

Larches Caravan Park, Mealsgate CA7 1LQ ☎ (016973) 71379/71803 *Prop: Mr & Mrs Elliott* OS map 85/206416 2m NE of Bothel on right of A595 (Carlisle) Open Mar-Oct 173 pitches (100 static)–adults only Grass and hard standing, sheltered ᕦ ▣ ⬭ ⚡ ⊕ ∅ ⊡ ⬚ ⚡ ⌑ ♿ £10.40-£15.40*

Skiddaw View Caravan Park, Sunderland CA7 2JG ☎ (01697) 320919 OS map 89/90/180370 1m S of Bothel off A591 (Keswick) on Sunderland road Open Apr 11-Oct 31 96 pitches (76 static) ⟋ ▣ ⬭ ⚡ ⊕ ∅ ⊕ ↩ ⚡ ⌑

BOWNESS ON SOLWAY, Cumbria   **Map B3**
SEE remains of Hadrian's Wall, mudflats and marshes
✗ Crown and Mitre 10m SE at Carlisle ☎ (01228) 25491

Cottage Caravan Park, Port Carlisle CA5 5DJ ☎ (01697) 351317 OS map 85/242612 2m E of Bowness on Solway off coast road Open Mar-Oct 237 pitches (200 static) Grass, level, sheltered, some hard standing ᕦ ⚲ ⟋ ▣ ⬭ ⚡ ⊕ ∅ ⊕ ↩ ⚡ ⌑ bar meals, beer garden

BOWNESS ON WINDERMERE–see Windermere

BRAITHWAITE–see Keswick

BRAMPTON, Cumbria **Map C3**
EC Thurs MD Wed SEE church with Burnes Jones windows, Moot Hall, Prince Charlie's house
◪ Moot Hall ✆ (016977) 3433
✗ Farlam Hall ✆ (01697) 773600
Irthing Vale Holiday Park, Old Church Lane CA8 2AA ✆ (016977) 3600 OS map 86/523614 ½m
N of Brampton off A6071 (Longtown) Open Mar-Oct 50 pitches (23 static) 4½ acres level grass
🏕🖥🎦🏬⊕∅🚻🚿 🏪🚋 £9.50 (min)* glenwndrby@aol.com www.ukparks.co.uk/irthingvale

CARK IN CARTMEL–see Grange over Sands

CARLISLE, Cumbria **Map B3**
EC Thurs MD all except Thurs SEE cathedral, castle, Tullie House museum, market cross, tithe
barn
◪ Old Town Hall, Green Market ✆ (01228) 625600
✗ The Pheasant Inn, Cumwhitton ✆ (01228) 560102 Open Tue-Sun 6-9
✗ The Bridge End Inn, Bridge End, Dalston ✆ (01228) 710161
Cairndale Caravan Park, Cumwhitton CA8 9BZ ✆ (01768) 896280 *Prop: Mr & Mrs Irving* OS map
86/519522 6m SE of Carlisle off A69 (Brampton) via Great Corby Open Mar-Oct 20 pitches (15
static) Hard standings, level, sheltered 🚿🖥⊕🚿🚋 £5.50-£6.00
Dalston Hall Caravan Park, Dalston CA5 7JX ✆ (01228) 710165 *Prop: NE Farthing* OS map
85/375517 3m W of Carlisle on B5299 (Dalston) Open Mar-Oct 60 pitches Level grass and hard
standing 🏕✗🛒🚿🖥🎦⊕∅🚻🚿🚋🔥 fishing, 9-hole golf £6.00-£12.00 (Visa/Mastercard/Switch)
nigel@etmanco.fsnet.co.uk www.dalstonhall.co.uk
Dandy Dinmont Caravan Site, Blackford CA6 4EA ✆ (01228) 674611 *Prop: B Inglis* OS map
85/397622 4m N of Carlisle off A7 (Longtown) Open Mar-Oct 47 pitches 4½ acres level grass
and hard standings 🖥🚿🎦⊕∅ £7.75-£9.25 dandydinmont@btopenworld.com
Orton Grange Caravan Park, Wigton Road CA5 6LA ✆ (01228) 710252 OS map 85/357517 4m
SW of Carlisle on A595 (Wigton) Open all year 72 pitches (22 static) 7 acres level, grass and
hard standings, sheltered 🏕🛒✗🖥🚿🎦⊕∅🔲 (heated) ⊕🚻🚿🚋 games room, accessory
shop
For other sites near Carlisle see Bowness on Solway, Brampton, Longtown and Wigton

COCKERMOUTH, Cumbria **Map A4**
EC Thurs MD Mon SEE Wordsworth House, ruined castle, Moorland Close, birthplace of Fletcher
Christian of Mutiny on the Bounty fame
◪ Town Hall, Market St ✆ (01900) 822634
✗ Hundith Hill Hotel, Lorton Vale ✆ 0845 45 66 399
Graysonside Farm Caravan Park, Lorton Road CA13 9TQ ✆ (01900) 822351 *Prop: Andrew &
Janette Likeman* OS map 89/134292 1m E of Cockermouth on B5292 (Buttermere) Open Mar-
Nov 12 pitches Grass and hard standing 🚿(5) ⊕🚿 (outdoor, £200 pa) £10.00-£15.00
janette@graysonside.freeserve.co.uk www.graysonside.co.uk
Inglenook Caravan Park, Fitzbridge, Lamplugh CA14 4SH ✆ (01946) 861240 Fax (01946) 861240
OS map 89/084205 6½m SSW of Cockermouth off A5086 (Egremont) Open all year 58 pitches
(28 static) Level/sloping grass and hard standings 🏕✗🖥🚿🎦⊕∅🚻🚋🔥 £7.00-£9.50*
enquiry@inglenookcaravanpark.co.uk www.inglenookcaravanpark.co.uk
Wheatsheaf Inn, Low Lorton CA13 9UW ✆ (01900) 85268 OS map 89/153263 4m SE of
Cockermouth on B5289 (Buttermere) Open Mar-Oct 15 pitches Level grass, sheltered
✗🚿🖥🚿🎦⊕∅
Whinfell Hall Caravan Park, Lorton CA13 0RQ ✆ (01900) 85057 OS map 89/150254 3½m SSE of
Cockermouth off B5289 (Borrowdale) Open Mar-Oct 55 pitches (16 static) 4 acres, level grass
and hard standing 🖥🚿🎦⊕🚿🔥 £7.00-£9.00*
Wyndham Caravan Park, Keswick Road CA13 9SF ✆ (01900) 822571/825238 OS map 89/133312
1m E of Cockermouth on old Keswick road Open Mar-Oct 132 pitches (102 static) Level grass
and hard standing, sheltered 🏕🚿🖥🚿🎦⊕∅🚻🚋🏠 dancing, snooker, family social club,
amusement arcade

CONISTON, Cumbria　　　　　　　　　　　　　　　　　　　　　Map B5
EC Wed SEE Ruskin Museum, parish church, Donald Campbell Memorial, Tennyson's home, Coniston Water, Coniston Old Man 2,633ft, Tarn Hows (NT)
🛈 Ruskin Ave ✆ (01539) 441533
✗ Crown Hotel, Tilberthwaite Avenue ✆ 0153 94 41243

Coniston Hall, Haws Bank LA21 8AS ✆ (01539) 441223 *Prop: A & B Wilson* OS map 96/304964
¾m S of Coniston off A593 (Millom) via Haws Bank by Coniston Water Open Mar-Oct 200 pitches–no trailer caravans 20 acres, level/gentle slope, grass 🐾 ✗ ▤ 𝌆 ⊕ boating, fishing £10.00

Pier Cottage Caravan Park LA21 8AJ ✆ (01539) 441497 Fax (01539) 441252 OS map 96/310973
¼m E of Coniston off B5285 (Hawkshead) by lake Open Mar-Oct 10 pitches–no tents–must book 1 acre, level, sheltered ⊕

DENT, Cumbria　　　　　　　　　　　　　　　　　　　　　　　Map D6
SEE Dentdale, Dales Way, St Andrew church
✗ Sun Inn, Main St ✆ (01539) 625208

Conder Farm LA10 5QT ✆ (01539) 625277 OS map 98/706868 In Dent off Deep Dale road Open all year 48 pitches Sloping grass

High Laning Caravan Camping Park LA10 5QJ ✆ (01539) 625239 OS map 98/738469 In two sections on W edge of Dent Open all year 85 pitches 3½ acres level grass and hard standing 🐾✗♀⚲⩘ ▤🅿𝌆⊕∅⤣ ▥⛽🏠& *email@highlaning.co.uk www.highlaning.co.uk*

EGREMONT, Cumbria　　　　　　　　　　　　　　　　　　　　Map A4
EC Wed MD Fri SEE castle ruins
🛈 12 Main St ✆ (01946) 820693 ✗ Roseneath 6m NW at Low Moresby ✆ (01946) 861572

Home Farm Caravan Park, Rothersyke CA22 2UD ✆ (01946) 820797 and 824023 OS map 89/993094 2m SW of Egremont on B5345 (Calder Bridge-St Bees) Open Mar-Nov 18 pitches Hard standings and grass, level, sheltered ▤🅿⊕∅🅂

Tarside Caravan Site, Braystone, Beckermet CA21 2YL ✆ (01946) 841308 OS map 89/005063 2m S of Egremont–signposted from B5345 Open all year 200 pitches (100 static) Level grass and hard standing ✗♀⩘⚲ ▤🅿𝌆⊕∅⤣▥⛽🏠& fishing

ESKDALE–see Gosforth

GILCRUX–see Cockermouth

GOSFORTH, Cumbria　　　　　　　　　　　　　　　　　　　　Map A5
SEE Gosforth Cross in churchyard
✗ Brook House Inn, Boot, Eskdale ✆ (01946) 723288 Open 12-8.30

Church Stile Farm, Wasdale, Seascale CA20 1ET ✆ (01946) 762252 Fax (01946) 726028 OS map 89/124040 4m E of Gosforth on unclass (Nether Wasdale) road Open Mar-Oct 50 pitches (40 static)–no touring caravans ▤🅿⊕⤣& £8.00-£11.00* (most cards) *churchstile@campfarm.fsnet.co.uk www.churchstile.com*

Fisherground Farm Campsite, Eskdale CA19 1TF ✆ (01946) 723349 *Prop: Mick Perkin & Alison Fenton* OS map 89/153002 7m SE of Gosforth on unclass (Eskdale Green/Boot) road Open Mar-Nov 200 pitches–no caravans Level grass, sheltered ▤🅿⊕∅⤣ adventure playground, miniature railway, camp fires permitted £8.00-£10.00* inc car *camping@fishergroundcampsite.co.uk www.fishergroundcampsite.co.uk*

Seven Acres Caravan Camping Park, Holmrook CA19 1YD ✆ (01524) 781698 OS map 89/073019 1m S of Gosforth centre off A595 (Broughton-Whitehaven) Open Mar-Oct 103 pitches (65 static) 7 acres level grass and hard standings, part sheltered ▤🅿𝌆⊕∅🅂⤣▥ (all major cards)

GRANGE OVER SANDS, Cumbria　　　　　　　　　　　　　　Map B6
EC Thurs SEE Cartmel Priory gatehouse 2m W, Holker Hall 3m SW
🛈 Victoria Hall, Main St ✆ (01539) 534026
✗ Grange, Lindale Rd ✆ (014484) 3666

Meathop Fell Caravan Club Site, Grange-over-Sands, Meathop LA11 6RB ✆ (01539) 532912 OS map 97/437804 5m N of Grange over Sands on A590 (Levens Bridge) Open all year, level 130 pitches part hard standings 🅿𝌆⊕∅⤣& £9.50-£25.10 (Mastercard/Visa) *www.caravanclub.co.uk*

CHECK BEFORE ENTERING
There's usually no objection to your walking onto a site to see if you might like it but always ask permission first. Remember that the person in charge is responsible for safeguarding the property of those staying there.

GREYSTOKE–see Penruddock

HAWKSHEAD, Cumbria   Map B5
EC Thurs SEE Esthwaite Water, forest, Theatre in the Forest 3m S of Grizedale
🅸 Main car park ✆ (01539) 436525
✘ Queen's Head ✆ (01539) 436271

Croft Caravan and Camp Site, North Lonsdale Road LA22 0NX ✆ (01539) 436374 Fax (01539)
436544 OS map 96/353982 ¼m SE of Hawkshead centre on B5286 (Near Sawrey) Open Mar-
Oct 100 pitches (20 static) Level grass sheltered 🅱🖥🖧⊕⌀🔌 TV room £12.50-£18.50*
(Mastercard/Visa/Delta/Switch) enquiries@hawkshead-croft.com www.hawkshead-croft.com

Hawkshead Hall Farm LA22 0NN ✆ (01539) 436221 OS map 96/351988 ½m N of Hawkshead
centre on right of B5286 (Ambleside) near junction with B5285 (Coniston) Open Mar-Oct 60
pitches 3½ acres gentle slope, grass and hard standings No showers

Waterson Ground Farm, Outgate LA22 0NJ ✆ (01539) 436225 OS map 96/351994 1m N of
Hawkshead on left of B5286 (Ambleside) near junction with Borwick Lodge road Open Mar 1-Oct
15 50 pitches 6 acres level grass

INGS–see Windermere

KENDAL, Cumbria   Map C5
MD Sat SEE parish church, museum, Sizergh castle (NT) 3m SW
🅸 Town Hall, Highgate ✆ (01593) 725758
✘ Woolpack, Stricklandgate ✆ (01539) 723852

Ashes Lane Camping Caravan Park, Ashes Lane, Staveley LA8 9JS ✆ (01539) 821119 OS map
97/479964 3m NW off Kendal off A591 (Windermere) Open Mar-Jan 300 pitches (50 static) 22
acres, part level 🅱✘🍴↩🖥🖧⌀⊕⌀🕒🔌⌴🍴🖧♿

Low Park Wood Caravan Club Site, Sedgwick LA8 0JZ ✆ (01539) 560186 OS map 97/509878
3m SSW of Kendal off M6 at Junction 36 Open Easter-Oct 180 pitches no tents Hard
standing 🅱⌀⊕⌀ £12.50-£17.60* (Mastercard/Visa/Switch/Delta) www.caravanclub.co.uk

Pound Farm, Crook LA8 8JZ ✆ (01539) 821220 OS map 97/471953 3m NW of Kendal off A591
(Windermere) on left of B5284 (Bowness) Open Mar 1-Nov 14 34 pitches–bkg advised 2 acres
level grass and hard standings, sheltered 🅱🖧⊕ £15.00*

Ratherheath Lane Camping Caravan Park, Chain House, Bonning Gate LA8 8JU ✆ (01539)
821119 OS map 97/479957 3m NW of Kendal off A5284 (Crook) in Ratherheath Lane Open Mar
1-Nov 15 20 pitches Level grass 🖧⌀⊕⌴

KESWICK, Cumbria   Map B4
EC Wed MD Sat SEE Derwentwater, Southey's grave, Castlerigg stone circle
🅸 Moot Hall, Market Sq ✆ (01768) 772645 ✘ Queen's, Main St ✆ (01768) 773333

Burns Farm, St Johns in the Vale CA12 4RR ✆ (01768) 779225/791112 OS map 90/308242 2½m
E of Keswick off A66 (Penrith) on Castlerigg Stone Circle road Open Mar-Nov 4 32 pitches 2
acres level grass 🅱🖥🖧⊕⌀🏠♿ £8.00-£14.00* info@burnsfarmcamping.co.uk www.burns-
farm.co.uk

Burnside Caravan Site, Underskiddaw CA12 4PF ✆ (01768) 72950 OS map 89/265245 1m NW
of Keswick on A591 (Bothel)–A66 roundabout Open Mar 15-Oct 31 49 pitches (25 static) 2½
acres level grass and hard standing 🅱🖥🖧⌀⊕

Castlerigg Hall, Castlerigg CA12 4TE ✆ (01768) 74499 Fax (01768) 74499 OS map 89/285225
1m SE of Keswick off A591 (Grasmere) Open March-Nov 15 150 pitches Level grass and hard
standing 🅱↩⌁🖥🖧⌀⊕⌀⌴🍴♿ breakfast, campers £9.60-£15.20*
(Mastercard/Switch/Visa) info@castlerigg.co.uk www.castlerigg.co.uk

Derwentwater Caravan Park, Crowe Park Rd CA12 5EN Quiet lakeside park in woodland 3 min
from town centre ✆ (01768) 772579 OS map 90/256235 ½m W of Keswick centre via Tithebarn
Street, by lake Open Mar 1-Nov 14 210 pitches (160 static) no tents, no awnings 17½ acres
hard standings, sheltered 🍴🅱🖥🖧⊕⌀🔌 private beach–pitches with all mains services

Scotgate Caravan Site, Braithwaite CA12 5TF ✆ (01768) 778343 Fax (01768) 778099 OS map
90/235236 2½m W of Keswick at junction of A66 (Cockermouth) and B5292 (High Lorton) Open
Mar-Oct 150 pitches (35 static) no adv bkg 9 acres level grass and hard standing
🅱✘⌁🖥🖧⌀⊕🕒🍴 (most cards) www.scotgateholidaypark.co.uk

For other sites near Keswick see Bassenthwaite

KIRKBY LONSDALE, Cumbria   Map C6
EC Wed MD Thurs SEE Devil's Bridge, St Mary's church
🅸 Main St ✆ (01524) 271437 ✘ Pheasant Inn 1m NE at Casterton ✆ (01524) 271230

Wood Close Caravan Park, Casterton LA6 2SE ✆ (01524) 271597 Fax (01524) 272301 OS map
97/619783 ½m SE of Kirkby Lonsdale centre off A65 (Skipton) opposite junction with A683
(Lancaster) Open Mar-Oct 84 pitches (54 static) Grass, some hard standings, part level,
sheltered 🅱🖥🖧⌀⊕⌀🔌🍴♿ fishing, golf
michellehodgkins@woodclosecaravanpark.fsnet.co.uk www.woodclosepark.com

KIRKBY STEPHEN, Cumbria   Map D5
EC Thurs MD Mon SEE Cloister, church, Wharton Hall
🖼 Market St ✆ (01768) 371199
✘ King's Arms, Market Sq ✆ (01768) 371378

Bowber Head, Ravenstonedale CA17 4NL ✆ (01539) 623254 OS map 91/740032 4½m SW of
Kirkby Stephen off A683 (Sedbergh) Open all year 26 pitches (19 static) Level/sloping grass
🎫🚐🌀☻🗲🏢 TV hook-ups (Mastercard/Visa/Switch)

Pennine View Caravan Park, Station Road CA17 4SZ ✆ (01768) 371717 OS map 91/772075 ¼m
S of Kirkby Stephen centre off A685 (Tebay) Open Mar-Nov 58 pitches Level grass and hard
standing, sheltered 🎫🚐🌀☻🗲➳🗲♿ £11.75-£15.80* (Delta/Mastercard/Switch/Visa)

LAMPLUGH–see Cockermouth

LEVENS, Cumbria   Map C5
EC Thurs SEE Levens Hall 1m SE, Sizergh Castle 1m NE
✘ Heaves ✆ (01539) 560396

Sampool Caravan Park LA8 8EQ ✆ (01539) 552265 *Prop: JA Dobson* OS map 97/479843 1m
SW of Levens off A590 (Levens Bridge-Lindale) near river Kent Open Mar-Oct 200 pitches (185
static)–no tents 18 acres level grass and hard standings 🛁🎫🚐🌀☻🗲➳ fishing £10.00 inc
elect

LONGTOWN, Cumbria   Map B2
EC Wed SEE church, St Michael's Well
🖼 Memorial Hall Community Centre ✆ (01228) 791876
✘ Graham Arms Hotel, English St ✆ (01228) 791213 Open 12-8.30

Camelot Caravan Park, Sandysike CA6 5SZ ✆ (01228) 791248 OS map 85/390667 1½m S of
Longtown on A7 (Carlisle) Open Mar-Oct 20 pitches 1½ acres level grass and hard standings,
sheltered 🚐🌀☻🗲 dog walk £6.00-£10.50

Oakbank Country Park CA6 5NA ✆ (01228) 791108 Fax (01228) 791108 OS map 85/368702 1m
N of Longtown off A7 (Langholm) on Chapelknowe road Open all year 24 pitches 60 acres
level/sloping grass and hard standing 🛁✘🚐☻☻➳🗲▢♿ fishing (trout, carp, salmon) £8.50
(min)* (most cards) oakbank@nlaq.globalnet.co.uk

MELMERBY, Cumbria   Map C4
✘ Shepherds Inn off A686 ✆ (01768) 881217

Cross Fell Caravan and Camping Park, Ousby CA10 1QA ✆ (01768) 881374 OS map 91/620350
1m S of Melmerby on Skirwith road in Ousby Open Mar-Jan 38 pitches Level grass
✘🍴⚡➤🎫🚐☻🌀

Melmerby Caravan Park CA10 1HE ✆ (01768) 881311 OS map 91/615373 In Melmerby on A686
(Alston) Open Mar-Oct 47 pitches (41 static) Level grass and hard standing, sheltered
🛁✘🎫🚐🌀☻🗲🗲 £8.50

See listing under Pooley Bridge

MILLOM, Cumbria **Map B6**
EC Wed SEE folk museum, Holy Trinity church
✗ Punchbowl Inn 2m N at The Green ☏ (01229) 772605

Butterflowers, Port Haverigg LA18 4HB ☏ (01229) 772880 OS map 96/158784 1½m SW of Millom off A5093 (Silecroft) Open all year 189 pitches (79 static) 9 acres level grass 🖬🎒⊛∅▱(heated) ⤙ 🎐🔾 (Mastercard/Visa/Switch)

Silecroft Caravan Site, Silecroft LA18 4NX ☏ (01229) 772659 OS map 96/124812 4m N of Millom off A5093 (Broughton in Furness) Open Mar-Oct 184 pitches (124 static) Level grass and hard standing 🖬🖬🎒⊛⊕⤙🔾

MILNTHORPE, Cumbria **Map C6**
SEE Milnthorpe Sands, Kent Valley
✗ Crooklands Hotel, Crooklands ☏ 0153 95 67432

Fell End Caravan Park, Slackhead Road, Hale LA7 7BS ☏ (01524) 781695 OS map 97/503778 3m S of Milnthorpe off A6 (Carnforth) Open all year 315 pitches (215 static) 28 acres; caravans, hard standing (shingle), sheltered; tents, level and sloping, grass, sheltered 🖬✗🍷⤙⤚🎒(10amp) 𝄞⊛∅⊕⤙🔾🎐 ♿ Satellite TV aerial hook-ups (all cards)

Hall More Caravan Park, Hale LA7 7BP ☏ (01524) 781695 Fax (01524) 784815 OS map 97/502771 2½m S of Milnthorpe off A6 (Kendal) Open Mar-Oct 100 pitches (56 static) 7 acres level grass, sheltered 🖬🖬🎒𝄞∅ fishing, pony trekking £5.00-£12.00* (most cards) *enquiries@southlakeland-caravans.co.uk www.southlakeland-caravans.co.uk*

Millness Hill Park, Crooklands LA7 7NU ☏ (01539) 567306 OS map 97/537826 2m E of Milnthorpe near junction 36 of M6 Open Mar-Oct 75 pitches (30 static) Caravans, grass, sheltered; tents, part sheltered 🖬🎒𝄞⊛∅▱(children's) ⊕⤙🔾🎐🏠

Water's Edge Caravan Park, Crooklands LA7 7NN ☏ (01539) 567708 OS map 97/535835 3m NE of Milnthorpe off B6385 (Endmoor) on A65 at Crooklands (M6 junction 36) Open Mar-Nov 48 pitches 3 acres level grass and hard standings 🖬🍷⤙🖬🎒⊛∅⊕🔾🎐♿ £7.50-£16.50 (Mastercard/Visa) *sandra@crooklandsmotorco.co.uk www.watersedgecaravanpark.co.uk*

NEWBY BRIDGE, Cumbria **Map B5**
SEE lake Windermere, Haverthwaite railway ✗ Swan Hotel ☏ (015395) 31681

Bigland Hall Caravan Park, Haverthwaite LA12 8PJ ☏ (01539) 531702 Fax (01539) 531702 OS map 96/339838 2½m SW of Newby Bridge on B5278 (Cark) Open Mar-Nov 16—must book peak periods 144 pitches (48 static) Hard standings 🖬🖬🎒𝄞⊛∅ £12.00-£15.00*

Black Beck Caravan Park, Bouth LA12 8JN ☏ (01229) 861274 Fax (01229) 861041 OS map 96/335853 3m SW of Newby Bridge off A590 (Ulverston) Open Mar-Nov 15 305 pitches (235 static) 38 acres level grass and hard standing, sheltered 🖬⤙🖬🎒⊛∅⤙🎐♿ £12.00-£21.00* (all cards) *reception@blackbeck.net*

Hill of Oaks and Blakeholm Caravan Estate, Tower Wood LA12 8NR ☏ (01539) 531578 Fax (01539) 530431 OS map 96/385894 2½m N of Newby Bridge on A592 (Windermere) Open Mar-Nov 16 258 pitches (215 static) Hard standings, sheltered 🖬🎒𝄞∅♿ bathing, fishing, boating (private lake frontage), lakeside picnic area £17.50-£19.50* *enquiries@hilloftoaks.co.uk www.hilloftoaks.co.uk*

Oak Head Caravan Park, Ayside LA11 6JA ☏ (01539) 531475 Prop: S Scott OS map 96/389839 1m SE of Newby Bridge off A590 (Grange over Sands) at Ayside Open Mar-Oct 130 pitches (70 static) 5 acres level/sloping grass, and hard standings, sheltered 🖬🎒𝄞⊛∅♿ £10.00-£12.00

Park Cliffe Camping and Caravan Estate, Birks Road LA23 3PG ☏ (01539) 531344 OS map 96/391911 3m NE of Newby Bridge off A592 (Windermere) Open Mar-Oct 200 pitches (50 static) 25 acres hard standings and level/sloping grass, sheltered 🖬✗🍷⤙⤚🖬🎒𝄞⊛∅⤙🎐 £17.50-£21.00 (Mastercard/Visa) *info@parkcliffe.co.uk www.parkcliffe.co.uk*

For other sites near Newby Bridge see also Ulverston and Windermere

PATTERDALE, Cumbria **Map B5**
SEE Aira Force, Helvellyn 3,200ft, Ullswater
🏛 2m NW at Glenridding ☏ (01768) 482414 ✗ Patterdale ☏ (01768) 482231

Gillside Farm, Glenridding CA11 0QQ ☏ (01768) 482346 Prop: Messrs Lightfoot OS map 90/385175 1m N of Patterdale on A592 (Penrith) Open Mar-Oct 90 pitches (25 static) Grass, level, some hard standings 🖬🎒𝄞⊛∅🎐 dairy produce £12.00-£14.50 *gillside@btconnect.com www.gillsidecaravanandcampingsite.co.uk*

Sykeside Camping Park, Brotherswater CA11 0NZ ☏ (01768) 482239 Fax (01768) 482558 OS map 90/408132 3m S of Patterdale on A592 (Windermere) Open all year 80 pitches Level grass and hard standing 🖬✗🍷⤙⤚🖬🎒𝄞⊛∅🏠 £13.50-£15.00 (all cards exc Amex) *info@sykeside.co.uk www.sykeside.co.uk*

PENRITH, Cumbria   Map C4
EC Wed MD Tues SEE castle ruins, monuments in St Andrew's church, old inns, Brougham castle 2m SE
⬛ Penrith museum, Middlegate ✆ (01768) 867466
✘ George, Devonshire St ✆ (01768) 862696
Lowther Caravan Park, Elysian Fields, Eamont Bridge CA10 2JB ✆ (01768) 863631 OS map 90/524282 1m S of Penrith on A6 (Shap) Open Mar-Oct–no adv booking 575 pitches (375 static) Level grass and hard standing, sheltered 🛁✘⚊↗⬛🔲⬰⊕∅⤵🛝♿ fishing
Thacka Lea Caravan Park, Thacka Lea CA11 9HX ✆ (01768) 863319 OS map 90/509308 ½m N of Penrith off A6 (Carlisle) Open Mar-Oct 25 pitches Grass and hard standing, level/sloping, sheltered 🔲⬰ £10.00
For other sites near Penrith see Melmerby, Penruddock, Pooley Bridge and Watermillock

PENRUDDOCK, Cumbria   Map C4
✘ Swiss Chalet 3m SE at Pooley Bridge ✆ (01768) 483215
Beckses Caravan Park CA11 0RX ✆ (01768) 483224 Fax (01768) 483006 OS map 90/418278 1m W of Penruddocck on B5288 (Greystoke-Keswick) adj Beckses Garage Open Easter-Oct 31 45 pitches (18 static) 3 acres level/sloping grass, hard standings, sheltered 🛁⬛🔲⬰⊕∅⬰🛝🅿🔲 £6.50 (min)*
Gill Head Farm, Troutbeck CA11 0ST ✆ (017687) 79652 Fax (017687) 79130 OS map 90/380269 3m SW of Penruddock off A66 (Keswick) on right of A5091 (Ullswater) Open April-Oct 55 pitches 15 acres level grass and hard standings, sheltered 🛁⚊⬛🔲⬰⊕∅ fishing £10.00 (min)* *gillhead@talk21.com www.gillheadfarm.co.uk*
Hopkinsons, Berrier CA11 0XB ✆ (01768) 483456 OS map 90/405289 3m NW of Penruddock off A66 (Keswick) at Sportsman Inn on Hutton Roof road–signposted Open Mar-Oct 248 pitches (167 static) Level grass and hard standing, sheltered 🛁🔲🔲⬰⊕∅⊕⤵♿ games room
Thanet Well Caravan Park, Greystoke CA11 0XX *Family site in rolling countryside* ✆ (01768) 484262 OS map 90/397351 5m N of Penruddock via Greystoke and Lamonby road (signposted) Open Mar-Oct 85 pitches (65 static) Grass and hard standings, part level, sheltered 🛁⬛🔲⬰⊕∅⤵🔲
For other sites near Penruddock see also Threlkeld

POOLEY BRIDGE, Cumbria   Map C4
SEE Ullswater, Iron Age fort W
⬛ Finkle St ✆ (01768) 486530
✘ Howtown 4m SW at Howtown ✆ (01768) 486514
Hill Croft Caravan Park CA10 2LT ✆ (01768) 486363 OS map 90/476243 ½m E of Pooley Bridge on Roehead road Open Mar-Oct 325 pitches (200 static) 10 acres, part sloping grass and hard standing 🛁↗⬛🔲⬰⊕∅⤵♿ £15.00-£20.00*
Park Foot Caravan Camping Park, Howtown Road CA10 2NA ✆ (017684) 86309 OS map 90/469235 1m S of Pooley Bridge on lakeside road Open Easter-Oct 430 pitches (130 static) Caravans, grass and hard standing; tents, grass, part level, sheltered 🛁✘⚊⬛🔲⬰⊕∅ ⊕⤵🔲📷♿ bar meals, lake access for water sports, tennis, pony trekking, fell walking, children's club, bike hire £10.00-£21.00 (most cards) *holidays@parkfootullswater.co.uk www.parkfootullswater.co.uk*
Waterfoot Caravan Park CA11 0JF ✆ (01768) 486302 Fax (01768) 486728 OS map 90/462243 ½m W of Pooley Bridge on A592 (Penrith-Ullswater) Open Mar-mid Nov 180 pitches (123 static)–no tents–adv booking by phone only Level/sloping grass and hard standing, sheltered 🛁🔲⬛🔲⬰⊕∅⤵📷♿ £12.00-£16.00* inc elect *enquiries@waterfootpark.co.uk www.waterfootpark.co.uk*

PORT CARLISLE–see Bowness on Solway

RAVENGLASS, Cumbria   Map A5
EC Sat SEE narrow gauge railway, Muncaster castle and gardens, museum
✘ Pennington Arms, Main St ✆ (01229) 717222
Walls Caravan-Camping Park CA18 1SR ✆ (01229) 717250 Fax (01229) 717250 OS map 96/088965 ½m E of Ravenglass off A595 Gosforth-Bootle road Open Mar-Oct 60 pitches 5 acres grass and hard standings, sheltered 🛁⬛🔲⬰⊕∅📷 £5.00-£13.00* *wallscaravanpark@ravenglass98.freeserve.co.uk www.ravenglass98.freeserve.co.uk*

SEDBERGH, Cumbria   Map C5
EC Thurs MD Wed SEE parish church, Quaker meeting house
⬛ 72 Main St ✆ (01539) 620125
✘ Oakdene Country, Garsdale Rd ✆ (01539) 620280
Pinfold Caravan Park LA10 5JL ✆ (01539) 620576 OS map 98/667919 ½m E of Sedbergh on Hawes road Open Mar-Oct 84 pitches (56 static)–adv bkg for caravans only Level grass and hard standing, sheltered 🔲⬛🔲⬰⊕∅ (all cards)

At fringe of Lake District

Seacote Caravan Park

On seafront by beach adjoining historic award-winning village

Headland walks, golf, hotel bar, restaurant, entertainment

Tourers, tents, caravan hire ☎(01946) 822777

SILLOTH, Cumbria   **Map A3**
EC Tues SEE Hadrian's Wall
🄰 10 Criffel St ☎(01697) 331944 ✗Golf, Criffel St ☎(01697) 331438

Hylton Park Holiday Centre, Eden Street CA5 4AY ☎(01697) 331707 Fax (01697) 325555 OS
   map 85/113534 ½m S of Silloth on B5300 (Maryport) Open Mar-Nov 15 257 pitches (213 static)
   Level grass, sheltered 🄑🄓🄐🄔🄖 £13.40-£16.50* (most cards) enquiries@stanwix.com
   www.stanwix.com

Moordale Caravan Park CA7 4JZ ☎(01697) 331375 Prop: A & M Ruckledge OS map 85/105518
   2m S of Silloth on B5300 (Maryport) adj golf course and beach Open Mar-Oct 118 pitches (65
   static) 7 acres level grass and hard standings 🄓🄐🄔🄖 £11.00-£13.00
   www.moordalepark.com

Rowanbank Caravan Park, Beckfoot CA7 4LA Quiet family run coastal site ☎(01697) 331653 Fax
   (01697) 331653 OS map 85/096497 2m SW of Silloth on B5300 (Maryport) in
   Beckfoot–signposted Open Mar 1-Nov 15 50 pitches 3½ acres level grass and hard standing,
   part sheltered 🄑🄓🄐🄔🄖 £6.50-10.00*

Seacote Caravan Park, Skinburness Road CA5 4QJ ☎(01697) 331121 OS map 85/105550 1m N
   of Silloth on Skirnburness road Open Mar 1-Nov 15 100 pitches (80 static)–no tents Level grass
   and hard standings sheltered 🄓🄐🄔🄖

The Solway Holiday Village CA7 4QQ ☎(01697) 331236 OS map 85/118548 ½m N of Silloth off
   Skinburness road Open Mar-Oct 300 pitches (200 static) 120 acres level grass and hard
   standing 🄑🄒🄓🄐🄔🄖(large screen) 🄷🄸 golf, pool and snooker, health studio,
   bowling alley, sports hall, tennis, kids

Stanwix Park Holiday Centre, Greenrow CA5 4HH ☎(01697) 332666 Fax (01697) 332555 OS
   map 85/108527 1m S of Silloth on B5300 (Maryport) Open all year exc Christmas 348 pitches
   (221 static) Level grass, sheltered 🄑✗🄒🄐🄔🄖(heated) 🄗🄘 indoor leisure centre, tenpin bowling, dancing, pony trekking £15.25-£18.55*
   (Mastercard/Visa/Switch) enquiries@stanwix.com www.stanwix.com

Tanglewood Caravan Park, Causeway Head CA5 4PE ☎(01697) 331253 OS map 85/131534 1m
   E of Silloth on B5302 (Wigton) Open Mar-Feb–must book peak periods 90 pitches (59 static)
   Level grass and hard standing, sheltered 🄑🄒🄓🄐🄔🄖 club house £12.00*
   tanglewoodcaravanpark@hotmail.com www.tanglewoodcaravanpark.co.ul

STAVELEY–see Kendal

TEBAY, Cumbria   **Map C5**
✗Tebay Mountain Lodge, Orton ☎(015396) 24351

Tebay Caravan Park, Orton CA10 3SB ☎(01539) 624511 OS map 91/608061 Signposted from
   Westmorland sevice areas on M6 between junctions 38 and 39 Open Mar-Oct 70 pitches–no
   tents Hard standings, sheltered 🄑✗🄓🄐🄔🄖 £10.50-£13.20 (most cards)
   caravans@westmorland.com www.tebaycaravanpark.co.uk

ULVERSTON, Cumbria   **Map B6**
EC Wed MD Thurs SEE parish church, crystal works, Laurel and Hardy museum, Swarthmoor Hall
🄰 Coronation Hall, County Sq ☎(01229) 587120
✗Bay Horse, Canal Foot ☎(01229) 53972

Bardsea Leisure Park, Priory Road LA12 9QE Former quarry attractively landscaped ☎(01229)
   584712 Fax (01229) 580413 OS map 97/296765 1m S of Ulverston on A5087 (Bardsea) Open
   all year 171 pitches (88 static) 10 acres level grass and hard standings, sheltered
   🄑🄓🄐🄔🄖 £7.00-£20.00* (all cards) reception@bardsealeisure.co.uk
   www.bardsealeisure.co.uk

For more up-to-date information, and for links to camping websites, visit our site at:
www.butford.co.uk/camping

WATERMILLOCK, Cumbria											Map C4
SEE Ullswater, Aira Force 2m SW
✗ Pooley Bridge Inn 3m NE at Pooley Bridge ☏(01768) 483215

Cove Caravan Camping Park CA11 0LS ☏(01768) 486549 Fax (01768) 486549 OS map 90/431236 1½m N of Watermillock off A592 (Penrith) at Brackenrigg Inn on Penruddock road Open Mar-Oct 89 pitches (38 static) 5 acres level/sloping grass and hard standings, sheltered ⛟🖥💷🅿♿⚡🅢✓🏪♿ £10.00-£15.00* info@cove-park.co.uk www.cove-park.co.uk

Knotts Hill Caravan Chalet Park CA11 0JR ☏(01768) 486328 OS map 90/435218 1m W of Watermillock off A592 (Windermere) at Gowbarrow Lodge Open Mar-Oct 45 pitches–no tents Level/gently sloping woodland, hard standings 💷🅿⚡🅢🏪🏠

Quiet Site CA11 0LS Good facilities, charming location ☏(01768) 486337 Fax (01768) 486610 OS map 90/431237 2m N of Watermillock off Penruddock road Open Mar-Nov 83 pitches Grass and hard standing, level/sloping, part sheltered ⛟🚻🖥💷🅿⚡🅢✓🏪🏪♿ tent storage, children's room £10.00-£18.00* info@thequietsite.co.uk www.thequietsite.co.uk

Ullswater Caravan Camping and Marine Park CA11 0LR ☏(01768) 486666 Fax (01768) 486095 OS map 90/436230 ½m SW of Watermillock off A592 (Windermere) near junct 40 of M6 Open Mar-Nov 210 pitches (sep area for tents) (55 static) 7 acres grass and hard standing, level/sloping, part sheltered ⛟🚻🛁🖥💷🅿⚡🅢✓🏪🏠♿ boat launching and mooring 1 mile £10.00-£15.00* (Mastercard/Visa/Switch/Delta) info@uccmp.co.uk www.uccmp.co.uk

WHITEHAVEN, Cumbria											Map A4
EC Wed MD Thurs, Sat SEE museum in market hall, pottery craft centre, St Bees Head
ℹ Market Place ☏(01946) 852939
✗ Roseneath, Low Moresby ☏(01946) 61572

Seacote Park CA27 0ET ☏(01946) 822777 Prop: Mr & Mrs Milburn OS map 89/962119 3m S of Whitehaven off B5345 (St Bees) Open all year 300 pitches (200 static) 22 acres level/sloping grass and hard standings ⛟🚻🖥💷✓ £7.00-£14.00 (most cards) reception@seacote.com www.seacote.com

Seven Acres Caravan Park, Holmrook CA19 1XD Situated at entrance to valleys of Eskdale and Wosdale ☏(01946) 822777 Prop: Mr & Mrs Milburn OS map 89/123456 Midway between Gosforth and Holmark on A595 Open all year 65 pitches Level grass 🖥💷💷⚡🅢✓🏪🏪♿ £12.00-£15.00 (most cards) reception@seacote.com www.sevenacres.info

WIGTON, Cumbria											Map B3
EC Wed MD Tues SEE St Mary's church
✗ Wheyrigg Hall 3m W on B5302 (Silloth) ☏(01697) 361242

Clea Hall Holiday Park, Westward CA7 8NQ ☏(01697) 342880 OS map 85/274499 4½m S of Wigton off B5305 (Penrith) Open Mar-Oct 106 pitches (90 static) Level/sloping grass ⛟🚻🅢🖥💷🏪🏪 baths, library, lounge

WINDERMERE, Cumbria											Map B5
EC Thurs SEE lake, steamboat museum, viewpoint of Orrest Head, aquarium, Belle Isle
ℹ Victoria St ☏(015394) 46499
✗ Applegarth, College Rd ☏(01539) 443206

Fallbarrow Park, Bowness on Windermere LA23 3DL ☏(01539) 444422 Fax (01539) 488736 OS map 96/402972 1m SW of Windermere centre on A592 (Ullswater-Newby Bridge) by lake Open Mar-Nov 15–must book peak periods 340 pitches (248 static)–no tents Level grass and hard standing, sheltered ⛟✗🚻🅢↗🖥💷💷⚡🅢✓🏪🏪 serviced pitches, slipway, boating, swimming £17.00-£24.00* (all major cards) enquiries@southlakeland-caravans.co.uk www.southlakeland-caravans.co.uk

Ings Caravan Park, Ings LA8 9QF ☏(01539) 821426 OS map 97/444990 2m E of Windermere off A591 (Kendal) near Ings Garage Open Mar-Oct 71 pitches (58 static) Level grass and hard standing 🖥💷💷⚡🅢🏪

Lambhowe Caravan Park, Lyth Valley, Crosthwaite LA8 8JE Well-run site within reach of lake ☏(01539) 568483 OS map 97/423915 5m SE of Windermere on A5074 (Howe) Open Mar-Nov 15–must book peak periods 125 pitches (111 static) Grass and hard standings, level, sheltered 🚻🖥💷🅢⚡🅢

Limefitt Park LA23 1PA ☏(01539) 432300 OS map 90/416030 4m N of Windermere on A592 (Ullswater) Open Easter-Oct 210 pitches (45 static) Grass and hard standing, level/sloping ⛟🚻🅢↗🖥💷💷⚡🅢✓🏪🏪 fishing £11.00-£17.00 inc elect (most cards) enquiries@southlakeland-caravans.co.uk www.southlakeland-caravans.co.uk/parks/1117/view

White Cross Bay Leisure Park and Marina, Ambleside Road LA23 1LF ☏(01539) 443937 OS map 90/393006 1½m NW of Windermere on A591 (Ambleside) Open Mar-Nov–must book public holidays 312 pitches (187 static)–no tents Level grass and hard standings, sheltered ⛟✗🚻🅢↗🖥💷💷⚡🅢✓🏪🏪🏠 lake access/slipway, marina, tennis (Mastercard/Visa)

For other sites near Windermere see Ambleside and Kendal

A striking feature of the region is still its diversity of landscape. In the east, between inland Northallerton and the boisterous coastal resorts of Whitby and Scarborough, are the spacious North York Moors, where flat topped heather-clad hills are separated by wooded dales. Since most roads go round rather than through them the

moors are strictly for walkers – who can cross the area in an east-west direction on the Lyke Wake Walk between Ravenscar and Osmotherley. A pleasant centre on the southern edge of the moors, now a national park, is Pickering. Almost as rewarding are the Cleveland and Hambleton Hills, the northern and western extensions of the moors. Sights which ought not to be missed are the majestic twelfth-century ruins of Rievaulx Abbey west of Helmsley and Wade's Causeway, a well-preserved section of Roman road near Hunt House south of Grosmont.

Looping down from seaside Filey to the Humber near industrial Hull are the Wolds, a chalk mass of dry uplands and steep-sided valleys, once used only for sheep grazing but now intensively farmed. In the western half of the region – mainly within the triangle linking Sedbergh, Aysgarth and Skipton – are the sparsely populated and scenic Yorkshire Dales, another national park bisected by the sixty miles long River Ure flowing through Wensleydale. Other dales or valleys, topped by wild fells and stretches of open moor, are Littondale, Wharfedale, Nidderdale, Airedale and – reached via the spectacular Buttertubs Pass – Swaledale. A well-known sight in Airedale is Malham Cove, a great natural amphitheatre 300ft high. Near Hawes In Wensleydale is Hardraw Force, England's

highest waterfall. Often windy and wet, the dales abound in potholes and caverns, the most striking probably being the Victoria Caves beneath Ingleborough Common near Ingleton. The park is crossed by the Dales Way, which follows riverside paths from Ilkley to Windermere.

The east-flowing streams of the dales drop down to the Vale of York, through which the Great North Road rides a ridge not far from the ancient capital and its superb minster.

The low shore of Holderness on the Humber estuary east of the Wolds slopes gradually to Spurn Head, a long spit of sand, but at Boulby near Saltburn in the north are England's highest cliffs. Along the wholly unspoiled coast between these two places are resorts large and small, most at the edge of firm sands. Near Bridlington is Flamborough Head, with its sea-girt caves and tiny bays enclosing pebble beaches.

Getting around in the east is now made much easier by the Humber bridge, a major feat of engineering which spans the river between Barton on the south and Hessle on the north bank.

Campsites are numerous in the northeast. Those inland are often simple; those on the coast, where the choice is greatest, often well equipped.

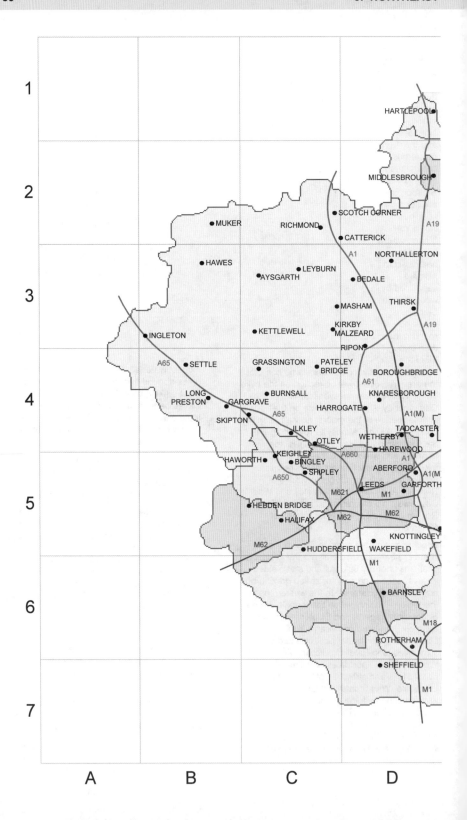

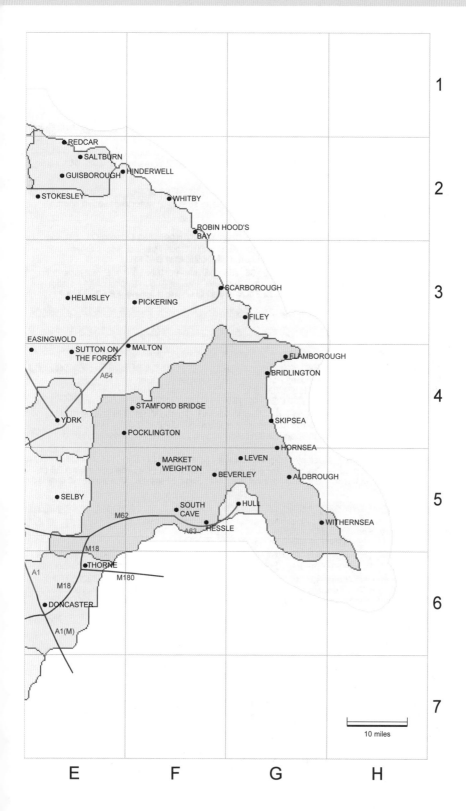

> ### FACTS CAN CHANGE
> We do our best to check the accuracy of the entries in this guide but changes can and do occur after publication. So if you plan to stay at a site some distance from home it makes sense to ring the manager or owner before setting off.

ACASTER MALBIS–see York

ALDBROUGH, E Yorks   Map G5
✗ Medio 10m W at Hull   ☎ (01482) 507070

Royal Hotel, Cliff Top, Seaside Road HU11 4SB   ☎ (01964) 527786   OS map 107/257395   1m NE of Aldbrough on road to beach, near sea   Open Apr-Sept   8 pitches   2 acres mainly level   ✗ (snack) ⚲◢

AYSGARTH, N Yorks   Map C3
EC Wed *Most popular village in Wensleydale* SEE mile long stretch of waterfalls, parish church, carriage museum, Nat Park centre
✗ George and Dragon   ☎ (01969) 663358

Street Head Caravan Site, Newbiggin, Bishopdale DL8 3TE   ☎ (01969) 663472/663571   OS map 98/998861   1½m S of Aysgarth on right of B6160 (Kettlewell)   Open Mar-Oct   100 pitches (50 static)   Grass and hard standing, level, sheltered   ⚲✗⚲⊟⚑◢◉∅⚑

Westholme Caravan Park DL8 3SP   ☎ (01969) 663268   OS map 98/106883   1m E of Aysgarth on A684 (Leyburn)   Open Mar-Oct–must book public holidays and Jul-Aug   113 pitches (44 static) Level grass and hard standing, sheltered   ⚲⚲⊟⚑◢◉∅◉↵   trout fishing   £8.50-£13.00*

ATWICK–see Hornsea

BARDSEY–see Leeds

BARMSTON–see Skipsea

BARNSLEY   Map D6
MD Mon, Wed, Fri, Sa   SEE Cannon Hall Park, Town Hall, Cooper art gallery
🛈 Central Library, Shambles St   ☎ (01266) 206757
✗ The Cock Inn, Pilley Hill, Birdwell   ☎ (01226) 742155

Earths Wood Caravan Park, Bank End Lane, Barnsley Road, Clayton West HD8 9LJ   ☎ (01484) 863211 and 864266   OS map 110/265102   6m NW of Barnsley off A636 (Denby Dale) on High Hoyland road (junction 38 of M1)   Open Mar-Oct   45 pitches   3 acres level grass, sheltered ⊟⚑◉∅⚭

Green Springs Touring Park, Rockley Lane, Worsbrough S75 3DS   ☎ (01226) 288298 *Prop: R Hodgson*   OS map 111/330019   2m S of Barnsley off A61 on Pilley road near junct 36 of M1   Open Apr-Oct   65 pitches   Grass, part level, hard standings, sheltered   ⚑(10 amp) ◢◉⚑🜨 TV hook-up   £9.50*

BEDALE, N Yorks   Map D3
SEE church of St Gregory, market place, Bedale Hall, Snape Castle 3m S
🛈 Bedale Hall, North End   ☎ (01677) 424604
✗ Leeming Motel 1m NE near A1 at Leeming Bar   ☎ (01677) 423611

Boot and Shoe Inn, Thirn HG4 4AU   ☎ (01677) 460219   OS map 99/217860   3m SW of Bedale off Thornton Watlass road   Open Apr-Oct   10 pitches   1 acre gentle slope   ✗ (snack) ⚲ *No showers*

Pembroke Caravan Park, Leases Road, Leeming Bar DL7 9BW   ☎ (01677) 422608/422652   OS map 99/285905   2m NE of Bedale off A684 (Northallerton) near A1 (good A1 stopover)   Open Apr-Sept   25 pitches   Level grass, sheltered, some hard standings   ⚲↵⚑◢◉∅⚑⊟   £8.00-12.00

BEVERLEY, E Yorks   Map F5
MD Wed, Sat   SEE Minster, North Bar Museum, market cross
🛈 Butcher Rd   ☎ (01482) 867430
✗ Beverley Arms, North Bar Within   ☎ (01482) 869241

Lakeminster Park, Hull Road, Woodmansey HU17 0PN   ☎ (01482) 882655   OS map 107/049384   1m SE of Beverley on A1174 (Hull)   Open all year   80 pitches (30 static)   Level grass, sheltered ⚲⚲↵⊟⚑◢◉∅⊠⚑✤🏠   fishing

BINGLEY, Bradford   Map C5
EC Tues MD Wed, Fri, Sat   SEE All Saints Church, stocks, cross and market house, Leeds-Liverpool canal locks
✗ Bankfield, Bradford Rd   ☎ (01274) 567123

Harden and Bingley Caravan Park, Harden BD16 1DF   ☎ (01535) 273810   OS map 104/089379   2m SW of Bingley off B6429 (Harden) near Malt Shovel Inn   Open Apr-Oct   96 pitches (81 static) 3 acres level/sloping grass and hard standing, sheltered   ⚲⊟⚑◢◉∅⚑   woodland walks

BISHOPTHORPE–see York

BOROUGHBRIDGE, N Yorks   **Map D4**
EC Thurs MD Mon SEE Roman Museum at Aldborough
🛈Fishergate ✆(01423) 323373
✗Crown, Horsefair ✆(01423) 322328
Bluebell Caravan Park, Kirby Hill YO5 9DN ✆(01423) 322380 OS map 99/392680 1m N of
   Boroughbridge on B6265 (Ripon) Open May-Sept 10 pitches Grass, sloping
Old Hall Caravan Park, Langthorpe YO5 9BZ ✆(01423) 322130/323190 OS map 99/391673 ½m
   W of Boroughbridge off B6265 (Ripon) Open Apr-Oct 120 pitches (98 static) Level grass
   🖪🚌🖊❂🖉❂🚻🛒🚰

BRIDLINGTON, E Yorks   **Map G4**
EC Thurs MD Wed, Sat SEE Bayle Gate, museum, zoo, Sewerby Hall and Park, Flamborough Head
2m NE
🛈Prince St ✆(01262) 673474
✗Martonian Inn, 35 Jewison Lane, Sewerby ✆(01262) 675179 Open 6-9.30
Poplars Touring Park, 45 Jewison Lane, Sewerby YO15 1DX ✆(01262) 677251 *Prop: Judith*
   Truelove OS map 101/196699 2m NE of Bridlington off Flamborough road adj motel Open Mar-
   Nov 30 pitches Grass and hard standing, sheltered 🚌🖉❂🖉 hotel and pub near £9.00-£14.50
   www.the-poplars.co.uk
Fir Tree Park, Jewison Lane YO16 5YG ✆(01262) 676442 Fax (01262) 676442 OS map
   101/192701 2m N of Bridlington off A165 (Scarborough) on B1255 (Flamborough) Open Apr-Oct
   446 pitches (401 static)–no tents 25 acres level grass and hard standing
   🛒✗🍴🏕🖪🚌🖉❂🖉🚰(indoor heated) ❂🍴🚻🚮🛒 *info@flowerofmay.com*
   www.flowerofmay.com
Thorpe Hall Caravan Camping Park, Rudston YO25 4JE ✆(01262) 420393/420574 *Prop: Sir Ian*
   MacDonald of Sleat OS map 101/109677 4½m W of Bridlington on B1253 (Rudston) Open Mar-
   Oct 90 pitches Grass, level, sheltered 🛒🖪🚌🖉❂🖉❂🍴🚻🛒 baths, fishing £7.00-£21.00
   (Mastercard, Visa, Maestro, Solo) *caravansite@thorpehall.co.uk www.thorpehall.co.uk*

CASTLE HOWARD–see Malton

CAWOOD–see Selby

CLAPHAM–see Ingleton

CONSTABLE BURTON–see Leyburn

EASINGWOLD, N Yorks   **Map E4**
EC Wed MD Fri SEE market cross, Bull Ring, Byland Abbey
🛈Chapel Lane ✆(01347) 821530
✗George, Market Pl ✆(01347) 821698
Easingwold Caravan Camping Park, Thirsk Road Y06 3NF ✆(01347) 821479 OS map
   100/510708 1m N of Easingwold on A19 (Thirsk) Open Mar-Oct 50 pitches (30 static) 5 acres
   grass, gentle slope/level, sheltered 🚌🖉❂
Holly Brook Caravan Park, Pennycarr Lane, off Stillington Road YO61 3EU ✆(01347) 821906 OS
   map 100/534684 1m SE of Easingwold off Stillington road Open Mar-Dec 30 pitches–adults only
   Level grass and hard standing, sheltered 🖪🚌🖉❂🖉🚻🛒🚮 fridge/freezer, microwave, small
   library
The Alders Caravan Park, Home Farm, Alne YO61 1RY ✆(01347) 838722 OS map 100/497654
   2m SW of Easingwold in Alne Open Mar-Oct 40 pitches 6 acres level grass 🚌🖉❂🖉🛒 £7.00-
   £10.25 *www.alderscaravanpark.co.uk*

FANGFOSS–see Stamford Bridge

FILEY, N Yorks   **Map G3**
EC Wed SEE Promenade Gardens, beach
🅸 John St ☎ (01723) 383637
✘ Crown 7½mNW at Scarborough ☎ (01723) 373491

Blue Dolphin Holiday Park, Gristhorpe Bay YO14 9PU ☎ (01723) 515155 OS map 101/090833
  2m N of Filey on A165 (Scarborough)–signposted Open all year 701 pitches (272 static) 12
  acres level grass 🅱✘♀⚲⌁⌂💧🅱⌀⊕∅⟋▭(heated) ⊕⌄🏠 disco, cabaret, putting green
  www.havenholidays.co.uk

Filey Brigg Touring Caravan Site and Country Park, North Cliff YO14 9ET ☎ (01723) 513852 OS
  map 101/120814 ½m N of Filey centre on Church Cliff Drive Open Mar 25-Oct 30 140 pitches
  🅱✘🅱⌀⌀⊕⊕♿ path to beach £6.50-£14.00* (all cards)

Lebberston Touring Caravan Park, Lebberston YO11 3PE ☎ (01723) 585723 OS map
  101/081822 3m NW of Filey off A165 (Scarborough) on B1261 (Lebberston) Open Mar-Oct 75
  pitches–no tents 7½ acres level/sloping grass and hard standing, sheltered 🅱(mobile)
  ⌁🅱🅱⌀⊕∅⊕
  dog walk, separate pitches £11.50-£17.00* (Mastercard/Visa/Switch/Delta)
  info@lebberstontouring.co.uk www.lebberstontouring.co.uk

Muston Grange Caravan Park YO14 0HU ☎ (01723) 512167 Prop: Bell Elliot Leisure Ltd OS map
  101/1137797 1½m SW of Filey on A1039 (Bridlington) Open Mar-Oct 240 pitches–no tents
  10 acres level, hard standing 🅱🅱🅱⌀⊕⌄♿ £9.50-£15.00* (most cards)
  www.mustongrange.co.uk

Reighton Sands Holiday Village, Reighton Gap YO14 9SJ ☎ (01723) 890476 OS map
  101/145759 4m SE of Filey off A165 (Bridlington) Open Mar-Sept 657 pitches (135 static)
  Grass, part level, hard standings 🅱✘♀⚲⌁⌂🅱🅱⌀⊕∅⟋▭⌄

Spring Willows Caravan Park, Main Road, Staxton YO12 4SB ☎ (01723) 891505 Fax (01723)
  892123 OS map 101/023799 3m W of Filey on A1039 (Staxton) via Muston Open Mar-Jan 184
  pitches Grass and hard standing, sheltered 🅱✘♀⌂🅱🅱⌀⊕∅⟋▭(indoor) ⊕⌄⬜🅱♿ sauna,
  solarium, games room, lounge, children (Mastercard/Switch/Delta/Visa)
  fun4all@springwillows.fsnet.co.uk www.springwillows.co.uk

For other sites near Filey see Scarborough

FLAMBOROUGH, E Yorks   **Map G4**
SEE St Oswald's church, lighthouse, museum, Flamborough Head 5m NE, Danes Dyke 3m NE
✘ Royal Dog and Duck, Tower St ☎ (01262) 850206

Old Mill Caravan Park, Bempton YO16 5XD ☎ (01262) 673565 OS map 101/183705 2m W of
  Flamborough off B1255 (Bridlington) at Marton Open Apr-Oct 55 pitches–no tents Level grass
  and hard standing, sheltered 🅱🅱⊕∅🅱⌄

FYLINGDALES–see Whitby

FYLINGTHORPE–see Robin Hood

GALPHAY–see Kirkby Malzeard

GARGRAVE, N Yorks   **Map B4**
SEE Eshton Hall N
✘ Masons Arms, Marton Rd ☎ (01756) 749304

Eshton Road Caravan Park, Eshton Road BD23 3PN ☎ (01756) 749229 Prop: Fred Green & Son
  Ltd OS map 103/936546 ¼m NE of Gargrave centre on Hetton road by Liverpool–Leeds canal
  Open all year 40 pitches (20 static) 1 acre level grass and hard standing, sheltered 🅱🅱⌀⊕
  £10.00-£15.00

GRASSINGTON, N Yorks   **Map C4**
EC Thurs SEE old moorland lead mines, museum, Linton church
🅸 National Park Centre, Hebden Rd ☎ (01756) 752774
✘ The Devonshire Arms, Grassington Rd, Cracoe ☎ (01756) 730237 Open 12-2/6.30-9

Howgill Lodge, Barden BD23 6DJ ☎ (01756) 720655 OS map 104/065592 6m SE of Grassington
  off B6160 (Ilkley) Open Mar-Oct 40 pitches Level grass and hard standing 🅱✘🅱🅱⌀⊕∅⟋⊡
  B&B £12.50-£18.00* (all cards) info@howgill-lodge.co.uk www@howgill-lodge.co.uk

Threaplands House Farm, Cracoe BD23 6LD ☎ (01756) 730248 Prop: JC Wade OS map
  98/986606 2m S of Grassington off B6265 (Skipton) Open Mar-Oct 30 pitches 8 acres level
  grass 🅱🅱⌀⊕🅱⌂♿ £8.50

Wood Nook Caravan Site, Skirethorns, Threshfield BD23 5NU ☎ (01756) 752412 Fax (01756)
  752946 OS map 98/974641 1¾m W of Grassington off Threshfield road Open Mar-Oct 40
  pitches (10 static) Level/sloping grass and hard standings, sheltered 🅱🅱🅱⌀⊕∅⌄⊡ (most
  cards) bookings@woodnook.net www.woodnook.net

MUSTON GRANGE CARAVAN PARK

Muston Grange has much to offer the Caravanner.
A quiet friendly touring park within easy walking distance of
the picturesque seaside resort of Filey.

Muston Road, Filey North Yorkshire YO14 OHU. Tel: (01723) 512167

GREAT BROUGHTON–see Stokesley

GUISBOROUGH, Redcar & Cleveland   Map E2
EC Wed MD Thurs, Sat SEE Upleathen Church, smallest in England
✗ Moor Cock, West End Rd ✆ (01287) 632342

Tocketts Mill Caravan Park, off Skelton Road TS14 6QA ✆ (01287) 610182 OS map 94/626182
2m NE of Guisborough off A173 (Skelton) Open Mar-Oct 100 pitches (75 static) Level grass,
sheltered ⚑🅱🎪⌀❀⌀↩

HAREWOOD, N Yorks   Map D4
SEE Harewood House 1m SW
✗ Ladbroke 6m E at Wetherby ✆ (01937) 563881

Maustin Caravan Park, Kearby cum Netherby LS22 4DP ✆ (0113) 288 6234 OS map 104/344474
3m NE of Harewood on A61 Harrogate road Open Mar-Oct 100 pitches (80 static)–no facs for
children Level grass, sheltered ✗⚑⌀⌀🅱🎪❀⌀⌷🏠⛟ bowling green
(Mastercard/Visa/Switch)

HARROGATE, N Yorks   Map D4
EC Wed MD daily SEE Valley Gardens, The Stray, Pump Room Museum, moors and dales, Ripley
Castle 4m NW
🅸 Royal Baths Assembly Rooms, Crescent Rd ✆ (01423) 537300
✗ Bay Horse Inn, Burnt Yates ✆ (01423) 770230

Bilton Park, Village Farm, Bilton Lane HG1 4DH ✆ (01423) 863121/565070 OS map 104/318573
2m NE of Harrogate off A59 ring road at Skipton Hotel Open Apr-Oct 95 pitches (70 static) Level
grass 🛢🎪⌀❀↩🏠 farm produce, fishing biltonpark@tcsmail.net

Chequers Inn Motor Lodge, Bishop Thornton HG3 3JN ✆ (01423) 770173 OS map 99/268638
6m NNW of Harrogate off A59 (Knaresborough) and B6165 (Ripley) Open Apr-Oct 70 pitches
(50 static) Level grass, sheltered ✗⚑🅱🎪⌀❀ horse riding

High Moor Farm, Skipton Road HG3 2LT ✆ (01423) 563637/564955 Fax (01423) 529449 OS map
104/244559 4m W of Harrogate on A59 (Skipton) Open Apr-Oct 340 pitches (180 static) Level
grass and hard standing 🛢✗⚑⌀↗🅱🎪⌀❀⌀⌷❀↩🏠⛟ lic club, golf £12.00-£14.00*
(most cards)

Ripley Caravan Park, Ripley HG3 3AU ✆ (01423) 770050 OS map 104/291599 3½m N of
Harrogate off A61 (Ripon) on B6165 (Knaresborough) Open Easter-Oct 100 pitches Level grass
and hard standings 🛢🅱🎪⌀❀⌀⌀⌷(indoor-heated) ❀↩🏠⛟ nursery playroom, sauna
£11.00-£13.50* (most cards) ripleycaravanpark@talk21.com

Rudding Holiday Park, Follifoot HG3 1JH Set in grounds of Rudding Park ✆ (01423) 870439
Prop: S Mackaness OS map 104/345302 2m SE of Harrogate off A661 (Wetherby) Open Mar-
Jan 141 pitches (80 static) Level/sloping grass and hard standing, sheltered
🛢✗⚑🎪↗🅱🎪⌀❀⌀⌀⌷(outdoor-heated) ❀↩🏠⛟ 18 hole golf course, serviced pitches
£8.50-£28.00 (all cards) holiday-park@ruddingpark.com www.ruddingpark.com

Shaws Trailer Park, Knaresborough Road HG2 7NE ✆ (01423) 884432 OS map 104/325557 1m
E of Harrogate on A59 (Knaresborough) Open all year 211 pitches (146 static) Level/sloping
grass and hard standings 🅱🎪⌀❀🏠 £8.00-£10.00

HATFIELD–see Thorne

HAWES, N Yorks   Map B3
EC Wed MD Tues SEE Waterfalls
🅸 Dales Countryside Museum, Station Yard ✆ (01969) 666210
✗ Simonstone Hall, Simonstone ✆ (01969) 667255

Bainbridge Ings Caravan Camping Site DL8 3NU ✆ (01969) 667354 Prop: Mark & Janet Facer
OS map 98/875894 ½m E of Hawes off A684 (Leyburn) Open Apr-Oct 85 pitches (15 static)
Level grass and hard standings 🅱🎪⌀❀⌷ £9.50-£10.00 janet@bainbridge-ings.co.uk
www.bainbridge-ings.co.uk

Shaw Ghyll, Simonstone DL8 3LY ✆ (01969) 667359 Prop: Roger Stott OS map 98/865933 2m N
of Hawes on Muker road Open Mar-Oct 30 pitches 3 acres level grass, sheltered 🎪❀⌀⌀↩
£10.00 rogerstott@aol.com

✕ RESTAURANTS

The restaurants recommended in this guide are of three kinds – pubs, independent restaurants and those forming part of hotels and motels. They all serve lunch and dinner – at a reasonable price – say under £10 a head. We shall be glad to have your comments on any you use this season and if you think they are not up to standard, please let us have your suggestions for alternatives.

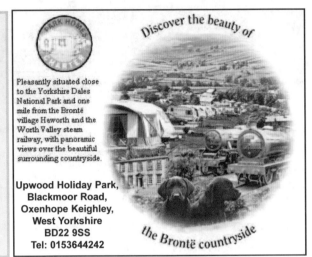

HAWORTH, Bradford   Map C5
SEE Old Vicarage (home of Bronte sisters), Keighley steam railway
ℹ️ 2 West Lane ☎ (01535) 642313
✕ Old White Lion ☎ (01535) 642313

Upwood Holiday Park, Blackmoor Rd, Oxenhope BD22 9SS ☎ (01535) 644242 OS map 104/044355 1m SE of Haworth at Oxenhope Open Mar 1-Jan 4 150 pitches (45 static) Grass and hard standings, gentle slope, open ✕♀➝🚿🚽⌀⊕∅⊡⊗⤴💧🚰🦽 £9.00-£16.50 (Mastercard/Visa/Switch) caravan@upwoodholidaypark.fsnet.co.uk www.upwoodholidaypark.fsnet.co.uk

HEBDEN BRIDGE, Calderdale   Map C5
SEE Weavers' cottages, Hardcastle Crags 3m NW
ℹ️ Bridge Gate ☎ (01422) 843831
✕ Pack Horse Inn, Widdop ☎ (01422) 842803

High Greenwood House, Heptonstall HX7 7AZ ☎ (01422) 842287 OS map 103/969308 3½m NW of Hebden Bridge off A646 (Todmorden) on Widdop road Open Apr-Oct 50 pitches 5 acres, level/sloping grass and hard standings 🚽⌀🚰 £8.00-£10.00*

HELMSLEY, N Yorks   Map E3
EC Wed MD Fri SEE Castle ruins, Rievaulx Terrace frescoes 2m NW, Rievaulx Abbey 3m NW, N Yorks moors
ℹ️ Helmsley Castle ☎ (01439) 770173
✕ Gepetto's Restaurant, 8 Bridge St ☎ (01439) 770479

Foxholme Touring Caravan and Camping Park, Harome YO62 5JG Peaceful site in wooded countryside ☎ (01439) 770416 Prop: KJR Binks & Sons OS map 100/661831 4m SE of Helmsley off A170 (Pickering) Open Apr-Oct 60 pitches–adults only Level grass, some hard standings, sheltered 🛁🚽🚰⌀⊕∅ £12.50

Golden Square Caravan Park, Golden Square, Oswaldkirk YO6 5YQ ☎ (01439) 788269 Fax (01439) 788236 OS map 100/605798 2m S of Helmsley off B1257 (Malton) on Ampleforth road Open Mar-Oct 129 pitches Level grass and hard standing, sheltered
🛁➝🏹🚽🚰⌀⊕∅⊗⤴🚰(25-45) ⊡🏠🦽🚿 luxury toilet block, fishing, swimming, pony trekking near £9.00-£13.00* barbara@goldensquarecaravanpark.com www.goldensquarecaravanpark.com

Wombleton Caravan Park, Moorfield Lane, Wombleton YO62 5RY ☎ (01751) 431684 OS map 100/665827 3m SE of Helmsley off A170 (Pickering) on Wombleton road Open Mar-Oct 118 pitches Level grass and hard standing, sheltered 🛁🚽🚰⌀⊕∅🚰

Wren's of Ryedale Touring Park, Nawton YO62 7SD ☎ (01439) 771260 Prop: GD & LJ Smith OS map 100/656841 3m E of Helmsley off A170 (Pickering) Open Mar-Oct 45 pitches Level grass, sheltered 🛁🚽🚰⌀⊕∅⤴🚰 bike hire £8.50-£12.50 5% discount with this guide dave@wrensofryedale.fsnet.co.uk www.wrensofryedale.fsnet.co.uk

HIGH HAWSKER–see Whitby

CAUSE FOR COMPLAINT
If you have cause for complaint while staying on a site take the matter up with the manager or owner. If you are still not satisfied set the facts down in writing and send photocopies to anyone you think might be able to help, such as the local (licensing) authority for the area where the site is located.

HINDERWELL, N Yorks   **Map E2**
✗ Ellerby Country Inn 1½ S at Ellerby 📞 (01947) 840342

Fern Farm, High Street TS13 5JH 📞 (01947) 840350 OS map 94/792168 On A174 in Hinderwell opposite Badger and Hounds Inn Open Mar-Oct 20 pitches Level/sloping grass, sheltered 🔲⊕

Runswick Bay Caravan Park, Runswick Bay TS13 5HR 📞 (01947) 840997 OS map 94/804163 1m S of Hinderwell on Runswick Bay road Open Mar-Oct 40 pitches 5 acres level grass sheltered 🔲⊕

Serenity Touring Caravan Camping Park, High St TS13 5JH *Quiet mainly adult, family run park near Runswick Bay and Staithes* 📞 (01947) 841122 OS map 94/793166 In village on A174 (Whitby-Saltburn) Open Mar-Oct 40 pitches 3 acres level/sloping grass, sheltered 🔲🔶⊕

HOLMFIRTH–see Huddersfield

HORNSEA, E Yorks   **Map G5**
EC Wed MD Sun SEE Hornsea Mere (freshwater lake now bird sanctuary), Holderness museum of village life, Hornsea pottery
ℹ 120 Newbegin 📞 (01964) 536404
✗ Dacre Arms 5m W at Brandesburton 📞 (01964) 542392

Four Acres Caravan Park, Hornsea Road, Atwick YO25 8DG 📞 (01964) 536940 *Prop: Anthony & Ann Dove* OS map 107/193506 2m N of Hornsea on B1242 (Skipsea) Open Mar-Oct 93 pitches 4 acres level grass 🔲🔶⊕🔶✦🔲 £9.00-£15.00*

Longbeach Leisure Park, South Cliff HU18 1TL *Landscaped park overlooking Bridlington bay with direct beach access* 📞 (01964) 532506 OS map 107/213465 ¼m S of Hornsea centre at South Cliff, by sea Open Mar-Oct 450 pitches (400 static) 90 acres level grass and hard standings, sheltered 🔧🔲🔶⊕∅🔶✦🔲♿ 9 hole pitch and putt, fishing lake (all cards)

Springfield Farm, Atwick Road HU18 1EJ 📞 (01964) 532112 OS map 107/195484 ¾m N of Hornsea on B1242 (Bridlington) Open Mar 28-Oct 31 30 pitches Level grass and hard standing, part sheltered 🔲🔶✦

HUDDERSFIELD, Kirklees   **Map C5**
EC Wed MD Mon, Thurs SEE town hall, Roman relics, Castle Hill Tower, Kirklees Hall, Holmfirth postcard museum
ℹ 3 Albion St 📞 (01484) 223200
✗ Solo Mio (Italian), Imperial Arcade, Market St 📞 (01484) 542828

Holme Valley Camping Caravan Park, Thongsbridge, Holmfirth HD7 2TD 📞 (01484) 665819 Fax (01484) 663870 OS map 110/153104 6m S of Huddersfield off A6024 (Holmfirth) Open all year 62 pitches 4½ acres level grass and hard standing, sheltered 🔧✦🔲🔶⊕∅✦🔲♿ Autogas filling station, covered washing up area, fishing (Mastercard/Visa/Amex/Solo/Switch)

HULL   **Map G5**
EC Thurs MD Tues, Fri, Sat SEE Wilberforce House Museum, St Mary's Curch, Humber Bridge at Hessle 2m W
ℹ 1 Paragon St 📞 (01482) 223559
✗ Waterfront, Dagger Lane, Old Town 📞 (01482) 227222

Burton Constable Holiday Park and Arboretum, Old Lodges, Sproatley HU11 4LN 📞 (01964) 562508 *Prop: JR Chichester Constable* OS map 107/186357 7m NE of Hull off A165 (Bridlington) Open Mar-Oct (tourers/tents), Mar-Feb (static) 398 pitches (228 static, 62 lodges) 70 acres level/sloping grass, sheltered 🔲🔶🔶⊕∅🔶✦♿ boating, fishing, shop £12 (min)* inc elect (Mastercard/Visa/Amex) info@burtonconstable.co.uk www.burtonconstable.co.uk

For other sites near Hull see also Barton upon Humber, Beverley, Hornsea, South Cave and Withernsea

INGLETON, N Yorks   Map B3
EC Thurs MD Fri *Tourist village where in 1884 the Ingleton improvement society christened the wooded gorges of the Doe and Twiss the ingleton Glens and built the bridges and paths that now make up the Falls Walk* SEE Norman church, Ingleborough Mountain (2,373ft) with subterranean lake, White Scar Cave, Thornton Force
🛈 Community Centre Car Park ✆(01524) 241049
✗ Royal 7m NW at Kirkby Lonsdale ✆(01524) 271217

Flying Horseshoe Hotel, Clapham LA2 8ES ✆(015242) 51229 OS map 98/733679 4m SE of Ingleton off A65 (Settle) on Keasden road near rail station Open Mar-Oct 46 pitches Level grass and hard standing ✗⚲⊷🢒🞄⊘🞄 fishing near (Mastercard/Visa)

Goat Gap Inn, Clapham LA2 8JB ✆(01524) 241230 OS map 98/714703 2m E of Ingleton on A65 (Kirkby Lonsdale-Settle) Open Mar-Oct 15 pitches Level/sloping grass and hard standing, sheltered ✗⚲⊷🢒🞄🢒🞄🞄 (Mastercard/Visa)

Goodenbergh Caravan Park, Bentham LA2 7EW ✆(01524) 262022 OS map 97/638705 3m SW of Ingleton via Burton in Lonsdale off Low Bentham road Open Apr-Oct 140 pitches (130 static) Level grass and hard standing, sheltered 🛊🢒🞄🞄⊘🞄⊡ pony trekking

Riverside Caravan Park, High Bentham LA2 7HS ✆(01524) 261272 OS map 98/666688 3m SW of Ingleton off High Bentham road Open Mar-Oct 200 pitches (170 static) 20 acres level grass, sheltered 🞄🢒🞄🞄⊘🞄✔⊟🞄 fishing

Trees Caravan Park, Westhouse LA6 3NZ ✆(01524) 241511 *Prop: RW & JA Stocks* OS map 98/672737 1m W of Ingleton on left of A65 (Kendal) Open Apr-Oct 29 pitches (20 static)–no tents–booking advisable 2½ acres level grass and hard standings, sheltered 🢒🞄🞄⊘🞄🞄 £8.50 *stocks@greenwoodleghe.co.uk www.caravancampingsites.co.uk/northyorks/thetrees*

KEIGHLEY, Bradford   Map C5
EC Tues MD Wed, Fri, Sat SEE Cliffe Castle Museum, Keighley-Worth Valley Railway
✗ Bridge Inn 3m NW at Silsden ✆(01535) 653144

Dales Bank Holiday Park, Low lane, Horn Lane (off Bradley Road), Silsden BD20 9JH ✆(01535) 653321 OS map 104/036483 5m N of Keighley off A629 (Skipton) Open Apr-Oct 52 pitches Level grass, sheltered 🛊✗⚲🢒🞄🢒🞄⊘🞄

Springs Farm Caravan Park, Lothersdale BD20 8HH ✆(01535) 632533 OS map 103/944450 10m NW of Keighley off A629 (Skipton) on Lothersdale Road Open Apr-Oct 37 pitches (18 static) 3½ acres grass, gentle slope, hard standing; must book tents and m/caravans–preferred for caravans 🢒🞄⊘🞄 fly fishing

See also Haworth

KETTLEWELL, N Yorks   Map C3
EC Thurs SEE Wharfedale, Great Whernside (2,310ft), Kilnsey Crag, moors
✗ Racehorses ✆(01756) 760233

Fold Farm BD23 5RH ✆(01756) 760886 OS map 98/975725 ¼m NE of Kettlewell centre Open all year 20 pitches–no caravans–booking advisable ½ acre grass, sloping

KINGSTON UPON HULL–see Hull

KIRKBY MALZEARD, N Yorks   Map C3
✗ King's Head 4m N at Masham ✆(01765) 689295

Gold Coin Farm, Galphay HG4 3NJ ✆(01765) 658508 OS map 99/253724 1m SE of Kirkby Malzeard on Ripon road Open Apr-Sept 6 pitches Level grass 🢒🞄 *No showers*

Woodhouse Farm Caravan and Camping Park, Winksley HG4 3PG ✆(01765) 658309 OS map 99/240715 2m S of Kirkby Malzeard off Grantley road Open Apr-Oct 200 pitches (25 static) Grass and hard standing, level, sheltered 🛊✗⚲🢒🞄🞄🢒🞄🞄⊘🞄✔⊟🞄 paddling pool, fishing lake £9.50-£15.00* (Mastercard/Visa/Switch) *woodhouse.farm@talk21.com www.woodhousewinksley.com*

KNARESBOROUGH, N Yorks   Map D4
EC Thurs MD Wed SEE castle ruins, St Roberts' chapel, old manor house and chemist shop, Mother Shipton's Cave, Nidderdale NW
🛈 Market Place ✆(01423) 537300
✗ Bond End Wine Bar, Bond End ✆(01423) 863899

Allerton Park, Allerton Mauleverer HG5 0SE ✆(01423) 330569 Fax (01759) 371377 OS map 105/416576 4m E of Knaresborough on A59 (Harrogate-York) near junct with A1 Open Feb-Jan 180 pitches (130 static) Grass and hard standings, sloping, sheltered 🛊🞄🢒🞄🞄⊘🞄⊙✔⊡🞄 11.00-£13.00 *enquiries@yorkshireholidayparks.co.uk www.yorkshireholidayparks.co.uk*

Kingfisher Caravan Park, Low Moor Lane, Farnham HG5 9DQ ✆(01423) 869411 Fax (01423) 869411 OS map 104/350606 2m NW of Knaresborough off B6055 (Boroughbridge) Open Mar-Oct 135 pitches (60 static) Level grass and hard standing, sheltered 🛊🞄🢒🞄🞄⊘🞄✔🞄⊡🞄 £10.00 (min)*

KNOTTINGLEY, Wakefield   Map D5
SEE Old Pump, 14c arcade and racecourse at Pontefract 2m NW
✗ Wentbridge House, 4m S at Wentbridge ☎ (01977) 620444

West Park, Great North Road, Darrington WF8 3HY ☎ (01977) 620382 OS map 111/486167 2½m S of Knottingley on A1 (Doncaster) Open all year 30 pitches 🔲

LEEDS   Map D5
MD daily SEE Cathedral (RC), town hall, museum, City square, Kirkstall Abbey and Abbey House Museum, Middleton Railway, Roundhay Park, Tropical World, Royal Armouries
🆔 The Arcade, City Station ☎ (01132) 425242
✗ Metropole, King St ☎ (0113) 245 0841

Moor Lodge Caravan Park, Blackmoor Lane, Bardsey LS17 9DZ ☎ (01937) 572424 Fax (01937) 572424 OS map 104/355425 6m NE of Leeds off A58 (Wetherby) Open all year 72 pitches (60 static)–adults only Level grass 🛒🔲🔌🔧⊕∅↩ £9.00 (min)* (all cards) rodatmlcp@aol.com www.ukparks.co.uk/moorlodge

LEEMING BAR–see Bedale

LEVEN, E Yorks   Map G5
✗ Esplanade 6m E at Hornsea ☎ (01964) 532616

Dacre Lakeside Park, Brandesburton YO25 8SA ☎ (01964) 543704 Fax (01964) 543851 OS map 107/118468 3m N of Leven off A165 (Bridlington) Open Mar-Oct 120 marked pitches 6 acres level grass by lake 🛒🍺🔲🔧⊕∅♿ late arrivals enclosure, wind surfing, canoeing, dinghy sailing www.dacrepark.co.uk

LEYBURN, N Yorks   Map C3
🆔 4 Central Chambers ☎ (01969) 23069
✗ Golden Lion, Market Pl ☎ (01969) 622161

Constable Burton Hall Caravan Park DL8 5LJ Walled site in grounds near country house ☎ (01677) 450428 OS map 99/161911 3½m E of Leyburn on A684 (Bedale) Open Easter-Oct 120 pitches Level/sloping grass, sheltered 🔲🔧🔌⊕∅ £9.00-£13.00*

Lower Wensleydale Caravan Park, Harmby DL8 5NU ☎ (01969) 623366 OS map 99/128901 1m E of Leyburn off A684 (Bedale) on Bellerby road Open Apr-Nov 100 pitches–no tents (exc trailer tents) 10 acres level/sloping grass and hard standing, sheltered 🔲🔧⊕

LINTON ON OUSE–see York

LOTHERDALE–see Skipton

MALTON, N Yorks   Map F4
EC Thurs MD Tues, Fri, Sat SEE St Michael's church, Roman Museum, Old Malton Priory, Flamingoland zoo
🆔 58 Market Place ☎ (01653) 600048 ✗ Green Man, Market St ☎ (01653) 602662

Castle Howard Caravan and Camping Park, Coneysthorpe YO60 7DD ☎ (01653) 648316 OS map 100/705710 5m W of Malton off A64 (York) Open Mar-Oct 192 pitches (120 static) Level grass, sheltered 🛒🔲🔧🔌⊕∅ fishing £4.50-£12.50* inc hot water lakeside@castlehoward.co.uk www.castlehoward.co.uk

Robin Hood Caravan and Camping Park, Green Dyke Lane, Slingsby YO62 7AP ☎ (01653) 628391 Fax (01653) 628391 OS map 100/700749 6m NW of Malton off B1257 (Slingsby) Open Apr-Oct 62 pitches Level grass and hard standings, sheltered 🛒🏹🔲🔧🔌⊕∅😊↩🏪📺♿ battery charging £10.00-£18.00* info@robinhoodcaravanpark.co.uk www.robinhoodcaravanpark.co.uk

MASHAM, N Yorks   Map C3
EC Thurs MD Wed SEE Norman church, Saxon cross, brewery
✖ King's Head, Market Pl ☎ (01765) 689295

Black Swan Caravan and Camping, Black Swan Hotel, Fearby HG4 4NF ☎ (01765) 689477 Fax
   (01765) 689477 OS map 99/194809 1m W of Masham off A6108 (Ripon-Leyburn) on Fearby
   road at rear of Black Swan hotel Open Mar-Oct 100 pitches Grass, level, part sheltered
   🐾 ✖ 🍴 🛢 🌀 🕭 📮 🎪 🏪 🏧 £4.50-£15.00* (all cards) info@blackswanholiday.co.uk
   www.blackswanholiday.co.uk

MIDDLESBROUGH   Map D2
MD daily Once village on S bank of river Tees now heart of conurbation of Teesside born in 1830s
with extension of Stockton-Darlington railway SEE parks, bridges, museum, cathedral (RC),
Newham Grange Farm Museum, Capt Cook's Birthplace Museum, Stockton Transport Museum 4m
NW
🛈 125 Albert Rd ☎ (01642) 358086
✖ Blue Bell 4m SE at Marton ☎ (01642) 593939

Middlesbrough Caravan Park, Prissick Sports Centre, Marton Road TS4 3SA ☎ (01642) 311911
   OS map 93/512166 ½m S of Middlesbrough on A172 (York) Open Easter-Oct 22 pitches Level
   grass ✿

MUKER, N Yorks   Map B2
SEE Swaledale, waterfalls
✖ The Farmers Arms ☎ (01748) 886297

Usha Gap DL11 6DW ☎ (01748) 886214 OS map 98/900980 ½m W of Muker on right of B6270
   (Hawes) by river Open all year 24 pitches 1 acre level grass, fishing £10.00
   ushagap@btinternet.com www.ushagap.btinternet.co.uk

NORTHALLERTON, N Yorks   Map D3
EC Thurs MD Wed, Sat SEE church, Porch House, old inns
🛈 Applegarth Car Park ☎ (01609) 776864
✖ Golden Lion, Market Pl ☎ (01609) 772404

Cote Ghyll Caravan Camping Park, Osmotherley DL6 3AH Park in sheltered picturesque valley
   with outstanding walking/cycling close at hand ☎ (01609) 883425 Fax (01609) 883425 OS map
   99/459979 5¾m NE of Northallerton off junction of A684 (Osmotherly) and A19 (Thirsk-
   Middlesbrough)–signposted Open Mar-Oct 95 pitches (18 static) Grass level/sloping, sheltered
   🐾 🛢 🌀 ✿ 🌀 🕭 🎪 🏪 £10.50-£13.00 hills@coteghyll.com www.coteghyll.com

Hutton Bonville Caravan Park, Church Lane, Hutton Bonville DL7 0NR ☎ (01609) 881416 OS
   map 93/356005 4m N of Northallerton off A167 (Darlington) Open Apr-Oct 75 pitches (70 static)
   Grass, sloping 🍴 🛢 🌀 ✿ 🌀 🕭

OTLEY, Leeds   Map C4
SEE Chevin Hill (900ft), medieval bridge, old inns, Bramhope chapel SE
🛈 The Library, Nelson St ☎ (01943) 462485
✖ Chevin Lodge, York Gate ☎ (01493) 467818

Yorkshire Clarion Clubhouse, Chevin End, West Chevin Road, Menston LS29 6BL OS map
   104/187442 1m SW of Otley on Menston road Open Apr-Oct 20 pitches–no adv booking 1 acre
   level grass, sheltered ✿

FOLLOW THE COUNTRY CODE

Guard against all risk of fire. Fasten all gates.
Keep dogs under proper control. Keep to the
paths across farmland. Avoid damaging
fences, hedges and walls. Leave no litter.
Safeguard water supplies. Protect wildlife,
plants and trees. Go carefully on country
roads and be prepared for slow-moving
vehicles like tractors. Respect the life of the
countryside.

PATELEY BRIDGE, N Yorks   Map C4
EC Thurs SEE Bronze Age relics, Stump Cross Caverns 4m W, How Stean Gorge in Upper Nidderdale
🛈 14 High St ✆ (01423) 537300
✗ Sportman's Arms 3m N at Wath in Nidderdale ✆ (01423) 711306

Heathfield Caravan Park, Wath Rd HG3 5PY ✆ (01423) 711652 OS map 99/150670 1½m NW of Pateley Bridge off Ramsgill road in Nidderdale Open Mar-Oct 180 pitches (170 static)–no tents
🛒🖥🎫🅿◉🚿🌀

Manor House Farm, Summerbridge HG3 4JS ✆ (01423) 780322 OS map 99/203605 3½m SE of Pateley Bridge off B6165 (Knaresborough) Open Mar 21-Oct 31 60 pitches (50 static) Hard standings, sheltered 🖥🎫🅿🌀 baths

Riverside Caravan Park HG3 5HL ✆ (01423) 711383 OS map 99/154658 ½m N of Pateley Bridge on Low Wath road Open Apr-Oct–booking (3 nights or more) 158 pitches (110 static) Level grass and hard standings, sheltered 🖥🎫🅿◉🌀

Studfold Farm, Lofthouse in Nidderdale HG3 5SG ✆ (01423) 755210 OS map 99/099733 7m NW of Pateley Bridge on Stean road at head of Nidderdale Open Apr-Oct–must book 80 pitches (60 static) Level grass, sheltered 🛒🌀🚐 farm produce

Westfield Farm, Heathfield HG3 5BX ✆ (01423) 711880 *Prop: E Simpson* OS map 99/133666 1½m NW of Pateley Bridge off Ramsgill road via Heathfield Open Apr-Oct 30 pitches–family camping only 1½ acres level/sloping grass, sheltered 🎫🌀◉ £10.00*
See also Harrogate

PICKERING, N Yorks   Map F3
EC Wed MD Mon SEE church (15c murals), castle ruins, steam railway, Beck Isle Museum of Rural Life
🛈 The Ropery ✆ (01751) 473791
✗ Black Bull Inn, Malton Rd ✆ (01751) 475258
✗ The Cayley Arms, Allerston ✆ (01723) 859338

Black Bull Inn, Malton Road YO18 8EA ✆ (01751) 472528 OS map 100/802815 1m S of Pickering on A169 (Malton) at rear of inn Open Mar-Oct 36 pitches (33 static) 4 acres level grass
✗🍴🖥🎫🅿◉🌀🅿↩🚐🏠

Overbrook Caravan Park, Maltongate, Thornton Dale YO18 7SE *4 star-David Bellamy Gold Award* ✆ (01751) 474417 *Prop: Hilary Scales & Graham Hoyland* OS map 100/834822 2½m E of Pickering off A170 (Scarborough) Open Mar-Oct 50 pitches–no children 2½ acres level grass, sheltered, hard standings 🎫🌀◉🅿🏠 £12.00-£17.00 enquire@overbrookcaravanpark.co.uk www.overbrookcaravanpark.co.uk

Rosedale Caravan and Camping Parks, Rosedale Abbey YO18 8SA ✆ (01751) 417272 OS map 100/723960 9m NW of Pickering off A170 (Helmsley) via Wrelton Open Mar-Oct–no adv booking for tents on public holidays 225 pitches Grass and hard standings 🛒🖥🎫🌀◉🅿↩🅿🚻 fishing info@flowerofmay.com www.flowerofmay.com

Spiers House Caravan and Camp Site, Forestry Commission, Cropton YO18 8ES ✆ (01751) 417591 OS map 100/758918 5m NW of Pickering off Rosedale Abbey road Open Apr-Oct 150 pitches Grass sloping and hard standings 🛒🖥🎫🌀◉🌀🅿↩🚻 forest trail

Sun Inn, Normanby YO62 6RH ✆ (01751) 431051 OS map 100/736816 6m SW of Pickering off A170 (Helmsley) via Marton by River Severn Open Apr-Oct–adv booking preferred 15 pitches ✗🍴↩🖥🚐 fishing

Upper Carr Caravan Park, Malton Road YO18 7JP ✆ (01751) 473115 OS map 100/802815 1½m S of Pickering off A169 (Malton) Open Mar-Oct 80 pitches Grass and hard standing, level, sheltered 🛒↗🖥🎫🌀◉🅿↩🅿🏠🚻 pets corner, nature trail £9.50-£16.50 (Mastercard/Visa/Switch/Solo/Electron) harker@uppercarr.demon.co.uk www.uppercarr.demon.co.uk

Vale of Pickering Caravan Park, Carr House Farm, Allerston YO18 7PQ *Outstanding site in lovely country* ✆ (01723) 859280 OS map 101/879808 4½m E of Pickering off A170 (Scarborough) on B1415 (Malton) Open Mar-Jan 8 120 pitches 8 acres level grass and hard standing, sheltered 🛒↗🖥🎫🌀◉🅿↩🅿🏠🚻 £12.00-£15.00 (Mastercard/Visa/Debit) tony@valeofpickering.co.uk www.valeofpickering.co.uk

Wayside Caravan Park, Wrelton YO18 8PG ✆ (01751) 472608 Fax (01751) 472608 OS map 100/764858 2½m W of Pickering off A170 (Helmsley) Open Easter-Oct 160 pitches (80 static) 10 acres level grass 🛒🖥🎫🌀◉🌀🚻 £8.50-£14.00 (Mastercard/Visa/Delta/Switch) waysideparks@freenet.co.uk www.waysideparks.co.uk

---

CHECK BEFORE ENTERING
There's usually no objection to your walking onto a site to see if you might like it but always ask permission first. Remember that the person in charge is responsible for safeguarding the property of those staying there.

RICHMOND, N Yorks   Map C2
EC Wed MD Sat SEE Holy Trinity church, Green Howards' regimental museum, castle ruins,
Greyfriars Tower, Georgian Theatre
🗓 Friary Garden, Victoria Rd ☏ (01748) 850252
✘ Frenchgate, Frenchgate ☏ (01748) 852067

Brompton Caravan Park DL10 7EZ *Well maintained riverside park* ☏ (01748) 824629 Fax (01748)
826383 OS map 93/201004 1½m E of Richmond on B6271 (Catterick Bridge) by river Swale
Open Apr-Oct–must book peak periods 150 pitches (23 static) Level grass 🛁⚡▣🂡∅❋
∅❂↵▣(40 not on site) 🚐🏠♿ on site fishing, scenic walks £12.50-£19.50*
(Delta/Mastercard/Switch/Visa) *bromptoncaravanpark@btinternet.com*
www.bromptoncaravanpark.co.uk

Fox Hall Caravan Park, Ravensworth DL11 7JZ *Separate gravelled pitches in woodland setting*
☏ (01325) 718344 OS map 93/545678 5m NW of Richmond on Ravensworth road Open Apr-Oct
65 pitches (55 static) 3½ acres level grass and hard standings, sheltered ▣🂡❋↵ £10.00
inc elect

Swaleview Caravan Park, Reeth Road DL10 4SF ☏ (01748) 823106 Fax (01748) 823106 OS map
92/134013 2½m W of Richmond on A6108 (Leyburn) by River Swale Open Mar-Jan 150 pitches
(100 static) Grass, level, sheltered 🛁▣🂡∅❂↵🚐♿ (Mastercard/Switch/Delta)
swalview@teesdaleonline.co.uk

RIPLEY–see Harrogate

RIPON, N Yorks   Map D3
EC Wed MD Thurs SEE Cathedral, St Wilfrid's church, almshouses, racecourse, Fountains Abbey
3m SW, Newby Hall 3m SE
🗓 Minster Rd ☏ (01423) 537300
✘ Black A Moor Hotel, Boroughbridge Rd, Bridge Hewick ☏ (01765) 603511

River Laver Holiday Park, Studley Rd HG4 2QR ☏ (01765) 690508 *Prop: Glen & Helen Scholey*
OS map 99/297708 1m W of Ripon on B6265 (Fountains Abbey) Open Mar-Dec 100 pitches
(50 static)–no tents 5 acres level hard standing, sheltered 🛁▣🂡∅❋∅♿ £14.50-£17.25 inc
elect *riverlaver@lineone.net www.riverlaver.co.uk*

Riverside Meadows Caravan-Camping Park, Ure Bank Top HG4 1JD ☏ (01765) 602964 Fax
(01765) 604045 OS map 99/317726 1m NE of Ripon off A61 (Thirsk) Open Easter-Oct 401
pitches (200 static)–no single sex groups Hard standing, level/sloping grass, sheltered
🛁❢🂡▣🂡∅❋∅❂↵🗆🚐📶♿ *info@flowerofmay.com www.flowerofmay.com*

Sleningford Watermill Caravan Park, North Stainley HG4 3HQ ☏ (01765) 635201 OS map
99/280783 5m NNW of Ripon on A6108 (Leyburn) Open Apr-Oct 90 pitches (25 static) Grass
and hard standing, level, sheltered 🛁↵🂡▣🂡∅❋∅❂↵🚐🏠♿ fly fishing, canoeing
www.ukparks.co.uk/sleningford

Yorkshire Hussar Inn Holiday Caravan Park, Markington HG3 3NR ☏ (01765) 677327 *Prop: JS
Brayshaw (Caravans) Ltd.* OS map 99/287649 5m S of Ripon off A61 (Harrogate) Open Mar-Oct
146 pitches (75 static) Level grass and hard standing, sheltered 🂡▣🂡∅❋❂↵🚐🚐 horse
riding £12.00-£15.00 *yorkshirehussar@yahoo.co.uk*

For other sites near Ripon see also Kirkby Malzeard

ROBIN HOOD'S BAY, N Yorks   Map F2
*Attractive old fishing and smuggling village, with main street feeding intricate maze of alleys and
steps.* SEE Fylingdales Moor W
✘ Victoria, Station Rd ☏ (01947) 880205

Middlewood Farm Holiday Park, Fylingthorpe Y022 4UF *Small family park with luxury facs and
magnificent views* ☏ (01947) 880414 Fax (01947) 880871 OS map 94/945045 ¼m SW of Robin
Hood's Bay in Fylingthorpe Open Mar 1-Jan 4 150 pitches (30 static) 7 acres level grass,
sheltered ▣🂡∅❋∅❂↵🚐 £7.50-£13.50* (Mastercard/Visa/Switch/Solo)
info@middlewoodfarm.com www.middlewoodfarm.com

COMMENTS

We would be pleased to hear your comments about the sites featured in this guide or your suggestions for future editions. Comments and suggestions may be emailed to ccb@butford.co.uk. Alternatively, write to The Editor, CCB, Butford Technical Publishing Ltd at the address given at the front of the book.

Scarborough Camping and Caravanning Club Site, Scarborough

🛡 CARAVAN STORAGE

Many sites in this guide offer caravan storage in winter but some will also store your caravan in summer, which for those of us able to tour several times a year saves towing over long distances. Sites most conveniently placed for this are those on or near popular routes to the West Country and Scotland.

ROSEDALE ABBEY–see Pickering

ROTHERHAM   **Map D6**
EC Thurs MD Mon, Fri, Sat SEE ancient bridge with chapel, All Saints church, museum and art gallery
🛈 Central Library, Walker Pl ☎ (01709) 835904
✗ Moat House, Moorgate Road ☎ (01709) 364902
Thrybergh Country Park,, Doncaster Road, Thrybergh S65 4NU ☎ (01709) 850353 OS map 111/474963 3m NE of Rotherham on A630 (Doncaster) Open all year 26 pitches booking advisable 3 acres, level grass and hard standing, sheltered 🛒✗⊷🖭⊕🎮⤵♿🌳 trout fishing £5.00-£8.25* *thrybergh.countrypark@rotherham.gov.uk*

SALTBURN BY THE SEA, Redcar & Cleveland   **Map E2**
Once a superior Victorian seaside resort, with traces of those times in the Italianate garden and sloping tramway near the pier
✗ Ship Inn overlooking beach
Margrove Park Holidays, Boosbeck TS12 3BZ ☎ (01287) 653616 OS map 94/652156 2m S of Saltburn by the Sea at Boosbeck Open Apr-Oct 100 pitches (80 static) Level grass ⊕🎮🛡

KEY TO SYMBOLS

🛒	shop	⊕	games area
✗	restaurant	⤵	playground
🍺	bar	📺	TV
⊷	takeaway food	🛡	winter storage
🏹	off licence	🅿	parking oblig.
🔲	laundrette	🚫	no dogs
🔌	elec hook-ups	🚐	caravan hire
🔵	gas supplies	🏨	bungalow hire
⊕	chem. disposal	♿	disabled facs.
∅	payphone	🌳	shaded
🏊	swimming pool		

Dogs are usually allowed but must be kept on a lead.
Sometimes they have to be paid for.

SCARBOROUGH, N Yorks   Map F3
EC Wed MD Thurs SEE St Mary's church, spa, ballroom theatre and concert hall, zoo and
marineland, miniature railway
🖼 Brunswick Shopping Centre ✆ (01723) 283636
✗ Denison Arms, 40 Main St, East Ayton ✆ (01723) 862131

Arosa Caravan and Camping Park, Ratten Row, Seamer YO12 4QB ✆ (01723) 862166 Fax
(01723) 862166 OS map 101/012830 4m S of Scarborough off A64 (Malton) Open Mar 1-Jan 4
105 pitches 🅿️🚿♨️➕⚡✔️❓ farm produce, B&B, lic club, bar meals (Mastercard/Visa/Switch/Delta)
suebird@arosa131.fsnet.co.uk

Brown's Caravan Park, Cayton Bay YO11 3NN ✆ (01723) 582303 OS map 101/065840 3m SE of
Scarborough off A165 (Filey) Open Apr-Sept 145 pitches (110 static) Level grass ✗ (bar snacks)
♀➤🚿♨️➕⚡✔️❓ £12.00-£18.00 (Mastercard/Visa/Solo/Switch/Delta/Electron)

Cayton Village Caravan Park, Mill Lane, Cayton Bay YO11 3NN ✆ (01723) 583171 *Prop: Carol
Croft* OS map 101/058834 3m S of Scarborough off A165 (Filey) in Cayton village Mar-Jan
200 pitches Level grass, supersites and hard standing, sheltered 🅿️➤🚿♨️➕⚡✔️⚡♨️👍 dog
walk £8.50-£22.00 (Mastercard/Visa/Switch) info@caytontouring.co.uk www.caytontouring.co.uk

Flower of May Holiday Park, Lebberston Cliff YO11 3NU ✆ (01723) 584311 Fax (01723) 581361
OS map 101/084833 4½m S of Scarborough off A165 (Filey) Open Easter-Oct–booking advisable
491 pitches (191 static) Level grass and hard standing 🅿️♀➕🚿♨️➕⚡❓ (indoor heated)
⚡✔️❓ (peak season) 🚐👍 bowling, squash, golf, skateboard ramps, basketball, conservatory
bar for families £9.00-£16.50 info@flowerofmay.com www.flowerofmay.com

Jacob's Mount Caravan Camping Park, Stepney Road YO12 5NL ✆ (01723) 361178 OS map
101/013870 2m SW of Scarborough on A170 (Pickering) Open Mar-Nov 140 pitches (60 static)
Level grass and hard standings, sheltered 🅿️♀➕➤🚿♨️➕⚡✔️❓🚐 serviced pitches
£11.00-£17.00 (Mastercard/Visa/Solo) jacobsmount@yahoo.co.uk www.jacobsmount.co.uk

Jasmine Caravan Park, Snainton YO13 9BE ✆ (01723) 859240 OS map 101/930813 9m SW of
Scarborough off A170 (Pickering) Open Mar-Jan 94 pitches Grass, level, sheltered
🅿️➤🚿♨️➕⚡🚐❓👍 £10.00-£18.00 (Mastercard/Visa/Switch) info@jasminepark.co.uk
www.jasminepark.co.uk

Merry Lees Caravan Park, Staxton YO12 4NN *Woodland park overlooking lake popular with 60
species of birds* ✆ (01944) 710080 OS map 101/020800 6m S of Scarborough on right off A64
(Malton) Open Mar-Oct 80 pitches 8 acres level grass, sheltered 🚿♨️➕⚡♨️ (Mastercard/Visa)

Scalby Close Park, Burniston Road YO13 0DA ✆ (01723) 365908 OS map 101/026913 2m N of
Scarborough on A165 (Burniston) Open Mar-Oct 50 pitches 3 acres level grass and hard
standing, sheltered 🅿️🚿♨️♨️➕⚡🚐 £8.50-£14.00 (Mastercard/Visa)
info@scalbyclosepark.co.uk www.scalbyclosepark.co.uk

Scarborough Camping and Caravanning Club Site, Burniston Rd YO13 0DA ✆ (01723) 366212
(day) *Prop: The Camping & Caravanning Club* OS map 101/025911 2m N of Scarborough centre
on A165 (Whitby) coast road Open Apr-Oct 300 pitches 20 acres level grass
🅿️➕➤🚿♨️➕⚡✔️👍 (Mastercard/Visa/Switch) www.campingandcaravanningclub.co.uk

SCOTCH CORNER, N Yorks   Map C2
EC Wed SEE Easby Abbey ruins, Richmond Castle 4m SW, Stanwick Fort
✗ Scotch Corner, Gt North Rd ✆ (01748) 822943

Scotch Corner Caravan Park DL10 6NS *Well equipped, well maintained* ✆ (01748) 824424
(winter) 822530 (summer) OS map 93/214047 ¼m SW of Scotch Corner on A6108 (Richmond)
Open Easter-mid Oct 96 pitches Level grass 🅿️✗♀🚿♨️➕⚡👍 £10.00-£13.00* (all cards)

Scalby Close Park, Scarborough

FACTS CAN CHANGE

We do our best to check the accuracy of the
entries in this guide but changes can and do
occur after publication. So if you plan to stay
at a site some distance from home it makes
sense to ring the manager or owner before
setting off.

SELBY, N Yorks   **Map E5**
EC Thurs MD Mon SEE Abbey Church, market cross, toll bridge
☒ 52 Micklegate ☎ (01757) 212181
✘ Londesborough Arms, Market Pl ☎ (01757) 707355

Bay Horse Inn, York Road, Barlby YO8 5JH ☎ (01757) 703878 OS map 105/630340 2m N of
  Selby on A19 (York) in Barlby Open all year 10 pitches Level grass, sheltered ☗ ∅ ✪ ▣

Cawood Holiday Park Caravan and Camping Centre, Ryther Road, Cawood YO8 3TT ☎ (01757)
  268450 Fax (01757) 268537 OS map 105/571380 4m NNW of Selby on B1223 (Tadcaster) near
  junction with B1222 (York) Open all year 60 pitches–adults only Level/sloping grass and hard
  standing, sheltered ☗ ✘ ♀ ⌁ ▱ ▣ ✪ ∅ ⊗ ⏚ (indoor) ⊗ ⤳ ☐ ⊡ ▦ ♿ fishing, entertainment, pool
  room £10.00-£20.00* inc elect (all cards) cawoodpark@aol.com www.cawoodpark.com

SETTLE, N Yorks   **Map B4**
EC Wed MD Tues SEE museum, Flowing Well at Giggleswick, Stainforth Foss at Stainforth 3m N
☒ Town Hall, Cheapside ☎ (01729) 825192
✘ Royal Oak, Market Pl ☎ (01729) 822561

Knight Stainforth Hall BD24 ODP ☎ (01729) 822200 Fax (01729) 823387 OS map 98/815672
  2½m N of Settle off A65 (Kirkby Lonsdale) at Stackhouse Lane beside River Ribble Open Mar-Oct
  160 pitches (60 static) Level/sloping grass, hard standings ☗ ▣ ▱ ∅ ✪ ∅ ⊗ ⤳ ☐ £10.00-£12.00*
  (most cards) info@knightstainforth.co.uk www.kinghtstainforth.co.uk

Langcliffe Caravan Park, Langcliffe Place, Langcliffe BD24 9LX ☎ (01729) 822387 OS map
  98/818652 ½m N of Settle off A65 (Ingleton) and B6479 (Horton in Ribblesdale) Open Mar-Oct
  122 pitches (53 static) 5 acres mainly level grass and hard standing ▣ ▱ ∅ ✪ ∅ ⤳ ⊡ fishing
  (Mastercard/Visa)

SHEFFIELD   **Map D7**
EC Thurs MD daily except Thur SEE cathedral, city museum, Cutlers' Hall, New Crucible Theatre,
Abbeydale Industral Hamlet (18c), Kelham Industrial Museum
☒ Winter Gardens ☎ (01142) 211900
✘ Crosspool, 468 Manchester Rd ☎ 0114 266 2113

Fox Hagg Farm, Lodge Lane, Rivelin S6 5SN ☎ (0114) 2305589 Prop: M Dyson & Son OS map
  110/292868 3m W of Sheffield off A57 (Glossop) near Bell Hagg Inn Open Apr-Oct 30 pitches
  (20 static) Level grass and hard standing ▣ ▱ ✪ ⤳ ⊡ £10.00

SHIPLEY, Bradford   **Map C5**
✘ Aagrah (Indian), Westgate ☎ (01274) 594660

Crook Farm, Shipley Glen Rd, Baildon BD17 5ED ☎ (01274) 584339 OS map 104/135393 2½m
  NW of Shipley off Glen road Open Mar-Jan 160 pitches (100 static) Grass and hard standing
  ♀ ▣ ▱ ∅ ∅ ⊗ ⤳ ☐ bar meals, mobile shop calls, childrens room

SILSDEN–see Keighley

SKIPSEA, E Yorks   **Map G4**
Small seaside resort overlooking extensive sandy beach SEE castle ruins, 12c church, All Saints
church 2m N at Barmston
✘ The Board Inn, Back St ☎ (01262) 468342

Beach Bank Caravan Park, South Field Lane, Ulrome YO25 8TU ☎ (01262) 468491 OS map
  107/175565 1½m NE of Skipsea on coast road Open Mar-Oct 60 pitches 2½ acres level/sloping
  grass, on cliff top ☗ ✘ ⌁ ▱ ∅ ✪ ∅

Far Grange Park YO25 8SY ☎ (01262)468010 OS map 107/187531 1½m S of Skipsea off B1242
  (Hornsea) by sea Open Mar-Oct 743 pitches (700 static) 63 acres level grass
  ☗ ✘ ♀ ⌁ ⤚ ▣ ▱ ∅ ∅ ⏚ ⊗ ⤳ ☐ ▦ ♿ tennis amusements, beach near, 18-hole golf course,
  clubhouse £11.00-£14.00 (most cards) enquiries@fargrangepark.co.uk www.fargrangepark.co.uk

Low Skirlington Caravan Park YO25 8SY ☎ (01262) 468213 and 468358 OS map 107/185525
  1½m S of Skipsea off B1242 (Hornsea) by sea Open Mar-Oct 725 pitches (450 static) Level
  grass and hard standings ☗ ✘ ▣ ▱ ⏚ ⊗ ▦ ⊞ (Mastercard/Visa)

Mill Farm Country Park, Mill Lane, Skipsea YO25 8SS ☎ (01262) 468211 OS map 107/166555
  ¼m N of Skipsea centre off B1242 (Bridlington) via Cross St Open Mar-Oct 54 pitches 6 acres
  level grass and hard standing, sheltered ▱ ✪ ∅ ▣ farm walk £8.25-£11.40

Skipsea Sands Caravan Park, Mill Lane YO25 8TZ ☎ (01262) 468210 OS map 107/175563 1m E
  of Skipsea by sea Open Mar-Nov 740 pitches (650 static) 36 acres level grass
  ☗ ✘ ♀ ⌁ ▣ ▱ ∅ ✪ ∅ ⏚ (indoor) ⊗ ⤳ ⊞

SHOWERS
Except where marked, all sites in this guide have flush lavatories and showers. Symbols for these
amenities have therefore been omitted from site entries.

SKIPTON, N Yorks   **Map C4**
EC Tues MD Mon SEE castle, church, Craven museum, old corn mill
▉9 Sheep St ☎(01756) 792809
✖Black Horse, Market Place ☎(01756) 792145

Springs Caravan Park, Lothersdale BD20 8HH ☎(01535) 632533 OS map 103/944450 5m S of
   Skipton off A629 (Keighley) and A6068 (Colne) at Cross Hills Open Apr-Oct–adv booking
   preferred 37 pitches–must book m/vans and tents Grass and hard standing ▨◿⊕▨◿☎
   fishing

Tarn Caravan Park, Stirton BD23 3LQ ☎(01756) 795309 OS map 103/977534 1¼m NW of
   Skipton off B6265 (Grassington) Open Apr-Oct 260 pitches (226 static)–no tents Level/sloping
   grass and hard standings ✖⌇▨◿⊕◿☻ one dog (no alsatians, rottweilers, dobermans, etc.)
   (Mastercard/Visa/Switch)

SLINGSBY–see Malton

STAMFORD BRIDGE, E Yorks   **Map F4**
SEE stone bridge and weir
✖Feathers 7m SE at Pocklington ☎(01759) 303155

Fangfoss Old Station Caravan Park, Fangfoss YO41 5QB ☎(01759) 380491 Fax (01759) 388497
   OS map 105/748528 3m SE of Stamford Bridge off A1079 (York-Hull) on Fangfoss road at
   Wilberfoss–signposted Open Mar-Jan 1 75 pitches Level grass and hard standing, sheltered
   ⌇⋌▤▨◿⊕◿☻◡▨⊟◔ £8.50-£15.50* (Mastercard/Visa)
   info@fangfosspark.fsbusiness.co.uk

Weir Caravan Park, Stamford Bridge YO41 1AN ☎(01759) 371377 Fax (01759) 371377 OS map
   105/710557 ¼m NW of Stamford Bridge centre off A166 (York) Open Mar-Oct 120 pitches (90
   static) Level grass and hard standing, sheltered ▤▨◿◿⊟ fishing, boating £11.00-£13.00*
   enquiries@yorkshireholidayparks.co.uk www.yorkshireholidayparks.co.uk

STILLINGFLEET–see York

STOKESLEY, N Yorks   **Map E2**
SEE church of SS Peter and Paul, town hall, packhorse bridge, Cleveland Hills
✖The Bay Horse, 88 High St, Great Broughton ☎(01642) 712319

Carlton Caravan Park, The Elms, Carlton in Cleveland TS9 7DJ ☎(01642) 712550 OS map
   93/509042 4m SW of Stokesley off A172 (Thirsk) Open Mar-Oct 25 pitches Level grass,
   sheltered ⌇✖◿⊕◡⊟ pets corner, post office

Toft Hill Farm, Kirkby in Cleveland TS9 7HJ ☎(01642) 712469 OS map 93/540043 3m S of
   Stokesley via Kirkby Open Apr-Oct 60 pitches 4 acres level/sloping grass, sheltered ⊕

White House Farm, Little Broughton TS9 7DF ☎(01642) 712148 OS map 93/555071 3m SE of
   Stokesley off B1257 (Helmsley) on Ingleby Greenhow road Open Mar-Oct 60 pitches (40 static)
   10 acres level grass ▤▨⊕◿◡⬙ fishing £10.00

STRENSALL–see York

SUTTON ON THE FOREST, N Yorks   **Map E4**
SEE Georgian houses, Sutton Hall and gardens, vicarage where Sterne wrote Tristram Shandy
✖ The White Bear Inn, Main St, Stillington ✆ (01347) 810338
Goosewood Caravan Park YO61 1ET ✆ (01347) 810829 OS map 100/599627 1½m SE of Sutton
on the Forest off York road Open Mar-Jan 75 pitches–booking advisable–no tents 20 acres level,
woodland setting, grass and hard standings, sheltered 🛒 ⚲ 🗑 🔌 𝚥 ⊕ ∅ 🎮 ⌣ 🏪 🏠 on site fishing,
leisure suite £15.50-£18.50 (most cards) enquiries@goosewood.co.uk www.goosewood.co.uk

THIRSK, N Yorks   **Map D3**
EC Wed MD Mon SEE church, Thirsk Hall, Golden Fleece Inn, Byland Abbey ruins
🛈 14 Kirkgate ✆ (01845) 522755
✖ Golden Fleece, Market Pl ✆ (01845) 523108
Carlton Minniott Park, Carlton Minniott YO7 4NJ ✆ (01845) 523106 OS map 99/40816 2m W of
Thirsk off A61 (Ripon) on right of Sandhutton road Open Apr-Oct 40 pitches 5 acres level grass,
sheltered 🔌 🎮 fishing and boating lake
Nursery Garden Caravan Park, Rainton YO7 3PG ✆ (01845) 577277 OS map 99/388756 5m SW
of Thirsk off A168 (Boroughbridge) via Asenby near junct 49 of A1M Open Mar-Oct 74 pitches
(52 static) Level grass, sheltered 🗑 🔌 𝚥 ⊕ ∅ 🎮 ⌣ 🅚
Quernhow Cafe Camping Park, Great North Road, Sinderby YO7 4LG ✆ (01845) 567221 OS map
99/337813 8m W of Thirsk on northbound carriageway of A1, 3m N of junction with A61 Open all
year 40 pitches Grass, level, sheltered ✖ ⌐ ⚲ 🔌 𝚥 ⊕ 🎮 🏠 tennis
Sowerby Caravan Park, Sowerby YO7 3AG ✆ (01845) 522753 Fax (01845) 574520 OS map
99/437804 ½m SE of Thirsk on Dalton road beyond bridge under A168, by river Open Mar-Oct
110 pitches (85 static) 6 acres level grass and hard standings 🛒 🗑 🔌 𝚥 ⊕ 🎮 ⌣ ♿ £8.5-£9.50*
White Rose Leisure Park, Hutton Sessay YO7 3BA ✆ (01845) 501215 OS map 100/476763 5m
SE of Thirsk off A19 (York) near inn Open Mar-Oct 220 pitches (120 static) Level grass,
sheltered 🛒 ✖ 🍸 ⊷ 🗑 🔌 𝚥 ⊕ ∅ ⊡ 🎮 ⌣ 🏪 🏠 ♿
York House Caravan Park, Balk, Sutton under Whitestonecliffe YO7 2AQ ✆ (01845) 597495 OS
map 100/476808 3m E of Thirsk off A170 (Pickering) on Bagby-Sutton road Open Apr-Oct
195 pitches Level grass 🛒 🗑 🔌 𝚥 ⊕ ⌣ 🏪 farm produce

THORNE, Doncaster   **Map E6**
EC Thurs MD Tues, Fri, Sat SEE parish church
✖ Belmont, Horsefair Green ✆ (01405) 812320
Hatfield Waterpark DN7 6EQ Watersports centre in delightful setting ✆ (01302) 841572/737343
Fax (01302) 846368 OS map 111/668097 3m SW of Thorne off A18 (Doncaster) Open all year
75 pitches Level grass, sheltered 🛒 🗑 🔌 ⊕ ∅ ⌣ ♿ fishing, rowing & windsurfing
(Mastercard/Visa)

THRESHFIELD–see Grassington

ULROME–see Skipsea

WAKEFIELD   **Map D5**
EC Wed MD daily except Wed, SEE cathedral, old bridge with chantry chapel, museum, Heath Hall
1½m E
🛈 The Bull Ring ✆ (01924) 305000
✖ Swallow, Queen St ✆ (01924) 837211
Nostell Priory Holiday Park, Top Park Wood, Nostell WF4 1QD Friendly site in mature woodland
✆ (01924) 863938 OS map 111/420175 6m SE of Wakefield off A638 (Doncaster) Open Apr-Sept
140 pitches (80 static) Grass and hard standings, level, sheltered 🗑 🔌 𝚥 ⊕ ∅ ⌣ 🏪 (30) 🚐
fishing

WENSLEYDALE–see Leyburn

KEY TO SYMBOLS

🛒	shop	𝚥	gas supplies	🏪	winter storage for caravans
✖	restaurant	⊕	chemical disposal point	🅿	parking obligatory
🍸	bar	∅	payphone	🎮	no dogs
⊷	takeaway food	⊡	swimming pool	🚐	caravan hire
⚲	off licence	🎮	games area	🏠	bungalow hire
🗑	laundrette	⌣	children's playground	♿	facilities for disabled
🔌	mains electric hook-ups	🖵	TV	🅚	shaded

CHARGES
Charges quoted are the minimum and maximum for two people with car and caravan or tent. They are given only as a guide and should be checked with the owner of the site.
Charges markded * are the prices for last year. Otherwise, the prices are those quoted for the current season.
Remember to ask whether hot water or use of the pool is extra and make sure that VAT is included.

WHITBY, N Yorks   **Map F2**
EC Wed MD Sat SEE abbey ruins, Pannett Park aviary and museum, Capt Cook's house, town hall, promenade
🛈 Langborne Rd ✆ (01723) 383637
✗ Magpie, Pier Rd ✆ (01947) 602058

Burnt House Caravan Park, Ugthorpe YO21 2BG ✆ (01947) 840448 OS map 94/783112 6m W of Whitby on right of A171 (Guiesborough) Open Mar-Oct 130 pitches (50 static) 7 acres level grass and hard standing 🖃🔲🔅❄⊘↩

Grouse Hill Caravan Park, Flask Bungalow Farm, Fylingdales YO22 4QH ✆ (01947) 880543/880560 Fax (01947) 880543 OS map 94/929003 8m SE of Whitby off A171 (Scarborough) Open Easter-Oct–must book peak periods 285 pitches 14 acres level/sloping grass and hard standings, sheltered 🔋🔲🔅❄⊘🅾🔅🔲🚗👤 serviced pitches

Ladycross Plantation Caravan Park, Egton YO21 1UA *Peaceful woodland site convenient for coast and North York Moors* ✆ (01947) 895502 *Prop: DH & L Miller* OS map 94/821080 5m W of Whitby off A171 (Guisborough) Open Mar-Oct 122 pitches 28 acres level grass and hard standing, sheltered 🔋🔲🔅❄⊘🅾🔲 £13.00-£16.00 inc elect (Mastercard/Visa/Maestro) *enquiries@ladycrossplantation.co.uk www.ladycrossplantation.co.uk*

Northcliffe Holiday Park,, High Hawsker YO22 4LL *Clifftop location with fine views* ✆ (01947) 880477 OS map 94/940080 4m S of Whitby off A171 (Scarborough) on B1447 (Robin Hood's Bay) Open Easter-Oct 200 pitches (170 static) Level grass and hard standing 🔋↩🏃🔲🔲 ❄❄🅾🔅↩🔅🚗👤 tea room, football pitch (Mastercard/Visa)

Rigg Farm Caravan Park, Stainsacre YO22 4LP ✆ (01947) 880430 *Prop: DA & AE Stuart* OS map 94/915062 3m SE of Whitby off B1416 (Ruswarp-Scarborough) Open Mar-Oct 29 pitches 3 acres grass and hard standing, level, sheltered 🔅❄⊘↩🔲🚗 games room, laundry £11.50-£15.50

Sandfield House Farm, Sandsend Road YO21 3SR ✆ (01947) 602660 *Prop: Martin & Chrissie Warner* OS map 94/879116 1m NW of Whitby on left of A174 (Sandsend) opp golf course Open Mar 15-Oct 30–no tents 50 pitches 10 acres level grass and hard standing 🔲🔅❄⊘🅾🔅 £12.00-£14.60 *info@sandfieldhousefarm.co.uk www.sandfieldhousefarm.co.uk*

Ugthorpe Caravan Park, Ugthorpe YO21 2BE ✆ (01947) 840518 OS map 94/785115 6m NW of Whitby off A171 (Guisborough) Open Apr-Oct 90 pitches (70 static) Level grass 🔋✗👤🔅❄⊘🅾🔅↩🔲

Whitby Holiday Park, Saltwick Bay YO22 4JX ✆ (01947) 602664 OS map 94/916108 1m E of Whitby at Saltwick Bay Open Easter-Oct 175 pitches 🔋✗👤🔲🔅❄⊘↩🚗 beach access

York House Caravan Park, High Hawsker YO22 4LW ✆ (01947) 880354 Fax (01947) 880354 OS map 94/927074 3m SE of Whitby on Sneaton Thorpe road Open Mar-Oct 100 pitches (41 static) Level/sloping grass and hard standing, sheltered 🔋🔲🔅❄⊘🅾🔅↩🔲 £8.00-£10.00*

See also Robin Hood

For more up-to-date information, and for links to camping websites, visit our site at:
www.butford.co.uk/camping

FOLLOW THE COUNTRY CODE

Guard against all risk of fire. Fasten all gates. Keep dogs under proper control. Keep to the paths across farmland. Avoid damaging fences, hedges and walls. Leave no litter. Safeguard water supplies. Protect wildlife, plants and trees. Go carefully on country roads and be prepared for slow-moving vehicles like tractors. Respect the life of the countryside.

WITHERNSEA, E Yorks   Map G5
SEE medieval church, Spurn Point 10m SE
✗ Shakespeare Inn 9m W at Hedon ☎ (01482) 898371

Easington Beach Caravan Park, Easington HU12 0TY ☎ (01964) 650293 OS map 113/410188
  8m SE of Withernsea off B1445 (Easington) Open Mar-Dec 350 pitches (300 static)
  (indoor) club, pets corner, badminton, putting green

Sandy Beach Caravan Park, Kilnsea HU12 0UB ☎ (01964) 650256 and 650372 OS map
  113/415158 9m SE of Withernsea off B1445 (Easington) near Spurn Point Open Mar-Oct
  420 pitches (350 static) Level grass and hard standing

YORK, N Yorks   Map E4
EC Wed MD daily SEE Minster, Nat Railway museum, castle museum, city walls, The Shambles
▣ De Grey Rooms, Exhibition Sq ☎ (01904) 621756
✗ Blacksmiths Arms, Farlington ☎ (01347) 810581

Chestnut Farm Caravan Park, Acaster Malbis YO23 2UQ ☎ (01904) 704676 OS map 105/588461
  3m SW of York off A64 (Leeds) via Copmanthorpe Open Apr-Oct 81 pitches (56 static) Level
  grass, sheltered

Home Farm Camping Caravan Park, Moreby, Stillingfleet YO19 6HN *Small working farm
  overlooking river Ouse* ☎ (01904) 728263 *Prop: G Coward* OS map 105/596438 4m S of York
  off A19 (Selby) on B1222 (Cawood) Open Feb-Dec 25 pitches Level grass, sheltered
  log cabin hire £8.00-£10.00* *home_farm@hotmail.co.uk*

Hundred Acre Farm Caravan Park, Pottery Lane, Strensall YO3 5TW ☎ (01904) 490020 OS map
  100/618622 7m N of York off A64 (Malton) via Strensall Open Mar-Oct 21 pitches 1 acre level
  grass sheltered nature reserve

Linton Leisureways, Linton Lock, Linton on Ouse YO30 2AZ *Secluded site in lovely countryside*
  ☎ (01347) 848486 OS map 100/502604 6m NW of York off A19 (Northallerton) at Shipton, by
  river Ouse Open Mar-Oct 90 pitches Level grass, sheltered

Moor End Farm, Acaster Malbis YO23 2UQ ☎ (01904) 706727 OS map 105/589457 4m S of York
  off A64 (Leeds) via Bishopthorpe or Copmanthorpe Open Apr-Oct 15 pitches Level grass,
  sheltered £9.00-£13.00* *moorendfarm@acaster99.fsnet.co.uk*
  www.ukparks.co.uk/moorend

Moorside Caravan Park, Lordsmoor Lane, Strensall YO32 5XJ ☎ (01904) 491865 *Prop: Mr Smith*
  OS map 100/647614 6m NE of York off A1237 (northern bypass) on Strensall road Open Easter-
  Oct 55 pitches–no children under 16, area for adults only 5 acres level grass and hard standing
  fishing £7.50-£14.00* *www.moorsidecaravanpark.co.uk*

Mount Pleasant Holiday Park, Acaster Malbis YO23 2UA ☎ (01904) 707078 OS map 105/583443
  5m S of York off A64 (Leeds) via Bishopthorpe Open Mar-Nov–no adv booking 284 pitches (224
  static) Level grass and hard standing first aid (Mastercard/Visa/Switch)

Naburn Lock Caravan Camping Park, Naburn YO19 4RU ☎ (01904) 728697 OS map 105/599453
  4m S of York off A19 (Selby) on B1222 (Stillingfleet) Open Apr-Oct 100 pitches 7 acres level
  grass, sheltered fishing, horse riding, bike hire, river bus to York £13.00-
  £16.00* (all cards) *www.naburnlock.co.uk*

Poplar Farm, Acaster Malbis YO23 2UH ☎ (01904) 706548 OS map 105/591455 3m S of York off
  A64 (Leeds) via Bishopthorpe Open Apr-Sept 130 pitches (80 static) Level grass and hard
  standing fishing, boating, regular river bus to York

Post Office Caravan Park, Acaster Malbis YO2 1UL ☎ (01904) 702448 OS map 105/582433 4m S
  of York off A64 (Leeds) via Bishopthorpe by River Ouse Open Apr-Oct 72 pitches (62 static)
  Level grass, sheltered

Rawcliffe Caravans, Manor Lane, Shipton Road YO3 6TZ ☎ (01904) 624422 OS map 105/582551
  2m NW of York off A19 (Thirsk) Open all year 120 pitches Level grass and hard standing
  petanque pitches, invalid room (Mastercard/Visa)

Riverside Caravan Camping Park, Ferry Lane, Bishopthorpe YO23 2SB *Secluded riverside
  location on level grass* ☎ (01904) 704442 Fax (01904) 705824 OS map 105/600475 2m S of
  York at Bishopthorpe on W bank of river Ouse Open Apr-Oct 25 pitches 1 acre grass, level,
  sheltered boat hire, slipway, fishing £7.00-£14.00* (Mastercard/Visa)
  info@yorkmarine.co.uk www.yorkmarine.co.uk

Swallow Hall, Crockey Hill YO19 4SG ☎ (01904) 448219 OS map 105/657462 5m S of York off
  A19 (Selby) on Wheldrake road Open Mar-Oct 40 pitches 5 acres level grass, sheltered
  18-hole golf, driving range, tennis (Mastercard/Visa)

See also Robin Hood

Help us make CAMPING CARAVANNING BRITAIN better known to site operators – and thereby
more informative – by showing them your copy when booking in.

KEY TO SYMBOLS

⚏	shop	∂	gas supplies	⚑	winter storage for caravans
✕	restaurant	✪	chemical disposal point	Ⓟ	parking obligatory
⚈	bar	∅	payphone	✿	no dogs
⚲	takeaway food	▱	swimming pool	⇔	caravan hire
⚓	off licence	☻	games area	⌂	bungalow hire
▣	laundrette	⚘	children's playground	♿	facilities for disabled
⚡	mains electric hook-ups	⊡	TV	☘	shaded

Lancashire may no longer be the most densely populated county in Europe, now that it has lost ground to newly created metropolitan authorities. Yet in the south, at least, industrial towns are still more numerous than villages. Cheshire consists mainly of a rolling plain centred on the medieval walled city of Chester, as famous for its Rows, or arcaded streets, as for its Roman relics.

The largest single open space in the region is the Forest of Bowland northeast of Preston, southern gateway to which is Clitheroe in the Ribble Valley. Fell and moor rather than forest, Bowland is fine walking country with few human settlements. North of Chester is the Wirral Peninsula, ridge and vale country in the centre but wholly industrial on either side. Between Northwich and Chester is the small Delamere Forest, dotted with lakes. Elsewhere, apart from the Cheshire farmlands, there is little but built up areas and industrialized moorland.

The coast of Lancashire is probably most scenic around Morecambe Bay, noted for its sunsets. Pleasant coastal resorts are Southport and Lytham St Annes, out of earshot of the funfairs and bingo halls of Blackpool, the pleasure ground for people living in the nearby industrial towns, with their staggered holidays or 'wakes'. West of Bowland is Lancaster, topped by its magnificent castle (part prison), housing a superb collection of armorial bearings. The Lune flows south into Lancaster along the Trough of Bowland. West of the river is the only undeveloped corner of the Lancashire coast, a wooded district between Carnforth and Silverdale on the Cumbrian border, isolated behind its saltings at the edge of Morecambe Bay.

Other sights in the region are the castles of Chester, Hawarden and Beeston, and the country houses of Moreton Old Hall, Bramhall, Tatton Park and Tabley Hall.

Most campsites in the region, often well equipped, are – like the town – grouped together rather than dispersed. So the choice is usually wide at the larger centres and resorts but non-existent elsewhere.

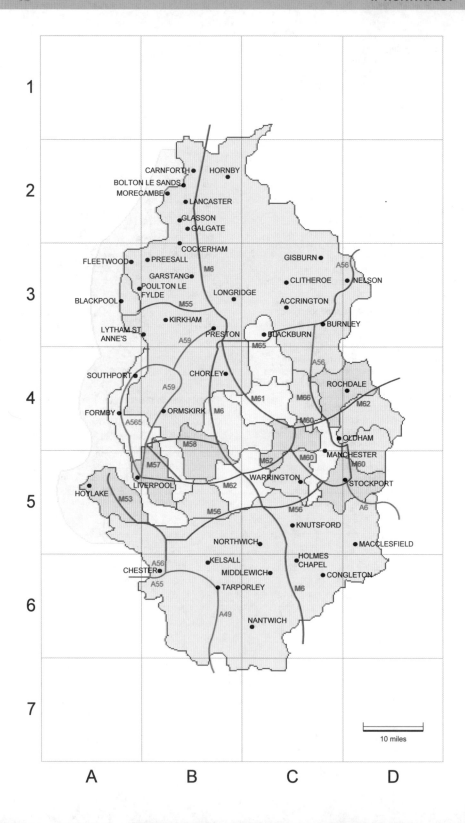

1

2

3

4

5

6

7

A   B   C   D

CARNFORTH ● HORNBY ●
BOLTON LE SANDS ●
MORECAMBE ●
● LANCASTER
● GLASSON
● GALGATE
COCKERHAM ●
FLEETWOOD ● ● PREESALL
GARSTANG ●
POULTON LE
FYLDE
BLACKPOOL ●
● KIRKHAM
LYTHAM ST
ANNE'S ●
SOUTHPORT ●
FORMBY ●
● ORMSKIRK
HOYLAKE ●
● LIVERPOOL
CHESTER ●
KELSALL ●
MIDDLEWICH ●
TARPORLEY ●
NANTWICH ●
GISBURN ●
CLITHEROE ● NELSON ●
LONGRIDGE ● ACCRINGTON ●
PRESTON ● BLACKBURN ●
BURNLEY ●
CHORLEY ●
ROCHDALE ●
OLDHAM ●
MANCHESTER ●
WARRINGTON ●
STOCKPORT ●
KNUTSFORD ●
MACCLESFIELD ●
NORTHWICH ●
HOLMES
CHAPEL ●
CONGLETON ●

M6
A56
M55
A59
A59
A565
A56
A56
M65
M61
M66
M62
M60
M57
M58
M62
M60
M53
M56
M62
M56
A6
A56
A55
A49
M6

10 miles

ACCRINGTON, Lancs   Map C3
EC Wed MD Tues, Fri, Sat
🛈 Town Hall, Blackburn Rd ✆(01254) 872595
✗ Abbey, Bank St ✆(01254) 235727

Harwood Bar Caravan Park, Mill Lane, Great Harwood BB6 7UQ ✆(01254) 884853 OS map
103/752338 2½m N of Accrington off A680 (Whalley) at Sunnyside Open Feb-Dec–must book
peak periods 143 pitches (117 static) Hard standing, sloping, sheltered 🗗🐾🞑🞉🞉⊘☺↩

ACTON BRIDGE–see Northwich

BLACKPOOL, Lancs   Map A3
EC Wed SEE seafront, Tower (518ft), winter gardens, zoo park, model village (Stanley park), electric
trams, illuminations (Sept-Oct)
🛈 1 Clifton St ✆(01253) 478222
✗ Cottage, Newhouse Rd ✆(01253) 464081

Gillett Farm, Peel Road, Peel FY4 5JU ✆(01253) 761676 OS map 102/356323 2m E of Blackpool
off A583 (Kirkham) on Peel road near junct 4 of M55 Open Mar-Oct 175 pitches (100 static)
12 acres level grass and hard standings 🐾🗗🞑🞉⊘☺☺↩🖳 (Mastercard/Visa)

Mariclough Hampsfield Camp Site, Preston New Road, Peel FY4 5JR Small friendly site in open
countryside ✆(01253) 761034 (before 8pm) OS map 102/357327 4m E of Blackpool on A583
(Preston) Open Easter-Oct–caravans must book peak periods 70 pitches Level grass and hard
standing, sheltered 🞉🞑☺ £9.00 www.maricloughhampsfieldcamping.com

Marton Mere Park, Mythop Road FY4 4XN ✆(01253) 760771 Fax (01253) 767544 OS map
102/337354 2½m E of Blackpool off junction 4 of M55 (Preston) Open Mar-Oct 1351 pitches
(920 static) no tents 93 acres hard standings, sheltered 🐾✗🍴🗗🞑🞑🖾(indoor heated) 🚐👦
tennis, bowling green (most cards)

Newton Hall Holiday Centre, Staining Road, Staining FY3 0AX ✆(01253) 882512 OS map
102/338366 2½m NE of Blackpool off B5266 (Singleton) at Newton Arms hotel Open Mar-Oct
525 pitches–no tents Level grass and hard standings 🐾🍴🗗🞑🞉⊘☺🖾(indoor) ↩🞉🞉🚐👦
fishing, amusement arcade

Pipers Height Caravan Camping Park, Peel Road, Peel FY4 5JT ✆(01253) 763767 OS map
102/355325 2½m SE of Blackpool off A583 (Kirkham) on Peel road Open Mar-Nov
154 pitches–families only Grass and hard standing, level, sheltered ✗🍴🗗🞑🞉☺🖳🏠👦
family room, entertainment mid and peak season

Redleigh Orchard Touring Caravan Park, Cropper Road FY4 5LB ✆(01253) 691459 OS map
102/347324 3m SE of Blackpool off A583 (Preston) Open Mar-Oct–must book peak periods
15 pitches–no tents Level grass and hard standing, sheltered 🗗🞑

Richmond Hill Caravan Park, 352 St Anne's Road FY4 2QN ✆(01253) 344266 OS map
102/320332 ½m S of Blackpool off A584 (Lytham) Open Mar-Oct 20 pitches Grass and hard
standing, level, sheltered 🞉🞑☺☺🚐 (weekly rates at discount)

BOLTON LE SANDS, Lancs   Map B2
SEE Sands of Morecambe Bay
✗ The Royal Hotel, Main Rd ✆(01524) 732057
✗ Ricky's Cantonese Restaurant, 26 Slyne Rd ✆(01524) 823888

Bolton Holmes Farm, off Mill Lane LA5 8ES ✆(01524) 732854 Prop: T Mason & Sons OS map
97/480693 1m NW of Bolton le Sands off A6 (Carnforth) Open Apr-Sept 75 pitches (42 static)
Level/sloping grass 🞉🞑☺ £9.00*

Detron Gate Farm LA5 9TN ✆(01524) 732842/733617 OS map 97/485685 ½m W of Bolton le
Sands off A6 (Lancaster) Open Mar-Oct 150 pitches (42 static) Level/sloping grass
🐾🗗🞑🞉⊘☺↩🖳

Morecambe Lodge Caravan Park LA5 8JP ✆(01524) 824361 Prop: JL Towers & BE Halhead OS
map 97/471674 1m SW of Bolton le Sands off A5105 (Morecambe) Open Mar-Oct 211 pitches
(178 static)–no tents 13 acres level grass and hard standing, sheltered 🗗🞑🞑☺☺ serviced
pitches, access to beach £7.00-£14.00 andrew@morecambe-lodge.co.uk www.morecambe-
lodge.co.uk

Sandside Farm Caravan Site, Sandside Farm, St Michael's Lane LA5 8JS ✆(01524) 822311 OS
map 97/475680 ½m SW of Bolton le Sands off A6 (Lancaster) Open Mar-Oct 165 pitches
(35 static) Level/sloping grass, sheltered, some hard standings 🐾🗗🞑🞉⊘☺↩

✆(01524) 824361

Morecambe Lodge Caravan Park

CARNFORTH, Lancs   Map B2
SEE Steamtown Railway Museum, Halton church 5m S, Borwick Hall 2m NE, Leighton Hall 3m N
✗ Holmere Hall, Yealand Conyers ☎ (01524) 735353

Capernwray House Caravan Site, Capernwray LA6 1AE ☎ (01524) 732363 OS map 97/530718
2½m NE of Carnforth off B6254 (Over Kellet) Open Mar-Oct—66 pitches 17 acres, level/sloping, grass and hard standings, sheltered ▣▤▧▨▩▪▫▬▭▮ B&B

Hawthorns Caravan Park, Nether Kellet LA6 1EA ☎ (01524) 732079 OS map 97/514686 2m SE of Carnforth off B6254 (Kirkby Lonsdale) via Over Kellet Open Mar-Oct 70 pitches (50 static)
Level grass and hard standing ▣▤▧▨▩▪▫▬ 9 hole putting green, library

Holgates Caravan Park, Cove Road, Silverdale LA5 0SH ☎ (01524) 701508 OS map 97/455759
5m NW of Carnforth on Arnside road Open Dec-Nov—must book peak periods 420 pitches
(350 static) Hard standings, level, part sheltered ▣✗▨▩▪▫▬▭▮(heated) ▬▭▮
gym, sauna, spa pool, pitch and putt £29.50-£31.00 (Mastercard/Visa) caravan@holgates.co.uk
www.holgates.co.uk

Old Hall Caravan Park, Capernwray LA6 1AD ☎ (01524) 733276 Fax (01524) 734488 OS map
97/533707 2½m NE of Carnforth off B6254 (Kirkby Lonsdale) on Capernwray road
Open Mar-Oct—advisable to book 198 pitches (160 static) Level hard standings, sheltered
▣▤▧▨▩▪▫▬▭▮ £15.50-£17.50* (most cards) oldhall@charis.co.uk www.oldhall.co.uk

CHESTER, Cheshire   Map B6
EC Wed MD daily except Wed SEE The Rows, cathedral, city walls, gates and towers, High Cross, Roman amphitheatre, Dee Bridge, old inns, Grosvenor museum, zoo and gardens, river and canal (boat trips)
▣ Town Hall, Northgate St ☎ (01244) 317962
✗ Blossoms, St John St ☎ (01244) 323186

Chester Southerly Caravan Park, Balderton Lane, Marlston-cum-Lache CH4 9LF ☎ (01244)
671308 and (07976) 743888 Fax (01244) 659804 OS map 117/385624 3m S of Chester off
A55/A483 (Wrexham) Open Mar-Nov—adv booking advisable 90 pitches Level grass and hard standings ▣▤▧▨▩▪▫▬ £12.00 (min)* www.chestersoutherlytouringpark.co.uk

Fairoaks Camping Caravan Park, Rake Lane, Little Stanney CH2 4HS ☎ 0151-355 1600 OS map
117/410738 4m N of Chester on A5117 (Mold) Open Mar-Oct 130 pitches 8 acres level grass and hard standings, sheltered ▣▤▧▨▩▪▫▬

Netherwood House, Whitchurch Road CH3 6AF ☎ (01244) 335583 Prop: A Broad-Davies OS map
117/447648 2m SE of Chester on A41 (Whitchurch) Open Mar-Oct 15 pitches, must book
1½ acres level grass, sheltered ▣▤ £10.00-£15.00* netherwood.chester@btinternet.com
www.netherwoodtouringsite.co.uk

See also Kelsall

CLITHEROE, Lancs   Map C3
EC Wed MD Mon, Tues, Fri, S SEE Pendle Hill (1,830ft), castle keep, Sawley Abbey, Castle House Museum
▣ Market Pl ☎ (01200) 425566
✗ Swan and Royal, Castle St ☎ (01200) 23130

Shireburn Caravan Park, Waddington Road, near Edisford Bridge BB7 3LB ☎ (01200) 423422 OS
map 103/727418 1½m W of Clitheroe off B6243 (Longridge) Open Mar-Oct 200 pitches
(180 static) Level grass and hard standings, sheltered ▣▤▧▨▩ fishing, lic club

Three Rivers Park, Eaves Hall Lane, West Bradford BB7 3JG ☎ (01200) 423523 Fax (01200)
442383 OS map 103/736451 2m N of Clitheroe off B6478 (Slaidburn) at Waddington Open all
year 250 pitches (150 static) Grass, level, hard standings, sheltered ▣▨▧▨▩▪(indoor)
▬▭▮ lic club, entertainment w/ends (Mastercard/Visa)

COCKERHAM, Lancs   Map B3
✗ Victoria 2m N at Glasson Dock ☎ (01524) 751423

Cockerham Sands Country Park LA2 0BB ☎ (01524) 751387 OS map 102/430544 3m NW of
Cockerham off A588 (Lancaster) at Upper Thurnham on Cockersand Abbey road, near sea
Open Mar-Oct 270 pitches (261 static) Grass and hard standings ▣▨▧▨▩▪▫▬▭(Jun-Sep)
▬▭

Moss Wood Caravan Park, Crimbles Lane LA2 0ES ☎ (01524) 791041 Fax (01524) 792444 OS
map 102/455513 1m SW of Cockerham on A588 (Poulton le Fylde) Open Mar-Oct 200 pitches
(175 static) 2½ acres hard standings, sheltered ▣▤▧▨▩▪▫ (most cards)
info@mosswood.co.uk www.mosswood.co.uk

GALGATE, Lancs   Map B2
✗ Hampson House ☎ (01524) 751158

Laundfields, Stoney Lane LA2 0JZ ☎ (01524) 751763 OS map 102/485553 E of Galgate centre
on right of Dolpinholme road, near junction 33 of M6 Open Mar-Oct 20 pitches—booking advisable
½ acre level grass ▣▤ £7.00

GARSTANG, Lancs   Map B3

EC Wed MD Thurs SEE castle ruins, parish church, Wyre bridge
🆔 Discovery Centre, Council offices, High St ✆ (01995) 602125
✗ Owd Tithebarn, Church St ✆ (01995) 602923

Bridge House Marina, Nateby Crossing Lane, Nateby PR3 0JJ ✆ (01995) 603207 Fax (01995) 601612 OS map 102/483457 ½m W of Garstang off Nateby road by Lancaster canal Open Mar-Jan 70 pitches (20 static)–no tents Level grass and hard standing 🛒🖥🛏🅿🚿✔ (most cards) edwin@bridgehousemarina.co.uk www.birdgehousemarina.co.uk

Claylands Farm, Cabus PR3 1AJ *Well maintained park close to river and woodland walks* ✆ (01524) 791242 *Prop: F & M & A Robinson* OS map 102/496485 2m N of Garstang off A6 (Lancaster)–signposted Open Mar-Jan 4 98 pitches (68 static) 4 acres gentle slope, grass and hard standing 🛒✗🖥🛏🅿🚿🚿✔♿ £15.00 (Mastercard/Visa) andrew@claylands.com www.claylands-caravan-park.co.uk

Six Arches Caravan Park, Scorton PR3 1AL ✆ (01524) 791683 OS map 102/502485 3m N of Garstang on A6 (Lancaster) Open Mar-Oct–must book 310 pitches (275 static)–no tents Grass and hard standing, level, sheltered 🛒🖾🧑🖥🛏🅿🚿🖳🚿✔🍽🏠 paddling pool, fishing, lic club

Smithy Caravan Park, Cabus Nook Lane, Winmarleigh PR3 1AA ✆ (01995) 606200 OS map 102/482482 1½m N of Garstang off A6 (Lancaster) on Winmarleigh road via Cabus Open Mar-Jan 90 pitches (70 static) Grass and hard standing, part level 🛒🖥🛏🅿🚿🚿🍽 fishing lake

GISBURN, Lancs   Map C3

MD Thurs
✗ Stirk House ✆ (01200) 445581

Rimington Caravan Park, Hardacre Lane, Rimington BB7 4EE ✆ (01200) 445355 Fax (01200) 445355 OS map 103/862471 1m S of Gisburn off A682 (Nelson) Open Apr-Oct 150 pitches (130 static) Level grass and hard standing, sheltered 🛒🖥🛏🅿🚿🚿🖳🍽♿ lic club £10.00 (min)* lisa@rimington2004.freeserve.co.uk

GLASSON DOCK, Lancs   Map B2

✗ Victoria, Victoria Terr ✆ (01524) 751423

Marina Caravan Park, Glasson Dock LA2 0BP ✆ (01524) 751787 OS map 102/443560 In Glasson on B5290 Open Mar-Dec 143 pitches (123 static) Grass and hard standings 🖥🛏🅿🚿🚿🖳🚿🍽♿

HOLMES CHAPEL, Cheshire   Map C6

✗ Swan, Station Rd ✆ (01477) 532259

Mount Pleasant Caravan Site, Goostrey CW4 8JS ✆ (01477) 532263 OS map 118/768700 2m NNE of Holmes Chapel off A50 (Knutsford) Open all year 110 pitches (90 static) Grass, level, open, sheltered, some hard standings 🖥🛏🅿🚿

HOYLAKE, Merseyside   Map A5

EC Wed SEE promenade, Dee estuary
✗ Linos, Market St ✆ 0151 632 1408

Wirral Country Park, Station Road, Thurstaston, Wirral L61 0HN ✆ 0151-648 5228 OS map 108/234838 3m SE of Hoylake off A540 (Heswall) via Thurstaston Open Apr 2-Nov 1 90 pitches 8 acres 🖥🛏🅿🚿✔ £14.60-£20.60* (Mastercard/Visa/Delta/Switch) www.holidayclub.co.uk

KELSALL, Cheshire   Map B6

SEE Delamere forest NE
✗ Willington Hall 2m S at Willington ✆ (01829) 752321

Northwood Hall Country Touring Park CW6 0RP ✆ (01829) 752569 OS map 117/517680 1m W of Kelsall on A54 (Chester) Open all year 30 pitches–must book 5 acres level/gentle slope, some hard standings 🖥🛏🅿🚿🚿✔🍽🖳🏠

KIRKHAM, Lancs   Map B3

EC Wed MD Thurs SEE church, fish-stone circle
✗ Queens Arms, Poulton St (A585) ✆ (01772) 686705

Whitmore Caravan Park, Bradshaw Lane, Greenhalgh PR4 3HQ ✆ (01253) 836224 OS map 102/401356 2m NNW of Kirkham off A585 (Fleetwood) Open Mar-Oct 25 pitches Level grass and hard standing, sheltered 🛏🅿🚿🖳 coarse fishing

KNUTSFORD, Cheshire   Map C5

EC Wed MD Fri, Sat SEE 17c Unitarian chapel (Mrs Gaskell's grave), Gaskell memorial tower, Sessions House, 18c Georgian church
🆔 Council Offices, Toft Rd ✆ (01565) 632611
✗ White Lion, King St ✆ (01565) 632018

Woodlands Park, Wash Lane, Allostock WA16 9LG ✆ (01565) 723429 Fax (01332) 810818 OS map 118/736707 4m S of Knutsford off A50 (Holmes Chapel) on right of B5082 (Northwich) near lake Open Mar 1-Jan 6 50 pitches–no motor cycles Level grass 🛒🖥🛏🅿 11.00 (min)*

Help us make CAMPING CARAVANNING BRITAIN better known to site operators – and thereby more informative – by showing them your copy when booking in.

LYTHAM ST ANNE'S, Lancs   Map B3
EC Wed SEE St Anne's Pier, Lifeboat memorial, parish church, Lowther gardens, Motive Power Museum, Fairhaven Lake
🛈 St Annes Rd West ☎(01253) 725610
✗ Queens, Central Beach ☎(01253) 737316

Bank Lane Caravan Park, Warton PR4 1TB ☎(01772) 633513 OS map 102/403276 5m E of Lytham off A584 (Preston) at Warton Bank Open Mar-Oct 230 pitches (180 static) 14 acres level grass and hard standing, sheltered 🛢🗑🚻🅰🚿🅾↩🌮

Eastham Hall Caravan Park, Saltcotes Road FY8 4LS ☎(01253) 737907 OS map 102/380289 2½m E of Lytham St Anne's off A584 (Preston) Open Mar-Oct 370 pitches (200 static)–no tents Grass and hard standing, level, sheltered 🛢🗑🚻🅰🚿🅾🕒↩🌮 (most cards)

Seaview Caravan Park, Bank Lane Warton PR4 1TD ☎(01772) 679336 OS map 102/405273 3m E of Lytham St Anne's off A584 (Preston) Open Mar-Nov 192 pitches (76 static) 6 acres grass 🛢🗑🚻🅰

MACCLESFIELD, Cheshire   Map D5
EC Wed MD daily SEE Silk museum, market stone, St Michael's church, Capesthorne Hall 4½m W
🛈 Town Hall, Market Place ☎(01625) 504114
✗ Oliver's Bistro, Chestergate ☎(01625) 832003

Capesthorne Hall Caravan Park SK11 9JY ☎(01625) 861779/861221 Fax (01625) 861619 OS map 118/840728 4½m W of Macclesfield off A537 (Knutsford) on right of A34 (Congleton) in grounds of stately home Open March-Oct 30 pitches–no tents or trailer tents Level grass, part sheltered 🛢🗑🚻🅰🅾🚿♿ gardens £13.00-£15.00* info@capesthorne.com www.capeshthorne.com

MORECAMBE, Lancs   Map B2
EC Wed MD Tues, Sat SEE Marineland, autumn illuminations, sands (guided walks across)
🛈 Central Promenade ☎(01524) 582808/9
✗ Elms, Elms Rd ☎(01524) 411501

Glen Caravan Park, Westgate LA3 3EL ☎(01524) 423896 OS map 97/435629 1m E of Morecambe off B5321 (Skerton) on Westgate road Open Mar-Oct 70 pitches (51 static) 3 acres level grass and hard standing, sheltered 🗑🚻🅰🅾🚿🌮

Greendales Farm Caravan Park, Carr Lane, Middleton LA3 3LH ☎(01524) 852616 OS map 102/418584 5m S of Morecambe off A589 (Heysham) and Overton road Open Mar-Oct 20 pitches 1 acre hard standing and level grass 🚻🅰↩

Hawthorne Camping Site, Carr Lane, Middleton Sands LA3 3LL ☎(01524) 852074 OS map 102/415573 3½m SW of Morecambe off A589 (Heysham) via Middleton and coast road Open Apr-Sept 73 pitches Level grass and hard standings 🎣⚲🗑🚻🅰🅾🕒🍴🌮 £10.00

Melbreak Camp, Carr Lane, Middleton LA3 3LH ☎(01524) 852430 OS map 102/418584 3m S of Morecambe off A683 (Middleton) on Carr Lane near holiday camp Open Mar-Oct 42 pitches (32 static) 2 acres level grass and hard standing 🛢↩🗑🚻🅰🅾 £8.20-£10.50*

Regent Leisure Park, Westgate LA3 3DF ☎(01524) 413940 OS map 97/428630 ½m SE of Morecambe off B5273 (Lancaster) Open Mar-Jan 324 pitches (300 static) Hard standing, level, sheltered 🛢✗⚲↩🗑🚻🅰🅾🚿📺↩🍴🌮🍽♿ lic club, evening entertainment, snooker, pool, children's indoor adventureland

Riverside Caravan Park, Oxcliffe Hall Farm, Heaton with Oxcliffe LA3 3ER Small friendly farm site on river estuary ☎(01524) 844193 OS map 97/448617 2m E of Morecambe off B5273 (Scale Hall) on Heaton road Open Mar-Oct 70 pitches (20 static) Level grass 🛢🚻🅰🅾🕒🚿🌮🍽 £8.00-£10.00* (Mastercard/Visa/Switch) info@riverside-morecambe.co.uk www.riverside-morecambe.co.uk

Venture Caravan Park, Langridge Way, Westgate LA4 4TQ ☎(01524) 412986 Prop: Mahdeen Leisure Ltd OS map 97/435632 ¼m S of Morecambe off A589 (Heysham) Open all year 316 pitches (260 static) 17 acres level grass 🛢⚲↩🎣🗑🚻🅰🅾📺↩🍴🌮🍽♿ amusements £10.10-£12.10 (Maestro/Visa/Electron/Solo) mark@venturecaravanpark.co.uk www.venturecaravanpark.co.uk

NANTWICH, Cheshire   Map C6
EC Wed Old market town still with medieval street pattern SEE St Mary's church, Welsh Row, museum
🛈 Church House, Church Walk ☎(01270) 610983/610880 ✗ Crown, High St ☎(01270) 625283

Brookfield Caravan Park, Shrewbridge Road CW5 7AD ☎(01270) 569176 OS map 118/652516 ½m S of Nantwich centre off A530 (Whitchurch) adj park and river Open Easter-Sept 25 pitches–no adv booking 1 acre, level grass fishing

NORTHWICH, Cheshire   Map C5
EC Wed MD Tue, Fri, Sat SEE Budworth Mere, Anderton Lift linking river Weaver and Trent and
Mersey Canal, Marbury Country Park
✘ Quincey's, London Rd ✆ (01606) 845524

Daleford Manor Caravan Park, Dalefords Lane, Sandiway CW8 2BT ✆ (01606) 883391 OS map
   118/605698 4m SW of Northwich off A556 (Manchester-Chester) and Foxwist Green road Open
   Mar-Oct 42 pitches (30 static)–no tents Level grass and hard standing, sheltered 🅾 ⊕

Lamb Cottage, Dalefords Lane, Whitegate CW8 2BN ✆ (01606) 882302 Fax (01606) 888491 OS
   map 118/614693 4m SW of Northwich off A556 (Manchester-Chester) Open Mar-Oct 100 pitches
   Grass, level, sheltered 🔲🅰⊕∅🔲& £15.00-£17.00* (most cards) lynn@lccp.fsworld.co.uk
   www.lambcottage.co.uk

Woodbine Cottage, Warrington Road, Acton Bridge CW8 3QB ✆ (01606) 852319 and 77900 OS
   map 117/590755 4m NW of Northwich on A49 (Warrington) via Weaverham Open Mar 1-Oct
   21–must book public holidays 50 pitches Grass and hard standing 🔲🅾🔲🅰⊕🔲🔲(40) 🔲

OLDHAM, Gtr Manchester   Map C4
EC Thurs MD Mon, Fri, Sat SEE art gallery, crypt of parish church, Town hall, Bluecoat school
🔲 12 Albion St ✆ 0161 627 1024
✘ King George, Hollins Rd ✆ 0161 624 5170

Moorlands Caravan Park, Ripponden Rd, Denshaw OL3 5UN Good touring centre with splendid
   moorland views ✆ (01457) 874348 OS map 109/977120 5m NE of Oldham on A672
   (Huddersfield) near junct 22 of M62 Open all year 42 pitches 2½ acres level, hard standings and
   level grass 🅾🔲🅰⊕🔲🔲

ORMSKIRK, Lancs   Map B4
SEE church of SS Peter and Paul
✘ Bull & Dog Inn, Liverpool Rd South, Burscough ✆ (01704) 895798

Abbey Farm, Dark Lane L40 5TX ✆ (01695) 572686 Prop: R & J Perkins OS map 108/433099
   1½ NE of Ormskirk via Derby Street amd Greetby Hill, near Burscough Abbey Open all
   year–must book peak periods 104 pitches (44 static) Level grass and hard standings, sheltered
   🔲🔲🅾🔲🅰⊕∅⊕🔲& library, games room, fishing £8.50-£15.80 (Mastercard/Visa)
   abbeyfarm@yahoo.com www.abbeyfarmcaravanpark.co.uk

Shaw Hall Caravan Park, off Smithy Lane, Scarisbrick L40 8HJ ✆ (01704) 840298 Fax (01704)
   840539 OS map 108/397115 3m NW of Ormskirk off A570 (Southport) Open Mar-Jan
   345 pitches (300 static) Level grass and hard standing 🔲🔲🅾🔲🅰⊕∅🔲🔲& lic club with
   entertainment, bowling green £16.00-£21.00* (most cards) shawhall@btconnect.com
   www.shawhall.co.uk

POULTON LE FYLDE, Lancs   Map A3
SEE St Chad's church
✘ Anna's Bistro, Breck Rd ✆ (01253) 882336

Kneps Farm Holiday Park, River Road, Thornton Cleveleys FY5 5LR ✆ (01253) 823632 OS map
   102/354430 2m N of Poulton le Fylde off B5412 (Thornton) Open Mar-Nov 15–must book peak
   periods 150 pitches (80 static) 10 acres level grass and hard standing 🔲🅾🔲🅰⊕🔲🔲🔲&
   sep pitches £13.00-£17.00 (Mastercard/Visa) enquiries@knepsfarm.co.uk www.knepsfarm.co.uk

Meadowcroft and Queensgate Caravan Park, Garstang Road, Great Eccleston PR3 0ZQ
   ✆ (01995) 670266 OS map 102/415403 3m E of Poulton le Fylde on A586 (Garstang-Blackpool)
   Open Mar-Oct 91 pitches (83 static) Level grass and hard standing 🅾🔲🅰⊕∅

PREESALL, Lancs   Map B3
✘ Saracens Head, Park Lane (B5377) ✆ (01253) 810346

Glenfield Caravan Park, Smallwood Hey Rd, Pilling PR3 6HE ✆ (01253) 790782 OS map
   102/399483 2m E of Preesall off A588 (Cockerham) in Pilling village Open Mar-Oct 257 pitches
   (125 static) 8½ acres level grass 🅾🔲🅰⊕∅

Maaruig Touring Caravan Park, 71 Pilling Lane FY6 0HB ✆ (01253) 810404 Prop: PR & A Woods
   OS map 102/364490 1m N of Preesall off B5377 (Knott End) Open Mar 1-Jan 4 28 pitches
   Grass, level, sheltered 🅾🔲⊕ from £11.00

Sunset Park, Sower Carr Lane, Hambleton FY6 9EQ ✆ (01253) 700222 OS map 102/373425 3m
   S of Preesall off A588 (Poulton) Open Mar-Oct 105 pitches (70 static) Level grass and hard
   standing 🔲🔲🅾🔲🅰⊕∅🔲(indoor children's) ⊕🔲🔲 spa bath, sauna, fishing (Mastercard/Visa)

Willowgrove Caravan Park, Sandy Lane FY6 0EJ ✆ (01253) 811306 OS map 102/366480 1m N
   of Preesall off B5377 (Knott End) Open Mar-Oct 200 pitches (137 static) Level grass
   🔲🅾🔲🅰⊕∅🔲& coarse fishing, bird watching

For more up-to-date information, and for links to camping websites, visit our site at:
www.butford.co.uk/camping

PRESTON, Lancs   Map B3
MD Daily except Thur SEE Roman Museum (Ribchester), Crown Court Hall, parish church,
shopping precinct, Harris museum, Fulwood barracks (military museum)
🛈 Guildhall, Lancaster Rd ✆ (01772) 253731
✗ Tiggi's (Italian), Guildhall St ✆ (01772) 658527

Royal Umpire Touring Park, Croston PR5 7JB ✆ (01772) 600257 OS map 108/504190 5m S of
Preston on A581 (Chorley-Southport) at Croston Open all year 201 pitches 60 acres grass and
hard standing, part sheltered 🛒✗ ⊷ ⚲ 🗋🢒🗐 🖴 ⊕∅ ☻ ↵ ⅋

ROCHDALE, Gtr Manchester   Map D4
EC Tues MD daily except Tues SEE St Chad's church, town hall, museum, John Bright's grave, Co-
op museum
🛈 The Esplanade ✆ (01706) 864928
✗ Millers Pub & Restaurant, Hollingworth Lake, Littleborough ✆ (01706) 378163

Hollingworth Lake Caravan Park, Rakewood, Littleborough OL15 0AT ✆ (01706) 378661 OS map
109/943146 4m NE of Rochdale off A68 (Milnrow) and B6225 (Littleborough) at The Fish Inn on
Rakewood road (junct 21 of M62) Open all year 75 pitches (40 static) 5 acres, grass and hard
standing, sheltered 🛒 🗐🢒🗐 🖴 ⊕∅ ⊏▱⅋ pony trekking for park £6.00-£14.00

SANDIWAY–see Northwich

SILVERDALE–see Carnforth

SOUTHPORT, Merseyside   Map A4
EC Tues SEE St Cuthbert's church, Floral Hall and gardens, zoo, Birkdale Sands, Ribble estuary
🛈 112 Lord St ✆ (01704) 533333
✗ Legh Arms, 5m NE at Mere Brow ✆ (01772) 812225

Brooklyn Caravan Park and Country Club, Gravel Lane, Banks PR9 8BU ✆ (01704) 228534 OS
map 108/392198 4m NE of Southport on A565 (Preston) Open Mar 1-Jan 7 250 pitches
(150 static) Level grass, sheltered 🛒 ✗ ♨ 🗐🢒🗐🖴 ⊕∅↵ ▰▱

Leisure Lakes Caravan Park, Mere Brow PR4 6JX *Well equipped site in spacious parkland with
facs for watersports* ✆ (01772) 813446 OS map 108/415187 5m NE of Southport off A565
(Preston) at Mere Brow Open all year 86 pitches 8 acres level grass and hard standings
✗ ♨ ⊷ 🗐🢒🗐🖴 ⊕∅ ☻↵⅋ golf driving range (Mastercard/Visa/Switch)

STOCKPORT, Gtr Manchester   Map D5
EC Thurs MD Tues, Fri, Sat SEE Art Gallery Museum, Bramall Hall 2½m S
🛈 Staircase, Marketplace ✆ 0161 474 4444
✗ Alma Lodge, Buxton Rd ✆ 0161-483 4431

Elmbeds Caravan and Camping Park, Elmbeds Road, Higher Poynton SK12 1TG ✆ (01625)
872370 *Prop: P Whittaker* OS map 109/945829 5m SE of Stockport off A523 (Macclesfield)
Open Apr-Oct 70 pitches (50 static) Level/sloping grass and hard standing, sheltered 🢒🗐🖴 ⊕∅
£6.00-£12.50

THORNTON CLEVELEYS–see Poulton le Fylde

WARRINGTON, Cheshire   Map C5
EC Thurs MD daily except Thur SEE parish church, museum and library, town hall, Barley Mow inn
🛈 The Market Hall ✆ (01925) 632571
✗ Patten Arms, Parker St ✆ (01925) 436602

Holly Bank Caravan Park, Warburton Bridge Road, Rixton WA3 6HU ✆ 0161 775 2842 OS map
109/692904 5½m E of Warrington off A57 (Irlam) near Junction 21 of M6 Open all year
75 pitches Level grass and hard standing, sheltered 🛒 🗋🢒🗐🖴 ⊕∅ ☻↵▰ £13.00-£17.00*

WARTON–see Lytham

WEETON–see Poulton le Fylde

WINSFORD–see Middlewich

Kneps Farm Holiday Park,
River Road, Stanah,
Thornton-Cleveleys,
Lancashire, FY5 5LR

Tel: 01253 823632
enquiries@knepsfarm.co.uk

The essentially rural East Midlands consists of the five shires of Derby, Leicester, Lincoln, Northampton and Nottingham. Derbyshire is the most scenic of this group, containing as it does much of the Peak District, dramatic in the upper half, softer and more gentle in the lower, with its high fells and beautiful dales, homely villages, handsome spa towns and subterranean rivers and caves, The three main rivers – Dane, Dove and Manifold – rise at Axe Edge to flow through the well known valleys to which they give their names. Chapel en le Frith is a handy base for the northern half, and Buxton – where the Pennines roll down into the dales – for the southern. Some of the most impressive scenery can be reached only on foot, for example on the trail between Tissington and Buxton, or the ridge walk from Mam Tor near Castleton to Lose Hill. Peak Pathfinder bus services operate in season from Buxton and Ashbourne to Dovedale. Two historic Derbyshire buildings not to be missed are Peveril Castle near Castleton and, farther south, Chatsworth House.

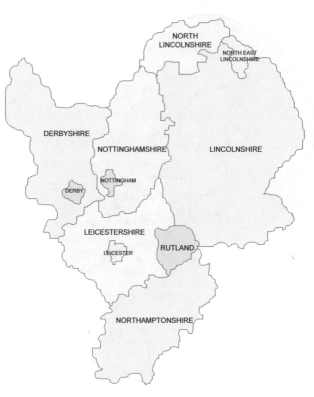

Adjoining Derbyshire on the east is Nottinghamshire. Its distinctive and appealing scenery includes the central plateau cut by treelined valleys, the wolds in the southeast, the Trent Valley in the east, with steep buffs lining the river at Gunthorpe and Hazelford, and the glades and clearings of gently rolling Sherwood Forest around Edwinstowe. Routes for walkers include the Fosse Way, the Trent Ridgeway between Radcliffe and East Bridgeford and the Soar Ridgeway above Thrumpton. Important sights are the castles of Nottingham and Newark, the houses of Newstead Abbey and Wollaton Hall and the parks of Thoresby and Welbeck.

Nottinghamshire's neighbour on the east is Lincolnshire, in which the landscape shifts from the Belvoir Hills, forming the western border, to the limestone ridge from Barrowby Hill to Lincoln and the low ground around the Wash, which is patterned with canals and flood banks and appropriately called Holland. In the south is flat and fertile farmland, some of it around Spalding dazzling with tulips in spring. Along the coast are firm sands sheltered by dunes; south of Skegness is an extensive nature reserve. The two most historic buildings in the county are probably the cathedral and Norman castle of Lincoln.

Leicestershire, a small county famed for its hunting, is most pastoral in the east and south, where the tow-paths of its canals provide excellent routes for walkers. Between Leicester, Ashby and Loughborough is Charnwood Forest, where crags and moorland alternate with woods. There are grand churches at Kelton, Empingham, Market Harborough and Staunton Harold.

Southernmost county in the region is Northamptonshire, green and peaceful away from the industrial towns of Kettering, Rothwell, Wellingborough and Corby. As well as Yardley Chase and the Forest of Rockingham round the Welland Valley there are numerous Saxon churches and country houses worth seeing.

Campsites are well distributed throughout the region in the Peak and dales, the Trent Valley and Sherwood Forest, on the Lincolnshire coast and the main transit routes.

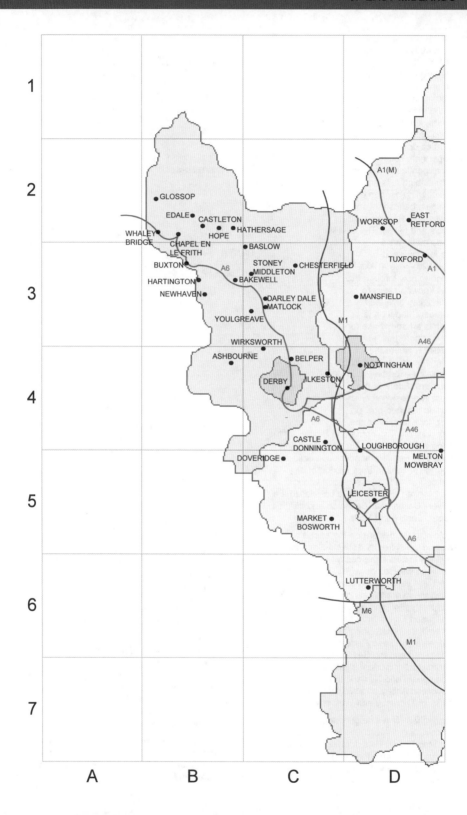

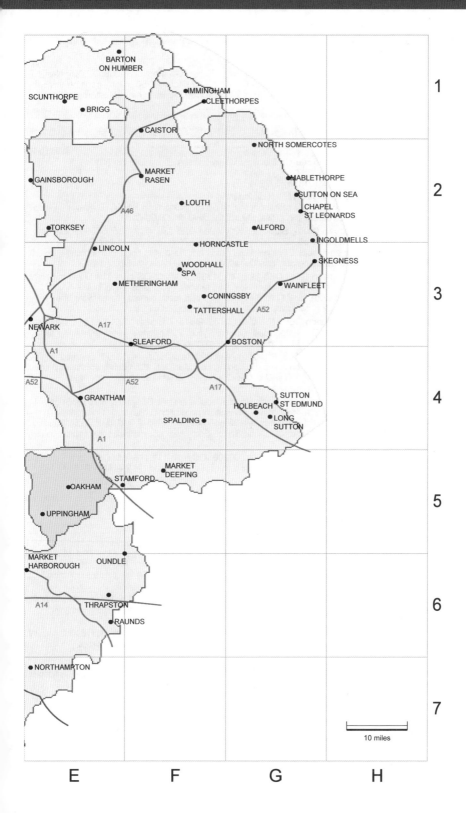

ALFORD, Lincs   Map G2
SEE museum, church
✗ Half Moon, West St ☎ (01507) 463477

Woodthorpe Hall Leisure Park LN13 0DD ☎ (01507) 450294 OS map 122/436803 3½m N of Alford on left of A1104-B1373 (Withern) Open Mar-Oct 200 pitches (150 static)–booking advisable Level grass and hard standings, sheltered ▭✗♀▢❽◍ ▭☗ golf, fishing (Mastercard/Visa)

ALPORT–see Youlgreave

ANCASTER–see Sleaford and Grantham

ASHBOURNE, Derbys   Map B4
EC Wed MD Thurs, Sat SEE 13c church, Manifold Valley 3m NW, Dovedale 2m NW
▨ 13 Market Place ☎ (01335) 343666
✗ Smiths Tavern, St Johns St ☎ (01335) 342264

Bank Top Farm, Fenny Bentley DE6 1LF *Working dairy farm with viewing gallery* ☎ (01335) 350250 OS map 119/183498 2m N of Ashbourne off A515 (Buxton) on B5056 (Bakewell) Open Easter-Sept 50 pitches Level/sloping grass, sheltered ▭❽◉ £8.00-£13.00*

Blackwall Plantation (Caravan Club), Blackwall, Kirk Ireton DE6 3JL ☎ (01335) 370903 OS map 119/253498 6m E of Ashbourne off A517 (Belper) and Kirk Ireton road Open Apr-Oct 134 pitches–adv booking advisable 25 acres level grass and hard standings in woodland ❽◍◉ ▭ £14.60-£20.60* (Mastercard/Visa/Delta/Switch) www.caravanclub.co.uk

Callow Top Holiday Park, Buxton Road DE6 2AQ ☎ (01335) 344020 OS map 119/172477 ½m N of Ashbourne on A515 (Buxton) Open Easter-Nov 150 pitches (40 static) Level grass ▭✗♀↩▢❽◍◉∅▭(heated) ◉↩▢☗↺ pub and pub food, games room, cycle hire, fishing (most cards) enquiries@callowtop.co.uk www.callowtop.co.uk

Gateway Caravan Park, Osmaston DE6 1NA ☎ (01335) 344643 OS map 119/193451 1½m SE of Ashbourne off A52 (Derby) on Osmaston road Open all year 200 pitches Level grass and hard standings, sheltered ▭♀▢❽◍▭↺ games room, club room, squash court

Highfield Farm, Fenny Bentley DE6 1LE ☎ (0870) 741 8000 Fax (0870) 741 2000 OS map 119/174510 2½m N of Ashbourne on A515 (Buxton) Open Mar-Oct 105 pitches (55 static) Level grass and hard standing, sheltered ▭▢❽◍◉∅▭(indoor) ◉↩▢▣▭ farm produce £12.00-£15.00* (most cards)

Rivendale Caravan and Leisure Park, Buxton Road, Alsop in le Dale DE6 1QU ☎ (01335) 310441 *Prop: Greg Potter* OS map 119/164562 6m N of Ashbourne off A515 (Buxton) Open Mar-Jan 105 pitches Level grass and hard standings, sheltered ▭✗♀↗▢❽◍◉◉↩▭↺ games room, lounge, dog walk £9.50 (Mastercard/Visa/Switch/Solo) vicky@riverdalecaravanpark.co.uk www.rivendalecaravanpark.co.uk

Sandybrook Country Park DE6 2AQ ☎ (01335) 300000 OS map 119/178483 1m N of Ashbourne on A515 (Buxton) Open Apr-Oct 30 pitches Sloping grass, sheltered ✗♀↩❽◍◉∅◉↩☗ (most cards if prepaid)

BAKEWELL, Derbys   Map B3
EC Thurs MD Mon SEE Vernon monuments in church, Saxon cross, almshouses, old bridge, Old House museum, Haddon Hall 2m SE, Chatsworth House 3m NE
▨ Old Market Hall, Bridge St ☎ (01629) 813227
✗ Aitch's Wine Bar ☎ (01629) 813895

Greenhills Holiday Park, Crow Hill Lane DE45 1PX ☎ (01629) 813467 *Prop: Mr & Mrs JA Green* OS map 119/195698 1m NW of Bakewell off A6 (Buxton) Open Mar-Oct 170 pitches (65 static) Level grass, sheltered ▭♀▢❽◍◉∅↩▭↺ lic club £10.00-£17.50 (all cards exc Amex & Diners) info@greenhillsholidaypark.co.uk www.greenhillsholidaypark.co.uk

Haddon Grove Farm, Over Haddon DE4 1JF ☎ (01629) 812343 OS map 119/177663 4m SW of Bakewell off B5055 (Monyash) Open Mar-Oct 19 pitches Grass, partly level, sheltered ❽◍◉∅▭ £5.50

Mill Farm, Haddon Grove, Over Haddon DE45 1JF ☎ (01629) 812013 OS map 119/180662 3m W of Bakewell off B5055 (Monyash) at Haddon Grove Open all year 10 pitches 2 acres level/sloping grass and hard standings ◉▭

BARTON UPON HUMBER, N Lincs   Map E1
EC Thurs SEE suspension bridge, churches, museum, country park
▨ Humber Bridge Viewing Area, (North Bank) ☎ (01482) 640852
✗ The Sloop Inn, 81 Waterside Rd ☎ (01652) 637287

Barton Broads, Chemical Lane DN18 5JW ☎ (01652) 634742 OS map 112/035225 ½m E of Barton upon Humber on A1077 (Barrow) Open all year 35 pitches ▭↗◍◉◉▭ fishing

Silver Birches Tourist Park, Waterside Road DN18 5BA ☎ (01652) 632509 *Prop: Tom and Sybil Prior* OS map 112/028247 ½m N of Barton upon Humber on Waterside Road Open all year 25 pitches Level grass, sheltered ▢❽◍∅◉↩ £12.00 sybilprior@yahoo.co.uk www.silverbirchescaravanpark.co.uk

White Cat
Caravan and Camping Park
Shaw Lane
Old Leake
Boston
Lincolnshire
PE22 9LQ

Telephone +44 (0)1205 870121

THE WHITE CAT CARAVAN & CAMPING PARK

TOURIST BOARD REGISTERED

AA
▶▶▶

BASLOW, Derbys
Map C3

SEE St Anne's church, 17c bridge, Derwent valley, Chatsworth House 2m S
✘ Cavendish ✆ (01246) 882311

Stocking Farm, Calver S30 1XA ✆ (01433) 630516 OS map 119/247747 2m NW of Baslow off A623 (Chapel en le Frith) on Calver Mill road Open Apr-Oct 20 pitches–bkg adv 1 acre gentle slope grass, hard standing

See also Stoney Middleton

BELPER, Derbys
Map C4

SEE Alport Height NW, Wirksworth parish church NW
✘ The Spanker Inn, Spanker Lane, Nether Heage ✆ (01773) 853222

The First Farm, Crich Lane, Nether Heage, Ambergate DE56 2JH ✆ (01773) 852913 *Prop: Stella Ragsdale* OS map 119/355507 ½m N of Belper off A6–signposted Open all year–adults only 60 pitches Level grass, some hard standings ✘🔌⊕∅🛢 gas supplies nearby £11.00-£12.50 *www.thefirstfarmcaravanpark.btinternet.co.uk*

BOSTON, Lincs
Map G3

EC Thurs MD Wed, Sat SEE St Botolph's church, Guildhall museum, Dominican Friary
ℹ Market Place ✆ (01205) 356656
✘ Three Horseshoes, Main Rd, Leverton ✆ (01205) 870420 Open 12-2/6-9

Oak Tree Caravan Park, Firth Bank, Anton's Gowt PE22 7BG ✆ (01205) 860369 OS map 131/280435 2m W of Boston off A1121 (Swineshead Bridge) Open Mar 16-Oct 30 40 pitches (32 static) Level grass, sheltered ✘♀🔌🛢∅⊕🛢 children's room, games room (most cards)

Orchard Park, Frampton Lane, Hubberts Bridge PE20 3QU ✆ (01205) 290328 Fax (01205) 290247 OS map 131/273433 3½m W of Boston off A1121 (Sleaford) on B1192 (Kirton End) Open all year 188 pitches (128 static) Level grass, sheltered 🛒✘♀🔌🛢∅⊕∅🛝🖥🛢🚐♿ £12.00-£14.00 (all major cards) *www.orchardpark.co.uk*

Plough Inn, Swineshead Bridge PE20 3PT ✆ (01205) 820300 OS map 131/219428 7m W of Boston on left of A17 (Sleaford-Spalding) near junction with A1121 Open Apr-Sept 30 pitches Level grass, sheltered ⊕🛝 fishing

White Cat Caravan and Camping Park, Shaw Lane, Old Leake PE22 9LQ ✆ (01205) 870121 *Prop: Mr & Mrs Lannen* OS map 122/415512 8m NE of Boston on A52 (Skegness) Open Apr-Oct 40 pitches Level grass, sheltered 🛒🔌∅⊕∅🛝🛢🚐 £9.00-£12.00 *kevin@klannen.freeserve.co.uk www.whitecatpark.com*

Pomeroy Caravan Park, Buxton

KEY TO SYMBOLS

🛒	shop	⊕	games area
✘	restaurant	🛝	playground
♀	bar	🖵	TV
🍴	takeaway food	🛢	winter storage
🔑	off licence	🅿	parking oblig.
🔲	laundrette	⊘	no dogs
🔌	elec hook-ups	🚐	caravan hire
∅	gas supplies	🏠	bungalow hire
⊕	chem. disposal	♿	disabled facs.
∅	payphone	⋈	shaded
🏊	swimming pool		

BUXTON, Derbys   Map B3
EC Wed MD Tues, Sat SEE The Crescent (of 18c houses), Pavilion gardens, Corbar Woods,
Grimlow Woods, Peak Rail Steam Centre, Cat and Fiddle Inn 4m NW
🛈 The Crescent ☎(01298) 25106
✗ Robin Hood Inn, 131 London Rd ☎(01298) 24335
✗ Wanted Inn, Sparrow Pit ☎(01298) 812862

Cold Springs Farm SK17 6SS ☎(01298) 22762 OS map 119/044747 1m NW of Buxton on left of
A5002/5004 (Whaley Bridge) Open Mar-Nov 40 pitches 4 acres grass, gentle slope 🆗🌢🖉🌣
flat rental

Cottage Farm Caravan Park, Blackwell SK17 9TQ ☎(01298) 85330 OS map 119/126717 6m E of
Buxton off A6 (Bakewell) on Blackwell road Open Mar-Oct 30 pitches 3 acres level grass and
hard standings 🅺🖥🖉🌢🖉 £7.00 email@cottagefarmsite.co.uk www.cottagefarmsite.co.uk

Limetree Park, Dukes Drive SK17 9RP ☎(01298) 22988 OS map 119/068726 1m S of Buxton off
A6 (Bakewell) and A515 (Ashbourne) Open Mar-Oct 135 pitches (36 static) 9 acres, Level/gentle
slope grass and hard standings 🅺🆗🖥🖉🌢🖉🌣🗘🖵🖷(35) 🚐🏠🖧 £13.00-£16.00 (most cards)

Pomeroy Caravan Camping Park, Street House Farm, Flagg SK17 9QG ☎(01298) 83259 Prop:
Messrs Melland OS map 119/116675 5m SE of Buxton on A515 (Ashbourne) Open Easter-
Oct–must book public holidays 40 pitches Level grass and hard standing, sheltered 🆗🖥🖉🌢
£6.00-£9.50

Thornheyes Farm, Longridge Lane, Peak Dale SK17 8AD ☎(01298) 26421 Prop: Bernard Kenney
OS map 119/078756 1½m N of Buxton off A6 (Chapel en le Frith) Open Easter-Nov–not suitable
for children 15 pitches 2 acres level/sloping grass 🖥🖉🌢 £6.00*

CASTLE DONINGTON, Leics   Map C4
SEE Donington Hall, church, Old Key House, Kings Mills village, motor racing circuit
✗ Priest House 1m W at Kings Mills by river Trent ☎(01332) 810649

Park Farmhouse Caravan Park, Melbourne Rd, Isley Walton DE74 2RN ☎(01332) 862409 OS
map 129/418253 1½m SW of Castle Donington off Ashby de la Zouch road at Isley Walton near
junct 24 of M1 Open Mar-Nov 65 pitches 5 acres mainly level grass, sheltered
✗🍴🖥🖉🌢🖉🗘🖷🖧 (all cards)

CASTLETON, Derbys   Map B2
EC Wed SEE Peveril Castle ruins, Peak, Blue John and Treak Cliff caverns, Winnats Gorge and
Speedwell cavern 3m W
✗ Castle ☎(01433) 620578

Rowter Farm S33 8WA ☎(01433) 620271 OS map 110/132820 2½m W of Castleton off Buxton
road via Winnats Pass Open Easter-Oct 35 pitches 4 acres level grass £8.00-£10.00

CHAPEL EN LE FRITH, Derbys   Map B2
SEE church, stocks, Market cross, old inns
✗ King's Arms, Market Pl ☎(01298) 812105

Hayfield Campsite, Kinder Road, Hayfield SK22 2LE ☎(01663) 745394 OS map 110/052875 4m
N of Chapel en le Frith off A624 (Glossop) at Hayfield Open Mar-Nov 90 pitches–no caravans
Grass, level 🅺🖉🌢🖉 drying room £11.75-£15.35* (most cards)
www.campingandcaravanningclub.co.uk

CHAPEL ST LEONARDS, Lincs   Map G2
SEE Hogsthorpe church 1m W
✗ Trafalgar Inn & Restaurant, 101 St Leonards Drive ☎(01754) 871354

Eastfields Touring Park, Chapel Point PE24 5UX ☎(01754) 874499 Prop: P Kirk OS map
122/563733 ½m N of Chapel St Leonards centre at Chapel Point near beach Open Easter-Oct
60 pitches–no tents 3 acres level grass 🆗🖥🌢🖉🖷🖧 fishing lake £20.00-£30.00

Hill View Lakes Touring Caravan Park, Skegness Road, Hogsthorpe PE24 5NR ☎(01754) 872979
Prop: K Palmer OS map 122/541714 1m SW of Chapel St Leonards on left of A52 (Mablethorpe)
Open Mar 15-Oct 31 90 pitches Level grass 🗘🆗🖥🌢🖉🖷🗗 coarse fishing adj, dogs welcome
but not around lakes £15.00-£20.00 inc elect, awning

Robin Hood Leisure Park, South Rd PE24 5TR ☎(01754) 874444 OS map 122/560715 On S
edge of Chapel St Leonards in South Road Open Mar-Oct 815 pitches (680 static)–no tents–no
adv booking 40 acres level grass and hard standings 🅺✗🍴🗘🏹🆗🖥🖉🌢🖉🖵🗗🗘🖷🚐🏠🖧
betting shop, theatre club (most cards)

CHATSWORTH–see Baslow

SHOWERS
Except where marked, all sites in this guide have flush lavatories and showers. Symbols for these
amenities have therefore been omitted from site entries.

For more up-to-date information, and for links to camping websites, visit our site at:
www.butford.co.uk/camping

CHESTERFIELD, Derbys   Map C3
EC Wed (not town cen MD Mon, Fri, Sat SEE parish church, Bolsover Castle 6m E, Hardwick Hall
8m SE
🖥 Rykneld Sq ☎ (01246) 3457777
✖ Portland, West Bars ☎ (01246) 234502

Batemans Mill Holiday Park, Old Tupton S42 6AE ☎ (01246) 861082 OS map 119/370641 4½m
   S of Chesterfield off A61 (Alfreton) and Ashover road at Old Tupton Open all year 30 pitches
   ✖♀🗑🛒🕭✦∅

CLEETHORPES, NE Lincs   Map F1
EC Thurs (winter) MD Wed SEE leisure park, beacon
🖥 43 Alexandra Rd ☎ (01472) 323111
✖ Kingsway, Kingsway ☎ (01472) 601122

Municipal Camping Park, Humberston DN36 4HG ☎ (01472) 813395 OS map 113/372063 2m S
   of Cleethorpes off A1031 (Mablethorpe) Open Apr-Sept 50 pitches 🖥♀🗑↩

DARLEY DALE, Derbys   Map C3
Famous Peak District beauty spot in Derwent valley
✖ Grouse Inn, Dale Road North ☎ (01629) 734357

Darwin Forest Country Park, Darley Moor DE4 5LN ☎ (01629) 732428 OS map 119/302649 2m
   NE of Darley Dale on left of B5057 (Chesterfield) Open all year 48 pitches Level grass and hard
   standings sheltered by woodland 🖥✖♀↩⊹🗑🛒🕭✦∅🖵🕂↩🗆🏠♿ tennis, mini golf
   (Mastercard/Visa/Switch)

Grouse and Claret, Station Yard, Station Rd, Rowsley DE4 2EL ☎ (01629) 733233 Fax (01629)
   735194 OS map 119/258660 2m N of Darley Dale on A6 (Bakewell) at junction with B6012
   (Baslow) at rear of eating house adj river Open all year 29 pitches Level standing, sheltered
   🖥✖♀🛒∅↩ £7.00 (min)* (all cards)

DERBY   Map C4
MD Tues, Thurs, Fri, SEE Cathedral, RC church of St Mary by Pugin, St Mary's bridge and chapel,
Crown Derby Works and Museum, Kedleston Hall 3½m NW, Elvaston Castle, Country Park 4m SE
🖥 Assembly Rooms, Market Place ☎ (01332) 255802
✖ Gondola (Italian), Osmaston Rd ☎ (01332) 332895

Shardlow Marina, London Road, Shardlow DE7 2GL ☎ (01332) 792832 OS map 129/444303 7m
   SE of Derby on left of A6 (Loughborough) at Shardlow Open Mar-Oct 70 pitches Level grass and
   hard standings, sheltered 🖥✖♀🗑🛒🕭✦🕂 fishing £8.00-£10.75

DOVERIDGE, Derbys   Map C5
✖ Cavendish Arms ☎ (01889) 563820

Cavendish Caravan Camping, Derby Rd DE6 5JR ☎ (01889) 562092 OS map 128/122342 ½m
   NE of Doveridge centre on old A50 (Derby-Stoke on Trent) Open Apr-Oct 15 pitches 2 acres part
   level grass 🛒 *No showers*

EAST RETFORD–see Retford

EDALE, Derbys   Map B2
Moorland village at start of long distance (250m) Pennine way. SEE Mam Tor, Edale valley
✖ Castle 3m SE at Castleton ☎ (01433) 620578

Coopers Caravan and Campsite, Newfold Farm S30 2ZD ☎ (01433) 670372 OS map 110/121859
   In Edale adj post office Open all year 25 pitches Sloping grass 🖥✖🛒🕭✦🖪 £7.50 (min)*

Fieldhead Campsite S33 7ZA ☎ (01433) 670386 Prop: Mark & Samatha Reeves OS map
   110/124856 In Edale betw station and church Open all year 45 pitches Level grass, sheltered
   🅿♿ £8.00-£10.00 bookings@fieldhead-campsite.co.uk www.fieldhead-campsite.co.uk

Upper Booth Farm S33 7ZS ☎ (01433) 670250 OS map 110/103853 2m W of Edale on Jacobs
   Ladder road, by stream and Pennine Way Open all year 40 pitches–no trailer or motor caravans
   3 acres level grass ∅

FENNY BENTLEY–see Ashbourne

GRANTHAM, Lincs   Map E4
EC Wed MD Thurs, Sat SEE market cross, St Wulfram's church, old inns, Belton House 2½m NE
🖥 Guild Hall Centre, St Peters Hill ☎ (01476) 566444
✖ Angel and Royal, High St ☎ (01476) 565816

Old Hall Farm, Sudbrook, Ancaster NG32 3RY ☎ (01400) 230262 OS map 130/984455 6m NE of
   Grantham on B6403 (Colsterworth-Newark) Open all year 10 pitches 2½ acres level grass

HARTINGTON, Derbys   Map B3
SEE Beresford Dale, Dovedale S
✗ Charles Cotton, Market pl ☎ (01298) 84229

Barracks Farm, Beresford Dale SK17 0HQ ☎ (01298) 84261 OS map 119/118575 2m S of
Hartington off B5054 (Warslow) Open Apr-Oct 100 pitches (35 static) 10 acres level grass

Chapel Farm, Heathcote SK17 0AY ☎ (01298) 84312 OS map 119/147602 1m SE of Hartington in
Heathcote village Open Mar-Oct 20 pitches–booking advisable 3 acres gentle slope *No
showers*, farm produce

HATHERSAGE, Derbys   Map B2
SEE Castle earthworks, Iron Age Fort, church with Robin Hood associations
✗ Hathersage Inn, Main St ☎ (01433) 650259

North Lees Campsite, Birley Lane S12 3BP ☎ (01433) 650838 OS map 110/235832 1½m N of
Hathersage off A625 via Jaggers Lane Open Apr-Sept 45 pitches–booking advisable 1½ acres
gentle slope

Swallow Holme Caravan Park, Station Road, Bamford S33 0BN ☎ (01433) 650981 *Prop: John
Froggatt* OS map 110/207825 2m NW of Hathersage on A6013 (Bamford) Open Easter-Oct
60 pitches (40 static) Level grass and hard standings, sheltered 🛇🔲⊕ £12.00-£16.00

HOLBEACH, Lincs   Map G4
EC Wed MD Thurs SEE church, bulbfields (Apr-May)
✗ Rose and Crown, West End ☎ (01406) 423941

Delph Bank Touring Park Just for Adults, Old Main Rd, Fleet Hargate PE12 8LL ☎ (01406)
422910 OS map 131/393248 2m E of Holbeach on B1515 (Fleet Hargate) Open Mar-Nov 45
pitches Grass and hard standings, sheltered 🛇🔲🗕⊕⊘🔲 dog walk
enquiries@delphbank.co.uk www.delphbank.co.uk

HOPE, Derbys   Map B2
Moorland village in Hope valley at heart of Northern Peak district. SEE caves, Roman fort S,
Ladybower reservoir N
✗ Poachers Arms, Castleton Rd ☎ (01433) 620380

Laneside Caravan Park S30 2RR ☎ (01433) 620215 OS map 110/180830 ¼m E of Hope on
A6187 (Hathersage) Open Apr-Oct–must book peak periods 120 pitches Level grass and hard
standing, sheltered 🔋🛇🔲🗕⊕⊘🏠 (Mastercard/Visa/Delta/Switch)

HORNCASTLE, Lincs   Map F3
EC Wed MD Thurs, Sat SEE St Mary's church, Bain valley
🖪 14 Bull Ring ☎ (01507) 526636
✗ Fighting Cocks, West St ☎ (01507) 527307

Ashby Park, West Ashby LN9 5PP *Well run park in 70 acres of Lincolnshire Wolds* ☎ (01507)
527966 OS map 122/251726 2m N of Horncastle between A153 (Louth) and A158 (Lincoln)
Open Mar-Nov 90 pitches Level grass, sheltered ✗🗕🔲🛇🗕⊕⊘⛊ fishing (all cards)

HUBBERTS BRIDGE–see Boston

INGOLDMELLS, Lincs   Map G2
Modest resort N of Skegness overlooking extensive beaches of fine sand backed by dunes SEE
Gunby Hall (NT) 6m W, Burgh le Marsh church and windmill 4m SW
✗ County 3m S at Skegness ☎ (01754) 612461

Country Meadows Holiday Park, Anchor Lane PE25 1LZ ☎ (01754) 874455 and 873351 *Prop: J &
G Hardy* OS map 122/565697 1m N of Ingoldmells off A52 (Mablethorpe) and road to beach on
right Open Easter-Oct 200 pitches (100 static) 6 acres level grass 🛇🔲🗕⊕⊘🕂🗕🔲⛊ £11.00
(Mastercard/Visa) www.countrymeadows.co.uk

Hardy's Tourer Park, Sea Lane PE25 1PG ☎ (01754) 874071 OS map 122/566688 ¼m E of
Ingoldmells centre on road to Ingoldmells Point Open Mar 15-Oct 15 100 pitches 10 acres level
grass 🔋🗕🛇🔲🗕⊕⊘🕂

Valetta Farm, Mill Lane, Addlethorpe PE24 4TB ☎ (01754) 763758 *Prop: J & P Leeman* OS map
122/553674 1m SW of Ingoldmells off A52 (Skegness) and Burgh le Marsh road, in Mill Lane
Open Mar 15-Oct 15 55 pitches 2 acres mainly level grass 🔲⊕⊘🔲 £12.00

LINCOLN, Lincs   Map E3
EC Wed MD daily SEE cathedral, castle, courthouse, Stonebow with Guildhall above, county
museum
🖪 9 Castle Hill ☎ (01522) 873213
✗ White Hart, Bailgate ☎ (01522) 526222

Hartsholme Country Park, Skellingthorpe Road LN6 0EY ☎ (01522) 873578 OS map 121/943691
3m SW of Lincoln off A46 bypass on Skellingthorpe road Open Mar-Oct 50 pitches Grass, level,
sheltered ✗🍴🗕🔲⊕🕂🗕🔲🗕 lake fishing (permit) £6.00-£16.00* www.lincoln.gov.uk

LONG SUTTON, Lincs **Map G4**
SEE church, Sutton Bridge river port E
✗ Rose and Crown 7m S at Wisbech ✆ (01945) 583187

Foreman's Bridge Caravan Park, Sutton Road, Sutton St James PE12 0HU ✆ (01945) 440346 Fax (01945) 440346 OS map 131/412196 2m SW of Long Sutton off B1390 (Sutton St James) by river Open Mar-Nov 40 pitches 2 acres part level grass and hard standing 🛢🕿🖉🌳✇🅿🚐🔲⚹ cycle hire £6.00-£8.50* www.foremans-bridge.co.uk

Laurel Park, Huntsgate, Gedney Broadgate PE12 0DJ ✆ (01406) 364369 OS map 131/405222 2m W of Long Sutton off A17 (Holbeach) at Gedney roundabout on Gedney Broadgate road Open Apr-Dec 14 pitches 2 acres, grass, mainly level 🛢🕿🖉🌳😊⚹🚐

LOUTH, Lincs **Map F2**
EC Thurs MD Wed SEE church, town hall, market hall
✗ Priory, Eastgate ✆ (01507) 602930

Manby Caravan Park, Manby LN11 8SX ✆ (01507) 328232 Fax (01507) 327867 OS map 122/395876 3m E of Louth on B1200 (Saltfleet) at Manby Open Apr-Oct 31 125 pitches Level grass and hard standing, sheltered 🏕✗🍴🔌🛢🕿🖉🌳🖂😊⚹⚹ (Mastercard/Visa)

MABLETHORPE, Lincs **Map G2**
EC Wed (winter) MD Thurs SEE church, sands, Queens Park
🛈 Louth Hotel ✆ (01507) 474939
✗ Dave's Restaurant, 92 High St ✆ (01507) 473659

Denehurst Hotel Caravan Camping, Alford Road LN12 1PX ✆ (01507) 472951 OS map 122/496846 ¾m W of Mablethorpe on right of A1104 (Alford) past junct with A1031 Open Mar-Oct 20 pitches Level grass, sheltered ✗🍴🔌🖉 tea gardens (Mastercard/Visa)

Holivans, Quebec Road LN12 1QH ✆ (01507) 473327 OS map 122/498865 1m N of Mablethorpe on coast road Open Easter-Sept 192 pitches (165 static) Level grass 🍴⚹🛢🕿🖉🌳😊🔲 lic club

Kirkstead Holiday Park, North Road, Trusthorpe LN12 2QD ✆ (01507) 441483 Prop: Mark & Anita Pittam OS map 122/515838 1m S of Mablethorpe on A52 (Skegness) Open Mar-Nov 105 pitches (75 static) 6 acres level grass 🏕🍴🔌🛢🕿🖉🌳😊⚹🔲🚐🔲⚹ children's room, clubhouse, bar meals £10.00-£16.00 (all cards) mark@kirkstead.co.uk www.kirkstead.co.uk

Mermaid Caravan and Tent Park, Seaholme Road LN12 2NX ✆ (01507) 473273 OS map 122/500846 ½m SW of Mablethorpe off Seacroft Road Open Mar 15-Oct 20 600 pitches (300 static) Level grass 🏕🍴⚹🛢🕿🖉🌳😊🖉⚹⚹ lic club/bar

Seacroft Holiday Estate, Mainbridge, Trusthorpe LN12 2PN ✆ (01507) 472421 Prop: R Sutherland OS map 122/513830 1½m SE of Mablethorpe on A52 (Skegness) Open Mar-Nov 245 pitches (230 static)–no tents 20 acres level grass 🏕✗🛢🕿🖉🌳😊🖉🚐🔲⚹ clubhouse, fishing lake £11.50-£16.00 (Mastercard, Visa, Switch) info@seacroftcaravanpark.com www.seacroftcaravanpark.com

Trusthorpe Springs Leisure Park, Trusthorpe Hall, Mile Lane, Trusthorpe LN12 2QQ ✆ (01507) 441384 OS map 122/500838 1m S of Mablethorpe off A1104 at Cross Inn in Mile Lane Level grass and hard standings, sheltered Open Mar-Oct 152 pitches (130 static)–no tents 🏕✗⚹🛢🖉🌳😊🖉🖂⚹🚐⚹

St Vincents Caravan Camping Park, Seaholme Rd LN12 2NX ✆ (01507) 472287 OS map 122/505842 In South Mablethorpe off Seaholme Road Open Mar-Oct 48 pitches–no adv bkg 1½ acres level grass ✗⚹🕿🖉🌳🖉

MANSFIELD, Notts **Map D3**
EC Wed MD Mon, Thurs, Fri, SEE parish church, Moot hall, Clumber Park, Newstead Abbey (Byron assoc) 4m S, Sherwood Forest
✗ Bella Napoli (Italian), Leeming St ✆ (01623) 652376

Shardaroba, Silverhill Lane, Teversal NG17 3JJ ✆ (01623) 551838 Fax (01623) 552174 OS map 120/472615 3m W of Mansfield off A38 (Alfreton) and B6014 (Tibshelf) Open Mar-Oct 100 pitches 6 acres level grass and hard standings 🏕🛢🕿🖉🖉⚹⚹ late arrivals area £12.00-£16.00* (Amex/Mastercard/Switch/Visa) stay@shardaroba.co.uk www.shardaroba.co.uk

Sherwood Forest Caravan Park, Edwinstowe NG21 9HW ✆ (0800) 146505 OS map 120/593651 5m NE of Mansfield off A6075 (Edwinstowe) on B6030 Open Feb-Nov 150 pitches 20 acres level grass 🏕🛢🕿🖉🌳😊🖉⚹🔲🚐⚹

MARKET BOSWORTH, Leics **Map C5**
SEE Bosworth battlefield 1m S (now country park)
✗ Olde Red Lion, Park St ✆ (01455) 291713

Bosworth Water Trust, Far Coton Lane CV13 6PD Park with 20 acres of lakes for sailing and fishing ✆ (01455) 291876 OS map 140/385030 1m SW of Market Bosworth off B585 (Sheepy Magna) by Ashby canal Open all year 76 pitches 5 acres level grass and hard standings ✗🕿⚹ 20 acre lake for windsurfing, sailing and fishing

MARKET DEEPING, Lincs   Map F5
✗ Deeping Stage, Market Pl ✆ (01778) 343234

Deepings Caravan Camping Park, Outgang Road, Towngate East PE6 8LQ ✆ (01778) 344335 OS map 142/166116 2m NE of Market Deeping off A16 (Spalding) Open Feb-Dec 45 pitches Level grass and hard standings ▣ ◢ ⊕ ▣ ⌂

Tallington Lakes Leisure Park, Tallington PE9 4RJ ✆ (01778) 347000 OS map 142/095095 3m W of Market Deeping off A16 (Stamford) on Barholm road Open Mar-Jan 341 pitches (241 static) Level grass and hard standings ✗ � ↝ ⚆ ▣ ▣ ◢ ⊕ ↲ ▭ ⌂ ⬠ wind surfing, water skiing, canoeing, jet skiing, dinghy sailing, dry slope skiing, tennis court £9.00-£11.00 (Mastercard/Visa/Switch) info@tallington.com www.tallington.com

MARKET HARBOROUGH–see Lutterworth

MARKET RASEN, Lincs   Map F2
EC Thurs MD Tues, Wed SEE St Thomas's church, racecourse
✗ White Hart 5m E at Ludford ✆ (01507) 313489

The Racecourse, Legsby Road LN8 3EA ✆ (01673) 842307 OS map 121/115880 1m SE of Market Rasen off A631 (Louth) Open Mar 31-Oct 1 55 pitches Level grass ▣ ▣ ◢ ⊕ ∅ ⊙ ↲ ▭ golf (Mastercard/Visa)

Walesby Woodland Caravan Park, Walesby Rd LN8 3UN ✆ (01673) 843285 OS map 113/117906 1½m N of Market Rasen off B1203 (Tealby) Open Mar-Oct 64 pitches Level grass, sheltered ▤ ▣ ▣ ◢ ⊕ ∅ ↲ ▣ ▭ ⬠ (Mastercard/Visa)

MATLOCK, Derbys   Map C3
EC Thurs MD Tues, Fri SEE High Tor (673ft), Hall Leys Park, Riber castle, Fauna Reserve, Heights of Abraham by cable car, Tramway Museum 4m SE at Crich, Haddon Hall 5m NW
🄸 The Pavillion, Matlock Bath ✆ (01629) 55082
✗ New Bath 1m S on A6 at Matlock Bath ✆ (01629) 583275

Birchwood Farm, Wirksworth Road, Whatstandwell DE4 5HS ✆ (01629) 822280 OS map 119/315551 6m S of Matlock off A6 (Belper) on B5035 (Wirksworth) adj Midshires Way Open Mar-Oct 44 pitches (20 static) 4 acres level/sloping grass ▤ ▣ ▣ ◢ ⊕ ▣ ▭ table tennis

Haytop Country Park, Whatstandwell DE4 5HP ✆ (01773) 852063 OS map 119/331538 6m SE of Matlock off A6 (Derby) at Whatstandwell bridge Open all year 60 pitches (30 static) 65 acres level/sloping grass and hard standings ▣ ◢ ⊕ ∅ farm produce, fishing, canoeing (own boats)

Merebrook Caravan Park, Whatstandwell DE4 5HH ✆ (01773) 857010/852154 OS map 119/332555 5m S of Matlock on A6 (Derby) beside River Derwent Open all year 196 pitches (116 static) Grass, part level, sheltered ▣ ▣ ◢ ⊕ ∅ ⬠ fishing

Middle Hills Farm, Grangemill DE4 4HY ✆ (01629) 650368 OS map 119/230595 4m W of Matlock on A5012 (Buxton) beyond Holly Bush Inn Open all year 60 pitches 4 acres level grass, sheltered ▣ ⊕ ∅ ▣ ▭ ⌂

Packhorse Farm, Matlock Moor DE4 5LF ✆ (01629) 582781 OS map 119/322517 2m NE of Matlock off A615 (Alfreton) Open all year–must book public holidays 47 pitches Grass and hard standing ▣ ⊕ sep pitches, farm produce

Pine Groves Caravan Park, High Lane, Tansley DE4 5BG ✆ (01629) 534815 and 534670 OS map 119/343586 2½m E of Matlock off A615 (Alfreton) Open Apr-Oct 100 pitches (40 static) 8 acres level grass, sheltered ▣ ▣ ⊕ ∅ ▣ ▭ ⬠

Sycamore Country Park, Lant Lane, Tansley DE4 5LF ✆ (01629) 55760 OS map 119/327617 2½m NE of Matlock off A632 (Chesterfield) Open Mar 15-Oct 31 87 pitches (52 static) Level grass ▣ ◢ ⊕ ∅ ↲

Wayside Farm, Matlock Moor DE4 5LF ✆ (01629) 582967 OS map 119/322620 2m NE of Matlock off A632 (Chesterfield) at site sign Open all year 30 pitches Level/sloping grass, hard standing, sheltered ▤ ↝ ▣ ◢ ⊕ ⊙ ↲ ⌂ ⬠ children's pet corner

For other sites near Matlock see Wirksworth and Youlgreave

METHERINGHAM, Lincs   Map E3
✗ Harvey's 9m NW at Lincoln ✆ (01522) 21886

White Horse Inn Holiday Park, Dunston Fen LN4 3AP ✆ (01526) 399919 Fax (01526) 399919 OS map 121/130660 6m ENE of Metheringham off B1188 (Lincoln) on unclass via Dunston by river Open Feb-Dec 42 pitches (32 static) Level grass, sheltered ✗ � ▣ ▣ ▣ ◢ ⊕ ∅ ↲ ▭ fishing, moorings, games room £4.00-£13.00* whitehorse@dunstonefen.co.uk www.dunstonfen.co.uk

---

⬛ CARAVAN STORAGE

Many sites offer caravan storage in winter but some will also store your caravan in summer, which for those of us able to tour several times a year saves towing over long distances. Sites most conveniently placed for this are those on or near popular routes to the West Country and Scotland.

t: 01778 34 7000
e: info@tallington.com

NEWARK, Notts   Map E3
EC Thurs MD Wed, Fri, Sat SEE Church of St Mary Magdalene, Beaumond Cross, Town Hall,
facades of Market Square, old inns, folk museum
🆔 Gilstrap Centre, Castlegate ✆ (01636) 655765
✘ Great Northern Inn, Ossington Rd, Carlton-on-Trent ✆ (01636) 821348

Carlton Touring Park, Ossington Road, Carlton on Trent NG23 6NW ✆ (01530) 835662 Mobile
07854595387 Prop: SAC Goodman OS map 120/791641 7m N of Newark on A1 (Doncaster)
facing hotel Open Easter-Oct 22 pitches Hard standings and level grass, sheltered 🚐⊕∅🚐🔱
fishing £10.00 inc elect

Milestone Caravan Park, Cromwell NG23 6JE ✆ (01636) 821244 OS map 120/798622 5½m N of
Newark off A1 (Doncaster) in village Open all year 60 pitches 8 acres level grass and hard
standing 🔋🚐𝌆⊕∅🔥

NEWHAVEN, Derbys   Map B3
✘ Jug & Glass Inn, Hartington ✆ (01298) 84848 Open 12-Sep
✘ The Waterloo Inn, Main St, Biggin ✆ (01298) 84284

Newhaven Caravan Camping Park SK17 0DT ✆ (01298) 84300 Prop: Bob Macara OS map
119/166603 ¼m N of Newhaven at junction of A515 (Buxton) and A5012 (Grangemill) Open Mar-
Oct 198 pitches (73 static) Level grass and hard standing, sheltered 🛒➤🔋🚐𝌆⊕∅🔥🌱
sep pitches £9.00-£10.25 (most cards) newhavencaravanpark.co.uk

Waterloo Inn, Biggin SK17 0DH ✆ (01298) 84284 Prop: Stephen & Karen Compton OS map
119/153595 ½m SW of Newhaven off A515 (Ashbourne) near Biggin church Open all year
20 pitches–booking advisable 2 acres grass, part level ♀➤➤🚐⊕ bar meals, washing up sink
£5.00-£12.50 (all major cards)

NORTHAMPTON, Northants   Map E7
EC Thurs MD Wed, Fri, Sat SEE Abingdon Park Museum, church of Holy Sepulchre, Lamport Hall
and garden, Queen Eleanor cross 2m S, Althorp House 5m NW
🆔 Visitor Centre, St Giles Sq ✆ (01604) 838800
✘ Napoleon, Welford Rd ✆ (01604) 713899

Billing Aquadrome, Little Billing NN3 4DA ✆ (01604) 408181 OS map 152/808615 3m E of
Northampton off A45 (Wellingborough) Open Mar 21-Oct 30 1990 pitches (995 static) Level
grass, sheltered 🛒✘♀➤🔋🚐𝌆∅🖻🌱🚐🔥 club rooms, fishing, lakes

SITE DIRECTIONS

The distance and direction of a campsite is given from the centre of the town under which it
appears.

KEY TO SYMBOLS

🛒	shop	𝌆	gas supplies	🚐	winter storage for caravans
✘	restaurant	⊕	chemical disposal point	🅿	parking obligatory
♀	bar	∅	payphone	❀	no dogs
➤	takeaway food	🖻	swimming pool	🚐	caravan hire
➤	off licence	🎯	games area	🏠	bungalow hire
🔋	laundrette	🌱	children's playground	♿	facilities for disabled
🚐	mains electric hook-ups	📺	TV	🔱	shaded

> ❧ DOGS
> Dogs are usually allowed but must be kept on a lead. Sometimes they have to be paid for.

NORTH SOMERCOTES, Lincs   Map G2
✗ Priory 8m W at Louth ✆ (01507) 602930

Lakeside Park LN11 7RB ✆ (01507) 358428/358315 OS map 113/432960 ½m SE of North
  Somercotes on A1031 (Mablethorpe) Open Apr-Oct 450 pitches (300 static) Level grass and
  hard standing ⚏✗⚎⟷◨▨⌀⊛⌀▱(indoor) ⊛⌄⚲ lic club, sauna, steam room, tennis courts,
  golf course (most cards)

NOTTINGHAM   Map D4
EC Mon (large stores MD daily SEE parish church, cathedral, castle, arboretum, Trip to Jerusalem
Inn, Salutation Inn (13c), annual Goose Fair
ℹ Smithy Row ✆ (0115)9155330
✗ Cafe Royal, Upper Parliament St ✆ (0115) 941 3444

Holme Pierrepont Caravan Camping Park, National Water Sports Centre, Adbolton Lane, Holme
  Pierrepont NG12 2LU ✆ (0115) 982 4721 OS map 129/620390 5m SE of Nottingham off A52
  (Grantham) Open Apr-Oct 360 pitches Grass, level ⚏◨▨⌀⌀⚲⚲ fishing, boating

New Moor Farm Trailer Park, Calverton NG14 6FZ ✆ (0115) 965 2426 OS map 129/615490 7m N
  of Nottingham off A614 (Ollerton) Open all year 140 pitches (80 static) Level grass ⚏◨⚲
  fishing

Thornton's Holt, Stragglethorpe, Radcliffe on Trent NG12 2JZ ✆ (0115) 933 2125 Fax (0115) 933
  3318 Prop: PE Taylor & SD Jones OS map 129/636337 3½m E of Nottingham off A52
  (Grantham) on Cotgrave/Cropwell Bishop road Open all year (limited facs Nov 2-Mar 31)
  155 pitches Level grass and hard standings, sheltered ⚏◨▨⌀⊛⌀▱(indoor heated) ⊛⚲⌄
  first aid, barbecue, games room £10.00-£15.00 camping@thorntons-holt.co.uk www.thorntons-
  holt.co.uk

OAKHAM, Rutland   Map E5
EC Thurs MD Wed, Sat SEE Castle ruins, horseshoe collection, Rutland County Museum, Butter
cross, stocks, parish church
ℹ Victoria Hall ✆ (01572) 724329
✗ Wheatsheaf, Northgate ✆ (01572) 723458

Ranksborough Hall Leisure Centre, Milton Road, Langham LE15 7ER ✆ (01572) 722984 OS map
  130/833115 2m N of Oakham on A606 (Melton Mowbray) Open all year 273 pitches (84 static)
  Level grass and hard standing ⚏◨⌀▱ crazy golf, squash, solarium

See also Uppingham

OUNDLE, Northants   Map E6
EC Wed MD Thurs SEE public school, St Peter's church, old Talbot inn, almshouses, Barnwell
Country Park and Marina 1m S
ℹ West St ✆ (01832) 274333
✗ Talbot, New St ✆ (01832) 273621

The George, Glapthorn Road PE8 4PR ✆ (01832) 272324 OS map 141/035890 ½m N of Oundle
  on Glapthorn road Open all year 23 pitches 1 acre No showers

Woodland Waters Ltd
Willoughby Road, Ancaster, Grantham,
Lincs NG32 3RT. Tel/Fax 01400 230888

CHARGES

Charges quoted are the minimum and
maximum for two people with car and
caravan or tent. They are given only as a
guide and should be checked with the owner
of any site at which you plan to stay.
Charges markded * are the prices for last
year. Otherwise, the prices are those quoted
for the current season.
Remember to ask whether hot water or use
of the pool (if any) is extra and make sure
that VAT is included.

RETFORD, Notts   Map D2
EC Wd MD Thurs SEE St Swithin's church,
🛈 Amcott House, Grove St ☎(01777) 860780
✗ White Hart, The Square ☎(01777) 703761

Ferry Boat Inn, Church Laneham DN22 0NQ ☎(01777) 703350 OS map 121/815767 6m E of
    Retford off A57 (Saxilby) Open Apr-Sept 40 pitches ✗♀

Manor House Caravan Park, Laneham DN22 2NJ ☎(01777) 228428 OS map 121/819771 6m E
    of Retford off A57 (Saxilby) Open Mar-Oct 190 pitches (170 static) 15 acres level grass
    🗗🗕🗕🗕🗕

SKEGNESS, Lincs   Map G3
EC Thurs (Oct-May) MD daily (summer) SEE St Clement's church, Natureland (aquarium and
marine zoo)
🛈 Embassy Centre, Grand Parade ☎(01754) 899887
✗ Vine Hotel, Vine Rd ☎(01754) 763018

Elms Touring Park, Addlethorpe PE24 4TR ☎(01754) 872266 OS map 122/546690 3½m NW of
    Skegness off A158 (Horncastle) at Gunby Open Mar 15-Oct 15–must book peak periods 200
    pitches Level grass and hard standing, sheltered 🗗🗕🗕🗕🗕& fishing, super pitches £14.00

North Shore Holiday Centre, Elmhirst Avenue, off Roman Bank PE25 1SN ☎(01754) 763815 OS
    map 122/566646 ½m N of Skegness off A52 (Sutton on Sea) Open Apr-early Oct 625 pitches
    (375 static) Level grass and hard standing 🗕🗕🗕🗕🗕🗕🗕🗕🗕🗕🗕🗕🗕& lic club, mini-golf,
    tennis, bowls

Richmond Holiday Centre, Richmond Drive PE25 3TQ ☎(01754) 762097 OS map 122/559624
    ¼m SW of Skegness off A52 near station Open Mar-Nov–must book public holidays 724 pitches
    (550 static) Level grass 🗕✗♀🗕🗕🗕🗕🗕🗕🗕(indoor heated) 🗕🗕🗕🗕& post office,
    amusements, lic hotel (Mastercard/Visa)

Southview Leisure Park, Burgh Road PE25 2LA ☎(01754) 874893 OS map 122/543647 1m W of
    Skegness off A158 (Burgh le Marsh) Open mid Mar-mid Oct 300 pitches (225 static) 🗗🗕🗕🗕
    fishing lake, lic club, cabaret, bowling green, amusement arcade

SLEAFORD, Lincs   Map F3
EC Thurs MD Mon, Fri, Sat SEE St Denis church, Carre Hospital (almhouses), Handley monument
🛈 The Mill, Money's Yard, 76 Carre St ☎(01529) 414294
✗ Rose and Crown, Watergate ☎(01529) 303350

Low Farm Touring Park, Spring Lane, Folkingham NG34 0SJ ☎(01529) 497322 Prop: N & J
    Stevens OS map 130/070333 9m S of Sleaford off A15 (Bourne) Open Easter-Oct 36 pitches
    2½ acres level/sloping grass, sheltered 🗕🗕🗕🗕 £8.00-£12.00*

Woodland Waters, Willoughby Road, Ancaster NG32 3RT Picturesque park set in 72 acres of
    woods and lakes ☎(01400) 230888 Prop: Malcolm & Denise Carradine OS map 130/977436
    5m W of Sleaford on A153 (Grantham) Open all year 64 pitches with elect hook-up Level grass,
    sheltered ✗♀🗕🗕🗕🗕🗕🗕🗕 5 well-stocked fishing lakes, bar/restaurant on site £9.00-£11.00
    (most cards) info@woodlandwaters.co.uk www.woodlandwaters.co.uk

SOUTHWELL–see Newark

SPALDING, Lincs   Map F4
EC Thurs MD Tues SEE church, Ayscoughfee Hall with bird museum and gardens, White Horse Inn,
bulbfields (Apr-May)
🛈 Ayscoughfee Hall, Churchgate ☎(01775) 725468
✗ Lincolnshire Poacher, Double St ☎(01775) 766490

Lake Ross Caravan Park, Dozens Bank, West Pinchbeck PE11 3NA ☎(01775) 761690 OS map
    131/211223 2¼m W of Spalding on A151 (Bourne) near Pode Hole Bridge Open Apr-Oct
    28 pitches Level grass, sheltered 🗕♀🗕🗕🗕🗕🗕🗕🗕 fishing

STONEY MIDDLETON, Derbys   Map C3
✗ Bridge ¼m SE at Calver Bridge ☎(01433) 630415

Peakland Caravan Park, High St S32 4TL ☎(01433) 631414 OS map 119/223754 ¼m SW of
    Stoney Middleton centre in High Street Open Apr-Oct 32 pitches–no trailer caravans Level grass
    🗕🗕🗕

CAUSE FOR COMPLAINT
If you have cause for complaint while staying on a site take the matter up with the manager or
owner. If you are still not satisfied set the facts down in writing and send photocopies to anyone
you think might be able to help, such as the local (licensing) authority for the area where the site
is located.

**Rivendale Caravan & Leisure Park,
Buxton Road, Alsop-en-le-Dale,
Ashbourne, Derbyshire.
Bookings: 01332 843000 or 01335 310311
e-mail: enquiries@rivendalecaravanpark.co.uk**

See listing under Ashbourne

✘ RESTAURANTS

The restaurants recommended in this guide are of three kinds – pubs, independent restaurants and those forming part of hotels and motels. They all serve lunch and dinner – at a reasonable price – say under £10 a head. We shall be glad to have your comments on any you use this season and if you think they are not up to standard, please let us have your suggestions for alternatives.

CHECK BEFORE ENTERING

There's usually no objection to your walking onto a site to see if you might like it but always ask permission first. Remember that the person in charge is responsible for safeguarding the property of those staying there.

SUTTON ON SEA, Lincs   **Map G2**
EC Thurs SEE sands, Huttoft windmill and granary
✘ Bacchus Hotel, 17 High St, Mablethorpe ☎ (01507) 441204
Cherry Tree Touring Site Adults only, Huttoft Road LN12 2RU ☎ (01507) 441626 *Prop: G & M Murray* OS map 122/525802 1½m S of Sutton on Sea on left of A52 (Skegness) near beach Open Mar-Oct–no tents 60 pitches 3½ acres, level grass and hard standing 🏠🅿◍❂♿♨⚓ motorhome service point £12.00-£15.00 (all major cards) info@cherrytreesite.co.uk www.cherrytreesite.co.uk
Jolly Common, Sea Lane, Huttoft LN13 9RW ☎ (01507) 490236 OS map 122/524776 3m S of Sutton on Sea off A52 (Skegness) Open Mar 15-Oct 31 55 pitches 9 acres, level fishing lake

SUTTON ST EDMUND, Lincs   **Map G4**
SEE Crowland Abbey 8m W
✘ Queens 5m SE at Wisbech ☎ (01945) 583933
Orchard View Caravan Camping Park, Broadgate PE12 OLT ☎ (01945) 700482 OS map 142/365108 1m S of Sutton St Edmund via Parson Drove Open Apr-Oct 37 pitches 6 acres level grass ⚑♀↗🅿◍❂♨⚓♿ dog walk £5.50-£9.70* raymariaorchardview@btinternet.com

SUTTON ST JAMES–see Long Sutton

TATTERSHALL, Lincs   **Map F3**
SEE church (with largest clock in Eng), village of Tumby 1m N, Tattershall castle
✘ Leagate Inn, Leagate Rd ☎ (01526) 342370
Orchard Caravans, Chapel Hill LN4 4PZ ☎ (01526) 342414 OS map 122/207540 2m S of Tattershall off A153 (Sleaford) at Chapel Hill Open all year–must book peak periods 48 pitches Level grass, sheltered ♀⚑🅿◍❂🖥❂♨⚓♿ boat moorings, fishing
Tattershall Park Country Club LN4 4LR ☎ (01526) 343193 OS map 122/207573 1m SW of Tattershall on left of A153 (Sleaford) Open Easter-Oct 150 pitches (90 static) Level grass and hard standing, sheltered ⚑✘🅿◍❂◍❂♨⚓♨⚓♿ boating, fishing, pony trekking, squash, windsurfing, riding school, nature walks, gym, sauna, solarium

THRAPSTON, Northants   **Map E6**
SEE Nene Valley lakes to N
✘ Woolpack on A604 near main bridge ☎ (01832) 732578
Mill Marina, Midland Road NN14 4JR ☎ (01832) 732850 OS map 141/994781 ½m S of Thrapston on Denford road Open Apr-Dec–must book summer weekends 75 pitches Level grass, part sheltered ⚑♀🅿◍❂◍❂♨⚓ fishing, slipway www.mill-marina.co.uk

TORKSEY, Lincs   Map E2
✗ White Swan at Torksey Lock ☎ (01427) 71653

Little London Caravan Park LN1 2EL ☎ (01427) 71322 OS map 121/840778 1m S of Torksey on A156 (Lincoln) near junction with A1133 Open Mar-Oct 400 pitches 7½ acres
✗ ⚑ 🅿 ⊟ 🅰 ⊘ ⊗ ⊘ ⊟ 🗔 lic club

TUXFORD, Notts   Map D3
EC Wed SEE parish church, grammar school, ancient lock-up
✗ Newcastle Arms, Market pl ☎ (01777) 870208

Greenacres Caravan & Touring Park, Lincoln Road NG22 0JN ☎ (01777) 870264 Fax (01777) 870264 Prop: S & M Bailey OS map 120/755720 1m ENE of Tuxford on A6075 (Lincoln) Open Apr-Oct 79 pitches (39 static) Grass and hard standing 🔦 🅿 🅰 ⊗ ⊘ ⊕ ⟲ 🅰 🗔 ⅙ £14.00 inc elect bailey_security@freezone.co.uk www.members.freezone.co.uk/bailey_security

Longbow Caravan Park, Milton NG22 0PP ☎ (01777) 838067 OS map 120/717736 2m N of Tuxford off A1 (Doncaster) on Milton/Walesby road Open all year 20 pitches 1 acre
🅿 🅰 ⊗ ⟲ ⊟ 🗔 Grass and hard standing, level

Orchard Park Caravan Camping Park, Marnham Road NG22 0PY *Quiet sheltered park in old orchard* ☎ (01777) 870228 Fax (01777) 870320 OS map 120/753708 1m E of Tuxford off A6075 (Lincoln) Open Mar 15-Oct 31 65 pitches 5 acres level grass, sheltered 🅿 🅰 ⊗ ⊘ 🅰 ⅙ £10.00-£12.00* (most cards) info@orchardcaravanpark.co.uk www.orchardcaravanpark.co.uk

UPPINGHAM, Rutland   Map E5
EC Thurs MD Fri SEE Uppingham School, church, Lyddington village (Bede House) 2m S, Rutland Water 3m N
✗ Vaults, High St ☎ (01572) 823259

Old Rectory, Belton in Rutland LE15 9LE ☎ (01572) 717279 Prop: Richard & Vanessa Peach OS map 141/819009 3m W of Uppingham off A47 (Peterborough-Leicester) on New road Open Jan-Dec 15 pitches Level/sloping grass 🅿 🅰 ⊗ ⊘ 🏠 £8.00-£12.00 richard@iep.uk.com

WAINFLEET ALL SAINTS, Lincs   Map G3
SEE 15c turreted Magdalen school, Croft church (interior) 2m NE, nature reserve 5m E
✗ Red Lion, High St ☎ (01754) 880301

Riverside Caravan Park, Wainfleet Bank PE24 4ND ☎ (01754) 880205 OS map 122/480593 2m W of Wainfleet All Saints on B1195 (Spilsby) at Wainfleet Bank Open Mar 15-Oct 31 30 pitches Grass, sheltered 🅿 🅰 ⊗ 🅰 (30) ⊗

Swan Lake Leisure Park, Culvert Road, Thorpe Culvert PE24 4NJ ☎ (01754) 881456 OS map 122/464606 2m NW of Wainfleet All Saints off B1195 (Spilsby) on Thorpe Culvert road Open Mar-Nov 35 pitches 7 acres level grass 🅿 🅰 ⊗ ⟲ 🅰 (25) ⊗ 🗔 fishing swan.lake@talk21.com www.swanlake.co.uk

WHALEY BRIDGE, Derbys   Map B2
SEE Goyt valley
✗ White Horse, Lower Macclesfield Rd, Horwich End ☎ (01663) 732617

Ringstones Caravan Park, Yeardsley Lane, Furness Vale SK23 7EB ☎ (01663) 747042 (Mobile) 07790 428773 Prop: Mrs M Hallworth OS map 110/005824 1½m N of Whaley Bridge off A6 (Stockport) Open Mar-Oct 65 pitches (45 static) Level grass, sheltered ⊗ 🅰 £8.00 mo@ringstones.demon.co.uk

WHATSTANDWELL–see Matlock

FOLLOW THE COUNTRY CODE
Guard against all risk of fire. Fasten all gates. Keep dogs under proper control. Keep to the paths across farmland. Avoid damaging fences, hedges and walls. Leave no litter. Safeguard water supplies. Protect wildlife, plants and trees. Go carefully on country roads and be prepared for slow-moving vehicles like tractors. Respect the life of the countryside.

Orchard Park, Marnham Road Tuxford, Nottinghamshire NG22 0PY Tel: 01777 870228

WOODHALL SPA, Lincs   Map F3
EC Wed SEE springs and mineral baths, Wellington monument, Tower on the Moor
🄸Cottage Museum, Iddesleigh Rd ✆(01526) 353775
✖Petwood, Stixwould Rd ✆(01526) 352411

Bainland Country Park, Horncastle Road LN10 6UX ✆(01526) 352903 Fax (01526) 353730 OS
   map 122/215640 1m NE of Woodhall Spa on B1191 (Horncastle) Open all year 150 pitches
   Level grass and hard standing 🛒✖🍴♨🏕🅿🖊🚿🏊⊘☐(heated) 🐕⚓☎(satellite) 🛢🎣🏠♿
   tennis, golf, sauna, jacuzzi, croquet, boules, sunbed, trampoline, bowling green £9.50-£24.50
   (Mastercard/Visa/Switch/Delta) bookings@bainland.com www.bainland.com

Jubilee Park, Stixwould Road LN10 6QH ✆(01526) 352448 Prop: East Lindsey District Council
   OS map 122/192635 ½m N of Woodhall Spa on Stixwould road Open Apr-Nov 1 75
   pitches–must book high season Level grass ✖(café) ♨🖊☐(heated) ⚓🎣♿ bowling, putting
   greens, tennis, cycle hire £13.00-£17.00*

Roughton Moor Caravan Park LN10 6UU ✆(01526) 352312 OS map 122/205663 2m NE of
   Woodhall Spa on B1191 (Horncastle) Open all year 120 pitches (70 static) 🛒🖊

See also Tattershall

WORKSOP, Notts   Map D2
EC Thurs MD Wed, Fri, Sat SEE Priory Church, 13c Lady Chapel, 14c gatehouse, old market cross
🄸Library, Memorial Ave ✆(01909) 501148
✖Cottage, 30 Park St ✆(01909) 474379

Clumber Park Caravan Club Site, Lime Tree Ave, Clumber Park S80 3AE ✆(01909) 484758 OS
   map 120/628728 4½m SE of Worksop off A57 (Newark)–signposted Open Mar-Oct 162
   pitches–must book w/ends and BH–no tents Level grass and hard standing 🖊🏊⚓
   £17.00-£22.00* (Mastercard/Visa/Delta/Switch) www.caravanclub.co.uk

Riverside Caravan Park, Central Ave S80 1ER ✆(01909) 474118 Prop: Gill Price OS map
   120/583791 ½m SW of Worksop centre off junction of A60 and A57–signposted Open all year
   60 pitches 5 acres, level grass, hardstanding 🖊🏊⊘ clubhouse, coarse fishing £12.00

YOULGREAVE, Derbys   Map C3
SEE church, Arbor Low 3m W, Bradford Dale
✖George Inn, Church St ✆(01629) 636292

Harthill Hall Farm, Alport DE4 1LH ✆(01629) 636203 OS map 119/227646 1m NE of Youlgreave
   off Rowsley road at junct with B5056 (no access for caravans via Alport) Open Mar-Nov
   32 pitches 🖊

Hopping Farm DE4 1NA ✆(01629) 636302 OS map 119/209631 1m S of Youlgreave off Dale End
   road Open Apr-Sept 15 pitches–must book 1½ acres 🖊

Central England is made up of Shropshire and Staffordshire in the north, Warwickshire, Herefordshire and Worcestershire in the centre and Gloucestershire in the south. To these are added the new unitary authorities, embracing Coventry, Birmingham and Wolverhampton, which is wholly industrial. Yet the region retains enough unspoiled landscape to make it one of the most attractive in Britain.

Divided by the Severn and bordered on the west by Wales, Shropshire is wild in the northwest, soft in the south. West and south of Shrewsbury are the scenic uplands: the geological freak of the Wrekin, the oldest mountain in Britain which takes only an hour to climb; the 1600ft high Long Mynd above Church Stretton; the narrow spine of wooded Wenlock Edge extending from Craven Arms to Ironbridge and famed for its views, and to the southwest the Clee Hills, topped by ancient British camps. Around these heights are the fascinating old towns of Shrewsbury, with its half timbered houses and inns; medieval Much Wenlock and ancient Ludlow, moated by the Teme and dominated by its great castle. Long Mynd is traversed by the venerable Portway track and near Newcastle one of the best preserved sections of Offa's Dyke cuts across the treeless Clun Forest.

In adjoining Staffordshire is Cannock Chase near Rugeley, a vast area of woods and moorland, and east of Stoke on Trent is Hawksmoor nature reserve.

Fine walking country exists In the rich countryside of Herefordshire and Worcestershire, from Bewdley in the west high above the Severn to the pleasant reaches of other rivers: the willow hung Avon winding down to Pershore and Bredon Hill, and the Teme flowing through hopfields and orchards to its junction with the Severn. West of the plain of Malvern are the Malvern Hills, with a nine-mile walk on the saddleback ridge to the Herefordshire Beacon, 1114ft high. From the cathedral city of Hereford the River Wye flows south into Gloucestershire, most striking feature of which is the Cotswold Hills, rising up from the Severn and rolling east into Oxfordshire. Ross on Wye is an acknowledged centre for the Wye Valley, with its famous beauty spots of Symonds Yat and

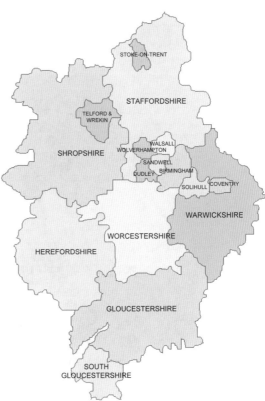

the reaches below Goodrich castle. On the left bank of the river is the Forest of Dean, with is magnificent woods of oak and birch. The Teme Valley northwest of Worcester forms part of a forty-five mile waymarked drive through attractive scenery. A popular centre in the Cotswolds is Cirencester, where the old roads Icknield Way and Ermine Street join the equally ancient Fosse Way. The Cotswold Way also crosses the district, on an escarpment from Chipping Campden to Bath via Duntisbourne and Slimbridge.

Southwest of Stratford on Avon in Warwickshire charming villages line the Stour; and Stratford itself is the heart of Shakespeare country; his birthplace is in Henley Street, his grave in the churchyard by the river and Anne Hathaway's cottage at Shottery. Not far away are the beautiful reaches of the Avon south of Kenilworth, its castle is almost as imposing as Warwick's, further south.

Most campsites in the region are recommended more for their setting than for their amenities.

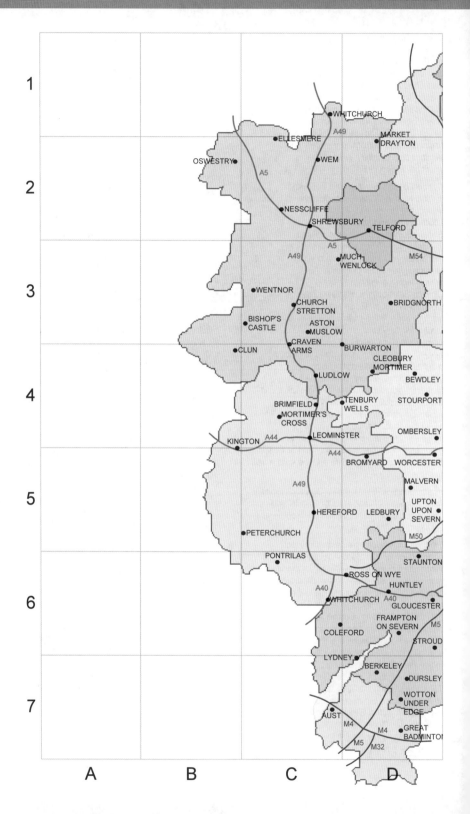

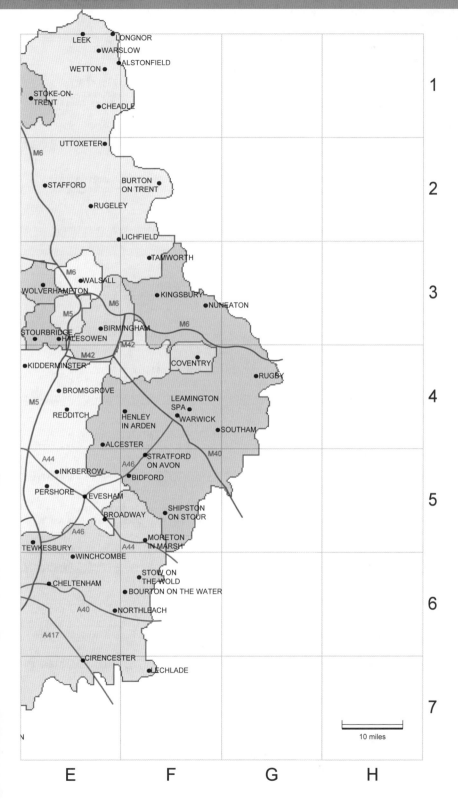

ALCESTER, Warwicks   Map E4
EC Thurs SEE town hall and houses in Butter, Church and Henley streets, 1 Malt Mill Lane (Shakespeare assns), Ragley Hall and Park (adventure trails) 2m SW
✘ Arrow Mill on Evesham road at Arrow ✆ (01789) 762419

Island Meadow Caravan Park, The Mill House, Aston Cantlow B95 6JP ✆ (01789) 488273 Fax (01789) 488273 OS map 151/135597 3m NE of Alcester off B4089 (Wootton Wawen)–access via Little Alne advisable Open Mar-Oct–must book peak periods 80 pitches (56 static) Grass, level, sheltered 🐾⚡💧⊕∅⊕😊⊑⚓ fishing £11.00-£15.00*
holiday@islandmeadowcaravanpark.co.uk www.islandmeadowcaravanpark.co.uk

ALSTONEFIELD, Staffs   Map E1
SEE Manifold Valley SW, Dove Dale S
✘ Dales 3m N at Hartington ✆ (01298) 84235

The George DE6 2FX ✆ (01335) 310205 OS map 119/132556 ¼m E of Alstonefield centre on Tissington road at rear of hotel Open all year 12 pitches–no adv booking–no trailer caravans 1 acre level grass, walled ⚲ (Mastercard/Visa)
See also Longnor and Warslow

ASTON CANTLOW–see Alcester

ASTON MUNSLOW, Shrops   Map C3
SEE Millichope Park NE, nature trail (Wolverton Wood)
✘ Sun Inn at Corfton ✆ (01584) 861239

Glebe Farm, Diddlebury SY7 9DH Secluded wooded paddock on farm ✆ (01584) 841221 OS map 137/508855 ½m SW of Aston Munslow off B4368 (Craven Arms) on Peaton road Open all year 6 pitches Level grass, sheltered

AUST, S Gloucestershire   Map C7
For those travelling by motorway between Wales and England, a popular place to stop, only ½m from junct 21 of M4 SEE Severn Bridge
✘ Boar's Head ✆ (01454) 632278

Boar's Head Campsite BS12 3AX ✆ (01454) 632278 OS map 172/575890 ¼m SE of Aust off A403 (Avonmouth) by inn Open Mar-Oct 20 pitches Grass level/sloping ✘ (snack) ⚲🍺

BADMINTON, S Gloucestershire   Map D7
SEE Badminton House and Kennels, old Beaufort Arms inn
✘ Petty France 3m NW on A46 ✆ (01454) 238361

Petty France Farm, Dunkirk GL9 1AF ✆ (01454) 238665 OS map 172/787855 4m NW of Badminton on A46 (Stroud-Bath) near junct 18 of M4 Open Easter-Sep 12 pitches Grass, level, part sheltered ⊕

BERKELEY, Glos   Map D7
EC Wed SEE parish church, castle, Slimbridge Wildfowl Trust 6m NE
✘ Old School House, Canonbury St ✆ (01453) 811711

Hogsdown Farm, Lower Wick GL11 6DD ✆ (01453) 810224 OS map 162/710973 1½m SE of Berkeley off B4066 (Dursley) on Lower Wick road Open all year 40 pitches Level grass and hard standing, sheltered 🐾💧⊕∅⊕😊🍴🚿⊑ B&B

BERROW–see Tewkesbury

BEWDLEY, Worcs   Map D4
EC Wed MD Tues, Sat SEE Wyre Forst, Tudor houses and inns, Telford bridge, Severn valley Rly to Bridgnorth
🛈 St George's Hall, Load St ✆ (01299) 404740
✘ Black Boy, Kidderminster Rd ✆ (01299) 403523

Woodlands Holiday Home Park, Dowles Road DY12 3AE ✆ (01299) 403208/403294 OS map 138/773767 1½m NW of Bewdley on left of B4194 (Bridgnorth) by Wyre Forest Open Mar-Jan 158 pitches (150 static)–no tents 💧⊕∅⊕∅🍴

BIDFORD ON AVON, Warwicks   Map F5
SEE 13c church, 15c bridge
✘ Arrow Mill 3m N on A422 at Arrow ✆ (01789) 762419

Cottage of Content Inn, Barton B50 4NP ✆ (01789) 772279 OS map 150/107511 1m SE of Bidford on Avon off B4085 (Evesham) in Barton village Open Mar-Oct 25 pitches Grass, sloping, sheltered ✘⚲🍴∅⊕🍴 No showers (most cards)

Help us make CAMPING CARAVANNING BRITAIN better known to site operators – and thereby more informative – by showing them your copy when booking in.

BISHOP'S CASTLE, Shrops **Map C3**
✘Castle, Market Sq ☎(01588) 638403

The Old School Caravan Park, Shelve, Minsterley SY5 0JQ ☎(01588) 650410 *Prop: T Ward* OS map 137/336990 6m N of Bishops Castle on A488 (Shrewsbury) Open Mar-Jan 22 pitches ▣◉∅▣ TV hook-up £11.00

Powis Arms, Lydbury North SY7 8AU ☎(01588) 680254 OS map 137/349858 3m SE of Bishop's Castle on right of B4385 (Leintwardine) in grounds of 18c coaching inn Open Apr-Oct 15 pitches 1 acre level grass ✘�▣∅

See also Wentnor

BOURTON ON THE WATER, Glos **Map F6**
EC Sat SEE aquarium, Birdland, model village
✘Old New Inn, High St ☎(01451) 820467

Folly Farm, Notgrove GL54 3BY *Basic site in area of outstanding natural beauty* ☎(01451) 820285 OS map 163/124206 2½m W of Bourton on the Water on A436 (Andoversford) Open Mar-Oct 20 pitches Level grass and hard standing, sheltered ▣◉ *j.kenwright@virgin.net www.cotswoldcamping.net*

BRIDGNORTH, Shrops **Map D3**
EC Thurs MD Mon, Sat SEE Bishop Percy's House, cliff railway, castle ruins, town hall, Northgate museum, Severn Valley Rly to Bewdley
▤Library, Listley St ☎(01746) 763257
✘Bear Inn, Northgate (High Town) ☎(01746) 763250

Stanmore Hall Touring Park, Stourbridge Road WV15 6DT ☎(01746) 761761 Fax (01746) 768069 OS map 138/922742 2m E of Bridgnorth on A458 (Stourbridge) Open all year 131 pitches (all weather, serviced) Grass and hard standing, sheltered ▤⚲▣▣◉∅❸⤳◻ᵫ £13.80-£16.30* (Mastercard/Switch/Visa) *stanmore@morris-leisure.co.uk www.morris-leisure.co.uk*

See also Burwarton

BRILLEY–see Kington

BROADWAY, Worcs **Map E5**
EC Thurs SEE Lygon Arms, Elizabethan houses, Fish Inn, church, Broadway Tower country park
▤Cotswold Court ☎(01386) 852937
✘Crown and Trumpet, Church St (Snowshill road) ☎(01386) 853202

Leedons Park, Childswickham Road WR12 7HB ☎(01386) 852423 Fax (01386) 853655 OS map 150/080385 1m NW of Broadway off A44 (Evesham) Open all year 420 pitches Grass, level, part sheltered ▤⚲▣▣⊘∅◻(outdoor heated in season) ❸⤳◻⌸ᵫ kitchen facs (most cards)

BROMYARD, Hfds **Map D5**
SEE Norman church, Lower Brockhampton House 2m E, Bromyard Downs NE
▤The Bromyard Centre ☎(01432) 260621
✘The Nelson Inn, Longley Green, Suckley ☎(01886) 884530

Boyce Caravan Park, Stanford Bishop, Bringsty WR6 5UB ☎(01886) 884248 *Prop: Richards & Bateson* OS map 149/697526 3m E of Bromyard off A44 (Worcester) and B4220 (Malvern) Open Mar-Oct 168 pitches (150 static) Level grass, part sheltered ▣▣⊘∅❸⤳⌂ coarse fishing £10.00 *enquires@boyceholidaypark.co.uk www.boyceholidaypark.co.uk*

BROOME–see Craven Arms

CHEADLE, Staffs **Map E1**
EC Wed MD Fri, Sat *Attractive market town amid rolling hills and moorland* SEE church (RC), Hawksmoor nature reserve 2m E
✘Royal Oak, High St ☎(01538) 753116

Hales Hall Caravan Camping Park, Oakamoor Road ST10 4QR ☎(01538) 753305 *Prop: Cristina Clare* OS map 119/021441 1m NE of Cheadle on B5417 (Oakamoor) Open Easter-Oct–must book public holidays 80 pitches (30 static) Level/sloping grass and hard standing, sheltered ▤✘床⤳⚲▣▣∅◉∅◻(heated) ❸⤳◻▣ £12.00-£14.00

Quarry Walk Park, Coppice Lane, Freehay ST10 1RQ ☎(01538) 723412 Fax (01538) 723495 OS map 128/045404 2m S of Cheadle off A522 (Uttoxeter) in Freehay on Great Gate road Open all year 40 pitches 46 acres level grass and hard standings, sheltered ▤▣▣⊘◉❸⤳ᵫ *quarry@quarrywalkpark.co.uk www.quarrywalkpark.co.uk*

Star Caravan Camping Park, Cotton, Oakamoor ST10 3DW *1½m from Alton Towers, 5 star ETB* ☎(01538) 702219 *Prop: MA Mellor* OS map 119/067456 3m NE of Cheadle on B5417 (Cotton) near Star Inn Open Feb-Nov 170 pitches (50 static) Level/sloping grass and hard standing, sheltered ✘▣▣⊘◉∅❸⤳▣⌸ᵫ⚬ parent & baby room, 5 star ETB £12.00 *www.starcaravanpark.co.uk*

CHELTENHAM, Glos   Map E6
EC Wed MD Thurs SEE Pittville Park, museum, colleges, Rotunda, Regency houses, mineral springs
🅩 The Promenade ✆ (01242) 522878
✘ Bayhill Inn, St Georges Place (behind bus station) ✆ (01242) 524388

Cheltenham Racecourse (Caravan Club), Prestbury Park GL50 4SH ✆ (01242) 523102 OS map 163/960250 1½m NE of Cheltenham on A436 (Evesham) Open Mar-Oct 84 pitches Grass and hard standing 🗑🚐🗲⊕∅

CHURCH STRETTON, Shrops   Map C3
EC Wed MD Thurs SEE parish church, Long Mynd (NT), Cardingmill Valley, Acton Scott Farm Museum 2m S off A49
🅩 Church St ✆ (01694) 723133
✘ Green Dragon SW at Little Stretton ✆ (01694) 722925

Small Batch Caravan and Camping Site, Ashes Valley, Little Stretton SY6 6PW *Basic site in fine walking country* ✆ (01694) 723358 OS map 137/441920 1½m SW of Church Stretton off A49 (Craven Arms) on B5477 Open Easter-Sept 37 pitches Grass, level 🚐⊕ £10.00

Wayside Inn, Marshbrook SY6 6QE ✆ (01694) 781208 OS map 137/441898 2½m S of Church Stretton at junc of A49 (Ludlow) and B4370 (Bishops Castle) Open all year 40 pitches 2 acres, level grass, sheltered ✘ bar meals, No showers

CIRENCESTER, Glos   Map E7
EC Thurs MD Mon, Tues, Fri SEE parish church, Corinium museum, Roman wall, Chedworth Roman Villa 7m N
🅩 Corn Hall, Market Place ✆ (01285) 654180
✘ King's Head, Market Pl ✆ (01285) 653322

Cotswold Hoburne, Broadway Lane, South Cerney GL7 5UQ ✆ (01285) 860216 OS map 163/055958 4m SE of Cirencester off A419 (Swindon) Open Easter-Oct–must book peak periods 540 pitches (154 static) Hard standings 🖢✘♀⬖🗑🚐🗲⊕∅🖵(2) ⊕⤸🗖⊛�🏠👢 club house, tennis courts

Mayfield Touring Park, Perrott's Brook GL7 7BH ✆ (01285) 831301 OS map 163/020055 2m N of Cirencester on A435 (Cheltenham) Open all year 72 pitches Grass, part sloping, and hard standing 🖢🗑🚐🗲⊕∅⊕⤸⊛🚻 Take-away food from £9.00* (Mastercard/Visa/Switch) *mayfieldparkcirencester.fsbusiness.co.uk www.mayfieldpark.co.uk*

CLUN, Shrops   Map B4
✘ The Old Post Office, The Square ✆ (01743) 236019

Bush Farm, Clunton SY7 0HU ✆ (01588) 660330 OS map 137/337811 2m E of Clun off B4368 (Craven Arms) at Clunton, by river Clun Open Apr-Oct 25 pitches 2 acres level grass and hard standings, sheltered 🚐⊕🚐👢🏴 fishing

COLEFORD, Glos   Map C6
EC Thurs SEE ruined 14c church, Forest of Dean
🅩 High St ✆ (01594) 812388
✘ Dog and Muffler 1m N at Joyford (off B4432) ✆ (01594) 832444

Braceland Site, (Forest Enterprise) GL16 8BA ✆ (01594) 833376 OS map 162/569129 1½m N of Coleford off B4432 (Ross) at Berry Hill Open Mar-Oct 600 pitches 20 acres level grass, sheltered 🚐⊕🚐

Forest of Dean Camping Ground, Christchurch GL16 7NN ✆ (01594) 833057 OS map 162/569129 2m N of Coleford off B4432 (Ross) Open all year 280 pitches Level/sloping grass and hard standing 🖢🗑🚐🗲⊕∅⤸🚐⊛👢

Woodland View Camping Park, Sling GL16 8JA ✆ (01594) 835127 OS map 162/582085 1½m S of Coleford on B4228 (Chepstow) near Lambsquay Hotel Open Mar 1-Oct 31 20 pitches 1½ acres, part level grass and hard standing 🖢🚐🗲⊕ £8.00-£12.75 (all major cards)

COVENTRY   Map F4
MD daily exc Thurs SEE cathedral remains and new cathedral, St Mary's Hall, Holy Trinity church, Lady Godiva statue, art gallery, new city centre
🅩 Bayley Lane ✆ 0247 622 7264
✘ Campanile, Wigston Road, Walsgrave ✆ (01203) 622311

Hollyfast Caravan Park, Wall Hill Road, Allesley CV5 9EL ✆ (02476) 336411 OS map 140/300833 2m NW of Coventry off A4114 (Birmingham) Open all year 75 pitches 10 acres level grass and hard standings, sheltered 🚐⊕⊕⤸🗖👢

For more up-to-date information, and for links to camping websites, visit our site at:
www.butford.co.uk/camping

Mayfield Touring Park, Cirencester

CRAVEN ARMS, Shrops — Map C4
EC Wed MD Fri, Sat SEE Stokesay Castle, Iron Age hill fort
✘ The Engine & Tender, Broome ☎ (01588) 660275

Engine and Tender Inn, Broome SY7 0NT ☎ (01588) 660275 OS map 137/401812 2½m SW of Craven Arms off B4367 (Clungunford) Open all year 30 pitches Level/sloping grass, sheltered 🔋 ✘ ⚲ ⚌ 🗑 🔲 ∅ 🔌 🚉 (most cards)

Kevindale, Broome SY7 0NT ☎ (01588) 660199 *Prop: KJ Rudd* OS map 137/403809 2m SW of Craven Arms on B4367 (Bucknell) in Broome village Open Apr-Sep 12 pitches 4 acres level grass ⚙ £7.00-£7.50

CROSSWAY GREEN–see Stourport on Severn

DURSLEY, Glos — Map D7
EC Thurs
✘ Tudor Arms, Shepherds Patch, Slimbridge ☎ (01453) 890306

Tudor Caravan and Camping Site, Shepherds Patch, Slimbridge GL2 7BP ☎ (01453) 890483 *Prop: KI & EJ Fairall* OS map 162/728041 4½m NW of Dursley off A4135 (Slimbridge) Open all year–must book peak periods 75 pitches Level grass and hard standing, sheltered 🔋 ✘ 🔲 ∅ ⚙ £10.00-£12.00 *info@tudorcaravanpark.co.uk www.tudorcaravanpark.com*

EDGERLEY–see Nesscliffe

ELLESMERE, Shrops — Map C2
EC Thurs MD Tues SEE Kynaston Monument, half timbered houses, The Mere (lake)
▪ The Mereside, Ellesmore ☎ (01691) 622981
✘ Grange 1m N on A528 ☎ (01691) 623495

Fernwood Caravan Park, Lyneal SY12 0QF ☎ (01948) 710221 OS map 126/453338 4m SE of Ellesmere off B5063 (Wem) Open Mar-Nov 225 pitches (165 static) no tents 66 acres level grass and hard standings 🔋 🔲 ⚌ ∅ ⚙ ∅ ⚡ 🚉 ♿ coarse fishing (40 acres woodland) £15.50-£19.50 inc elect (Mastercard/Visa) *enquiries@fernwoodpark.co.uk www.fernwoodpark.co.uk*

Tudor Caravan and Camping Site, Dursley

EVESHAM, Worcs   **Map E5**
EC Wed SEE abbey ruins, churches, local history museum, Abbey park and gardens, riverside
🖾 Almonry Museum, Abbey Gate ☏ (01386) 446944
✗ Waterside on A44 ☏ (01386) 442420

Ranch Caravan Park, Honeybourne WR11 7PR ☏ (01386) 830744 Fax (01386) 833503 OS map
     150/115445 5m E of Evesham off B4035 (Bretforton) Open Mar-Nov 300 pitches (180 static) no
     tents Level grass, sheltered–some hard standing 🛒🖥🛢🖎⊕∅🖵(heated) ⌇🚐 lic club
     £13.50-£18.00* (Mastercard/Visa/Delta/Switch) enquiries@ranch.co.uk www.ranch.co.uk

Weir Meadow Holiday and Touring Park, Lower Leys WR11 5AB ☏ (01386) 442417 OS map
     150/044439 In Evesham off A44 (Chipping Norton) by River Avon Open Mar-Nov 185 pitches
     (125 static)–no tents Level grass 🖥🖎🛢∅⌇🚐🖧 boating, fishing (all cards)

GLOUCESTER, Glos   **Map D6**
MD daily SEE cathedral, folk museum, New Inn, canal, Prinknash Abbey 5m SE, regimental
museum
🖾 28 Southgate St ☏ (01452) 396572
✗ Swan Inn, Ledbury Rd, Staunton ☏ (01452) 840323

Gable Farm, Moreton Valence GL2 7ND ☏ (01452) 720331 OS map 162/787100 6m S of
     Gloucester on A38 (Bristol) near Junction 13 of M5 Open Mar-Nov 30 pitches Level grass,
     sheltered 🖎🛢⊕🖧

Red Lion, Wainlodes Hill, Norton GL2 9LW ☏ (01452) 730251 Prop: M Loveridge OS map
     162/848258 5m N of Gloucester off A38 (Tewkesbury) by River Severn Open all year 105 pitches
     Grass, level 🛒✗🍴⌇🖥🛢🖎⊕🖧🖵🖧 bar snacks, fishing £9.00-£11.00
     (Mastercard/Visa/Switch) www.redlioninn-caravancamping.co.uk

Staunton Court, Ledbury Rd, Staunton GL19 3QS ☏ (01452) 840230 OS map 150/782292 7m
     NW of Gloucester on A417 (Ledbury) Open all year 50 pitches 4½ acres level/sloping grass,
     sheltered 🖎⊕🖧 fishing, tackle shop £5.50-£7.00 inc elect www.stauntoncourt.co.uk

See also Huntley and Tewkesbury

HANLEY SWAN–see Malvern

HAY ON WYE–see Central and South Wales

HEREFORD, Hfds   **Map C5**
EC Thurs MD daily except Tues SEE cathedral, The Old House, 15c Wye Bridge
🖾 1 King St ☏ (01432) 268430
✗ Bunch of Carrots Inn 2m SE at Hampton Bishop ☏ (01432) 870237

Lucks-All Caravan and Camping Park, Mordiford HR1 4LP ☏ (01432) 870213 Fax (01432) 870213
     OS map 149/567362 5m SE of Hereford off B4077 (Ledbury) on B4224 (Mordiford) by River Wye
     Open Mar-Nov 80 pitches 10 acres level grass and hard standing 🛒🖥🛢🖎⊕∅🖧⌇🖥🖧🖧
     £9.00-£12.00* (Mastercard/Switch/Visa) www.lucksallpark.co.uk

HONEYBOURNE–see Evesham

HUGHLEY–see Much Wenlock

HUNTLEY, Glos   **Map D6**
SEE Newent Wood 1m NW, falconry centre 3m N at Newent
✗ Red Lion ☏ (01452) 870251

Forest Gate GL19 3EU *Convenient base for Forest of Dean and Severn Vale* ☏ (01452) 831192
     OS map 162/718194 In Huntley near junct of A40 and A4136 (Mitcheldean) Open Mar-Oct
     30 pitches 3 acres level grass, sheltered 🛒🖥🛢⊕∅ B&B (Mastercard/Visa)
     forestgate@huntley.glos.demon.co.uk www.forestgate-huntley.co.uk

SHOWERS

Except where marked, all sites in this guide
have flush lavatories and showers. Symbols
for these amenities have therefore been
omitted from site entries.

Pearl Lake Leisure Park,
Mortimers Cross

KINGTON, Hfds   **Map B5**
EC Wed MD Tues SEE Hergest Ridge 1m W
▯ Council Offices, Mill St ✆ (01544) 230778
✘ Royal Oak, Church St ✆ (01544) 230484

Penlan Caravan Park, Brilley HR3 6JW ✆ (01497) 831485 OS map 148/272515 4½m SW of
Kington off Brilley road Open Easter-Oct 12 pitches–must book 2 acres level/sloping grass,
sheltered 🛢🔌⊕∅ £10.00-£15.00 peter@penlan.org.uk www.penlancaravanpark.co.uk

KNIGHTON ON TEME–see Tenbury Wells

LECHLADE, Glos   **Map F7**
SEE Georgian houses, church, river Isis
✘ Royal Oak, Oak St ✆ (01367) 252261

Bridge House GL7 3AG ✆ (01367) 252348 Prop: R Cooper OS map 163/219991 ¼m S of
Lechlade on A361 (Swindon) near river bridge Open Mar-Oct 51 pitches 4½ acres level grass,
open 🛢🔌⊕∅🔌⅄ £8.00-£10.00

St John's Priory Caravans, Faringdon Road GL7 3EZ ✆ (01367) 252360 OS map 163/224989
½m E of Lechlade on A417 (Faringdon) Open Mar-Oct 100 pitches (74 static) Level grass,
sheltered 🔌∅⊕

LEDBURY, Hfds   **Map D5**
EC Wed MD Tues, Wed SEE Church Lane, Birtsmorton Court SE 7m
▯ 3 The Homend ✆ (01531) 636147
✘ Feathers ✆ (01531) 635266

Russells End Caravan Park, Bromsberrow HR8 1PB ✆ (01531) 650687 OS map 150/755330
4½m SE of Ledbury on A417 (Gloucester) near junct 2 of M50 Open Mar-Oct 60 pitches
🛢🔌∅⊕∅⊕

See also Gloucester

LEEK, Staffs   **Map E1**
EC Thurs MD Wed SEE parish church, Nicholson Institute, Prince Charlie's house, 17c almshouses,
Rudyard lake 3m NW, N Staffs Railway Museum 2m S
▯ Market Place ✆ (01538) 483741
✘ Flintlock ✆ (01538) 361032

Glencote Caravan Park, Churnet Valley, Station Road, Cheddleton ST13 7EE ✆ (01538) 360745
Fax (01538) 361788 Prop: Mr & Mrs Birch OS map 118/982524 3m S of Leek off A520 (Stone)
near canal-side pub Open Mar-Oct 60 pitches 6 acres grass and hard standing, level, sheltered
🛢🔌∅⊕∅⅄🔌 fishing, BBQ area £15.00 (Mastercard/Visa/Switch) canistay@glencote.co.uk
www.glencote.co.uk

LICHFIELD, Staffs   **Map E2**
EC Wed MD Mon, Fri, Sat SEE cathedral, Birthplace of Dr Samuel Johnson, Museum, St John's
Hospital (almshouses) with church adj
▯ Donegal House, Bore St ✆ (01543) 308209
✘ George, Bird St ✆ (01543) 414822

Willowbrook Farm, Alrewas DE13 7BA ✆ (01283) 790217 OS map 128/183157 5m NE of Lichfield
on E side of (dual carriageway) A38 (Burton on Trent) Open all year 20 pitches 3 acres, level
grass 🔌⊕∅ No showers fishing

LONGNOR, Staffs   **Map E1**
SEE church, Dovedale E, Manifold Valley S
✘ Old Cheshire Cheese, High St ✆ (01298) 83218

Longnor Wood Just for Adults Caravan Park, Newtown, Fawfieldhead SK17 0NG Secluded
haven for mature tourist ✆ (01298) 83648 OS map 119/072641 1m SW of Longnor off Leek road
Open Apr or Easter-Oct 46 pitches (14 static) 11 acres, grass, level 🛒ⅉ🛢🔌∅⊕∅🔌🏠🔌
putting, croquet, boules

LUDLOW, Shrops   **Map C4**
EC Thurs MD Mon, Fri, Sat SEE castle, old inns, museum, craft centre
▯ Castle St ✆ (01584) 875053
✘ Church Inn, Buttercross ✆ (01584) 872174

Orleton Rise Holiday Home Park, Green Lane, Orleton SY8 4JE ✆ (01584) 831617 Fax (01584)
831617 OS map 137/138/477680 5m S of Ludlow off B4361 (Leominster), ½m from Maidenhead
Inn Open Mar-Jan 104 pitches (87 static)–no tents Level grass and hard standing, sheltered
🔌∅⊕∅ £9.00-£14.00* www.lucksallpark.co.uk

LYNEAL–see Ellesmere

MALVERN, Worcs   Map D5
EC Wed MD Fri SEE College, Priory church, St Anne's well, grave of Elgar at Little Malvern,
Malvern Hills
🖪21 Church St ✆(01684) 892289
✘Cottage in the Wood 2m S at Malvern Wells ✆(01684) 573487

Oakmere Caravan Park, Hanley Swan WR8 0DZ ✆(01684) 310375 OS map 150/803428 3m SE
of Malvern on B4209 (Upton on Severn) Open Easter-Oct 90 pitches (70 static) Hard standings
and level grass, sheltered 🌣🖉⊕🌀⊖↩🖭

Riverside Caravan Park, Little Clevelode WR13 6PE ✆(01684) 310475 OS map 150/832462
3½m E of Malvern on B4424 (Worcester) by River Severn Open Apr-Oct 200 pitches (130 static)
Level grass, sheltered 🖪🌣🏹🖥🖭🖉🌀⊖↩🗂🖭🎦 fishing, tennis

See also Tewkesbury and Upton on Severn

MORTIMERS CROSS, Hfds   Map C4
Famous as site of decisive battle in Wars of Roses SEE battle museum
✘The Riverside Inn, Aymestry ✆(01568) 708440 Open 12-2.15/7-9

Pearl Lake Leisure Park, Shobdon HR6 9NQ *Picturesque lakeside park with golf course, lovely on-
site walks* ✆(01568) 708326 OS map 149/394623 1m W of Mortimer's Cross on right of B4362
(Presteigne) Open Mar 1-Nov 30 165 pitches (150 static)–must book Level grass and hard
standings ✘🌣↩🖥🖭🖉⊕🌀↩ TV hook-up, serviced pitches, 9 hole golf course, bowling green,
15-acre lake and 20-acre woodland £12.00-£16.00* inc elect (Mastercard/Visa)
info@pearllake.co.uk www.bestparks.co.uk

Shobdon Airfield Touring Park, Shobdon HR6 9NR ✆(01568) 708369 OS map 149/400610 3m
W of Mortimer's Cross off B4362 (Presteigne) and Pembridge road Open Mar-Oct 25 pitches
level grass and hard standing 3 acres ✘🌣⊕ gliding, flying lessons inc microlight (most cards)

MUCH WENLOCK, Shrops   Map C3
Small town which grew up round priory founded 680 and twice demolished SEE ruined priory,
Guildhall, old houses, Benthall Hall 4m NE, Shipton Hall 6m SW, Corvedale 2m S, Wenlock Edge
SW
🖪Museum, High St ✆(01952) 727679
✘George and Dragon, High St ✆(01952) 727312

Mill Farm, Hughley SY5 6NT ✆(01746) 785208/785255 Fax (01746) 785211 OS map 138/563982
4m SW of Much Wenlock off A458 (Shrewsbury) via Harley Open Mar-Jan–must book peak
periods 125 pitches (88 static) Level grass and hard standing, sheltered 🖥🖭🖉⊕🌀⊖🖭🎦
pony trekking, fishing, bowling green info@millfarmcaravanpark.co.uk
www.millfarmcaravanpark.co.uk

NESSCLIFFE, Shrops   Map C2
SEE Earthwork on hill, half-timbered church at Melverley 4m SW on Severn
✘Old Three Pigeons opp Kynaston Cave ✆(01743) 741279

Cranberry Moss Camping and Caravan Site, Kinnerley SY10 8DY ✆(01743) 741444 OS map
126/365212 2m NW of Nesscliffe off A5 (Oswestry) on left of B4396 (Knockin) Open Apr-Sep
60 pitches 4 acres level/sloping grass 🖪🖥🖭🖉⊕🌀↩

Royal Hill Camping, Edgerley SY10 8ES ✆(01743) 741242 OS map 126/352175 2m SW of
Nesscliffe on Melverley road Open Apr-Oct 30 pitches Level grass 🌣🖥🖭🖉⊕🌀↩🎦 freezer
pack service

NOTGROVE–see Bourton on the Water

NUNEATON, Warwicks   Map F3
MD Sat SEE churches, museum, Arbury Hall 3m SW
🖪Library, Church St ✆0247 634 7006
✘Railway Tavern, Bond St ✆(01203) 382015

Wolvey Villa Farm Caravan Camping Park, Wolvey LE10 3HF ✆(01455) 220493/220630 OS
map 140/428869 6m SE of Nuneaton off B4114 (Rugby)–Wolvey signed from Junct 2 of M6 and
Junct 1 of M69 Open all year–must book peak periods 110 pitches Level grass and hard
standing (winter), sheltered 🖪🏹🖥🖭🖉⊕🌀🖭🖭🎦♿ putting green, fishing

OAKAMOOR–see Cheadle

OMBERSLEY, Worcs **Map D4**
SEE timbered cottages and inns, Holt Fleet lock on river Severn W
✘Crown and Sandys Arms ✆(01905) 620252

Holt Fleet Farm, Ombersley WR6 6NW ✆(01905) 620512 OS map 150/825634 1m W of
   Ombersley off A4133 near Holt Fleet lock by river Severn Open Apr-Oct 338 pitches (188 static)
   Level grass ⚑✘▣⌀✿ lic club

Lenchford Meadow Park, Lenchford, Shrawley WR6 6TB ✆(01905) 620246 OS map 150/813643
   2m W of Ombersley off A443 (Great Witley) on right of B4196 (Stourport) Open Mar 7-Jan 6
   72 pitches 5 acres level grass, sheltered ✘♀▣▣⌀✿

OSWESTRY, Shrops **Map B2**
EC Thurs MD Wed SEE parish church, King Oswald's Well, Llwyd Mansion, Offa's Dyke
▣Mile End Services (A5) ✆(01691) 662488
✘Wynnstay, Church Street ✆(01691)655261

Royal Oak, Treflach SY10 9HE ✆(01691) 652455 OS map 126/258254 3m SW of Oswestry off
   A483 (Welshpool) via Trefonen by Offa's Dyke Open Apr-Oct 12 pitches–no adv booking 1 acre,
   level ✘♀

PERSHORE, Worcs **Map E5**
EC Thurs SEE abbey, 14c bridge over river Avon
▣19 High St ✆(01386) 556591
✘Angel, High St ✆(01386) 552046

Eckington Riverside Caravan Park, Eckington WR10 3DD ✆(01386) 750985 OS map
   150/922423 2m S of Pershore off A4104 (Upton) on B4080 (Tewkesbury) Open Mar 1-Nov 85
   pitches (50 static) 5 acres level grass, sheltered ▣✿ fishing

PETERCHURCH, Hfds **Map C5**
SEE Golden Valley
✘Mill Restaurant & Bar, The Mill ✆(01981) 550151

Bridge Inn, Michaelchurch Escley HR2 0JW ✆(01981) 510646 Prop: NJ & K Maddy OS map
   161/317341 5m SW of Peterchurch off B4348 (Kingstone) Open Mar-Oct 12 pitches Grass and
   hard standings ✘♀⇀▣⌀ children £10.00 nickmaddy@aol.com

Poston Mill Park, Vowchurch HR2 0SF ✆(01981) 550225 Fax (01981) 550885 OS map
   161/356371 1½m SE of Peterchurch on B4348 (Kingstone) Open all year 164 pitches (82 static)
   Level grass and hard standings, sheltered ✘♀⇀♪▣▣⌀✿⌀✿⌴▣▭&. serviced pitches,
   TV hook-ups £12.00-£16.00* (Mastercard/Visa)

REDDITCH, Worcs **Map E4**
EC Wed MD daily exc Sun SEE National Needle Museum in Forge Mill, Bordesley abbey ruins
▣Civic Sq, Alcester St ✆(01527) 60806
✘Old Washford Mill 2m S on B4497 at Washford by river Arrow ✆(01527) 23068

Outhill Caravan Park, Outhill, Studley B80 7DY ✆(01527) 852160 Prop: Mrs D Wofford OS map
   150/107663 3m E of Redditch off A4189 (Henley in Arden) on left of Studley road Open Apr-Oct
   15 pitches–no tents 10 acres level grass–cold water only £3.00-£5.00

ROSS ON WYE, Hfds **Map D6**
EC Wed MD Thurs, Sat SEE House of
▣The Swan, Edde Cross St ✆(01989) 562768
✘Orles Barn 1m W at Wilton ✆(01989) 762155

Broadmeadow Caravan Park, Broadmeadow HR9 7BH ✆(01989) 768076 Fax (01989) 566030
   Prop: Brian & Elizabeth Edwards OS map 162/607246 On E edge of Ross on Wye, access via
   Station Approach off Gloucester road Open Apr-Sept 150 pitches Level grass and hard standing
   ▣▣⌀✿⌀✿⌴&. (all cards) broadm4811@aol.com www.broadmeadow.info

RUGBY, Warwicks **Map G4**
EC Wed MD Mon, Fri, Sat Birthplace of football SEE Rugby School, Stanford castle and park NE
5m
▣4 Lawrence Sheriff St ✆(01788) 534970
✘The Bear, Bilton Lane, Long Lawford ✆(01788) 522297

Lodge Farm Caravan Site, Bilton Lane, Long Lawford CV23 9DU ✆(01788) 560193 OS map
   140/477749 1½m W of Rugby off A428 (Coventry) at Long Lawford on Bilton Lane Open Apr-Oct
   35 pitches 5 acres level grass sheltered ▣⌀✿▣▭▦ £8.00-£10.00 (all cards)
   alec@lodgefarm.com www.lodgefarm.com

The distance and direction of a campsite is given from the centre of the town under which it appears.

SHIPSTON ON STOUR, Warwicks   **Map F5**
EC Thurs *Small town on Stour in typical Cotswold countryside*
✖ White Bear, High St ☎ (01608) 661558

Mill Farm, Long Compton CV36 5NZ ☎ (01608) 684663 OS map 151/280332 4m S of Shipston on
Stour off A34 (Oxford) on Barton on the Heath road Open Easter-Oct 10 pitches 3½ acres level
grass 🔲⊕ No showers

SHOBDON–see Mortimers Cross

SHREWSBURY, Shrops   **Map C2**
EC Thurs MD Tues, Wed, Fri, S SEE abbey church, 15c Grope Lane, St Mary's church, Roman city
of Wroxeter 6m SE, Condover Hall 5m S
🎫 The Square ☎ (01743) 281200
✖ The Hare & Hounds, Cruckton ☎ (01743) 860230

Bridge Inn, Dorrington SY5 7ED ☎ (01743) 718209 OS map 126/475037 6m S of Shrewsbury on
left of A49 (Ludlow) Open all year 10 pitches 2 acres level/sloping grass ✖🍴🍽⊕∅🔌🔲⚓
(all major cards)

Cartref Shrewsbury, Fords Heath SY5 9GD ☎ (01743) 821688 *Prop: AD & P Edwards* OS map
126/415116 4m W of Shrewsbury on A458 (Welshpool)–signposted from bypass Open May-Oct
35 pitches Level grass, sheltered 🔲🔲⊕∅🔵⊕🔌⚓ £7.00-£10.00
www.caravancampingsites.co.uk

Oxon Touring Park, Welshpool Road SY3 5FB ☎ (01743) 340868 Fax (01743) 340869 OS map
126/455138 2m W of Shrewsbury off A458 (Welshpool) near junct with A5–follow signs for Oxon
Park and Ride Open all year 120 pitches with mains services Level grass and hard standing,
sheltered 🏪🔌🔲∅⊕∅🔵🔌🔳⚓ £9.00-£16.00* (all major cards) info@townsend-farm.co.uk
www.townsend-farm.co.uk

Severn House, Montford Bridge SY4 1ED ☎ (01743) 850229 OS map 126/435155 4m NW of
Shrewsbury off A458 (Welshpool) on B4380 (Oswestry) by river Severn Open Apr-Oct 25 pitches
1¼ acres grass and hard standings, sheltered 🏪✖🍴🔲∅⊕

SLIMBRIDGE–see Dursley

SOUTHAM, Warwicks   **Map F4**
SEE old bridge, 'Mint' House, Grand Union and Oxford Canals
✖ Old Mint, Coventry St (A423) ☎ (01926) 812339

Holt Farm, Welsh Road East CV47 1NJ ☎ (01926) 812225 *Prop: Neil Adkins* OS map 151/455593
3m SE of Southam off Priors Marston road–signposted from A423 bypass Open Mar-Oct
45 pitches 1½ acres level grass part sheltered 🔲⊕ fishing £8.00-£10.00

STAUNTON–see Gloucester

STOKE ON TRENT   **Map E1**
EC Thurs MD Wed, Fri, Sat SEE St Peter's church, town hall, Arnold Bennett museum at Corbridge,
Wedgewood, mining and potteries museums, canal by boat
🎫 Potteries Shopping Centre, Quadrant Rd, Hanley ☎ (01782) 236600
✖ Victoria Inn 2m W at Newcastle under Lyme ☎ (01782) 615569

Trentham Gardens, Stone Rd, Trentham ST4 8AX ☎ (01782) 657341 OS map 118/863407 4m S
of Stoke on Trent on right of A34 (Stafford) near junct 15 of M6–signposted Open all year
250 pitches–bkg advisable 30 acres level wooded meadowland, secluded 🏪✖🍴🍽🔲∅
⊕∅🔌⚓ fishing

STOURPORT, Worcs   **Map D4**
EC Wed MD Fri SEE canal basin and locks, caves, nature reserve, Harrington Hall 5m E
✖ Bird in Hand, Holly Rd ☎ (01299) 822385

Lickhill Manor Caravan Park DY13 8RL ☎ (01299) 877820 *Prop: Lickhill Manor Ltd* OS map
138/797718 ½m W of Stourport off B4195 (Bewdley) on Lickhill road Open all year 240 pitches
(120 static) Level grass and hard standings 🔲∅⊕∅🔵🔌⚓🔲⚓🔷 fishing £10.00-£17.50
(Mastercard/Visa/Switch/Delta) www.lickhillmanor.co.uk

Lincomb Lock Caravan Park, Worcester Road, Titton DY13 9QR ☎ (01299) 823836 OS map
138/825690 ½m SE of Stourport off A4025 (Worcester) at signs Open Mar-Nov 132 pitches
(118 static)–no tents Level grass, sheltered 🔲∅⊕∅🔵🔌🔲🔷 fishing

Shorthill Caravan Camping Centre, Kidderminster Road, Crossway Green DY13 9SH ☎ (01299)
250571 OS map 138/841689 3m SE of Stourport on A449 (Kidderminster-Worcester) at rear of
Little Chef Open all year 25 pitches Level grass and hard standing ✖🔲∅⊕🔲🔵🔌

For more up-to-date information, and for links to camping websites, visit our site at:
www.butford.co.uk/camping

STOW ON THE WOLD, Glos   **Map F6**
EC Wed SEE town hall, St Edward's hall and church, market cross, Cotswold Farm Park (Guiting Power)
ⓘ Hollis House, The Square ✆ (01451) 831082
✗ Queens Head, The Square ✆ (01451) 830563

New Inn, Nether Westcote OX7 6SD ✆ (01993) 830827 OS map 163/227205 4m SE of Stow on
    the Wold off A424 (Burford) on Nether Westcote road Open all year 25 pitches
    ✗♀⚲🗑🔌⊕∅🌀 farm produce

STRATFORD ON AVON, Warwicks   **Map F5**
EC Thurs MD Tues, Fri SEE Shakespeare's birthplace (Henley St), Holy Trinity church, old inns,
almshouses, Mary Arden's house at Wilmcote 3m NW, Anne Hathaway's cottage at Shottery
ⓘ Bridgefoot ✆ (01789) 293127 ✗ White Swan, Rother St ✆ (01789) 297022

Dodwell Park, Evesham Road CV37 9ST ✆ (01789) 204957 OS map 151/168537 1m SW of
    Stratford on Avon on B439 (Bidford) Open all year 50 pitches Grass and hard standings, part
    level, part sheltered ⚱⚲🗑🔌⊘⊕∅🌀 (Mastercard/Visa/Switch)
The Racecourse, Luddington Road CV37 9SE ✆ (01789) 201063 OS map 151/187536 1m SW of
    Stratford on Avon off B439 (Evesham) Open Mar-Sept 250 pitches Level grass 🗑🔌⊕∅🌀⛺
    £10.00-£12.00 (Mastercard/Visa/Switch) info@stratfordracecourse.net
    www.stratfordracecourse.net
See also Alcester

SYMONDS YAT–see Coleford

TELFORD   **Map D2**
SEE Ironbridge Gorge (various ex of industrial archaeology) 3m S, Wrekin hill 3m SW
ⓘ Telford Centre ✆ (01952) 230032
✗ Falcon 2m W at Wellington ✆ (01952) 255011

Church Farm, Rowton TF6 6QY ✆ (01952) 770381 OS map 127/615199 6m NW of Telford on
    A442 (Whitchurch) Open all year 12 pitches Level grass, part sheltered 🔌⊕🌀🚻🏠 children
Severn Gorge Park, Bridgnorth Road, Tweedale TF7 4JB ✆ (01952) 684789 OS map 127/704052
    3m S of Telford off A442 (Bridgnorth) at Tweedale Open all year 50 pitches 6 acres, level grass
    and hard standings, secluded woodland ⚱🗑🔌⊘⊕∅🌀⚲🌀🚻 £10.15-£16.25* inc elect
    (most cards)

TENBURY WELLS, Worcs   **Map D4**
EC Thurs MD Tues, Fri SEE Burford House Gardens W, Teme Valley
✗ Peacock Inn 2m E on A456 at Newnham Bridge ✆ (01584) 810506

Knighton on Teme Caravan Park WR15 8NA ✆ (01584) 781246 OS map 138/633698 3m E of
    Tenbury Wells off A456 (Bewdley) at Newnham Bridge on Knighton on Teme road Open Mar-Dec
    95 pitches (90 static) Level grass, sheltered 🔌∅⊕∅⚲
Westbrook Park, Little Hereford SY8 9AU ✆ (01584) 711280 OS map 138/547680 3m W of
    Tenbury Wells off A456 (Ludlow) on Leysters road by river Teme Open Mar-Oct 50 pitches
    Level grass, sheltered 🗑🔌∅⊕

TEWKESBURY, Glos   **Map E5**
EC Thurs MD Wed, Sat SEE Norman abbey, museum, medieval merchants' houses
ⓘ Tewkesbury Museum, 64 Barton St ✆ (01684) 295027
✗ Duke of York Inn, Berrow, Malvern ✆ (01684) 833449

Croft Farm Leisure and Water Park, Bredons Hardwick GL20 7EE ✆ (01684) 772321 OS map
    150/911354 2m NE of Tewkesbury on Bredons Hardwick road (B4080) opp Cross Keys Inn Open
    Mar-Dec 76 pitches 6 acres, part sloping grass and hard standing ✗♀🗑🔌∅⊕⊘🌀⚲🌀 fishing,
    boating, boardsailing, health and fitness centre (most cards) www.croftfarmleisure.co.uk
Dawleys Caravan Park, Owls Lane, Shuthonger GL20 6EQ ✆ (01684) 292622 OS map
    150/886353 2m N of Tewkesbury off A38 (Worc) Open Apr-Sept 110 pitches (90 static)
    Level/sloping grass and hard standing, sheltered 🗑🔌⊕∅🌀 £10.00-£20.00
Mill Avon Holiday Park, Gloucester Road GL20 5SW ✆ (01684) 296876 Prop: Les Stamp OS
    map 150/888323 ¼m S of Tewkesbury on A38 (Gloucester), at rear of car park Open Mar-
    Oct–must book public holidays 55 pitches (24 static) Part hard standing, level grass, open
    🗑🔌∅⊕∅🌀 fishing £20.00 millavon@quinweb.net www.millavonholidaypark.com
Sunset View Touring Park, Church End Lane, Twyning GL20 6EH ✆ (01684) 292145 Prop:
    Andrew & Cheryl Goulstone OS map 150/889357 1½m N of Tewkesbury off A38 (Worcester) near
    Junction 1 of M50 Open all year 45 pitches Level grass 🔌∅⊕∅🌀🌀🚍 horse riding £10.00
    cherylgoulstone@hotmail.com
Three Counties Caravan Park, Sledge Green, Berrow WR13 6JW ✆ (01684) 833439 (Mobile)
    07812 059622 Prop: J & E Fury OS map 150/809347 6m W of Tewkesbury on A438 (Ledbury)
    near bridge under M50 Open Mar 18-Oct 21 50 pitches Grass, level/sloping, sheltered
    🔌⊕∅🌀 £12.00 shthebar@yahoo.co.uk
See also Winchcombe and Upton on Severn

UPTON ON SEVERN, Worcs   **Map D5**
EC Thurs SEE church, bridge, old houses
ℹ Pepperpot, Church St ✆(01684) 594200 ✘ White Lion, High St ✆(01684) 592551

Anchor Inn, Welland WR13 6LN ✆(01684) 592317 OS map 150/813403 2½m W of Upton on
    Severn on A4104 (Little Malvern) in village Open all year 19 pitches 1 acre level grass and hard
    standing ✘♀🚐❀∅ (most cards)

WARWICK, Warwicks   **Map F4**
EC Thurs MD Sat *County town founded in Saxon times on spur above river Avon* SEE 14c castle,
Lord Leycester's Hospital, St Mary's church
ℹ Court House, 2 Jury St ✆(01926) 492212 ✘ Woolpack, Market Pl ✆(01926) 496191

The Racecourse (Caravan Club), Hampton Street CV34 6HA ✆(01926) 495448 OS map
    151/277647 ½m W of Warwick off A429 (Stratford) on B4095 (Henley) Open Apr-Nov
    55 pitches–no tents Level grass and hard standing 🗗 (all cards)

The Racecourse, Hampton Street CV34 6HN ✆(01926) 495448 OS map 151/277645 ¼m SW of
    Warwick centre on right of B4095 (Henley) in centre of racecourse Open Mar-Nov 60 pitches
    2 acres level grass and hard standings 🚐𝄐❀∅↩🔥

WELLAND–see Upton on Severn

WEM, Shrops   **Map C2**
SEE parish church, Lowe Hall
✘ Grange 6m W at Ellesmere ✆(01691) 623495

Lower Lacon Caravan Park, Lower Lacon SY4 5RP ✆(01939) 232376 *Prop: CH Shingler* OS
    map 126/532302 1m NE of Wem on B5065 (Prees) Open all year 270 pitches (50 static) Level
    grass and hard standing, sheltered 🝤✘(café) ♀↩↗🗗🚐𝄐❀∅⊟🔥↩🔥☖(35) 🔥 £14.50–
    £19.00 (all cards) info@llcp.co.uk www.llcp.co.uk

WENTNOR, Shrops   **Map C3**
SEE Long Mynd 1m E, Linley Woods W
✘ The Inn on the Green ✆(01588) 650105

Cwnd House Farm SY9 5EQ ✆(01588) 650237 OS map 137/383950 1½m NE of Wentnor off
    Bridges road Open May-Oct 10 pitches level grass

Green Caravan and Camping Park SY9 5EF ✆(01588) 650605 *Prop: Mrs B Turley* OS map
    137/382933 ½m NW of Wentnor at The Green on Bridges road Open Easter-Oct 140 pitches
    Level grass and hard standing, sheltered 🝤✘♀🗗🚐𝄐❀↩🔥 £10.00 (Mastercard/Visa)
    karen@greencaravanpark.co.uk www.greencaravanpark.co.uk

WHITCHURCH, Shrops   **Map C1**
EC Wed MD Fri SEE parish church (with tomb of John Talbot in porch), almshouses
ℹ 12 St Mary's St ✆(01948) 664577
✘ Willey Moor Lock Tavern, Tarporley Rd (A49) ✆(01948) 663274

Brook House Farm, Grindley Brook SY13 4QJ ✆(01948) 664557 OS map 117/526425 1m N of
    Whitchurch on A41 (Chester) Open Mar-Nov 25 pitches Level grass, sheltered 🚐❀

Green Lane Farm Caravan Park, Prees SY13 2AH ✆(01948) 840460 OS map 126/568347 4½m
    SE of Whitchurch off A41-A442 (Telford) on Prees road Open Apr-Oct 20 pitches 3 acres level
    grass sheltered 🚐❀ www.greenlanefarm.northshropshire.biz

WOLVEY–see Nuneaton

WOODMANCOTE–see Cheltenham

WORCESTER, Worcs   **Map D5**
EC Thurs MD Wed, Fri, Sat *Industrial town cut in two by river Severn, here a navigable waterway*
SEE Cathedral, Commandery, Guildhall, 15c Greyfriars, Royal Porcelain Works, Elgar museum 2m
NW at Broadheath
ℹ Guildhall, High St ✆(01905) 726311 ✘ Star, Foregate St ✆(01905) 24308

Coppice Leisure Park, Ockeridge Wood, Wichenford WR6 6YP ✆(018866) 888305 OS map
    150/791625 8m NW of Worcester off A443 (Tenbury) Open Mar 1-Jan 6 150 pitches
    (138 static)–no tents ♀↗🗗🚐𝄐❀∅⊟🔥↩ lic club

Mill House, Hawford WR3 7SE ✆(01905) 451283 OS map 150/847601 3½m N of Worcester on
    A449 (Kidderminster) near river bridge Open Easter-Oct 100 pitches 10 acres level grass
    🝤✘↩🚐𝄐❀ fishing £7.00 (min)* millhousecaravansite@yahoo.co.uk

Seaborne Leisure Caravan Park, Court Meadow, Kempsey WR5 3JL ✆(01905) 820295 *Prop:
    Seaborne Leisure Centre* OS map 150/848495 2m S of Worcester off A38 (Tewkesbury)
    at Kempsey Open Easter-Oct 105 pitches (70 static)–no tents (Children over 14 welcome)
    ♀🗗🚐❀🔥🎣 slipway, moorings £12.00 (all major cards)

See also Ombersley

East Anglia is composed of Norfolk, Suffolk, Essex and Cambridgeshire, the last increased in size since it absorbed the former Huntingdonshire.

Beyond the metropolitan area southernmost Essex has a varied landscape of field and river and a deeply indented coast line. The mudflats of the deep river estuaries, the habitat of many species of wildfowl, give way to sandy beaches at Southend, Clacton and Frinton. Highlights of inland Essex are the glades and uplands of Epping Forest, the villages of the Rodings, the town of Saffron Walden, the most attractive in the county, and ancient Colchester, oldest recorded town in Britain. There are also the stately homes of Audley End and Steeple Bumpstead, the pretty villages of Finchingfield, Cavendish and Newport and the churches of Greensted and Thaxted. A long distance footpath, the Essex Way, runs for fifty-five miles from Epping to Dedham.

The secretive charm of rural Suffolk, with its moated farmhouses, can be discovered in the Constable country around East Bergholt near the Essex border and the ancient wool district around Lavenham. Uncommercialized resorts along the constantly-eroded coastline include charming Aldeburgh and Southwold and Dunwich, slowly being devoured by the sea.

North Norfolk is best known for its Broads between Norwich and Yarmouth, a sprawling network of rivers and shallow reed fringed lakes formed from age-old peat diggings. Popular centres for cruising on the Broads are Hickling, Potter Heigham and Wroxham. Important nature reserves line the coast between the attractive resorts of Cromer and Hunstanton on the Wash. notably on the saltings east of Wells. Also on the Wash is the graceful port of King's Lynn. Thetford Forest, spilling over into Suffolk, encloses the wild heaths of Breckland, but the neolithic flint mines of Grimes Graves are definitely in Norfolk. Antique Norwich has a wealth of historic buildings and a long tradition of immigration from the Low Countries. Two walkers' routes in Norfolk are the ancient roads of Peddars Way and Icknield Way. Important buildings include the abbey church of Wymondham, the ruined fortress of Castle Rising where Edward III imprisoned his mother Isabella, and the stately homes of Felbrigg Blickling, Oxburgh and Holkham.

Cambridgeshire encloses part of the Great Fen, marshland which until reclaimed from the sea stretched from Lincoln to Cambridge. The heart of Fenland is the Isle of Ely, its great cathedral like a tall ship in the flat landscape. Here sections of the original marshland have been preserved in their primeval state at Wood Walton Fen and Wicken Fen. Northwest of Cambridge the 60ft high Devil's Dyke bisects the equally old Icknield Way. Major sights in Cambridge itself are the medieval King's and Trinity Colleges and the Backs by the river Cam. The superb Norman cathedral of Peterborough is worth a detour, as are the country houses of Wimpole and Hinchingbrooke and the pretty villages of Alconbury, Grantchester and Haslingfield.

The greatest concentrations of campsites are at the popular coast resorts, with less of a choice in the Broads, the Essex estuaries and inland Suffolk. Amenities are not usually extensive, even on the coast.

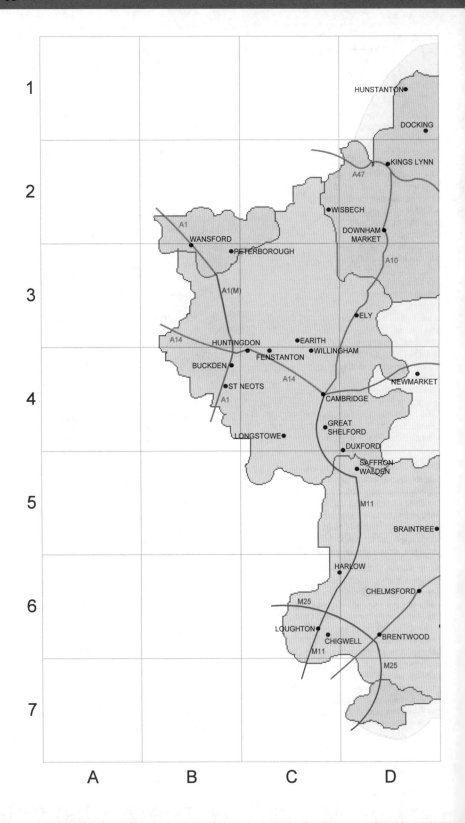

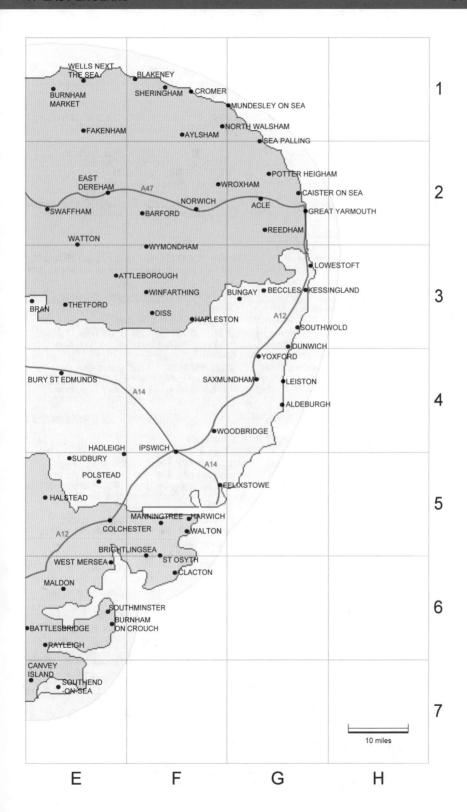

10 miles

ACLE, Norfolk   Map G2
Pleasant market town near river Bure
✗ Bridge by river Bure ✆ (01493) 750288

Broad Farm Trailer Park, Main Road, Burgh St Margaret NR29 3AF ✆ (01493) 369273 OS map
134/446142 3m NE of Acle off A1064 (Caister on Sea) Open Easter-Sept 480 pitches Level
grass, sheltered ⚑✗♀⌂◨▨◪⬛(outdoor heated) ☺⚘
(Mastercard/Visa/Delta/JCB/Electron/Solo)

Bureside Holiday Park, Boundary Farm, Oby NR29 3BW ✆ (01493) 369233 OS map 134/405151
3m N of Acle off B1152 (Martham) Open Whitsun-Sept 175 pitches Level grass ⚑◨◪
⬛(heated) ⤸ boating (slipway) fishing lake

Clippesby Holidays, Clippesby NR29 3BL ✆ (01493) 367800 Fax (01493)367809 OS map
134/423144 3m NE of Acle off A1064 (Caister) and B1152 (Martham) Open Easter-Sept
100 pitches 34 acres, level grass, sheltered ⚑✗♀◨▨◪⊘◫⬛(heated) ☺⤸⌂⛪ putting,
tennis £13.00-£19.50* (all cards) *holidays@clippesby.com www.clippesby.com*

ALDEBURGH, Suffolk   Map G4
EC Wed *Quiet unspoiled resort with long pebble beach* SEE church with memorial to George
Crabbe, 16c Moot Hall
ℹ The Cinema, High St ✆ (01728) 453637
✗ White Lion, Market Pl ✆ (01728) 452720

Church Farm Caravan Site, Thorpeness Road IP15 5BH ✆ (01728) 453433 OS map 156/463569
¼m N of Aldeburgh off A1094 (Snape) Open Apr-Oct 112 pitches Grass, level, open ◪⊡ farm
produce

ATTLEBOROUGH, Norfolk   Map E3
EC Wed MD Thurs SEE parish church, Attleborough Hall
✗ The White Lodge, London Rd ✆ (01953) 452474 Open Mon-Fri 11-2.30, Sat-Sun all day

Applewood, Banham Zoo, The Grove, Banham NR16 2HE ✆ (01953) 888370 OS map 144/058876
5m S of Attleborough on B1113 (Stowmarket) Open all year 100 pitches 8 acres level grass
⚑✗♀⌂⤔◨▨◪⊘◫⤸⛪ farm shop (most cards)

Oak Tree Caravan Park, Norwich Road NR17 2JX ✆ (01953) 455565 *Prop: Don & Carol
Birkinshaw* OS map 144/057690 ½m NE of Attleborough on old A11 (Norwich) Open March-Dec
38 pitches 5 acres, level grass ▨◪⊘ £9.00 *oaktree.cp@virgin.net www.oaktree-caravan-
park.co.uk*

AYLSHAM, Norfolk   Map F1
EC Wed MD Mon, Fri SEE Blickling Hall 1½m NW
✗ Marsham Arms, 40 Holt Rd, Hevingham ✆ (01603) 754268
✗ The Plough Inn, Norwich Rd, Marsham ✆ (01263) 735000

Haveringland Hall Park, Cawston NR10 4PN ✆ (01603) 871302 *Prop: D Hopkins* OS map
133/156214 4m SW of Aylsham off B1145 (Cawston) Open Apr-Oct 100 pitches (60 static)
25 acres grass, level, sheltered ◨▨◪⊘◫☺⬛⊡⛪ fishing by permit in 12 acre lake, woodland
walks, holiday lodges for sale £7.00-£14.00 (most cards) *info@haveringlandhall.co.uk
www.haveringlandhall.co.uk*

Landguard House, Erpingham NR11 7QB ✆ (01263) 761219 OS map 133/204324 4m N of
Aylsham on Erpingham rd Open Apr-Oct 25 pitches 1½ acres, mainly level grass ✗(snack) ♀▨

Top Farm, Kittles Lane, Marsham NR10 5QF *Spacious site adjoining heathland and meadows*
✆ (01263) 733962 OS map 133/182244 2m SW of Aylsham off A140 (Norwich-Cromer) Open all
year–booking advised 25 pitches 5 acres level grass and hard standing, sheltered ▨◫☺☺⛪⛪⤸
dog walking area, baby-changing area £4.00-£8.00 *www.top-farm.info*

BACTON–see Mundesley

Old Manor Caravan Park

Close to
GRAFHAM WATER
fishing
sailing windsurfing

COUNTRYSIDE
DISCOVERY

Twenty miles from
CAMBRIDGE
historic
university city

BARFORD, Norfolk Map F2
SEE abbey and market cross at Wymondham 3m S
✖Abbey 3m S at Wyndmondham ✆(01953) 602148

Swans Harbour, Barford Road, Marlingford NR9 4BE ✆(01603) 759658 OS map 144/123086 1m NE of Barford on left of Marlingford road beyond river bridge Open all year 30 pitches 4 acres level grass and hard standing, sheltered 🚻⊕∅😊 £10.50 www.swansharbour.co.uk

BATTLESBRIDGE, Essex Map E6
✖Barge, Hawk Hill ✆(01268) 732622

Hayes Farm Caravan Park, Hayes Chase, Burnham Road SS11 7QT ✆(01245) 320309 OS map 167/788957 2m NE of Battlesbridge off A130 (Chelmsford) on A132 (South Woodham Ferrers) Open Apr-Oct 389 pitches (314 static)–no tents–no adv booking 26 acres level grass, sheltered 🚻♀🚽🚐∅⊕∅😊⌁🔌 club, dancing

BECCLES, Suffolk Map G3
EC Wed MD Fri *Georgian town on Waveney once busy river port* SEE church, East Anglia Transport Museum 5m E
🛈The Quay, Fen Lane ✆(01502) 713196
✖Kings Head, New Market ✆(01502) 712147

Waveney River Centre, Staithe, Burgh St Peter NR34 0BT ✆(01502) 677343 OS map 134/491934 6m NE of Beccles off A143 (Great Yarmouth) via Burgh St Peter, at Staithe, by river Waveney Open Mar-Oct 100 pitches (40 static) 20 acres level grass 🚻✖♀🚐∅⊕∅🖵😊⌁♿ fishing, boating, sauna, solarium, day boat hire, gym, spa bath

BELTON–see Great Yarmouth

BRANDON, Suffolk Map E3
EC Wed MD Thurs, Sat SEE 15c bridge, St Peter's church
✖The Crown Hotel, Crown Rd, Mundford ✆(01842) 878233 Open 12-3/7-10

Warren House Caravan Park, Brandon Road, Methwold IP26 4RL ✆(01366) 728238 *Prop: Jane Scarrott* OS map 143/46931 4m NW of Brandon on B1112 (Methwold) Open Mar-Oct–must book public holidays 40 pitches *No showers* £5.00-£10.00

BRIGHTLINGSEA, Essex Map F5
Modest resort in loop of river Colne a short way from sea
✖Railway Tavern, Station Rd (off B1029 near Waterfront) ✆(01206) 302581

Lakeside Touring Caravan Park, Promenade Way CO7 0HH ✆(01206) 303421 OS map 168/082164 ½m SW of Brightlingsea centre off road to Westmarsh Point Open Mar-Oct 270 pitches (240 static) 🚽∅⊕

BUCKDEN, Cambs Map B4
SEE church, bishop's palace, old posting inns, Grafham Water 1m W
✖The Mermaid Inn, High St, Ellington ✆(01480) 891450

Old Manor Caravan Park, Grafham PE28 0BB ✆(01480) 810264 *Prop: Mr & Mrs D Howes* OS map 153/155695 2m NW of Buckden off B661 (West Perry) Open all year exc Xmas/New Year 80 pitches 6 acres level grass and hard standing 🚻🚽🚐∅⊕∅🖵(heated) ⌁♿♿♿ off licence £13.00-£20.00 (most cards) camping@old-manor.co.uk www.old-manor.co.uk

BUNGAY, Suffolk Map G3
EC Wed MD Thurs *Georgian town in loop of river Waveney* SEE castle ruins, churches, market cross, aviation museum 3m SW
✖Green Dragon, Broad St ✆(01986) 892681

Outney Meadow Caravan Park, Outney Meadow NR35 1HG ✆(01986) 892338 Fax (01986) 896627 OS map 134/333905 ¼m N of Bungay off A143 (Great Yarmouth) on Outney Common Open all year 45 pitches Grass, level, hard standings, part sheltered 🚻🚽🚐∅⊕∅🚐 boating, canoe and bike hire, fishing £9.00-£14.00* c.r.hancy@ukgateway.net www.outneymeadow.co.uk

BURGH CASTLE–see Great Yarmouth

BURNHAM MARKET, Norfolk Map E1
SEE St Mary's church, windmill, Burnham Thorpe (birthplace of Nelson) and church 1m SE
✖Fishes, Market Place ✆(01328) 738588

Burnham Market Caravan Park, Back Lane PE31 8EY ✆(01485) 570595 OS map 132/832428 ½m N of Burnham Market centre off B1355 (Burnham Norton) Open Apr-Oct–no adv booking 30 pitches Grass, level, sheltered 🚐

Help us make CAMPING CARAVANNING BRITAIN better known to site operators – and thereby more informative – by showing them your copy when booking in.

BURNHAM ON CROUCH, Essex   Map E6
EC Wed   SEE St Mary's church
✗ Olde White Harte, The Quay   ☎ (01621) 782106

Creeksea Place Caravan Park, Ferry Road CM0 8PJ   ☎ (01621) 782387/782675   OS map 168/935962   ½m W of Burnham off B1010 (Althorne)   Open Mar-Nov   150 pitches (100 static) Level grass sheltered   🅿🚶♿Ⓞ☺↩🚽   fishing lake

BURWELL–see Newmarket

BURY ST EDMUNDS, Suffolk   Map E4
EC Thurs   SEE abbey, St Mary church (Angel roof)
ℹ 6 Angel Hill   ☎ (01284) 764667
✗ Angel, Angel Hill   ☎ (01284) 753926

The Dell Caravan Camping Park, Beyton Road, Thurston IP31 3RB   ☎ (01284) 270121 Fax (01359) 270121   OS map 155/930650   5m E of Bury St Edmunds off A14 (Ipswich) at Thurston Open all year   100 pitches   5 acres level grass and hard standing, part sheltered 🅿🚶♿Ⓞ↩🚽♿   £12.00   thedellcaravanpark@btinternet.com

CAISTER ON SEA, Norfolk   Map G2
EC Wed   SEE ruined Caister castle, motor museum
✗ Blue Dolphin, Beach Rd, Hemsby   ☎ (01493) 732665

California Cliffs Caravan Park, California, Ormesby NR29 3QU   ☎ (01493) 730584   OS map 134/518148   1½m N of Caister off B1159 (Winterton on Sea) near beach   Open Apr-Sept–must book peak periods   690 pitches   🅿✗↩Ⓞ♿▭   lic club

The Grange Touring Park, Ormesby St Margaret NR29 3QG   ☎ (01493) 730306   Prop: J Groat   OS map 134/512143   1m N of Caister at junction of A149 (North Walsham) and B1159 (Winterton) Open Apr-Sept   70 pitches   Grass, level, sheltered   🍴🅿🚶♿Ⓞ↩   £7.00-£12.00 info@grangetouring.co.uk www.grangetouring.co.uk

Grasmere Caravan Park, Bultitudes Loke NR30 5DH   ☎ (01493) 720382   OS map 134/522117   ½m S of Caister off A149 (Great Yarmouth) near stadium   Open Apr 1-Oct 28   109 pitches (63 static) 5 acres level grass and hard standing   🅿🚶♿Ⓞ↩♿▭🏠♿   £10.00-£13.00 (all cards) www.grasmere-wentworth.co.uk

Green Farm Caravan Park, Beach Road, Scratby, California NR29 3NW   ☎ (01493) 730440   OS map 134/512155   3m N of Caister off A149 (North Walsham) and B1159 (Hembsby)   Open Mar-Nov   240 pitches (200 static)   Level grass   🅿✗🍴↩Ⓞ🚶♿Ⓞ▭(indoor) ☺↩🚪🚲 www.greenfarmcaravanpark.com

Long Beach Estate Caravan Park, Hemsby NR29 4JD   ☎ (01493) 730023   Prop: JM Groat   OS map 134/503178   4m NNW of Caister off B1159 (Winterton on Sea)   Open Apr-Oct   200 pitches (120 static)   Grass, level, part sheltered   🅿✗🍴↗Ⓞ🚶♿(£30) ♿Ⓞ☺↩   club room, private beach   £6.50-£12.00   info@long-beach.co.uk www.long-beach.co.uk

Newport Caravan-Camping Park, Hemsby NR29 4NW   ☎ (01493) 730405   OS map 134/502169 3m N of Caister off B1159) (Hemsby)   Open Apr-Oct   270 pitches (180 static)   Level grass sheltered   🅿✗Ⓞ🚶♿☺🚽▭   lic club

Old Hall Leisure Park, High Street NR30 5JL   ☎ (01493) 720400   OS map 134/518124   ¼m N of Caister centre on A149 (North Walsham)   Open Apr-Oct   81 pitches   Grass, level sheltered ✗↩Ⓞ♿▭(heated) ♿🚲🚪

Scratby Hall Caravan Park, Scratby NR29 3PH   ☎ (01493) 730283   OS map 134/502155   3m N of Caister off B1159 (Hemsby)   Open Easter-Oct 7   108 pitches   Grass, level, sheltered 🅿Ⓞ🚶♿Ⓞ↩🚶♿   £5.50-£13.00

Sundowner Holiday Park, Newport Road, Hemsby NR29 4NW   ☎ (01493) 730159/731554   OS map 134/501168   3m N of Caister off A149 (Stalham) and B1159 (Mundesley) on Newport road Open Apr-Sept   100 pitches   Grass, level, part sheltered   🅿🍴↗Ⓞ🚶♿Ⓞ▭↩🏠♿

CAMBRIDGE, Cambs   Map C4
MD daily   Charming university city on river   SEE Colleges and garden, bridges, Fitzwilliam museum, King's College chapel, botanic garden
ℹ Wheeler St   ☎ 0871 226 8006
✗ Three Horseshoes, 22 South St, Comberton   ☎ (01223) 262252

Highfield Farm Touring Park, Long Road, Comberton CB3 7DG   ☎ (01223) 262308   Prop: Mr & Mrs BH Chapman   OS map 154/389572   4¼m WSW of Cambridge off A1303-A428 (St Neots) on Comberton road–from M11 jnc 12 via A603 (Sandy) and B1046 (Comberton)   Open Apr-Oct 120 pitches   8 acres level grass and hard standing, sheltered   🅿Ⓞ🚶♿Ⓞ↩   battery charging, freezer pack service, post box, farm walk   £9.00-£13.50   enquiries@highfieldfarmtouringpark.co.uk www.highfieldfarmtouringpark.co.uk

Travellers Rest Caravan Site, Chittering CB5 9PH   ☎ (01223) 860751   OS map 154/700499   8m NE of Cambridge on A10 (Ely)   Open Apr-Sept   40 pitches   Grass, level, sheltered ✗🚶♿↩ bar meals

CANVEY ISLAND, Essex   Map E7
EC Thurs MD Sat SEE Dutch Cottage museum, Lobster Smack inn, nature reserve
✗ Pipe of Port 6m E at Southend on Sea ✆ (01702) 614606

Kings Park, Hindles Road SS8 8HE ✆ (01268) 511555 OS map 178/816835 ½m W of Canvey
Island off B1014 (South Benfleet) Open Mar-Oct 450 pitches (250 static) 🅿 ✗ ♀ ⟷ ⚲ ▣
🅿 ⊘ ⊘ ⊟ ⊕ ↵ ⌂ night club, fishing lake

CHITTERING–see Cambridge

CLACTON ON SEA, Essex   Map F6
EC Wed MD Tues, Sat SEE Norman church, Martello Tower, St Osyth's Priory 3m W
🅸 Town Hall, Station Rd ✆ (01255) 423400
✗ King's Cliff 1m NE at Holland on Sea ✆ (01255) 812343

Ashley Holiday Park, London Rd, Little Clacton CO16 9RN ✆ (01255) 860200 OS map
169/165189 2m N of Clacton on left of A133 (Colchester) Open Mar 1-Oct 15 125 pitches
♀ 🅿 ⊘ ⊕ ⊘ ↵ ⚘

Highfield Holiday Park, London Rd CO16 9QY ✆ (01255) 424244 OS map 169/166178 2m N of
Clacton on A133 (Colchester) Open Easter-Oct 725 pitches (400 static)–no tents 45 acres grass,
gentle slope 🅿 ✗ ♀ ⟷ ▣ 🅿 ⊘ ⊕ ⊘ ⊟ ⊕ ↵ ⊡ 🅿 ⚘ ⊏ ⌂ (most cards)

Silver Dawn Touring Park, Jaywick Lane CO16 8BB ✆ (01255) 421856 OS map 168/150153 3m
W of Clacton off B1027 (Colchester) Open Easter-Oct 15–adv booking preferred 86 pitches
(56 static)–no tents ♀ 🅿 paddling pool, lic club

Tower Caravan Park, Jaywick CO15 2LF *Resort's only site by the sea* ✆ (01255) 820372 OS map
168/132136 2½m SW of Clacton at Jaywick Sands Open Apr-Oct 625 pitches (525 static)
Grass, level, open 🅿 ✗ (cafe)♀ ↵ ▣ 🅿 ⊘ ⊕ ⊘ ⊟ ⊕ ↵ ⚘ ⊏ lic club

Weeley Bridge Caravan Park, Weeley CO16 9DH ✆ (01255) 830403 OS map 168/147219 5½m
NNW of Clacton on A133 (Weeley) near station Open Mar 27-Oct 11 90 pitches–no tents Grass,
level, open 🅿 ⊘ ⊕ 🅿

See also St Osyth

CLIPPESBY–see Acle

COLCHESTER, Essex   Map E5
EC Thurs MD Tues, Sat *Oldest recorded town in England, now thriving regional centre* SEE
Colchester and Essex museum, Roman Walls, St Martin's church, oyster fisheries, Bourne mill
🅸 Queen St ✆ (01206) 282920 ✗ George, High St ✆ (01206) 578494

Colchester Camping Caravan Park, Cymbeline Way CO3 4AG ✆ (01206) 545551 Fax (01206)
710443 OS map 168/971255 1m W of Colchester near junction of A12 (Chelmsford) and A133
(town centre)–signposted Open all year 251 pitches Grass and hard standing, level, part
sheltered 🅿 ↵ ▣ 🅿 ⊘ ⊕ ⊘ ⊕ ↵ 🅿 ⊟ & caravan/m-home wash, 8 serviced pitches £10.00-£16.10*
(all major cards) *enquiries@colchestercamping.co.uk www.colchestercamping.co.uk*

Mill Farm, Harwich Road, Great Bromley CO7 7JQ ✆ (01206) 250485 OS map 168/076246 4m E
of Colchester on A604 (Harwich) via Elmstead Market Open Mar-Oct 40 pitches 4 acres, gentle
slope ⊕

Seven Arches Farm, Lexden CO3 5SX ✆ (01206) 574896 OS map 168/969255 2m W of
Colchester off A604 on old Halstead road by level crossing Open all year 12 pitches Level grass,
sheltered

CROMER, Norfolk   Map F1
EC Wed SEE 14c church, lifeboat museum, Birdland, lighthouse
🅸 Bus Stn, Prince of Wales Rd ✆ (01263) 512497
✗ Bath House, The Promenade ✆ (01263) 514260

Forest Park Caravan Site, Northrepps Road NR27 0JR ✆ (01263) 513290 *Prop: S Gurney* OS
map 133/233405 1½m SE of Cromer off B1159 (Mundesley) Open Mar-Jan 801 pitches (325
static) Grass, part level 🅿 ✗ ♀ ⟷ ↵ ▣ 🅿 ⊘ ⊕ ⊘ ⊟ (heated indoor) ⊕ ↵ Q clubhouse, bar
meals, woodland walks, hair-dresser £9.50-£18.00 (Visa/Mastercard/Switch)
info@forestpark.co.uk www.forest-park.co.uk

Manor Farm Caravan and Camping Site, East Runton NR27 9PR ✆ (01263) 512858 OS map
133/198418 1½m W of Cromer off A148 (Holt) on East Runton road Open Easter-Sep–no motor
cycles 200 pitches Level/sloping grass, sheltered 🅿 ▣ 🅿 ⊘ ⊕ ⊘ ↵ & £8.50-£10.00* *manor-
farm@ukf.net www.manorfarmcaravansite.co.uk*

Seacroft Camping Park, Runton Road NR27 9NJ ✆ (01263) 511722 Fax (01263) 511512 OS map
133/199426 ½m W of Cromer on A149 (Sheringham) near beach Open Mar-Oct 120 pitches
5 acres level grass, pitches screened by shrubs, sheltered 🅿 ✗ ♀ ▣ 🅿 🅿 ⊘ ⊕ ⊘ ⊟ ⊕ ↵ ⊏ &
£11.00-£18.00* (all cards) *www.ukparks.co.uk/seacroft*

Woodhill Caravan and Camping Park, East Runton NR27 9PX ✆ (01263) 512242 OS map
133/197428 1m W of Cromer on A149 (Sheringham) Open Mar-Oct 394 pitches (132 static)
Grass and hard standings, part level, part open 🅿 ↵ ▣ 🅿 ⊘ ⊕ ⊘ ⊕ ↵ ⊏ ⊏ & (most cards)

DEREHAM–see East Dereham

DISS, Norfolk   **Map F3**
EC Tues MD Fri SEE St Mary's church, Diss Mere, 17c Scole Inn 2m E
🛈 Meres Mouth, Mere St ☎(01379) 650523
✗ Greyhound, Nicholas St ☎(01379) 651613

Honeypot Camp and Caravan Park, Wortham IP22 1PW ☎(01379) 783312 OS map 144/086771
3m SW of Diss on A143 (Bury St Edmunds) at Wortham Open Apr-Sept 35 pitches (some at
lakeside) Grass, level, sheltered 🛒🕳🔌🅰⊕∅☻⌣🏕 freezer pack service, fishing (inc hot
water)

Willows Camping Caravan Park, Diss Road, Scole IP21 4DH ☎(01379) 740271 Fax (01379)
740271 OS map 144/147788 1½m E of Diss on A1066 (Scole) beside river Waveney Open
Easter-Oct 35 pitches Grass, level, sheltered 🛒🕳🔌🅰⊕☻⌣

See also Harleston

DOCKING, Norfolk   **Map D1**
✗ Pilgrims' Reach ☎(01485) 518383

Garden Caravan Site, Barmer Hall, Syderstone PE31 8SR *Secluded site in walled garden*
☎(01485) 578220 OS map 132/810335 3m SE of Docking on B1454 (Fakenham) Open Mar-Nov
33 pitches Level/sloping grass, sheltered 🕳🔌🅰⊕∅⌣🅰 TV hook-up £10.00-£12.00*

The Rickells, Bircham Road, Stanhoe PE31 8PU ☎(01485) 518671 *Prop: Heather Crown* OS map
132/793353 1½m SE of Docking on right of B1454 (Fakenham) near junct with B1155 (Stanhoe-
Great Bircham) Open Mar 15-Oct 31 30 pitches Level/sloping grass, sheltered
🕳🔌🅰⊕∅☻⌣🔲🏕 £8.50-£10.00

DOWNHAM MARKET, Norfolk   **Map D2**
EC Wed MD Fri, Sat SEE parish church
✗ Castle, High St ☎(01366) 382157

Woodlakes Leisure, Holme Rd, Stowbridge PE34 3PX ☎(01553) 810414 OS map 143/617075
3m N of Downham Market off A10 (Kings Lynn) and Stowbridge road Open Mar-Oct 100 pitches
66 acres of woods and lakes, level grass, sheltered 🛒🕳🔌🅰⊕∅⌣🏕 fishing, woodland walks

DUNWICH, Suffolk   **Map G3**
SEE museum, Minsmere nature reserve, Dunwich forest, Blythburgh church 3m NW
✗ Ship Inn, St James' Street ☎(01728) 648219

Cliff House Holiday Park, Minsmere Road IP17 3DQ ☎(01728) 648282/648808 OS map
156/477688 1m S of Dunwich centre on coast road adj bird sanctuary Open Apr-Oct 208 pitches
(108 static) booking advisable 30 acres, grass and hard standings, sheltered, level woodland
🛒✗♀⚲🕳🔌🅰⊕∅☻⌣🔲🏕 beach access (most cards)

DUXFORD, Cambs   **Map D4**
SEE 15c St Peter's church, Duxford chapel, Imperial War museum (RAF)
✗ Duxford Lodge, Ickleton Road ☎(01223) 836444

Appleacre Park, London Road, Fowlmere SG8 7RU ☎(01763) 208354 OS map 154/422452 3m
W of Duxford off A505 (Royston) on Fowlmere road near junct 10 of M11 Open all year 30
pitches
3 acres level grass and hard standing, sheltered 🕳🔌⊕⌣ *www.ukparks.co.uk/appleacre*

EARITH, Cambs   **Map C3**
SEE New Bedford River, dug in 17c at start of reclamation of Fens
✗ Slepe Hall 3m W at St Ives ☎(01480) 463122

Westview Marina, High Street, Earith PE28 3PN ☎(01487) 841627 OS map 142/143/382750 ¼m
W of Earith centre on left of A1123 (Huntingdon) by river Great Ouse Open Apr-Oct 28 pitches
Level grass, sheltered 🔌🅰⊕ £10.25 inc elect and awning

EAST BERGHOLT–see Hadleigh

EAST RUNTON–see Cromer

KEY TO SYMBOLS

🛒	shop	🅰	gas supplies	🏕	winter storage for caravans
✗	restaurant	⊕	chemical disposal point	🅿	parking obligatory
♀	bar	∅	payphone	⊗	no dogs
⇌	takeaway food	🔲	swimming pool	🚐	caravan hire
⚲	off licence	☻	games area	🏠	bungalow hire
🕳	laundrette	⌣	children's playground	♿	facilities for disabled
🔌	mains electric hook-ups	🔲	TV	☀	shaded

ELY, Cambs   **Map D3**
EC Tues MD Thurs SEE Cathedral, Bishop's Palace, Ely Porta school, Monks' Granary (15c), St Mary's church, Museums, Brass Rubbing Centre
🔲 Oliver Cromwells House, St Mary's St ✆ (01353) 668518
✘ The Lamb and Flag, Main Street, Welney ✆ (01354) 610242 Open Tue-Sat 12-2.30/6.30-9, Sun 12-4

Riverside Caravan Camping Park, New River Bank, Littleport CB7 4TA ✆ (01353) 860255 *Prop: Steve & Vanessa Wood* OS map 143/577858 3m N of Ely off A10 (Littleport) near river Great Ouse Open Jan-Dec–no children at bank holidays 49 pitches (12 static) 4½ acres, mainly level 🔋🖾∅⊕🖾🔾 boating, fishing £10.00-£12.00 *riversideccp@btopenworld.com www.riversideccp.co.uk*

FAKENHAM, Norfolk   **Map E1**
EC Wed MD Thurs SEE parish church, ruins of Walsingham Abbey 4m N
✘ The Crown Inn, Crown Rd, Colkirk ✆ (01328) 862172

Little Snoring Caravan Camping Park, Holt Road, Little Snoring NR21 0AX ✆ (01328) 878335 OS map 132/962322 3m NE of Fakenham on A148 (Cromer) Open all year 30 pitches Hard standings and grass, level, sheltered 🔋🖾🖾∅⊕∅🖾 sauna, spa bath, sunbed

Fakenham Racecourse NR21 7NY ✆ (01328) 862388 Fax (01328) 855908 OS map 132/916287 1m SE of Fakenham on A1065 (Swaffham) Open all year 120 pitches Grass and hard standings, level, sheltered 🔋✘🖾🖾🖾∅⊕∅⊡🔾🖔 mothercare unit, table tennis, squash, tennis, bowls, golf, 3 star hostel rooms avail £11.00-£18.00 (most major cards-not Amex) *caravan@fakenhamracecourse.co.uk www.fakenhamracecourse.co.uk*

Old Brick Kilns Caravan Camping Park, Little Barney NR21 0NL ✆ (01328) 878305 Fax (01328) 878948 *Prop: Mrs A Strahan* OS map 132/133/004332 6m NE of Fakenham off B1354 (Aylsham) Open Feb 20-Jan 6 60 pitches Grass and hard standings, level, part sheltered 🔋✘🖾🖔🗡 🖾🖾∅⊕∅🔾🗸⊡🖾🖔🔾 first aid, battery charging £13.50-£23.00 (most cards) *enquiries@old-brick-kilns.co.uk www.old-brick-kilns.co.uk*

Fakenahm Racecourse, Fakenham

✘ RESTAURANTS

The restaurants recommended in this guide are of three kinds – pubs, independent restaurants and those forming part of hotels and motels. They all serve lunch and dinner – at a reasonable price – say under £10 a head. We shall be glad to have your comments on any you use this season and if you think they are not up to standard, please let us have your suggestions for alternatives.

FELIXSTOWE, Suffolk   **Map F5**
EC Wed MD Thurs SEE St Andrew's church, St Peter's church
🔲 The Seafront, Felixstowe ✆ (01394) 276770
✘ Ferryboat, Felixstowe Ferry ✆ (01394) 284203

Peewit Caravan Park, Walton Avenue IP11 2HB ✆ (01394) 284511 Fax (01473) 659824 OS map 169/289337 ½m SW of Felixstowe off A45 to port Open Easter-Oct 260 pitches (200 static) Grass, level, sheltered, some hard standings 🔋🖾🖾∅⊕∅🗸🖔 £9.00-£16.00* *peewitpark@aol.com www.peewitcaravanpark.co.uk*

Suffolk Sands Holiday Park, Carr Rd, Landguard Common IP11 8TS ✆ (01394) 273434 OS map 169/292340 1m W of Felixstowe centre off A45 Open Mar-Nov 400 pitches (350 static)–no tents 🔋✘🖾🖾🖾∅⊕∅🗸🖾

FENSTANTON, Cambs   **Map C4**
SEE river Great Ouse N
✘ King William, High St (off A604) ✆ (01480) 462467

Crystal Lakes Touring Caravan Park, Low Rd PE18 9VV ✆ (01480) 497728 OS map 153/314687 ¼m NW of Fenstanton on St Ives road Open all year 80 pitches 40 acres level grass and lakes, sheltered 🔋✘🖔🖾🖾∅⊕∅🗸⊡🖾 fishing

GISLEHAM–see Kessingland

GOSFIELD–see Halstead

GRAFHAM–see Buckden

GREAT YARMOUTH, Norfolk   **Map G2**
EC Thurs MD Wed, Sat SEE The Rows, 17c Fisherman's Hospital, Nelson monument, parish church, medieval tollhouse
🛈 Marine Parade ✆ (01493) 842195
✗ Clipper Schooner, Friars Lane (off South Quay) ✆ (01493) 854926

Burgh Castle Marina, Butt Lane NR31 9PZ ✆ (01493) 780331 OS map 134/474042 5m W of Great Yarmouth off A143 (Bungay) near south shore of Breydon Water Open all year 200 pitches (180 static) Hard standing and grass, level, sheltered 🗒✗🍴⚡⚓➤🗓🗓🖋⊕⊘🗙🗖↵🗖🗙🗖 harbour and slipway, fishing

Liffens Holiday Park, Burgh Castle NR31 9QB ✆ (01493) 780357 Fax (01493) 782383 OS map 134/489036 3m SW of Great Yarmouth off A143 (Bungay) at Belton–signposted Open Apr-Oct 300 pitches (150 static) 22 acres level grass 🗒✗🍴⚡⚓➤🗓🗓🖋⊕⊘🗙🗙↵🗖🗖🖨 post office, tennis court, crazy golf £10.00-£21.00* (all cards) www.liffens.co.uk

Rose Farm Touring Park, Stepshort, Belton NR31 9JS ✆ (01493) 780896 Fax (01493) 780896 OS map 134/488035 4m SW of Great Yarmouth off A143 (Beccles) and Belton road Open all year 80 pitches 7 acres level grass sheltered 🗒🗓🗙🗖⊕↵🗖🗙 £8.00-£10.00* www.members@aol.com/rosefarm04

Seashore Caravan Holiday Village, North Denes NR30 4HG ✆ (01493) 851131 (bookings) OS map 134/525103 1m N of Great Yarmouth on A149 (North Walsham) Open Easter-Sept 198 pitches Grass, level 🗒✗🗓🖋🗖🖨 lic club, hairdressing

Sunfield Holiday Park, Station Road, Belton NR31 9NB ✆ (01493) 781144 OS map 134/478026 4m SW of Great Yarmouth off A143 (Diss) via Belton Open Easter-Sept–no adv booking in peak season 400 pitches (250 static) Level/sloping grass, sheltered 🗒✗🍴⚡➤🗓🗓🖋⊕⊘🗙(heated)↵🗖🗖🖨 lic club, bowling/putting greens

Yarmouth Racecourse, Jellicoe Road NR30 4AU ✆ (01493) 855223 (0800-2000 hrs) OS map 134/526103 1m N of Great Yarmouth off A149 (Caister) Open Apr-Mid Oct 122 pitches 🗓🗙🗖⊕⊘

HADLEIGH, Suffolk   **Map E5**
MD Fri SEE Deanery Tower, Guildhall, 15c almshouses, ancient church
✗ Weavers, High St ✆ (01473) 827247

Grange Country Park, East Bergholt CO7 6UX ✆ (01206) 298567 OS map 155/097352 6m SE of Hadleigh on B1070 (East Bergholt) Open Feb 1-Jan 3 180 pitches (55 static) 🗒🍴🗓🗙🗖⊘🗖↵ sauna, snacks, games room

HALSTEAD, Essex   **Map E5**
EC Wed SEE St Andrew's church, Gosfield Hall 2m SW
✗ Dog Inn, Hedingham Rd ✆ (01787) 477774

Gosfield Leisure Park, Church Road, Gosfield CO9 1YD ✆ (01787) 475043 OS map 167/778295 2½m SW of Halstead off A131 (Braintree) Open all year 25 pitches Level grass, sheltered ✗ (lic) 🍴🗙⊕ fishing in adjoining lake, water skiing (Mastercard/Visa)

HARLESTON, Norfolk   **Map F3**
SEE Waveney valley NE/SW, pretty valley of Mendham E
✗ Swan, The Thoroughfare ✆ (01379) 852221

Little Lakeland Caravan Park, Wortwell IP20 0EL ✆ (01986) 788646 Fax (01986) 788646 *Prop: Jean & Peter Leatherbarrow* OS map 156/280850 2m NE of Harleston off A143 (Bungay) Open Mar-Oct 58 pitches (20 static) Level grass, sheltered 🗒🗓🗙🗖⊕↵🗖🗖 library, fishing £9.80-£14.20 inc awning info@littlelakeland.co.uk www.littlelakeland.co.uk

Waveney Valley Holiday Park, Airstation Lane, Rushall IP21 4QF ✆ (01379) 741228 OS map 156/198831 3m W of Harleston off B1134 (Pulham Market) on Rushall road Open Apr-Oct 65 pitches (20 static) Level grass and hard standing, sheltered 🗒✗🍴🗓🗙🗖🗙⊕⊘🗖🖨 lic club, horse riding waveneyvalleyholidaypark@compuserve.com www.caravanparksnorfolk.co.uk

HARLOW, Essex   **Map C6**
EC Wed MD Tues, Thurs, Fri, *Designed as new town in 1947 around village of Old Harlow* SEE museum housed in Georgian manor house
✗ Churchgate Manor, Old Harlow ✆ (01279) 420246

Roydon Mill Caravan Park, Roydon CM19 5EJ ✆ (01279) 792777 Fax (01279) 792695 OS map 167/405095 3m W of Harlow on B181 (Roydon) near River Stort Open all year 217 pitches (106 static)–adv booking advisable Hard standings and grass, level, open 🗒✗🍴⚡🗓🗙🗖🗙 ⊕⊘↵🗖🗙🖨 club, fishing, water ski school £11.00-£12.00* (most cards) info@roydonpark.com www.roydonpark.com

HARWICH, Essex   **Map F5**
EC Wed MD Fri *Seafaring town on N tip of Essex coast and ferry port to Holland* SEE old houses,
Guildhall, Redoubt Fort, Treadmill crane on green
🛈 Iconfield Park ✆ (01255) 506139
✘ The Pier at Harwich, The Quay ✆ (01255) 241212

Dovercourt Caravan Park, Low Road, Dovercourt CO12 3TZ ✆ (01255) 243433 *Prop: Hammerton
  Leisure Ltd* OS map 169/242301 2m SW of Harwich off A120 (Colchester) near memorial in
  Upper Dovercourt Open Mar-Oct 650 pitches (600 static) Grass, level, open 🔋✘🗑🅰🔌🔲⤴
  🚩(50) 🚃 lic club £13.00-£22.00* inc elect (Mastercard/Visa) *enquiries@dovercourtcp.com*
  www.dovercourtcp.com

HEACHAM–see Hunstanton

HEMSBY–see Caister

HOPTON ON SEA–see Great Yarmouth

HUNSTANTON, Norfolk   **Map D1**
EC Thurs MD Wed SEE ruined St Edmund's chapel, lighthouse, church of St Mary
🛈 The Green ✆ (01485) 532610
✘ Lodge, Cromer Rd ✆ (01485) 523896

Heacham Beach Holiday Park, South Beach Rd, Heacham PE31 7DD ✆ (01485) 570270 OS map
  132/663369 3m S of Hunstanton off A149 (Kings Lynn) at Heacham South Beach Open Easter-
  Oct 250 pitches (200 static) 🔋♿🗑🔲🅰⊕∅⤴

Manor Park Holiday Village, Manor Road PE36 5AZ ✆ (01485) 532300 OS map 132/670398 ½m
  S of Hunstanton off A149 (King's Lynn) Open Apr-Oct 536 pitches (470 static)–no tents Grass,
  level 🔋🔌🗑🔲🅰⊕∅🔲⤴🚉🏠 lic club, entertainment (most cards)

Riverside Caravan Park, Jubilee Rd, Heacham PE31 0BB ✆ (01485) 570676/572206 OS map
  132/664373 3m S of Hunstanton off A149 (Kings Lynn) near Heacham North beach Open Mar-
  Oct 175 pitches (155 static) booking advisable–no tents 15 acres level grass and hard standings
  🗑🔲🅰⊕∅

Searles Holiday Centre, South Beach Road PE36 5BB ✆ (01485) 534211 Fax (01485) 533815 OS
  map 132/678422 ¼m S of of Hunstanton off A149 (King's Lynn) near South Beach Open Feb-
  New Year 800 pitches (450 static) Grass, level, open 🔋✘♿🗑🔲🅰∅🔲(heated) 🚃♿ lic club,
  barbecue £11.00-£30.00* (most cards) *www.searles.co.uk*

HUNTINGDON, Cambs   **Map C4**
EC Wed MD Sat SEE Cromwell museum, old inns, town hall, 14c bridge, Cowpers House, Pepys's
House 1m SW at Brampton
🛈 The Library, Princes St ✆ (01480) 388588
✘ Axe & Compass, High St, Hemingford Abbots ✆ (01480) 463605 Open Mon-Fri 12-2.30/6-7,
Sat-Sun 12-3/6-7
✘ Out & Out Restaurant, Brampton Mill, Bromholme Lane, Brampton ✆ (01480) 459758 Open Mon-
Sat 12-10, Sun 12-9

Hartford Marina, Banks End, Wyton PE17 2AA ✆ (01480) 454677 OS map 153/267725 2m E of
  Huntingdon on A1123 (St Ives) Open Mar-Oct 30 pitches Level grass, sheltered
  🔋✘♿🏹🗑🅰⊕∅

Houghton Mill Camping Park, Mill Street, Houghton PE17 2BJ ✆ (01480) 462413 OS map
  53/284720 4m E of Huntingdon off A1123 (St Ives) by river Great Ouse Open Easter-Sept
  65 pitches Grass, level, sheltered 🔲🅰∅🅾♿ river fishing

Park Lane Touring Park, Park Lane, Godmanchester PE18 8AF ✆ (01480) 453740 Fax (01480)
  453740 OS map 153/245709 2m SE of Huntingdon off B1043 (Godmanchester) at Black Bull Inn
  Open Mar-Oct 50 pitches Grass and hard standing, level, part sheltered 🔋✘🗑🔲🅰∅⊕∅♿♿

Quiet Waters Caravan Park, Hemingford Abbots PE28 9AJ ✆ (01480) 463405 *Prop: Tony & Linda
  Coulson* OS map 53/283710 3m E of Huntingdon off A14 (Cambridge) at junct 25 Open Apr-Oct
  20 pitches (9 static) Grass and hard standing, level, sheltered 🗑🔲🅰∅⊕∅🚃🏠♿ boating,
  angling £11.50-£14.50 (Mastercard/Visa/Delta/Switch) *quietwaters.park@btopenworld.com*
  www.quietwaterscaravanpark.co.uk

Willows Caravan Park, Bromholme Lane, Brampton PE28 4NE ✆ (01480) 437566 *Prop: G Carter*
  OS map 153/212705 2m SW of Huntingdon off A14 (St Neots) on B1514 (Brampton) Open all
  year 55 pitches 4 acres level grass and hard standing ✘🗑🔲🅰⊕🅾⤴♿ £14.00-£17.00 inc elect
  willows@willows33.freeserve.co.uk *www.willowscaravanpark.com*

See also Fenstanton

For more up-to-date information, and for links to camping websites, visit our site at:
www.butford.co.uk/camping

IPSWICH, Suffolk   Map F5
MD Tues, Wed, Fri, S *County town of Suffolk and one of oldest settlements in England* SEE
Christchurch mansion, Great White Horse Hotel (assoc with Dickens), old churches
🛈 Town Hall, Princes St ✆ (01473) 258070 ✘ County, St Helens St ✆ (01473) 255153

Low House Touring Caravan Centre, Bucklesham Road, Foxhall IP10 0AU ✆ (01473) 659437 Fax
(01473) 659880 OS map 169/222423 3½m SE of Ipswich off A14 ring road (south) and A1156
(East Ipswich) on Bucklesham road Open all year 30 pitches 3½ acres level grass sheltered
🛇🔲🖴🗐❀∅↙ pets corner £9.00 (min)* low.house@btopenworld.com

Orwell Meadows Leisure Park, Priory Farm, Nacton IP10 0JS ✆ (01473) 726666 OS map
169/192402 2m SE of Ipswich off southern bypass (A14) via Ransomes Europark exit Open Mar-
Jan 140 pitches (40 static) 30 acres level grass, sheltered 🛇✘♀🖴🗐❀∅🔲↙🖥🚐🅳 family
room (Mastercard/Visa) recept@orwellmeadows.co.uk

Priory Park IP10 0JT ✆ (01473) 727393 Fax (01473) 278372 OS map 169/195405 2m SE of
Ipswich off A12/A45 Southern bypass Open Apr-Oct 280 pitches (160 static) Grass and hard
standing, level/sloping, sheltered 🛇✘♀🔲🖴🗐❀∅🔲(heated) ↙🔲🅰 lic club, golf course
(9-hole), beach frontage, hard tennis courts, nature trails, tidal boat launching £16.00-£24.00*
jwl@priory-park.com www.priory-park.com
See also Manningtree and Woodbridge

KESSINGLAND, Suffolk   Map G3
EC Thurs SEE 17c church, wildlife park and marshlands S, Benacre Broad, Kessingland Cliffs N
✘ Pier Avenue 3m S at Southwold ✆ (01502) 722632

Chestnut Farm, Gisleham NR33 8EE ✆ (01502) 740227 OS map 156/510875 1m W of
Kessingland on Mutford-Rushmere road Open Apr-Oct 40 pitches Grass, level, sheltered 🖴❀

Heathland Beach Caravan Park, London Road NR33 7PJ ✆ (01502) 740337 Fax (01502) 742355
OS map 156/533878 1m N of Kessingland off A12 (Lowestoft) Open Apr-Oct 274 pitches
(211 static) 30 acres level grass 🛇✘♀🔲🖴❀🔲(heated) ↙🖥🚐🅳 tennis, beach access
£8.00-£20.50* (Delta/Mastercard/Switch/Visa) heathlandbeach@btinternet.com
www.heathlandbeach.co.uk

White House Farm, Gisleham NR33 8DX ✆ (01502) 740248 OS map 156/517880 1m NW of
Kessingland on Carlton Colville road Open Apr-Oct 40 pitches Grass, level, open 🖴🗐❀∅↙🖥
fishing
See also Lowestoft

KINGS LYNN, Norfolk   Map D2
EC Wed MD Tues, Fri, Sat *Ancient port on river Ouse rich in medieval architecture* SEE Guildhall,
Customs House, Museum, Walsingham Shrine (RC church), Castle Rising 4m NE, four Wiggenhall
villages by river Ouse S
🛈 The Custom House, Saturday Market ✆ (01553) 763044
✘ Dukes Head, The Market Place ✆ (01553) 774996

Gatton Waters Caravan Park, Hillington PE31 6BJ ✆ (01485) 600643 OS map 132/705255 4m
NE of Kings Lynn off A148 (Cromer) Open Easter-Oct–adult only 90 pitches Level grass
✘♀🖴🗐❀∅ fishing (lake) gattonwaters@virgin.net www.gattonwaters.co.uk

King, Parkside House, New Rd, North Runcton PE33 0QR ✆ (01553) 840004 *Prop: Paul & Claire
Yallop* OS map 132/646165 2m SE of Kings Lynn off A47 (Norwich) Open all year 35 pitches
5 acres grass, sheltered parkland 🖴❀ £5.00-£12.00 (all major cards) klcc@btconnect.com

LEISTON, Suffolk   Map G4
EC Wed SEE ruins of St Mary's Abbey, Minsmere bird sanctuary, Long Shop museum
✘ White Horse, Station Rd ✆ (01728) 830694

Cakes and Ale Camping Park IP16 4TE ✆ (01728) 831655 Fax (01473) 736270 *Prop: Fergus
Little* OS map 156/432637 1m W of Leiston off B1119 (Saxmundham) Open Easter-Oct 250
pitches (200 static) Grass, some hard standings, level, part sheltered
🛇♀🔲🖴🗐❀∅🕓↙🖥🅰 tennis, clubhouse £15.00-£22.00 (Maestro/Visa/Mastercard)
cake.ale@virgin.net

LITTLEPORT–see Ely

LOUGHTON, Essex   Map C6
EC Thurs ✘ The Owl, Lippitts Hill ✆ 020 8502 0663

Debden House Camping, Debden Green IG10 2PA ✆ (0181) 508 3008 OS map 167/438982 1½m
N of Loughton off road to Theydon Bois near golf course and junct 26 of M25 Open May-Sep
225 pitches Grass, part level 🛇∅❀↙🅳

Elms Caravan Park, Lippits Hill, High Beach IG10 4AW *Family run park within easy reach of
London* ✆ (0208) 502 5652 *Prop: Terry & Pat Farr* OS map 177/399971 3m NW of Loughton off
A112 (Waltham Abbey-Chingford) at Lippitts Hill Open Mar-Oct 50 pitches 3 acres level grass
and hard standings, sheltered 🛇✘🖴🗐❀∅🅰 horse riding, golf, cycling £14.00*
info@theelmscampsite.co.uk www.theelmscampsite.co.uk

Beach Farm, Lowestoft

> ### FOLLOW THE COUNTRY CODE
>
> Guard against all risk of fire. Fasten all gates. Keep dogs under proper control. Keep to the paths across farmland. Avoid damaging fences, hedges and walls. Leave no litter. Safeguard water supplies. Protect wildlife, plants and trees. Go carefully on country roads and be prepared for slow-moving vehicles like tractors. Respect the life of the countryside.

LOWESTOFT, Suffolk   **Map G3**
EC Thurs MD Fri, Sat, Sun SEE lighthouse, St Margaret's church, Somerleyton Hall 4m NW
i East Point Pavilion, Royal Plain *C* (01502) 533600
✘ Jolly Sailors, Pakefield St, Pakefield *C* (01502) 561398

Azure Seas Caravan Park, The Street, Corton NR32 5HN *C* (01502) 731403 OS map 134/546968 3m N of Lowestoft off A12 (Great Yarmouth) on B1358 (Corton) Open Apr-Oct 100 pitches (70 static) 10 acres, level, wooded ▢ ▣ ∂ beach adjoining *admin@azureseas.co.uk www.azureseas.co.uk*

Beach Farm, Arbor Lane, Pakefield NR33 7BD *C* (01502) 572794 *Prop: G Westgate* OS map 156/537898 2m S of Lowestoft off A12 (Kessingland) at junction with A1117 (Great Yarmouth) Open Mar-Dec 100 pitches (95 static) Level grass, sheltered ✘ ♀ ⊷ ▢ ▣ ∂ ⊕ ∅ ⊟ (heated) ⤳ ⊐ ▣ ⊟ ઙ Ⴈ beer garden, hire of holiday homes and lodges from £150 (7 nights) £15.00-£20.00 (all main cards) *beachfarmpark@aol.com www.beachfarmpark.co.uk*

Carlton Manor, Chapel Road, Carlton Colville NR33 8BL *C* (01502) 566511 OS map 156/521903 2m SW of Lowestoft off A146 (Beccles) Open Apr-Oct 90 pitches Grass, level ✘ ♀ ⊷ ⟋ ▢ ▣ ∂ ∅ ⊕ ⤳ ⊐ ▣ ઙ putting green
See also Kessingland

MALDON, Essex   **Map E6**
EC Wed MD Thurs, Sat SEE old inns, Moot Hall, Plume library, Chelmer and Blackwater Navigation
i Coach Lane *C* (01621) 856503
✘ Swan, High St *C* (01621) 853170

Beacon Hill Leisure Park, St Lawrence Bay, Southminster CM0 7LS *C* (01621) 779248 (24 hrs) OS map 168/964050 9m E of Maldon off A1010 (Bradwell) Open Apr-Oct 250 pitches (120 static) 25 acres level grass ᒪ ♀ ⟋ ▢ ▣ ∂ ⊕ ∅ ⊟ ⤳ ▣ slipway, battery charging, club house, leisure complex, sauna, bubble spa (Mastercard/Visa)

MANNINGTREE, Essex   **Map F5**
EC Wed MD Sat SEE Swannery, Mistley Towers, Constable country (Dedham Vale) 3m W
✘ Station Buffet *C* (01206) 564777

Strangers Home Inn, Bradfield CO11 2US *C* (01255) 870304 OS map 168/142308 3m E of Manningtree off B1352 (Harwich) Open Mar-Oct 70 pitches 2 acres level grass ᒪ ✘ ♀ ▣ ∂ ∅ ⤳
See also Hadleigh

MARLINGFORD–see Barford

MUNDESLEY ON SEA, Norfolk   **Map G1**
EC Wed *Quiet holiday village with sands and safe bathing* SEE Paston windmill, St Margaret's church, 16c barn
✘ Royal, Paston Rd *C* (01263) 720096

Sandy Gulls Clifftop Touring Park, Cromer Road NR11 8DF *C* (01263) 720513 *Prop: S Hicks* OS map 133/303376 1m NW of Mundesley on B1159 (Cromer) coast road Open Mar-Nov 140 pitches (100 static) 16 acres level grass sheltered ᒪ ▣ ∂ ⊕ ∅ ⊟ £18.00

Woodlands Leisure Park, Trimingham NR11 8AL *C* (01263) 579208 Fax (01263) 833144 OS map 133/274388 3m NW of Mundesley on B1159 (Cromer) Open Apr-Oct 300 pitches (190 static)–no tents Grass, level, sheltered ᒪ ✘ ♀ ⟋ ▢ ▣ ∂ ⊕ ∅ ⊟ (indoor) ⊕ ▣ ઙ (Mastercard/Visa)

Woodlands Leisure Park, Mundesley on Sea

> ### FACTS CAN CHANGE
>
> We do our best to check the accuracy of the entries in this guide but changes can and do occur after publication. So if you plan to stay at a site some distance from home it makes sense to ring the manager or owner before setting off.

NEWMARKET, Suffolk   Map D4
EC Wed MD Tues, Sat SEE Devil's Dyke prehistoric earthworks, Nell Gwynne's House, racecourse
🏰 Palace House ✆ (01638) 667200
✖ White Hart, High St ✆ (01638) 663051

Stanford Park, Weirs Drove, Burwell CB5 0BP ✆ (01638) 741547 OS map 154/585661 3m NW of Newmarket off B1103 (Burwell) Open all year 150 pitches Grass and hard standing, level, sheltered 🛆🔲🟫🔷⊕⊘🔵↵🟥🔳🔄🔳 £10.00* *enquiries@stanfordcaravanpark.co.uk www.stanfordcaravanpark.co.uk*

NORTH WALSHAM, Norfolk   Map F1
EC Wed MD Thurs SEE church, market cross, Paston school
✖ Scarborough Hill House, Yarmouth Rd ✆ (01692) 402151

Two Mills Touring Park, Old Yarmouth Road NR28 9NA ✆ (01692) 405829 Fax (01692) 405829 *Prop: Mr & Mrs RA Barnes* OS map 133/134/291286 1m SE of North Walsham on Old Yarmouth Road (former A149) opposite Scarborough Hill Hotel Open Mar 1-Jan 3 55 pitches–adults only–no tents exc trailer tents 6 acres level grass and hard standings, sheltered
🏧🛆🟫🔷⊕⊘🟥🔳 £13.00-£18.00 (most cards) *enquiries@twomills.co.uk www.twomills.co.uk*

NORWICH, Norfolk   Map F2
EC Thurs MD daily SEE cathedral, city churches, Erpingham gate, old buildings and streets
🏰 The Forum, Millennium Plain ✆ (01603) 727927
✖ Maid's Head, Tombland ✆ (01603) 628821

Buck Inn, Honingham NR9 5BL ✆ (01603) 880393 OS map 133/103118 7½m NW of Norwich off A47 (East Dereham) Open Mar-Oct 6 pitches Grass, part level, sheltered 🟥↵ *No showers*, bar meals

Norfolk Showground Caravan Club Site, Long Lane, Bawburgh NR9 3LX ✆ (01603) 742708 OS map 133/153103 3m W of Norwich off A47 (East Dereham) at Roundwell Inn on Bawburgh road Open Mar-Oct 60 pitches–must book Jul-Aug 5 acres, level 🔷⊘ £9.50-£21.40 (most cards) *www.caravanclub.co.uk*

OBY–see Acle

POLSTEAD, Suffolk   Map E5
Village centred on its green in heart of Constable country.
✖ Cock Inn, The Green ✆ (01206) 263150

Polstead Touring Park, Holt Rd CO6 5BZ ✆ (01787) 211969 Fax (01787) 211969 OS map 155/987404 2m N of Polstead off A1071 (Hadleigh-Sudbury) opposite Brewers Arms inn Open all year 30 pitches 3½ acres grass and hard standings 🏧🛆🟫🔷⊕⊘🔵↵🔳 dog walk £8.00-£11.00*

POTTER HEIGHAM, Norfolk   Map G2
Holiday village between river Thurne and Hickling Broad SEE 13c bridge, St Nicholas church, boatyard
✖ Horse & Groom Hotel, Main Rd, Rollesby ✆ (01493) 740624

Causeway Cottage, Bridge Road NR29 5JB ✆ (01692) 670238 (Mobile) 07867 974143 *Prop: Trevor & Sue Chaplin* OS map 134/416187 ½m S of Potter Heigham centre off A149 (Gt Yarmouth) near river Open Mar 27-Oct 2 15 pitches Level grass, sheltered 🟥🔷⊕🔵🔳 pets welcome £5.00-£10.00

Willowcroft, Staithe Road, Repps with Bastwick NR29 5JU ✆ (01692) 670380 *Prop: Kendy Trigg-Dudley* OS map 134/414173 2m S of Potter Heigham off A149 (Great Yarmouth) on Thurne road Open Easter-Oct 40 pitches 2 acres, level grass, sheltered 🟥🔷⊕ boating, fishing £12.00-£15.00* *kandy.willowcroftsite@btinternet.com www.willocroftsite.btinternet.com*

REEDHAM, Norfolk   Map G2
*Marshland village at only crossing of river Yare between Norwich and coast at Great Yarmouth (£2
per car)* SEE chain ferry across river Yare, church of St John the Baptist, Berney Arms Mill 3m NE
✗ Ferry ☏ (01493) 700429

Pampas Lodge, The Street, Haddiscoe NR14 6AA ☏ (01502) 677265 OS map 134/447971 4m SE
of Reedham on A143 (Great Yarmouth-Beccles) at Haddiscoe Open Apr-Oct 50 pitches Grass
and hard standing, level, sheltered ⛺🅿🔌🚿🚽🎮🏪🏠

Reedham Ferry Camping and Caravan Park NR13 3HA ☏ (01493) 700999 Fax (01493) 700999
OS map 134/407015 ½m SW of Reedham on B1140 (Beccles) adjoining Ferry Inn Open Easter-
Oct 20 pitches Grass, level, part sheltered ✗⛽🔌🚿🚽🎮 fishing, boating, slipway £11.00-
£16.50* (Mastercard/Visa/Delta/Switch) *reedhamferry@aol.com www.archerstouringpark.co.uk*

ST OSYTH, Essex   Map F6
SEE priory ruins and gatehouse, parish church with 16c beamed roof
✗ White Hart, Mill St ☏ (01255) 820318

Hutley's Caravan Park, St Osyth Beach, St Osyth CO16 8TB ☏ (01255) 820712 OS map
168/122155 On W edge of St Osyth on road to beach Open Easter-Oct 750 pitches
(730 static)–no tents Grass, level, open 🏪✗⛽🔌🚿🚽🔌🎮 children's room, naturist
beach (all major cards)

Orchards Holiday Village, Point Clear CO16 8LJ ☏ (01255) 820651 OS map 168/093153 2m W
of St Osyth at Point Clear Open Mar-Oct 1360 pitches (1320 static)
🏪✗⛽🔌🚿🚽🔌🎮🏠 bowling

SAXMUNDHAM, Suffolk   Map G4
EC Wed MD Thurs SEE church
✗ The White Horse, Bruisyard Rd, Bendham ☏ (01728) 663497 Open 12-2/6.30-9
✗ The Lion Inn, Main Road, Little Glemham ☏ (01728) 746505 Open Tue-Sat 12-2/6.30-9,
Sun 12-3/7-9 (closed Mon exc bank hols)

Carlton Meres Country Park IP17 2QP ☏ (01728) 603344 *Prop: Mr & Mrs MA Walker* OS map
156/366651 1½m NW of Saxmundham off B1119 (Framlingham) Open Easter-Sept
275 seasonal pitches Grass and hard standing ✗⛽🔌🚿🚽🎮🏪 fishing (price on request)
(most cards) *enquiries@carlton-meres.co.uk www.carlton-meres.co.uk*

Marsh Farm, Sternfield IP17 1HW ☏ (01728) 602168 *Prop: Mrs M Bloomfield* OS map 156/387607
1m S of Saxmundham off A12-B1121 (Aldeburgh) at Sternfield–signposted Open all year
45 pitches 30 acres level grass 🔌🎮 £8.00-£14.00

Whitearch, Main Road, Benhall IP17 1NA ☏ (01728) 604646 *Prop: MV Rowe* OS map 156/385615
1m S of Saxmundham near junction of A12 (Woodbridge) and B1121 (Aldeburgh)–signposted
Open Apr-Sep 50 pitches 14 acres level/sloping grass and hard standings 🏪🔌🚿🚽🔌
fishing, tennis, TV hook-ups £10.00

See also Yoxford

SEA PALLING, Norfolk   Map G2
✗ Fisherman's Return 3m SE at Winterton on Sea ☏ (01493) 393305

Golden Beach Holiday Centre, Beach Road NR12 0AL ☏ (01692) 598269 Fax (01692) 598693
OS map 134/430272 ¼m N of Sea Palling off road to beach Open Mar 21-Oct 31 147 pitches
(110 static) Grass, level, some hard standings 🏪✗⛽🔌🚿🚽🔌🎮🏪 £8.50-£12.50

SHERINGHAM, Norfolk   Map F1
EC Wed MD Sat SEE priory ruins at Beeston Regis, North Norfolk steam railway
ℹ Station Approach ☏ (01263) 824329
✗ The Village Inn, Water Lane, West Runton ☏ (01263) 838000

Beeston Regis Caravan Park, West Runton NR27 9NG ☏ (01263) 823614 OS map 133/175432
1m E of Sheringham off A149 (Cromer) Open Mar-Oct 400 pitches (300 static)–adv booking
advisable 15 acres level grass, clifftop location 🏪🔌🎮 beach access, coarse fishing
(MastercardVisa/Switch/Delta) *info@beestonregis.co.uk www.beestonregis.co.uk*

Woodlands Caravan Park, Holt Road, Upper Sheringham NR26 8TU ☏ (01263) 823802 Fax
(01263) 825797 OS map 133/136408 1½m S of Sheringham on A148 (Cromer-Fakenham) Open
Mar 15-Oct 31 376 pitches (160 static) 21 acres, level grass, sheltered
🏪✗⛽🔌🚿🚽🎮(indoor)🎮🔌 fishing (all main cards)

SHOEBURYNESS–see Southend

SNETTISHAM–see Hunstanton

SITE DIRECTIONS
The distance and direction of a campsite is given from the centre of the town under which it appears.

D B Bloomfield
Marsh Farm
Sternfield
Saxmundham

Tel 01728 602168

A pretty site overlooking reed-fringed lakes which offer excellent coarse fishing

THE BROADS

A low-lying area east of Norwich laced by a network of rivers is notable for its wide shallow lakes fringed by reeds. The Broads, as these stretches of water are called, are the home of many rare birds, animals and plants, including the marsh harrier, the otter, the royal fern and the water parsnip. To anglers these lakes mean pike, some of the largest found anywhere, but fishing on a wider scale is freely available. There are three important nature reserves in the Broads. The Bure Marshes between Wroxham and Ranworth take in Hoveton Great Broad and Ranworth Broad, with several heronries and roosts of cormorants. There is a nature trail open May to September at Hoveton, accessible only by boat. A half-day water trail visiting seven hides is organised by the Norfolk Wildlife Trust (contact the warden at Stubb Road, Hickling NR12 0BW; ☎(01692) 598276). Horsey Mere, the third reserve and a famous haunt of birds, lies near the coast and is owned by the National Trust. Access is only by boat.

See listing under Saxmundham

SOUTHEND ON SEA
Map E7

MD Thurs, Fri, Sat SEE 13c South church Hall, Civic House, Pier, 12c Prittlewall Priory and museum, Planetarium

🅸 Western Esplanade ☎(01702) 215120

✗ Bakers Bar, Alexandra St (off High St) ☎(01702) 390403

East Beach Caravan Park, Shoeburyness SS3 9SG ☎(01702) 292466 OS map 178/943842 3m E of Southend off A13 near Shoeburyness station and beach–signposted Open Mar-Oct 160 pitches (75 static) 🛒🎾🗑🛢🌀⊛∅↩

Riverside Village Holiday Park, Creeksea Ferry Rd, Wallasea Island, Rochford SS4 2EY ☎(01702) 258297 OS map 178/932952 6m NE of Southend off A127 (Romford) and B1013 (Rochford) via Ashingdon Open Mar-Oct 220 pitches (160 static) Level grass, part sheltered 🛒🎾🗑🛢🌀⊛∅⊖↩🏮 boules

SOUTHMINSTER, Essex
Map E6

✗ Station Arms, Station Rd ☎(01621) 772225

Steeple Bay Caravan Park, Steeple CM0 7RS ☎(01621) 773991 OS map 168/933050 3m N of Southminster at Steeple Bay via Steeple Open Apr-Oct 360 pitches (300 static) Level grass and hard standing 🛒✗🎾⌐↗🗑🛢🌀⊛∅⊟↩🏮 launching facs (all cards)

See also Maldon

SOUTHWOLD, Suffolk
Map G3

EC Wed MD Mon, Thurs SEE town hall, St Edmund's church, museum, lighthouse

🅸 Town Hall, Market Place ☎(01502) 724729

✗ Crown, High St ☎(01502) 722275

Harbour Caravan and Camping Park, Ferry Road IP18 6ND ☎(01502) 722486 OS map 156/504750 ½m S of Southwold off A1095 (Blythburgh) on harbour road Open Apr-Oct 150 pitches Grass, level, part open 🛢∅♿

CHECK BEFORE ENTERING

There's usually no objection to your walking onto a site to see if you might like it but always ask permission first. Remember that the person in charge is responsible for safeguarding the property of those staying there.

SUDBURY, Suffolk   Map E5
EC Wed MD Thurs, Sat SEE churches, Corn Exchange, Gainsborough's house, Old Moot Hall, Salter's Hall
🖥 Town Hall, Market Hill ☎(01787) 881320
✗ Fords Bistro, Gainsborough St ☎(01787) 374298

Willowmere Caravan Park, Bures Road, Little Cornard CO10 0NN ☎(01787) 375559 Fax (01787) 375559 *Prop: Mrs A Wilson* OS map 155/886390 1½m S of Sudbury on B1508 (Colchester) Open Apr-Oct 40 pitches Grass, level, sheltered 🗐🗗🖉🅰⊘ £8.00-£11.00

SWAFFHAM, Norfolk   Map E2
EC Thurs MD Sat SEE church, market cross, Pedlar Sign
✗ George, Station St ☎(01760) 721238

Breckland Meadows Touring Park, Lynn Road PE37 7PT ☎(01760) 721246 OS map 144/809094 ¾m W of Swaffham centre on old King's Lynn road Open all year (must book Nov-Feb) 45 pitches 3½ acres level grass and hard standing 🗓🗐🗗🖉🅰⊘🗗 heated amenity block £6.00-£12.00* (most cards) info@brecklandmeadows.co.uk www.brecklandmeadows.co.uk

Pentney Park, Pentney PE32 1HU ☎(01760) 337479 OS map 132/743142 7m NW of Swaffham off A47 (King's Lynn) at junction with B1153 (Gayton) Open all year 200 pitches Grass, level, sheltered 🗓✗↩↗🗐🗗🖉🅰⊘🖉🗔(heated) 🟢↩🖼(40) 🗛 gym, miniature railway £15.95 (Mastercard/Visa/Switch/Solo)

THETFORD, Norfolk   Map E3
EC Wed MD Tues, Sat SEE churches, King's House, Old Bell Hotel, Ancient House (museum), Euston Hall 3m SE
✗ Bell, King St ☎(01842) 754455

Dower House, East Harling NR16 2SE ☎(01953) 717314 *Prop: David & Karin Bushell* OS map 144/969852 8m E of Thetford off A1066 (Diss) Open Mar-Oct 140 pitches Grass, level, part sheltered 🗓🗓↗🗐🗗🖉🅰⊘🗔🟢↩🗖🖼🗗 £10.30-£16.95 (Mastercard/Visa/Switch/Solo) *info@dowerhouse.co.uk www.dowerhouse.co.uk*

TRIMINGHAM–see Mundesley

WANSFORD, Peterborough   Map B3
SEE packhorse bridge, church
✗ Falcon Inn 3m S at Fotheringhay ☎(01832) 226254

Yarwell Mill Caravan Park, Yarwell PE8 6PS ☎(01780) 782344 OS map 142/074973 1m S of Wansford off Fotheringhay road by river Nene Open Mar-Oct 148 pitches (24 static) Level grass, sheltered 🗗🖉🅰⊘🟢↩🖼🗗 fishing, boating

WELLS NEXT THE SEA, Norfolk   Map E1
EC Thurs *Old-world fishing port of flint cottages and Georgian houses* SEE Quay, miniature railways, Holkham Hall 2m W
🖥 Staithe St ☎(01328) 710885 ✗ Crown, The Buttlands ☎(01328) 710209

High Sandcreek Camping, Stiffkey NR23 1QP ☎(01328) 830235 OS map 132/965438 3m E of Wells off A149 (Sheringham) Open Apr-Oct 80 pitches 2 acres, gentle slope 🗓🖉 boating, fishing, bird watching £5.00-£10.50

Pinewoods Holiday Park, Beach Road NR23 1DR ☎(01328) 710439 OS map 132/914453 1m N of Wells on road to beach Open Mar 15-Oct 31 900 pitches (530 static) 75 acres, level grass and hard standing 🗓✗(snack) ↩↗🗐🗗🖉🅰⊘🟢↩🗖🖙🖼🗗 boating, fishing, pitch and putt, miniature railway, trampolines (Mastercard/Visa/Switch)

WEST MERSEA, Essex   Map E6
SEE Georgian cottages, fishing museum
✗ The Fox, East Rd ☎(01206) 383391
✗ The Granary Restaurant, Waldegrave Holiday Park ☎(01206) 383909

Fen Farm, East Mersea CO5 8UA ☎(01206) 383275 *Prop: Ralph & Wenda Lord* OS map 168/058144 4m E of West Mersea off B1025 (Colchester) and East Mersea road Open Apr-Oct 130 pitches (85 static) 10 acres level grass 🗐🗗🖉🅰⊘🖉↩🖼🗗 mobile shop, £15.00-£23.50 (Mastercard/Visa/Switch) fenfarm@talk21.com www.merseaisland.com/fenfarm

Seaview Holiday Park, Seaview Avenue CO5 8DA ☎(01206) 382534 *Prop: Andrew Dixon* OS map 168/020148 1m N of West Mersea off B1025 (Colchester) by sea Open Mar-Oct 370 pitches (250 static) Level/sloping grass adj beach 🗓✗🗓🗐🗗🖉🅰⊘ £13.00-£20.00 www.westmersea.com

Waldegraves Farm CO5 8SE ☎(01206) 382898 OS map 168/033128 1m E of West Mersea off B1025 (Colchester) by sea Open Mar-Nov 309 pitches (249 static) Grass, level, part sheltered 🗓✗🖙↩🗐🗗🖉🅰⊘🖉🗔🟢↩🖼(50) 🗖 boating and fishing lakes, satellite TV, golf range, pitch and putt £17.00-£25.00 (all cards) holidays@waldegraves.co.uk www.waldegraves.co.uk

WEST RUNTON–see Sheringham

WILLINGHAM, Cambs　　　　　　　　　　　　　　　　　　　Map C4
✖ Three Tuns, Church St ☏ (01954) 260437

Alwyn Camping Caravan Site, Over Road CB4 5EV ☏ (01954) 260977 OS map 154/396701 ¼m W of Willingham on Over road Open Mar-Oct 90 pitches 5 acres level grass, sheltered
🛒♀🗓🗐⌀⊕∅☻↩⛶🛅

Roseberry Tourist Park, Earith Road CB4 5LT ☏ (01954) 260346 OS map 154/407723 1m N of Willingham on B1050 (Chatteris) Open all year 80 pitches Grass and hard standing, level, sheltered 🗐🗓⌀⊕↩🛅

WINFARTHING, Norfolk　　　　　　　　　　　　　　　　　　Map F3
✖ The Greyhound, The Street, Tibenham ☏ (01379) 677676 Open Wed-Fri 6.30-8.30, Sat-Sun 12-3/6-8.30

The Greyhound, Tibenham NR16 1PZ ☏ (01379) 677676 Prop: David Hughes & Colleen Hughes OS map 144/136895 3m NE of Winfarthing off Bunwell road in Tibenham Open Mar-Oct 10 pitches 2 acres, level grass ✖♀↩ No showers £5.00 mail@thetibenhamgreyhound.co.uk www.thetibenhamgreyhound.co.uk

WISBECH, Cambs　　　　　　　　　　　　　　　　　　　　　Map C2
EC Wed MD Thurs, Sat SEE North and South Brinks (Georgian houses), Peckover House, Wisbech and Fenland museum
🗓 2-3 Bridge St ☏ (01945) 583263
✖ Rose Tavern, North Brink ☏ (01945) 588335

Friday Bridge International Farm Camp, March Road PE14 0LR ☏ (01945) 860255 OS map 143/455040 3m S of Wisbech on B1101 (March) beyond Friday Bridge Open May-Oct 20 pitches Grass, level, sheltered 🛒🏊 lic club, disco, tennis, pool, volley ball, Sky TV

WOODBRIDGE, Suffolk　　　　　　　　　　　　　　　　　　Map F4
EC Wed MD Thurs SEE St Mary's church, Shire Hall, tide mill, marina, old houses and inns
✖ Seckford Arms, Seckford St ☏ (01394) 384446

Forest Camping, Tangham Camp Site, Butley IP12 3NF ☏ (01394) 450707 OS map 169/355485 7½m E of Woodbridge off B1084 (Orford) on forest road via Butley Open Apr-Oct 90 pitches Grass, level, open 🛒🗓🗓⌀⊕∅⊕🛅 forest walks £13.00-£15.00* (most cards) admin@forestcamping.co.uk www.forestcamping.co.uk

Moat Barn Touring, Dallinghoo Rd, Bredfield IP13 6BD ☏ (01473) 737520 Prop: MJ Allen OS map 156/270535 2m N of Woodbridge off A12 (Lowestoft) Open Easter-Jan 25 pitches 2 acres level grass 🛒🗓🗓⊕🛅 £12.00* www.moatbarn.co.uk

Moon and Sixpence, Waldringfield IP12 4PP ☏ (01473) 736650 Fax (01473) 736270 OS map 169/262456 2m S of Woodbridge off A12 (Ipswich) eastern bypass on Newbourn road Open Apr-Oct 275 pitches (200 static) Grass, level, terraced, sheltered 🛒✖♀➳🗓🗓⌀⊕∅☻↩⛶ tennis courts, basketball, petanque, volley ball, lic club, 2 acre lake with beach, woodland walks £16.00-£26.00 (Mastercard/Visa) moonsix@dircon.co.uk www.moonsix.dircon.co.uk

St Margaret's House, Shottisham IP12 3HD ☏ (01394) 411247 OS map 169/322446 6m SE of Wood-bridge off B1083 (Shottisham) Open Apr-Oct 30 pitches Grass, level, sheltered 🛒🗓⌀⊕↩ £7.50-£10.00* ken.norton@virgin.net

The Sandlings Centre, Lodge Road, Hollesley IP12 3RR ☏ (01394) 411202 OS map 169/338434 6m SE of Woodbridge off B1083 (Shottisham) Open Mar-Jan 61 pitches (36 static)—no caravans Grass, level, sheltered 🗐🗓⌀⊕∅🛅🚃🏠

YOXFORD, Suffolk　　　　　　　　　　　　　　　　　　　　Map G4
SEE Minsmere bird reserve and Ipswich forest E, Sibton Park W
✖ Crown on B1125 2m E at Westleton ☏ (01728) 660777

Haw Wood Caravan Park, Haw Wood, Hinton IP17 3QT ☏ (01986) 784248 Prop: Andrew Blois OS map 156/423716 2m NE of Yoxford off A12 (Lowestoft) Open Apr-Oct 90 pitches (25 static) Grass, level, sheltered 🗓⌀⊕↩🛅🚃 £12.00-£14.00

See also Maldon

KEY TO SYMBOLS

🛒	shop	⌀	gas supplies	🛅	winter storage for caravans
✖	restaurant	⊕	chemical disposal point	🅿	parking obligatory
♀	bar	∅	payphone	⊗	no dogs
↩	takeaway food	🏊	swimming pool	🚃	caravan hire
➳	off licence	☻	games area	🏠	bungalow hire
🗐	laundrette	↩	children's playground	♿	facilities for disabled
🗓	mains electric hook-ups	⛶	TV	🌳	shaded

Adjoining Greater London on the north and west, the five Home Counties of Hertford, Bedford, Buckingham, Oxford and Berkshire have withstood population pressures enough to retain a fair share of unspoiled scenery.

Hertfordshlre occupies the northern part of the Thames basin which slopes gently up to the Chiltern escarpment extending from Royston to Tring. The main sights are the Roman relics at St Albans, the castle at Hertford and the stately homes of Gorhambury, Hatfield and Knebworth.

Adjoining Hertfordshire on the north, Bedfordshire is best known for the broad scenic valley of the Ouse, for which Bedford is a good centre. There are notable churches at Dunstable, Leighton Buzzard and Eaton, the country houses of Woburn and Luton Hoo and the pretty villages of Chalgrave near Dunstable and Upper Dean near Bedford.

Ivinghoe Beacon, at 904ft the highest point in the Chilterns, is in the southern half of Buckinghamshire. Famed for the beauty of their beech woods, the Chilterns are crossed by two routes for walkers. The North Bucks Way begins near Princes Risborough and ends at Wolverton, and the Ridgeway, which starts at Ivinghoe Beacon, follows the escarpment all the way to Avebury in Wiltshire. In the north is the Vale of Aylesbury, patterned with rivers and streams. Wendover is a pleasant town, and Haddenham, Hambledon and Latimer are attractive villages. Hughenden Manor is one of several interesting country houses to visit.

Buckinghamshire's neighbour is Berkshire, still threequarters pasture, farmland and woods. Where the Thames flows through the gap at Goring the lush beauty of its valley contrasts with the austerity of the Berkshire Downs on one side and the Chilterns on the other. The Berkshire Ridgeway can still be followed the twenty miles between Thameside Streatley and Ashbury. Windsor Castle is probably the most important building in the county.

Wedged in between Berkshire and Buckinghamshire, Oxfordshire is centred on the Thames basin between the Chilterns on the north and the Cotswolds on the west, where the river flows through remote and peaceful water meadows and past riverside pubs – most inviting between Oxford and Lechlade. Other sights in the county are the university buildings of Oxford, the pretty town of Abingdon, the stately home of Blenheim and the delightful villages of Stanton Harcourt, Minster Lovell and Ewelme.

Although it is no longer the largest city in the world, London covers a vast area. The most important buildings are St Paul's Cathedral, Westminster Abbey, the Tower of London, Westminster Hall, the Royal Hospital, the fine house of Syon Park and the Tudor palace of Hampton Court.

Campsites in the region are few. The only ones in London itself are invariably crowded and campers and caravanners visiting the capital do so more easily by staying at a campsite on the perimeter and travelling to and in the central area by public transport. Campsites exist at several places along the Thames but there are few elsewhere.

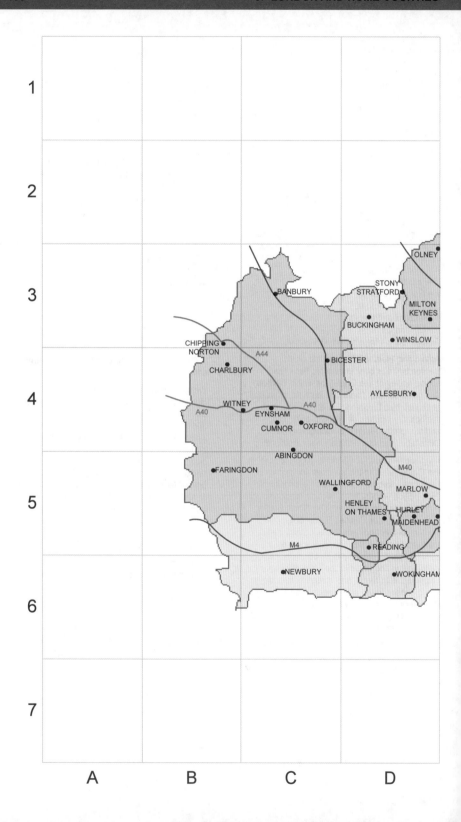

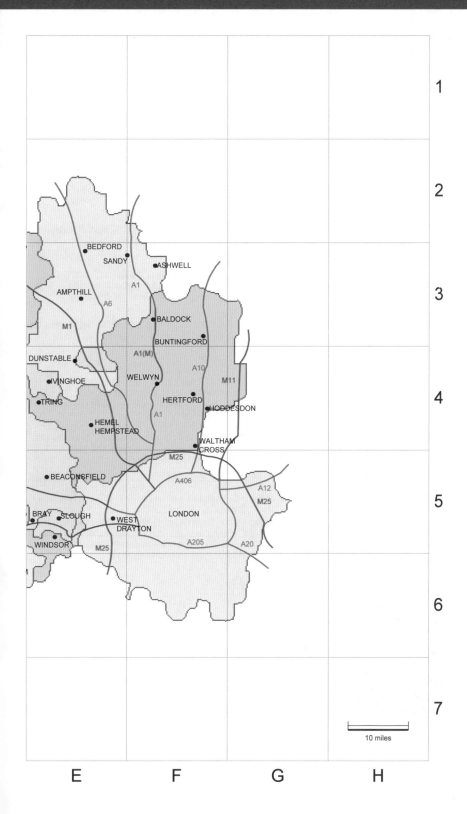

1

2

3

BEDFORD
SANDY
ASHWELL
A1
AMPTHILL
A6
M1
BALDOCK
BUNTINGFORD
A1(M)
DUNSTABLE
A10
M11
IVINGHOE
WELWYN
TRING
HERTFORD
HODDESDON
A1
HEMEL
HEMPSTEAD
WALTHAM
CROSS
M25
BEACONSFIELD
A406
A12
M25
BRAY SLOUGH
WEST
DRAYTON
LONDON
WINDSOR
M25
A205
A20

4

5

6

7

10 miles

E   F   G   H

ABINGDON, Oxon   Map C4

EC Thurs MD Mon *Attractive market town on loop of river Thames (Isis)* SEE 17c county hall (museum), guildhall (portraits, plate), abbey ruins, St Helens and St Nicholas churches, river Thames from towpath

☑ Bridge St ✆ (01235) 522711

✗ Old Anchor, St Helens Wharf ✆ (01235) 521726

Bridge House, Clifton Hampden OX14 3EH ✆ (01865) 407725 OS map 164/547953 3m E of Abingdon off A415 (Henley) at Clifton Hampden on Long Wittenham road by river Thames Open Apr-Oct 40 pitches 3½ acres level grass, sheltered ▯▯▨▨▨

AMPTHILL, Beds   Map E3

SEE Georgian houses, St Andrew's church, White Hart Hotel (18c)

☑ 12 Dunstable St ✆ (01525) 402051

✗ Upstairs Downstairs, King's Arms Yd ✆ (01525) 404303

Rose and Crown, Ridgmont MK43 0TY ✆ (01525) 280245 OS map 153/977363 4m W of Ampthill on right of A507 (Woburn) Open all year 15 pitches Level grass, sheltered ▨✗▨▨▨▨▨▨ No showers (all cards)

BALDOCK, Herts   Map F3

EC Thurs *Ancient town with Georgian houses lining High St* SEE Wynn almshouses, Ashwell village 4m NE

✗ Forte Travelodge on A1 southbound ✆ (01462) 835329

Radwell Mill Lake, Radwell Mill SG7 5ET *Quiet orchard site with easy access to A1(M)* ✆ (01462) 730253 OS map 153/229358 2m NW of Baldock off A507 (Ampthill) via Radwell (beyond village) near junct 10 of A1(M) Open Easter-Nov 10 pitches Level grass, sheltered ▨▨ lake, full motorway services ½m £5.00* (£4.00 CC members)

BANBURY, Oxon   Map C3

EC Tues MD Thurs, Sat SEE church, Calthorpe Manor, Broughton castle and church 3m SW, Wroxton cottages 3m NW

☑ Banbury Museum, 8 Horsefair ✆ (01295) 259855

✗ Cromwell Lodge, North Bar ✆ (01295) 259781

Anita's Touring Caravan Park, The Yews, Mollington OX17 1AZ *Central for touring Cotswolds* ✆ (01295) 750731 Fax (01295) 750731 OS map 151/440475 4m N of Banbury on A423 (Coventry) near junct 11 of M40 Open all year 36 pitches 2 acres level/sloping grass and hard standings, sheltered ▨▨▨ £7.00* *anitagail@btopenworld.com*

Barnstones Caravan Park, Great Bourton OX17 1QU ✆ (01295) 750289 *Prop: Dave Boddington* OS map 151/455453 3m N of Banbury off A423 (Coventry) on Great Bourton road Open all year 49 pitches with mains electricity (20 with all mains services) 4 acres, level grass and hard standing, sheltered ▨▨▨▨▨▨▨▨▨ heated toilet block £8.50

BEACONSFIELD, Bucks   Map E5

EC Wed, Sat *Busy town on wide main street (A40) in lovely wooded countryside* SEE Model Village, Friends' Meeting House at Jordans, Milton's Cottage at Chalfont St Giles, Chiltern Hills

✗ The White Hart, Three Households, Chalfont St Giles ✆ (01494) 872441

Highclere Farm Country Touring Park, New Barn Lane, Seer Green HP9 2QZ ✆ (01494) 874505 *Prop: NF Penfold Ltd* OS map 176/976928 3m E of Beaconsfield off A335 (Amersham) on Seer Green road (signposted) (M40 junct 2) Open Mar-Jan 95 pitches 3 acres level grass and hard standing sheltered ▨▨▨▨▨▨▨▨ £15.00-£18.00 (most cards exc Diners) *highclerepark@aol.com www.highclerepark.co.uk*

Highclere Farm Country Touring Park, Beaconsfield

COMMENTS

We would be pleased to hear your comments about the sites featured in this guide or your suggestions for future editions. Comments and suggestions may be emailed to ccb@butford.co.uk. Alternatively, write to The Editor, CCB, Butford Technical Publishing Ltd at the address given at the front of the book.

BICESTER, Oxon   Map C4
Noted fox-hunting centre enclosing wide market square
✗ Greyhound Inn 4m E at Marsh Gibbon ☎ (01869) 277365

Heyford Leys Farm, Upper Heyford OX6 3LU ☎ (01869) 232048 OS map 164/513245 3m NW of Bicester off B4030 (Chipping Norton) between junct 9 and 10 of M40 Open Mar-Oct 100 pitches (55 static) 🛁🚻🚾🅿🚐⚡🐾🛗♿

CHARLBURY, Oxon   Map B4
EC Wed or Thurs
✗ Bell, Church St ☎ (01608) 810278

Cotswold View Caravan and Camping Site OX7 3JH ☎ (01608) 810314 Fax (01608) 811891 OS map 164/363209 1m NNW of Charlbury on B4022 (Enstone) Open Easter-Oct 125 pitches Grass, part level 🛁🏹🚻🚾🅿⚡🚮⚡🐾🏪♿ hard tennis court, bike hire

CHIPPING NORTON, Oxon   Map B3
EC Thurs MD Wed *Small Cotswold town still with several old inns, the relics of coaching days* SEE church, almshouses, Guildhall, White Hart Inn (17c)
🛈 Guildhall ☎ (01608) 644379
✗ White Hart, High St ☎ (01608) 642572

Churchill Heath Caravan Site, Kingham OX7 6UJ ☎ (01608) 658317 OS map 163/256227 4½m SW of Chipping Norton on left of B4450 (Stow on the Wold) Open all year 50 pitches Grass and hard standing, level, sheltered 🛁🔌🏹🚻🚾🅿⚡🚮⚡🐾🏪

CUMNOR, Oxon   Map C4
SEE view from summit of Hurst Hill, church (interior)
✗ Bear and Ragged Staff, Appleton Rd ☎ (01865) 862329

Spring Farm, Faringdon Rd OX2 9QY ☎ (01865) 863028 OS map 164/462032 ½m SW of Cumnor on right of A420 (Faringdon)–signposted Open Apr-Oct 20 pitches–booking advisable Level/sloping grass, sheltered ⚡🐾

FARINGDON, Oxon   Map B5
EC Thurs MD Tues SEE church, arcaded library, Folly Tower, Great Barn (NT) at Great Coxwell 2m SE, Buscot House 3m NW
🛈 7a Market Place ☎ (01367) 242191
✗ Swan Hotel, Radcot-On-Thames, Bampton ☎ (01367) 810220 Open 08-Sep

Swan Hotel, Radcot, Bampton OX18 2SX ☎ (01367) 810220 *Prop: Alan & Linda Mitchell* OS map 163/286995 2m N of Faringdon on A4095 (Witney) by river Thames Open all year 25 pitches 2 acres, level ✗🍴 fishing (permits avail), boating, B&B No showers £4.00-£6.00 (all major cards) lm.mitchell@ntlworld.com www.swanhotelradcot.co.uk

HENLEY ON THAMES, Oxon   Map D5
EC Wed MD Thurs SEE Thames bridge, church, Kenton Theatre, royal regatta (Jun-Jul)
🛈 King's Arm Barn, Kings Rd ☎ (01491) 578034
✗ Red Lion, Hart St ☎ (01491) 572161

Swiss Farm International Caravan Park, Marlow Road RG9 2HY ☎ (01491) 573419 OS map 175/760834 ¼m N of Henley on Thames on left of A4155 (Marlow) Open Mar-Oct 180 pitches Grass level, sloping, sheltered 🛁🍴🔌🚻🚾🅿⚡🚮⚡🏊⚡🚮🏪♿ fishing, social club £10.00-£11.00* (Mastercard/Delta/Switch/Debit) enquiries@swissfarmcamping.co.uk www.swissfarmcamping.co.uk

HODDESDON, Herts   Map F4
EC Thurs MD Wed
✗ New Rose and Crown 3m N at Ware ☎ (01920) 462572

Lee Valley Caravan Park, Essex Road EN11 0AS ☎ (01992) 462090 OS map 166/383082 1m SE of Hoddesdon off A1107 (Cheshunt) near weir pool in Lee Valley Regional Park Open Easter-Oct 200 pitches (100 static) 24 acres, level grass 🛁🚻🚾🅿⚡🚮⚡🐾♿ boating, fishing, model railway club

HURLEY, Windsor & Maidenhead   Map D5
EC Wed SEE Thames (islands, lock, weir), parish church, ruined priory, cottages
✗ Dew Drop off A423 ☎ (01628) 824327

Hurley Riverside Park, Shepherds Lane SL6 5NE *Surrounded by farmland close to Thames Path* ☎ (01628) 824493/823501 OS map 175/815840 ¾m W of Hurley centre off A4130 (Henley) by river Thames Open Mar-Oct 490 pitches (290 static) 72 acres grass, level, part sheltered 🛁 (peak periods) 🚻🚾🅿⚡🚮🏊🚮♿ multi-service hook-ups, river fishing, slipway £8.00-£15.25* (Mastercard/Visa/Maestro) info@hurleyriversidepark.co.uk www.hurleyriversidepark.co.uk

For more up-to-date information, visit our site at: **www.butford.co.uk/camping**

HURLEY
RIVERSIDE PARK

Tel: 01628 823501
Email: info@hurleyriversidepark.co.uk

Hurley Church   *Above the lock at Hurley*

IVINGHOE, Bucks   Map E4
✗ King's Head, Station Rd ☎ (01296) 668388

Silver Birch Cafe, Dunstable Road, Pitstone LU7 9EN ☎ (01296) 668348 OS map 165/947152
1½m SW of Ivinghoe on B488 (Tring) Open Mar-Nov 14 pitches Grass, sheltered ✗
No showers

LONDON E4
Lee Valley Campsite, Sewardstone Road, Chingford E4 7RA ☎ (0208) 529 5689 OS map
177/380970 10m N of central London on A112 (Waltham Abbey) Open Apr-Oct 200 pitches
12½ acres, level grass and hard standing 🛒⚲🗑🛢🔌❋∅🔫♿ ironing room

LONDON E15
Lee Valley Park, Eastway Camping Caravan Park, Temple Mills Lane, Stratford E15 2EN ☎ (0208)
534 6085 OS map 177/372852 6 m NE of Central London off A112 (Stratford) Open Apr-Sept
80 pitches Grass, level ✗🗑🛢❋∅✪ tennis, squash, cycle hire

LONDON N9
Lee Valley Leisure Centre, Meridian Way, Edmonton N9 0AS ☎ (0208) 345 6666 OS map
177/360944 8m N of Central London off A406 (North Circular) near junct 25 of M25 Open all year
160 pitches 4½ acres grass (tents) hard standing (caravans), level 🛒✗🍴🗑🛢🔌❋∅🖂🔫♿
creche, sauna, golf, tennis, badminton, squash, cinema (Mastercard/Visa/Euro)

MAIDENHEAD, Berks   Map D5
EC Thurs MD Fri, Sat SEE Oldfield House, river Thames, 18c bridge, Courage Shire Horse Centre
2m W on A4
🛈 Central Library, St Ives Rd ☎ (01628) 796502
✗ Harvester, Bath Rd, Taplow ☎ (01628) 630817

Amerden Camping Caravan Park, Old Marsh Lane, Dorney Reach SL6 0EE ☎ (01628) 627461
Prop: Mrs Hakesley OS map 175/918797 4m SE of Maidenhead off A4 (Slough) adjoining Bray
Lock Open Apr-Oct 50 pitches Level grass 🗑🛢❋🔫🖂♿ fishing, riverside walks
£12.00-£16.00 inc elect *beverly@amerdencaravanpark.co.uk*

*W*ellington *C*ountry *P*ark
It's much much more than a family day out

☎ (0118) 9326444

NEWBURY, Berks   Map C6

EC Wed MD Thurs, Sat SEE 16c church, 16c Cloth Hall, St Bartholomew's Hospital (almshouses) Kennet and Avon Canal (barge trips), racecourse
🔲 The Wharf ☎ (01635) 30267
✗ Coopers Arms, Bartholomew St ☎ (01635) 247469

Oakley Farm Caravan Camping Park, Oakley Farm House, Wash Water RG20 0LP ☎ (01635) 36581 OS map 174/455630 2½m SW of Newbury off A34 (Winchester) on A343 Highclere/Wash Common road Open Mar-Oct 30 pitches 3 acres level grass and hard standing 🔲🔲🔲🔲🔲 tennis court £7.50-£9.50 www.oakleyfarm.co.uk

---

OLNEY, Milton Keynes   Map D3

EC Wed MD Thurs *Small town famous for pancake race and as place where Cowper and Newton published the 300 Olney hymns*
✗ Bull, Market Pl ☎ (01234) 355719

Emberton Country Park MK46 5DB ☎ (01234) 711575 *Prop: Milton Keynes Council* OS map 152/886505 1m S of Olney on A509 (Newport Pagnell) beside river Ouse Open Apr-Oct–must book peak periods 315 pitches (115 static) Grass, level, sheltered 🔲✗🔲🔲🔲🔲🔲 fishing, boating (40 acres of lakes), nature trail £11.50-£17.50* (most cards) embertonpark@miltonkeynes.gov.uk www.mkweb.co.uk/embertonpark

---

OXFORD, Oxon   Map C4

MD Wed *Industrial and university city where teaching began in 12c* SEE colleges, High Street, Bodleian library, Ashmolean museum, All Souls College chapel, Radcliffe camera, churches, old inns, towpath walks
🔲 The Old School, Gloucester Green ☎ (01865) 726871
✗ Turf Tavern, Bath Place via St Helens Passage ☎ (01865) 243235

Diamond Farm Caravan Camping Park, Bletchingdon OX5 3DR ☎ (01869) 350909 OS map 164/513169 5m N of Oxford off A423 (Banbury) and A34 (Bicester) on B4027 (Bletchingdon) Open Mar-Oct 37 pitches 4 acres, level grass, sheltered, some hard standing
🔲🔲🔲🔲🔲🔲🔲(heated) 🔲🔲🔲🔲

READING   Map D5

MD Mon, Wed, Fri, Sa *Major county town on river Kennet where ancient centre still stands* SEE art gallery and museum, churches, Mapledurham House 3m NW, Stratfield Saye House 7m S
🔲 Town Hall, Blagrave St ☎ (0118) 956 6226
✗ Butler, Chatham St ☎ (0118) 939 1635

Loddon Court Farm, Beech Hill Road, Spencers Wood RG7 1HT ☎ (0118) 988 3153 OS map 175/710653 4½m S of Reading off A33 (Basingstoke) at Doubles Garage near junction 11 of M4 Open all year 100 pitches (60 static) Grass, level, part sheltered 🔲🔲🔲🔲🔲🔲

Wellington Country Park, Riseley GU17 7TA ☎ (0118) 9326444 Fax (0118) 9323445 OS map 175/724626 6m S of Reading off A33 (Basingstoke) on A32 (Alton) Open all year exc Christmas & New Year 58 pitches Grass, level, part sheltered ✗🔲🔲🔲🔲🔲🔲 £16.00-£25.00* (Mastercard/Switch/Visa) camping@wellington-country-park.co.uk www.wellington-country-park.co.uk

---

STANDLAKE–see Witney

STONY STRATFORD, Bucks   Map D3

EC Thurs SEE Georgian High Street, Cock inn, Grand Union Canal
✗ Stratford, St Paul's Court, High St ☎ (01908) 566577

Cosgrove Leisure Park, Cosgrove MK19 7JP ☎ (01908) 563360 and 562846 OS map 152/798424 2m N of Stony Stratford off A5-A508 (Northampton) via Cosgrove Open Apr-Oct 806 pitches (343 static) 🔲🔲🔲🔲🔲🔲🔲🔲🔲🔲 boating, water skiing

---

FACTS CAN CHANGE
We do our best to check the accuracy of the entries in this guide but changes can and do occur after publication. So if you plan to stay at a site some distance from home it makes sense to ring the manager or owner before setting off.

KEY TO SYMBOLS

♨	shop	∂	gas supplies	⌨	winter storage for caravans
✗	restaurant	⊕	chemical disposal point	℗	parking obligatory
ⵂ	bar	∅	payphone	✤	no dogs
⌁	takeaway food	▱	swimming pool	⛟	caravan hire
⟆	off licence	☻	games area	⌂	bungalow hire
▣	laundrette	⚲	children's playground	♿	facilities for disabled
▨	mains electric hook-ups	⊟	TV	⌀	shaded

WALLINGFORD, Oxon   Map C5
EC Wed MD Fri SEE churches, Thames bridge, town hall, old houses and inns, Flint House museum
▨ Town Hall, St Martins St ☏ (01491) 826972
✗ The Bell, 79 The Street, Crowmarsh Gifford ☏ (01491) 835324

Benson Waterfront, Benson OX10 6SJ ☏ (01491) 838304 OS map 164/175/613916 1½m N of Wallingford off A423 (Oxford) by river Thames Open Apr-Oct 50 pitches (25 static) 4 acres, level grass, sheltered ♨ ✗ ⵂ ⌁ ▣ ∂ ⊕ ∅ boating, fishing (Mastercard/Visa)

Bridge Villa International, Crowmarsh Gifford OX10 8HB ☏ (01491) 836860 *Prop: Lindsay Towsend* OS map 175/612895 ½m E of Wallingford by bridge over river Thames Open Feb-Dec—must book peak periods 111 pitches Grass, level, sheltered ♨ ▨ ∂ ⊕ ∅ ⌨ £11.00-£14.00 (Mastercard/Visa/Delta/Switch) *bridge.villa@btinternet.com*

Riverside Park OX10 8EB ☏ (01491) 835232 and (01865) 341035 OS map 175/612895 ¼m E of Wallingford on A4130 (Henley) by river Thames—best approached from E Open May-Sept—must book 28 pitches Grass, level ∅ ▱ ✤ ♿ boating, fishing

WITNEY, Oxon   Map C4
EC Wed MD Thurs, Sat SEE Blanket Hall, Butter cross, church
▨ Town Hall, Market Sq ☏ (01993) 775802
✗ The Black Horse, 81 High St, Standlake ☏ (01865) 300307

Hardwick Park, Downs Road, Standlake OX29 7PZ ☏ (01865) 300501 *Prop: Hardwick Parks Ltd* OS map 164/392045 4m SE of Witney off A415 (Abingdon) by lake Open Apr-Oct 367 pitches (153 static) Level grass ♨ ✗ ⵂ ▣ ▨ ∂ ⊕ ∅ ⚲ ⵂ ⛟ ♿ lake fishing, swimming, windsurfing, waterskiing, jetskiing £9.50-£11.75 (Mastercard/Visa/Switch) *info@hardwickparks.co.uk* *www.hardwickparks.co.uk*

Lincoln Farm Park, High Street, Standlake OX29 7RH ☏ (01865) 300239 Fax (01865) 300127 OS map 164/394028 5m SE of Witney near junction of A415 (Abingdon) and B4449 (Bampton) Open Feb-Nov 90 pitches Grass and hard standing, level, sheltered ♨ ▣ ▨ ∂ ⊕ ∅ ▱ ⚲ ♿ pitch and putt, leisure centre with pool, spa and sauna £10.70-£17.45* (most cards)

WOKINGHAM, Berks   Map D6
EC Wed MD Tues, Thurs, Fri,
✗ Crooked Billet, Honey Hill (off B3430 2m SE) ☏ (0118) 9733928

California Chalet and Touring Park, Finchampstead RG40 4HU ☏ (01189) 733928 Fax (01189) 328720 OS map 175/785650 3½m SW of Wokingham off A321 (Sandhurst) and B3016 (Finchampstead) Open Mar-Dec 35 pitches Grass and hard standings, level, sheltered ♨ ▣ ▨ ⚲ ⌂ ♿ lake fishing, paddling pool, nature trail £7.00-£15.00* *california.dodd@virgin.net* *www.californiapark.co.uk*

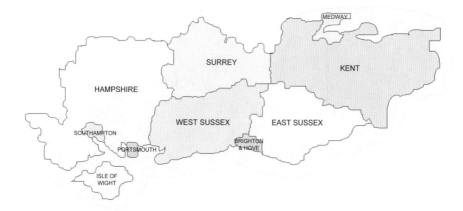

Kent, Surrey, Sussex, Hampshire and the Isle of Wight form the extensive region of Southern England.

The most striking geographical feature of Kent is the North Downs, extending from Greater London to the white cliffs of Dover and broken only by the rivers Medway, Darent and the Stour. The silted-up shore of the Thames Estuary on the north gives Way to the sandy beaches of North Foreland, fronted on one side by Margate and on the other by Ramsgate. Along the south coast, high cliffs alternate with sandbanks and reclaimed saltings like flat and secretive Romney Marsh. Places of interest include the walled city of Canterbury, historic Rochester, the stately home of Knole, Dover Castle and the smugglers' prison of Dymchurch, from which a miniature railway operates as far as Romney.

Romney Marsh crosses the boundary into East Sussex, where the coast is strung with resorts. Stretching across the northern part of the county is the Weald, covered by the great Ashdown Forest southwest of East Grinstead. Backing the western half of the coast between Eastbourne and Brighton are the South Downs, cut by the sea into tall cliffs.

An unusual feature of the coast of West Sussex is the headland of Selsey Bill, south of Chichester. At this point the South Downs are well inland, the coast west of Chichester being indented by tidal creeks and inlets forming a natural harbour. Near Chichester is the Weald and Downland Museum at Singleton, the Roman palace of Fishbourne and the Kingsley Vale Nature Reserve. Historical buildings include the castles of Arundel, Bodlam and ruined Pevensey and

the fanciful Regency Pavilion at Brighton.

Green belt Surrey retains miles of chalk downs and woodlands cut by rich valleys. The North Downs extend east and west, with Box Hill and Leith Hill and the Hog's Back forming the heights. Some of Surrey's most charming villages are Ripley, Shere, Farnham and Brockham Green. Other important sights are the gardens of Wisley, and Polesden Lacey.

The best known natural feature of Hampshire is the New Forest, centred on Lyndhurst, with its chalk uplands, deep woods and sandy wastelands. Guarding the entrance to Southampton Water is the Isle of Wight, twenty-two miles wide and thirteen miles from north to south, wooded down to the water's edge in many places and rising to an east-west ridge of chalk downs. The rural west around Freshwater is probably the most inviting, being less populated. Ferries carrying passengers operate from Portsmouth to Ryde, and carrying cars and passengers from Portsmouth to Fishbourne, Lymington to Yarmouth and Southampton to Cowes. Bus services are comprehensive but the only railway runs between Ryde and Shanklin. Major sights in Hampshire include Osborne House on the Isle of Wight, the castle and magnificent cathedral of Winchester, the maritime museum at Buckler's Hard and Nelson's *Victory* in Portsmouth Dockyard.

Campsites in Southern England are usually well equipped. Biggest concentrations are around Chichester, Lymington and Sandown in the south and Whitstable in the north. Many cater for campers and caravanners going to and from the cross-Channel ports, though few exist at the ports themselves.

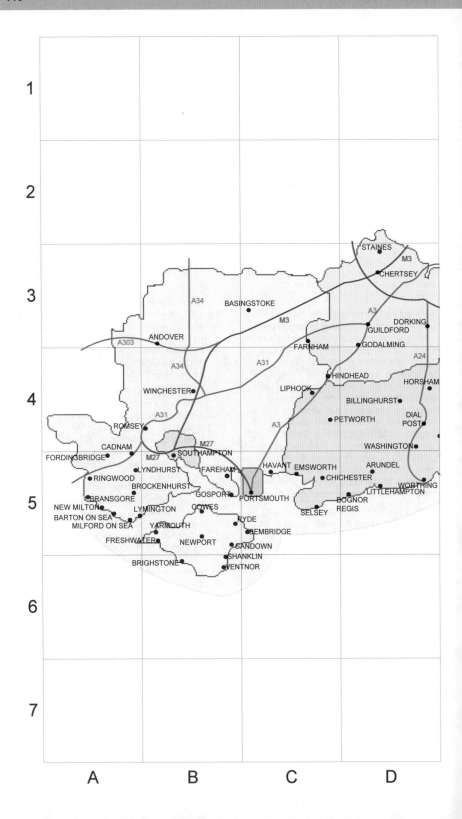

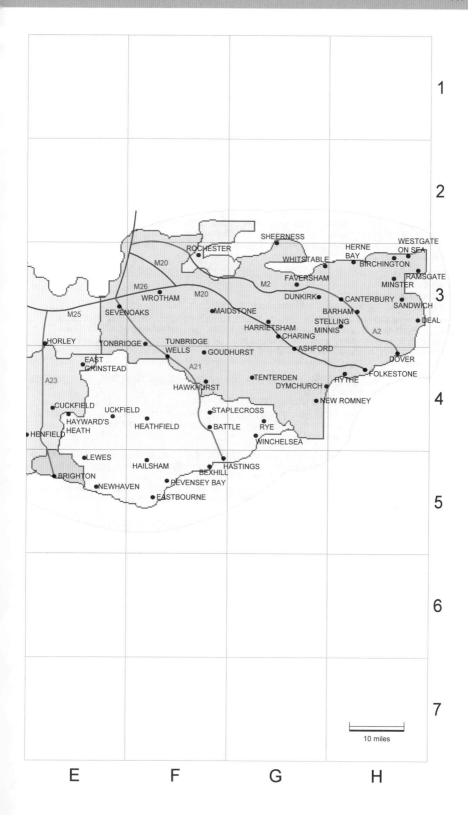

1

2

SHEERNESS

HERNE   WESTGATE
ROCHESTER   BAY   ON SEA
M20   WHITSTABLE   BIRCHINGTON
        FAVERSHAM   RAMSGATE
M26   M2   MINSTER
WROTHAM   M20   DUNKIRK   CANTERBURY   SANDWICH

3

M25   SEVENOAKS   MAIDSTONE   BARHAM   DEAL
                   STELLING
          HARRIETSHAM   MINNIS
HORLEY   CHARING   A2
    TONBRIDGE   TUNBRIDGE
EAST   WELLS   GOUDHURST   ASHFORD   DOVER
GRINSTEAD   FOLKESTONE
A23   A21   TENTERDEN   HYTHE
            HAWKHURST   DYMCHURCH

4

CUCKFIELD   UCKFIELD   STAPLECROSS   NEW ROMNEY
HAYWARD'S   HEATHFIELD   BATTLE   RYE
HENFIELD HEATH   WINCHELSEA

LEWES   HASTINGS
     HAILSHAM   BEXHILL
BRIGHTON   PEVENSEY BAY
NEWHAVEN
      EASTBOURNE

5

6

7

10 miles

E   F   G   H

ANDOVER, Hants   Map B3

EC Wed MD Thurs, Sat SEE Guildhall, church
🖼 Town Mill House, Bridge St ☎(01264) 324320
✖ Globe, High St ☎(01264) 323415

Wyke Down Touring Caravan Camping Park, Picket Piece SP11 6LX ☎(01264) 352048 *Prop: Mr & Mrs P Read* OS map 185/403476 3m E of Andover off A303 (signposted) Open all year 69 pitches Part hard standing, level grass, part sheltered ✖♀-⊷ᗒ◑∅▢⊕↩🗖 golf driving range £12.00-£16.00 (Mastercard/Visa) *p.read@wykedown.co.uk www.wykedown.co.uk*

ARUNDEL, W Sussex   Map D5

EC Wed SEE castle, Swanbourne Lake, St Nicholas church, museum, Wildfowl Trust
🖼 61 High St ☎(01903) 882268
✖ Out & Out, Crossbush ☎(01903) 882655

Maynards Caravan Camping Park, Crossbush BN18 9PQ *Busy site with good access to A27* ☎(01903) 882075 Fax (01903) 885547 *Prop: R Hewitt* OS map 197/035065 ¾m E of Arundel off A27 (Worthing) at restaurant car park Open all year 70 pitches 2½ acres level grass, sheltered 🛒✖♀-⊷ᗒ◑⊕♿

Ship and Anchor Marina, Station Road, Ford BN18 0BJ ☎(01243) 551262 *Prop: Heywood & Bryett Ltd* OS map 197/002040 2½m S of Arundel on Ford road by river Open Mar-Oct 160 pitches 12 acres, level grass, sheltered 🛒✖♀-⊷ᗒ◑∅⊕↩♿ lic premises £11.50-£13.50 *ysm36@dial.pipex.com*

ASHFORD, Kent   Map G4

EC Wed MD Tues, Wed, Sat SEE St Mary church, Windmill, memorial gardens
🖼 The Churchyard ☎(01233) 629165
✖ The Kings Head, Woodchurch Rd, Shadoxhurst ☎(01233) 732243

Broadhembury Caravan and Camping Park, Steeds Lane, Kingsnorth TN26 1NQ ☎(01233) 620859 *Prop: Keith & Jenny Taylor* OS map 189/012381 3m S of Ashford off A2070 (New Romney) in Kingsnorth (M20 junct 10) Open all year 60 pitches (25 static) 5 acres, level grass and hard standing, sheltered 🛒➶🗐ᗒ◑⊕∅⊕↩▢⊑♿ first aid £10.00-£17.00 (Mastercard/Visa) *holidays@broadhembury.co.uk www.broadhembury.co.uk*

BARHAM, Kent   Map H3

EC Wed SEE church, Downs
✖ Dolls House, on Elham Valley Rd (B2065) ☎(01227) 831241

Ropersole Farm, Dover Road CT4 6SA ☎(01227) 831352 OS map 179/228486 1m SE of Barham on southbound carriageway of A2 (Canterbury-Dover) Open Mar-Oct 85 pitches 5 acres, level, woodland setting 🛒✖(snack) ♀ᗒ◑

BARTON ON SEA, Hants   Map A5

EC Wed *Modern resort noted for its low cliffs (haunt of fossil hunters) and sand/shingle beach*
✖ Old Coastguard, Marine Drive East ☎(01425) 612987

Bunny Creek Caravan Park, Milford Rd, New Milton BH25 5PB ☎(01425) 612270 OS map 195/252936 1m E of Barton on Sea on B3058 (Milford on Sea) Open all year 10 pitches 1½ acres level grass ᗒ◑ £9.00-£10.50

BASINGSTOKE, Hants   Map C3

EC Thurs MD Wed, Sat *One-time market town massively expanded by London overspill* SEE 15c church, museum, war memorial park, the Vyne (NT) 3m N, Old Basing 3m E, Steventon (birthplace of Jane Austen) 5m SW
🖼 Willis Museum, Old Town Hall, Market Place ☎(01256) 817618
✖ Bounty, Bounty Rd ☎(01256) 820071

Jolly Farmer Inn, Cliddesden RG25 2JL ☎(01256) 473073 OS map 185/632493 2m S of Basingstoke off A339 (Alton) on right of B3046 (Alresford) in Cliddesden, near junct 6 of M3 Open all year 6 pitches 7 acres level/sloping grass ✖♀⊕∅↩

KEY TO SYMBOLS

🛒	shop	ᗒ	gas supplies	ᗒ	winter storage for caravans
✖	restaurant	⊕	chemical disposal point	🅿	parking obligatory
♀	bar	∅	payphone	⊗	no dogs
-⊷	takeaway food	▢	swimming pool	⊑	caravan hire
➶	off licence	⊕	games area	🏠	bungalow hire
🗐	laundrette	↩	children's playground	♿	facilities for disabled
ᗒ	mains electric hook-ups	▢	TV	◑	shaded

BATTLE, E Sussex   **Map F4**
EC Wed MD Fri SEE Abbey ruins, Deanery, Bull Ring, Langton House museum
🏰 Battle Abbey ✆ (01424) 773721
✗ George, High St ✆ (01424) 774466

Brakes Coppice Park, Forewood Lane, Crowhurst TN33 9AB ✆ (01424) 830322 OS map
   199/765134 2m SE of Battle off A2100 (Hastings) and Crowhurst road Open Mar-Oct
   30 pitches–must book 4 acres, level/gentle slope on woodland estate, grass and hard standing
   🔋📺🍴⊘❋⊘⊖↩🍴 fishing £9.00-£11.50* (Mastercard/Visa/Switch) *brakesco@btinternet.com*

Crazy Lane Tourist Park, Whydown Farm, Crazy Lane, Sedlescombe TN33 0QT ✆ (01424) 870147
   OS map 199/782170 2½m NE of Battle near junction of A21 (Hastings–Hurst Green) and B2244
   (Maidstone) Open Mar-Oct 36 pitches 3 acres, grass, level, sheltered 🔋📺🍴⊘❋⊘🍴♿
   £11.00-£14.00 *www.crazylane.co.uk*

Senlac Park, Main Road, Catsfield TN33 9DU ✆ (01424) 773969 OS map 199/719151 2m W of
   Battle off A269 (Bexhill) on B2204 (Ninfield) Open Mar-Oct 32 pitches Level grass and hard
   standings, sheltered by secluded woodland 🍴⊘❋ heated toilet block (Mastercard/Visa)

Tellis Coppice Touring Caravan Park, Catsfield TN33 9LP ✆ (01424) 773969 OS map
   199/719151 2m W of Battle on A269 (Bexhill) Open Mar-Nov 32 pitches Grass, level, sheltered
   ⊘❋ sep pitches, woodland

BEMBRIDGE, Isle of Wight   **Map C5**
EC Thurs SEE harbour, windmill
✗ Row Barge, Station Rd ✆ (01983) 872874

Carpenters Farm, St Helens PO33 1YL ✆ (01983) 872450 OS map 196/618886 3m W of
   Bembridge off B3330 (Ryde) Open May-Oct 70 pitches Grass, sloping, sheltered 📺🍴⊘❋⊘

Guildford Park Holiday Camping and Caravan Site, Guildford Road, St Helens PO33 1UH
   ✆ (01983) 872821 OS map 196/627893 3m NW of Bembridge off B3330 (Ryde) Open Easter-
   Sep 130 pitches 5 acres, level 🔋⊘❋🗆

Nodes Point Holiday Village, St Helens PO33 1YA ✆ (01983) 872401 Fax (01983) 874696 OS
   map 196/637899 2m NW of Bembridge off B3395–B3340 (Ryde) Open Apr-Oct 500 pitches (211
   static) Grass, sloping 🔋✗🍴📺🍴⊘❋⊘🗁↩✿🏠 £3.00-£24.00* (most cards)
   gm.nodespoint@park-resorts.com www.park-resorts.com

Whitecliff Bay Holiday Park PO35 5PL ✆ (01983) 872671 OS map 196/637867 1½m S of
   Bembridge off B3395 (Sandown) Open Easter-Oct 400 pitches (230 static) Grass, part level hard
   standings 🔋✗🍴↩☇📺🍴⊘❋⊘🗁🗆↩✿🗆🏠♿ lic club, leisure centre, super pitches,
   motorhome dump station £9.20-£15.90 (most cards) *holiday@whitecliff-bay.com www.whitecliff-
   bay.com*

BEXHILL ON SEA, E Sussex   **Map F5**
EC Wed SEE St Peter's church, De la Warr Pavilion, Manor House gardens in Old Town
🏰 De La Warr Pavillion, Marina ✆ (01424) 732208
✗ Southlands Court, Hastings Rd ✆ (01424) 210628

Cobbs Hill Farm, Watermill Lane, Sidley TN39 5JA ✆ (01424) 213460 *Prop: Barry & Lynne Claxton*
   OS map 199/735107 1m N of Bexhill off A269 (Ninfield) on Watermill Lane Open Apr-Oct–must
   book public holidays 55 pitches (15 static) Level grass and hard standing, sheltered
   🔋🍴⊘❋⊘↩🍴🗆 £7.00-£7.80 *cobbshillfarmuk@hotmail.com www.cobbshillfarm.co.uk*

Kloofs Caravan Park, Sandhurst Lane, Whydown TN39 4RG ✆ (01424) 842839 Fax (01424)
   845669 OS map 199/708091 2m W of Bexhill off A259 (Eastbourne) at Little
   Common–signposted Open all year 125 pitches (75 static) 3 acres level/sloping grass and hard
   standing, sheltered 🔋📺🍴⊘❋⊘❋↩🍴🗆🗆♿🔧 heated toilet block £12.50-£15.00*
   camping@kloofs.com www.kloofs.com

BIDDENDEN–see Tenterden

BILLINGSHURST, W Sussex   **Map D4**
EC Wed SEE church
✗ The Olde Six Bells, High St ✆ (01403) 782124

Limeburners Arms Camp site, Newbridge RH14 9JA ✆ (01403) 782311 OS map 197/074255 1½
   W of Billingshurst off A272 (Petworth) on B2133 (Ashington) Open Apr-Oct 42 pitches Grass,
   level, sheltered 🔋✗🍴⊘❋⊘🍴 £10.00 (min)* (Mastercard/Visa/Switch/Delta)

For more up-to-date information, visit our site at: **www.butford.co.uk/camping**

BIRCHINGTON, Kent   **Map H3**
EC Wed SEE DG Rossetti's grave, Quex Park
✗ Seaview, Station Rd ✆ (01843) 841702

Quex Caravan Park, Park Road CT7 0BL ✆ (01843) 841273 OS map 179/310683 1m SE of
  Birchington off A28 (Margate) Open Mar-Oct 208 pitches (120 static) 13½ acres, level grass
  ▮▯▯▯▯▯▯▯▯ £10.00-£15.00* (Mastercard/Visa/Delta/Switch) info@keatfarm.co.uk
  www.keatfarm.co.uk

St Nicholas at Wade Camping, Court Road, St Nicholas at Wade CT7 0NH ✆ (01843) 847245 OS
  map 179/263667 2½m SW of Birchington off A28/A299 (Canterbury) Open Apr-Oct 75 pitches
  Grass, level, sheltered ▮▯▯▯▯ £7.00-£14.00*

Thanet Way Caravan Park, Frost Farm, St Nicholas at Wade CT7 0NA ✆ (01843) 847219 OS map
  179/269671 2m SW of Birchington on A299 (Herne Bay) Open Mar-Oct 60 pitches (48 static)–no
  tents Grass, part level, open ▯▯▯▯▯▯

Two Chimneys Caravan Park, Shottendane Road CT7 0HD ✆ (01843) 841068/843157
  Prop: L Sullivan, A Godden & M Godden OS map 179/320684 2m SE of Birchington off Manston
  road near Two Chimneys Open Mar-Oct 430 pitches (90 static) Grass, level, sheltered
  ▮▯▯▯▯▯▯▯▯▯▯▯▯▯▯ club house, amusements, tennis court £12.00-£20.00
  (Mastercard/Visa/Eurocard) info@twochimneys.co.uk www.twochimneys.co.uk

BODIAM–see Staplecross

BOGNOR REGIS, W Sussex   **Map D5**
EC Wed MD Fri SEE Hotham Park arboretum, Dome House
▯ Place St Maur des Fosses, Belmont St ✆ (01243) 823140
✗ The Olive Branch, North End Rd, Yapton ✆ (01243) 551310

The Lillies Caravan Park, Yapton Rd, Barnham PO22 0AY ✆ (01243) 552081 Fax (01243) 552081
  Prop: Mr & Mrs PJ Kennett OS map 197/963041 4m N of Bognor Regis on B2233 (Eastergate-
  Climping) in Barnham Open all year 40 pitches Level grass and hard standing, sheltered
  ▮▯▯▯▯▯▯▯▯▯ £10.00-£14.00* (most cards) thelillies@hotmail.com
  www.lilliescaravanpark.co.uk

BOLNEY–see Haywards Heath

BRANSGORE, Hants   **Map A5**
SEE church, New Forest ✗ Three Tuns, Ringwood Rd ✆ (01425) 672232

Harrow Wood Farm, Poplar Lane BH23 8JE ✆ (01425) 672487 Prop: Richard Frampton OS map
  195/193978 ¼m SE of Bransgore off Hinton Admiral road Open Mar-Dec 60 pitches 6 acres,
  hard standings ▯▯▯▯▯▯▯ £11.50-£16.50 (Mastercard/Visa) harrowwood@caravan-
  sites.co.uk www.caravan-sites.co.uk

Heathfield Caravan Park BH23 8LA ✆ (01425) 672397 OS map 195/208895 1½m E of Bransgore
  off Hinton Admiral road Open Mar-Oct 200 pitches–must book peak periods 14 acres, level grass
  and hard standings ▮▯▯▯▯▯▯ farm produce

Holmsley Campsite (Forestry Commission), Forest Road, Thorney Hill BH23 7EQ ✆ (0131) 314
  6505 OS map 195/215991 2m E of Bransgore on A35 (Southampton-Christchurch) Open Mar
  20-Nov 2 700 pitches 89 acres level mainly open ▮▯▯▯▯▯▯▯▯ (Mastercard/Visa)

BRIGHSTONE, Isle of Wight   **Map B6**
✗ Wight Mouse Inn 6m SE at Chale ✆ (01983) 730431

Chine Farm Camping, Military Road, Atherfield Bay PO38 2JH ✆ (01983) 740228 Prop: HM Goody
  OS map 196/445804 2m SE of Brighstone on A3055 (Ventnor) Open May-Sept 80 pitches
  Grass, level, open ▯▯▯▯ beach £7.00-£10.00 www.chinefarm.co.uk

Grange Farm Brighstone Bay PO30 4DA ✆ (01983) 740296 OS map 196/420820 1m SW of
  Brighstone on A3055 (Freshwater–Ventnor) Open Mar-Oct 60 pitches Grass, level, open
  ▮▯▯▯▯▯▯▯▯▯ (most cards)

BROCKENHURST, Hants　　　　　　　　　　　　　　　　　　　**Map A5**
EC Wed　SEE parish church, New Forest
✗ Snakecatcher, Lyndhurst Rd　☏(01590) 622348

Hollands Wood Campsite (Forestry Commission), Lyndhurst Road SO42 7QH　☏(01703) 283771
　　OS map 196/303034　½m N of Brockenhurst on A337 (Lyndhurst) near Balmer Lawn Hotel
　　Open Mar 21-Sept 29　600 pitches　168 acres level oak woodland 🗑⊕∅

CADNAM, Hants　　　　　　　　　　　　　　　　　　　　　**Map A5**
EC Wed　SEE Rufus Stone
✗ Bell Inn 1m W at Brook　☏(01703) 812214

Ocknell Camping, Fritham SO43 7HH　☏(01703) 813771　OS map 195/255127　3m SW of Cadnam
　　off A31 (Ringwood) at Stoney Cross–access for westbound traffic only via A3078 (Fordingbridge) &
　　Brook　Open Easter-Sept　300 pitches　🖉⊕∅

CAMBER SANDS–see Rye

CANTERBURY, Kent　　　　　　　　　　　　　　　　　　　**Map H3**
EC Thurs MD Wed, (cattle Mon)　SEE Cathedral, churches, King's School, Eastbridge Hospital
(almshouses), city walls, Dane John gardens, castle keep, museum
🛈 12-13 Sun St, The Buttermarket　☏(01227) 378100
✗ The Chequers Inn, Stone St　☏(01227) 700734

Yew Tree Park, Stone Street, Petham CT4 5PL　☏(01227) 700306　*Prop: D Zanders*　OS map
　　179/137508　5 m S of Canterbury off B2068 (Hythe) by Chequers Inn　Open Mar-Oct　45 pitches
　　4 acres, grass, level/sloping 🗑🏠🖉⊕∅⌧⤙⊗🚐🏠🛆　£11.00 (Mastercard/Visa)
　　info@yewtreepark.com www.yewtreepark.com

CAPEL LE FERNE–see Folkestone

CHARING, Kent　　　　　　　　　　　　　　　　　　　　　**Map G3**
SEE North Downs Way SE
✗ Red Lion 1m W at Charing Heath　☏(01233) 712418

Dean Court Farm, Westwell TN25 4NH　☏(01233) 712924　OS map 189/950489　2m E of Charing
　　off A252 (Canterbury) at Challock on Westwell Lane　Open all year　20 pitches　Level/sloping grass
　　⊕　*No showers*

CHATHAM–see Rochester

CHICHESTER, W Sussex　　　　　　　　　　　　　　　　　**Map C5**
EC Thurs MD Wed, Sat　*One-time Roman town, still with its ancient street pattern*　SEE cathedral,
market cross, city walls, Council House (corporation plate), Greyfriars monastery ruins, Festival
Theatre, Roman Palace and Theatre at Fishbourne
🛈 29a South St　☏(01243) 775888
✗ Bell Inn, Bell Lane, Birdham　☏(01243) 514338　Open 12-3/6-9.30

Bell Caravan Park, Bell Lane, Birdham PO20 7HY　☏(01243) 512264　OS map 197/819992　4½m
　　SW of Chichester off A268 (West Wittering) on B2198 (Bracklesham)　Open Mar-Oct　75 pitches
　　(60 static)　Level grass, sheltered 🏠🖉⊕∅　£13.00

Gees Camp, Stocks Lane, East Wittering PO20 8NY　(01243) 670223　6m SW of Chichester on
　　A286/B2198 (Bracklesham)　Open Mar-Oct　25 pitches　1 acre, level grass, sheltered 🏠⊕🏠🅿

Nunnington Farm, West Wittering PO20 8LZ　OS map 197/787988　6m SW of Chichester off A286
　　(West Wittering)　Open Easter-Oct–no adv booking　112 pitches–couples and families only　Grass,
　　level, part sheltered 🛒🗑🖉⊕

Red House Farm Camping Site, Bookers Lane, Earnley PO20 7JG　☏(01243) 512959　*Prop: E
　　Clay*　OS map 197/815979　5m SW of Chichester off B2198 (Bracklesham Bay)　Open Easter-Oct
　　80 pitches　Grass, level 🏠⊕∅🕀🛆　£12.00-£14.00　*clayredhouse@hotmail.com*

Southern Leisure Centre, Vinnetrow Road PO19 6LB　*Big touring site in rural setting surrounded by
　　several lakes*　☏(01243) 787715　OS map 197/878039　1½m SE of Chichester off junction of A259
　　(Bognor) and A27 on Pagham road　Open Mar-Oct　1500 pitches　Grass, level, sheltered
　　🛒🍴⤙🏠🖉∅⌧(heated) 🕀🍴　fishing, water skiing

Wicks Farm Camping Park, Redlands Lane, West Wittering PO20 8QD　☏(01243) 513116　*Prop: R
　　Shrubb*　OS map 197/797996　5m SW of Chichester off A286/B2179 (West Wittering)　Open Mar-
　　Oct　44 pitches　Grass, level, sheltered 🛒🗑🖉⊕∅🕀⤙　tennis court　£13.00-£18.50
　　(most cards)　*www.wicksfarm.co.uk*

COWES, Isle of Wight   **Map B5**
EC Wed SEE Osborne House (royal apartments), Cowes Castle, Whippingham church 2m SE
⚹The Arcade, Fountain Quay ☏(01983) 813818
✗Waverley Park Holiday Centre, 51 Old Rd, East Cowes ☏(01983) 293452

Comforts Farm, Pallance Road, Northwood PO31 8LS ☏(01983) 293888 OS map 196/478938
1m SW of Cowes off A3020 (Newport) Open Mar-Oct 55 pitches Grass, part level, part sheltered
🅿🗑⌀⟁⊙🚻 horse riding school

Gurnard Pines Holiday Village, Cockleton Lane, Gurnard PO31 8QE ☏(01983) 292395 OS map
196/470950 1m SW of Cowes off B3325 (Northwood) Open Mar-Nov (camping), all year (village)
155 pitches 🅿✗🍴⎯🗑🍹⌀⊙⟁🍽⊙⤳❀🏪🏠♿ lic club/bar

Thorness Bay Holiday Park, Thorness PO31 8NJ ☏(01983) 523109 Fax (01983) 822213 OS map
196/452927 1m SW of Cowes off A3020 (Newport) on Thorness road Open Easter-Oct
458 pitches (258 static) 🅿✗🍴⎯🗑🍹⌀⊙⟁🍽⊙⤳🏪🏠 lic club, riding school, beach access
(most cards) holidaysales.thornessbay@park-resorts.com www.park-resorts.com

Waverley Park, Old Road, East Cowes PO32 6AW ☏(01983) 293452 Prop: Peter & Susan Adams
OS map 196/505958 ¼m E of Cowes off A3021 (Newport) Open Mar-Oct 126 pitches (81 static)
12 acres sloping grass ✗🍴🗑🍹⌀⟁⌀🍽⊙⤳⤳🏪🏠♿ club house £11.00-£15.50 inc elect
(most cards) sue@waverley-park.co.uk www.waverley-park.co.uk

CROWBOROUGH–see Tunbridge Wells

CROWHURST–see Battle

DEAL, Kent   **Map H3**
EC Thurs MD Sat SEE churches, lifeboat station, Deal castle, Walmer castle
⚹Deal Library, Broad St ☏(01304) 369576
✗Trogs, 114 High St ☏(01304) 374089

Clifford Park, Thompson Close, Walmer CT14 7PB ☏(01304) 373373 OS map 179/366499 2m S
of Deal on right of A258 (Dover) Open Mar-Oct 174 pitches (161 static) 9 acres level grass and
hard standings sheltered 🍹⌀⟁⌀❀

Sutton Vale Caravan Park, Sutton CT15 5DH ☏(01304) 366233 OS map 179/339496 3m SW of
Deal off A258 (Dover) Open Mar-Jan–must book peak periods 121 pitches–no tents Level grass
and hard standings, sheltered 🅿✗🗑🍹⌀⊙⌀🍽⊙🚻🅿 lic club (Mastercard/Delta/Switch)
office@suttonvale.co.uk www.suttonvale.co.uk

DENSOLE–see Folkestone

DIAL POST, W Sussex   **Map D4**
✗Red Lion 2m S at Ashington ☏(01903) 892226

Honeybridge Park, Honeybridge Lane RH13 8NX ☏(01403) 710923 Fax (01403) 710923 OS map
198/153184 ¼m SE of Dial Post off A24 (Worthing) on Ashurst road Open all year 100 pitches
15 acres level grass and hard standing, sheltered 🅿🗑🍹⌀⊙⌀⊙⤳🅿♿ £13.00-£20.00* (most
cards) enquiries@honeybridgepark.co.uk www.honeybridgepark.co.uk

DOVER, Kent   **Map H4**
EC Wed MD Sat SEE castle, Roman lighthouse, church, town hall, museum
⚹Old Town Gaol, Biggin St ☏(01304) 205108
✗Blakes, Castle St (near market square) ☏(01304) 202194

Hawthorn Farm International, Martin Mill CT15 5LA ☏(01304) 852658 OS map 179/341465 4m
NNE of Dover off A258 (Deal) near Martin Mill station Open Mar-Oct–no adv booking 410 pitches
(160 static) Grass, sheltered 🅿⎯➶🗑🍹⌀⊙⌀ rose garden (Mastercard/Visa)
For other sites near Dover see Folkestone and Hythe

DUNKIRK, Kent   **Map G3**
✘ White Horse 1½m W at Boughton Street ☎ (01227) 751343

Red Lion, Old London Road ME13 9LL ☎ (01227) 750661 OS map 179/084489 ½m E of Dunkirk on left of old A2 (Canterbury)–access via A2 Open Mar-Oct 25 pitches–no tents 1 acre, level grass, sheltered ✘ (snack), ♀⊟◉◪ farm shop

DYMCHURCH, Kent   **Map G4**
EC Wed *Modest family resort backing sandy beach* SEE 12c church, Smugglers Inn, Martello Towers, Romney, Hythe and Dymchurch railway
✘ Ship Inn, High St ☎ (01303) 872122

New Beach Touring Park, Hythe Rd TN29 0JX ☎ (01303) 872234 OS map 189/110303 ½m NE of Dymchurch on right of A259 (Hythe) near beach Open Mar 1-Jan 11 250 pitches Level grass
⚑✘♀⇠⊟⊟∅◉⊘◻(indoor) ↵

EASTBOURNE–see Pevensey Bay

EAST GRINSTEAD, W Sussex   **Map E4**
EC Wed MD Sat SEE Sackville College (17c almshouses) museum, High Street, St Swithin's church
✘ The Old Cage 3m N at Lingfield ☎ (01342) 834271

Long Acres Farm Caravan Park, Newchapel Road, Lingfield RH7 6LE ☎ (01342) 833205 *Prop: J Pilkington* OS map 187/368425 3m NW of East Grinstead off A22 (Croydon) on B2028 (Lingfield) Open all year 60 pitches 20 acres level grass and hard standings sheltered
⚑⇠⊟⊟∅◉⊘↵◪ fishing £11.50

FAVERSHAM, Kent   **Map G3**
EC Thurs MD Wed, Fri, Sat SEE town hall, houses in Abbey St, Globe House
ℹ Fleur de Lis Heritage Centre, Preston St ☎ (01795) 534542
✘ Read 2m S at Painters Forstal ☎ (01795) 535344

Painters Farm Caravan Camping Park, Painters Farm, Painters Forstal ME13 0EG ☎ (01795) 532995 OS map 178/990591 2m SW of Faversham off A2 (London–Canterbury) on Painters Forstal road Open Mar-Oct 50 pitches Grass, level, part sheltered ⚑⊟⊟∅◉

FOLKESTONE, Kent   **Map H4**
EC Wed MD Thurs, Sun SEE St Mary's church, Kingsworth gardens, The Leas, New Metropole arts centre
ℹ Harbour St ☎ (01303) 258594
✘ Paul's, Bouverie Rd West ☎ (01303) 259697

Black Horse Farm, Densole, Swingfield CT18 7BG ☎ (01303) 892665 OS map 179/211418 4m N of Folkestone on left of A260 (Canterbury) in Densole near Black Horse Inn Open all year 126 pitches Grass and hard standing, level, part open ⚑⤳⊟⊟∅◉⊘◪⚲ (Mastercard/Visa/Switch/Delta)

Little Satmar Holiday Park, Winehouse Lane, Capel le Ferne CT18 7JF ☎ (01303) 251188 Fax (01303) 251188 OS map 179/256392 2½m NE of Folkestone off B2011 (Dover) just past Capel le Ferne Open Mar-Oct 110 pitches (70 static) Level grass ⚑⇠⊟⊟∅◉⊘⊛↵◪▱ games room £10.00-£15.00* (Mastercard/Visa/Delta/Switch) *info@keatfarm.co.uk www.keatfarm.co.uk/touringparks/littlesatmar.htm*

Little Switzerland Camping Caravan Park, off Wear Bay Road CT19 6PS ☎ (01303) 252168 OS map 179/243375 1m E of Folkestone off A20 (Dover) via Wear Bay road Mar-Oct–must book peak periods 32 pitches Grass, level, sheltered ⚑✘♀⇠⊟⊟∅◉⊘ *littleswitzerland@lineone.net www.caravancampingsites.co.uk*

Varne Ridge Caravan Park, 145 Old Dover Road, Capel le Ferne CT18 7HX ☎ (01303) 251765 OS map 179/260390 4m E of Folkestone off B2011 (Dover) Open Mar-Nov 18 pitches (12 static)–no tents Level grass ⊟⊟∅◉⊘▱

Warren Camping Site, The Warren CT19 6PT ☎ (01303) 255093 OS map 179/246376 1m E of Folkestone off A20 (Dover) and road to harbour Open Apr-Sept 82 pitches–no trailer caravans ⚑⊟◉

White Cliffs Park, New Dover Road, Capel le Ferne CT18 7JA ☎ (01303) 250192 OS map 179/245383 3m NE of Folkestone on A20 (Dover) Open Feb-Jan 289 pitches (138 static) Level/sloping grass, hard standings, sheltered ⚑⊟⊟∅◉⊘◪

See also Hythe

FORDINGBRIDGE, Hants   **Map A5**
EC Thurs SEE Augustus John statue, Breamore House 3m N
ℹ Salisbury St ☎ (01425) 654560
✘ Ashburn, Station Rd ☎ (01725) 652060

Sandy Balls Holiday Centre, Godshill SP6 2JZ *Mainly wooded site central for walking and touring* ☎ (01425) 653042 *Prop: Sandy Balls Estate* OS map 195/169146 2m NE of Fordingbridge off B3078 (Cadnam) Open all year 357 pitches (122 static) Hard standing, level, sheltered ⚑✘♀⇠⤳⊟⊟∅◉⊘◻(indoor/outdoor) ⊛↵▱🏠⛋ fishing, horse riding, cycle hire £14.00-£28.00 (Mastercard/Visa) *post@sandy-balls.co.uk www.sandy-balls.co.uk*

A family run park very close to the sea. Club, restaurant, children's games room. Tel: 02392 502611 **Kingfisher Park**

GODALMING, Surrey   **Map D3**
EC Wed MD Fri SEE Charterhouse School, church, local interest museum, Winkworth Arboretum 2m SE
✘The Red Lion, Portsmouth Rd, Milford ✆(01483) 424342

The Merry Harriers Camping and Caravan Site, Hambledon GU8 4DR ✆(01428) 682883 *Prop:
Colin Beasley* OS map 186/965380 4m S of Godalming off B3100 (Milford) via Milford Station and
Hydestile Open all year 20 pitches 1 acre level grass ♀❷♥∅↩ pub food £6.00
(Mastercard/Visa/Maestro)

GOSPORT, Hants   **Map B5**
EC Wed MD Tues SEE 17c Holy Trinity church, Submarine Museum
🅵Bus Station Complex, South St ✆0239 252 2944
✘Old Lodge near sea at Alverstoke ✆(01705) 581865

Kingfisher Park, Browndown Road, Stokes Bay PO13 9BE ✆(02392) 502611 *Prop: R Davies* OS
map 196/585993 2m W of Gosport centre off B3333 (Lee on Solent) Open all year 220 pitches
(100 static) Level grass and hard standing ⚓✘♀↩⤴♪❶∅❷❷❸▢⚏♿ £10.00-£19.00
(Visa) info@kingfisher-caravan-park.co.uk www.kingfisher-caravan-park.co.uk

GOUDHURST, Kent   **Map F4**
EC Wed SEE parish church, Bedgebury Nat Pinetum 2½m S
✘Star and Eagle, High St ✆(01580) 211512

Tanner Farm Park, Goudhurst Road, Marden TN12 9ND ✆(01622) 832399 OS map 188/734414
3m N of Goudhurst on left of B2079 (Marden) Open all year 100 pitches–must book Jun-Sep
15 acres, grass and hard standing, level/sloping, part sheltered ⚓❶❷∅❸♥↩♿♿
(Mastercard/Visa/Delta/Switch)

HAILSHAM, E Sussex   **Map F5**
EC Thurs MD Wed SEE church, Michelham Priory 2m SW
✘Golden Cross Inn ✆(01825) 872216

Old Mill Holiday Park, Chalvington Road, Golden Cross BN27 3SS ✆(01825) 872532 *Prop: Lucy
& James Clow* OS map 199/541139 4m NW of Hailsham off A22 (East Grinstead) before Golden
Cross Inn Open Apr-Oct 26 pitches (18 static) Grass, sheltered ❷∅❸🏠 £9.00-£12.50
lucy@jasminewindmill.com www.jasminewindmill.com

Peel House Farm Caravan Park, Polegate BN26 6QX ✆(01323) 845629 Fax (01323) 845629 OS
map 199/592070 1m S of Hailsham on B2104 (Friday Street) Open Mar-Oct 20 pitches Level
grass, sheltered ⚓❶❷∅❸∅⚏ garden produce, games room £4.00-£12.00*
peelhocp@tesco.net

HAMBLE–see Southampton

HARRIETSHAM, Kent   **Map G3**
✘Harrow Inn 4m SE at Lenham ✆(01622) 858727

Hogbarn Caravan Park, Hogbarn Lane ME17 1NZ ✆(01622) 859648 OS map 189/884550 2m
NE of Harrietsham on right of Frinsted road Open Apr-mid Oct 200 pitches (80 static) Grass and
hard standing ❶❷∅❸▢(indoor)❹ lounge

HASTINGS, E Sussex   **Map F5**
EC Wed MD Wed, Sat SEE castle ruins, museum, St Clement's caves, Fisherman's church,
Hastings Historical Embroidery, Fishermen's museum, country park
🅵Queens Sq ✆(01424) 781111 ✘Roser's, Eversfield Pl ✆(01424) 712218

Carters Farm, Pett TN35 4JD ✆(01424) 813206 OS map 199/884144 5½m E of Hastings off
A259 (Rye) via Pett Open Mar-Oct 100 pitches–no adv booking Grass, part level, part sheltered
⚓❶∅❸∅

Shear Barn Holiday Park, Barley Lane TN35 5DX ✆(01424) 423583 OS map 199/842107 1½m E
of Hastings off A259 (Rye) Open Mar-Jan 750 pitches (200 static) Grass, part level
⚓↩⤴❶∅❸∅❹❺(£2/wk) ⚏ lic club £6.50-£17.50 (Mastercard/Visa) www.haulfryn.co.uk

Spindlewood Country Holiday Park, Rock Lane, Ore TN35 4JN ✆(01424) 720825 OS map
199/835120 1½m NE of Hastings off A259 (Rye) on left of Three Oaks road (Rock Lane) Open
Mar-Oct 125 pitches (75 static) 14 acres level grass, sheltered ✘♀❶❷∅❸∅⚏ fishing lake
(Mastercard/Visa)

Stalkhurst Camping, Stalkhurst Cottage, Ivyhouse Lane TN35 4NN ✆(01424) 439015 Fax (01424)
445206 OS map 199/829123 2½m NE of Hastings off A259 (Rye) and B2093 (Baldslow)
Open Mar 1-Jan 15–booking advised 39 pitches Grass, sloping, sheltered ⚓❷∅❸▢❹❺⚏
table tennis

HAVANT, Hants   **Map C5**
EC Wed MD Tues, Sat SEE parish church, old houses
🛈 1 Park Rd South ☎ 0239 248 0024
✖ Yew Tree Inn, 42 Havant Rd, Hayling Island ☎ 023 9246 5258

Fishery Creek Park, Fishery Lane, Hayling Island PO11 9NR ☎(02392) 462164 OS map
197/736987 5m S of Havant off A3023 (Hayling Island) via Church Road Open Mar-Oct
165 pitches–families only 7½ acres level grass 🛒✖⚡🔌🅿🚿🏪🅿🎣🚽🚻♿ boat storage, tidal
slipway, games room (Delta/Switch)

Fleet Farm, Yewtree Road, Hayling Island PO11 0QE ☎(02392) 463684 *Prop: CS Good* OS map
197/727017 4m S of Havant off A3023 at Yew Tree Inn Open Mar-Oct 75 pitches Hard
standings and grass, level, part sheltered, 🛒⚡🔌🚿🅿🅿 boat launch £10.00
www.haylingcampsites.co.uk

Lower Tye Family Campsite, Copse Lane, Hayling Island PO11 0RQ ☎(02392) 462479 *Prop: Zita
Good* OS map 197/731020 4m S of Havant off A3023 Open Mar-Nov 175 pitches Grass, level,
sheltered 🚿⚡🔌🚽🅿🎣🅿🚻 year round parking £11.75 *lowertye@aol.com*
www.haylingcampingsites.co.uk

Oven Camping Site, Manor Road, South Hayling PO11 0QX ☎(02392) 464695 OS map
197/719005 4½m S of Havant off A3023 at Mill Rythe roundabout Open Mar-Jan 300 pitches
Grass level, part sheltered 🛒⚡🚿🔌🅿🎣🚿(heated) 🎣🚽🏪♿ games room

HAYLING ISLAND–see Havant

HEATHFIELD, E Sussex   **Map F4**
SEE Gibraltar Tower, parish church
✖ The May Garland Inn, Horam ☎(01435) 812249 Open summer Mon-Thu 11-3/6-9, Sat-Sun all
day; winter 11-3/6-9

Greenviews Caravan Park, Broad Oak TN21 8RT ☎(01435) 863531 Fax (01435) 863531 OS map
199/597219 1m E of Heathfield on A265 (Hawkhurst) Open Apr-Oct 60 pitches (50 static) Grass,
level, open 🍴🚿⚡🔌🚿♿ club house

Horam Manor Touring Park, Horam TN21 0YD ☎(01435) 813662 OS map 199/576173 3m S of
Heathfield on A267 (Eastbourne) Open Mar-Oct 90 pitches–booking advisable 7 acres
level/sloping grass, sheltered 🚿⚡🔌🚿🅿🎣 £12.50 *camp@horam-manor.co.uk www.horam-manor.co.uk*

HENFIELD, W Sussex   **Map E4**
✖ Shepherd and Dog 4m SE via A281 at Fulking ☎(01273) 857382

Downsview Caravan Park, Bramlands Lane, Woodmancote BN5 9TG ☎(01273) 492801 Fax
(01273) 495214 OS map 198/238138 2m SE of Henfield off A281 (Brighton) Open Apr-Oct
57 pitches–no facs for children Grass and hard standing, level, sheltered 🛒🚿⚡🔌🚿🅿 £9.00-
£16.00* inc elect (most cards) *phr.peter@lineone.net*

HERNE BAY, Kent   **Map H3**
EC Thurs MD Sat SEE remains of Roman fort at Reculver, clock tower, windmill
🛈 Central Parade ☎(01227) 361911
✖ L'Escargot, High St ☎(01227) 372876

Southview Caravan Park, Maypole Lane, Hoath CT3 4LL ☎(01227) 860280 OS map 179/203647
2½m SE of Herne Bay off A299 (Thanet Way) via Maypole Open Apr-Oct 45 pitches Grass,
level, hard standings, sheltered 🚿⚡🔌♿(Jul-Aug) 🅿♿ £14.00-£16.00
southviewcamping@aol.com

HINDHEAD, Surrey   **Map C4**
SEE Devil's Punchbowl 1m E Waggoners Wells (NT) 2m SW, Frensham Common 3m N
✖ Devil's Punchbowl, London Road ☎(01428) 606565

Symondstone Farm, Churt GU10 2QL ☎(01428) 712090 OS map 186/844389 2½m NW of
Hindhead off A287 (Farnham) Open Apr-Oct 70 pitches 8 acres, part sloping 🔌🚿 *No showers*

HOLLINGBOURNE–see Maidstone

HORSHAM, W Sussex   Map D4
EC Thurs SEE St Mary's church, North chapel, museum, Leonardslee gardens 4m SE
🄸9 Causeway ✆(01403) 211661
✘Olde King's Head, Carfax ✆(01403) 753126

Raylands Caravan Park, Jackrells Lane, Southwater RH13 7DH ✆(01403) 731822 and 730218
OS map 198/170265 3m S of Horsham off A24 (Worthing) and Copsale road Open Mar-Oct
145 pitches (65 static) Grass, level, sheltered ✘🖾🛱🖉🛇🕀⛬ tennis, bar/clubhouse at
weekends (Mastercard/Visa)

HYTHE, Kent   Map H4
EC Wed SEE St Leonard's church and crypt, Romney, Hythe and Dymchurch light railway, military
canal, zoo park and gardens at Lympne 2m W
🄸Red Lion Sq ✆(01303) 267799
✘Stade Court, West Par ✆(01303) 268263

Folkestone Racecourse, Westenhanger CT21 4HX ✆(01303) 261761 (8am-8pm) OS map
179/128370 2m NW of Hythe off A20 (Maidstone-Dover) and B2068 (Canterbury) Open Mar 26-
Oct 4 50 pitches Level grass, open 🛱🖉🛇 free access to racing (Mastercard/Visa)

ISLE OF WIGHT–see Bembridge, Cowes, Freshwater, Newport, Ryde, Sandown, Shanklin,
Ventnor, Yarmouth

LEWES–see Newhaven

LEYSDOWN–see Sheerness

LINGFIELD–see East Grinstead

LITTLEHAMPTON, W Sussex   Map D5
EC Wed MD Fri, Sat SEE museum, miniature railway, mill and church at Clymping 2m W
🄸The Look & Sea Centre ✆(01903) 721866
✘The Locomotive, 74 Lyminster Rd ✆(01903) 716658

Rutherfords Touring Park, Cornfield Close, Worthing Road BN17 6LD Central site with clean safe
beach for children ✆(01903) 714240 Fax (01903) 714240 OS map 197/043030 In Littlehampton
on A259 (Worthing) Open all year 80 pitches 6 acres level grass 🖳🖾🛱🖉🕀🛇🕀💦🖴🅿 tennis,
badminton

White Rose Touring Park, Mill Lane, Wick BN17 7PH ✆(01903) 716176 Prop: Mr & Mrs D
Snowdon OS map 197/043029 1½m N of Littlehampton on A284 (Arundel) Open Mar-
Dec–booking public holidays essential 140 pitches 6 acres, level grass 🖳🖾🛱🖉🕀🛇🕀💦🖪🕭
serviced pitches (1000 sq ft), seasonal pitches avail £12.00-£18.00 (Mastercard/Visa)
snowdondavid@hotmail.com www.whiterosetouringpark.co.uk

LYNDHURST, Hants   Map A5
EC Wed SEE church, Queen's House, New Forest
🄸New Forest Museum, Main Car Park ✆0238 028 2269
✘Mailmans Arms, High St ✆(01703) 284196

Ashurst Campsite, Lyndhurst Road, Ashurst SO42 2AA ✆(01703) 283771 OS map 196/332102 2
NE of Lyndhurst on A35 (Southampton) Open Easter-Oct–booking public holidays advisable 280
pitches 🖾🖉🕀🛇🕭(exc Oct) 🕭 Level, part sheltered

Decoy Pond Farm, Beaulieu Rd SO42 7YQ Simple site in heart of New Forest ✆(02380) 292652
OS map 196/356073 3m E of Lyndhurst off B3056 (Beaulieu) after bridge Open Mar-Oct
4 pitches ½ acre level grass 🛱🕀

MAIDSTONE, Kent   Map F3
EC Wed MD Mon, Tues SEE All Saints church, Carriage Museum, Leeds castle 1m SW
🄸Town Hall, Middle Row ✆(01622) 602169
✘Grange Moor, St Michael's Road ✆(01622) 677623

Cold Blow Camping, Cold Blow Lane, Thurnham ME14 3LR ✆(01622) 735038 OS map
188/805578 2m NE of Maidstone off A249 (Sittingbourne) near junct 7 of M20 adj North Downs
Way Open all year 10 pitches Level grass and hard standing 🖾🛱🖉🕀🛇🕿 self-catering, B&B,
camping barn

Pine Lodge Caravan Park, Ashford Road, Hollingbourne ME17 1XH ✆(01622) 730018 Fax
(01622) 734498 OS map 188/818549 5m SE of Maidstone on A20 (Ashford) near junct 8 of M20
Open all year 100 pitches Level grass and hard standings 🖳🖾🛱🖉🕀🛇💦🕭🕭 £10.00-
£14.25* (most cards) booking@pinelodgetouringpark.co.uk www.pinelodgetouring.co.uk

NEW FOREST–see Bransgore, Brockenhurst, Cadnam, Fordingbridge, Lymington, Lyndhurst,
Milford on Sea, New Milton, Ringwood

NEWHAVEN, E Sussex   Map E5
EC Wed SEE St Michael's church, Fort Museum, cliffs
✘Hope Inn, West Pier ☎(01273) 515389

Buckle Caravan Camping Park, Marine Parade, Seaford BN25 2QR ☎(01323) 897801 Fax
(01323) 873767 OS map 198/467998 1½m SE of Newhaven off A259 (Eastbourne) at Abbots
Lodge Motel adj beach Open Mar 1-Jan 2 150 pitches 9 acres, level grass and hard standings
🔋🗑🚿⊕∅🚰 adults-only section available

Rushey Hill Caravan Park, The Highway BN9 8XH ☎(01273) 582344 OS map 198/425007 1½m
W of Newhaven centre off A259 (Brighton) at Brighton Motel Open Mar-Oct 297 pitches
(250 static)–no trailer caravans 15 acres, grass, sloping 🗑🚰🚐

NEW MILTON, Hants   Map A5
EC Wed SEE parish church
✘Cliff House 2m S at Barton on Sea ☎(01425) 619333

Bashley Park, Sway Road BH25 5QR ☎(01425) 612340 OS map 195/249969 1½m N of New
Milton off B3058 (Wootton) on B3055 (Sway) Open Mar-Oct–must book 420 pitches (350 static)
Hard standing, level, sheltered 🔋✘🚮🗑🚿🗑⊕∅🏊🎮😊🛝🖵🚐 lic club/bar, golf, snooker/pool,
table tennis, indoor leisure complex and outdoor pool

See also Barton on Sea

NEW ROMNEY, Kent   Map G4
EC Wed SEE church, ruined priory, Romney, Hythe and Dymchurch Light Railway
✘Blue Dolphins, Dymchurch Rd ☎(01797) 363224

Marlie Farm Holiday Village, Dymchurch Road TN28 8UE ☎(01797) 363060 OS map 189/075263
¼m E of New Romney on A259 (Hythe) Open Mar-Oct 450 pitches (250 static) Grass and hard
standing, level, part sheltered 🔋✘(snack) 🍺🚮🗑🗑🚿🗑⊕∅🏊😊🛝🖵🚐🚐♿

OWER–see Romsey

PETT–see Hastings

PEVENSEY BAY, E Sussex   Map F5
EC Thurs SEE parish church, Old Court House, Martello Towers, ruined Normal castle
✘Smugglers Inn, High St ☎(01323) 762112

Bay View Camping Caravan Park, Old Martello Road BN24 6DX ☎(01323) 768688 Fax (01323)
769637 OS map 199/649027 1m S of Pevensey Bay on private road off A259
(Eastbourne)–signposted Open Apr 4-Oct 5 84 pitches 3½ acres level grass and hard standings
🔋🗑🗑🚿⊕🛝🗑🚐 £10.00-£14.25* holidays@bay-view.co.uk www.bay-view.co.uk

Castle View Caravan-Camping Park, Eastbourne Road BN24 6DT ☎(01323) 763038 OS map
199/646032 1¼m W of Pevensey Bay on A259 (Eastbourne) Open Mar-Nov–must book peak
periods 146 pitches 🔋🚮🏹🗑🗑🚿⊕∅🏊🛝🗑🚐 baths

Fairfields Farm, Eastbourne Road, Westham BN24 5NG ☎(01323) 763165 OS map 199/639039
1½m SW of Pevensey Bay on B2191 (Langney) Open Apr-Oct 60 pitches 3 acres, level grass,
sheltered 🔋🗑🗑🚿⊕🗑 fishing, farm walk £10.50-£12.00 (Mastercard/Visa/Amex)
enquiries@fairfieldsfarm.com www.fairfieldsfarm.com

Martello Beach Caravan Park BN24 6DH ☎(01323) 761424 OS map 199/649035 1m SW of
Pevensey Bay on A259 (Eastbourne) Open Mar-Oct–must book peak periods 360 pitches
(320 static) 🔋✘🚮🗑🗑🚿⊕ lic club, private beach

PORTSMOUTH   Map C5
MD Thurs, Fri, Sat SEE Dicken's birthplace, Nelson's flagship Victory in dockyard, cathedral,
Cumberland House Museum, garrison church, Point Battery and Round Tower, Royal Naval
Museum, Royal Marines Museum ◀The Hard ☎(02392) 826722
✘Still and West, Bath Sq (near Isle of Wight ferry) ☎(02392) 821567

Southsea Caravan Park, Melville Road, Southsea PO4 9TB ☎(02392) 735070 OS map
196/677990 3m E of Portsmouth off A2030 (Southsea) and A288, on seafront Open all year 188
pitches (22 static) Grass, level, sheltered 🔋✘🍺🚮🗑🗑🚿🗑⊕∅🏊😊🛝🖵🚐♿

KEY TO SYMBOLS

🔋	shop	🗑	gas supplies	🮽	winter storage for caravans
✘	restaurant	⊕	chemical disposal point	🅿	parking obligatory
🍺	bar	∅	payphone	🚫🐕	no dogs
🚮	takeaway food	🏊	swimming pool	🚐	caravan hire
🏹	off licence	😊	games area	🏠	bungalow hire
🗑	laundrette	🛝	children's playground	♿	facilities for disabled
🗑	mains electric hook-ups	🖵	TV	🌳	shaded

RAMSGATE, Kent   Map H3
EC Thurs MD Fri SEE churches, model Tudor village, replica of Viking ship, harbour, and yacht marina
🏛 17 Albert Court ☎ (01843) 583333
✕ Churchill Tavern, The Paragon (by Royal Harbour) ☎ (01843) 587862

Manston Caravan Camping Park, Manston Court Road, Manston CT12 5AU ☎ (01843) 823442
   OS map 179/345665 2m NW of Ramsgate off A253 (Sarre) on B2050 (Birchington) near airfield
   Open Easter-Oct 130 pitches (46 static) Level grass 🔋🗞🔌🌀⊕∅🌀🚰 dog walk
   (Mastercard/Visa/Delta/Switch) roy@manston-park.co.uk www.manston-park.co.uk

Nethercourt Park, Nethercourt Hill CT11 0RZ ☎ (01843) 595485 OS map 179/363650 ¾m W of
   Ramsgate off A253 (Sarre) Open Apr-Oct 51 pitches Grass, level/sloping, hard standings
   sheltered 🔋↩🗞🔌⊕∅🌀🚰🔲♿

RINGWOOD, Hants   Map A5
EC Thurs MD Wed SEE parish church, old cottages, New Forest
🏛 The Furlong ☎ (01425) 470896
✕ The Red Shoot Inn & Brewery, Linwood ☎ (01425) 475792

Red Shoot Camping Park, Linwood BH24 3QT ☎ (01425) 473789 Prop: Mrs S Foulds & Mr & Mrs
   N Oldfield OS map 195/188094 4m N of Ringwood off A338 (Salisbury) via Moyles Court Open
   Mar-Oct 130 pitches Grass, level, part sheltered 🔋✕♀🏹🗞🔌🌀⊕∅🌀🚰♿ mountain bike
   hire £10.16-£15.20* enquires@redshoot-campingpark.com www.redshoot-campingpark.com

ROCHESTER   Map F3
EC Wed MD Fri SEE castle, cathedral, Guildhall, Eastgate House museum, 16c blockhouse, Upnor castle
🏛 Eastgate Cottage, Eastgate High St ☎ (01634) 843666
✕ The Tiger Moth, Highview Drive, Chatham ☎ (01634) 861653

Woolmans Wood Tourist Caravan Park, Bridgewood ME5 9SB ☎ (01634) 867685 OS map
   178/188/745640 3m S of Rochester off junct 3 of M2 on B2097 near airfield Open all year
   60 pitches–adults only 5 acres level grass and hard standings 🔋↩🗞🔌🌀⊕∅🚰 £9.00-£15.00
   (Mastercard) johnbedrock@aol.com www.woolmans-wood.co.uk

ROMSEY, Hants   Map B4
EC Wed SEE abbey church, King John's House, White Horse Hotel (16c), Broadlands (home of late Earl Mountbatten)
🏛 13 Church St ☎ (01794) 512987
✕ The Compass Inn, Winsor Rd, Winsor ☎ (02380) 812237 Open 12-2/6.30-9

Green Pastures Farm, Ower SO51 6AJ ☎ (02380) 814444 Prop: Tony & Jane Pitt OS map
   185/323158 4m SW of Romsey off A3090 (Totton) near Junction 2 of M27–signposted near
   Paultons Park Open Mar 15-Oct 31 45 pitches Grass, level, part sheltered 🔋🗞🔌🌀⊕∅🌀♿
   £12.00-£14.00 enquiries@greenpasturesfarm.com www.greenpasturesfarm.com

Hill Farm Caravan Park, Sherfield English SO51 6FH ☎ (01794) 340402 Fax (01794) 342358 OS
   map 185/295225 4m W of Romsey off A27 (Salisbury) on Lockerley road Open Mar-Oct
   140 pitches Grass, level, open 🔋✕🏹🗞🔌🌀⊕🚰🌀🚰🔲 ice pack service £11.00-£24.00*
   gjb@hillfarmpark.com www.hillfarmpark.com

RYDE, Isle of Wight   Map B5
EC Thurs SEE pier, Shell museum, bird sanctuary, I of Wight Steam Railway at Haven Street, Spithead
🏛 Western Esplanade ☎ (01983) 813818
✕ Yelfs Hotel, Union St ☎ (01983) 564062

Pondwell Holidays, Seaview PO34 5AQ ☎ (01983) 612330 OS map 196/623913 2m E of Ryde
   on B3330 (St Helens) Open May-Sept 200 pitches (36 static) Grass, part level, sheltered
   🔋🗞🔌🌀⊕∅🌀🚰🔲🎾🏠 (Mastercard/Visa)

RYE, E Sussex   Map G4
EC Tues MD Thurs SEE Ypres Tower Museum, Cinque Port, Flushing Inn (15c), St Mary's church,
George Hotel, Royal Military Canal, The Salts, Martello Tower at harbour
🏛 Heritage Centre, Strand Quay ☎ (01797) 226696
✕ Ypres Castle, Gun Gardens ☎ (01797) 223248

Cock Horse Inn, Peasmarsh TN31 6YD ☎ (01797) 230281 OS map 189/896229 3m NW of Rye
   on A268 (Tonbridge) Open Mar-Oct 6 pitches–caravans only 1½ acres, grass, level
   🔋✕♀🔌⊕∅🌀

Camber Sands Leisure Park, Lydd Road, Camber Sands TN31 7RX ☎ (01797) 225282 OS map
   189/975186 3½m SE of Rye off A259 (New Romney) in Camber near beach Open Mar-Oct
   860 pitches (800 static) Level grass 🔋✕♀(5) 🗞🔌∅🔲🌀🔲🏠 (all cards)

ST HELENS–see Bembridge

ST NICHOLAS AT WADE–see Birchington

SANDOWN, Isle of Wight **Map B5**
EC Wed MD Mon *Coast resort on SE of island noted for safe bathing from fine sandy beaches* SEE Snake and Reptile Centre, Yaverland church, Geological museum
🖪 8 High St ✆ (01983) 813818
✘ The Fighting Cocks Roadhouse, Hale Common, Arreton ✆ (01983) 865254

Adgestone Camping Park, Adgestone PO36 0HL ✆ (01983) 403432 OS map 196/591855 1½m N of Sandown off A3055 (Lake) at Manor House pub Open Mar-Oct 250 pitches 15 acres, level grass 🛒🔌🗄🖪🕹◎❂⌀🖾(heated) ⊕🔧♿ picnic garden, river and pond fishing, table tennis, petanque, volley ball, accessory shop (Mastercard/Visa)

Cheverton Copse Holiday Park PO36 0JP ✆ (01983) 403161 Fax (01983) 402861 OS map 196/5768 1½m SW of Sandown on A3056 (Newport) Open Apr-Sept 83 pitches (57 static) 4½ acres, part level 🖪🔌◎⌀🔧❂🖾🏠 lic club £7.00-£10.00* (most cards) berriesdandm@aol.com www.cheverton-copse.co.uk

Fairway Caravan-Camping Park, Fairway PO36 9PS ✆ (01983) 403462 OS map 196/589842 1m N of Sandown off A3055 (Ryde) at railway bridge Open Mar-Oct 150 pitches (110 static) Grass, level, sheltered 🛒🔌🗄🖪🔌◎⌀🔧🖾 lic club (Mastercard/Visa/Switch)

Old Barn Touring Park, Cheverton Farm, Newport Road PO36 9PJ ✆ (01983) 866414 Fax (01983) 865988 OS map 196/573833 1½m W of Sandown on A3056 (Newport) Open May-Sept 60 pitches Grass, part level hard standings, sheltered 🛒🖪🔌◎⌀🔧⌀🖾♿ games room, super pitches £9.60-£13.50* (Mastercard/Visa/Switch/Delta) oldbarn@weltinet.com www.oldbarntouring.co.uk

Queen Bower Dairy, Alverstone Road, Queen Bower PO36 0NZ ✆ (01983) 403840 OS map 196/569846 3m W of Sandown off A3056 (Newport) at Apse Heath Open May-Oct 20 pitches 2½ acres, level grass, sheltered 🔌❂ farm produce £4.00-£6.50 queenbowerdairy@aol.com www.queenbowerdairy.co.uk

Southland Camping Park, Newchurch PO36 0LZ *Secluded site on outskirts of rural village with good access* ✆ (01983) 865385 *Prop: Viv & Vanessa McGuinness* OS map 196/558847 2m W of Sandown off A3056 onto Winford Road Open Apr-Sept 120 pitches Level grass, sheltered 🛒🖪🔌◎⌀❂⊕🔧♿ m/van dump station, sep pitches, internet hotspot for wireless computers £10.20-£15.20 inc elect (Mastercard/Visa/Maestro/Delta) info@southland.co.uk www.southland.co.uk

Village Way, Newport Road PO36 9PJ ✆ (01983) 863279 *Prop: NM Smith* OS map 196/573833 1½m W of Sandown on A3056 (Newport) Open all year 12 pitches Level grass 🖪🔌⌀◎⌀ 🔌🖾🏠 free coarse fishing £6.00-£7.50

SANDWICH, Kent **Map H3**
EC Wed MD Thurs SEE port, Barbican, Guildhall, old houses, town walls
🖪 The Guildhall, Cattle Market ✆ (01304) 613565
✘ Bell, The Quay ✆ (01304) 613388

Homing Park, Church Lane, Seasalter CT5 4BU ✆ (01227) 771777 *Prop: Coast & Country Caravans* OS map TR095644 ¼ mile from A299 (signposted) Open Mar-Oct 238 pitches (195 static) 14 acres, grassy pitches all with mains services ⛲🖪🔌◎❂⌀🔧♿ £9.50-£16.75 (Mastercard/Visa/Switch) info@homingpark.co.uk www.coastandcountryleisure.com

SEAFORD–see Newhaven

SEDLESCOMBE–see Battle

Southland Camping Park, Sandown

5 Star Caravan and Camping
Holidays
Tel: 01243 604499

See listing under Selsey

SELSEY, W Sussex   Map C5
Quiet holiday resort with sandy beach SEE Selsey Bill S
✗ Crab and Lobster on B2145 3m N at Sidlesham ☎(01243) 641233
Warner Farm Touring Park, Warner Lane PO20 9EL ☎(01243) 604121 OS map 197/845939 ½m NW of Selsey centre off B2145–signposted Open Mar-Oct 250 pitches (200 static) Grass and hard standings, part sheltered ⚑✗♀⌂⚲⚊▥⚙⊘⊙⊡⚙⌇⚏♿ sun beds, steam room £15.50-£40.00 (most cards-not Electron) *touring@bunnleisure.co.uk www.bunnleisure.co.uk*

SEVENOAKS, Kent   Map E3
EC Wed MD Mon, Wed SEE church, Knole (NT)
ℹ Buckhurst Lane ☎(01732) 450305
✗ Royal Oak, Upper High St ☎(01732) 451109
East Hill Farm, East Hill Rd, Kemsing TN15 6YD ☎(01959) 522347 OS map 188/560623 4m N of Sevenoaks off A225 (Dartford) via Otford Mount–phone for directions Open Apr-Oct 110 pitches (80 static) 8 acres level grass ⚊⊙⌇

SHANKLIN, Isle of Wight   Map B6
EC Wed SEE The Chine, old cottages, church, Crab Inn, Luccombe Common, Roman villa 3m N at Brading
ℹ 67 High St ☎(01983) 813818
✗ Fishermans Cottage, Shanklin Chine ☎(01983) 863882
Landguard Camping, Landguard Manor Road PO37 7PH ☎(01983) 867028 Fax (01983) 865988 OS map 196/581826 ½m NW of Shanklin off A3056 (Newport) Open Easter-Sept 150 pitches 7 acres, level grass and hard standing, sheltered ⚑✗♀⌂⚲▥⚙⚊⊙⊘⊡(heated) ⊡♨♿ £10.00-£14.00* (Mastercard/Visa/Delta/Switch) *landguard@weltinet.com www.landguard-camping.co.uk*
Lower Hyde Leisure Park PO37 7LL ☎(01983) 866131 Fax (01983) 862532 OS map 196/575819 1m W of Shanklin via Landguard road Open Apr 17-Nov 1 365 pitches (237 static)–families only 50 acres, grass, level/sloping and hard standings ⚑✗(snack) ♀⌂≀▥⚙⚊⊙⊘⊡(heated) ⊙♨⚏🏠♿ tennis, cabaret (most cards) *holidaysale.lowerhyde@park-resorts.com www.park-resorts.com*
Ninham Country Holidays, Ninham PO37 7PL ☎(01983) 864243 Fax (01983) 868881 OS map 196/572827 1m NW of Shanklin off A3056 (Newport) Open Easter-Sep 98 pitches (families and couples only) 18 acres, grass, level/gentle slope, sheltered ⚑⌂≀▥⚙⚊⊙⊘⊡(outdoor heated) ⊙⌇⚏♨ baby care cubicles, barbecues, games room, water sports, mountain biking (most cards) *info@ninham.fsnet.co.uk www.ninham-holiday.co.uk*
See also Ventnor

SHEERNESS, Kent   Map G3
EC Wed MD Tues SEE promenade, pier (view), Minster abbey church 1m S
✗ Royal, The Broadway ☎(01795) 662626
Plough Leisure, Plough Road, Minster in Sheppey ME12 4JF ☎(01795) 872895 *Prop: Dennis Aldridge* OS map 178/972725 1½m E of Sheerness off Eastchurch road Open Mar-Oct 105 pitches (85 static) ▥⚙⚊⊙⊡(heated) ⊙⌇ £14.00*
Priory Hill Holiday Park, Wing Road, Leysdown on Sea ME12 4QT ☎(01795) 510267 OS map 178/039702 8m E of Sheerness via Eastchurch and B2231 (Leysdown) on left of Wing Road by sea Open Mar-Oct 50 pitches 1½ acres level grass ⚑♀▥⚙⚊⊙⊡(heated, indoor) ⚙⚏ clubhouse, entertainment £11.00-£20.00 (Mastercard/Visa) *enquiries@prioryhill.co.uk www.prioryhill.co.uk*
Riverbank Park, The Broadway, Minster on Sea ME12 2DB ☎(01795) 870300 OS map 178/960735 2m E of Sheerness in Minster by sea Open Mar-Oct 100 pitches 6 acres level grass ⚑♀▥⚙⚊⊙⊘⚙⚏🏠 (all cards)
Sheerness Holiday Park, Halfway Rd ME12 3AA ☎(01795) 662638 OS map 178/927736 ½m SE of Sheerness on A250 (Halfway Houses) Open Easter-Oct 330 pitches (250 static) Level grass ⚑✗♀⌂⚊▥⚙⚊⊙⊘⊡⌇⚏ games room (Mastercard/Visa/Switch/Solo)

SOUTHAMPTON   Map B5
MD Thurs, Fri, Sat *One-time transatlantic port on harbour noted for its double tide* SEE docks, Tudor House Museum, God's House Tower, Netley abbey 3m SE
ℹ 9 Civic Centre Rd ☎(02380) 833333
✗ Dolphin, High St ☎(02380) 226178
Riverside Holidays, Satchell Lane, Hamble SO31 4HR ☎(02380) 453220 *Prop: Davidson Leisure Resorts Ltd* OS map 196/483082 7m SE of Southampton off A27 (Fareham) and B3397 (Hamble) near junct 8 of M27 Open Mar-Oct 77 pitches (30 static)–adv booking advisable Grass, level, sheltered ✗♀▥⚙⚊⊙⊘⚙⚏🏠 £11.00-£28.00 (Mastercard/Visa) *enquiries@riversideholidays.co.uk www.riversideholidays.co.uk*

SOUTHSEA–see Portsmouth

STANSTED–see Wrotham

STAPLECROSS, E Sussex   **Map F4**
SEE Bodiam Castle 2m N
✘ Curlew 3m N at Bodiam ✆ (01424) 214214

Lordine Court Caravan Camping Park TN32 5TS ✆ (01580) 830209 OS map 199/802227 1½m E of Staplecross off B2165 (Horns Cross/Clayhill) Open Apr-Oct 270 pitches (150 static) Grass, part level, hard standings, part sheltered ⛽✘♀⊶🅱🚱🄌⊘🔲🕒↩🆓🏕 lic club/bars (Mastercard/Visa/Switch)

Park Farm, Bodiam TN32 5XA ✆ (01580) 830514 *Prop: Richard Bailey* OS map 199/766245 3m N of Staplecross off B2165 (Cripps Corner) on B2244 (Maidstone) Open Easter-Oct 50 pitches Grass, level, part sheltered, some hard standing 🚱⊕🕒↩🆓 fishing, riverside walks to Bodiam Castle, camp fires, beautiful rural setting £10.00 £10.00 *www.parkfarmcamping.co.uk*

STELLING MINNIS, Kent   **Map H3**
✘ Rose and Crown ✆ (01227) 709265

Rose and Crown CT4 6AS ✆ (01227) 709265 OS map 179/142469 ¼m W of Stelling Minnis centre adj common Open Mar-Oct 30 pitches 2 acres level grass ✘♀⊶🄌 *No showers*

STORRINGTON–see Arundel

TENTERDEN, Kent   **Map G4**
EC Wed MD Fri SEE St Mildred's church, steam railway, Smallhythe Place 2m S
🅸 Town Hall, High St ✆ (01580) 763572
✘ White Lion, High St ✆ (01580) 292921

Spill Land Caravan Park, Biddenden TN27 8BX ✆ (01580) 291379 *Prop: DS & AK Waite* OS map 188/849369 4m NW of Tenterden off A262 (Biddenden) on Benenden hospital road Open Apr-Sept 130 pitches (65 static)–last arrival 6pm–no motorvans–no under 18s or groups Grass, sloping, sheltered 🚱🄌⊕ £10.00-£12.00 *www.ukparks.co.uk/spillland*

Woodlands Caravan-Camping Park, Tenterden Road, Biddenden TN27 8BT ✆ (01580) 291216 Fax (01580) 291216 OS map 189/865371 3m NW of Tenterden on A262 (Biddenden) Open Mar-Oct 200 pitches Grass, level, part sheltered ⛽🅱🚱🄌⊕🄌↩🆓♿ £10.00-£12.00* *woodlandspark@aol.com www.campingsite.co.uk*

UCKFIELD, E Sussex   **Map E4**
EC Wed
✘ Ye Maiden's Head, High St ✆ (01825) 762019

Honeys Green Farm, Easons Green, Framfield TN22 5RE ✆ (01825) 840334 OS map 199/504177 3m SE of Uckfield off A22 (Eastbourne) at Halland Open Easter-Oct 30 pitches 2 acres level grass, sheltered 🚱⊕🄌🔲 coarse fishing, walks

WARSASH–see Fareham

WASHINGTON, W Sussex   **Map D4**
SEE Chanctonbury Ring 1m SE on South Downs
✘ Mill House 2m N at Ashington ✆ (01903) 892426

Washington Caravan Camping Park RH20 4AJ ✆ (01903) 892869 Fax (01903) 893252 OS map 198/123135 ½m N of Washington on A283 (Shoreham–Petersfield) near junction with A24 (Dorking–Worthing) Open all year 80 pitches 4 acres, level grass and hard standing 🅱🚱🄌⊕♿ £9.00

WESTHAM–see Pevensey Bay

WEST WITTERING–see Chichester

WHITSTABLE, Kent   **Map G3**
EC Wed MD Thurs SEE castle, All Saints church
▨7 Oxford St ℰ (01227) 275482
✕ Tankerton Arms, Tower Hill ℰ (01227) 272024

Primrose Cottage Caravan Park, Golden Hill CT5 3AR ℰ (01227) 273694 *Prop: Brian Campbell*
    OS map 179/118653 1m S of Whitstable on A2990 (Faversham–Herne Bay) Open Mar-Oct
    60 pitches (48 static)–no adv booking Grass, level, sheltered ▣▤▨▨◒◓⊘◍▣▱
    £10.00-£14.00 *brian@primrosepark.wanadoo.co.uk*

WINCHELSEA, E Sussex   **Map G4**
SEE church, town walls, old houses
✕ New Inn off A259 ℰ (01797) 226252

Rye Bay Caravan Park, Pett Level Road TN36 4NE ℰ (01797) 226340 OS map 189/913157 2m S
    of Winchelsea off A259 (Rye) at Winchelsea beach Open Mar-Oct 335 pitches (265 static)
    ✕▨▤◒◓⊘◒⤸

WINCHESTER, Hants   **Map B4**
MD Mon, Wed, Fri, Sa SEE cathedral, Guildhall, college, Great Hall in castle, West gate museum,
Greenjackets museum
▨ Guildhall, The Broadway ℰ (01962) 840500
✕ Wykeham Arms, Kingsgate St ℰ (01962) 853834

Morn Hill Park Caravan Club Site) SO21 1HL ℰ (01962) 869877 OS map 185/522295 3m E of
    Winchester at junction of A31 (London) and B3404 Open Mar 27-Oct 12 150 pitches Level grass,
    sheltered ▤▨▨◒⊘ £12.50-£17.60* (Delta/Mastercard/Switch/Visa) *www.caravanclub.co.uk*

WITTERING, E and W–see Chichester

WORTHING, W Sussex   **Map D5**
EC Wed MD Sat SEE cottages at West Tarring, Cissbury Ring, Salvington Mill
▨ Marine Parade ℰ (01903) 210022
✕ Rose and Crown ℰ (01903) 201623

Brook Lane Caravan Park, Brook Lane, Ferring BN12 5JD *Peaceful site for mid- to upper age
    group* ℰ (01903) 242802 OS map 198/090025 4m W of Worthing off A259 (Littlehampton) and
    road to South Ferring Open Mar-Oct 82 pitches (76 static)–no tents or awnings Hard standings
    and grass, sheltered ▤▨▨◒⊘

Northbrook Farm (Caravan Club), Titnore Way BN13 3RT ℰ (01903) 502962 OS map 198/106046
    2½m NW of Worthing off A259 (Littlehampton) Open Mar 25-Nov 2 122 pitches Level grass
    ▤▨▨◒⊘⤸ £13.35-£17.60* (Mastercard/Visa/Switch/Delta) *www.caravanclub.co.uk*

Onslow Caravan Park, Onslow Drive, Ferring BN12 5RX ℰ (01903) 243170 OS map 198/092029
    4m W of Worthing off A259 (Littlehampton) Open Mar-Oct 133 pitches (129 static)–no tents
    Grass and hard standing, level, sheltered ▤▨▨◒⊘

WROTHAM, Kent   **Map F3**
✕ Bull ℰ (01732) 883092

Thriftwood Caravan Camping Park, Plaxdale Green Road, Stansted TN15 7PB ℰ (01732) 822261
    Fax (01732) 824636 OS map 188/598608 1½m NNW of Wrotham off A20 (London) on Stansted
    road Open Mar-Feb 170 pitches 20 acres, level/gentle slope, grass and hard standing, sheltered
    ▣▤⌁▨▨◒⊘▱⤸▤▨⛊ cooking facs for campers (all cards)

To the Woods Camping, Botsham Lane, West Kingsdown TN15 6BN ℰ (01322) 863751 *Prop:
    EHE Helsdon* OS map 188/567637 2m NW of Wrotham off A20 (London) Open all year
    40 pitches–no adv booking Grass, part level, sheltered ▱◍ £7.00-£9.00 inc hook-up

YARMOUTH, Isle of Wight   **Map B5**
EC Wed *Resort on estuary of Yar with sandy beach accessible only at low tide* SEE castle, old inns
▨ The Quay ℰ (01983) 813818
✕ Wheatsheaf, Bridge Rd ℰ (01983) 760456

Orchard Park, Newbridge PO41 0TS ℰ (01983) 531331 Fax (01983) 531666 OS map 196/411878
    4m E of Yarmouth on B3041 (Newport) Open Feb 17-Jan 2 240 pitches (65 static) Grass, part
    level, sheltered, some hard standings ▣⤸⚲▤▨▨◒⊘▱(indoor and outdoor) ◓⤸⛊▱⛊
    battery charging, coarse fishing, pool, tennis £11.00-£14.80 inc elect (Mastercard/Visa)

Three counties between the two coasts facing the Bristol and English Channels make up the Southwest. They include the old counties of Somerset, Dorset and Wiltshire.

The widest open space in the region is the breezy plateau of Salisbury Plain in lonely Wiltshire, centred on the 4000 years old stone circle of Stonehenge and bordered on the south by the valley of the Wylye which flows into Salisbury; the city is dominated by the 400ft spire of its ancient cathedral. Beyond the Vale of Pewsey in the north are the Marlborough Downs, covered on the southwest by the Savernake Forest, patterned with ancient tracks and earthworks and dominated by the great Avebury circle. Other sights in the county are the artificial mound of Silbury Hill, the Saxon-Norman site of Old Sarum and the stately home of Wilton House.

Sandwiched between Wiltshire and the Bristol Channel is the ancient seaport of Bristol, with the beautiful Avon Gorge spanned by Brunel's famous suspension bridge to the northwest. A notable sight in Bristol is SS *Great Britain*, the first ocean going iron ship. There are pleasant valleys in the Cotswold escarpment in the north; Georgian Bath is on the east and the vast sands of Weston super Mare on the west. Worth a detour are the three great

houses of Badminton, Dodington and Dyrham.

The rolling green hills of Somerset rise up to the heathlands of the Mendip Hills near the stalactite caves of Cheddar. Between Taunton and the coast, which is at its best between Minehead and Porlock, are the wooded Quantocks. Below them is Exmoor, bounded on the north by great cliffs. Other sights are the charming old town of Dunster, the cathedral at Wells and the ruined Glastonbury Abbey in the Vale of Avalon.

Rural England remains much as it ever was in Dorset, the southernmost county in the region. The chalk downs extending southeast of Shaftesbury are cut by deep valleys and topped by prehistoric earthworks, most important of which is Maiden Castle, covering 115 acres. The coastline stretches from the vast natural harbour of Poole to Chesil Bank, a seventeen miles long line of pebbles which forms a causeway leading to the Isle of Portland, ending in the rock mass of Portland Bill.

All the major centres in the region possess several campsites, the highest densities being along the Dorset coast and the lowest in Wiltshire. Most coastal campsites cater for static as well as mobile caravanners and campers; many of those inland are on farms.

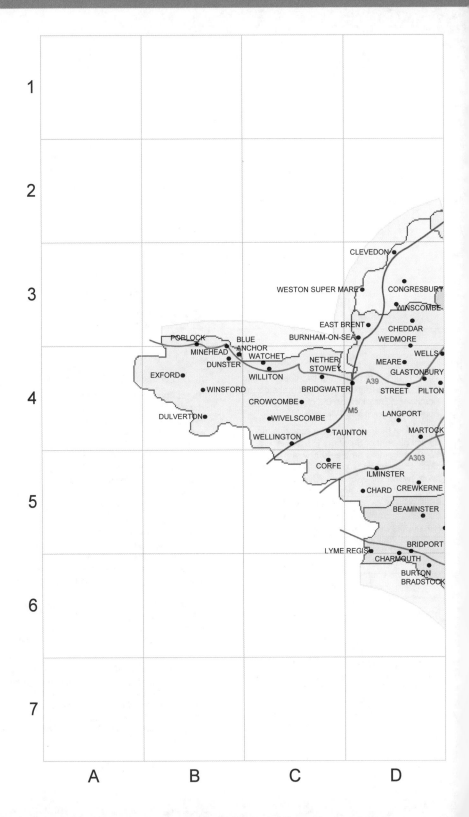

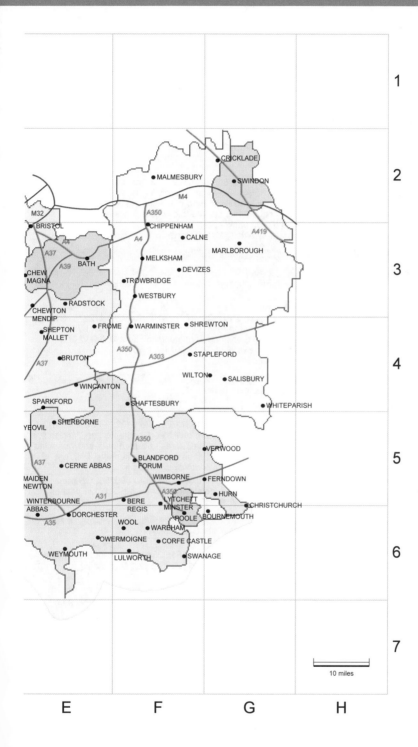

1

2

3

4

5

6

7

CRICKLADE

MALMESBURY ● SWINDON

M4

A350

M32 A419

BRISTOL CHIPPENHAM
A4
A4 CALNE
A37 MARLBOROUGH
MELKSHAM
A39 BATH
DEVIZES
CHEW
MAGNA TROWBRIDGE
WESTBURY
RADSTOCK
CHEWTON
MENDIP
SHEPTON FROME WARMINSTER SHREWTON
MALLET
A350
BRUTON A303 STAPLEFORD
A37
WILTON SALISBURY
WINCANTON
SPARKFORD SHAFTESBURY
WHITEPARISH
YEOVIL SHERBORNE
A350
VERWOOD
A37 CERNE ABBAS BLANDFORD
FORUM
MAIDEN WIMBORNE FERNDOWN
NEWTON
A350 HURN
WINTERBOURNE A31 BERE LYTCHETT CHRISTCHURCH
ABBAS REGIS MINSTER
DORCHESTER POOLE BOURNEMOUTH
A35 WOOL WAREHAM
OWERMOIGNE CORFE CASTLE
WEYMOUTH SWANAGE
LULWORTH

10 miles

E F G H

BATH   Map E3
MD Mon, Wed *Elegant city and spa since Roman times, famous for its Regency architecture* SEE Pump Room and Hot Springs, Roman Baths, Assembly Rooms and Museum of Costume, Royal Crescent, Pulteney Bridge, Claverton Manor (American Museum) 2m E
🖪 Abbey Church Yard ☏ (01225) 477101
✘ Crystal Palace, Abbey Green (via Church St) ☏ (01225) 423944

Bath Marina and Caravan Park, Brassmill Lane BA1 3JT ☏ (01225) 424301 *Prop: BWML* OS map 172/720655 1½m W of Bath off A4 (Bristol) by river Avon Open all year 88 pitches–no tents Hard standings ✘ ♀ 🖫 🔌 🔥 ⊕ ∅ ↩ & £18.50 (all cards exc Amex) *arthur.currie@bwml.co.uk www.bathcaravanpark.com*

Bury View Farm, Corston Fields BA2 9HD ☏ (01225) 873672 OS map 172/670643 4m W of Bath on right of A39 (Weston super Mare) Open all year 21 pitches 2 acres level grass 🔌 🔥 ⊕ *salbowden@btinternet.com*

Newton Mill Camping Park, Newton Road, Bath BA2 9JF ☏ (01225) 333909 Fax (01225) 461556 *Prop: Keith & Louise Davies* OS map 172/715645 3m W of Bath off A4 (Bristol) at Globe Inn Open all year 195 pitches 43 acres, terraced, grass and hard standing 🖫 ✘ ♀ ↩ 🏹 🖫 🔌 🔥 ∅ ⊕ ↩ & satellite TV, fishing, frequent bus service to city centre, superior heated amenities inc bathrooms £15.00-£19.50 (£6.00 backpacker) (Mastercard/Visa/Solo/Electron/Maestro) *newtonmill@hotmail.com www.campinginbath.co.uk*

BAYFORD–see Wincanton

BERE REGIS, Dorset   Map F5
Pleasant village in Thomas Hardy country SEE view from Woodbury Hill E, Clouds Hill (NT) former home of Lawrence of Arabia 3m SW
✘ Royal Oak, West St ☏ (01929) 471203

Rowlands Wait Touring Park, Rye Hill BH20 7LP ☏ (01929) 472727 Fax (01929) 472275 OS map 194/844930 1m S of Bere Regis off Wool/Bovington road Open Mar-Oct and winter by arrangement 71 pitches 8 acres, level/sloping grass and hard standing 🖫 🖫 🔌 🔥 ⊕ ∅ ⊕ ↩ games room, crazy golf, bike hire, woodland walks £7.50-£12.50* (all cards) *bta@rowlandswait.co.uk www.rowlandswait.co.uk*

BLANDFORD FORUM, Dorset   Map F5
EC Wed MD Thurs, Sat SEE parish church, Georgian houses
🖪 Market Place ☏ (01258) 454770
✘ Crown, West St ☏ (01258) 456626

The Inside Park, Down House Estate DT11 9AD ☏ (01258) 453719/07778 313293 Fax (01258) 459921 OS map 194/864052 1½m SW of Blandford Forum off A354 (Dorchester) on Winterborne Stickland road Open Easter-Oct 125 pitches Level grass, 12 acres secluded park and woodland 🖫 🏹 🖫 🔌 🔥 ⊕ ↩ 🔥 & games room, farm tours, woodland walks, dog kennels £10.00-£15.00 (Mastercard/Visa) *inspark@aol.com www.members.aol.com/inspark/inspark*

Lady Bailey Caravan Park, Winterborne Whitechurch DT11 0HS ☏ (01258) 880786 OS map 194/838001 4½m SW of Blandford Forum on A354 (Puddletown) Open Mar-Oct 121 pitches (32 static) 17 acres, grass, part sloping 🖫 🖫 🔥 ⊕ ∅ 🔥 🚐

BLUE ANCHOR, Somerset   Map B4
SEE West Somerset Railway, Cleeve Abbey 2m SE, Dunster Castle 3m W
✘ Luttrell Arms 3m W at Dunster ☏ (01643) 821555

Beeches Holiday Park TA24 6JW ☏ (01984) 840391 OS map 181/035435 1m E of Blue Anchor off B3191 (Watchet) on Old Cleeve road Open Mar 27-Oct 31 285 pitches (215 static) 🖫 🖫 ∅ 🖾 (heated outdoor) ↩

Blue Anchor Park TA24 6JT ☏ (01643) 821360 OS map 181/024435 ½m E of Blue Anchor on right of B3191 (Watchet) Open Mar-Oct 426 pitches (321 static) 29 acres, hard standings and level grass 🖫 🖫 🔌 🔥 ⊕ ∅ 🖾 (indoor) ↩ 🐕 🚐

KEY TO SYMBOLS

🖫	shop	∅	gas supplies	🔥	winter storage for caravans
✘	restaurant	⊕	chemical disposal point	🅿	parking obligatory
♀	bar	∅	payphone	🐕	no dogs
↩	takeaway food	🖾	swimming pool	🚐	caravan hire
🏹	off licence	⊕	games area	🏠	bungalow hire
🖫	laundrette	↩	children's playground	&	facilities for disabled
🔌	mains electric hook-ups	🖵	TV	♉	shaded

BATH

Newton Road
Bath BA2 9JF
Tel: 01225 333 909
www.campinginbath.co.uk

COMMENTS

We would be pleased to hear your comments about the sites featured in this guide or your suggestions for future editions. Comments and suggestions may be emailed to ccb@butford.co.uk. Alternatively, write to The Editor, CCB, Butford Technical Publishing Ltd at the address given at the front of the book.

BOURNEMOUTH
Map G6

SEE Winter gardens, chines, Pavilion, Hengistbury Head, Compton Acres gardens 2m SW
🖸 Westover Rd ☏ 0906 802 0234
✘ Crust, Bourne Ave, The Square ☏ (01202) 421430

Cara Touring Park, Old Bridge Road, Iford BH6 5RQ ☏ (01202) 482121 OS map 195/138937 3m E of Bournemouth on right of A35 (Christchurch) Open all year–must book 120 pitches (83 static)–no tents 6 acres level grass and hard standing 🏕️🗄️🗄️🗄️⊕⊘⊗🚐

BREAN–see Burnham

BRIDGWATER, Somerset
Map C4

EC Thurs MD Wed, Sat SEE Town Hall (tapestry, portraits), Admiral Blake House, Sedgemoor Battlefield 4m E
🖸 High St ☏ (01278) 427652
✘ Admirals Table, Bristol Rd ☏ (01278) 685671 Open Mon-Sat 12-9.30, Sun 12-9

Fairways International Touring Park, Bath Road, Bawdrip TA7 8PP ☏ (01278) 685569 Prop: Fairways Partnership OS map 182/348403 3½m NE of Bridgwater off A39 (Glastonbury) on right of B3141 (Woolavington) Open Mar 1-Nov 15 200 pitches 6 acres level grass 🏕️🗄️🗄️🗄️⊕ ⊘⊕🍴🗄️🛁 games room, rallies welcome, off licence nearby £6.00-£14.50 (all cards) fairwaysint@btinternet.com www.fairways.btinternet.co.uk

---

BRIDPORT, Dorset
Map D5

EC Thurs MD Wed, Sat SEE almshouses, museum, Golden Cap cliffs SW
🖸 32 South St ☏ (01308) 424901
✘ Anchor Inn, Seatown, Chideock ☏ (01297) 489215
✘ The New Inn, Eype ☏ (01308) 423254 Open 12-2/6.30-9

Binghams Farm Touring Caravan Park, Melplash DT6 3TT ☏ (01308) 488234 OS map 193/478963 1½m N of Bridport on A3066 (Beaminster) Open Easter-Oct 100+ pitches–adults only 5 acres level grass and hard standing, sheltered ✘🍴🗄️🗄️🗄️⊕⊘⊡🍴🛁🗄️ £10.00-£18.50 (all cards) enquiries@binghamsfarm.co.uk www.binghamsfarm.co.uk

Eype House Caravan Camping Park, Eype DT6 6AL ☏ (01308) 424903 Fax (01308) 424903 OS map 193/446911 2m SW of Bridport off A35 (Charmouth) Open Apr-Oct 55 pitches (35 static)–no touring caravans 4 acres, level grass 🏕️🗄️⊕⊘⊗🚐 £8.50-£14.50* enquiries@eypehouse.co.uk www.eypehouse.co.uk

Golden Cap Caravan Park, Seatown, Chideock DT6 6JX ☏ (01308) 422139 Prop: Mr & Mrs Cox OS map 193/422918 3m W of Bridport off A35 (Chideock) on Seatown road Open Mar-Nov 328 pitches (220 static) 28 acres level/sloping grass and hard standings 🏕️🍴🗄️🛁🚐 fishing lake £12.00-£25.00 (Mastercard/Visa) holidays@wdlh.co.uk www.wdlh.co.uk

Highlands End Farm Caravan Park, Eype DT6 6AR ☏ (01308) 422139 Prop: Mr & Mrs Cox OS map 193/453915 1m W of Bridport off A35 (Charmouth) on Eype Mouth road Open Mar-Nov 515 pitches (160 static) 28 acres, level grass and hard standings 🏕️✘🍴🛁🍴🗄️🗄️⊕⊘ (indoor, heated) ⊕🛁🗄️🚐🏠🛁 tennis court, pitch and putt £9.00-£21.50 (Mastercard/Visa) holidays@wdlh.co.uk www.wdlh.co.uk

Travellers' Rest Inn, Dorchester Road DT6 4PJ ☏ (01308) 458538 OS map 194/515926 3m E of Bridport on A35 (Dorchester) Open Mar-Oct 26 pitches Level/sloping grass and hard standing, sheltered ✘ (snack) 🍴🗄️⊕🛁 games room, children's room (most cards)

See also Burton Bradstock

For more up-to-date information, and for links to camping websites, visit our site at:
www.butford.co.uk/camping

WEST DORSET LEISURE HOLIDAYS

A World Heritage Site on your doorstep

Highlands End Holiday Park, Eype, Bridport, Dorset DT6 6AR
Tel: 01308 422139 Fax: 01308 425672 E-mail: holidays@wdlh.co.uk

BRISTOL   Map E3
EC Wed MD Sun SEE Merchant Venturer's almshouses, cathedral, Temple church, old Vandodger
Trow Inn, Theatre Royal, Clifton suspension bridge, SS Great Britain at Great Western Dock,
Maritime Heritage Centre
🛈 Wildscreen Walk, Harbourside ☎ 0906 711 2191
✘ Barbizon, Corn St ☎ (01272) 222658

Baltic Wharf (Caravan Club), Cumberland Road BS1 6XG ☎ (0117) 926 8030 OS map
   172/573722 ½m W of Bristol centre off A370 (Weston super Mare) Open all year 58
   pitches–booking advisable 2½ acres, hard standings and level grass ⏚⊕∅ £17.00-£22.00*
   (Delta/Mastercard/Switch/Visa) www.caravanclub.co.uk

Brook Lodge Country Touring and Camping Park, Cowslip Green, Redhill BS40 5RD ☎ (01934)
   862311 OS map 172/485620 8m SW of Bristol off A38 (Bridgwater) Open Mar-Oct 29 pitches
   Level grass and hard standings, sheltered 🛢🖥⏚⊕∅🗔(Jun 15-Aug) ⊕↩🔲🅿🌀🚽🍴

BRUTON, Somerset   Map E4
EC Thurs SEE church, packhorse bridge, 16c dovecote (NT), 17c Sexeys hospital (almshouses)
✘ Three Horseshoes 2m NE at Batcombe ☎ (01749) 850359

Batcombe Vale Caravan & Camping Park, Batcombe BA4 6BW ☎ (01749) 830246 OS map
   183/681379 2m N of Bruton off B3081 (Shepton Mallet) Open Apr-Sept 32 pitches Level grass,
   sheltered 🖥⏚⊕∅⊕🛢 fishing, boating donaldsage@compuserve.com
   www.batcombevale.co.uk

BUCKNOWLE–see Corfe Castle

BURNHAM ON SEA, Somerset   Map D3
EC Wed MD Mon SEE St Andrew's church, Gore Sands, Brean Down bird sanctuary
🛈 South Esplanade ☎ (01278) 787852
✘ Dunstan House Inn, 8 Love Lane ☎ (01278) 784343

Burnham Association of Sports Clubs, Stoddens Road TA8 2NZ ☎ (01278) 788355 OS map
   182/315502 1m NE of Burnham centre off B3140 (East Brent) at Middle Burnham–signposted
   Open all year 20 pitches–must book 30 acres sportsground, level grass 🖥⊕🌀 lic club
   (evenings) £8.00-£12.00

Channel View Camping Caravan Park, Brean Down TA8 2RR ☎ (01278) 751241/760485 OS map
   182/297554 2½m N of Burnham off B3140 (Berrow) on coast road beyond Brean Open Easter-
   Oct 90 pitches 🛢⊕

Diamond Farm Caravan Touring Park, Diamond Farm, Weston Rd, Brean TA8 2RL ☎ (01278)
   751041 Prop: MHR Hicks Ltd OS map 182/308560 4m N of Burnham on Sea on Lympsham
   road via Brean Open Mar-Oct 220 pitches 6 acres level grass 🛢✘↩🛢🖥⏚⊕∅↩🔲🏠⭡
   fishing, caravan spares £6.00-£12.00 trevor@diamondfarm42.freeserve.co.uk
   www.diamondfarm.co.uk

New House Farm, Mark Road, Highbridge TA9 4RA ☎ (01278) 782218 OS map 182/327473 3m
   SE of Burnham on right of B3139 (Wedmore) near motorway bridge Open Mar-Oct 30 pitches
   4 acres level grass 🛢🛢🖥⏚⊕↩

Northam Farm Caravan Park, Brean TA8 2SE ☎ (01278) 751244 Fax (01278) 751150 OS map
   182/297561 4m N of Burnham off B3140 (Berrow) on coast road to Brean Open Easter-Oct
   350 pitches Level grass and hard standing 🛢✘↩🛢🖥⏚⊕∅↩🔲⭡ fishing lake
   £5.00-£16.50 (Mastercard/Visa) enquiries@northamfarm.co.uk www.northamfarm.co.uk

Southfield Farm Camp Site, Brean TA8 2RL ☎ (01278) 751233 OS map 182/295561 4m N of
   Burnham off B3140 (Berrow) on coast road in Brean by sandy beach Open Spring Holiday-Oct
   475 pitches (275 static) Level grass part, sheltered 🛢🛢⏚⊕⭡ (Mastercard/Visa)

SITE DIRECTIONS
The distance and direction of a campsite is given from the centre of the town under which it appears.

BURTON BRADSTOCK, Dorset   **Map D6**
Village noted for its thatched houses and banded cliffs on E
✘ Three Horseshoes, Mill St ✆ (01308) 897259

Coastal Caravans, Annings Lane DT6 4QP ✆ (01308) 422139 *Prop: Mr & Mrs Cox* OS map
   193/494898 On E edge of Burton Bradstock in Annings Lane Open April-Sept 110 pitches
   (94 static) 10 acres level grass, sheltered 🅱🆘⊘⛽🅚 £8.00-£17.50 *holidays@wdlh.co.uk*
   www.wdlh.co.uk

Freshwater Beach Holiday Park, Burton Bradstock DT6 4PT ✆ (01308) 897317 OS map
   193/491883 ½m W of Burton Bradstock on left of B3157 (Bridport) Open mid Mar-mid Oct
   550 pitches (289 static) Level/sloping grass, sheltered 🅱✘🅨⊷⤟🅱🆘⊘⊕⊘🖵 (heated)
   ⊕⤻⌂⛽⛓ lic club, private beach, horse riding £8.00-£28.00 (Mastercard/Visa)
   www.freshwaterbeach.co.uk

CALNE, Wilts   **Map F3**
EC Wed MD Fri SEE almshouses, Adam church
✘ Lansdowne Strand, The Strand ✆ (01249) 812488

Blackland Lakes Holiday Centre, Knights Marsh Farm, Stockley Lane SN11 0NQ ✆ (01249)
   813672 Fax (01249) 811346 OS map 173/005689 1½m SSE of Calne off A4 (Marlborough) on
   Heddington road (signposted) Open all year–adv booking preferable 180 pitches 17 acres, grass
   and hard standing, level/sloping, sheltered 🅱⤟🅱🆘⊘⊕⊘🖵 (indoor) ⤻⛓ lake fishing, bird
   sanctuary, £10.00 (min)* (Mastercard/Switch/Delta/Visa) *info@blacklandlakes.co.uk*
   www.blacklandlakes.co.uk

CANNARDS GRAVE–see Shepton Mallet

CERNE ABBAS, Dorset   **Map E5**
SEE Cerme Abbas Giant N
✘ Red Lion, Long St ✆ (01300) 341441

Giants Head Farm, Old Sherborne Road DT2 7TR ✆ (01300) 341242 OS map 194/675029 2m NE
   of Cerne Abbas on Buckland Newton road Open Easter-Oct 50 pitches 3½ acres, level grass,
   sheltered 🅱🆘⊘⊕⌂🅟🖵⌂ £7.00-£11.00* *holidays@giantshead.co.uk www.giantshead.co.uk*

Lyons Gate Caravan Park, Lyons Gate DT2 7AZ ✆ (01300) 341260 OS map 194/662060 3m N of
   Cerne Abbas on A352 (Sherborne) Open all year 60 pitches 🅱🅨🅱🆘⊘⊕⊘🖵 (indoor) ⊕⤻
   🚽 (70) ⛽ lake fishing, golf course £12.00 (min)* *info@lyons-gate.co.uk www.lyons-gate.co.uk*

CHARD, Somerset   **Map D5**
EC Wed MD Sat *Market town of Saxon origin* SEE Choughs Inn, Manor House, wildlife park 3m E
at Cricket St Thomas
🅸 The Guildhall, Fore St ✆ (01460) 65710
✘ George, Fore St ✆ (01460) 63413

Alpine Grove Touring Park, Forton TA20 4HD ✆ (01460) 63479 Fax (01460) 63479 OS map
   193/342070 1½m SE of Chard off B3167 (Axminster-Crewkerne)–signposted Open April-Oct
   40 pitches 7½ acres, level, oak woodland 🅱🆘🆘⊘⊕⊘🖵 (heated) ⊕⤻ Grass and hard
   standings £8.00-£12.50* *stay@alpinegrovetouringpark.com www.alpinegrovetouringpark.com*

South Somerset Holiday Park, Exeter Road, Howley TA20 3EA ✆ (01460) 62221/66036 OS map
   193/275095 2½m W of Chard on A30 (Honiton) Open all year 140 pitches Level grass and hard
   standing, sheltered ⤟🅱🆘⊘⊘⤻⛓ lic club

CHARMOUTH, Dorset   **Map D6**
EC Thurs SEE 16c Queen's Armes, fossil exhibition, Blue Lias cliffs
✘ Queen's Armes, The Street ✆ (01297) 560339

Monkton Wylde Farm Touring Caravan Park DT6 6DB ✆ (01297) 34525 Fax (01297) 33594 OS
   map 193/328967 3m NW of Charmouth off A35 (Axminster) on left of B3165 (Marshwood) Open
   Easter-Nov 14 60 pitches 6 acres level grass sheltered–some hard standing 🅱🅱🆘⊘⊕⊘⤻⛽
   £7.40-£15.40* (Mastercard/Visa/Switch) *holidays@monktonwyld.co.uk www.monktonwyld.co.uk*

Newlands Caravan and Camping Park DT6 6RB ✆ (01297) 560259 Fax (01297) 560787 OS map
   193/375936 ½m E of Charmouth centre on right of A35 (Bridport) Open all year 280 pitches
   (80 static) Level grass and hard standing 🅱✘🅨⊷⤟🅱🆘⊘⊕⊘🖵 (indoor) ⊕⤻⛽⌂⛓ club
   bar, fish and chip bar (all cards) *enq@newlandsholidays.co.uk www.newlandsholidays.co.uk*

Wood Farm Caravan and Camping Park, Axminster Road DT6 6BT ✆ (01297) 560697 Fax
   (01297) 561243 OS map 193/355940 1m NW of Charmouth centre on right of A35 (Axminster)
   Open Apr-Oct 216 pitches (80 static) Level/sloping grass and hard standing, sheltered
   🅱⊷🅱🆘⊘⊘🖵 (heated indoor) ⊕⤻⌂ tennis, fishing lake £10.50-£18.00*
   (Delta/Mastercard/Switch/Visa) *holidays@woodfarm.co.uk www.woodfarm.co.uk*

❖ DOGS
Dogs are usually allowed but must be kept on a lead. Sometimes they have to be paid for.

CHEDDAR, Somerset   **Map D3**
EC & MD Wed SEE gorge, caves, Jacob's Ladder
🄸 The Gorge ☏ (01934) 744071
✘ Poacher's Table, Cliff St ☏ (01934) 742271

Broadway House Caravan and Camping Park BS27 3DB ☏ (01934) 742610 OS map 182/448546
  1m NW of Cheddar on A371 (Axbridge) Open Mar-Nov 200 pitches (35 static) Level/sloping
  grass, some hard standings, sheltered 🔒♀⌣⋏🗑🅱⌀⊕⌀☐⊕↵☐🖾🔥 babies' room, table
  tennis, crazy golf, activity programme, bicycle hire, nature trail, skateboard park, BMX track £5.50-
  £13.50 (all cards)

Bucklegrove Caravan Park, Rodney Stoke BS27 3UZ ☏ (01749) 870261 Fax (01749) 870101 OS
  map 182/488502 3½m SE of Cheddar on A371 (Wells) Open Mar-Jan—must book peak periods
  160 pitches (35 static) Level/sloping grass and hard standings, sheltered
  🔒✘♀⌣⋏🗑🅱⌀⊕⌀☐⊕↵☐🖥(50) ⊕🖾🔥 £5.00-£17.00* (Mastercard/Visa/Switch/Delta)
  info@bucklegrove.co.uk www.bucklegrove.co.uk

Church Farm Caravan and Camping Site BS27 3RF ☏ (01934) 743048 OS map 182/460530 ¼m
  S of Cheddar off A371 (Axbridge) Open Easter-Oct 155 pitches 5 acres, level grass and hard
  standings, sheltered 🔒🗑🅱⌀⊕⌀🖾🔥

Froglands Farm, Draycott Road BS27 3RH ☏ (01934) 742058 OS map 182/463530 ½m SE edge
  of Cheddar on A371 (Wells) Open Apr-Oct 68 pitches Level grass and hard standings, sheltered
  🗑🅱⌀⊕⌀

Longbottom Farm, Shipham BS25 1RW ☏ (01934) 743166 OS map 182/459567 3m N of
  Cheddar off A371 (Axbridge) and Shipham road Open all year 16 pitches Level/sloping grass,
  sheltered No showers

Ragwood Farm, Clewer BS28 4JG ☏ (01934) 742254 OS map 182/442510 2m SW of Cheddar on
  B3151 (Wedmore) Open Whitsun-Aug 60 pitches 🔒🗑⊕☐↵🖪

Rodney Stoke Inn, Rodney Stoke BS27 3XB ☏ (01749) 870209 OS map 182/483502 2m SE of
  Cheddar on right of A371 (Wells) in Rodney Stoke Open all year 30 pitches 1½ acres level grass
  sheltered ✘♀⌣⋏🅱⌀⌣↵ £8.50-£12.00 inc elect (Mastercard/Visa)

CHEW MAGNA, NE Somerset   **Map E3**
SEE 15c church and adj ale house, Tun bridge over river Chew, Chew Valley lake 1m S (bird
watching, sailing)
✘ The Red Lion, Sutton Hill Rd, Bishop Sutton ☏ (01275) 332689

Bath Chew Valley Caravan Park, Ham Lane, Bishop Sutton BS39 5TZ ☏ (01275) 332127 (8am-
  8pm) Prop: Keith Betton OS map 172/585599 2m SE of Chew Magna on Bishop Sutton road
  Open all year 35 pitches—no children—must book Level grass and hard standing 🗑🅱⌀⊕⌀🔥
  fully serviced pitches set among gardens, shop and bar nearby, pets, TV hook-up £12.00-£18.00
  inc elect and awning (Visa/Mastercard/Maestro/Electron) *enquiries@bathchewvalley.co.uk*
  www.bathchewvalley.co.uk

CHIDEOCK–see Bridport

CHIPPENHAM, Wilts   **Map F3**
EC Wed MD Fri, Sat SEE Maud Heath's Causeway, Yelde Hall museum, parish church, Lacock
Abbey 3m S
🄸 The Citadel, Bath Rd ☏ (01249) 706333
✘ Angel, Market Pl ☏ (01249) 652615

Piccadilly Caravan Park, Folly Lane West, Lacock SN15 2LP Family site above Lacock village
  ☏ (01249) 730260 Prop: Peter Williams OS map 173/912682 3½m S of Chippenham off A350
  (Melksham) on Gastard road Open Apr-Oct 47 pitches 2½ acres, grass, level/sloping, some hard
  standings 🗑🅱⌀⊕⌀⊕↵ £11.00-£13.00 *piccadillylacock@aol.com*

FACTS CAN CHANGE

We do our best to check the accuracy of the
entries in this guide but changes can and do
occur after publication. So if you plan to stay
at a site some distance from home it makes
sense to ring the manager or owner before
setting off.

Bath Chew Valley Caravan Park, Chew Magna

CHRISTCHURCH, Dorset   **Map G6**
EC Wed MD Mon SEE priory church, Red House museum, Hengistbury Head, Tucktonia model village
✗ King's Arms, Castle St ✆ (01202) 484117

Grove Farm Meadow Holiday Park, Stour Way BH23 2PQ *Well-run site by river Stour* ✆ (01202) 483597 Fax (01202) 483878 OS map 195/136947 2m NW of Christchurch off A35 (Bournemouth) on Hurn road Open Mar-Oct 250 pitches (193 static)–no tents 10 acres, level grass, sheltered ⚿⛽⚓🚿⚙⚡🔌⚓♨🚻🚽♿ first aid, fishing, games room £7.00-£25.00* (all major cards) *enquiries@meadowbank-holidays.co.uk*

CLEVEDON, N Somerset   **Map D3**
EC Wed SEE church, Clevedon Court Manor 1m E
✗ Walton Park, Wellington Terr ✆ (01272) 874253

Warrens Holiday Park, Lake Farm, Colehouse Lane, Kenn BS21 6TQ ✆ (01275) 871666 OS map 171/172/405695 1m S of Clevedon off B3133 (Yatton) Open Mar-Jan 100 pitches (53 static) 13 acres, level grass and hard standings, sheltered ✗⛽⚓♨⚡🔌 club house, fishing

CONGRESBURY, N Somerset   **Map D3**
SEE Yatton church 1m N, Cadbury Hill (views) 1m N
✗ Old Inn, St Paul's Causeway ✆ (01934) 832270

Oak Farm Touring Park, Weston Road BS49 5EB ✆ (01934) 833246 Mobile (07889) 319686 *Prop: BA Sweet* OS map 182/433640 ½m W of Congresbury on A370 (Weston super Mare)–M5 junct 21 Open Mar-Oct 27 pitches 2 acres, level grass, sheltered ⚡♨⚓ takeaway ½ mile £12.50-£15.00

CORFE, Somerset   **Map C5**
SEE Widcombe bird gardens
✗ Greyhound Inn 3m SE at Staple Fitzpaine ✆ (01823) 480227

Holly Bush Park, Culmhead TA3 7EA *Homely site in lovely country* ✆ (01823) 421515 OS map 193/222162 3m S of Corfe off B3170 (Honiton) Open all year 40 pitches 2 acres level grass and hard standings, sheltered ⚿⛽⚓♨⚡🔌⚓♨⚡♨ £9.00-£12.00* (most cards) *info@hollybushpark.com www.hollybushpark.com*

CORFE CASTLE, Dorset   **Map F6**
SEE castle ruins, model village
✗ Fox Inn, West St ✆ (01929) 480449

Burnbake Campsite, Rempstone BH20 5JH ✆ (01929) 480570 OS map 195/993832 2m E of Corfe Castle off B3351 (Studland) Open Apr-Sept–no adv booking 130 pitches–no caravans Level grass sheltered ⚿⛽⚓♨⚡🔌⚓♨ £8.50-£12.00 *info@burnbake.com www.burnbake.com*

East Creech Farm BH20 5AP ✆ (01929) 480519 *Prop: Mrs V Best* OS map 195/928827 2m W of Corfe Castle off A351 (Wareham) on Blue Pool road Open Apr-Oct 80 pitches 3 acres, grass, level/sloping, part sheltered ⛽♨⚡♨⚓ £7.50-£13.00 *east.creech@virgin.net www.eastcreechfarm.co.uk*

Woodlands Camping Caravan Park, Glebe Farm, Bucknowle BH20 5NG ✆ (01929) 480280 Fax (01929) 480280 OS map 195/948817 1m W of Corfe Castle off Church Knowle road Open Easter-Oct (pref 5 nights or multiples in peak periods) 65 pitches–no adv booking 7 acres, grass, level/sloping, sheltered ⚿⛽⚓♨⚡🔌♨♿ £10.00-£12.00*

Woodhyde Farm BH20 5HT ✆ (01929) 480274 OS map 195/973804 ½m S of Corfe Castle on right of A351 (Swanage) Open Easter-Oct 150 pitches 15 acres, level ⚿⚓

CORFE MULLEN–see Wimborne

CRICKLADE, Wilts   **Map G2**
EC Wed, Sat SEE Inglesham church, North Meadow nature reserve
✗ The Red Lion, The Street, Castle Eaton ✆ (01285) 810280 Open 12-2.30/6-9 (closed Tue lunch)

Second Chance Touring Park, Marston Meysey SN6 6SZ ✆ (01285) 810675/810939 *Prop: B Stroud* OS map 163/140960 3m NE of Cricklade off A419 (Swindon) on Kempsford road via Castle Eaton Open Mar-Nov 30 pitches 2 acres mainly level grass and hard standings, sheltered ⚡⚓♨♨ fishing, canoeing £8.00-£10.00 inc elect

CROWCOMBE, Somerset   **Map C4**
SEE church, Church House, Quantock Forest 2m E
✗ White Horse Inn 3m W at Stogumber ✆ (01984) 656277

Quantock Orchard Caravan Park TA4 4AW ✆ (01984) 618618 Fax (01984) 618618 OS map 181/142350 1m S of Crowcombe on A358 (Taunton-Minehead) by Flaxpool Garage Open all year 75 pitches 4 acres, level grass, some hard standings, sheltered ⚿⛽⚓♨⚡🔌⚓♨(heated) ♨⚓♿ games room, mountain bike hire (most cards) *qocp@flaxpool.freeserve.co.uk www.flaxpool.freeserve.co.uk*

DEVIZES, Wilts   **Map F3**
EC Wed MD Thurs, Sat *Pleasant old market town in fertile countryside* SEE market cross, museum,
St Mary's church, St John's Alley
🛈 Cromwell House ☏ (01380) 729408
✗ Bear, Market Pl ☏ (01380) 722444

Bell Caravan and Camp Site, Lydeway SN10 3PS *Peaceful site with easy access to Stonehenge,
Salisbury and Bath* ☏ (01380) 840230 OS map 173/050583 3m SE of Devizes on A342
(Andover) Open Apr-Oct 30 pitches Level grass and hard standing, sheltered
🛒 ⇌ ⤢ 🗑 🔌 🔌 ⊕ Ø ⌧ (heated) ⊛ ⤸ ⛛ 🔲 table tennis, covered barbecue area (all cards exc
Amex)

Lower Foxhanger Farm, Rowde SN10 1SS ☏ (01380) 828254 OS map 173/969613 2m W of
Devizes on A361 (Trowbridge) adj Kennet and Avon canal Open Apr-Oct 10 pitches Grass,
sloping, sheltered 🔌 Ø ⊕ Ø ⌧ (Mastercard/Visa) colin@foxhangers.co.uk www.foxhangers.com

DULVERTON, Somerset   **Map B4**
EC Thurs *Tourist resort beautifully set on river Barle at edge of Exmoor* SEE church tower,
earthworks, Tarr steps 5m NW
✗ Badgers Holt, Bridgetown ☏ (01643) 851204

Exe Valley Site, Mill House, Bridgetown TA22 9JR ☏ (01643) 851432 *Prop: Mrs Christine Matthews*
OS map 181/923333 7m N of Dulverton off A396 (Dunster) by river Exe Open Mar-Oct
50 pitches–no children Grass, level, hard standings, sheltered 🛒 🗑 🔌 Ø ⊕ Ø ♿ fly fishing
£7.50-£12.50 paul@paulmatt.fsnet.co.uk www.exevalleycamping.co.uk

Lakeside Touring Caravan Park, Higher Grants, Exebridge TA22 9BE ☏ (01398) 324068 OS map
181/932241 3m S of Dulverton on A396 (Dunster-Tiverton) Open Mar-Oct 50 pitches 4 acres
grass and hard standing, level/sloping, sheltered ✗ ⇌ 🗑 🔌 ⊕ Ø ♿ dog walk

Zeacombe House (Caravan Club), Anstey Mills EX16 9JU ☏ (01398) 341279 (8am-8pm) *Prop: Mr
& Mrs P Keeble* OS map 181/862241 3m SW of Dulverton on B3227 (old A361: Bampton-South
Molton) Open mid Mar-Oct 50 pitches 4½ acres level grass and hard standings, sheltered
🛒 ⇌ 🗑 🔌 Ø ⊕ Ø dog walk £14.00-£18.00 (Mastercard/Visa)

DUNKIRK–see Badminton

DUNSTER, Somerset   **Map B4**
EC Wed *Ancient village dominated by Conygar Hill, a landmark for shipping.* SEE historic castle,
Yarn Market, church, dovecote, nunnery, grist mill, Cleeve abbey 4m SE
✗ Luttrell Arms ☏ (01643) 821555

Totterdown Farm, Timberscombe TA24 7TA ☏ (01643) 841317 OS map 181/957424 2m SW of
Dunster on left of A396 (Tiverton) Open Jul 15-Sept 15 22 pitches Level grass

EAST BRENT, Somerset   **Map D3**
✗ Brent House Restaurant, Bridgwater Rd ☏ (01278) 760246

Dulhorn Farm, Weston Road, Lympsham BS24 0JQ ☏ (01934) 750298 Fax (01934) 750913 OS
map 182/349534 1m N of East Brent on left of A370 (Weston super Mare) Open Mar-Oct
57 pitches 3½ acres, level grass 🔌 Ø ⊕ ⤸ 🏠 £8.00-£14.00 garybowden@btconnect.com
www.dulhornfarmholiday.park.co.uk

EAST STOKE–see Wool

EXEBRIDGE–see Dulverton

EXFORD, Somerset   **Map B4**
At heart of Exmoor, unspoiled moorland village in hollow by river Exe
✗ Crown ☏ (01643) 831554

Westermill Farm TA24 7NJ ☏ (01643) 831238 *Prop: Oliver & Jill Edwards* OS map 181/824398
2½m W of Exford off Porlock road, by river–signposted Open all year 60 pitches–unsuitable for
trailer caravans 6 acres, level grass, sheltered 🛒 🗑 Ø ⊕ Ø 🏠 bathing, fishing, waymarked
walks, campfires, free showers/dishwashing £10.00

KEY TO SYMBOLS

🛒	shop	⌀	gas supplies	🔩	winter storage for caravans
✗	restaurant	⊕	chemical disposal point	Ⓟ	parking obligatory
🍺	bar	Ø	payphone	⊗	no dogs
⇌	takeaway food	⌧	swimming pool	⌫	caravan hire
⤢	off licence	⊛	games area	🏠	bungalow hire
🗑	laundrette	⤸	children's playground	♿	facilities for disabled
🔌	mains electric hook-ups	⛛	TV	🔲	shaded

FERNDOWN, Dorset — Map G5

EC Wed SEE church

✗ Bridge House 1m SW on A348 at Longham ☎ (01202) 578828

Back of Beyond Touring Park, St Leonards BH24 2SB ☎ (01202) 876968 *Prop: Mel & Sue Pike* OS map 195/107021 3m NE of Ferndown off A31 (Ringwood) Open Easter-Oct 80 pitches–adults only 28 acres level grass, sheltered 🔲🔲🔲🔲🔲🔲🔲 9-hole golf, seasonal pitches, fishing lakes/river £7.00-£15.50 (Mastercard/Visa) *melandsuepike@aol.com* *www.backofbeyondtouringpark.co.uk*

Oakdene Forest Park, St Leonards BH24 2RZ ☎ (01590) 648331 OS map 195/105030 2m E of Ferndown off A31 (Ringwood) Open Feb 1-Jan 5 128 pitches (90 static) 55 acres level grass and hard standing 🔲🔲🔲🔲🔲🔲🔲 paddling pools, disco, lic club, gym, sauna, adventure playground £9.50-£31.00 (Mastercard/Visa/Connect/Delta/Switch)

St Leonards Farm Caravan and Camping Park, West Moors BH22 0AQ ☎ (01202) 872637 OS map 195/095020 2m NE of Ferndown on A31 (Ringwood) Open Apr-Sept 175 pitches Level grass, sheltered 🔲🔲🔲🔲🔲🔲

Shamba Holidays, St Leonards BH20 2SB ☎ (01202) 873302 *Prop: Karen Gray* OS map 195/104026 2m NE of Ferndown off A31 (Ringwood) on East Moors Farm lane Open March-Oct 150 pitches 6 acres, level grass and hard standings 🔲 ✗ (snack) 🔲🔲🔲🔲🔲🔲🔲🔲🔲🔲🔲 £15.00-£25.00 (Visa/Access/Switch/Delta) *enquiries@shambaholidays.co.uk* *www.shambaholidays.co.uk*

GLASTONBURY, Somerset — Map D4

EC Wed MD Tues SEE Benedictine abbey ruins (oldest religious foundation in Britain), almshouses, St Michael's Tower on Glastonbury Tor, Tribunal House with relics of prehistoric lake village

ℹ The Tribunal, High St ☎ (01458) 832954

✗ George and Pilgrims, High St ☎ (01458) 831146

Ashwell Farm House, Ashwell Lane, Edgarley BA6 8LB ☎ (01458) 832313 OS map 182/514382 ¾m E of Glastonbury on A361 (Shepton Mallet) Open all year 80 pitches (15 static) 2 acres, gentle slope/level grass 🔲🔲🔲🔲

Isle of Avalon Touring Caravan Park, Godney Road BA6 9AF ☎ (01458) 833618 OS map 182/493396 ½m W of Glastonbury centre off B3151 (Wedmore) Open all year 120 pitches 8 acres, level grass and hard standings, sheltered 🔲🔲🔲🔲🔲🔲🔲🔲🔲 bike hire (all cards)

The Old Oaks Touring Caravan Camping Park, Wick Farm, Wick BA6 8JS ☎ (01458) 831437 Fax (01458) 833238 OS map 182/522394 2m NE of Glastonbury off A361 (Shepton Mallet) and A39 (Wells) Open mid Mar-early Oct 80 pitches–adults only 10 acres, grass and hard standings, level/sloping, sheltered 🔲🔲🔲🔲🔲🔲 fishing £9.00-£13.00* (Mastercard/Visa/Delta/Switch/Debit) *info@theoldoaks.co.uk www.theoldoaks.co.uk*

For other sites near Glastonbury see also Street

HARMANS CROSS–see Swanage

HIGHBRIDGE–see Burnham

HURN, Dorset — Map G5

✗ Avon Causeway ☎ (01202) 482714

Longfield Caravan Park, Matchams Lane BH23 6AW ☎ (01202) 485214 OS map 195/128997 2m N of Hurn on left of Matchams Lane Open all year–must book peak periods 29 pitches 2 acres, level grass and hard standings 🔲🔲 (all pitches) 🔲🔲🔲 farm produce

Mount Pleasant Touring Park, Matchams Lane BH23 6AW ☎ (01202) 475474 OS map 195/130990 1m N of Hurn on right of Matchams Lane Open Mar-Oct 170 pitches 7 acres grass, part sloping 🔲🔲🔲🔲🔲🔲🔲🔲🔲 £7.00-£14.00* (most cards) *enq@mount-pleasant-cc.co.uk* *www.mount-pleasant-cc.co.uk*

Port View, Matchams Lane BH23 6AW ☎ (01202) 474214 OS map 195/129991 1½m N of Hurn on right of Matchams Lane Open Easter-Oct 35 pitches Grass, part level, part sheltered 🔲🔲🔲

ILMINSTER, Somerset — Map D5

EC Thurs MD alt Wed SEE Barrington Court 3m N (NT)

✗ The Five Dials, Goose Lane, Horton ☎ (01460) 55359

Stewley Cross Caravan Park, Stewley Cross, Ashill TA19 9NP ☎ (01823) 480314 OS map 193/312180 3m NW of Ilminster off A303 (Honiton) on left of A358 (Taunton) at Stewley Cross Open Apr-Oct 20 pitches ½ acre level grass

Thornleigh Caravan Park, Thornleigh, Horton TA19 9QH ☎ (01460) 53450 *Prop: Ken & Shirley White* OS map 193/329151 1m W of Ilminster off A303 in village of Horton opp church Open Mar-Oct 20 pitches 1½ acres level grass 🔲🔲🔲 sauna £7.50-£9.25 inc elect *ken-shirl@supanet.com*

LACOCK–see Chippenham

LANGPORT, Somerset   Map D4
EC Wed SEE parish church, Hanging Chapel
✘ Langport Arms, Cheapside ✆ (01458) 250530

Bowdens Crest Caravan Camping Park, Bowdens TA10 0DD ✆ (01458) 250553 *Prop: Mrs May*
    OS map 193/413289 1½m N of Langport off A372 (Bridgwater) on Bowdens road Open all year
    60 pitches (30 static) 15 acres grass, some hard standing, sheltered
    🛒✘♀⇦⅃🖊🗑⊘⊗⦸↙🏳🗑🗑⚿ lic clubhouse £5.00-£16.00 (Mastercard/Visa/Access/Delta)
    bowcrest@btconnect.com www.bowdenscrest.co.uk

Thorney Lakes Caravan Park, Muchelney TA10 0DW ✆ (01458) 250811 OS map 193/429228 2m
    S of Langport on Kingsbury Episcopi road by river Parrett Open Mar-Jan 40 pitches Level grass,
    sheltered 🗑⊗ fishing lakes £10.00-£12.00* enquiries@thorneylakes.co.uk
    www.thorneylakes.co.uk

LANGTON MATRAVERS–see Swanage

LONGLEAT–see Warminster

LULWORTH, Dorset   Map F6
SEE cove, Durdle Door (natural cliff arch), Fossil Forest (access at certain times), Lulworth Castle,
church, Dorset coast path
✘ Castle on B3070 ✆ (01929) 400311

Durdle Door Holiday Park, West Lulworth BH20 5PU ✆ (01929) 400200 Fax (01929) 400260
    Prop: Weld Enterprises Ltd OS map 194/812809 1m W of Lulworth on Daggers Gate road
    Open Mar-Oct 555 pitches (400 static) 45 acres grass, level/sloping, sheltered 🛒✘♀⇦↙
    🖊🗑🗑⊗⊘⊗⦸↙🗑⚿⚿ mountain bike hire £10.00-£30.00 (all cards) durdle.door@lulworth.com
    www.lulworth.com

LYME REGIS–see Bridport

LYTCHETT MINSTER, Dorset   Map F5
Village close by Poole harbour
✘ Chequers 1½m NW at Lytchett Matravers ✆ (01202) 622215

Beacon Hill Touring Park, Blandford Road North BH16 6AB *Well equipped and quiet site in
    woodland setting* ✆ (01202) 631631 Fax (01202) 625749 OS map 195/975940 1½m NE of
    Lytchett Minster on A350 (Poole–Blandford) just N of junction with A35 Open Easter-Sep
    170 pitches 30 acres, mainly level grass, some hard standings, sheltered 🛒✘♀⇦↙🖊🗑🗑🖊
    ⊘🖂(heated) ⊗↙🗑⚿ tennis, fishing £10.00-£23.00* bookings@beaconhilltouringpark.co.uk
    www.beaconhilltouringpark.co.uk

Huntick Farm, Lytchett Matravers BH16 6BB ✆ (01202) 622222 OS map 195/957949 1m N of
    Lytchett Minster off Lytchett Matravers road at Rose and Crown Open Apr-Oct 30 pitches Level
    grass, sheltered 🗑🖊⊗⊘⊗↙🖊 boat and storage

Organford Manor, Organford BH16 6ES *Secluded site in grounds of manor* ✆ (01202) 622202 OS
    map 195/945925 2m SW of Lytchett Minster off B3067/A35 (Dorchester) on right of Organford
    road Open Mar 15-Oct 31 120 pitches (45 static) 8 acres, level grass, sheltered 🛒(high
    season) 🗑🖊🖊⊗⊘⊗🗑⚿⚿ £8.50-£10.00 organford@lds.co.uk www.organfordmanor.co.uk

Pear Tree Touring Park, Organford BH16 6LA ✆ (01202) 622434 OS map 195/940915 1½m SW
    of Lytchett Minster off A3067/A351 (Wareham) on left of Organford road Open Apr-Oct 15
    125 pitches 7½ acres, level grass and hard standings 🛒🖊🗑🖊⊗⊘↙🖊⚿ riding stables
    £10.00-£17.00* (most cards) info@visitpeartree.co.uk www.visitpeartree.co.uk

Sandford Park, Holton Heath BH16 6JZ *Family site with lots of entertainment set in secluded
    woodland with direct access to A351* ✆ (01202) 622513/(0870) 0667793 Fax (01202) 625678
    OS map 195/941912 1½m SW of Lytchett Minster on right of A351 (Wareham) Open Mar-Nov
    500 pitches (295 static)–adv booking advisable 60 acres, level grass, sheltered 🛒✘♀⇦↙
    🖊🗑🖊⊗⊘⊗🖂(indoor, heated) ⊗↙🗑🖊🗑🗑⚿ crazy golf, tennis, barbecues, paddling pool,
    ballroom, ladies hairdresser £12.50-£28.50* (most cards) bookings@weststarholidays.co.uk
    www.weststarholidays.co.uk

South Lytchett Manor Caravan Park, Lytchett Minster BH16 6JB ✆ (01202) 622577 Fax (01202)
    622620 OS map 195/964932 ¼m NE of Lytchett Minster on B3067 (Upton) Open Apr-Oct
    15–must book peak periods 150 pitches Level/sloping grass and hard standing, sheltered
    🛒⇦↙🖊🗑🖊⊗⊘↙🗑🖊⚿ £10.00-£16.50* (Mastercard/Visa/Delta/Switch) slmcpetalk21.com
    www.eluk.co.uk/camping/dorset/slytchett

MAIDEN NEWTON, Dorset   Map E5
SEE church with Norman chancel
✘ Old Market House 4m NE at Cerne Abbas ✆ (01300) 341680

Clay Pigeon Tourist Park, Wardon Hill DT2 9PW ✆ (01935) 83492 OS map 194/610023 3m N of
    Maiden Newton on A37 (Dorchester–Yeovil) Open all year 60 pitches 3½ acres, level grass and
    hard standing ✘🗑🗑🖊⊗⊘⊗↙🗑⚿

MALMESBURY, Wilts   Map F2
EC Thurs SEE abbey, market cross, almshouses, museum, Abbey Hall gardens
🛈 Town Hall, Market Lane ✆(01666) 823748
✗ The Smoking Dog, 62 High St ✆(01666) 825823

Burton Hill Caravan and Camping Park, Arches Lane SN16 0EH ✆(01666) 826880 *Prop: Warren
& Audrey Hateley* OS map 173/933872 ¼m S of Malmesbury off A429 (Chippenham) opposite
hospital Open Apr-Nov 30 pitches 2 acres, level grass, sheltered 🔲🔁🅰️🔅🅱️🔆🆒🅰️
£10.00-£12.00* (Mastercard/Visa/Maestro) *stay@burtonhill.co.uk www.burtonhill.co.uk*

MARLBOROUGH, Wilts   Map G3
EC Wed MD Wed, Sat SEE college, old houses and inns, White Horse, Savernake Forest
🛈 Car Park, George Lane ✆(01672) 513989
✗ Castle and Ball, High St ✆(01672) 515201

Hill View Caravan Park, Oare SN8 4JE ✆(01672) 563151 OS map 173/156623 6m SW of
Marlborough on A345 (Pewsey) Open Apr-Sept 46 pitches (36 static) 4 acres level grass,
sheltered 🔁🔆 (inc hot water)

Postern Hill, (Forest Enterprise) SN8 4ND ✆(01672) 515195 OS map 173/197680 1m S of
Marlborough on left of A346 (Andover) Open Mar 15-Oct 15 170 pitches–no adv booking
20 acres level grass, sheltered 🔁🅰️🔆⊘ (Mastercard/Visa)

MARTOCK, Somerset   Map D4
EC Thurs SEE 15-16c church (interior), Treasurer's House (NT), 17c Church House, East Lambrook
Manor 2m W
✗ White Hart, East St ✆(01935) 822005

Southfork Caravan Park, Parrett Works TA12 6AE ✆(01935) 825661 *Prop: Mr & Mrs Broadley*
OS map 193/443190 ½m W of Martock off South Petherton road by river Parrett Open all year
25 pitches 2 acres level grass 🔁⚓🔲🔁🅰️🔆⊘🔆🆒🚐 fishing, caravan spares and service
£9.00-£12.00 (all major cards) *southforkcaravans@btconnect.com www.southforkcaravans.co.uk*

MEARE, Somerset   Map D4
SEE peat moors visitor centre, nature reserve, Fish House (enq at Manor Farm)
✘ The Inn, Burtle Bar & Restaurant, Catcott Rd, Burtle ✆(01278) 722269 Open Sat-Sun all day

Orchard Camping, The Inn, Burtle, Burtle TA7 8NG ✆(01278) 722269 OS map 182/402429 2m W
of Meare off Shapwick road Open all year 30 pitches 1 acre level grass
✘♀⬚⚲♦∅⌁⬛🅿♿🔌 skittle alley, washing up sink £8.95-£10.95 (all cards)
chris@theburtleinn.co.uk www.theburtleinn.co.uk

MINEHEAD, Somerset   Map B4
EC Wed SEE old houses, model village, Dunster village and castle 2m SE, West Somerset Railway,
Exmoor
🆔 17 Friday St ✆(01643) 702624
✘ Luttrell Arms 2m SE at Dunster ✆(01643) 821555

Minehead and Exmoor Caravan and Camping Park, Porlock Road TA24 8SW ✆(01643) 703074
OS map 181/951458 1m W of Minehead centre on right of A39 (Porlock) Open Mar-Oct
50 pitches Grass and hard standing, level, part sheltered 🅱⬛🅱⊘♦∅⌁🅱♿ £10.00 (min)*
See also Dunster

NETHER STOWEY, Somerset   Map C4
SEE Coleridge's cottage
✘ Cottage Inn at Keenthorne on A39 (Cannington) ✆(01278) 732355

Currypool Mills, Cannington TA5 2NH ✆(01278) 671135 OS map 182/231383 2m E of Nether
Stowey off A39 (Bridgwater) on Spaxton road Open Easter-mid Nov 35 pitches 1½ acres level
grass and hard standing, sheltered 🅱⬛🅱⊘♦∅⬚(indoor)⌁🅱🏠
currypoolmills@btopenworld.com

Mill Farm Caravan Camping Park, Fiddington TA5 1JQ ✆(01278) 732286 OS map 182/218407
2½m E of Nether Stowey off A39 (Bridgwater) Open all year 125 pitches 15 acres level grass
and hard standings, sheltered 🅱⚲⬛🅱⊘♦∅⬚(heated)♿⌁⬚🅱🔌 farm produce, canoe
hire, pony rides, pets corner, free boating (all cards) *www.mill-farm-uk.com*

NORTH WOOTTON–see Pilton

ORCHESTON–see Shrewton

ORGANFORD–see Lytchett Minster

OWERMOIGNE, Dorset   Map E6
✘ Frampton Arms, Hurst Rd, Moreton ✆(01305) 852253

Moreton Camping and Caravanning Club Site, Station Road, Moreton DT2 8BB ✆(01305)
853801 *Prop: The Camping and Caravanning Club* OS map 194/782892 3m N of Owermoigne
on B3390 (Warmwell–Affpuddle) adj Moreton station Open Mar-Nov 130 pitches Level grass and
hard standings 🅱⚲⬛🅱⊘♦∅⌁🅱♿ (Mastercard/Visa/Switch)
www.campingandcaravanningclub.co.uk

Sandyholme Holiday Park, Moreton Road DT2 8HZ ✆(01305) 852677 *Prop: Mike & Libby
Smeaton* OS map 194/768867 1m N of Owermoigne on Moreton road Open Apr 1-Oct 31 100
pitches (52 static) 5 acres level grass 🅱✘♀⬚⚲⬛🅱⊘♦∅⌁⬚🅱⬚♿ bar meals £8.50-
£16.00* (Mastercard/Visa/Switch/Maestro) *smeatons@sandyholme.co.uk www.sandyholme.co.uk*

Warmwell Touring Park, Warmwell DT2 8JD ✆(01305) 852313 Fax (01305) 851824 OS map
194/735871 2m W of Owermoigne on B3390 (Warmwell-Affpuddle) near Warmwell Open Mar-
Dec 190 pitches Grass and hard standing, level/sloping, sheltered 🅱♀⬚⚲⬛🅱⊘♦∅⌁⬚🅱
lic club £11.55-£15.55* (Mastercard/Visa/Delta/Switch)

PILTON, Somerset   Map D4
SEE church (roof, screen), tithe barn, Pilton Manor Vineyards
✘ Camelot Inn, Glastonbury Rd, Polsham ✆(01749) 673783

Greenacres Camping, Barrow Lane, North Wootton BA4 4HL ✆(01749) 890497 *Prop: D Harvie*
OS map 182/183/553416 2m W of Pilton via North Wootton Open Apr-Oct 30 pitches–tents,
trailer tents and motorhomes only 4½ acres level grass 🅱⊘♿⌁⚙ free use of fridges &
freezers £12.00

POOLE   Map F6
EC Wed MD Tues, Sat SEE Guildhall museum, park and zoo, largest natural harbour in Britain with
Brownsea Island (NT)
🆔 Poole Quay ✆(01202)253253
✘ Dolphin, High St ✆(01202) 673612

Rockley Park, Hamworthy BH15 4LZ ✆(01202) 679393 Fax (01202) 683159 OS map 195/976910
2m W of Poole off Blandford road Open Mar-Oct 1178 pitches (1077 static) 🅱✘♀⬚⚲⬛🅱
⊘♦∅⬚♿⌁⬚♿ club, dancing (most cards) *www.british-holidays.co.uk*
See also Lytchett Minster

PORLOCK, Somerset   **Map B3**
EC Wed SEE church, Porlock Weir, Porlock Hill (one of steepest in Britain)
✘ Anchor and Ship 1m NW at Porlock Weir ☎ (01643) 862636

Burrowhayes Farm Caravan and Camping Site, West Luccombe TA24 8HT ☎ (01643) 862463
 OS map 181/898459 1m E of Porlock off A39 (Minehead) Open Mar-Oct–booking advisable in
 peak periods 140 pitches (20 static) 8 acres, grass, level/sloping, sheltered, hard standings
 ▣⬚◨◪✱∅� horses and ponies for hire (Mastercard/Visa)

Porlock Caravan Park TA24 8ND ☎ (01643) 862269 Fax (01643) 862269 *Prop: C Macey* OS map
 181/885470 ½m N of Porlock on B3225 (Porlock Weir) Open Apr-Oct 96 pitches (56 static)
 Level grass, sheltered ▣⬚◨◪✱∅◨⌂ £11.00-£15.00* *info@porlockcaravanpark.co.uk*
 www.porlockcaravanpark.co.uk

Porlock Caravan Park, Porlock, Minehead, Somerset TA24 8ND | Tel: +44 (01643) 862 269 | Email: info@porlockcaravanpark.co.uk

RADSTOCK, Somerset   **Map E3**
SEE Ammerdown Park yew gardens 2m SE
✘ Old Malt House 2m NW at Timsbury ☎ (01761) 470106

Pitcote Farm, Stratton on the Fosse BA3 4SX ☎ (01761) 232265 OS map 183/656494 3m S of
 Radstock off A367 (Shepton Mallett) Open all year 30 pitches 2 acres, level *No showers*

RODNEY STOKE–see Wells

ROWDE–see Devizes

ST LEONARDS–see Ferndown

SALISBURY, Wilts   **Map G4**
EC Wed MD Tues, Sat SEE cathedral with 404ft spire, Salisbury and S Wilts museum, Joiners' Hall,
old inns, Old Sarum (pre-Roman settlement) 2m N
🛈 Fish Row ☎ (01722) 334956
✘ Kings Arms, St John's St ☎ (01722) 327629

Alderbury Caravan Camping Park, Old Southampton Rd, Whaddon SP5 3HB ☎ (01722) 710125
 OS map 184/198264 3m SE of Salisbury off A36 (Southampton) in Whaddon Open all year
 40 pitches 1½ acres level grass and hard standings, sheltered ⬚◨◪✱◨⌂♿ £11.00-£13.00
 inc elect *alderbury@aol.com*

Coombe Touring Park, Combe Nurseries, Race Plain, Netherhampton SP2 8PN ☎ (01722) 328451
 Fax (01722) 328451 OS map 184/093283 4m W of Salisbury off A36 (Warminster) and A3094
 (Netherhampton) Open all year 50 pitches 3 acres, level grass, part sheltered ▣⬚◨◪✱∅⌂
 children £8.00-£11.00*

See also Whiteparish

SEVERN BRIDGE–see Aust

SHAFTESBURY, Dorset   **Map F4**
EC Wed MD Thurs *Only hilltop town in Dorset, perched above Blackmore Vale* SEE abbey ruins,
museum, Castle Hill, cobbled and much photographed Gold Hill
🛈 Bell St ☎ (01747) 853514
✘ Ship, Bleke St ☎ (01747) 853219

Blackmore Vale Caravan Park, Sherborne Causeway SP7 9PX ☎ (01747) 851523/852573 Fax
 (01747) 851671 OS map 183/836230 1m W of Shaftesbury on A30 (Yeovil) Open all year
 50 pitches Level grass and hard standing, sheltered ▣◨◪✱∅ £7.50-£10.00*
 (Mastercard/Visa/Switch/Solo/Electron) *www.caravancampingsites.co.uk*

CHARGES

Charges quoted are the minimum and maximum for two people with car and caravan or tent. They
are given only as a guide and should be checked with the owner of the site.
Charges markded * are the prices for last year. Otherwise, the prices are those quoted for the
current season.
Remember to ask whether hot water or use of the pool is extra and make sure that VAT is included.

Long Hazel International C & C, Sparkford

🚐 CARAVAN STORAGE

Many sites in this guide offer caravan storage in winter but some will also store your caravan in summer, which for those of us able to tour several times a year saves towing over long distances. Sites most conveniently placed for this are those on or near popular routes to the West Country and Scotland.

SHEPTON MALLET, Somerset   **Map E4**
EC Wed MD Fri SEE market cross, almshouses, church, museum
🛈 48 High St ✆ (01749) 345258
✗ Oakhill House 3m NE at Oakhill ✆ (01749) 840180

Manleaze Caravan Park, Cannards Grave BA4 4LY ✆ (01749) 342404 OS map 183/626423 1m S of Shepton Mallett on A371 (Castle Cary) Open all year 25 pitches 3 acres, level grass
🛒 ⇥ 🗐 🔌 🗑 ⊕ 📺

Old Down Touring Park, Emborough, Radstock BA3 4SA ✆ (01761) 232355 Fax (01761) 232355 OS map 183/626513 6m N of Shepton Mallet at junction of A37 (Bristol) and B3139 (Radstock-Wells) opp Old Down Inn Open Mar-Nov 35 pitches 5 acres, level grass and hard standings
🛒 🗐 🔌 🗑 ⊕ ⊘ ⊛ 📺   £8.00-£12.00* *olddown@talk21.com www.ukparks.com/olddown*

Phippens Farm, Stoke St Michael, Oakhill BA3 5JH ✆ (01749) 840395 OS map 183/649472 2m N of Shepton Mallet off A367 (Bath) on right of Stoke St Michael road Open Apr-Oct 25 pitches 7 acres level grass 🔌 ⊕ 📺 📺   £7.00

See also Chewton Mendip and Pilton

SHREWTON, Wilts   **Map F4**
✗ George Inn, London Rd ✆ (01980) 620341

Brades Acre Camping Park, Tilshead SP3 4RX ✆ (01980) 620402 OS map 184/034477 3m NW of Shrewton on left of A360 (Devizes) Open Apr-Nov 26 pitches Level grass, sheltered
🛒 ⓟ 🔌 🗑 ⊘ ⊕ ⊘ 📺   £10.00-£12.00

Stonehenge Touring Park, Orcheston SP3 4SH ✆ (01980) 620304 *Prop: JL Young* OS map 184/060455 1m NW of Shrewton off A360 (Devizes) on Orcheston road Open all year 30 pitches 2 acres level grass and hard standing, sheltered 🛒 🗐 🔌 🗑 ⊕ ⊘ ⊛ ⌣   £6.50-£11.50 (most cards)
stay@stonehengetouringpark.com www.stonehengetouringpark.com

SPARKFORD, Somerset   **Map E4**
✗ George N 4m at Castle Cary ✆ (01963) 450761

Long Hazel International Caravan and Camping Park, High Street BA22 7JH ✆ (01963) 440002 Fax (01963) 440002 OS map 183/602262 ¼m SW of Sparkford centre on A359 (Yeovil) Open Feb 16-Jan 16 75 pitches Level grass and hard standing, sheltered 🛒 🗐 🔌 🗑 ⊕ ⊘ ⊛ ⌣ 📺 ⓑ ⊛   £12.00-£14.00* *longhazelpark@hotmail.com www.sparkford.f9.co.uk/lhi.htm*

STREET, Somerset   **Map D4**
EC Wed *Shoe-making town within reach of several viewpoints–Windmill Hill SE, Ivythorn and Walton Hills S*
✗ Bear, High St ✆ (01458) 442021

Bramble Hill Camping Park, Walton BA16 9RQ ✆ (01458) 442548 OS map 182/454362 1m W of Street on A361-A39 (Taunton) Open Mar-Oct 40 pitches 3½ acres, level grass, sheltered 🔌 ⊕

KEY TO SYMBOLS

🛒	shop	⊘	gas supplies	🚐	winter storage for caravans
✗	restaurant	⊕	chemical disposal point	ⓟ	parking obligatory
ⓟ	bar	⊘	payphone	⊛	no dogs
⇥	takeaway food	🗑	swimming pool	📺	caravan hire
⚲	off licence	⊛	games area	🏠	bungalow hire
🗐	laundrette	⌣	children's playground	♿	facilities for disabled
🔌	mains electric hook-ups	📺	TV	⊛	shaded

Ulwell Cottage CARAVAN PARK

Ulwell, Swanage, Dorset BH19 3DG Tel: 01929 422823 e-mail: enq@ulwellcottagepark.co.uk

SWANAGE, Dorset   Map F6
EC Thurs (winter) *Quiet family resort on Isle of Purbeck with good sandy beaches* SEE parish
church and mill pond, clock tower, town hall, Tilly Whim caves
🛈 The White House, Shore Rd ☏ (01929) 422885
✗ Pines, Burlington Rd ☏ (01929) 425211

Flower Meadow Caravan Park, Haycrafts Lane, Harmans Cross BH19 3EB ☏ (01929) 480035 OS
map 195/984800 2½m W of Swanage off A351 (Wareham) at Harmans Cross on left of Haycrafts
Lane Open Apr-Oct 28 pitches Level/sloping grass and hard standing 🔲🔲🔲🔲🔲🔲🔲

Haycrafts Farm, Haycrafts Lane, Harmans Cross BH19 3EB ☏ (01929) 480572 OS map
195/965798 3m W of Swanage off A351 (Wareham) at Harmans Cross Open Easter-Sept–must
book peak periods 50 pitches–families and couples only 5 acres, grass, level/sloping, some hard
standings 🔲🔲🔲🔲🔲🔲 £16.80-£21.50* (Delta/Mastercard/Switch/Visa) www.caravanclub.co.uk

Herston Yards Farm, Washpond Lane BH19 3DJ ☏ (01929) 422932 OS map 195/015796 1½m W
of Swanage off A351 (Wareham) at Herston Cross Open Apr-Oct 80 pitches Level grass,
sheltered 🔲🔲🔲🔲

Ponderosa Camping Caravan Park, Valley Rd BH19 3DX ☏ (01929) 426130/480258 OS map
195/002795 2m W of Swanage on A351 (Wareham) Open Jul-Sept 70 pitches–no adv booking
6 acres level/sloping grass, sheltered 🔲

Priest's Way Holiday Park, off Steer Road BH19 2RS ☏ (01929) 422747 OS map 195/018785 1m
W of Swanage off A351 (Wareham) Open Apr-Sept 170 pitches (108 static) 12 acres
level/sloping grass and hard standing, sheltered 🔲🔲🔲🔲🔲🔲🔲

Tom's Field Campsite and Shop, Tom's Field Road, Langton Matravers BH19 3HN ☏ (01929)
427110 Fax (01929) 427110 OS map 195/995788 2½m W of Swanage off A351 (Wareham) and
B3069 (Kingston) Open Easter-Oct–100 pitches–no trailer caravans 4 acres, grass, level/sloping,
sheltered 🔲🔲🔲🔲🔲🔲🔲 walkers' barn avail year round by arrangement £7.00-£10.50*
(Amex/Delta/Switch/Visa) tomsfield@hotmail.com www.tomsfieldcamping.co.uk

Ulwell Cottage Caravan Park, Ulwell BH19 3DG ☏ (01929) 422823 Fax (01929) 421500 *Prop: J
Scadden & J Orchard* OS map 195/022808 1½m NW of Swanage off A351 (Wareham) Open
Mar 1-Jan 7 217 pitches (140 static) 13 acres, hard standings and grass, level/sloping, sheltered
🔲✗(snack) 🔲🔲🔲🔲🔲🔲🔲🔲🔲🔲🔲🔲 £10.00-£30.00 (Mastercard/Visa)
enquiries@ulwellcottagepark.co.uk www.ulwellcottagepark.co.uk

TAUNTON, Somerset   Map C4
Cider-making town in Tone valley SEE castle, county museum, public school, Priory gatehouse,
West Somerset Railway
🛈 Library,Paul St ☏ (01823) 336344
✗ Nags Head Tavern, Thornfalcon ☏ (01823) 442258 Open 12-3/6.30-9.30

Ashe Farm, Thornfalcon TA3 5NW ☏ (01823) 442567 *Prop: Mrs JM Small* OS map 193/280224
4m SE of Taunton off A358 (Chard) Open Apr-Oct 40 pitches 7 acres, level grass and hard
standing, sheltered 🔲🔲🔲🔲🔲🔲🔲🔲🔲🔲 games room, tennis court, dog walk £9.00-£11.00

Tanpits Cider Farm, Dyers Lane, Bathpool TA2 8BZ ☏ (01823) 270663 OS map 193/254258 2m
NE of Taunton off A38 (Bridgwater)–signposted Open Mar-Nov 20 pitches 1 acre level grass and
hard standings, sheltered 🔲🔲🔲🔲 £4.00-£6.50

THREE LEGGED CROSS–see Verwood

TILSHEAD–see Shrewton

TROWBRIDGE, Wilts   Map F3
EC Wed MD Tues, Fri, Sat SEE 18c lock up, town hall, The Courts at Holt 3m N, Tropical Bird
Gardens at Rode 4m W
🛈 St Stephen's Place ☏ (01225) 777054
✗ Polebarn, Polebarn Rd ☏ (01225) 777006

Stowford Mill Caravan Park, Wingfield BA14 9LH ☏ (01225) 752253 OS map 173/810576 3m W
of Trowbridge on left of A366 (Radstock) past junct with B3109 Open Apr-Oct 20 pitches Level
grass, sheltered 🔲 fishing

For more up-to-date information, visit our site at: **www.butford.co.uk/camping**

VERWOOD, Dorset   Map G5
SEE Ringwood Forest, Moors Valley country park
✗ Albion Inn, Station Rd ☏ (01202) 825267

Woolsbridge Manor Farm Caravan Park, Three Legged Cross BH21 6RA ☏ (01202) 826369 Fax
(01202) 820603 OS map 195/102049 3m S of Verwood off B3072 (West Moors) on left of Ashley
Heath road Open Easter-Oct 60 pitches 7 acres level grass, part sheltered 🅿🗑🚿🅰⊕∅⏚ఈ
£10.00-£15.00* (all major cards) *woolsbridge@btconnect.com*
www.woolsbridgemanorfarmcaravanpark.co.uk

WAREHAM, Dorset   Map F6
EC Wed (winter) MD Thurs *Old town on river Frome ringed by Anglo-Saxon earthworks* SEE St
Martin's church (Lawrence of Arabia associations)
🛈 Town Hall, East St ☏ (01929) 552740
✗ Quay, South St ☏ (01929) 552735

Birchwood Tourist Park, North Trigon BH20 7PA ☏ (01929) 554763 Fax (01929) 556635 OS map
195/899902 2m NW of Wareham on right of Bere Regis road Open Mar-Oct 175 pitches Grass,
level, sheltered 🅿🚮🏕🗑🚿🅰⊕❸⏚🚪ఈ putting, tennis, mountain bike hire
(Mastercard/Switch/Delta/Visa) *www.birchwoodtouristpark.co.uk*

Hunter's Moon Caravan Camping Park, Cold Harbour BH20 7PA ☏ (01929) 556605 OS map
195/899902 2½m NW of Wareham on Bere Regis road Open Easter-Oct 90 pitches 5 acres,
level grass, sheltered 🗑🚿🅰⊕∅❸⏚🏠

Lookout Park, Stoborough BH20 5AZ ☏ (01929) 552546 OS map 195/927856 1m S of Wareham
on left of A351 (Swanage) Open Feb-Nov 240 pitches (90 static) Grass and hard standing, level,
sheltered 🅿🚮🏕🗑🚿🅰⊕❸⊙⏚🚪❀🚃 games room £9.00-£11.00 *enquiries@caravan-
sites.co.uk*

Redcliffe Farm, Ridge BH20 5BE ☏ (01929) 552225 OS map 195/931867 2m SE of Wareham off
A351 (Swanage) by river Frome Open Easter-Oct 154 pitches 8 acres gentle slope, grass,
sheltered 🗑🚿⊕⏚ slipway to river Frome and Poole harbour

Ridge Farm Camping and Caravan Park, Barnhill Rd, Ridge BH20 5BG ☏ (01929) 556444 OS
map 195/938866 2m SE of Wareham off A351 (Swanage) in Ridge Open Easter-Sept 60 pitches
4 acres, level grass, sheltered 🅿🗑🚿🅰⊕∅🚿❀ £8.50-£10.50 *info@ridgefarm.co.uk*
www.ridgefarm.co.uk

Wareham Forest Tourist Park, North Trigon BH20 7NZ ☏ (01929) 551393 Fax (01929) 558321
OS map 195/895912 3m N of Wareham on Bere Regis road Open all year 200 pitches–some
with all mains services 43 acres, level grass and hard standings, sheltered
🅿🚮🗑🚿🅰⊡❸⏚🚿❀ఈ forest walks £11.00-£16.00 (Mastercard/Visa/Switch/Delta)
holiday@wareham-forest.co.uk www.wareham-forest.co.uk

See also Corfe Castle and Wool

WARMWELL–see Owermoigne

WATCHET, Somerset   Map C4
EC Wed *Bristol Channel port and resort with rock and sand beach, handy base for exploring
Quantock Hills to SE* SEE St Decuman's Well and church, West Somerset Steam Railway
✗ West Somerset Hotel, Swain St ☏ (01984) 634434

Warren Farm TA23 0JP ☏ (01984) 631220 OS map 181/048432 1½m W of Watchet on right of
B3191 (Blue Anchor) near beach Open Easter-Sept 100 pitches 13 acres, grass, level/sloping,
sheltered 🅿🅰⊕∅🚿ఈ

For other sites near Watchet see also Blue Anchor and Williton

---

WEDMORE, Somerset   Map D4
Village on N edge of Sedgemoor, a wilderness once, lush country now SEE church (Jacobean
pulpit), stone-built Ashton windmill
✗ The Pack Horse Inn, Church St, Mark ☏ (01278) 641209

Splott Farm, Blackford BS28 4PD ☏ (01278) 641522 OS map 182/410480 1m W of Wedmore on
B3139 (Highbridge) Open Mar-Nov 32 pitches enclosed by hedges 4½ acres level/sloping grass,
hedged 🗑🚿⊕❸⏚🚿 £10.00

See also Wells and Burnham

WELLINGTON, Somerset   Map C4
EC Thurs *Wool town from which the Iron Duke took his title* SEE 15c church (stair turret, tombs),
Wellington School, Wellington monument built 1817 on crest of Blackdown Hills 2m S
✗ The Prince of Wales Inn, Holcombe Rogus ☏ (01823) 672070 Open 12-2/6-9.30

Gamlins Farm, Greenham TA21 0LZ ☏ (01823) 672859 OS map 181/080197 3m W of Wellington
off A38 (Exeter) and Greenham road (junct 26 of M5) Open Easter-Sep 20 pitches 3 acres
terraced, part hard standing 🗑🚿⊕ £5.50-£10.00

Help us make CAMPING CARAVANNING BRITAIN better known to site operators – and thereby more informative – by showing them your copy when booking in.

WELLS, Somerset   Map D4
EC Wed MD Wed, Sat SEE cathedral, bishop's palace, town hall, tithe barn, museum, Wookey Hole caves 1½m NW
🛈 Town Hall, Market Sq ✆ (01749) 672552
✘ The Burcott Inn, Wookey Rd, Burcott ✆ (01749) 673874

Ebborlands Farm and Riding Centre, Wookey Hole BA5 1AY ✆ (01749) 672550 *Prop: Mrs EA Gibbs* OS map 182/525478 2m NW of Wells off A371 (Cheddar) at Easton or Haybridge Open May-Oct–adv booking only 6 pitches, sheltered riding lessons, hacking, shop & bar nearby eileen.gibbs@btinternet.com www.ebborlandsridingcentre.co.uk

Haybridge Caravan Park, Haybridge BA5 1AJ ✆ (01749) 673681 *Prop: Mrs D Vowles* OS map 183/531460 1m W of Wells on left of A371 (Cheddar) past junct with B3139 (Burnham) Open all year 35 pitches 4 acres hard standings and part sloping part level grass 🚻⊕🛁🏠🅿 £10.00

Homestead Park, Wookey Hole BA5 1BW ✆ (01749) 673022 *Prop: Ingledene Ltd* OS map 181/532475 1½m NW of Wells off A371 (Cheddar) Open Easter-Oct 30 pitches–adults only–tents only 4 acres, level grass, sheltered ⊘ £12.50 enquiries@homesteadpark.co.uk www.homesteadpark.co.uk

Cheddar Mendip Heights Camping and Caravanning Club Site, Townsend, Priddy BA5 3BP ✆ (01749) 870241 *Prop: Alan & Kate Sefton* OS map 182/523518 4m N of Wells off A39 (Bath) on B3135 (Cheddar) Open Mar 1-Nov 15 90 pitches Grass and hard standing, level/sloping, sheltered 🛒🏹🛁🚻⊘⊕⊘↩🅿 £6.50-£9.90 (all cards exc Amex) cheddar@campingandcaravanningclub.co.uk www.campingandcaravanningclub.co.uk

WESTHAY–see Meare

WEST LULWORTH–see Lulworth

WESTON SUPER MARE, N Somerset   Map D3
EC Thurs MD Sun SEE Winter gardens, Floral clock, model village, British Camp on Worlebury Hill, St Kew steps, church and woods at Kewstoke, Steepholm and Flatholm islands
🛈 Beach Lawns ✆ (01934) 888800
✘ The Bucket & Spade, Yew Tree Drive ✆ (01934) 521235

Ardnave Caravan Park, Kewstoke BS22 9XJ ✆ (01934) 622319 OS map 182/335635 2m N of Weston super Mare off A370 (Worle) near junction 21 of M5 Open Mar-Oct 120 pitches (110 static) Level grass 🛒🛁🚻⊘⊕⊘🅿 (Mastercard/Visa)

Country View Caravan Park, Sand Road, Sand Bay BS22 9UJ ✆ (01934) 627595 OS map 182/334646 4m N of Weston super Mare off A370 (Bristol) via Kewstoke Open Mar-Jan 120 pitches (66 static) Grass and hard standing, level 🛒🚻🛁🚻⊘⊕⊘🅿(heated) ↩🚻🅿♿ £10.00-£21.00*

Manor Farm, Grange Road, Uphill BS23 4TU ✆ (01934) 627873 OS map 182/362585 1m S of Weston super Mare off A370 (East Brent) Open Apr 1-Oct 20 60 pitches Grass, level 🛁⊘

Purn International Holiday Park, Bleadon BS24 0AN ✆ (01934) 812342 Fax (01934) 811104 OS map 182/330570 2m S of Weston super Mare on A370 (Bridgwater) adj Anchor Inn Open Mar-Nov 280 pitches (120 static) 11 acres level grass and hard standing, sheltered 🛒✘🚻🏹🛁 🛁⊘⊕⊘🅿↩🅿 lic club, entertainment, children's club £8.50-£17.00* (all cards) purninternational@snootyfoxresorts.co.uk www.snootyfoxresorts.co.uk

West End Farm Touring Park, Locking BS24 8RH ✆ (01934) 822529 Fax (01934) 822529 OS map 182/354600 2m E of Weston super Mare off A371 (Cheddar) near helicopter museum Open all year 75 pitches Level grass and hard standing, sheltered 🛁⊘⊕🚻↩♿ £8.00-£12.00*

Weston Gateway Tourist Caravan Park, West Wick BS24 7TF ✆ (01934) 510344 OS map 182/370621 3m NE of Weston super Mare off A370 (West Wick) Open Mar-Oct 180 pitches Level grass and hard standing, sheltered 🚻🛁🚻⊘⊕⊘🚻↩🔲🚻♿ lic club, children's room £9.00-£12.00

See also East Brent

✘ RESTAURANTS
The restaurants recommended in this guide are of three kinds – pubs, independent restaurants and those forming part of hotels and motels. They all serve lunch and dinner – at a reasonable price – say under £10 a head. We shall be glad to have your comments on any you use this season and if you think they are not up to standard, please let us have your suggestions for alternatives.

Bagwell Farm

TOURING PARK

Chickerell, Weymouth,
Dorset, England DT3 4EA

Telephone: 01305 782575
Fax: 01305 780554
e mail: enquire@bagwellfarm.co.uk

WEYMOUTH, Dorset   Map E6

EC Wed MD Thurs *Ferry port (Channel Islands and France) and resort occupying the area between Weymouth Bay and Portland. The town is noted for its fine Georgian houses.* SEE houses in Trinity St (17c), Chesil Beach pebble breakwater 11m long W

🖪 The Esplanade 📞(01305) 785747

✘ Glenburn 2m NE at Overcombe 📞(01305) 832353

Bagwell Farm Touring Park, Chickerell DT3 4EA 📞(01305) 782575 *Prop: Mrs K Kennedy* OS map 194/625816 4m NW of Weymouth on B3157 (Abbotsbury) Open all year 320 pitches 14 acres, level grass and hard standing, sheltered 🛁✘💇⚡🏍️🔋🛢🚿⚙️Ø♨️🚻👩‍🦽 pets' corner, barbecue area, camper's shelter £8.00-£25.00 (Mastercard/Visa/Electron) *enquiries@bagwellfarm.co.uk www.bagwellfarm.co.uk*

East Fleet Touring Park, Fleet DT3 4DW 📞(01305) 785768 OS map 194/636800 3m NW of Weymouth off B3157 (Bridport) at Chickerell Open Mar 15-Jan 15 350 pitches–booking advisable 20 acres grass and hard standing, level/gentle slope 🛁✘💇💇🏍️🔋🛢🚿⚙️Ø♨️👩‍🦽 £5.50-£13.50* (all major cards) *enquiries@eastfleet.co.uk www.eastfleet.co.uk*

Littlesea Holiday Park, Lynch Lane DT4 9DT 📞(01305) 774414 OS map 194/639822 1½m W of Weymouth off B3157 (Abbotsbury) Open Mar-Oct 900 pitches (690 static) Grass, part level 🛁✘💇🛢🚿⚙️🚻♨️🚂 bowling, lic club, amusements (all cards) *www.havenholidays.com*

Osmington Mills Holidays, East Farm Dairy, Osmington Mills DT3 6HB 📞(01305) 832311 Fax (01305) 835251 OS map 194/733822 5m E of Weymouth off A353 (Wareham) Open mid Mar-mid Nov 225 pitches–tents only Grass, part level, sheltered 🛁⚡🛢🚿⚙️Ø🚻 club house, bar food, horse riding, fishing £10.00-£18.00* (Mastercard/Visa/Switch/Delta) *holidays@osmingtonmills.fsnet.co.uk www.osmington-mills-holidays.co.uk*

Pebble Bank Caravan Park, Camp Road, Wyke Regis DT4 9HF 📞(01305) 774844 OS map 194/655775 2m W of Weymouth centre off A354 (Portland) Open Easter-Oct 10 180 pitches (90 static) 7 acres level/sloping grass sheltered 🛁⚡🛢🚿⚙️Ø♨️🚻 £6.50-£16.00* (most cards) *info@pebblebank.co.uk www.pebblebank.co.uk*

Portesham Dairy Farm, Bramdon Lane, Portesham DT3 4HG 📞(01305) 871297 OS map 194/604855 6m NW of Weymouth on left of B3157 (Bridport) Open mid Mar-Oct 60 pitches 3 acres, level grass, sheltered 🛁🛢🚿⚙️♨️🚻👩‍🦽

Sea Barn Farm, Fleet DT3 4EF 📞(01305) 782218 Fax (01305) 775396 OS map 194/626815 3m W of Weymouth off B3157 (Abbotsbury) Open Easter-Nov 250 pitches Grass, level, open 🛁⚡💇🏍️🔋🛢🚿⚙️Ø♨️🚻🚂 £8.50-£11.50* *fleetcamp@lineone.net www.seabarnfarm.co.uk*

Seaview Holiday Village, Preston DT3 6XZ 📞(01305) 833037 OS map 194/710830 3m NE of Weymouth on right of A353 (Bere Regis) beyond Preston Open Apr 1-Nov 1 80 pitches Level/sloping grass and woodland 🛁✘⚡🛢🚿Ø🚻♨️

Waterside Holiday Park, Bowleaze Cove DT3 6PP 📞(01305) 833103 Fax (01305) 832830 OS map 194/704825 2m NE of Weymouth off A353 (Bere Regis) at Bowleaze cove near beach Open Apr-Oct 123 pitches–booking advisable 35 acres level/sloping grass 🛁✘💇🛢🚿⚙️Ø🚻🔋♨️🚻🚂👩‍🦽 £17.00-£28.00* (Mastercard/Visa/Delta/Switch) *info@watersideholidays.co.uk www.watersideholidays.co.uk*

West Fleet Holiday Farm DT3 4ED 📞(01305) 782218 Fax (01305) 775396 OS map 194/625812 3m W of Weymouth off B3157 (Fleet) Open Easter-Oct 250 pitches–tents only 12 acres, grass, level, sheltered 🛁⚡💇🏍️🔋🛢🚿⚙️Ø🚻(heated) 🔋♨️🚻🏠 club house £10.00-£13.50* *fleetcamp@lineone.net www.westfleetholidays.co.uk*

⊗ DOGS

Dogs are usually allowed but must be kept on a lead. Sometimes they have to be paid for.

WHITEPARISH, Wilts **Map G4**
SEE Newhouse 2m W, rare example of country house built in form of Y, with Jacobean centre and Georgian wings
✗ Kings Head ✆ (01794) 884287

Hillcrest, Southampton Road SP5 2QW ✆ (01794) 884471 OS map 184/240223 1m SW of Whiteparish on A36 (Southampton-Salisbury) near Newton Open all year 35 pitches Grass, level/sloping, sheltered ▣▣✿

WICK–see Glastonbury

WILLITON, Somerset **Map C4**
EC Sat
✗ The Notley Arms Inn, Monksilver, Taunton ✆ (01984) 656217

Home Farm Holiday Park, St Audries Bay TA4 4DP ✆ (01984) 632487 *Prop: Mr & Mrs Nethercott* OS map 181/105430 3m NE of Williton off A39 (W. Quantoxhead) Open all year 270 pitches (230 static) Level/sloping grass and hard standing, sheltered ▣▣▣▣✿▣▣(indoor) ▣▣▣ lic club, private beach £10.00-£15.00 (Mastercard/Visa/Delta) www.homefarmholidaycentre.co.uk

WIMBORNE, Dorset **Map F5**
EC Wed MD Fri SEE Minster, St Margaret's chapel and hospital, museum, Badbury Rings 3m NW
▐ 29 High St ✆ (01202) 886116
✗ Lambs Green Inn, Lambs Green Lane, Corfe Mullen ✆ (01202) 843900

Charris Camping Caravan Park, Candys Lane, Corfe Mullen BH21 3EF ✆ (01202) 885970 OS map 195/995990 1m WSW of Wimborne on A31 (Dorchester) Open Mar-Oct 45 pitches 3 acres, grass level/sloping, sheltered ▣▣▣▣✿▣▣

Merley Court Touring Park, Merley BH21 3AA ✆ (01202) 881488 OS map 195/013984 2m S of Wimborne off A31 bypass Open Mar-Jan–booking essential 160 pitches 20 acres, level grass and hard standings, sheltered ▣▣▣▣▣▣✿▣▣(heated) ▣▣▣(Jul-Aug) ▣ tennis court, woodland walk, crazy golf, croquet, table tennis, mini-football, games room £11.00-£16.00* (Mastercard/Visa) holidays@merley-court.co.uk www.merley-court.co.uk

Springfield Touring Park, Candys Lane, Corfe Mullen BH21 3EF ✆ (01202) 881719 *Prop: Sheila & John Clark* OS map 195/993989 1¼m SW of Wimborne on left of A31 (Dorchester) Open Mar 15-Oct 31 45 pitches 3½ acres, level/sloping grass and hard standing ▣▣▣▣✿▣▣▣ £7.00-£14.00 (2 adults £50 any 7 days low season)

Wilksworth Farm Caravan Park, Cranborne Road BH21 4HW ✆ (01202) 885467 *Prop: Mr & Mrs R Lovell* OS map 195/008019 1m N of Wimborne on B3078 (Cranborne) Open Mar-Oct 162 pitches (77 static) 11 acres, level grass and hard standings, sheltered ▣✗▣▣▣▣✿ ▣▣(heated) ▣▣▣▣▣ serviced pitches, tennis £10.00-£20.00 rayandwendy@wilksworthfarmcaravanpark.co.uk www.wilksworthfarmcaravanpark.co.uk

WINCANTON, Somerset **Map E4**
EC Thurs MD Tues *Thriving market town, major staging post in coaching days*
▐ The Library, 7 Carrington Way ✆ (01963) 31693
✗ Dolphin, High St ✆ (01963) 32215

Sunny Hill Caravan Park, Sunny Hill Farm, Riding Gate, Bayford BA9 8NG ✆ (01963) 33281 OS map 183/733303 2m NE of Wincanton on old A303 (Bayford) Open Apr-Oct 20 pitches 2 acres level grass ▣✿ table tennis, pool

Wincanton Racecourse BA9 8BJ ✆ (01963) 32344 OS map 183/711294 ½m N of Wincanton on B3081 (Bruton) Open Apr 8-Sept 30 50 pitches Level grass ▣▣▣✿▣▣▣▣ golf £6.20-£7.50 (Mastercard/Visa)

WINSCOMBE, N Somerset **Map D3**
✗ Penscot Farmhouse ✆ (01934) 842659

Netherdale Caravan and Camping Park, Bridgwater Road, Sidcot BS25 1NH ✆ (01934) 843007 OS map 182/426567 1m SE of Winscombe on left of A38 (3m NW of Cheddar) Mar-Oct 30 pitches (37 static) 4 acres, level grass, sheltered ▣▣✿▣▣▣ filling station, restaurant, bar & shops nearby £10.00-£12.00 camping@netherdale.net www.netherdale.net

SHOWERS

Except where marked, all sites in this guide have flush lavatories and showers. Symbols for these amenities have therefore been omitted from site entries.

See listing under Wimborne

WINSFORD, Somerset   Map B4
SEE Devil's Punchbowl
✗ Royal Oak ☎ (01643) 851455

Halse Farm Camping Caravan Park TA24 7JL *David Bellamy Gold Conservation Award* ☎ (01643) 851259 Fax (01643) 851592 OS map 181/898342 1½m SW of Winsford off B3223 at Royal Oak pub in Halse Lane Open Mar 21-Oct 31 44 pitches 3 acres level grass and hard standing
▣ ▣ ∅ ⊛ ∅ ⤳ ⊡ ₺ £8.50-£10.50* (Mastercard/Visa/Switch/Delta) *brown@halsefarm.co.uk www.halsefarm.co.uk*
See also Dulverton

WIVELISCOMBE, Somerset   Map C4
EC Thurs SEE Brendon Hills and lakes NW
✗ Rock Inn 2m SW on B3227 at Waterrow ☎ (01984) 623293

Waterrow Touring Park, Bouchers Farm, Waterrow TA4 2AZ ☎ (01984) 623464 Fax (01984) 624280 OS map 181/053248 3m SW of Wiveliscombe on left of B3227 (Taunton) after Waterrow, by river Tone Open all year 45 pitches 4 acres level grass and hard standings
₺ ▣ ▣ ⊛ ∅ ▣ ⊡ ₺ landscaped pitches, short mat bowling, fishing, painting holidays, classes in photography and Spanish £10.50-£17.00* (Mastercard/Visa/Switch/Delta)
www.waterrowpark.co.uk

WOOKEY HOLE–see Wells

WOOL, Dorset   Map F6
Old town on S bank of river Frome. SEE Bindon Abbey ruins, Clouds Hill (Lawrence of Arabia cottage) 4m NW, Bovington tank museum 2m NW
✗ Lulworth 3m S at West Lulworth ☎ (01929) 400230

Manor Farm, East Stoke BH20 6AW ☎ (01929) 462870 OS map 194/875864 2m E of Wool off A352 East Stoke road Open Easter-Sept 50 pitches 2½ acres level grass, sheltered
₺ ▣ ▣ ∅ ⊛ ∅ ⊛ ⤳ ▣ ₺ ◑ *info@manorfarmcp.co.uk www.manorfarmcp.co.uk*

Whitemead Caravan Park, East Burton Road BH20 6HG ☎ (01929) 462241 Fax (01929) 462241 OS map 194/842868 ½m W of Wool on East Burton road Open Apr-Oct 95 pitches Level grass, sheltered, some hard standings ₺ ⤳ ⤻ ▣ ▣ ∅ ⊛ ∅ ⊛ ⤳ ▣ £7.20-£11.50*
whitemeadcp@aol.com www.whitemeadcaravanpark.co.uk

Woodlands Camping Park, Bindon Lane, East Stoke BH20 6AS ☎ (01929) 462327 OS map 194/862863 2m E of Wool on East Stoke road via Bindon Abbey Open Apr-Oct 40 pitches–tents only 2 acres level grass, sheltered ₺ ▣ ⊛ ₺ ◑ *stay@woodlandscampingpark.co.uk www.resortguide.co.uk/woodlands*

Most popular holiday region in England, the West Country of Devon and Cornwall is overrun in July and August. The region's main attractions are its coasts, lined with sandy beaches, and its mild climate, May and June often being sunnier than mid-season.

Inland Devon retains great tracts of peaceful country crossed by wooded valleys and high-banked lanes. Tall headlands and forested river mouths line the north coast, more gentle scenery the south – the highlight of which is the lovely Dart Estuary from which steamers regularly sail upstream to Totnes. The largest city on the south coast is Plymouth, more a port than a resort, but to the east on either side of the Salcombe headland are many unspoilt bays. Farther east is Torbay, some twenty miles round, with a climate mild enough for palm trees to flourish and its three big resorts of Torquay, Paignton and Brixham.

The granite mass of Dartmoor, a 1000ft high plateau bounded by Okehamptom, Plymouth, Tavistock and Bovey Tracey, is relatively uncrowded. The same goes for that part of Exmoor spilling over into North Devon from Somerset, for which South Molton is a handy base. The coast on either side of nearby Ilfracombe is one of the most attractive in the county. Between Dartmoor and Exmoor is a little-visited region centred on the Torridge and Taw Valleys. Two interesting sights in Devon are the country houses of Saltram and Buckland Abbey.

Despite the influx of tourists, Cornwall retains a secretive charm symbolised by unfamiliar place names, Celtic crosses and holy wells. For touring, the short distance between the north and south coasts, the north bold and rugged, the south sheltered and with more luxuriant vegetation, is an advantage. The long rollers of the Atlantic coast on the north are ideal for experienced surfers, but their undertow can trap the unwary. Lining both coasts are wooded creeks and quaint fishing ports with a charm now more theatrical than real. The largest resort on the north coast is Newquay, and on the south the deepwater harbour of Falmouth.

Confirmation of the region's popularity are the number of campsites (over 300), though most of these are well distributed. Main concentrations are at Newquay, St Austell, Lynton, Ilfracombe, Looe and Paignton on the coast and at Okehampton, Newton Abbot and Helston inland. Some of the coastal campsites – full to overflowing in season – are the equal of holiday villages, but most of those inland are small and with only basic facilities.

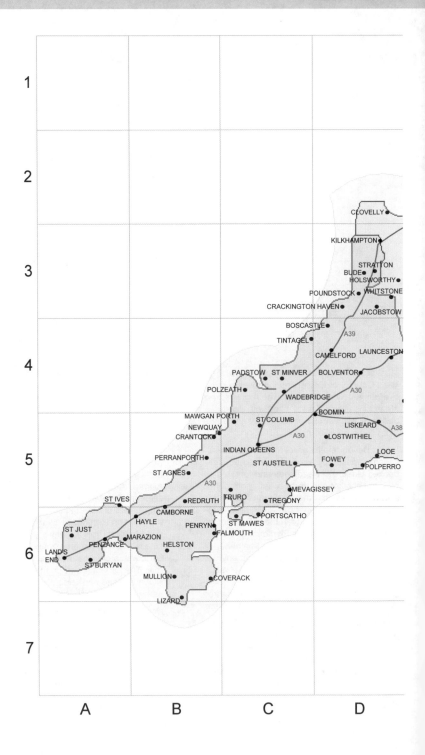

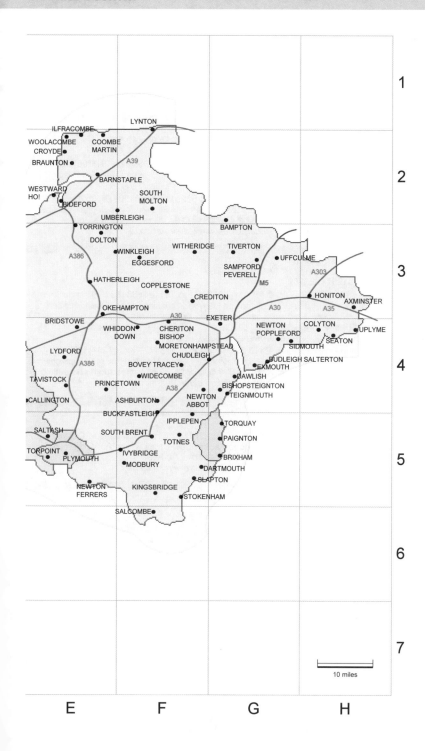

1

ILFRACOMBE
LYNTON
WOOLACOMBE
COOMBE
MARTIN
CROYDE
BRAUNTON
A39

2

BARNSTAPLE
WESTWARD
HO!
BIDEFORD
SOUTH
MOLTON
UMBERLEIGH
TORRINGTON
BAMPTON
DOLTON
A386
WINKLEIGH
WITHERIDGE
TIVERTON
EGGESFORD
UFFCULME
HATHERLEIGH
SAMPFORD
PEVERELL
A303

3

COPPLESTONE
M5
CREDITON
OKEHAMPTON
HONITON
AXMINSTER
BRIDSTOWE
A30
EXETER
A30
A35
WHIDDON
DOWN
CHERITON
BISHOP
NEWTON
POPPLEFORD
COLYTON
UPLYME
MORETONHAMPSTEAD
SIDMOUTH
SEATON
LYDFORD
CHUDLEIGH
A386
BOVEY TRACEY
BUDLEIGH SALTERTON
TAVISTOCK
WIDECOMBE
EXMOUTH

4

PRINCETOWN
DAWLISH
A38
BISHOPSTEIGNTON
CALLINGTON
ASHBURTON
NEWTON
ABBOT
TEIGNMOUTH
BUCKFASTLEIGH
SALTASH
IPPLEPEN
TORQUAY
SOUTH BRENT
PAIGNTON
TORPOINT
TOTNES
PLYMOUTH
IVYBRIDGE
BRIXHAM

5

MODBURY
DARTMOUTH
NEWTON
FERRERS
KINGSBRIDGE
SLAPTON
STOKENHAM
SALCOMBE

6

7

10 miles

E   F   G   H

ASHBURTON, Devon   **Map F4**
EC Wed SEE Little House museum, St Andrew's church, Buckfast Abbey 3m SW
✘ London Hotel, West St ✆ (01364) 652478

Ashburton Caravan Park, Waterleat TQ13 7HU ✆ (01364) 652552 Fax (01364) 652552 OS map
202/752721 1½m NE of Ashburton off A38 (Exeter) Open Easter-Sept 75 pitches (40 static)
Grass, level, sheltered ▯🅿◿◍◍◿ ⛉🅷 info@ashburtoncaravanpark.co.uk
www.ashburtoncaravanpark.co.uk

Lemonford Caravan Park, Bickington TQ12 6JR ✆ (01626) 821242 Prop: Mr & Mrs Halstead OS
map 191/794724 2m NE of Ashburton off A38/A383 (Newton Abbot) Open Mar 15-Oct 80 pitches
Level grass and hard standing, sheltered 🛒▯🅿◿◍◍◍◿🅷◑ £8.00-£12.50
mark@lemonford.co.uk www.lemonford.co.uk

Lower Aish Guest House, Poundsgate TQ13 7NY ✆ (01364) 631229 OS map 191/705725 4m
NW of Ashburton on B3357 (Tavistock) Open Mar-Oct 50 pitches (35 static) Level/sloping grass,
sheltered ✘ (snack) ◿ guided walks

River Dart Country Park, Holne Park TQ13 7NP ✆ (01364) 652511 Fax (01364) 652020 OS map
202/732700 2m W of Ashburton off Two Bridges road Open Apr-Sept–must book peak periods
185 pitches Level grass, sheltered 🛒✘🍴▯🅿◿◍◍◍◿🅷 nature and forest trails
£9.50-£16.50* (most cards) enquiries@irverdart.co.uk www.riverdart.co.uk

AXMINSTER, Devon   **Map H3**
EC Wed MD Thurs SEE parish church
🅸 Old Courthouse Complex, Church St ✆ (01297) 834386
✘ George, Trinity Sq ✆ (01297) 832209

Andrewshayes Caravan Park EX13 7DY ✆ (01404) 831225 Fax (01404) 831893 OS map
192/247988 3m W of Axminster off A35 (Honiton) on Dalwood-Stockland road Open Mar-Jan
170 pitches (80 static) 12 acres, grass and hard standings, sloping, sheltered
✘🍴◿▯🅿◿◍◿◿◿(heated) ◍◿◍◍🅷 bike hire £9.00-£15.50* (most cards)
enquiries@andrewshayes.co.uk www.andrewshayes.co.uk

Hunters Moon Holiday Park, Hawkchurch EX13 5UL ✆ (01297) 678402 Fax (01297) 678720 OS
map 193/347989 3m E of Axminster off B3165 (Crewkerne) Open Mar 15-Nov 14 179 pitches
11 acres, level grass, hard standings 🛒✘🍴◿▯🅿◿◍◍◍◿ club, games room and putting
green £8.00-£20.00* (Mastercard/Visa) www.ukparks.co.uk/huntersmoon

BAMPTON, Devon   **Map G2**
SEE 13c church, castle mound, town hall, Exmoor Pony Fair last Thurs in Oct
✘ Exeter Inn, Tiverton Rd ✆ (01398) 331345

Lowtrow Cross Caravan Site, Upton TA4 2DB ✆ (01398) 371199 Prop: Sue Tanser OS map
181/006292 6m NE of Bampton on B3190 (Watchet) at Lowtrow Cross Open Apr-Oct–adults only
23 pitches 4½ acres, part level grass ✘🍴◿▯🅿◿◍◿◿◿ £7.00-£9.75
(Visa/Mastercard/Switch) lowtrowcross@aol.com www.lowtrowcross.co.uk

BARNSTAPLE, Devon   **Map E2**
EC Wed MD Tues, Fri SEE arched bridge, almshouses, Queen Anne's Walk, museum, new civic
centre
🅸 36 Boutport St ✆ (01271) 375000
✘ Imperial, Taw Vale Parade ✆ (01271) 845861

Midland Holiday Park, Braunton Road EX31 4AU ✆ (01271) 343691 Fax (01271) 326355 OS map
180/540347 1½m W of Barnstaple on right of A361 (Ilfracombe) Open Easter-mid Nov
100 pitches (62 static) Level grass and hard standing, sheltered
🛒✘🍴◿▯🅿◿◍◿◍◿◿◿ dog exercise area £7.00-£16.00 (Mastercard/Visa)
info@tarkaholidaypark.co.uk www.tarkaholidaypark.co.uk

BERRYNARBOR–see Combe Martin

🚐 CARAVAN STORAGE

Many sites in this guide offer caravan storage
in winter but some will also store your caravan
in summer, which for those of us able to tour
several times a year saves towing over long
distances. Sites most conveniently placed for
this are those on or near popular routes to the
West Country and Scotland.

Ruthern Valley Caravan Park, Bodmin

BIDEFORD, Devon   **Map E2**
EC Wed MD Tues SEE Victoria Park (Armada guns), St Mary's Church, Chudleigh Fort
🛈 The Quay ☎ (01237) 477676
✗ Kings Arms, The Quay ☎ (01237) 472675
Knapp House, Churchill Way, Northam EX39 1NT ☎ (01237) 478843 OS map 180/458294 2m N
of Bideford off A386 (Appledore) Open Mar-Oct 70 pitches 70 acres level/sloping grass
🛒⬛🚿♦∅☐⤙🏕 assault course, bike hire

BISHOPSTEIGNTON, Devon   **Map G4**
EC Thurs SEE church, remains of bishops' palace
✗ Old Rydon 1½m W at Kingsteignton (Rydon Rd) ☎ (01626) 54626
Bishopsbrook Camping Park TQ14 9PT Site in area designated AONB ☎ (01626) 775249 OS
map 192/909730 ¼m S of Bishopsteignton on A381 (Teignmouth-Newton Abbot) near sea Open
Easter-Oct 77 pitches–no caravans 2 acres level/sloping grass

BLACKWATER–see St Agnes

BODMIN, Cornwall   **Map D5**
EC Wed MD Sat SEE St Petroc's church, chantry chapel ruins, regimental museum, Bodmin
Beacon, Lanhydrock House (NT) 2m SE
🛈 Shire Hall, Mount Folly Sq ☎ (01208) 76616 ✗ The Borough Arms, Dunmere ☎ (01208) 73118
Ruthern Valley Holidays, Ruthern Bridge PL30 5LU ☎ (01208) 831395 OS map 200/031666 4m
W of Bodmin off A389 (St Austell) via Nanstallon Open Apr-Sept 30 pitches 7½ acres level grass
and hard standings, sheltered 🛒🔥⬛🚿∅♦∅⤙🏕🏠 £10.00-£14.50 (most cards) www.self-
catering-ruthern.co.uk
Glenmorris Park, Longstone Road, St Mabyn PL30 3BY ☎ (01208) 841677 OS map 200/055734
4m N of Bodmin off B3266 (Camelford) at Longstone Open Easter-Oct–must book peak periods
80 pitches Level grass and hard standing, sheltered 🛒🔥⬛🚿∅♦∅☐(heated) ⊕⤙🖵🚿🏠
£4.00-£5.00 (Mastercard/Visa) info@glenmorris.co.uk www.glenmorris.co.uk
See also Bolventor

BOLVENTOR, Cornwall   **Map D4**
✗ Jamaica Inn ☎ (01566) 86250
Colliford Tavern PL14 6PZ ☎ (01208) 821335 Fax (01208) 821335 OS map 201/172740 2m W of
Bolventor off A30 (Bodmin) and St Neot road Open Easter-Sep 40 pitches–must book in peak
season 3 acres, level grass, sheltered 🛒✗⬛🚿∅♦∅👍 sep pitches, free house inn,
accommodation (all cards) info@colliford.com www.colliford.com

BOSCASTLE, Cornwall   **Map D4**
SEE harbour, witchcraft museum
✗ Cobweb Just E of harbour ☎ (01840) 250278
Lower Pennycrocker Camping, St Juliot PL35 0BY ☎ (01840) 250257 Prop: Brian Heard OS map
190/125929 2½m NE of Boscastle off B3263 (Bude) Open Easter-Sept 40 pitches 4 acres,
level/gentle slope, sheltered 🚿♦🚿 £8.00 www.pennycrocker.com

BRAUNTON, Devon   **Map E2**
EC Wed SEE museum, Saunton Sands 2m W
✗ Otters, Caen St ☎ (01271) 813633

Chivenor Caravan Park, Chivenor EX31 4BN ☎ (01271) 812217 *Prop: Rob & Su Massey* OS map
180/508350 2m SE of Braunton on A361 (Barnstaple) Open Mar-Jan 30 pitches Grass and hard
standing ▒ ⚲ ⬚ 🔌 ∅ ⊕ ∅ ⊗ ⤴ £7.50-£13.00 (most cards) *chivenorcp@lineone.net*
www.chivenorcaravanpark.co.uk

Hidden Valley Touring and Camping Park, West Down EX34 8NU ☎ (01271) 813837 Fax (01271)
814041 OS map 180/497406 2m N of Braunton on left of A361 (Ilfracombe) Open all year
120 pitches 25 acres, level grass and hard standings, sheltered ▒ ✗ ⚲ ⬚ 🔌 ∅ ⊕ ∅ ⤴ ⚲ lounge,
children's room, baby changing room, TV hook-ups £7.00-£18.00* (all cards exc Amex)
relax@hiddenvalleypark.com www.hiddenvalleypark.com

Lobb Fields Caravan and Camping Park, Saunton Road EX33 1EB ☎ (01271) 812090 OS map
180/473371 1m W of Braunton on right of B3231 (Croyde) Open Mar-Oct 180 pitches 14 acres
level grass and hard standing ⬚ 🔌 ⊕ ∅ ⊗ ⤴ ⚲ ⚲ £6.00-£21.00 (most cards)
info@lobbfields.com www.lobbfields.com

For other sites near Braunton see Barnstaple and Croyde

BRIDESTOWE, Devon   **Map E4**
SEE parish church
✗ The Prewley Moor Arms, Church Rd, Sourton Down ☎ (01837) 861178

Bridestowe Caravan Park EX20 4ER ☎ (01837) 861261 OS map 191/517892 ½m E of
Bridestowe centre on Lake road Open Mar-Dec 53 pitches (40 static) 5 acres, level grass,
sheltered ▒ ⬚ 🔌 ∅ ⊗ ⤴ ⚲ ⚲ £8.00-£12.00*

Bundu Caravan Camping Park, Sourton Cross EX20 4HT ☎ (01837) 861611 *Prop: M & F Sargent*
OS map 191/547916 2m NE of Bridestowe off junction of A30 (Okehampton) and A386 (Tavistock)
Open all year 39 pitches 4½ acres, level grass and hard standing ⬚ 🔌 ∅ ⊕ ⊗
£8.00-£12.00 inc elect *frances@bundusargent.wanadoo.co.uk www.bundu.co.uk*

BRIXHAM, Devon   **Map G5**
EC Wed SEE aquarium, Golden Hind replica, parish church, Berry Head fortifications, lighthouse
🛈 Old Market House, The Quay ☎ (01803) 852861
✗ Blue Anchor, Fore St ☎ (01803) 859373

Centry Touring Caravans and Tents, Gillard Road TQ5 9EY ☎ (01803) 853215 OS map
202/932558 1½m E of Brixham centre on right of Berry Head road Open Apr-Sept 80 pitches 8
acres level grass sheltered 🔌 ∅ ⊕ ∅

Galmpton Touring Park, Greenway Road, Galmpton TQ5 0EP ☎ (01803) 842066 Fax (01803)
844458 OS map 202/885558 3m W of Brixham off A3022 (Torbay) and road to Dittisham ferry
Open Apr-Sept 120 pitches 10 acres level/sloping grass, terraced, sheltered ▒ ⬚ 🔌 ∅ ⊕ ∅
⊗ ⤴ ⚲ (peak) ⚲ ⚲ £8.30-£14.80 (most cards) *galmptontouringpark@hotmail.com*
www.galmptontouringpark.co.uk

Hillhead Camp TQ5 0HH ☎ (01803) 853204 OS map 202/903538 2m W of Brixham on B3205
(Kingswear) Open Easter-Oct 330 pitches 20 acres level grass, sheltered ▒ ✗ ⚲ ⚲ ⬚ ⚲
⊕ ∅ ⬚ (heated) ⊗ ⤴ ⚲ ⚲ amusements, live entertainment in season £18.00-£23.00* inc
showers *www.caravanclub.co.uk*

Upton Manor Farm Camping Park, St Mary's Road TQ5 9QH ☎ (01803) 882384 *Prop: William,*
Jenny & Richard Hosking OS map 202/925548 1m SW of Brixham off B3205
(Kingswear)–signposted Open Easter-Oct 200 pitches Grass, level, sheltered ▒ ⬚ 🔌 ∅ ⊕
£10.00-£16.00 (most cards) *uptoncamp@aol.com www.uptonmanorfarm.co.uk*

BUCKFASTLEIGH, Devon   **Map F5**
EC Wed SEE Buckfast Abbey, church, caves, farm museum, Dart Valley Railway to Totnes
✗ Dartbridge Inn ☎ (01364) 642214

Beara Farm, Colston Road TQ11 0LW *Close by the River Dartmoor, within easy reach of the sea*
and Dartmoor ☎ (01364) 642234 *Prop: John Thorn* OS map 202/751645 1m SE of Buckfastleigh
off A384 (Totnes) on Colston road near river Dart Open all year 25 pitches 3½ acres, level grass
and hard standing ⊕ ⬚ spring water £8.00

Churchill Farm TQ11 0EZ ☎ (01364) 642844 OS map 202/743665 ½m NE of Buckfastleigh off
Buckfast road–access opp church Open May-Oct 25 pitches 2 acres level/sloping grass,
sheltered 🔌 ⊕ £8.00

CHECK BEFORE ENTERING
There's usually no objection to your walking onto a site to see if you might like it but always ask
permission first. Remember that the person in charge is responsible for safeguarding the property
of those staying there.

BUDE, Cornwall   Map D3
EC Thurs SEE Compass Hill, Poughill church 1½m NE
🛈 Visitor Centre, The Crescent ☎ (01288) 354240
✗ Falcon, Falcon Terrace ☎ (01288) 352005

Bude Holiday Park, Maer Lane EX23 9EE ☎ (01288) 355955 OS map 190/205072 1m N of Bude
on Maer road Open May-Sept–adv booking advisable 250 pitches (131 static) Grass and hard
standing 🛈✗♀⊸⟋🗑🏢⊘⊘🖾🕑⌁⊡⊠ lic club/bar (Mastercard/Visa)

Upper Lynstone Caravan and Camping Site EX23 0LP ☎ (01288) 352017 *Prop: JM & GA Cloke*
OS map 190/205054 ½m S of Bude on coast road (Widemouth Bay) Open Easter-Sept
112 pitches (42 static) Level/sloping grass 🛈🗑🏢⊘⊘🕑⌁⊠ £8.00-£15.00 (all major credit
cards) *reception@upperlynstone.co.uk www.upperlynstone.co.uk*

See also Kilkhampton, Poundstock and Stratton

BUDLEIGH SALTERTON, Devon   Map G4
EC Thurs SEE Octagon, Raleigh's birth place at Ware Barton 2m NW, Bicton gardens at East
Budleigh
🛈 Rolle Mews Car Park, Fore St ☎ (01395) 445275
✗ Salterton Arms, Chapel St ☎ (01395) 445048

Ladram Bay Caravan Site, Otterton EX9 7BX ☎ (01395) 568398 Fax (01395) 568338 OS map
192/096851 4m N of Budleigh Salterton off B3178 (Newton Poppleford) via Otterton Open Apr-
Sept–must book peak periods 309 pitches (120 static) Level/sloping grass 🛈♀⊸⟋🗑🏢⊘
⊘⊘🖾⌁⊠ fishing, boating, doctor's surgery £10.00-£22.00* (most cards)
welcome@ladrambay.co.uk www.ladrambay.co.uk

CAMBORNE, Cornwall   Map B6
EC Thurs MD Fri SEE 15c church, School of Mines,
✗ Tyacks Hotel, Commerical St ☎ (01209) 612424

Magor Farm, Tehidy TR14 0JF ☎ (01209) 713367 OS map 203/635425 1½m NNW of Camborne
off A30 (Hayle) via Coombe Open Mar-Oct 168 pitches 🗑🏢⊘🕑

CAMELFORD, Cornwall   Map D4
EC Wed SEE St Thomas's church, Brown Willy Hill
🛈 North Cornwall Museum, The Clease ☎ (01840) 212954
✗ Poldark Inn 2m W at Delabole ☎ (01840) 212565

Juliot's Well Holiday Park PL32 9RF ☎ (01840) 213302 Fax (01840) 212700 OS map 200/095829
2m S of Camelford off B3266 (Tintagel) Open Mar-Oct 80 pitches (50 static) 8½ acres
level/sloping grass and hard standings, sheltered 🛈✗♀⊸🗑🏢⊘⊘⊘🖾(heated) 🕑⌁🏢⊠
tennis £5.00-£10.00* (Delta/Mastercard/Switch/Visa) *juliotswell@holidaysincornwall.net
www.holidaysincornwall.net*

Lakefield Caravan Camping Park, Lower Pendavey PL32 9TX ☎ (01840) 213279 OS map
200/097853 1m N of Camelford on left of B3266 (Boscastle) Open Mar-Sept 40 pitches 5 acres,
level grass 🛈🗑🏢⊘⊘🕑⌁ dog walk, farm animal corner, riding school, tea room
£6.00-£10.50* *lakefield@pendavey.fsnet.co.uk www.lakefieldcaravanpark.co.uk*

Planet Caravan Park, Delabole PL33 9DT ☎ (01840) 213361 OS map 200/064834 3m NW of
Camelford on B3314 (Delabole) Open all year 40 pitches 3 acres level grass
🗑🏢⊘⊘⊘🖾🕑⌁⊡🏢⊠

CARLYON BAY–see St Austell

SPRINGFIELD *holiday park*
The ideal location for a holiday in the South West

Tedburn Road
Tedburn St Mary
Exeter, Devon
EX6 6EW

Tel: +44 (0) 1647 24242
Fax: +44 (0) 1647 24131
Email: Springfielddevon@aol.com

See listing under Cheriton Bishop

CHERITON BISHOP, Devon   Map F4
SEE 13c church, old well
✗ Old Thatch Inn ☎ (01647) 224204

Barley Meadow Caravan and Camping Park, Crockernwell EX6 6NR ☎ (01647) 281629 OS map 191/755935 1½m W of Cheriton Bishop on old A30 (Okehampton) Open Mar 15-Nov 15 40 pitches Grass and hard standings, level [icons] pool room £7.50-£11.00* angela.waldron1@btopenworld.com www.barleymeadow.co.uk

Springfield Holiday Park, Tedburn St Mary EX6 6EW ☎ (01647) 24242 Prop: P & D Goddard OS map 191/792936 exit Woodleigh Junction A30 (Cheriton Bishop) park signposted Open Easter-Oct 48 pitches Grass and hard standing, level, part sheltered [icons] free showers £11.00-£14.00 springfielddevon@aol.com www.springfieldholidaypark.co.uk

CHUDLEIGH, Devon   Map G4
✗ Riverside 3m SW at Bovey Tracey ☎ (01626) 832422

Finlake Holiday Park TQ13 0EJ ☎ (01626) 853833 OS map 191/855786 1m SW of Chudleigh near junct of B3344 (Chudleigh Knighton) and B3193 (Dunsford-Kingsteignton) Open Easter-Oct 450 pitches–no single sex groups 130 acres grass and hard standing, sheltered [icons] [icons](heated) [icons] lic club, games room, 9-hole golf, fishing, boating, horse riding £6.00-£16.50 www.haulfryn.co.uk

Holmans Wood Caravan Park, Harcombe Cross TQ13 0DZ ☎ (01626) 853785 Prop: Mr & Mrs A Barzilay OS map 192/883812 2m NE of Chudleigh on right of B3344 (Exeter) Open Mar-Oct 75 pitches Hard standings and level grass, sheltered [icons] forest walks, close to Dartmoor, camping meadow £10.50-£16.75 (Mastercard/Visa) enquiries@holmanswood.co.uk www.holmanswood.co.uk

CHUDLEIGH KNIGHTON–see Bovey Tracey

COLYTON, Devon   Map H4
EC Wed Market town of medieval charm in Coly valley 1m inland from coastal resort of Seaton, with picturesque winding streets and 14c river bridge SEE church (monuments), Great House in South St
✗ Kingfisher, Dolphin St ☎ (01297) 552471

Leacroft Touring Park EX24 6HY ☎ (01297) 552823 OS map 192/219923 2m SW of Colyton on Branscombe/Beer road via Colyton Hill Open Apr-Oct 138 pitches 10 acres level/sloping grass and hard standings [icons]

COMBE MARTIN, Devon   Map E2
EC Wed SEE church, Pack of Cards Inn
🛈 Sea Cottage, Cross St ☎ (01271) 883319
✗ Campo Casana at Berrynarbor ☎ (01271) 882557

Mill Park Touring Site, Berrynarbor EX34 9SH ☎ (01271) 882647 OS map 189/565472 1½m W of Combe Martin off A399 (Ilfracombe) Open Mar-Nov 160 pitches Grass, level, sheltered [icons] fishing (Mastercard/Visa)

Napps Camping Site, Old Coast Road, Berrynarbor EX34 9SW ☎ (01271) 882557 OS map 180/561476 2m W of Combe Martin on A399 (Ilfracombe) Open Easter-Oct 200 pitches Level grass and hard standings [icons] tennis court, games room, football pitch £6.00-£18.00 (all cards exc Amex) bookings@napps.fsnet.co.uk www.napps.co.uk

Newberry Farm Touring Caravans and Camping, Woodlands EX34 0AT ☎ (01271) 882334 OS map 180/574470 ½m W of Combe Martin on A399 (Ilfracombe) Open Easter-Oct 110 pitches 30 acres hard standing and level grass, sheltered [icons] coarse fishing, woodland walks (Mastercard/Visa) enq@newberrycampsite.co.uk www.newberrycampsite.co.uk

Sandaway Holiday Park, Berrynarbor EX34 9ST ☎ (01271) 866666 OS map 180/568473 ¼m W of Combe Martin off A399 (Ilfracombe) Open Mar 15-Oct 31 125 pitches (102 static) [icons](heated) [icons] lic club, own beach

Stowford Farm Meadows EX34 0PW ☎ (01271) 882476 Fax (01271) 883053 OS map 180/560426 4m SW of Combe Martin off A3123 (Ilfracombe) Open Easter-Oct 570 pitches Grass, level/sloping [icons](café) [icons] £6.50-£20.00* (Mastercard/Visa/Delta/Switch) enquiries@stowford.co.uk www.stowford.co.uk

Watermouth Cove Holiday Park, Berrynarbor EX34 9SJ ☎ (01271) 862504 OS map 180/550480 2m W of Combe Martin on A399 (Ilfracombe) Open Easter-Oct 90 pitches Level grass and hard standings, sheltered [icons] lic club, beach, fishing £8.00-£23.50* (Mastercard/Visa/Switch/Delta) info@watermouthcoveholidays.co.uk www.watermouthcoveholidays.co.uk

COPPLESTONE, Devon   Map F3
✗ Crediton Inn 4m SE at Crediton ☎ (01363) 772882

Nichols Nymett Holiday Park, North Tawton EX20 2BP ☎ (01837) 82484 OS map 191/693023 5m W of Copplestone off A3072 (Sampford Courtenay) Open Mar-Oct 25 pitches [icons]

COVERACK, Cornwall **Map B6**
SEE cliffs, Goonhilly Downs 3m W, 'raised beach' at Lowland Point 1½m NE
✘White Hart 3m E at St Keverne ☏(01326) 280325

Little Trevothen Caravan Park TR12 6SD ☏(01326) 280260 Fax (01326) 280260 OS map
203/775179 ¾m W of Coverack Open May-Sep 100 pitches (16 static) Grass, level
🛒🗑🚿🅿⊕✆☺⌁🚪🎣🚐 £6.50-£9.50* inc hot water mmita@btopenworld.com
www.littletrevothen.com

Penmarth Campsite, Penmarth Farm TR12 6SB Woodland walk to beach ☏(01326) 280389 OS
map 205/775179 ¼m W of Coverack Open Easter-Oct 35 pitches 2 acres, level grass £6.50
For other sites near Coverack see Mullion and Lizard

CRACKINGTON HAVEN, Cornwall **Map D3**
SEE cliffs, surfing beaches ✘Coombe Barton ☏(01840) 230345

Hentervene Caravan Camping Park EX23 0LF ☏(01840) 230365 Fax (01840) 230514 OS map
190/155944 1m SE of Crackington Haven off A39 (Wadebridge-Bude) at Otterham–signposted
Open all year 75 pitches (32 static) 8 acres, level grass and hard standings, sheltered
🛒🗑🚿🅿⊘✆☺⌁🚪🎣🚐🏠 barbecue, babycare room £10.00 (min)
(Mastercard/Visa/Delta/Switch/Solo) contact@hentervene.co.uk www.hentervene.co.uk

CRANTOCK, Cornwall **Map B5**
EC Wed SEE beach and dunes, 12c church, St Ambrose Well
✘The Pheasant Inn, Churchtown, St Newlyn East ☏(01872) 510237
✘Bowgie Inn, West Pentire ☏(01637) 830968 Open 11-2.30/6-9.30

Cottage Farm Tourist Park, Treworgans, Cubert TR8 5HH ☏(01637) 831083 Prop: Mr & Mrs
Harrison OS map 200/786589 1m S of Crantock off Cubert Road Open Easter-Oct 45 pitches
Level/sloping grass and hard standings 🗑🚿🅿⊕✆☺⌁🚐🏠 £9.50-£11.50
info@cottagefarmpark.co.uk www.cottagefarmpark.co.uk

Crantock Plains Tourist Park, Crantock Plains Farm TR8 5PH ☏(01637) 830955/831273 OS map
200/805589 1½m SE of Crantock off Newlyn East road and A3075 (Newquay-Redruth) Open all
year 40 pitches 6 acres, level grass, sheltered 🛒🗑🚿🅿⊘✆☺⌁🚪🎣⊘ www.crantock-
plains.co.uk

Holywell Bay Holiday Park, Holywell Bay TR8 5PR ☏(01637) 871111 OS map 200/600780 2m S
of Crantock on Cubert–Holywell road Open all year exc Christmas & New Year 225 pitches
(150 static) Grass, level, sheltered, some hard standings 🛒⌁🗑🚿🅿⊕✆⊘(outdoor)
☺⌁❀🚐🏠 access to sandy beach £7.00-£26.00 (Mastercard/Visa/Switch)
enquiries@parkdeanholidays.co.uk www.parkdeanholidays.co.uk

The Meadow, Holywell Bay TR8 5PP Quiet site 300 yds from sandy beach ☏(01872) 572752 OS
map 200/768588 3m S of Crantock on Cubert-Holywell road, at Holywell village Open Easter-Oct
16 pitches–no tents 1¼ acres level grass and hard standings, sheltered 🗑🚿🅿⊕✆🚐🏠

Quarryfield Caravan Camping Park TR8 5RJ ☏(01637) 872792 OS map 200/793608 ¼m N of
Crantock off road to Newquay Open Apr-Oct–must book (caravans) 145 pitches 10 acres level
grass 🛒✘🎱🗑🚿🅿⊘⊘🍴⊕🚪🚐 (Mastercard/Visa/Delta/Switch)

Treago Farm, West Pentire Road TR8 5QS ☏(01637) 830277 Prop: JA, PA, DT & S Eastlake OS
map 200/782601 1m W of Crantock on West Pantire road Open Apr-Oct 100 pitches 7 acres
grass, level/sloping, sheltered 🛒🎱🏹🗑🚿🅿⊘✆☺⌁🚪🎣🚐🏠♿ £10.00-£14.00 (most cards)
treagofarm@aol.com www.treagofarm.co.uk

Trebellan Tourist Park, Trebellan, Cubert TR8 5PY ☏(01637) 830522 Fax (01637) 830277 OS
map 200/790571 2m S of Crantock via Cubert Open May-Oct 150 pitches 11 acres, part level
grass, sheltered 🛒✘🎱🏹🗑🚿🅿⊘✆⊘(heated) ☺🚪🏠♿ fishing lakes £8.00-£12.00* (most
cards) treagofarm@aol.com www.treagofarm.co.uk

Trevella Caravan Park TR8 5EW ☏(01637) 830308 Fax (01637) 830155 OS map 200/801597
½m SE of Crantock off Newlyn East road Open Easter-Nov 1 320 pitches (270 static) 25 acres
level/sloping grass and hard standings, sheltered 🛒⌁🗑🚿🅿⊘✆☺⊘☺⌁🚪🎣♿ snack bar,
crazy golf, fishing £6.80-£13.00* (all major cards) trevellapark@aol.com www.trevella.co.uk

Trevornick Holiday Park, Holywell Bay TR8 5PW ☏(01637) 830531 Fax (01637) 831000 OS map
200/775587 1½m SW of Crantock on Cubert–Holywell road Open Easter-Sept 550 pitches
Sloping grass 🛒✘🎱⌁🏹🗑🚿🅿⊘✆⊘(heated) ☺⌁🚪♿ children's club, lic club, golf, coarse
fishing, pre-erected tent hire £8.60-£16.00* (most cards) info@trevornick.co.uk
www.trevornick.co.uk

CROCKERNWELL–see Cheriton Bishop

CROYDE, Devon   Map E2
Village of thatched cottages by a stream with sandy beach ½m away SEE Baggy Point cliffs and
rock garden 2m NW, Georgeham village 1m NE, Woolacombe Sands 2m N
✘Thatched Barn on B3231 ☎(01271) 890349

Bay View Farm, Croyde Bay EX33 1PN ☎(01271) 890501 *Prop: G & J Hakin* OS map
180/443388 ¼m SW of Croyde on left of B3231 (Braunton) Open May-Sept 70 pitches 10 acres
level grass and hard standing 🏕️⊷🔲🔌🌀⊘🌀💲⚡🍴♿ £12.00-£14.00
www.bayviewfarm.co.uk

Croyde Bay Holidays, Croyde Bay EX33 1NZ ☎(01271) 890351 OS map 163/434396 ½m W of
Croyde on road to beach Open Easter-Nov 162 pitches (50 static)–min stay 2 nights for tents in
season 10 acres level grass adj beach and sand dunes 🏕️✘♈🔲🔌🌀💲⚡ tennis, fishing

Putsborough Sands Caravan Park, The Anchorage, Putsborough EX33 1LB ☎(01271) 890230
Prop: Rob Tucker OS map 180/448409 1m N of Croyde on Putsborough Sands road–narrow
approach Open Easter-Oct 5 25 pitches–must book Whitsun-Sept 15–no tents 2 acres, gentle
slope/terraced 🏕️🔌🌀⊘🌀 adj sandy beach £19.00-£26.00 (all cards) *rob@putsborough.com*
www.putsborough.com

Ruda Holiday Park, Croyde Bay EX33 1NY ☎(01271) 890671 OS map 180/438397 ½m W of
Croyde off road to Baggy Point adj beach Open all year 495 pitches (280 static) Level grass
🏕️✘(snack) ♈⊷🔲🔌🌀⊘🌀⊘🖿🌀💲⚡🖵🍴♿ lic club, doctor, free entertainment
£7.00-£30.00* (Mastercard/Visa/Switch/Delta) *enquiries@parkdeanholidays.co.uk*
www.parkdeanholidays.co.uk

For other sites near Croyde see Braunton and Woolacombe

CULLOMPTON–see Honiton

DARTMOUTH, Devon   Map F5
EC Wed MD Tues, Fri SEE Butterwalk Museum, Castle, St Saviour church, Mayflower Stone,
borough museum, Newcomen Engine House
ℹ️Engine House, Mayor's Avenue ☎(01803) 834224
✘Deer Park Inn, Dartmouth Rd, Stoke Fleming ☎(01803) 770755
✘The Forces Tavern, Forces Cross, Blackawton ☎(01803) 712226

Deer Park Holiday Estate, Stoke Fleming TQ6 0RF ☎(01803) 770253 *Prop: Peter & Sara Keane*
OS map 202/864493 2m S of Dartmouth on A379 (Torcross) Open Mar 15-Oct 31–must book
160 pitches Grass, mainly level, open 🏕️✘♈🔲🔌🌀⊘🖿🌀💲♿ bar food £7.50-£16.00
(Mastercard/Visa) *info@deerparkinn.co.uk www.deerparkinn.co.uk*

Leonards Cove Holiday Estate, Stoke Fleming TQ6 0NR ☎(01803) 770206 OS map 202/865483
2m S of Dartmouth off A379 (Stoke Fleming) Open Easter-Oct 152 pitches (112 static)
🏕️✘⊷⚯🔲🔌🌀⊘🌀💲🖵🍴

Little Cotton Caravan Park, Little Cotton TQ6 0LB ☎(01803) 832558 *Prop: TP White* OS map
202/860508 2m W of Dartmouth on A3122 (Halwell) Open Mar-Nov 95 pitches Level/sloping
grass, part sheltered, hard standings 🏕️🔲🔌🌀⊘🌀⊘♿ adj Park & Ride £12.25 (Mastercard/Visa)
enquiries@littlecotton.co.uk www.littlecotton.co.uk

Start Bay Caravan Park, Strete TQ6 0RU ☎(01803) 770535 OS map 202/840473 5m SW of
Dartmouth off A379 (Kingsbridge) on Halwell road Open Easter-Oct 25 pitches 1¼ acres level
grass, part sheltered ⊷🔲🔌🌀⊘🌀🖿 barbecues (all cards exc Amex)

Woodland Leisure Park, TQ9 7DQ *'Best Family Campsite in Europe Alan Rogers Award* ☎(01803)
712598 OS map 202/813522 4½m W of Dartmouth on left of A3122 (Totnes) Open Easter-Nov 5
225 pitches 16 acres grass and hard standing, part sheltered 🏕️✘⊷🔲🔌🌀⊘🌀⊘🌀💲⚡♿
leisure park (free entry), water coasters, toboggan run, 14 play zones, indoor play complex,
falconry £11.00-£17.50 (Mastercard/Visa) *fun@woodlandspark.com www.woodlandspark.com*

DAWLISH, Devon   Map G4
EC Thurs SEE The Lawn, Manor House, Stonelands House, Dawlish Warren peninsula 2m NE
▨ The Lawn ✆ (01626) 215665
✗ Mount Pleasant Inn, Mount Pleasant Rd, Dawlish Warren ✆ (01626) 863151
✗ The Boathouse, The Main Beach ✆ (01626) 888899

Cofton Country Holidays, Starcross EX6 8RP ✆ (01626) 890111 OS map 192/967803 2m N of
  Dawlish on A379 (Exeter) Open Easter-Oct–must book peak periods 512 pitches (62 static)
  Grass, level/sloping, sheltered ▨▨▨▨▨▨▨▨▨▨▨▨▨▨▨▨▨▨▨ coarse fishing lakes
  (most cards)
Golden Sands Holiday Park, Week Lane EX7 0LZ ✆ (01626) 863099 Fax (01626) 867149 OS
  map 192/873783 1m NE of Dawlish off A379 (Exeter) Open Easter-Oct 270 pitches (188 static)
  Grass, level, sheltered ▨▨▨▨▨▨▨▨▨▨(indoor/outdoor) ▨▨▨(season) ▨▨▨ lic club,
  amusements, entertainment £9.00-£16.50* (all major cards) info@goldensands.co.uk
  www.goldensands.co.uk
Lady's Mile Touring and Camping Park, Shutterton EX7 9YZ ✆ (01626) 863411 Fax (01626)
  888689 OS map 192/968780 1m N of Dawlish on A379 (Exeter) Open Mar-Oct 600 pitches
  Level/sloping grass, sheltered ▨▨▨▨▨▨▨▨▨▨▨▨▨▨▨ 9-hole golf, disco
  £7.00-£11.50 (Mastercard/Visa/Eurocard) www.ladysmile.co.uk
Leadstone Camping, Warren Road EX7 0NG ✆ (01626) 864411 Prop: Ian & Jean Bulpin OS map
  192/974783 1m NE of Dawlish off A379 (Exeter) Open Jun 16-Sept 3 137 pitches Grass, part
  level, some hard standings, sheltered ▨▨▨▨▨▨▨▨▨ £11.00-£17.00 (all cards)
  post@leadstonecamping.co.uk www.leadstonecamping.co.uk
Peppermint Park, Warren Road, Dawlish Warren EX7 0PQ ✆ (01626) 863436 Prop: Crumpwood
  Ltd OS map 192/978788 2m NE of Dawlish off A379 (Exeter) Open Mar-Oct 250 pitches
  26 acres grass, part level ▨▨▨▨▨▨▨▨▨▨(heated) ▨▨▨▨▨▨ golf, beach,
  entertainment, coarse fishing, timber lodges, holiday home sales £12.00-£23.00 (Mastercard/Visa)
  info@peppermintpark.co.uk www.peppermintpark.co.uk

DOLTON, Devon   Map E3
SEE church, Iddesleigh village S
✗ Beaford House 2m N at Beaford ✆ (01805) 804503
Dolton Caravan Park EX19 8QF ✆ (01805) 804536 OS map 180/5 In Dolton off A3124–access
  between school and Royal Oak Inn Open Easter-Oct 4 25 pitches 2 acres level grass, sheltered
  ▨▨▨▨▨▨

DOWNDERRY–see Seaton (Cornwall)

DUNKESWELL–see Honiton

EXETER, Devon   Map G4
MD daily University city of Roman origin on river Exe and county town of Devon, with England's
oldest ship canal (16c) SEE cathedral, city walls, Customs House maritime museum, Northernhay
gardens, Rougemont castle
▨ Civic Centre, Paris St ✆ (01392) 265700
✗ Exeter and Devon Arts Centre, Bradninch Place, Gandy St ✆ (01392) 219741

Haldon Lodge Caravan Camping Park, Clapham, Kennford EX6 7YG ✆ (01392) 832312 OS map
  192/894868 5m SW of Exeter off A38 (Ashburton) at Kennford services on Dunchideock road
  (signposted) Open all year 90 pitches 4½ acres level/sloping grass and hard standings,
  sheltered ▨▨▨▨▨▨▨▨▨ horse riding
Kennford International Caravan Park, Kennford EX6 7YN ✆ (01392) 833046 Fax (01392) 833046
  OS map 192/911586 4m S of Exeter on A38 (Plymouth) opposite Kennford service area ½m from
  end of M5 Open all year 120 pitches Level grass and hard standings ▨▨▨▨▨▨▨▨▨▨
  ▨▨▨▨▨ serviced pitches (individually hedged), picnic tables, lounge bar £10.00-£12.70*
  (Mastercard/Visa/Switch) ian@kennfordint.fsbusiness.co.uk www.kennfordint.co.uk

EXMOUTH, Devon   Map G4
EC Wed SEE La Ronde house with shell gallery
▨ Alexandra Terrace ✆ (01395) 222299 ✗ Grand, Sea Front ✆ (01395) 263278
Castle Brake Holiday Park, Woodbury EX5 1HA ✆ (01395) 232431 OS map 192/028879 4m N of
  Exmouth off B3180 (Ottery St Mary) near Woodbury Castle Open Mar-Oct 80 pitches (38 static)
  9 acres level grass, sheltered ▨▨▨▨▨▨▨▨▨▨▨▨▨ (most cards)
Devon Cliffs Holiday Park, Sandy Bay EX8 5BT ✆ (01395) 226266 OS map 192/035800 2m E of
  Exmouth off A376 (Budleigh Salterton) via Littleham, at Sandy Bay, near junct 30 of M5
  Open Mar-Oct 775 pitches (575 static) 143 acres terraced ▨▨▨▨▨▨▨▨▨▨ (all cards)
  www.havenholidays.com
Webbers Farm, Castle Lane, Woodbury EX5 1EA ✆ (01395) 232276 Fax (01395) 233389 OS map
  192/018874 3m N of Exmouth off B3179 at Woodbury–signposted Open Easter-Sept
  115 pitches–must book Grass level/gentle slope ▨▨▨▨▨▨▨▨▨ freezer pack service
  £12.00-£16.00* reception@webberspark.co.uk www.webberspark.co.uk

KEY TO SYMBOLS

🦶	shop	⊘	gas supplies	🔋	winter storage for caravans
✖	restaurant	⊕	chemical disposal point	🅿	parking obligatory
⚥	bar	∅	payphone	❄	no dogs
⏚	takeaway food	▭	swimming pool	⊞	caravan hire
⚲	off licence	❸	games area	🏠	bungalow hire
🗓	laundrette	⤼	children's playground	ㄥ	facilities for disabled
⚡	mains electric hook-ups	⌺	TV	🝆	shaded

FALMOUTH, Cornwall   **Map B6**
SEE 17c church, Pendennis Castle, Jacob's Ladder, Maritime Museum
🦶Killigrew St ☎(01326) 312300
✖Trengilly Wartha Inn & Restaurant, Nancenoy, Constantine ☎(01326) 340332
✖Boslowick Inn, Prislow Lane ☎(01326) 312010

Menallack Farm, Treverva TR10 9BP *Rural site with fine views* ☎(01326) 340333 *Prop: John & Caryl Minson* OS map 204/752312 4m SW of Falmouth on Gweek road Open Apr-Oct
30 pitches Level/sloping grass 🦶⚡⊘❄❸ £7.50-£8.50 *menallack@fsbdial.co.uk*

Pennance Mill Farm, Maen Porth TR11 5HJ ☎(01326) 317431 *Prop: AJ Jewell* OS map
204/791307 3m SW of Falmouth on coast road to Maen Porth beach Open Easter-end Oct
75 pitches 4 acres level grass, sheltered 🦶🗓⚡⊘⊕∅❸⤼⌺⚡🏠ㄥ farm produce
£10.00-£13.00 *www.pennancemill.co.uk*

Tregedna Farm, Maenporth TR11 5HL ☎(01326) 250529 OS map 204/785305 2½m SW of
Falmouth on right of Maenporth road Open May-Sept 40 pitches 10 acres, grass, sloping
🦶🗓⚡⊘⊕∅❸ £10.00* *www.tregednafarmholidays.co.uk*

Tremorvah Tent Park, Swanpool TR11 5BE ☎(01326) 312103 OS map 204/798312 1m SW of
Falmouth off Mawnan road Open May 15-Sept 30 75 pitches 3 acres, gently sloping/terraced
🦶🗓⊘∅

FOWEY, Cornwall   **Map D5**
EC Wed *On W shore of natural harbour, a major port in medieval times and notorious centre of piracy* SEE church, museum, St Catherine's Point
🦶5 South St ☎(01726) 833616 ✖The Old Ferry Inn, Bodinnick-By-Fowey ☎(01726) 870237
Open Nov-Mar 2-2.30/6.30-8.30, Apr-Oct 12-3/6-9 (sandwiches all day)

Penhale Caravan Camping Park PL23 1JU ☎(01726) 833425 *Prop: Mrs M Berryman* OS map
200/104526 1½m NW of Fowey on left of A3082 (Par) Open Apr-Oct 56 pitches 9 acres level
and gentle slope, grass 🗓⚡⊘⊕∅⊞ £5.75-£11.00 *info@penhale-fowey.co.uk www.penhale-fowey.co.uk*

Polruan Holidays, Polruan PL23 1QH ☎(01726) 870263 *Prop: RJ & LJ Hemley* OS map
200/132507 3m SE of Fowey via Bodinnick (ferry) Open Apr-Oct 33 pitches (11 static) Grass
and hard standings, part level, part sheltered 🦶🗓⚡⊘⊕∅❸⊞ £7.25-£14.50
polholiday@aol.com

Penmarlam Caravan and Camping Park, Bodinnick by Fowey PL23 1LZ ☎(01726) 870088 *Prop: MR Wallace* OS map 200/133527 1m E of Fowey off Bodinnick road (ferry) Open Apr-Oct
33 pitches 4 acres level grass, sheltered, outstanding views, new amenity block 🦶⚲🗓⚡⊘⊕ㄥ
slipway, quay and limited moorings, internet access, fishing, serviced pitches £7.00-£15.50
(Mastercard/Visa) *info@penmarlampark.co.uk www.penmarlampark.co.uk*

GOON HAVERN–see Perranporth

GORRAN HAVEN–see Mevagissey

HAYLE, Cornwall   **Map B6**
EC Thurs *Port and market town on estuary in St Ives Bay, with find sands and dunes* SEE St
Felicitas church
✘ Bird in Hand, Trelissick Rd ✆ (01736) 753974

Atlantic Coast Caravan Park, 53 Upton Towans TR27 5BL ✆ (01736) 752071 OS map
203/580400 2m NE of Hayle on B3301 (Portreath) Open Apr-Oct 65 pitches (33 static) Grass,
level, part sheltered 🐾➔♿🖥🅿🌳⚡∅🚿📺 games room

Calloose Caravan Camping Park, Leedstown TR27 5ET ✆ (01736) 850431 Fax (01736) 850431
OS map 203/605353 3½m SE of Hayle off B3302 (Helston) Open March-Nov 120 pitches 12
acres, level grass and hard standings, sheltered 🐾🍴➔🖥🅿🌳⚡∅🔌(heated) ⚡✔🚻🚮♿
crazy golf, skittle alley, tennis court, sep pitches, snacks (most cards) *calloose@hotmail.com*
www.calloose.co.uk

Higher Trevaskis Touring Caravan Camping Park, Gwinear Road, Connor Downs TR27 5JQ
✆ (01209) 831736 OS map 203/610385 3m NE of Hayle off A30 (Camborne) on Carnhell Green
road Open Apr-Oct 82 pitches 5½ acres level grass and hard standings, sheltered
🐾🖥🅿🌳⚡∅⚡✔

Parbola Holiday Park, Wall, Gwinear TR27 5LE ✆ (01209) 831503 OS map 203/619368 2½m
ESE of Hayle off A30 (Camborne) Open Easter-Sept–must book peak periods 138 pitches
Woodland clearings and level field 🐾🖥🅿🌳⚡∅⚡✔🚮🚻♿ baby room, crazy golf £10.50-
£16.50* (most cards) *bookings@parbola.co.uk www.parbola.co.uk*

St Ives Bay Holiday Park, Upton Towans TR27 5BH *Site on sand dunes adj beach* ✆ (01736)
752274 Fax (01736) 754523 OS map 203/575388 1m NE of Hayle off A30 (Redruth) on B3301
(Portreath) by beach Open May-Sept 500 pitches (250 static) 🐾➔🖥🔌(indoor heated) ✔ pub,
children's room, beach access, petrol £6.50-£23.00* (Mastercard/Switch/Visa)
stivesbay@bt.connect.com www.stivesbay.co.uk

Sunnymeadow Holiday Caravan Park, Lelant Downs TR27 6LL ✆ (01736) 752243 OS map
203/528360 2m W of Hayle off A30 (Penzance) Open all year 11 pitches Grass, level, sheltered
🐾🖥🅿🌳⚡∅⚡🚻🚮 £7.00-£8.50 *sunnymeadow@tiscali.co.uk www.chycor.co.uk*

HELSTON, Cornwall   **Map B6**
EC Wed MD Mon, Sat *Market town on Lizard peninsula* SEE museum, St Michael's church,
Godolphin House 5m NW, Furry Day festival (May)
ℹ️ 79 Meneage St ✆ (01326) 565431
✘ Sand Bar, Praa Sands, Penzance ✆ (01736) 763516
✘ Queen's Arms Inn, Breage ✆ (01326) 573485

Boscrege Caravan Park, Ashton TR13 9TG ✆ (01736) 762231 *Prop: Tony Armstrong* OS map
203/590303 4½m NW of Helston off A394 (Penzance) Open Mar-Oct 50 pitches (26 static)
12 acres, level grass, sheltered 🖥🅿🌳∅⚡🚻🚮 microwave facs for campers £6.95-£14.25
(Mastercard/Visa) *enquiries@caravanparkcornwall.com www.caravanparkcornwall.com*

Gunwalloe Caravan Park TR12 7QP ✆ (01326) 572668 *Prop: K & E Wallis* OS map 203/658229
3m S of Helston off A3083 (Lizard) Open Apr-Oct 40 pitches 2½ acres, level grass, sheltered
🅿∅⚡ £6.50-£7.50*

Lower Polladras Caravan-Camping Site, Carleen TR13 9NX ✆ (01736) 762220 Fax (01736)
762220 OS map 203/617308 3½m NW of Helston off B3302 (Camborne) Open Apr-Oct 60
pitches 4 acres level, grass, part sheltered 🐾🖥🅿🌳∅⚡✔🚮 £6.50-£12.50*
polladras@hotmail.com www.lower-polladras.co.uk

Pengersick Caravan Site, Praa Sands TR20 9SH ✆ (01736) 762201 *Prop: The Haulfryn Group*
OS map 203/582285 5m W of Helston on A394 (Penzance) Open Easter-Oct 31
🍴🖥🅿🌳∅⚡✔🚻🚮 £12.00-24.00 (all major cards) *praa@haulfryn.co.uk www.haulfryn.co.uk*

Poldown Caravan Park, Carleen TR13 9NN ✆ (01326) 574560 OS map 203/629299 2½m NW of
Helston off A394 (Penzance) and B3302 (Hayle) Open Apr-Oct 20 pitches (7 static) 2 acres,
level grass, sheltered 🖥🅿⚡∅✔🚮 £7.75-£11.75 *info@poldown.co.uk www.poldown.co.uk*

Retanna Holiday Park, Edgcumbe TR13 0EJ ✆ (01326) 340643 Fax (01326) 340643 OS map
203/710327 3½m NE of Helston on A394 (Penryn) Open Apr-Oct 64 pitches (28 static) Level
grass and hard standings, sheltered 🐾➔🖥🅿🌳⚡∅⚡✔🚻🚮🚮♿ £9.00-£11.00*
(Mastercard/Visa/Switch/Delta) *retannaholpark@lineone.net www.retanna.co.uk*

HOLSWORTHY, Devon   **Map D3**
EC Tues MD Wed, Thurs SEE church, museum, St Peter's Fair (Jul)
✘ Kings Arms, The Square ✆ (01409) 253517

Lufflands Caravan Park, Soldon Cross, Bradworthy Road EX22 7PJ ✆ (01409) 253426 OS map
190/324099 4m NW of Holsworthy off A3072 (Bude) on Bradworthy road Open Mar 15-Oct 30
50 pitches 🐾🍴🖥🌳∅⚡🚮

HONITON, Devon   Map H3
EC Thurs MD Tues, Sat SEE Priory museum, Honiton Pottery
🆔Lace Walk ☎(01404) 43716 ✗Wyndham Arms, High St, Kentisbeare ☎(01884) 266327

Fishponds House Campsite, Dunkeswell EX14 0SH ☎(01404) 891287 OS map 192/154074 5m
N of Honiton off A30 (Chard) and Dunkeswell road in wildlife sanctuary Open all year 15 pitches
Level/sloping grass and hard standings 🔌✗🔌🔌🔌 tennis

Forest Glade Holiday Park, Cullompton EX15 2DT ☎(01404) 841381 Fax (01404) 841593 *Prop:*
Mr & Mrs Wellard OS map 192/100075 6m NW of Honiton off A373 (Cullompton) at Keepers
Cottage Inn Grass and hard standings, level, sheltered Open Mar-Nov–must book (caravans)
120 pitches (40 static) 🔌✗(snack) ⟿⟋🔌🔌🔌🔌🔌🔌🔌(heated indoor) 🔌🔌🔌🔌🔌🔌🔌 first aid,
tennis, mother and baby room, sauna, toddler's pool £9.30-£16.00 inc elect
(Mastercard/Visa/Switch) *enquiries@forest-glade.co.uk www.forest-glade.co.uk*

Honiton Golf Club, Middlehills EX14 9TR ☎(01404) 44422 Fax (01404) 46383 OS map
192/173992 2m SE of Honiton off A35 (Bridport) at Tower Cross Open Mar 15-Oct 31 10 pitches
Hard standings, sheltered ✗🔌🔌🔌🔌🔌 golf (one party member must play golf, no child under 16
unless a competent golfer) £12.00 *secretary@honitongolfclub.fsnet.co.uk*
www.honitongolfclub.co.uk

ILFRACOMBE, Devon   Map E2
EC Thurs MD Sat SEE church, museum, St Nicholas chapel on Lantern Hill, Torrs Walk,
🆔The Promenade ☎(01271) 863001
✗Coach House, Bicclescombe Park Rd (off A361) ☎(01271) 864160

Big Meadow Camping Park, Watermouth EX34 9SJ ☎(01271) 862282 OS map 180/554479 2m
E of Ilfracombe on A399 (Combe Martin) Open Easter-Sept–adv booking advisable 125 pitches
Level grass, sheltered 🔌🔌⟋🔌🔌🔌🔌🔌🔌🔌🔌 camp shop, games room £6.50-£12.00
bigmeadow@hotmail.co.uk www.bigmeadow.co.uk

Hele Valley Holiday Park, Hele Bay EX34 9RD ☎(01271) 862460 OS map 180/536474 1m E of
Ilfracombe off A399 (Combe Martin) Open Apr-Oct 139 pitches (80 static) Grass and hard
standings, level, sheltered 🔌🔌🔌🔌🔌🔌🔌🔌🔌🔌🔌🔌🔌 (all cards exc Amex)
holidays@helevalley.co.uk www.helevalley.co.uk

Little Meadow Camping, Lydford Farm EX34 9SJ ☎(01271) 866862 OS map 180/550480 2m E
of Ilfracombe off A399 (Combe Martin) at Watermouth Open Easter-Sept 50 pitches 6 acres level
grass 🔌🔌🔌🔌🔌🔌🔌🔌🔌 *info@littlemeadow.co.uk www.littlemeadow.co.uk*

Mullacott Cross Caravan Park, Mullacott Cross EX34 8NB ☎(01271) 862212 OS map
180/512445 2m S of Ilfracombe near junction of A361 (Braunton) and B3343 Open Easter-Oct
100 pitches (35 static) ✗🔌🔌🔌 £5.00-£10.00

See also Woolacombe and Combe Martin

INDIAN QUEENS, Cornwall   Map C5
✗Victoria 3m E at Roche ☎(01726) 890207

Resparva House Touring Park, Chapel Town, Summercourt TR8 5AH ☎(01872) 510332 OS map
200/881557 3m SW of Indian Queens off A30 (Redruth) on Summercourt road Open May-Sept
15 pitches–no children 1 acre, level grass 🔌🔌🔌

Summer Lodge Holiday Park, White Cross TR8 4LW ☎(01726) 860415 Fax (01726) 861490 OS
map 200/890597 2m W of Indian Queens on A392 (Newquay) Open Mar-Oct 166 pitches
(116 static) 10 acres level grass, sheltered 🔌✗🔌⟿⟋🔌🔌🔌🔌🔌🔌🔌🔌🔌🔌🔌🔌🔌
£6.00-£17.00* (most cards) *summer.lodge@snootyfoxresorts.co.uk www.snootyfoxresorts.co.uk*

White Acres Holiday Park, White Cross TR8 4LW ☎(01726) 862100 OS map 200/890600 2m W
of Indian Queens on A392 (Newquay) Open all year 309 pitches (209 static)
🔌✗🔌🔌🔌(heated) 🔌 fishing lakes £7.00-£26.00* (Delta/Mastercard/Switch/Visa)
enquiries@parkdeanholidays.co.uk www.parkdeanholidays.co.uk

IPPLEPEN, Devon   Map F5
✗Two Mile Oak Inn, Totnes Rd, Newton Abbot ☎(01803) 812411

Dornafield Farm, Two Mile Oak TQ12 6DD ☎(01803) 812732 *Prop: Dornafield Ltd* OS map
202/838683 1½m N of Ipplepen off A381 (Newton Abbot-Totnes) at Two Mile Oak Cross, near
Denbury road Open Mar 18-Jan 7 135 pitches 30 acres, hard standings and level grass,
sheltered 🔌⟿⟋🔌🔌🔌🔌🔌🔌🔌🔌 all-weather tennis court £11.50-£19.80
(Mastercard/Visa/Delta/Electron/Maestro/Solo) *enquiries@dornafield.com www.dornafield.com*

Ross Park Caravan Park, Park Hill Farm TQ12 5TT ☎(01803) 812983 Fax (01803) 812983 OS
map 202/845671 1m E of Ipplepen on A381 (Newton Abbot-Totnes) Open Mar-Jan 110 pitches
Level grass and hard standings, sheltered 🔌✗🔌⟿⟋🔌🔌🔌🔌🔌🔌🔌🔌🔌 £9.75-£15.75*
enquiries@rossparkcaravanpark.co.uk www.rossparkcaravanpark.co.uk

Woodville Park, Totnes Rd TQ12 5TN ☎(01803) 812240 OS map 202/845674 In village on A381
Open Mar 15-Oct 15 25 pitches–no tents, no facs for children 3½ acres, grass and hard standing,
sheltered 🔌🔌🔌🔌🔌 barbecue area, farm shop near

See also Newton Abbot and Totnes

IVYBRIDGE, Devon   Map F5
EC Wed
🄸 South Dartmoor, Leonards Rd ☏ (01752) 897035
✗ Imperial, Western Rd ☏ (01752) 892269

Smithaleigh Caravan and Camping Park PL7 5AX ☏ (01752) 893194 OS map 202/588554 2½m
   W of Ivybridge off A38 (Plymouth) Open all year–must book peak periods 90 pitches 7 acres,
   level grass and hard standings ▓🖫🖴🖉🖀🗗🖴🖳 family room, skittles, crazy golf

Whiteoaks Caravan Camping Park, Davey's Cross PL21 0DW ☏ (01752) 892340 OS map
   202/652562 1m E of Ivybridge off B3213 (Bittaford) Open Apr-Oct 16 pitches Grass, level
   🖫🖴🖉🖀🖳

JACOBSTOW, Cornwall   Map D3
Quiet village off A39 (Bude-Newquay) SEE church
✗ Combe Barton 3m W at Crackington Haven ☏ (01840) 230345

Edmore Tourist Park, Wainhouse Corner EX23 0BJ ☏ (01840) 230467 Fax (01840) 230467 OS
   map 190/187955 1m W of Jacobstow at Wainhouse Corner on A39 (Stratton-Newquay) Open
   Easter-Oct 30 pitches 3 acres grass, part sloping, part sheltered ▓🖫🖴🖉🖀🖂🖳🗗🖴🖳🗠
   £8.00-£10.00* *edmorepark@aol.com www.cornwallvisited.co.uk*

KENNACK SANDS–see Lizard

KILKHAMPTON, Cornwall   Map D3
North Cornwall village on A39 (Bideford-Bude) W of Tamar lake SEE church (carved bench ends)
✗ The New Inn ☏ (01288) 321488 Open 12-2/6-9.30

East Thorne Touring Park EX23 9RY ☏ (01288) 321654 *Prop: K Ovenden* OS map 190/260110
   ½m SE of Kilkhampton on right of B3254 (Launceston) Open Apr-Oct 29 pitches 2 acres, level
   grass sheltered 🖫🖴🖀🖂🗗🖴🖳 games room £6.00-£9.00

Sandymouth Bay Holiday Park, Sandymouth Bay EX23 9HW ☏ (01288) 352563 Fax (01288)
   354822 OS map 190/210104 2½m SW of Kilkhampton off A39 (Wadebridge) on road to Sandy
   Mouth Bay via Stibb Open Apr-Oct 200 pitches (150 static) ▓✗🛇🗝🖈🖫🖴🖉🖀🖂🖂🗗
   🗗🖴🗠🖴🖳 solarium, disco £7.50-£20.00* (most cards) *sandymouth@aol.com
   www.sandymouthbay.co.uk*

Tamar Lake Farm, Thurdon EX23 9SA ☏ (01288) 321712 OS map 190/287108 3m E of
   Kilkhampton on Tamar Lakes road Open Mar-Oct 15 pitches ½ acre, level grass, sheltered
   ▓✗🛇🗠🖳 fishing £10.00 (min)* (most cards) *www.swalakestrust.org.uk*

KINGSBRIDGE, Devon   Map F5
EC Thurs MD Wed, Fri SEE Shambles arcade, Kingsbridge Estuary, annual fair (Jul), Cookworthy
porcelain museum, local artists summer exhibition
🄸 The Quay ☏ (01548) 853195
✗ The Dodbrook Inn, Church St ☏ (01548) 852068
✗ Giovanni's, 1 Church St ☏ (01548) 856707

Island Lodge, Stumpy Post Cross TQ7 4BL ☏ (01548) 852956 *Prop: Kay Parker* OS map
   202/742470 1½m N of Kingsbridge on A381 (Totnes) Open all year 30 pitches Level grass
   🖫🖴🖀🖉🗗🖴🖳 seasonal pitches £10.00-£13.00

Mounts Farm Touring Park, The Mounts, East Allington TQ9 7QJ ☏ (01548) 521591 OS map
   202/753489 3m NE of Kingsbridge on A381 (Totnes) Open Mar 15-Oct 50 pitches 6 acres level
   grass, sheltered ▓🖫🖴🖀🖉🖂 £10.00-£13.00* (all cards) *mounts.farm@lifeone.net
   www.mountsfarm.co.uk*

Parkland Caravan & Camping Site, Sorley Green Cross TQ7 4AF ☏ (01548) 852723 *Prop: James
   Parker* OS map 202/730463 1m N of Kingsbridge on A381 (Totnes) Open all year 50 pitches
   Grass and hard standing 🖫🖴🖉🖀🖂🖂🖳🗗🖴🗠🖳 seasonal pitches £7.80-£14.25
   enquiries@parklandsite.co.uk www.parklandsite.co.uk

KINGSTEINTON–see Newton Abbot

LAND'S END, Cornwall   Map A6
✗ State House (Lands End complex) ☏ (01736) 871680

Cardinney Caravan and Camping Park, Crows an Wra TR19 6HJ ☏ (01736) 810880 Fax (01736)
   810998 OS map 203/375273 3m NE of Land's End on A30 (Penzance) Open Feb-Nov
   105 pitches 5 acres level grass and hard standings, sheltered ▓✗🗝🖫🖴🖉🖀🖂🖂🗗🗗🗠
   games room £8.00-£12.00* (Mastercard/Visa/Delta/Switch) *cardinney@btinternet.com
   www.cardinney-camping-park.co.uk*

Sea View Caravan Park, Sennen TR19 7AD ☏ (01736) 871266 OS map 203/357253 ¼m E of
   Land's End on right of A30 (Penzance) Open all year 100 pitches (75 static) Level grass
   ▓✗🗠🖈🖫🖴🖉🖀🖂🖳🗗🗠 (Mastercard/Visa)

For other sites near Land's End see St Buryan

THE LIZARD

A rugged peninsula with a central plateau ablaze with heather from spring to autumn, Lizard Point with its lighthouse is the southernmost place in England and one of the most dangerous for shipping. Along the coast are tall cliffs and caverns with beaches at only a few places, one of the most extensive – and most popular – being Kennack Sands.

Lydford Camping and Caravanning Club Site, Lydford

LAUNCESTON, Cornwall   Map D4
EC Thurs MD Tues
📋 Market House Arcade ☎ (01566) 772321
✘ Westgate Inn, Westgate St ☎ (01566) 772493

Chapmanswell Caravan Park, St Giles on the Heath PL15 9SG ☎ (01409) 211382 OS map 190/356932 7m N of Launceston on A388 (Holsworthy) Open Mar-Oct 81 pitches (30 static) 4 acres, level grass, part hard standings, sheltered by hedges 🅿️🗑️📶🅿️♿️⊘🅱️⊕♿️

LISKEARD, Cornwall   Map D5
EC Wed MD Mon, Thurs SEE Guildhall, Castle Park, Pipe Well
✘ The Manor Restaurant, Great Trethew Manor Hotel, Horwinetops ☎ (01503) 240663
Open summer 12-9, winter 12-2.30/6-9

Great Trethew Manor Campsite, Horningtops PL14 3PY ☎ (01503) 240663 *Prop: MJ Peacock* OS map 201/286601 3m SE of Liskeard off A38 (Plymouth) on B3251 (Looe) Open Mar-Sept 55 pitches 30 acres level/sloping grass, sheltered ✘♀🏃📶🗑️🅿️♿️⊘🅱️♿️🅱️🏨 pony rides, tennis, fishing lake £8.00-£14.00* (most cards) *great_trethew_manor@yahoo.com www.great-trethew-manor.co.uk*

Pine Green Caravan and Camping Park, Doublebois PL14 6LD ☎ (01579) 320183 OS map 201/195653 4m W of Liskeard off A38 (Bodmin) on B3360 (East Taphouse) Open Jan-Dec 50 pitches Hard standings and terraced grass 🗑️♿️⊕♿️🅱️🏪

Trenant Caravan Park, St Neot PL14 6RZ ☎ (01579) 320896 *Prop: C Parry* OS map 201/212685 2½m NW of Liskeard off A38 (Bodmin) via Dobwalls and Treverbyn Open Apr-Oct 12 pitches–phone before arrival 1½ acres, level grass, sheltered 🅱️⊕ £6.00-£7.00
See also Bolventor

LIZARD, Cornwall   Map B6
SEE lighthouse, cliffs, Cadgwith 2m NE
✘ Smugglers Fish & Chip Shop, 1 Kynance Terrace ☎ (01326) 290763

Chy-Carne Holiday Park, Kennack Sands, Ruan Minor TR12 7LX ☎ (01326) 290200 OS map 204/727164 4m NE of Lizard off A3083 (Helston) Open Apr-Oct 83 pitches Level/sloping grass, sheltered 🅿️🗑️📶🅿️♿️⊘🅱️⊕♿️🅱️🏪🏨 £7.00-£14.50* (all cards) *enquiries@chy-carne.co.uk www.chy-carne.co.uk*

Gwendreath Farm Caravan Park, Kennack Sands, Ruan Minor TR12 7LZ ☎ (01326) 290666 OS map 204/730169 3m NNE of Lizard off B3293 (Helston-St Keverne) Open Apr-Oct 40 pitches (30 static) 7 acres level grass, sheltered 🅿️🏃📶🗑️🅿️♿️⊘🅱️⊕🅱️🏪 £9.00 (min)* (Mastercard/Visa) *tom.gibson@virgin.net www.tomandlinda.co.uk*

Sea Acres Holiday Park, Kennack Sands TR12 7LT ☎ (01326) 290064 OS map 204/734164 3m NE of Lizard off A3083 (Helston) Open all year exc Christmas & New Year 150 pitches (100 static) 20 acres, level grass 🅿️✘♀🔌🏃📶🗑️🅿️♿️⊘🅿️📺⊕🅱️🏪 club, beach £6.50-£12.00 (Mastercard/Switch/Visa) *enquireis@parkdeanholidays.co.uk www.parkdeanholidays.co.uk*

Silver Sands Holiday Park, Gwendreath, Ruan Minor, Helston TR12 7LZ *Remote small site with woodland walk to beach* ☎ (01326) 290631 *Prop: Clive & Frankie Pullinger* OS map 204/731169 3m NE of Lizard off B3293 (St Keverne) Open May-Sept 50 pitches (16 static) 9 acres level grass, sheltered 🗑️🅱️♿️⊕⊘🅱️⊕♿️🅱️🏪♿️ £9.00-£16.50* (all major cards) *enquiries@silversandsholidaypark.co.uk www.silversandsholidaypark.co.uk*

❖ DOGS
Dogs are usually allowed but must be kept on a lead. Sometimes they have to be paid for.

LOOE, Cornwall   **Map D5**
EC Thurs SEE West Looe church, Guildhall museum, Cornish Museum, Deep Sea and Shark Angling Festival
☑ The Guildhall, Fore St, East Looe ✆ (01503) 262072
✘ Copley Arms, Hessenford, Torpoint ✆ (01503) 240209
✘ The Jubilee Inn, Jubilee Hill, Pelynt ✆ (01503) 220312

Camping Caradon Touring Park, Trelawne PL13 2NA ✆ (01503) 272388 OS map 201/219542 2m W of Looe off A387 (Polperro) and B3359 (Pelynt) Open Apr-Oct 85 pitches Grass, level ⚏♀↩🗑🅿🅰✪↵ £7.00-£10.00 (Mastercard/Visa) *www.campingcaradon.co.uk*

Looe Valley Touring Park, Polperro Road PL13 2JS ✆ (01503) 262425 OS map 201/228536 2m SW of Looe off A387 (Polperro) Open mid Apr-Sept 500 pitches (40 static) Level grass, sheltered ⚏♀↩⳾🗑🅿🅾⊠(heated) ✪↵🗆🅰🆎🏠 lic club, disco (most cards)

Polborder House Camping Caravan Park, St Martin's by Looe PL13 1NZ *Well run small site above Looe* ✆ (01503) 240265 *Prop: Josie & Ray Frankland* OS map 201/283555 2m NE of Looe off B3253 (Normansland) Open Apr-Oct 36 pitches 3 acres, level grass and hard standing, sheltered ⚏🗑🅿🅰✪🅾↵🆎& baby room £8.80-£12.40 (Mastercard/Visa) *reception@peaceful-polborder.co.uk www.peaceful-polborder.co.uk*

Tencreek Caravan-Camping Park PL13 2JR ✆ (01503) 262447 *Prop: Dolphin Holidays* OS map 201/233524 1½m WSW of Looe on A387 (Polperro) Open all year 245 pitches (62 static) –families and couples only 14 acres, level/part sloping grass ⚏✘♀↩⳾🗑🅿🅰✪ 🅾⊠(outdoor/indoor) ↵🗆🅰🆎& club room, solarium £8.90-£17.50 (most cards) *reception@tencreek.co.uk www.dolphinholidays.co.uk*

Tregoad Farm Touring Caravan Camping Park, St Martin's PL13 1PB ✆ (01503) 262718 Fax (01503) 264777 OS map 201/272560 1½m NE of Looe off B3253 (Widegates) Open Apr-Oct 150 pitches Level grass, sheltered ⚏✘♀↩🗑🅿🅰✪🅾↵🆎 lic club, fishing (Mastercard/Visa/Delta/Switch) *tregoadfarmccp@aol.com www.cornwall-online.co.uk/tregoad*

Trelawne Manor Holiday Estate PL13 2NA ✆ (01503) 272151 OS map 201/219538 2m W of Looe off A387 (Polperro) and B3359 (Pelynt) Open Easter, Mar-Oct–must book peak periods 317 pitches (200 static) ⚏✘↩⳾🗑🅿🅰✪🅾⊠(heated) ✪↵🗆 lic club/bar, ballroom

Trelay Farm Park, Pelynt PL13 2JX ✆ (01503) 220900 Fax (01503) 220900 OS map 201/210545 3m W of Looe off A387 (Polperro) and B3359 (Pelynt) Open Easter-Oct 75 pitches (20 static) Level/sloping grass ⚏🗑🅿🅰✪🅾✪🆎& £5.00-£10.50* *stay@trelay.co.uk www.trelay.co.uk*

LOSTWITHIEL, Cornwall   **Map D5**
EC Wed SEE Duchy Hall, bridge, museum, St Bartholomew's church, Restormel castle ruins 1m N
☑ Community Centre, Liddicoat Rd ✆ (01208) 872207
✘ Royal Oak, Duke St ✆ (01208) 872552

Powderham Castle Tourist Park, Lanlivery PL30 5BU ✆ (01208) 872277 OS map 200/083592 1½m SW of Lostwithiel off A390 (St Austell)–signposted Open Apr-Nov 75 pitches–adult only areas 10 acres level grass and hard standings, sheltered 🗑🅿🅰✪🅾✪↵🗆🅰 battery charging, freezer pack service, indoor badminton, 9-hole putting green, separate area for adults only £7.50-£14.50* *powderhamcastletp@tiscali.co.uk www.powderhamcastletouristpark.co.uk*

LYDFORD, Devon   **Map E4**
SEE St Petroc's church, Lydford Gorge and waterfall, ruined castle
✗ The Dartmoor Inn at Lydford ☎ (01822) 820221
✗ The Castle Inn ☎ (01822) 820242

Lydford Camping and Caravanning Club Site, The Croft EX20 4BE ☎ (01822) 820275 *Prop: The Camping and Caravanning Club* OS map 191/512853 ¼m N of Lydford centre on Bridestowe road Open Mar-Oct 70 pitches 4 acres, level grass, sheltered 🗓️🚿⊘◐∅⊘ (Mastercard/Visa/Switch) *www.campingandcaravanningclub.co.uk*

LYNTON, Devon   **Map F2**
EC Sat (winter) *Clifftop village which developed as resort in Victorian-Edwardian times. Linked with tiny harbour of Lynmouth below by steep winding Rd down wooded hillside and a cliff railway. Good centre for walks on Exmoor.* SEE Lyn and Exmoor museum, Watersmeet, Valley of Rocks, Countisbury church 2m E
🏴 Lee Rd ☎ (01598) 752225
✗ Rising Sun by harbour at Lynmouth ☎ (01598) 753223

Channel View Caravan Park, Manor Farm, West Lyn EX35 6LD *Easily accessible site with panoramic views* ☎ (01598) 753349 *Prop: RC Wren* OS map 180/724482 2m SE of Lynton on A39 (Barnstaple) Open Mar 15-Nov 15 80 pitches Level grass and hard standings, sheltered 🛒✗(cafe) ⚲🗓️🚿⊘⊛∅⊶🖛🚿 parent-baby room, family bathroom £8.00-£14.00 (Mastercard/Visa/Switch) *relax@channel-view.co.uk www.channel-view.co.uk*

Lorna Doone Farm, Parracombe EX31 4RJ ☎ (01598) 763576 OS map 180/675446 5m SW of Lynton on A39 (Barnstaple) Open Mar-Oct 40 pitches 2½ acres, level/sloping grass

Sunny Lyn Holiday Park, Lyn Bridge EX35 6NS ☎ (01598) 753384 Fax (01598) 753273 OS map 180/721486 ¼m S of Lynton on B3234 (Barbrook) Open Mar-Nov–no adv booking 38 pitches Grass and hard standings, level, sheltered 🛒✗🍴↩⚲🗓️🚿⊘⊛∅⊛🖛🚿🏠 fishing £10.00-£13.00* (Mastercard/Visa/Delta/Switch/Debit) *info@caravandevon.co.uk www.caravandevon.co.uk*

MALBOROUGH–see Salcombe

MARAZION, Cornwall   **Map A6**
EC Wed SEE St Michael's Mount, Age of Steam
✗ Coach & Horses Inn, Kenneggy Downs, Rosudgeon ☎ (01736) 762470

Kenneggy Cove Holiday Park, Higher Kenneggy, Rosudgeon TR20 9AU ☎ (01736) 763453 *Prop: L Garthwaite* OS map 203/568288 3m E of Marazion on A394 (Helston) near beach Open Apr-Oct 60 pitches Level grass, sheltered 🛒↩🗓️🚿⊘⊛∅⊛⊶🖛 £8.00-£13.50* *enquiries@kenneggycove.co.uk www.kenneggycove.co.uk*

River Valley Country Park, Relubbus TR20 9ER ☎ (01736) 763398 Fax (01736) 763398 OS map 203/566320 3m NE of Marazion off A394 (Helston) on B3280 (Leedstown) Open Mar-Dec 150 pitches Grass and hard standing, level, sheltered 🛒⚲🗓️🚿⊘⊛∅⊛🖛🚿 area reserved for adults only £7.00-£13.50* (all cards exc Amex) *rivervalley@surfbay.dircon.co.uk www.rivervalley.co.uk*

Trevair Touring Site, South Treveneague, St Hilary TR20 9BY ☎ (01736) 740647 OS map 203/548326 2m NE of Marazion off B3280 (Goldsithney) Open Easter-Oct 40 pitches 3 acres level grass sheltered 🗓️🚿⊛🖛🏠

Wayfarers Caravan Park, St Hillary TR20 9EF ☎ (01736) 763326 *Prop: Elaine Holding* OS map 203/551314 2m E of Marazion on B3280 (Goldsithney) Open Mar-Jan 60 pitches 5 acres level grass and hard standings sheltered 🛒🗓️🚿⊘⊛∅🖛 first aid, adults only park £10.00-£16.00 *www.wayfarerspark.co.uk*

Wheal Rodney Holiday Park TR17 0HL ☎ (01736) 710605 OS map 203/521329 ½m N of Marazion on Crowlas road Open all year 37 pitches Level grass, sheltered 🗓️🚿⊘⊛∅⊛☐(indoor heated) 🖛🏠 spa bath, sauna, solarium £9.00-£15.00* (Mastercard/Visa/Switch/Delta) *reception@whealrodney.co.uk www.whealrodney.co.uk*

MAWGAN PORTH, Cornwall   **Map C5**
SEE Mawgan Vale SE, Watergate Bay S ✗ The Merrymoor Inn ☎ (01637) 860258

Magic Cove Touring Park TR8 4BZ ☎ (01637) 860263 OS map 200/852672 ¼m S of Mawgan
Porth on B3276 (Newquay-Padstow) near beach Open Easter-Oct–adv booking (minimum 7
nights in season) 25 pitches Level grass, sheltered ▣⊕ £6.00-£12.00 magic@redcove.co.uk
www.redcove.co.uk

Marver Touring Park TR8 4BB ☎ (01637) 860493 OS map 200/855672 ½m E of Mawgan Porth
off B3276 (Newquay-Padstow) near beach Open Easter-Oct 25 pitches 1 acre level grass
▣▣⌀ sauna familyholidays@aol.com www.marverholidaypark.co.uk

Sun Haven Valley Caravan and Camping Park, Mawgan Porth TR8 4BQ ☎ (01637) 860373 Fax
(01637) 860373 OS map 200/860668 ½m SE of Mawgan Porth on left of St Mawgan road Open
Apr-Oct 118 pitches Grass and hard standing ▤↗▣▣⌀⊕∅▣⌂↲⊟🏠⮞ £9.00-£15.00*
(Mastercard/Visa/Switch/Delta/Debit) traceyhealey@hotmail.com www.sunhavenvalley.co.uk

Treporth Campsite, Porthcothan PL28 8LS ☎ (01841) 520479 OS map 200/860716 2m N of
Mawgan Porth on right of B3276 (Padstow) Open Apr-Oct 16 pitches 1 acre grass, gentle slope

Trevarrian Holiday Park, Trevarrian TR8 4AQ Holiday park overlooking beach ☎ (01637) 860381
OS map 200/851662 ½m S of Mawgan Porth on B3276 (Newquay) Open Easter-Sept
185 pitches 5 acres level grass, open ▤⌂▣▣⌀⊕∅▣⊟↲⌂ paddling pool, live
entertainment, tennis, pitch and putt, bar snacks (Delta/Visa)

Watergate Bay Holiday Park, Tregurrian, Watergate Bay TR8 4AD Well organised touring site
☎ (01637) 860387 Prop: B & GM Jennings OS map 200/849655 1½m S of Mawgan Porth off
B3276 (Newquay) at Tregurrian Open Easter-Oct 171 pitches 30 acres level grass and hard
standings ▤✗⌂↲↯▣▣⌀⊕∅▣⊟(heated) ⊕↲⌂▣🏠⮞ lic club, evening entertainment,
free minibus to beach, dog exercise area £8.50-£14.00 (all cards)
email@watergatebaytouringpark.co.uk www.watergatebaytouringpark.co.uk

See also Newquay and St Columb Major

MEVAGISSEY, Cornwall   **Map C5**
SEE harbour, museum, aquarium, model railway
✗ Polgooth Inn, Ricketts Lane, Polgooth ☎ (01726) 74089

Pengrugla Caravan and Camping Park, St Ewe PL26 6EL ☎ (01726) 842714 OS map
204/998470 2m NW of Mevagissey off B3273 (St Austell) on Sticker road Open Mar-Oct 112
pitches Level/sloping grass, hard standing ▤▣⌀⌀ dairy produce, beach access,
slipway (Mastercard/Visa/Switch)

Penhaven Touring Park, Pentewan PL26 6DL ☎ (01726) 843687 OS map 204/015475 2m N of
Mevagissey on right of B3273 (St Austell) Open Apr-Oct 105 marked pitches 13½ acres level
grass sheltered, some hard standings ▤↲↯▣▣⌀⊕∅▣⊟↲🏠⮞ bike hire (most cards)

Pentewan Sands Holiday Park PL26 6BT ☎ (01726) 843485 Fax (01726) 844142 OS map
204/017468 1m N of Mevagissey on B3273 (St Austell) Open Apr-Oct–must book peak periods
600 pitches (114 static) 26 acres, hard standings, level grass ▤✗🍴↲↯▣▣⌀⊕∅▣⊟(heated)
⊕↲⌂⌀▣🏠⮞ tennis, sailing club, private beach £9.95-£24.15*
(Mastercard/Visa/Switch/Delta) info@pentewan.co.uk www.pentewan.co.uk

Sea View International Holiday Park, Boswinger, Gorran Haven PL26 6LL Landscaped park above
Veryan Bay notable for its facilities ☎ (01726) 843425 Fax (01726) 843358 OS map 204/991412
3m S of Mevagissey off Gorran Haven road Open Easter-Sept–must book peak periods
210 pitches (38 static) Grass and hard standing ▤↲↯▣▣⌀⊕∅▣⊟(2 heated) ⊕↲⌂🏠⮞

Sun Valley Holiday Park, Pentewan Road PL26 6DJ ☎ (01726) 843266 Fax (01726) 843266 OS
map 204/006484 1½m N of Mevagissey on B3273 (St Austell) Open Apr-Oct–must book peak
periods 100 pitches (75 static) 20 acres, level grass and hard standings, sheltered
▤✗🍴↲↯▣▣⌀⊕∅▣⊟(heated indoor) ⊕↲⌂⌀🏠 children's room, tennis £12.00-£26.00*
(Mastercard/Visa/Switch/Delta) reception@sunvalley-holidays.co.uk www.sunvalley-holidays.co.uk

Tregarton Park, Gorran PL26 6NF ☎ (01726) 843666 OS map 204/985437 2m W of Mevagissey
off Gorran Haven road Open Apr-Sept–booking advisable 130 pitches Grass, part sloping, and
hard standings, sheltered ▤↯▣▣⌀⊕∅▣⊟(heated) ⊕↲ (Mastercard/Visa/Switch)

Trelispen Caravan and Camping Park, Gorran Haven PL26 6NT ☎ (01726) 843501 Prop: Dr
James Whetter OS map 204/008421 2m SW of Mevagissey off Gorran Haven road Open Apr-
Oct 40 pitches Level grass, sheltered ▣▣⌀⊕↲▣ nature reserve £8.00-£15.00
trelispen@care4free.net

Treveague Farm, Gorran PL26 6NY ☎ (01726) 842295 Prop: Steve & Myra Welsh OS map
204/001410 3m S of Mevagissey off coast road near Gorran Haven: follow signs Penare
Open Apr-Sept 30 pitches 8 acres level/sloping grass ▤▣▣⌀⊕⊗▣⮞ £10.00-£12.00
treveague@btconnect.com

Treveor Farm Caravan and Camping, Gorran PL26 6LW ☎ (01726) 842387 Fax (01726) 842387
OS map 204/988418 2½m SW of Mevagissey via Gorran Open Easter-Oct 50 pitches 4 acres
mainly level grass ▤▣▣⊕∅⌀↲ coarse fishing £5.00-£12.00* info@treveorfarm.co.uk
www.treveorfarm.co.uk

✗ RESTAURANTS

The restaurants recommended in this guide are of three kinds – pubs, independent restaurants and those forming part of hotels and motels. They all serve lunch and dinner – at a reasonable price – say under £10 a head. We shall be glad to have your comments on any you use this season and if you think they are not up to standard, please let us have your suggestions for alternatives.

California Cross Camping and Caravanning Club Site, Modbury

MODBURY, Devon   **Map F5**
Hilly town in region of South Hams, with Bigbury only feasible access to sea SEE church, Erme valley, Bigbury sands and Burgh Island 4m S
▸ 4 Modbury Court ☎(01548) 830159
✗ The California Country Inn, California Cross ☎(01548) 821449

California Cross Camping and Caravanning Club Site, Ivy Bridge PL21 0SG ☎(01548) 821297
Prop: The Camping and Caravanning Club OS map 202/705530 3m E of Modbury on B3207 (Halwell) near junction with B3196 (South Brent–Kingsbridge) Open Apr-Oct 80 pitches–adv booking min 2 nights 3½ acres, level grass, sheltered 🛒✗♀⚡🗓🚿🅿⊕∅↩♿ £13.40-£18.00 (Mastercard/Visa/Switch)

Moor View Touring Caravan Park, California Cross PL21 0SG ☎(01548) 821485 Fax (01548) 821485 OS map 202/701523 3m E of Modbury on B3207 (Dartmouth) Open Mar 15-Nov 15 68 pitches Level grass and hard standing, sheltered 🛒↩🗓🚿🅿⊕🅂↩🅿 £6.50-£12.90* (most cards) *info@moorviewtouringpark.co.uk www.moorviewtouringpark.co.uk*

Pennymoor Camping-Caravan Park PL21 0SB ☎(01548) 830542/830020 Fax (01548) 830542 OS map 202/685516 1½m E of Modbury off A379 (Kingsbridge) at Harraton Cross Open Mar 15-Nov 15 155 pitches (70 static) 11½ acres grass, level/gentle slope 🛒🗓🚿🅿⊕🅂♿↩🅿♿ £6.00-£12.00* *enquiries@pennymoor-camping.co.uk www.pennymoor-camping.co.uk*

South Leigh Caravan and Camping Park PL21 0SB ☎(01548) 830346 OS map 202/689514 1m E of Modbury off A379 (Kingsbridge) at Harraton Cross Open Mar 24-Oct 31 200 pitches (100 static) Level/sloping grass 🛒♀↩🗓🚿🅿⊕∅🔲🅿🅿♿ snack bar, live entertainment in season

MORTEHOE–see Woolacombe

MULLION, Cornwall   **Map B6**
EC Wed *Remote resort on Lizard Peninsula, one most scenic parts of wild and rocky coastline, the cliffs running S to isolated Predannack Head and N to coves of Polurrian and Poldhu* SEE church (carved bench ends), Mullion Cove 1m SW, Poldhu Point and Marconi Memorial 1m NW
✗ Wheel Inn, Cury Cross Lanes, Helston ☎(01326) 240412
✗ The Regent Cafe & Gift Shops, The Square, The Lizard ☎(01326) 290483

Franchis, Cury Cross Lanes TR12 7AZ ☎(01326) 240301 *Prop: Brian & Dawn Thompson* OS map 203/696204 1m NE of Mullion on A3083 (Helston-Lizard) Open Mar-Oct 70 pitches 17 acres, level grass, sheltered 🛒🗓🚿🅿⊕∅🅿🅿🏠 £8.00-£11.00 *enquiries@franchis.co.uk www.franchisholidays.co.uk*

The Friendly Camp and Caravan Park, Tregullas Farm, Penhale TR12 7LJ ☎(01326) 240387 *Prop: JBW Bennetts* OS map 203/698185 1m SE of Mullion on A3083 (Helston-Lizard) Open Apr-Oct 10 10 pitches 1½ acres level grass sheltered ∅🅿 £7.00-£10.00 (Mastercard/Visa)

Mullion Holiday Park, Penhale TR12 7LJ *Family site in lovely setting on Lizard peninsula* ☎(01326) 240428 & 0870 4445344 Fax (01326) 241141 OS map 203/698185 1½m SE of Mullion at junction of B3296 (Penhale) and A3083 (Helston-Lizard) Open May-Sept 498 pitches (348 static) Grass, level and hard standing 🛒✗♀↩↗🗓🚿🅿⊕∅🔲(indoor/outdoor) 🅂↩🅿🅿🅿🏠♿ lic club, solarium, amusements, crazy golf £12.50-£28.50* (Mastercard/Visa/debit cards) *bookings@weststarholidays.co.uk www.weststarholidays.co.uk*

Teneriffe Farm, Predannack TR12 7EZ ☎(01326) 240293 OS map 203/676169 2m S of Mullion off B3296 (Mullion Cove) on Predannack road Open Apr-Oct 20 pitches Grass, part level, open 🗓🚿🅿⊕∅🅿

NEWQUAY, Cornwall   **Map B5**
EC Wed (winter) *One-time port and fishing centre on N Cornish coast noted for its fine sands, surfing beaches and impressive cliff scenery N beyond Watergate Bay* SEE surfing beaches, zoo, St Columb Minor Church (15c), Trerice Manor 4m S, Kelsey Head 5m SW
Municipal Offices, Marcus Hill ℰ(01637) 854020
Mavericks, 70 Henver Rd ℰ(01637) 878089
The Fort Inn, 63 Fore St ℰ(01637) 875700

Hendra Holiday Park, Lane TR8 4NY ℰ(01637) 875778 Fax (01637) 879017 OS map 200/834606 1½m SE of Newquay on A392 (Indian Queens) Open Apr-Oct 788 pitches (160 static) 46 acres level grass and hard standings, sheltered (indoor/outdoor) lic club, disco, amusements, crazy golf, children's club £8.40-£14.00* (Mastercard/Switch/Visa) hendra.cornwall@dial.pipex.com www.hendra-holidays.com

Newquay Holiday Park TR8 4HS ℰ(01637) 871111 OS map 200/855626 2m E of Newquay on A3059 (St Columb) Open all year exc Chrismas & New Year 488 pitches (138 static) 23 acres, grass, part sloping, hard standings, sheltered (heated) paddling pool, lic club £7.00-£26.00* (Mastercard/Visa/Switch) enquiries@parkdeanholidays.co.uk www.parkdeanholidays.co.uk

Porth Beach Tourist Park, Porth TR7 3NH ℰ(01637) 876531 Fax (01637) 871227 OS map 200/832629 1½m N of Newquay on B3276 (Padstow) near beach Open Apr-Oct 201 pitches 7 acres level grass, sheltered ice packs £9.00-£26.00* (Delta/Mastercard/Switch/Visa) info@porthbeach.co.uk www.porthbeach.co.uk

Riverside Holiday Park, Lane TR8 4PE ℰ(01637) 873617 *Prop: P Miller* OS map 200/831593 2½m E of Newquay off A3075 (Redruth) and Quintrell Downs road Open Easter-Oct 150 pitches 14 acres level grass, sheltered fishing £8.00-£12.00 (all cards) info@riversideholidaypark.co.uk www.riversideholidaypark.co.uk

Rosecliston Tourist Park, Trevemper TR8 5JT *Well organised pitches for tourists* ℰ(01637) 830326 OS map 200/813593 2m S of Newquay on A3075 (Redruth) Open May-Oct 126 pitches 6 acres, level grass and hard standings (heated) sauna, solarium

Sunnyside Holiday Park, Quintrell Downs TR8 4PD *In beautiful countryside near coast exclusively for 17-35 age group* ℰ(01637) 873338 OS map 200/850602 2m E of Newquay on left of A392 (St Austell) beyond Quintrell Downs Open Apr-Oct 265 pitches–no trailer caravans 25 acres level grass, sheltered lic club with entertainment, whirlpool spa (Mastercard/Visa)

Trebarber Farm Camping Caravan Site, St Columb Minor TR8 4JT ℰ(01637) 873007 Fax (01637) 873007 OS map 200/864626 3m NE of Newquay off A3059 (St Columb Major) Open May-Oct 65 pitches level grass £6.00-£11.00 trebarberfarm@amserve.com www.trebarberfarmholidays.com

Tregustick Farm Holiday Park, Porth TR8 4AR ℰ(01637) 872478 OS map 200/845631 2m N of Newquay off B3276 (Padstow) Open Apr-Oct 120 pitches (100 static) 9 acres, part level

Treloy Tourist Park TR8 4JN ℰ(01637) 872063/876279 *Prop: Richard Paull* OS map 200/860636 3m E of Newquay off A3059 (St Columb) Open Apr-Sept 140 pitches 11½ acres, hard standings and grass, level/sloping golf course concession £8.00-£13.00* (Mastercard/Visa/Switch) treloytp@bt.connect.com www.treloy.co.uk

Trenance Caravan Park, Edgcumbe Avenue TR7 2JY *One of nearest sites to town centre* ℰ(01637) 873447 Fax (01637) 852677 OS map 200/816611 ½m S of Newquay on left of A3075 (Redruth) Open May-Oct 184 pitches (134 static) 10 acres, grass, sloping, sheltered £10.00-£13.00* (all cards) tony.hoyte@virgin.net www.mywebbpage.net/trenance

Trencreek Holiday Park TR8 4NS *Family park in village setting* ℰ(01637) 874210 OS map 200/829608 1m SE of Newquay off A392 (Indian Queens) Open Apr-Sept 150 pitches Level grass and hard standings children's room, coarse fishing, entertainment, paddling pool

Trethiggey Touring Park, Quintrell Downs TR8 4LG *Peaceful family-run site with country views* ℰ(01637) 877672 Fax (01637) 879706 OS map 200/848597 2m E of Newquay on A3058 (St Austell) Open Mar-Dec–must book peak periods 157 pitches 15 acres, level/sloping grass and hard standing, sheltered (all year) battery charging (most cards) enquiries@trethiggey.co.uk www.trethiggey.co.uk

Trevelgue Caravan Park, Porth TR8 4AS ℰ(01637) 873475/875905 OS map 200/837635 2m NE of Newquay off B3276 (Padstow) on Tregustick road Open Apr-Oct 399 pitches (142 static) 15 acres level grass (indoor heated) jacuzzi

See also Crantock, Mawgan Porth, Indian Queens and St Columb

SITE DIRECTIONS
The distance and direction of a campsite is given from the centre of the town under which it appears.

NEWTON ABBOT, Devon   **Map F4**
EC Thurs MD Wed, Sat *Busy market town beside river Teign and popular touring centre on E edge of Dartmoor* SEE Forde House, Wolborough church
🏫 Bridge House, Courtenay St ☎(01626) 215667
✗ Dartmouth Inn, East St ☎(01626) 853451

Twelveoaks Farm Caravan Park, Teigngrace TQ12 6QT *Family-managed rural site in quiet location* ☎(01626) 352769 Fax (01626) 352769 OS map 191/852735 1½m NW of Newton Abbot off A382 (Moretonhampstead) Open all year 25 pitches–no tents Hard standing and grass, sloping 🛢️🖥️🅿️🗑️🚿🔌🚻 £6.50-£10.00* (Mastercard/Switch/Visa) *info@twelveoaksfarm.co.uk www.twelveoaksfarm.co.uk*

Ware Barton, Kingsteignton TQ12 3QQ ☎(01626) 354025 OS map 192/884729 2½m NE of Newton Abbot on A381 (Teignmouth) Open May-Sept 90 pitches (40 static) Level/sloping grass, sheltered

See also Ipplepen

NEWTON POPPLEFORD, Devon   **Map G4**
✗ Coach House at Southerton ☎(01395) 68946

Popplefords, Exeter Road EX10 0DE ☎(01395) 568672 OS map 192/064895 1½m W of Newton Poppleford on right of A3052 (Exeter) Open Mar-Oct 6 pitches 10 acres grass and hard standing, level, sheltered ✗🅿️🚿

NORTHAM–see Bideford

OKEHAMPTON, Devon   **Map E3**
EC Wed MD Sat SEE town hall (17c) parish church, Fitz Well, Dartmoor (2028ft Yes Tor, 2039ft High Willhays, West Okement Valley)
🏫 3 West St ☎(01837) 53020
✗ Plume of Feathers, Fore St ☎(01837) 52815

Olditch Farm Caravan Park, Sticklepath EX20 2NT ☎(01837) 840734 Fax (01837) 840877 OS map 191/646935 4m E of Okehampton on left of old A30 (Exeter) before Sticklepath Open Mar-Nov 52 pitches (19 static) Level/sloping grass and hard standings, sheltered 🛢️✗🖥️🅿️🗑️🔌🚿🔌🚻(£2.00/wk) 🚽 meals (most cards) *stay@olditch.co.uk www.olditch.co.uk*

For other sites near Okehampton see Bridestowe and Whiddon Down

TRAVELLING TO THE WEST COUNTRY
Travelling to and from the West Country, try to avoid Friday evenings or Saturdays in July, August and September. On Saturdays in July and August there may well be traffic jams on M5 southbound between junctions 14 and 20. If you have to use the motorway on a Saturday during these months try to time your journey to be outside the peak hours of 0600 to 1400. Motorists should also avoid the Tamar Bridge at Saltash on the A38 west of Plymouth at peak times, particularly on Saturdays in July and August between 0900 and 1600.

*Beverley Park,
Paignton*

PADSTOW, Cornwall   **Map C4**
EC Wed MD Thurs *Popular resort on Camel estuary with ancient harbour* SEE St Petroc's church,
Tropical Bird and Butterfly garden, Hobby Horse festival (May Day)
◪ Red Brick Bldg, North Quay ☏ (01841) 533449
✖ Waves, Higher Harlyn, St Merryn ☏ (01841) 520096

Carnevas Farm Holiday Park, St Merryn PL28 8PN *Spacious site in open countryside* ☏ (01841)
520230 *Prop: Mrs Caroline Pawley* OS map 200/862728 3m SW of Padstow off B3276
(Newquay) Open Apr-Oct 198 pitches 8 acres, grass, level/sloping ▤✖♀➛⋏▤➋∅⊛∅
➛⌂⛺⛆ games room £7.50-£14.50 *carnevascampsite@aol.com*
www.carnevasholidaypark.co.uk

Dennis Cove Camping PL28 8DR *Site with access to Padstow beach* ☏ (01841) 532349 OS map
200/921744 ¼m S of Padstow off A389 (Wadebridge) by river Open Whitsun-Sept 43 pitches
Grass, level, part sheltered ▤▤➋∅⊛ fishing £10.00-£13.90* *denniscove@freeuk.com*
www.denniscove.co.uk

Harlyn Sands Holiday Park, Trevose Head, St Merryn PL28 8SQ ☏ (01841) 520720 OS map
200/869755 3m W of Padstow off B3276 (Newquay) Open Easter-Nov 425 pitches (300 static)
Level grass ▤✖♀➛▤➋∅⊛∅➛⌂⛺ club house, beach nearby

Higher Harlyn Park, St Merryn PL28 8SG ☏ (01841) 520022 OS map 200/877744 2½m SW of
Padstow off B3276 (Newquay) Open Mar-Sept 325 pitches (70 static)–no adv booking 30 acres,
level grass ▤✖♀➛⋏▤➋∅⊛∅⊡➛⌂⛺⛆ children's room (Mastercard/Visa/Delta/Switch)

Mother Ivey's Bay Caravan Park, Trevose Head PL28 8SL ☏ (01841) 520990 OS map
200/860762 5m W of Padstow off B3276 (Newquay) on Trevose Head–signposted Open Easter-
Oct 350 pitches (250 static)–booking advisable 13 acres level/sloping grass, open
▤⋏▤➋∅⊛∅➛⛺ (most cards)

Ponderosa Caravan Park, St Issey PL27 7QA ☏ (01841) 540359 OS map 200/927719 2½m S of
Padstow on left of A389 (Wadebridge) Open Easter-Oct 60 pitches 4 acres, level grass
▤▤➋⊛➛⛺⌂ dairy produce £5.00-£8.00

Seagull Tourist Park, Treginegar Farm, St Merryn PL28 8PT ☏ (01841) 520117 OS map
200/883713 3½m SW of Padstow off B3276 (Newquay) Open Apr-Oct 86 pitches (36 static) 5
acres, level grass and hard standings ▤➋∅⊛∅☉⛺⌂⛆

Tregavone Farm Touring Park, St Merryn PL28 8JZ ☏ (01841) 520148 OS map 200/897732 2m
S of Padstow off A389 (Wadebridge) and Shop road Open Mar-Oct 40 pitches 4 acres level
grass ▤➋⊛☉ £7.00-£9.00

Tregidier Caravan Park, Trevean Lane, St Merryn PL28 8PR ☏ (01841) 520264 OS map
200/875725 3½m SW of Padstow off B3276 (Trenance) Open Apr-Oct–must book peak periods
18 pitches 1 acre, level grass ▤✖♀➛▤➋⊛∅⛺

Padstow Touring Park PL28 8LE ☏ (01841) 532061 *Prop: P Barnes* OS map 200/912739 1m S
of Padstow on left of A389 (Wadebridge) Open all year 150 pitches 13½ acres level grass and
hard standings, sheltered ▤▤➋∅⊛∅➛⛺⌂ motorhome pumpout, serviced pitches £9.50-
£13.00 (most cards) *phil@padstowtouringpark.co.uk www.padstowtourngpark.co.uk*

Trethias Farm, St Merryn PL28 8PL *David Ballamy Gold Conservation Award* ☏ (01841) 520323
Prop: Mr & Mrs Chandler OS map 200/865734 4m WSW of Padstow off B3276 (Newquay) on
Treyarnon Beach road–signposted Open Apr-Sept 128 pitches (65 static) Level grass
▤▤➋∅⊛∅ recycling facility £10.50-£12.00

Trevean Farm Caravan and Camping, St Merryn PL28 8PR ☏ (01841) 520772 OS map
200/875724 4m SW of Padstow off B3276 (Newquay) on Rumford road–signposted Open Apr-
Oct 39 pitches 2 acres level grass ▤▤➋∅⊛∅➛⛺⌂

Trewince Farm Holiday Park, St Issey PL27 7RL ☏ (01208) 812830 Fax (01208) 812835 OS map
200/938714 3m SE of Padstow on right of A389 (Wadebridge) Open Easter-Oct 120 pitches
(30 static) 4½ acres grass and hard standings, level and terraced ▤➋∅⊛▣ (heated, outdoor)
⊛➛⛺⌂⛆⚑ woodland walks (most cards)

Treyarnon Bay Caravan Park, Treyarnon Bay, St Merryn PL28 8JR ☏ (01841) 520681 OS map
200/860737 3½m W of Padstow off B3276 (Newquay) near Treyarnon beach Open Apr-Sept
260 pitches (200 static) 22 acres grass part level/sloping part sheltered ▤▤∅⊛∅⛺

For other sites near Padstow see St Minver and Wadebridge

FOLLOW THE COUNTRY CODE
Guard against all risk of fire. Fasten all gates. Keep dogs under proper control. Keep to the paths
across farmland. Avoid damaging fences, hedges and walls. Leave no litter. Safeguard water
supplies. Protect wildlife, plants and trees. Go carefully on country roads and be prepared for slow-
moving vehicles like tractors. Respect the life of the countryside.

PAIGNTON, Devon   Map G5

EC Wed SEE zoo, Oldway Mansion, Kirkham House, St John's church, harbour, aquarium
⛳Esplanade ☎0906 6801268 ✗Indies Leisure Complex, Totnes Rd ☎(01803) 669191
✗The Blagdon Inn, Blagdon Barton ☎(01803) 521412

Barton Pines Inn, Blagdon Road, Higher Blagdon TQ3 3YG *Touring site in wooded grounds of charming inn with extensive views* ☎(01803) 553350 *Prop: DG McClarron* OS map 202/847612 2½m W of Paignton off A380 (Marldon)–signposted Open Mar-Oct–must book peak periods 33 pitches Level grass, sheltered 🔲🔳🔘⌗(heated) ⚐⛺ tennis £5.00-£14.00 *info@bartonpines.com www.bartonpines.com*

Beverley Park, Goodrington Road TQ4 7JE ☎(01803) 843887 OS map 202/886576 1½m S of Paignton off A379 (Dartmouth) Open Easter-Oct–must book 391 pitches (197 static) Grass, level, open, hard standings 🔲✗🔳⚐⌁🔲🔳🔘⌗(heated, in & out 🔘⚐⌁🔳🔲🏠⛺ tennis, ballroom, sauna,golf, indoor soft play area £9.30-£30.80 (Mastercard/Visa) *info@beverley-holidays.co.uk www.beverley-holidays.co.uk*

Byslades International Touring Park, Totnes Road TQ4 7PY *Well equipped site for tourers two miles from safe beaches* ☎(01803) 555072 *Prop: R & K Wedd* OS map 202/848602 2m W of Paignton on A385 (Totnes) Open Easter-Sept 190 pitches 23 acres, grass and hard standings 🔲🔳⚐⌁🔲🔳🔘⌗🔲(heated) 🔘⚐🔲⚐⛺🔲 children's room, tennis, crazy golf £6.00-£13.50 (Mastercard/Visa/Maestro/Solo) *info@byslades.co.uk www.byslades.co.uk*

Higher Well Farm Holiday Park, Stoke Gabriel TQ9 6RN ☎(01803) 782289 *Prop: John & Liz Ball* OS map 202/585856 4m W of Paignton off A385 (Totnes) at Parkers Arms on Stoke Gabriel road Open Easter-Oct 98 pitches Level/sloping grass, sheltered 🔲🔳⚐🔘⌗🔲(18) ⛺ new toilet/shower block inc family washrooms and dishwashing room £7.50-£12.50 (most cards) *www.higherwellfarmholidaypark.co.uk*

Hoburne Torbay, Grange Court, Grange Road, Goodrington TQ4 7JP ☎(01803) 558010 Fax (01803) 696286 OS map 202/888588 1½m S of Paignton on A379 (Dartmouth) Open Mar-Oct 677 pitches (520 static) Level/sloping grass and hard standings 🔲✗🔳⚐⌁🔲🔳⚐🔘⌗🔲🔘⚐⚐🔲 sep pitches, lic club/bar, steam room, solarium, snooker, boules £10.00-£25.00* (most cards) *enquiries@hobourne.com www.hobourne.com*

Lower Yalberton Caravan and Camping Park, Long Road TQ4 7PH ☎(01803) 558127 OS map 202/863586 2½m SW of Paignton off A380 (Brixham) ring road Open May-Sept 543 pitches 24 acres level/sloping grass 🔲✗🔳⚐⌁🔲🔳⚐🔘⌗🔲(heated) 🔘⚐🔲⚐🔲 disco (all cards)

Marine Park Holiday Centre, Grange Road, Goodrington TQ4 7JR ☎(01803) 843887 OS map 202/888582 1½m SW of Paignton off A3022 (Brixham) ring road Open May-Sept 88 pitches (66 static) Grass, level/sloping, hard standing, sheltered 🔲🔳⚐⛺⚐🔲 £10.50-£21.00 (all cards) *info@beverley-holidays.co.uk www.beverley-holidays.co.uk*

Orchard Park, Totnes Road TQ4 7PW ☎(01803) 550504 OS map 202/854601 1m W of Paignton on right of A385 (Totnes) in grounds of manor house Open mid Mar-Oct 200 pitches 17 acres, part level 🔲✗(snack) 🔳🔲⚐🔘🔘🔲

Paignton Holiday Park, Totnes Road TQ4 7PY ☎(01803) 550504 Fax (01803) 521684 OS map 202/855603 2m W of Paignton on right of A385 (Totnes) Open Mar-Oct 250 pitches (82 static)–must book Jul-Aug 14 acres, grass and hard standing 🔲✗🔳⚐⌁🔲🔳⚐🔘⌗🔲(heated) 🔘⚐🔲🔲⚐🔲 entertainment (Mastercard/Visa)

Ramslade Touring Park, Stoke Road, Stoke Gabriel TQ9 6QB ☎(01803) 782575 OS map 202/857588 3m SW of Paignton off A385 (Totnes) at Parkers Arms, Collaton Open mid Mar-end Oct 135 pitches 8 acres, grass, level/sloping, hard standings, sheltered ⌁🔲🔳⚐🔘⌗🔲🔘⚐🔲🔲⚐(Jul-Aug) ⛺ paddling pool, serviced pitches (all major cards)

Whitehill Holiday Park, Stoke Road TQ4 7PF ☎(01803) 782338 Fax (01803) 782722 OS map 202/857588 2m W of Paignton off A385 (Totnes) on Stoke Gabriel road Open May-Sept (families and couples only) 400 pitches (60 static) 20 acres, gentle slope and level grass 🔲🔳⚐🔲🔳⚐🔘⌗🔲(heated) 🔘⚐🔲⚐🔲 £8.50-£20.00 *info@whitehill-park.co.uk www.whitehill-park.co.uk*

Widend Caravan and Camping Park, Berry Pomeroy Road, Marldon TQ3 1RT *Prop: RJ Cowen & Family* Paignton (01803) 550116 2m NW of Paignton on right of Marldon-Berry Pomeroy road Open Easter-Oct 207 pitches 22 acres, level grass, sheltered, some hard standings 🔲🔳⚐🔲🔳⚐🔘⌗🔲(heated) 🔘⚐⚐(Jul Aug) 🔲🏠⛺ seasonal pitches £7.00-£15.00 (Mastercard/Visa/Delta/Switch)

PAR–see St Austell

PARRACOMBE–see Lynton

PENRYN, Cornwall   Map B6

EC Thurs SEE St Gluvias church, Seven Stars Inn, museum, town hall
✗The Stonemasons Arms, Longdowns ☎(01209) 860724

Calamankey Farm, Longdowns TR10 9DL ☎(01209) 860314 *Prop: CC Davidson* OS map 204/745342 2½m W of Penryn on A394 (Helston) Open Apr-Oct 60 pitches–no trailer caravans 3 acres, gentle slope 🔳🔘🔲 *chrisdavidson@calamankey.com www.calamankey.boltblue.net*

Whitehill Holiday Park, Paignton

> ### SHOWERS
>
> Except where marked, all sites in this guide have flush lavatories and showers. Symbols for these amenities have therefore been omitted from site entries.

PENZANCE, Cornwall **Map A6**

EC Wed MD Tues, Thurs, Sat SEE nautical museum, geological museum, Gulval church, Penlee memorial park, Chysauster prehistoric village 3m N, Trengwainton gardens 2m NW
 Station Rd *(01736) 362207 ✗ Fountain Tavern, St Clare St *(01736) 62673

Bone Valley Caravan Camping Park, Heamoor TR20 8UJ *(01736) 360313 Fax (01736) 360313 OS map 203/463313 1m N of Penzance on B3312 (Madron) Open Mar-Dec–booking advisable Jul-Aug 17 pitches Level grass and hard standing, sheltered ▙▄◻▣▨◈⦸◻▱ battery charging, campers room, ice pack service £9.50-£12.50* (all cards)
enquiries@bonvalleycandcpark.co.uk

For other sites near Penzance see Marazion and St Buryan

PERRANARWORTHAL–see Penryn

PERRANPORTH, Cornwall **Map B5**

SEE open air theatre, St Agnes Head, Perran Bay
✗ Beach Dunes 1m N at Reen Sands *(01872) 572263

Monkey Tree Holiday Park, Rejerrah TR8 5QR *(01872) 572032 *Prop: RJ Walker* OS map 200/802552 3m NE of Perranporth on A3075 (Redruth–Newquay) Open Apr-Oct 450 pitches (48 static) Grass and hard standing, level, part sheltered ▙✗▙▄◻▣▨◈⦸◻⦻◭◻▣▱◻▯ snack bar, sauna £7.00-£11.90 (all major cards) *enquiries@monkeytreeholidaypark.co.uk www.monkeytreeholidaypark.co.uk*

Newperran Tourist Park, Rejerrah TR8 5QJ *(01872) 572407 OS map 200/792543 2½m E of Perranporth off B3285 (Goonhavern) and A3075 (Newquay) Open May-Sept 270 pitches Level grass and hard standing ▙▄↗◻▣▨◈⦸◻(heated) ◈⦻◻▱ crazy golf

Penrose Farm Touring Park, Goonhavern TR4 9QF *(01872) 573185 Fax (01872) 573972 OS map 200/795534 2½m E of Perranporth on B3285 (Indian Queens) in Goonhavern Open Apr-Oct–families and couples only 150 pitches 9 acres level grass and hard standing, sheltered ▙◻▣◈⦸⦻◭▱▱ (all cards) *www.penrosefarm.co.uk*

Perranporth Camping Touring Park, Budnick Rd TR6 0DB *(01872) 572174 Fax (01872) 572174 OS map 200/190/758543 ¼ NE of Perranporth on B3285 (Goonhavern) Open Apr 17-Sept 30 235 pitches–booking advisable Grass and hard standing, level/sloping, sheltered ▙◻▣▨◈⦸(heated) ⦻▱ snack bar, club bar

Perran Quay Tourist Park, Hendra Croft, Rejerrah TR8 5QP *(01872) 572561 Fax (01872) 575043 OS map 200/800550 3m NE of Perranporth on A3075 (Redruth–Newquay) Open all year 135 pitches Grass and hard standings, level, sheltered ▙◻▣◻◻◈⦻◻▱ babies' room, lounge, first aid, barbecue, paddling pool, games room (most cards) *rose@perran-quay.co.uk*

Perran Sands Holiday Park TR6 0AQ *(01872) 573742 OS map 200/768548 ½m NE of Perranporth off B3285 (Goonhavern) Open mid May-Sept 950 pitches (450 static) 500 acres, hard standings, dunes and grass, mainly level ▙✗▙▄↗◻▣▨◈⦸◻◻⦻◻▱▱▣ tent hire, entertainment £9.00-£27.00 (all major cards) *lisa.spickett@bourne-leisure.co.uk www.havenholidays.co.uk/perransands*

Roseville Holiday Park, Goonhavern TR4 9LA *(01872) 572448 *Prop: John & Wendy Inkster* OS map 200/786539 2m E of Perranporth on B3285 (Goonhavern) Open Apr-Oct 65 pitches 7 acres level grass, sheltered ▙◻▣▨◈⦸◻◻◈⦻◻▱ £10.00
enquiries@rosevilleholidaypark.co.uk www.rosevilleholidaypark.co.uk

Silverbow Park, Goonhavern TR4 9NX *(01872) 572347 Fax (01872) 572347 OS map 200/781531 2m ESE of Perranporth on A3075 (Newquay-Redruth) Open May-Sep 100 pitches–no teenagers 24 acres, level/sloping grass, hard standings, sheltered ▙◻▣▨◈⦸◻(heated) ◈⦻◻▱◻◭▱ sep pitches, badminton, tennis, serviced pitches, short mat bowls
See also St Agnes and Crantock

PLYMOUTH, Devon   **Map E5**
SEE The Hoe, St Andrew's church, Smeaton's Tower (aquarium), cathedral (RC), Barbican (maze of alleys), Saltram House 3m E ◪ Island House, 9 The Barbican ✆(01752) 304849
✗ China House, Sutton Wharf (off Sutton Rd) ✆(01752) 260930

Brixton Camping Site, Venn Farm, Brixton PL8 2AX ✆(01752) 880378 OS map 202/548520 6m SE of Plymouth on A379 (Kingsbridge) Open Easter-Oct 43 pitches Grass, level, sheltered ▣ £4.25-£5.50

Riverside Caravan Park, Longbridge Road, Marshmills, Plympton PL6 8LD ✆(01752) 344122 *Prop: IWA Gray* OS map 201/517576 3m E of Plymouth near junction of A38 (Bodmin-Exeter) and A374 (Longridge-Plympton) Open all year 292 pitches Hard standings, level grass, sheltered ✗♀⌂▣▤◿⊗∅⊠(heated) ⊕⌁⊡▣✿⅋⊕ £11.00-£15.00 (all cards)
info@riversidecaravanpark.com www.riversidecaravanpark.com

POLPERRO, Cornwall   **Map D5**
EC Sat SEE museum (of smuggling), `The House on the Props', chapel cliff
✗ Three Pilchards, The Quay ✆(01503) 72233

Killigarth Manor Holiday Estate PL13 2JQ ✆(01503) 72216/272409 Fax (01503) 272065 OS map 201/215516 1m N of Polperro off A387 (Looe) Open Easter-Oct 350 pitches (150 static) 6½ acres level grass ▤✗♀⌂▣▤◿⊗∅⊠⌁⊡⅋▱⅋ lic club (most cards)
killigarthmanor@breathemail.net www.killigarth.co.uk

POLRUAN–see Fowey

POLZEATH, Cornwall   **Map C4**
Small resort on Padstow Bay SEE surfing beach, Pentire headland
✗ White Lodge, Old Polzeath ✆(01208) 862370

Southwinds Caravan Camping Park PL27 6QU ✆(01208) 863267 *Prop: Mr & Mrs B Harris* OS map 200/948791 ½m E of Polzeath on St Minver road Open Easter-Oct 100 pitches 10 acres level grass, sheltered ▣▤◿⊗∅⊕⌁⅋ path to beach £15.00-£30.00 (Mastercard/Visa)
paul@tristramcampsite.fsnet

Tristram Caravan Camping Park, Cliff Top PL27 6SR ✆(01208) 862215/863267 *Prop: R Harris* OS map 200/934790 On W outskirts of Polzeath overlooking Hayle Bay Open Mar-Nov 140 pitches 10 acres level grass, sheltered ▤✗⅊▣▤◿⊗∅⊕⌁⊡⅋ own access to beach £15.00-£40.00 (Mastercard/Visa) *paul@tristramcampsite.fsnet.co.uk*

PORTH–see Newquay

PORTHTOWAN–see Redruth

PORTSCATHO, Cornwall   **Map C6**
Attractive fishing village backed by lovely scenery SEE quay, Porthcurnick beach N, St Anthony Head 3m SW ✗ Plume of Feathers ✆(01872) 580321

Trewince Manor TR2 5ET ✆(01872) 580289 OS map 204/868339 ¾m S of Portscatho on St Anthony rd Open Jul-Aug 54 pitches 4 acres, level/sloping grass ▤✗♀⌂⅊▣▤◿⊗∅ ⊠(indoor) ⊕⊡▱⅋ spa bath, sauna, games room, moorings (own quay, river frontage) (most cards)

POUNDSTOCK, Cornwall   **Map D3**
SEE church, 14c guildhall (now barn), Penfound Manor 1m E on Longford Barton road
✗ Bay View Inn, Marine Drive, Widemouth Bay ✆(01288) 361273

Budemeadows Touring Holiday Park EX23 0NA ✆(01288) 361646 *Prop: Mr & Mrs Jones* OS map 190/215014 2m NE of Poundstock on right of A39 (Bideford) Open all year 145 pitches 9½ acres, grass and hard standings, part level ▤♀⌂▣▤◿⊗∅⊠(heated) ⊕⌁⊡▱⅋⊕ barbecues, games room £13.80-£18.00 (Mastercard/Visa/Switch) *holiday@budemeadows.com www.budemeadows.com*

Cornish Coasts Caravan Camping Park, Middle Penlean EX23 0EE ✆(01288) 361380 *Prop: Sue & Gary Cummings* OS map 190/204983 ½m S of Poundstock on coastal side of A39 (Widemouth Bay) Open Apr-Oct 45 pitches 4 acres, grass, part level, part sheltered, hard standings ▤▣▤◿⊗⌁⅋▱ £6.00-£10.00 *sue@cornishcoasts.co.uk www.cornishcoasts.co.uk*

Penhalt Farm Holiday Park EX23 0DG ✆(01288) 361210 Fax (01288) 361210 OS map 190/194003 ½m NW of Poundstock on Millook road Open Easter-Oct 100 pitches 8 acres, level/gentle slope, grass and hard standing ▤▣▤◿⊗∅⊕⌁⅋▱⅋⊕ £6.00-£15.00* (Delta/Mastercard/Switch/Visa) *denandjennie@penhaltfarm.fsnet.co.uk www.holidaybank.co.uk/penhaltfarmholidaypark*

Widemouth Bay Caravan Park, Great Wanson EX23 0DF ✆(01288) 361208 Fax (01288) 866791 OS map 190/199008 3m NW of Poundstock on Wanson road via Coppathorne Open Mar-Oct 467 pitches (132 static) ▤✗(snack) ⌁▣▤⊗∅⊠(heated) ⌁⅋ games room, lic club, entertainment (high season) £6.00-£20.00* (most cards) *bookings@jfhols.co.uk www.johnfowlerholidays.com*

See also Bude

Wheal Rose Camping and Caravan Park

Secluded family-run park ideal for touring central and west Cornwall.

Tel:01209 891496
www.whealrosecaravanpark.co.uk

PRAA SANDS–see Helston

PRINCETOWN, Devon **Map E4**
✗ Plume of Feathers ☎ (01822) 890240

Plume of Feathers Inn PL20 6QG ☎ (01822) 890240 OS map 191/587735 100m SE of Princetown centre near junction of B3212 (Yelverton) and Tavistock road Open all year 85 pitches–no trailer caravans 2½ acres level grass and hard standings sheltered
🐾✗♀⚲⊘⤴◻️&

REDRUTH, Cornwall **Map B5**
EC Thurs MD Fri SEE Murdoch's House, Carn Brea hill fort
✗ Fox and Hounds at Scorrier ☎ (01209) 820205

Cambrose Touring Park, Portreath Road TR16 4HT ☎ (01209) 890747 *Prop: Mr & Mrs Fitton* OS map 203/687455 2m W of Redruth on B3300 (Portreath) Open Mar-Oct 60 pitches Level grass, sheltered 🐾⤴⚲◻️🅿️⊘⊕⊘◻️(heated) ⊕⤴⊡🅿️⊡& £8.00-£13.00
cambrosetouringpark@supanet.com www.cambrosetouringpark.co.uk

Chacewater Camping Caravan Park, Cox Hill, Chacewater TR4 8LY ☎ (01209) 820762 *Prop: Miss AJ Peterken* OS map 204/738438 3m E of Redruth off A390 (Truro) Open May 1-Sep 30 100 pitches–adults over 30 only Level grass and hard standing, sheltered 🐾◻️🅿️⊘⊕ £11.00-£16.50 (most cards) *chacewaterpark@aol.com www.chacewaterpark.co.uk*

Lanyon Holiday Park, Loscombe Lane, Four Lanes TR16 6LP ☎ (01209) 313474 Fax (01209) 313422 OS map 203/685387 3m S of Redruth off B3297 (Helston) at Four Lanes–signposted Open mid Feb-mid Jan 75 pitches (35 static) Level grass ✗♀⤴⚲◻️🅿️⊘⊕⊘◻️(heated) ⤴⊡🅿️ games room £6.00-£18.00* (all cards) *jamierielly@btconnect.com www.lanonholidaypark.co.uk*

Porthtowan Tourist Park, Mile Hill, Porthtowan TR4 8TY ☎ (01209) 890256 Fax (01209) 890256 OS map 203/694465 2m N of Redruth off Porthtowan road Open Easter-Oct 50 pitches 5 acres, level grass, sheltered 🐾◻️🅿️⊘⊕⊘⊕⤴& table tennis £7.00-£11.50*
admin@porthtowantouristpark.co.uk www.porthtowantouristpark.co.uk

Rose Hill Touring Park, Rose Hill, Porthtowan TR4 8AR *Sheltered quiet woodland site 4 mins level walk to beach* ☎ (01209) 890802 OS map 203/693473 3½m N of Redruth at Porthtowan near beach Open Mar-Oct 50 pitches Level grass and hard standings, sheltered
🐾⤴⚲◻️🅿️⊘⊕⊘⊕& bakery £10.90-£16.90* (all cards) *reception@rosehillcamping.co.uk www.rosehillcamping.co.uk*

Tehidy Holiday Park, Harris Mill, Illogan TR16 4JQ ☎ (01209) 216489 *Prop: Mrs J Williams* OS map 203/682434 1½m NW of Redruth off B3300 (Portreath) Open Apr-Oct 38 pitches 4½ acres level/sloping grass, sheltered 🐾⚲◻️🅿️⊘⊕⊘⊕⤴⊡🅿️⊡🏠& £6.50-£10.00 (all cards exc Amex) *holiday@tehidy.co.uk www.tehidy.co.uk*

Tresaddern Holiday Park, St Day TR16 5JR ☎ (01209) 820459 OS map 204/733422 2m E of Redruth on B3298 (St Day) Open Apr-Oct 32 pitches 2 acres, grass, level/sloping, hard standings 🐾◻️🅿️⊘⊕⊘⊕🅿️⊡🏠 £10.00-£12.00* *holidays@tresaddern.com www.tresaddern.com*

Wheal Rose Caravan Camping Park, Wheal Rose, Scorrier TR16 5DD *Secluded family-run park with spotless facs central for West Cornwall* ☎ (01209) 891496 OS map 203/715448 1m NE of Redruth off A30 (Truro) on Porthtowan road Open Mar-Dec 50 pitches Level grass and hard standing, sheltered 🐾◻️🅿️⊘⊕⤴⊡🅿️⊡& £7.00-£12.00 *www.whealrosecaravanpark.co.uk*

RUAN MINOR–see Lizard

For more up-to-date information, and for links to camping websites, visit our site at:
www.butford.co.uk/camping

> **FACTS CAN CHANGE**
> We do our best to check the accuracy of the entries in this guide but changes can and do occur
> after publication. So if you plan to stay at a site some distance from home it makes sense to ring
> the manager or owner before setting off.

ST AGNES, Cornwall   Map B5

EC Wed SEE church, harbour, St Agnes Head, Trevaunance Cove, Tin mine engine houses, view
from St Agnes Beacon (700 ft) accessible by car
✗ Sally's Restaurant, 40 Vicarage Road ☎ (01872) 552194 Open Mon-Thu 5-10

Beacon Cottage Farm Touring Park, Beacon Drive TR5 0NU ☎ (01872) 552347 *Prop: Jane Sawle*
OS map 203/705501 2m W of St Agnes off Beacon Drive Open May-Oct 50 pitches 2 acres
level grass sheltered 🔋🗇🖃🗠⊗⊘⊙🗸🖃🏠 dog walk, 2 holiday cottages £10.00-£19.00
(Mastercard/Visa) beaconcottagefarm@lineone.net www.beaconcottagefarmholidays.co.uk

Chiverton Caravan and Touring Park, Blackwater TR4 8HS ☎ (01872) 560667 OS map
204/743468 2½m SE of St Agnes on B3277 (Three Burrows) near junction with A30-A390 Open
Feb-Jan 70 pitches (50 static) 4 acres level grass 🖈🖃⊗⊘🖃🗸🖾🕭 exclusive use of gym,
sauna and steamroom £8.00-£17.00 chivertonpark@btopenworld.com www.chivertonpark.co.uk

Presingoll Farm TR5 0PB ☎ (01872) 552333 Fax (01872) 552333 OS map 204/190/721494 1m S
of St Agnes on B3277 (Truro) Open Apr-Oct 90 pitches 3½acres, level grass 🔋🗇🖃⊗⊘🗸🕭
farm produce £10.00 (min)* pam@presingollfarm.fsbusiness.co.uk
www.presingollfarm.fsbusiness.co.uk

Trevarth Holiday Park, Blackwater TR4 8HR ☎ (01872) 560266 Fax (01872) 560379 OS map
204/743469 3m SE of St Agnes off B3277 (Truro) and Chiverton roundabout (A30) on Blackwater
road Open Apr-Oct 75 pitches (20 static) 4½ acres level grass, sheltered 🗇🖃⊘⊗⊘⊙🗸🖃🖾
£8.30-£11.50* (Mastercard/Visa/Switch/Delta) trevarth@lineone.net www.ukparks.co.uk/trevarth

ST AUSTELL, Cornwall   Map C5

EC Thurs SEE old inns, church, china clay quarries (tours), market house
✗ White Hart, Church St ☎ (01726) 872100

Carlyon Bay Caravan Camping Park, Cypress Avenue, Carlyon Bay PL25 3RE ☎ (01726) 812735
Fax (01726) 815496 OS map 200/052527 2½m E of St Austell on A390 (St Blazey) at Britannia
Inn roundabout Open Easter-Oct—must book peak periods 180 pitches 32 acres, grass, level,
sheltered 🔋🗠🗇🖃⊘⊗🖃(heated) 🗸🖾 footpath to beach £9.00-£20.00* (most cards)
holidays@carlyonbay.net www.carlyonbay.net

Par Sands Holiday Park, Par PL24 2AS *Sheltered site behind Par beach* ☎ (01726) 812868 OS
map 204/084535 4m E of St Austell off A3082 (Par Sands) near Eden Project Open Apr-Sept
375 pitches (210 static) Level grass 🗇🖃⊘⊗⊘🖃(indoor heated) ⊙🗸🖾🕭 crazy golf, tennis,
bowls, cycle hire £7.50-£21.00 (Mastercard/Visa) holidays@parsands.co.uk www.parsands.co.uk

Penhaven Touring Park, Pentewan PL26 6DL *Landscaped site in wooded valley* ☎ (01726)
843687 Fax (01726) 843870 OS map 204/015475 2m S of St Austell on left of B3273
(Mevagissey) Open Apr-Oct 105 pitches 13½ acres, level grass and hard standings, sheltered
🔋🗠🖈🗇🖃⊘⊗⊘🖃🗸🖃🕭 bike hire (most cards)

River Valley Holiday Park, London Apprentice PL26 7AP ☎ (01726) 73533 Fax (01726) 73533 OS
map 204/008504 1½m S of St Austell on B3273 (Mevagissey) Open Mar-Sep 45 pitches Level
grass and hard standing, sheltered 🔋🗇🖃⊘⊗⊘🖃(heated) ⊙🗸🖃🕭 bike hire
£7.00-£20.00* (Mastercard/Delta/Switch) river.valley@tesco.net www.cornwall-holidays.co.uk

Trencreek Farm Holiday Park, Hewaswater PL26 7JG ☎ (01726) 882540 Fax (01726) 883254 OS
map 204/965485 3m SW of St Austell on B3287 (Tregony) Open Apr-mid Sep—must book peak
periods 178 pitches (38 static) Grass, part level, sheltered 🔋🗠🖈🗇🖃⊘⊗⊘🖃(heated)
⊙🗸🖃🏠🕭 fishing, tennis court, pitch and putt £6.00-£15.00* (most cards)
trencreek@aol.com www.trencreek.co.uk

Trewhiddle Holiday Estate, Pentewan Road PL26 7AD *15 minutes from the Eden Project and
Heligan Gardens* ☎ (01726) 879420 Fax (01726) 879421 OS map 204/005512 1m S of St Austell
on B3273 (Mevagissey) Open all year 105 pitches (68 static) 16 acres level/sloping grass and
hard standings, sheltered ✗🍴🗠🗇🖃⊘⊗⊘🖃🗠⊙🗸🖃🖾 lic pub, games room £10.00-£20.00*
(Delta/Mastercard/Switch/Visa) dmcclelland@btconnect.com www.trewhiddle.co.uk

See also Mevagissey

Pentewan Road St. Austell Cornwall PL26 7AD
Tel: +44 (0)1726 879 420

ST BURYAN, Cornwall   Map A6
SEE granite church, Boscawen stone circle
✖ Old Success Inn 3m W at Sennen Cove ✆ (01736) 871232

Boleigh Farm, Lamorna TR19 6BN ✆ (01736) 810305 OS map 203/434249 1½m SE of St Buryan on B3315 (Penzance-Land's End) Open Easter-Oct 30 pitches 1½ acres level grass, sheltered ⌀ ✿

Lower Treave Caravan Park, Crows an Wra TR19 6HZ ✆ (01736) 810559 Fax 0870 0553647 OS map 203/387273 2m NW of St Buryan on A30 (Penzance-Land's End) Open Apr-Oct 85 pitches 4½ acres, terraced/level grass ⛴ ▣ ▬ ⌀ ✿ (most cards) camping@lowertreave.demon.co.uk www.lowertreave.demon.co.uk

Tower Park TR19 6BZ ✆ (01736) 810286 Prop: Mr & Mrs D J Green OS map 203/405263 ¼m NW of St Buryan on right of St Just road Open Easter-Oct 112 pitches 12 acres, level grass, sheltered ⛴↝▣▬⌀✿⌀↲▭⛝ও £6.75-£9.25 (all major cards) enquiries@towerparkcamping.co.uk www.towerparkcamping.co.uk

Treverven Touring Caravan and Camp Site TR19 6DL ✆ (01736) 810200 Fax (01736) 871977 OS map 203/413238 1m S of St Buryan on B3315 (Newlyn-Treen) Open Easter-Oct 115 pitches 6 acres level grass ⛴ (mobile) ▣▬⌀✿⌀↲ও (Mastercard/Switch/Visa) www.chycor.co.uk/camping/treverven

ST COLUMB, Cornwall   Map C5
EC Wed MD Mon
✖ Falcon 2½m N at St Mawgan ✆ (01637) 860225

Music Water Touring Site, Rumford PL27 7SJ ✆ (01841) 540257 Prop: FR Mabbley OS map 200/906685 3m N of St Columb off A39 (Wadebridge) and B3274 (Padstow) Open Apr-Oct 140 pitches 8 acres, grass, level/gentle slope, sheltered ⛴↝↗▣▬⌀✿▭⛝↲▭⛝ pet corner £8.00-£13.00* www.caravancampingsites.co.uk

Trekenning Tourist Park TR8 4JF Well equipped site in peaceful setting ✆ (01637) 880462 OS map 200/907625 ½m S of St Columb at junction of A39 (Truro) and A3059 (Newquay) Open Apr-Oct 75 pitches Grass and hard standings, level/sloping, sheltered ⛴ ✖ (café) ⛝↗▣▬⌀✿⌀▭⛝↲▭⛝ (all cards)

ST DAY–see Redruth

ST ISSEY–see Padstow

ST IVES, Cornwall   Map A5
EC Thurs MD Mon, Fri Old fishing port which became a centre for artists in the 1880s SEE All Saint's church, stone bridge and chapel, Norris Museum, Porthmeor surfing beach, Barbara Hepworth museum, Tate Gallery
🛈 The Guildhall, Street-an-Pol ✆ (01736) 796297
✖ Chy-an-Drea, The Terrace ✆ (01736) 795076

Ayr Holiday Park, Higher Ayr TR26 1EJ Nearest site to town centre, on cliffside above bay ✆ (01736) 795855 Fax (01736) 798797 OS map 203/515407 ½m W of St Ives off B3306 (St Just) Open all year 80 pitches (51 static) Level grass and hard standings ▣▬⌀✿⌀↲ £12.00-£21.00* (most cards) recept@ayrholidaypark.co.uk www.ayrholidaypark.co.uk

Balnoon Campsite, Halsetown TR26 3JA ✆ (01736) 795431 OS map 203/510390 2m SW of St Ives off B3311 (Penzance) after Halsetown Open Apr-Oct 25 pitches 1 acre level grass ⛴▬⌀✿ £7.00-£11.00* nat@balnoon.fsnet.co.uk

Hellesveor Caravan and Camping Site TR26 3AD ✆ (01736) 795738 OS map 203/503401 1m W of St Ives on right of B3306 (St Just) Open Easter-Oct 20 pitches 1 acre, level grass ⛴▣▬⌀⌀✿▭

Higher Chellew Campsite, Nancledra TR20 8BD ✆ (01736) 364532 OS map 203/498351 3m S of St Ives on B3311 (Penzance) Open Mar-Oct 30 pitches 1½ acres level grass, sheltered ▣✿⛺

Penderleath Caravan and Camping Park, Towednack TR26 3AF ✆ (01736) 798403 OS map 203/497375 2m SW of St Ives off B3311 (Penzance) Open May-Sep 75 pitches 10 acres level and sloping grass ⛴✖⛴↝↗▣▬⌀✿▭⛝↲▭⛝ও £8.50-£14.00* www.penderleath.co.uk

Polmanter Tourist Park, Halsetown TR26 3LX Inland site in quiet location ✆ (01736) 795640 Fax (01736) 793607 OS map 203/512388 1½m SW of St Ives off B3311 (Penzance) Open Apr-Oct 240 pitches 12 acres level grass and hard standings ⛴✖⛴↝↗▣▬⌀✿⌀▭(heated) ✿↲ paddling pools, tennis £10.00-£23.00* (most cards) reception@polmanter.com www.polmanter.com

Trevalgan Holiday Farm TR26 3BJ ✆ (01736) 796433 Fax (01736) 796433 OS map 203/490400 1½m W of St Ives off B3306 (Land's End) Open Easter-Sept 120 pitches 5 acres, level grass ⛴↝↗▣▬⌀✿⌀✿↲▭⛝ games room, pets corner, picnic area, farm trail, barbecue, crazy golf £11.00-£18.00* (Mastercard/Visa/Delta/Switch) recept@trevalgantouringpark.co.uk www.trevalgantouringpark.co.uk

Sennen Cove Camping and Caravanning Club
Site, St Justin in Penwith

CHARGES

Charges quoted are the minimum and maximum for two people with car and caravan or tent. They are given only as a guide and should be checked with the owner of any site at which you plan to stay.
Charges markded * are the prices for last year. Otherwise, the prices are those quoted for the current season.
Remember to ask whether hot water or use of the pool (if any) is extra and make sure that VAT is included.

ST JUST IN PENWITH, Cornwall   **Map A6**
EC Thurs *Quiet resort on cliffs of Penwith peninsula, most westerly in England, along rugged coast of which are sheltered coves accessible only on foot* SEE tin mining museum, 15c church, cape Cornwall 1m W, Pendeen Watch (view)
✗The Queens Arms, Botallack ☎(01736) 788318 Open 12-2/6-9
✗First & Last Inn, 24 Alverton Rd, Penzance ☎(01736) 364095

Bosavern House TR19 7RD *Small site in enclosed garden* ☎(01736) 788301 *Prop: Mr & Mrs A Collinson* OS map 203/371305 ½m S of St Just on left of B3306 (Land's End) in grounds of country house Open Mar-Oct 12 pitches 1 acre, level grass, sheltered ⚏⚏⚏⚏⚏⚏⚏⚏⚏ £13.00 inc elect, awning (most cards) *mail@bosavern.com www.secretbosavern.com*

Sennen Cove Camping and Caravanning Club Site, St Buryan TR19 6JB ☎(01736) 871588 *Prop: The Camping and Caravanning Club* OS map 203/378276 2m S of St Just on right of B3306 (Land's End) Open May-Sept 75 pitches–adv booking min 2 nights ⚏⚏⚏⚏⚏⚏⚏ £13.40-£18.00 (Mastercard/Visa/Switch) *www.campingandcaravanningclub.co.uk*

Kelynack Caravan Camping Park TR19 7RE ☎(01736) 787633 Fax (01736) 787633 OS map 203/373301 ¾m S of St Just off B3306 (Land's End) Open Apr-Oct 37 pitches Level grass and hard standing, sheltered ⚏⚏⚏⚏⚏⚏⚏⚏⚏⚏⚏⚏ camping barn £7.00 (min)* *kevin@kelynackholidays.co.uk www.ukparks.co.uk/kelynack*

Levant House Caravan Camping Park, Levant Road, Pendeen TR19 7SX ☎(01736) 788795 OS map 203/374337 2½m N of St Just off B3306 (St Ives) Open Apr-Oct 43 pitches Level/sloping grass ⚏⚏⚏⚏

Roselands Caravan Park, Dowran TR19 7RS *Small site in remote rural setting* ☎(01736) 788571 OS map 203/387305 1m SE of St Just off A3071 (Penzance) on Sancreed road Open Jan-Oct 30 pitches 3 acres level grass, sheltered ⚏⚏⚏⚏⚏⚏⚏⚏⚏⚏⚏ bike hire

Trevaylor Caravan Park, Truthwall TR19 7PU ☎(01736) 787016 *Prop: Bill & Angela Sanderson* OS map 203/368325 1m N of St Just on B3306 (St Ives) Open Easter-Oct 55 pitches 6 acres, level grass, sheltered ⚏⚏⚏⚏⚏⚏⚏⚏⚏ bar food £8.00-£10.00 *campingcornwall@yahoo.co.uk www.trevaylor.com*

ST KEW HIGHWAY–see Wadebridge

CHECK BEFORE ENTERING

There's usually no objection to your walking onto a site to see if you might like it but always ask permission first. Remember that the person in charge is responsible for safeguarding the property of those staying there.

Trevaylor Caravan Park, Wells

ST MABYN–see Bodmin

ST MAWES, Cornwall   **Map C6**
SEE castle, waterfront
✘ St Mawes, The Seafront ✆ (01326) 270266

Trethem Mill Touring Park, St Just in Roseland TR2 5JF ✆ (01872) 580504 OS map 204/862364
2m N of St Mawes on A3078 (Tregony) Open Apr-Oct 90 pitches Level/sloping grass and hard
standings ⬛🗄🔌🖉🕂Ø↲♿🖂 £8.00-£12.00 (most cards)

ST MERRYN–see Padstow

ST MINVER, Cornwall   **Map C4**
EC Thurs SEE church, beaches of Polzeath (2m NW) and Rock (2m SW)
✘ Four Ways ✆ (01208) 862384

Dinham Farm Caravan-Camping Park PL27 6RH ✆ (01208) 812878 OS map 200/971750 1m S
of St Minver off B3314 (Wadebridge) on Treganna road Open Apr-Oct 60 pitches Level/sloping
grass, sheltered 🗄🔌🕂Ø🖂(heated) 🕂↲🖵🖂🕭

Gunvenna Touring Caravan and Camping Park PL27 6QN ✆ (01208) 862405 OS map
200/968782 ½m N of St Minver on right of B3314 (Port Isaac) Open Apr-Oct (no groups of
singles unless members of a bona fide club) 75 pitches Level grass
⬛✘🍴↲🗄🔌🖉🕂Ø🖂(heated, indoor) 🕂↲🕭♿

St Minver House Holiday Estate PL27 6RR ✆ (01208) 862305 OS map 200/965767 1m S of St
Minver off B3314 (Delabole–Wadebridge) Open Easter/Apr-Oct 230 pitches (200 static)
⬛✘🍴🗄🔌🖉🕂🖂🕂🖵🔊 Level grass lic club, snack bar, amusements £7.00-£27.00*
(Mastercard/Visa/Switch) www.parkcleanholidays.com

See also Polzeath

ST TUDY–see Camelford

SALCOMBE, Devon   **Map F6**
EC Wed *Superb coastal scenery, a gentle climate and good beaches explain this resort's popularity*
SEE site, maritime museum, Bolt Head cliffs (400ft)
🛈 Council Hall, Market St ✆ (01548) 843927/842736
✘ The Winking Prawn, North Sands Beach ✆ (01548) 842326 Open 10.30-10

Alston Farm Caravan and Camping Site, Malborough TQ7 3BJ ✆ (01548) 561260 *Prop: PW
Shepherd* OS map 202/717407 2m N of Salcombe off A381 (Kingsbridge) Open Easter-Oct
200 pitches (40 static) Level/sloping grass, sheltered ⬛🗄🔌🖉🕂Ø🕂🅿 £7.00-£11.50
info@alstoncampsite.co.uk www.alstoncampsite.co.uk

Bolberry House Farm, Bolberry, Malborough TQ7 3DY *Family-run park near sandy beach*
✆ (01548) 561251 OS map 202/688394 3m W of Salcombe off A381 (Kingsbridge) at Malborough
Open Easter-Oct 70 pitches 5½ acres level grass ⬛🗄🔌🖉🕂Ø↲🖵 freezer pack service, dog
exercise area £7.50-£12.00* bolberry.house@virgin.net www.bolberryparks.co.uk

Higher Rew Touring Caravan Camping Park, Malborough TQ7 3BW ✆ (01548) 842681 *Prop: The
Squire Family* OS map 202/714383 3m W of Salcombe off A381 (Kings bridge) and Soar road via
Malborough Open Mar-Oct 90 pitches 4 acres, level/gentle slope, grass ⬛🗄🔌🖉🕂Ø🕂↲🖵
tennis court £7.00-£13.00 enquiries@higherrew.co.uk www.higherrew.co.uk

Karrageen Caravan and Camping Park, Bolberry, Malborough TQ7 3EN ✆ (01548) 561230 Fax
(01548) 560192 OS map 202/689394 3m W of Salcombe off A381 (Kingsbridge) at Malborough
on Bolberry road Open Mar 15-Sept 30 95 pitches 7½ acres grass, level/sloping, terraced
⬛↲🗄🔌🖉🕂Ø🖵♿ freezer pack service, baby room £8.00-£14.00* phil@karrageen.co.uk
www.karrageen.co.uk

Sun Park, Soar TQ7 3DS ✆ (01548) 561378 Fax (01548) 561378 OS map 202/708378 3m W of
Salcombe off A381 (Kingsbridge) at Malborough on Soar road Open Easter-Sept 60 pitches
(34 static) 5 acres, level grass ⬛🗄🔌🖉🕂Ø🕂↲🖵🔊 games room £6.00-£11.00*
bjsweetman@talk21.com www.sunpark.co.uk

SALCOMBE REGIS–see Sidmouth

SALTASH, Cornwall   Map E5
EC Thurs SEE Saltash Quay, Tamar bridge, Ince Castle 4m W
✖ Notter Bridge Inn, Notter ✆ (01752) 842259

Dolbeare Caravan Camping Park, St Ive Road, Landrake PL12 5AF ✆ (01752) 851332 Fax
(01752) 851332 OS map 201/364615 4m NW of Saltash off A38 (Liskeard) on Blunts road Open
all year 60 pitches Level/sloping grass and hard standings, sheltered 🄫🗎🔌🖉⊕∅🛇🔧🚻
£9.50-£15.50* dolbeare@btopenworld.com www.dolbeare.co.uk

Notter Bridge Caravan and Camping Park, Notter Bridge PL12 4RW ✆ (01752) 842318 OS map
201/385609 3½m NW of Saltash on A38 (Liskeard) Open Apr-Sept 29 pitches 5 acres, level
grass and hard standings, sheltered 🗎🔌⊕🚿🛒⛽🔧♿ fishing, canoeing £8.00-£11.00
holidays@notterbridge.co.uk www.notterbridge.co.uk

SAMPFORD PEVERELL, Devon   Map G3
EC Wed SEE 12c church
✖ Globe Inn, 16 Lower Town ✆ (01884) 821214

Minnows Caravan Camping Park EX16 7EN ✆ (01884) 821770 Prop: Zig & Krystyna Grochala
OS map 181/040147 ½m E of Sampford Peverell off A361 (Tiverton-Barnstaple) on Holcombe
Rogus rd by Grand Western canal, near jnc 27 of M5 Open Mar-Nov 45 pitches Grass, level,
hard standings 🗎🔌🖉⊕∅🛇🔧♿ service pitches, freezer pack service, fishing, boating £9.00-
£19.00 (most cards) www.ukparks.co.uk/minnows

SEATON, Cornwall   Map D5
✖ Dolphin Long Bar, Fore St, Beer ✆ (01297) 625800

Carbeil Holiday Park, Treliddon Lane, Downderry PL11 3LS ✆ (01503) 250636 OS map
201/318544 2m E of Seaton off B3247 (Millbrook) on Narkurs road–signposted Open Mar-Oct
22 pitches–booking advisable 1¼ acres sloping grass and hard standings, sheltered
🄫✖🍴🔌🗎🔌⊕∅🛒🔧🚻

Ashdown Touring Caravan Park EX13 6HY ✆ (01297) 22052 OS map 192/216922 3m NW of
Seaton off A3052 (Lyme Regis–Exeter) on Colyton road Open Apr-Oct 90 pitches 5 acres, level
grass 🄫🗎🔌🖉⊕∅🛒 £9.00-£11.00*

Manor Farm Camping Site EX12 2JA ✆ (01297) 21524 OS map 192/236917 1m N of Seaton on
A3052 (Sidmouth-Lyme Regis) Open Mar-Oct 274 pitches 22 acres, grass, level/sloping
🄫🗎🔌⊕∅🔧⛽

SEATON–see Sidmouth

SENNEN–see Land's End

SIDMOUTH, Devon   Map G4
EC Thurs Once fashionable watering place with wealth of Regency and Victorian architecture
backing long pebble beach SEE Esplanade, museum, Beer Head E, High Peak (view) 2m W,
Sidbury church 3m N
ℹ Ham Lane ✆ (01395) 516441
✖ The Blue Ball at Sidford ✆ (01395) 514062

Kings Down Tail Caravan and Camping Park, Salcombe Regis EX10 0PD ✆ (01297) 680313 Fax
(01297) 680313 OS map 192/172908 3m NE of Sidmouth on A3052 (Lyme Regis) Open Mar 15-
Nov 15 102 pitches Level grass and hard standings, sheltered 🄫🏹🗎🔌🖉⊕∅🛇🔧⛽ games
room £8.80-£13.30* (most cards) info@kingsdowntail.co.uk www.kingsdowntail.co.uk

Oakdown Touring and Holiday Home Park, Weston EX10 0PH ✆ (01297) 680387 Fax (01297)
680541 OS map 192/167903 2½m NE of Sidmouth on right of A3052 (Exeter-Lyme
Regis)–signposted Open Easter-Oct 162 pitches (62 static) 13½ acres, level grass and hard
standing, sheltered 🗎🔌🖉⊕∅🛇🔧🗆⛽🛒♿ serviced pitches, field trail to donkey sanctuary
(Mastercard/Visa)

Salcombe Regis Caravan and Camping Park, Salcombe Regis EX10 0JH ✆ (01395) 514303 Fax
(01395) 514314 OS map 192/150892 1½m E of Sidmouth off A3052 (Lyme Regis) Open Apr-Oct
110 pitches 16 acres, level grass and hard standings 🄫🏹🗎🔌🖉⊕∅🛇🔧⛽ £8.00-£13.50*
(Mastercard/Visa/Delta/Switch) info@salcombe-regis.co.uk www.salcombe-regis.co.uk

SOURTON CROSS–see Bridestow

SOUTH BRENT, Devon Map F5
EC Wed
✘ Royal Oak, Station Rd ☎ (01364) 72133

Cheston Caravan Park, Folly Cross, Wrangton Rd TQ10 9HF ☎ (01364) 72586 Fax (01364) 72586 OS map 202/683586 1m SW of South Brent off A38 (Plymouth) via Wrangton Cross at Cheston–signposted Open Mar 15-Jan 15 24 pitches 1½ acres level grass, sheltered, some hard standings 🏕🚿🅿⬤✆🚻🚮♿

Edeswell Farm, Rattery TQ10 9LN ☎ (01364) 72177 OS map 202/732605 2m E of South Brent on right of A385 (Cott) Open Apr-Oct 46 pitches Grass, terraced, sheltered 🏕🍴♿🚿🅿⬤⬤ ⊘🚿(indoor heated) ⬤✆🚻🚮🚮 fishing, animal centre (Mastercard/Visa/debit cards)

Great Palstone Caravan Park TQ10 9JP ☎ (01364) 72227 OS map 202/705601 1m E of South Brent on Exeter road (old A38) Open Mar 15-Nov 15 50 pitches Level grass, sheltered 🏕🚿⬤⬤🚿⬤🚮 guided walks (free)

SOUTH MOLTON, Devon Map F2
EC Wed MD Thurs SEE Guildhall, church
🛈 1 East St ☎ (01769) 574122
✘ Stumbles, East St ☎ (01769) 554145

Yeo Valley Holiday Park, Black Cock Inn EX36 3NW ☎ (01769) 550297 Fax (01769) 550101 OS map 180/788262 4m E of South Molton off B3227 (Bampton) Open all year 65 pitches 7 acres, level/gentle slope, grass and hard standing 🏕✘🍴⬤🚿🅿⬤⊘🚿(indoor) ⬤✆🚻🚮🚮🏠 bike hire, fishing £12.50-£15.00* (Mastercard/Visa/Switch/Delta) lorna@yeovalleyholidays.com www.yeovalleyholidays.com

STICKLEPATH–see Okehampton

STOKE FLEMING–see Dartmouth

STOKENHAM, Devon Map F5
✘ Church House ☎ (01548) 580253

Union Inn, Chillington TQ7 2LD ☎ (01548) 580241 OS map 202/793427 1m W of Stokenham off A379 (Kingsbridge) in Chillington Open Mar 15-Oct 31 10 pitches 1 acre level grass and gravel, sheltered 🏕 (mobile) ✘🍴🚿⬤✆

Old Cotmore Farm TQ7 2LR ☎ (01548) 580240 Fax (01548) 580875 OS map 202/804415 1m S of Stokenham on Start Point/East Prawle road Open Mar-Oct 30 pitches Grass and hard standings, sheltered 🏕🚿🅿⬤⊘⬤✆🚮🚮🏠♿ £8.25-£12.50* (most cards) graham.bowsher@btinternet.com www.oldcotmorefarm.co.uk

STOKE GABRIEL–see Paignton

STRATTON, Cornwall Map D3
SEE parish church, Tree Inn, Poughill church (15c wall paintings) 1m NW, Launcells church (15c interior) 1m SE
✘ Kings Arms Inn, Howells Rd (A3092) ☎ (01288) 352396

Red Post Inn and Holiday Park, Launcells EX23 9NW ☎ (01288) 381305 Fax (01288) 381305 OS map 190/265052 2m E of Stratton on A3072 (Holsworthy) at junction with B3254 (Kilkhampton–Launceston) Open all year 50 pitches 3½ acres, level grass and hard standings, sheltered 🏕✘🍴⬤🚿🅿⬤⬤✆🚮🚮 £9.00-£11.50* (all cards) redpostinn@aol.com

Red Post Meadows Tourist Park, Launcells EX23 9NW ☎ (01288) 381306 OS map 190/263051 2m E of Stratton on right of A3072 (Holsworthy) Open Easter-Oct 70 pitches 8 acres, level grass, sheltered 🏕🚿🅿⬤⬤⬤✆🚮🚮 farm produce, pets corner

Willow Valley Camping Park, Bush EX23 9LB ☎ (01288) 353104 OS map 190/236078 1m N of Stratton on left of A39 (Bideford) Open Apr-Dec 45 pitches 4 acres, level grass, sheltered 🏕🚿🅿🚿⬤⊘✆🏠 £6.00-£9.00* (Mastercard/Visa/Delta/Switch) willowvalley@talk21.com www.caravansitecornwall.co.uk

Wooda Caravan Park, Wooda Farm, Poughill EX23 9HJ ☎ (01288) 352069 Fax (01288) 355258 OS map 190/227079 1m N of Stratton on right of Stibb/Coombe Valley road Open Apr-Oct 200 pitches (54 static) 12 acres, grass, part level, some hard standings 🏕✘🚿🅿🚿⬤⊘✆🚮(£40) 🚮♿ fishing, pitch and putt, clay pigeon shooting, archery, pony trekking, woodland walks, pets corner £8.50-£13.50* (Mastercard/Visa/Switch/Delta) enquiries@wooda.co.uk www.wooda.co.uk
For other sites near Stratton see Bude, Kilkhampton and Poundstock

SUMMERCOURT–see Indian Queens

TAVISTOCK, Devon   **Map E4**
EC Wed MD Fri SEE Goose fair (Oct), canal port and copper mine at Morwellham 4m SW (tours),
Wheal Betsy mine and Gibbet Hill (1,158ft) 5m NE
⚫Bedford Sq ☎(01822) 612938
✖Trout 'N' Tipple, Parkwood Rd ☎(01822) 618886
✖The Cornish Arms & Monterey Jacks, West St ☎(01822) 612145

Harford Bridge Holiday Park, Peter Tavy PL19 9LS ☎(01822) 810349 Fax (01822) 810028 *Prop:*
G & I Williamson OS map 201/505767 2m N of Tavistock off A386 (Okehampton) on Peter Tavy
road Open Mar-Nov 200 pitches (60 static) 16 acres level grass 🔲📞🔌⊕∅⊖✓❑🔛🏠⚑ fly
fishing, tennis court £8.50-£15.75 (Mastercard/Visa/Switch/Solo) *enquiry@harfordbridge.co.uk*
www.harfordbridge.co.uk

Higher Longford Caravan Camping Park PL19 9LQ ☎(01822) 613360 OS map 201/518745 2m
E of Tavistock on B3357 (Princetown) Open all year 80 pitches 6 acres, level grass and hard
standings, sheltered 🔲🔶🔌📞∅⊕∅⊖✓❑🔛🏠👶🍴 multi-service pitches, summer storage,
seasonal pitches £9.00-£15.00 (most cards exc Amex) *stay@higherlongford.co.uk*
www.higherlongford.co.uk

Langstone Manor Caravan Camping Park, Moortown PL19 9JZ ☎(01822) 613371 *Prop: Jane &*
David Kellet OS map 201/525738 2m E of Tavistock off B3357 (Two Bridges) Open Mar-Nov
42 pitches Level grass and hard standing ✖♀🔌📞∅⊕∅✓❑🔛 £9.00-£11.00 (most cards)
web@langstone-manor.co.uk www.langstone-manor.co.uk

Magpie Leisure Park, Bedford Bridge, Horrabridge PL20 7RY ☎(01822) 852651 OS map
201/506704 3m SE of Tavistock on A386 (Plymouth) Open Mar-Jan 48 pitches Level grass,
sheltered 🔲📞∅⊕∅⊖✓🔛🏠 fishing

Woodovis Park PL19 8NY ☎(01822) 832968 *Prop: John & Dorothy Lewis* OS map 201/432744
4m W of Tavistock off A390 (Liskeard) Open Apr-Oct 84 pitches 14 acres, grass and hard
standing, level, sheltered 🔲🔶🔌📞⊕∅🔲(indoor heated) ⊖✓🔛🏠👶 mini-golf, sauna,
jacuzzi £17.00-£19.00 (most cards) *info@woodovis.com www.woodovis.com*

TEIGNMOUTH, Devon   **Map G4**
EC Thurs *Popular resort since early 19c* SEE seafront, Teign road bridge (view), Ness headland E
⚫The Den, seafront ☎(01626) 215666
✖Ship, Quayside ☎(01626) 772674

Coast View Country Club, Torquay Road, Shaldon TQ14 0BG ☎(01626) 772392 OS map
202/937718 1m S of Teignmouth on A379 (Torquay) over Shaldon Bridge Open Apr-Oct
162 pitches (50 static) 16 acres level/sloping grass and hard standings 🔲∅🔲 club, snack bar

Wear Farm, Bishopsteignton TQ14 9PT ☎(01626) 779265/775249 OS map 192/890732 2½m W
of Teignmouth on A381 (Newton Abbot) Open Easter-Oct 247 pitches (100 static) Level grass,
sheltered 🔲📞∅⊕∅⊖✓🔛 fishing, access to river for boats

See also Bishopsteignton

Tel: +44 (0)1769 550 297
Email: info@yeovalleyholidays.com
Yeo Valley
HOLIDAY PARK

See listing under South Molton

TINTAGEL, Cornwall Map C4
EC Wed MD Thurs SEE ruined castle on headland, Old Post Office, Bossiney beach and Rocky Valley NE
✗ Tintagel Arms, Fore St ✆ (01840) 770780

Bossiney Farm, Bossiney PL34 0AY ✆ (01840) 770481 OS map 200/066888 ¼m NE of Tintagel on B3263 (Boscastle) Open Apr-Oct 74 pitches Level grass, sheltered (Mastercard/Visa) www.bossineyfarm.co.uk

Headland Caravan and Camping Site, Atlantic Road PL34 0DE ✆ (01840) 770239 Fax (01840) 770925 OS map 200/058888 In village of Tintagel off B3263 (Boscastle)–signposted Open Easter-Oct 90 pitches (30 static) 5 acres, level/gentle slope, grass and hard standings £9.00-£12.50* (most cards) headland.cp@virgin.net www.headlandcaravanpark.co.uk

Ocean Cove Caravan Park, Bossiney PL34 0AY ✆ (01840) 770352 OS map 200/065890 1m NE of Tintagel on B3263 (Boscastle) Open Apr-Sept 171 pitches (150 static) sauna

Trewethett Farm, Trethevy PL34 0BQ ✆ (01840) 770222 OS map 190/200/074895 1½m NE of Tintagel off B3263 (Boscastle) Open Apr 2-Nov 1 75 pitches tennis £16.10-£21.50* (Delta/Mastercard/Switch/Visa) www.caravanclub.co.uk

TORPOINT, Cornwall Map E5
EC Wed SEE Antony House, Plymouth Sound
✗ Rising Sun on village green 4m S at Kingsand ✆ (01752) 822840

Whitsand Bay Holiday Park, Mill Brook PL10 1JZ ✆ (01752) 822597 Fax (01752) 823444 OS map 201/410514 3m S of Torpoint off A374 and B3247 (Mill Brook) on coast road Open all year 220 pitches (100 static) Level/sloping grass, sheltered (heated) lic club, crazy golf, barbecue £8.00-£20.00* (most cards) enquiries@whitesandbayholidays.co.uk www.whitesandbayholidays.co.uk

TORQUAY, Devon Map G5
EC Wed, Sat *Resort with gentle climate, sandy beaches and favoured location overlooking Tor Bay which developed in mid 19c after the arrival of the railway.* SEE Torre Abbey, Kent's Cavern (stalagmites and Stalactites), model village, Cockington village, museums, Torbay and Dartmouth Railway, Compton Castle 4m NW
ℹ Vaughan Parade ✆ 0906 680 1268
✗ The Hare & Hounds, Torquay Rd, Kingskerswell ✆ (01803) 873119 Open 12-2/6.30-10

Manor Farm, Daccombe TQ12 4ST ✆ (01803) 328294/862395 Fax (01803) 328294 OS map 202/903678 2m NE of Torquay off A380 (Newton Abbot) Open Easter-Oct 75 pitches 3 acres, gentle slope farm produce £10.00 (min)*

Widdicombe Farm, Marldon TQ3 1ST ✆ (01803) 558325 *Prop: Mr & Mrs Glynn* OS map 202/875634 2½m W of Torquay off A380 (Brixham) Open Mar 24-Oct 15 200 pitches–families and couples only Level grass and hard standings games room, club room, family bathroom, adult only fields, seperate family field, entertainment £9.00-£17.50 (Mastercard/Visa) info@widdicombefarm.co.uk www.widdicombefarm.co.uk

TORRINGTON, Devon Map E3
Market town on hill above river Torridge, a good centre for touring lovely Taw valley
ℹ Town Hall, High St ✆ (01805) 624324
✗ Black Horse, High St ✆ (01805) 622121

Greenways Valley EX38 7EW ✆ (01805) 622153 Fax (01805) 622320 OS map 180/505185 ½m NE of Torrington off B3227 (South Molton)–signposted Open Mar 15-Oct 31 22 pitches (19 static) Level grass, sheltered (heated) tennis, games room

Smytham Holiday Park, Little Torrington EX38 8PU ✆ (01805) 622110 *Prop: T Harper* OS map 180/485162 2m S of Torrington on right of A386 (Hatherleigh) Open Mar 15-Oct 31 80 pitches (40 static) Level/sloping grass and hard standing, sheltered £7.00-£16.00* (Mastercard/Visa) info@smytham.co.uk www.smytham.co.uk

TRURO, Cornwall Map C5
MD Wed *Georgian town which originated as major river port* SEE cathedral, county and pottery museums, Trelissick gardens 4m S
🛈 Municipal Buildings, Boscawen St ✆ (01872) 274555
✗ The Old Plough Inn, Church Rd, Shortlanesend ✆ (01872) 273001

Carnon Downs Caravan and Camping Park, Carnon Downs TR3 6JJ *Quiet landscaped site with good access* ✆ (01872) 862283 OS map 204/805408 3m SW of Truro on A39 (Falmouth) Open all year 110 pitches 30 acres, level grass and hard standings, sheltered ⌂♨ £10.00-£17.50* (most cards) info@carnon-downs-caravanpark.co.uk www.carnon-downs-caravanpark.co.uk

Leverton Place Caravan Camping Park TR4 8QW ✆ (01872) 560462 OS map 204/770451 3m W of Truro off A390 (Redruth) on Chacewater road Open all year 125 pitches 9½ acres level grass and hard standings, sheltered (heated) fishing

Liskey Holiday Park, Green Bottom, Chacewater TR4 8QN ✆ (01872) 560274 Fax (01872) 561413 OS map 204/769451 3½m W of Truro off A390 (Redruth) Open Apr-Sept–booking advisable Jul-Aug 85 pitches 8 acres, grass and hard standings, level/slightly sloping, sheltered bathroom, play barn, serviced pitches £11.50-£14.50* (most cards) enquiries@liskeyholidaypark.co.uk www.liskeyholidaypark.co.uk

Ringwell Valley Holiday Park, Bissoe Road, Carnon Downs TR3 6LQ ✆ (01872) 862194 OS map 204/794408 3m SW of Truro off A39 (Falmouth) at Carnon Downs Open Apr-Oct 122 pitches (44 static) Level/sloping grass, sheltered pub meals (Mastercard/Visa)

Summer Valley Touring Park, Shortlanesend TR4 9DW ✆ (01872) 877878 *Prop: CR & AJH Simpkins* OS map 204/802479 2m NW of Truro on B3284 (Perranporth) Open Apr-Oct 60 pitches 3 acres, grass, level/gentle slope campers lounge £9.50-£12.50 (Visa/Mastercard) info@summervalley.co.uk www.summervalley.co.uk

UFFCULME, Devon Map G3
SEE Coldharbour working mill museum
✗ Racehorse 6m W at Tiverton ✆ (01884) 252606

Old Well Camping Park, Waterloo Cross EX15 3ES ✆ (01884) 240873 OS map 181/058139 2m NW of Uffculme on A38 (Tiverton–Wellington) near junction 27 of M5 Open Mar-Nov 20 pitches

Waterloo Cross Camping and Caravan Park, Waterloo Inn, Waterloo Cross EX15 3ES ✆ (01884) 240317 OS map 181/055139 2m NW of Uffculme on B3191 near junction of A38 (Tiverton–Wellington) Open Mar 15-Nov 15 50 pitches

UPLYME, Devon Map H4
Quiet village N of Lyme Regis
✗ Harbour Inn, Church St, Axmouth ✆ (01297) 20371
✗ Talbot Arms, Lyme Rd, Uplyme ✆ (01297) 443136

Shrubbery Lyme Regis, Rousdon DT7 3XW ✆ (01297) 442227 *Prop: John Godfrey* OS map 193/269914 2m SW of Uplyme on right of A3052 (Lyme Regis–Colyford) Open Mar-Nov 120 pitches–must book peak periods 10½ acres, level grass, sheltered dairy produce £7.75-£12.25 (most cards) www.ukparks.co.uk/shrubbery

Hook Farm Caravan and Camping Park, Gore La DT7 3UU *Peaceful family-run site* ✆ (01297) 442801 OS map 193/323930 ½m S of Uplyme on right of Ware road Open Mar-Nov 117 pitches 5 acres, grass, level terraced, some hard standing, sheltered £6.00-£19.00

Westhayes Caravan Park, Rousdon DT7 3RD ✆ (01297) 23436 OS map 193/287917 3m SW of Uplyme on right of A3052 (Lyme Regis-Colyford) Open all year 150 pitches 7 acres level grass, sheltered (heated outdoor) (Mastercard/Visa)

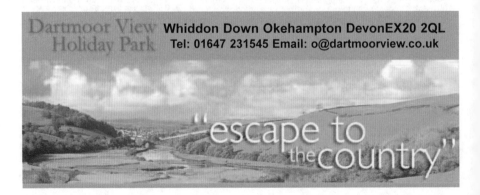

VERYAN–see Tregony

WADEBRIDGE, Cornwall   Map C4
EC Wed MD Mon SEE 15c bridge, Walmsley bird sanctuary 2m N
✗ Molesworth Arms, Molesworth St ☎ (01208) 812055

Lanarth Hotel Caravan Park, St Kew Highway PL30 3EE ☎ (01208) 841215 *Prop: Mrs JM Buckley*
  OS map 200/027749 3m NE of Wadebridge on right of A39 (Camelford) Open Apr-Oct
  86 pitches Level grass, sheltered ✗♀☂🔌⊕🖂⚡ £7.00-£9.50 *www.north-cornwall-accommodation.com/lanarth*

Laurels Holiday Park, Padstow Road, Whitecross PL27 7JQ ☎ (01208) 813341 Fax (01208)
  816590 OS map 200/959716 2m W of Wadebridge near junction of A39 (Truro) and A389
  (Padstow) Open Easter-Oct 30 separate pitches 3 acres, level grass, sheltered
  🔌🛢☂⊘⚡🏠 pets welcome £5.00-£14.00* *anicholson@thelaurelsholidaypark.co.uk*
  www.thelaurelsholidaypark.co.uk

Little Bodieve Holiday Park, Bodieve Rd PL27 6EG *Well equipped and well run site in quiet rural
  area* ☎ (01208) 812323 *Prop: Mr & Mrs Berry & Mrs B Hills* OS map 200/990734 1m N of
  Wadebridge off A39 (Camelford) on B3314 (St Minver) Open Apr-Oct 270 pitches (75 static)
  20 acres level grass 🛒♀☂🛢☂⊘⊕⊘🖂⚡🔌⚡🚻 bar meals, clubhouse, crazy golf, pets
  corner £8.80-£13.00* (Mastercard/Visa/Switch) *berry@littlevodieveholidaypark.fsnet.co.uk*
  www.littlebodievie.co.uk

For other sites near Wadebridge see Padstow, St Columb and St Minver

WATERGATE BAY–see Mawgan Porth

WATERLOO CROSS–see Uffculme

WHIDDON DOWN, Devon   Map F4
✗ Oxenham Arms 3m W at South Zeal ☎ (01837) 840244

Dartmoor View Holiday Park EX20 2QL ☎ (01647) 231545 Fax (01647) 231654 OS map
  191/684928 ¼m W of Whiddon Down on right of old A30 (Okehampton) Open Mar-Oct
  115 pitches (30 static) 5½ acres, part sloping grass and hard standing 🛒♀☂🛢☂⊘
  ⊕⊘🖂(heated) ⊕🔌⚡⚡🚻 £8.50-£14.00* (all cards) *injo@dartmoorview.co.uk*
  www.dartmoorview.co.uk

WHITSTONE, Cornwall   Map D3
SEE church, Swannacott Wood W
✗ The Countryman, Sampford Courtenay, Okehampton ☎ (01837) 82206

Hedley Wood Caravan Camping Park, Bridgerule EX22 7ED ☎ (01288) 381404 Fax (01288)
  382011 *Prop: Alan Bryant* OS map 190/262015 2m N of Whitstone off B3254 (Kilkhampton) on
  Widemouth Bay road Open all year 120 pitches 16 acres, level, open or woodland, grass and
  hard standings 🛒✗♀☂🔌🛢☂⊘⊕⊘⊕🔌⚡🚻♿ dog kennelling, dog walk, nature trail
  £7.00-£11.50 *alan@hedleywood.co.uk www.hudleywood.co.uk*

Keywood Caravan Park, Keywood Park EX22 6TW ☎ (01288) 381338 (bookings (01752) 707391)
  OS map 190/253997 2m NW of Whitstone on Whitstone Head road Open Easter-Oct–must book
  peak periods 75 pitches 5 acres, level woodland 🛒✗♀🛢☂☂⊘⊕⊘🔌⚡🚻

WIDECOMBE IN THE MOOR, Devon   Map F4
SEE church, Church House (NT), Widecombe Fair (Sept), Grimspound prehistoric village 3m W
✗ Olde Inne ☎ (01364) 621207

Cockingford Farm TQ13 7TG ☎ (01364) 252258 OS map 191/718751 1m S of Widecombe on
  Buckland road Open May-Oct–must book (caravans) 30 pitches 2½ acres, gentle slope

WIDEMOUTH BAY–see Poundstock

WINKLEIGH, Devon   Map E3
SEE Ashley Countryside Collection NE
✗ Kings Arms, The Square ☎ (01837) 83384

Wagon Wheels Holiday Park EX19 8DP ☎ (01837) 83456 OS map 191/624090 1m N of
  Winkleigh on left of B3220 (Torrington) Open Mar 17-Oct 26 120 pitches (100 static) 9½ acres,
  grass, level 🛒🔌🛢⊘🖂(heated) ⊕🔌🚻 lic club, amusements

See listing under Woolacombe

WITHERIDGE, Devon   Map F3
SEE church, thatched cottages
✗ Mount Pleasant Inn, Nomansland, Tiverton ☎(01884) 860271 Open Mon-Sat 12-10, Sun 12-9.30

West Middlewick Farm, Nomansland EX16 8NP *Working farm with panoramic views* ☎(01884)
861235 OS map 181/825138 1m E of Witheridge on left of B3137 (Tiverton) Open all year
30 pitches Level grass, hard standing, sheltered ▣◉◒&◱ farm produce £6.00-£9.00
stay@westmiddlewick.co.uk www.westmiddlewick.co.uk

Yeatheridge Farm Caravan Park, East Worlington EX17 4TN ☎(01884) 860330 OS map
191/768110 3m SW of Witheridge off B3042 (Eggesford) Open Easter-mid Sept–must book peak
periods 85 pitches 9 acres, level/gentle slope, grass, sheltered ▣↗▣◪◉◒☐(indoor
heated) ◒↙▢◪◱ fishing, woodland walks, horse riding, skittle alley £7.00-£11.50*
(Mastercard/Delta/Visa) *yeatheridge@talk21.com www.yeatheridge.co.uk*

WOODBURY–see Exmouth

WOOLACOMBE, Devon   Map E2
EC Wed SEE surfing beach, Mortehoe church 1m N, Morte Point cliffs 2m NW, Bull Point lighthouse
2½m N
▨ Red Barn Cafe, Car Park, Barton Rd ☎(01271) 870553
✗ The Old Mill Inn ☎(01271) 870237

Easewell Farm, Mortehoe EX34 7EH ☎(01271) 870343 *Prop: R Lancaster* OS map 180/465455
1½m N of Woolacombe centre off North Morte road 250 pitches Hard standings
and grass, part level, part sheltered ▣✗♀◪▣◪◉◒Ø☐(heated) ↙▢◪◱◈ lic club,
9-hole golf course, indoor bowls £15.00-£47.50 (most cards) *goodtimes@woolacombe.com
www.woolacombe.com*

Little Roadway Farm Camping EX34 7HL ☎(01271) 870313 OS map 180/470424 1m SE of
Woolacombe near junction of Challacombe Hill and B3231 (Ilfracombe–Croyde) Open March-Nov
100 pitches 10 acres, level/sloping grass ▣↗▣◪◉◒↙◪ games room £6.00-£12.00

North Morte Farm Caravan and Camping Park, Mortehoe EX34 7EG ☎(01271) 870381 OS map
180/462455 1½m N of Woolacombe centre off North Morte road Open Easter-Sept–must book
(caravans) 248 pitches (73 static) Level/sloping grass ▣↗▣◪◉◒Ø↙◱& £9.00-£13.00
(most cards) *info@northmortefarm.co.uk www.northmortefarm.co.uk*

Twitchen Parc, Mortehoe EX34 7ES ☎(01271) 870343 Fax (01271) 870089 OS map 180/465448
1m NE of Woolacombe centre off Mortehoe–Turnpike Cross road Open Easter-Oct 300 pitches
(280 static) Level/sloping grass and hard standing, sheltered ▣✗♀◪↗▣◪◉◒Ø☐(heated)
◒↙▢◪◱ children £4.50-£40.00* (most cards) *goodtimes@woolacombe.co
www.woolacombe.com*

Warcombe Farm Camping Park, Station Road, Mortehoe EX34 7EJ ☎(01271) 870690 Fax
(01271) 871070 OS map 180/478455 2m NE of Woolacombe off Mortehoe road Open Mar-Oct
100 pitches 19 acres, level grass, sheltered ▣♀▣◪◉◒Ø↙& fishing £7.00-£15.00*
(most cards) *info@warcombefarm.co.uk www.warcombefarm.co.uk*

Woolacombe Bay Holiday Village, Seymour EX34 7AH ☎(01271) 870343 OS map 180/468442
½m NE of Woolacombe centre off Mortehoe road Open Easter-Oct–tents only 386 pitches
(236 static) Grass, level ▣✗♀◪↗▣◪◉◒Ø☐(heated) ◒↙▢◪ snack bar, children's
club, health suite, beach bus, golf (most cards)

Woolacombe Sands Holiday Park, Station Road EX34 7AF ☎(01271) 870569 OS map
180/463438 ¼m E of Woolacombe on right of B3343 (Mullacott Cross) Open Apr-Oct 200
pitches (65 static) 30 acres, level/terraced grass, sheltered ▣✗♀◪▣◪◉◒Ø☐◒↙◪◱◈
£10.00-£27.50 (Mastercard/Visa)

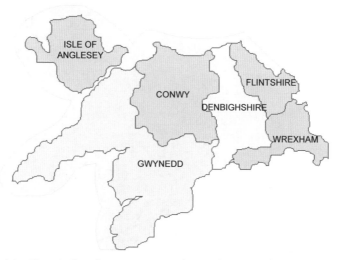

North Wales consists of the counties of Gwynedd, named from an ancient Welsh kingdom, Conwy (from the Vale of Conwy) and the areas around ancient Denbigh, Flint and Wrexham.

The dominant physical feature of the region is Snowdonia, a range of 3000ft high foldings, bounded on the east by the beautiful Vale of Conway and on the west by the Menai Straits separating Anglesey from the mainland. Betws y Coed is a popular centre for walks and climbs in Snowdonia. For the less energetic, lakeside Bala to the south is another.

Telford's Menai Bridge links Bangor with Anglesey, an island of unspectacular scenery ringed by an attractive coastline of quiet bays enclosing uncrowded beaches. Best known are Amlwch and Benllech in the north, Rhosneigr in the south. Below Anglesey is the long arm of the Lleyn Peninsula, its more hospitable and sandy eastern shore dotted with tiny resorts linked by often ultra-narrow roads. The most crowded place in summer is Abersoch.

West of Edwardian Llandudno modest resorts like Penmaenmawr and Llanfairfechan line the northern mainland coast, but more popular with campers are the long stretches of sand on the west between Porthmadog and the Dovey Estuary below Tywyn, linked to inland Abergynolwyn by a miniature railway.

More low-lying scenery forming the eastern half of the region is noted for the fine sands and sophisticated resorts along the coast west of the Dee Estuary and the purple moorlands flanking the picturesque vale of Clwyd. A large coalfield surrounds Wrecsam, Chirk and Ruabon near the border with England. Guarding the Vale of Llangollen to the southeast are the Berwyn Mountains, traversed by the northern section of Offa's Dyke Path, one of many routes for walkers in the region. North Wales may be a land of chapels yet it also has fine churches, like that of St Asaph, one of the smallest cathedrals in Britain. The finest castle in Wales is at Caernarfon – but those at Rhuddlan, Beaumaris, Chirk and Harlech are almost as impressive.

Campsite locations are most attractive inland. Many campsites along the coast are occupied mainly by static caravans and have a holiday camp atmosphere. Others are made noisy by the railway that runs close to the sea at many points. Campsite amenities vary from sophisticated on the coast to primitive inland.

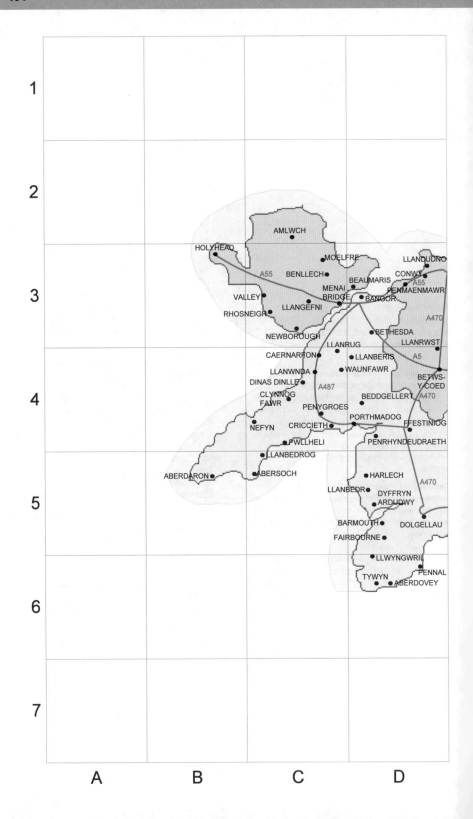

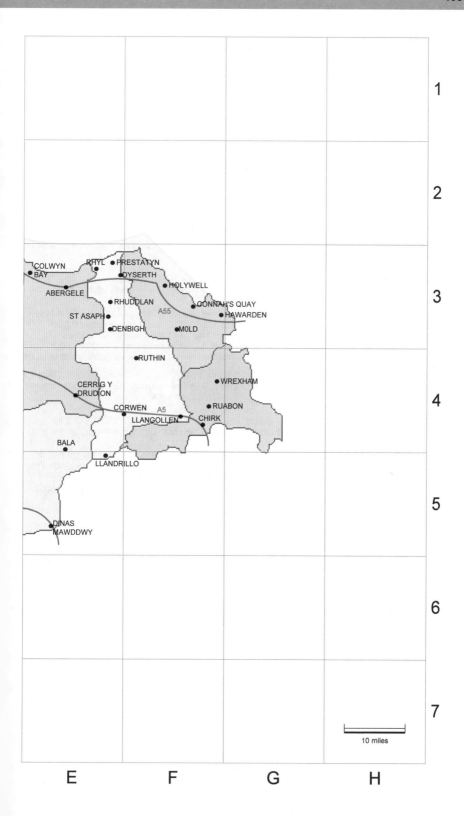

1

2

3

4

5

6

7

COLWYN BAY
RHYL
PRESTATYN
DYSERTH
HOLYWELL
ABERGELE
RHUDDLAN
CONNAH'S QUAY
A55
ST ASAPH
HAWARDEN
DENBIGH
MOLD
RUTHIN
CERRIG Y DRUDION
WREXHAM
CORWEN
A5
RUABON
LLANGOLLEN
CHIRK
BALA
LLANDRILLO
DINAS MAWDDWY

10 miles

E   F   G   H

ABERDARON, Gwynedd   Map B5
EC Wed SEE Wishing Well, Whistling Sands, Hell's mouth, Bardsey Island
✘ Ty Newydd ☎ (01758) 760207

Mur Melyn Camping, Mur Melyn LL53 8LW ☎ (01758) 760522 OS map 123/176289 2m N of
  Aberdaron off B4413 (Llanbedrog) on Whistling Sands road–signposted Open Whitsun-Sept–must
  book touring caravans 20 pitches 5 acres level grass, sheltered ⊕⊕ £4.00

Ty Mawr Caravan Park, Bryncroes, Sarn LL53 8EH ☎ (01248) 351537 (enqs) OS map 123/219317
  4m NE of Aberdaron off B4413 (Llanbedrog) Open Apr-Oct 25 pitches 2 acres level grass,
  sheltered 🗑♥⊕Ø⊕↙& roy@llyn-walls.co.uk www.tymawrcaravanpark.co.uk

ABERDOVEY, Gwynedd   Map D6
EC Wed SEE Happy Valley, Dolgoch Falls, Cader Idris (2,927ft)
🚩 The Wharf Gardens ☎ (01654) 767321
✘ Penhelig Arms, Terrace Rd ☎ (01654) 767215

Cefn Crib Caravan Park, Pennal SY20 9LB ☎ (01654) 791239 OS map 135/680990 4½m E of
  Aberdovey on A493 (Machynlleth) Open Mar 15-Sept 30 52 pitches 4 acres level grass,
  sheltered 🗑⊕

For other sites near Aberdovey see Machynlleth and Tywyn

ABERGELE, Conwy   Map E3
EC Thurs MD Mon SEE Gwrych Castle
✘ Oriel House 6m SE at St Asaph ☎ (01745) 582716

Henllys Farm, Towyn LL22 9HF ☎ (01745) 351208 Prop: GB & IM Kerfoot OS map 116/972792
  1½m NE of Abergele on A548 (Rhyl) Open Apr-Sept 280 pitches Level grass 🗑♥⌀⊕↙
  £11.00-£18.00 (Mastercard/Visa)

Hunter's Hamlet Touring Caravan Park, Sirior Goch Farm, Betws-yn-Rhos LL22 8PL ☎ (01745)
  832237 Prop: Mrs J Hunter & Ms S Hunter OS map 116/930736 3m S of Abergele off A548
  (Llanrwst) on left of B5381 (Llandudno Junction) Open Mar 21-Oct 3–no tents 23 pitches
  2½ acres grass and hard standings 🗑♥⌀⊕Ø⊕↙♥& family bathroom £10.00-£12.00*
  (£18.00-£20.00 serviced pitches) (most cards) huntershamlet@aol.com www.huntershamlet.co.uk

ABERSOCH, Gwynedd   Map C5
EC Wed One most attractive villages on Lleyn peninsula, with fine beaches SEE Llanengan church
2m W, Hell's Mouth 3m W
✘ White House ☎ (01758) 713427

Beach View Caravan and Camping Site, Bwlchtocyn LL53 7BT ☎ (01758) 712956 OS map
  123/306266 1½m SW of Abersoch on Bwlchtocyn road Open Mar-Oct 50 pitches 5 acres, level
  grass, sheltered 🛒🗑⊕⊕

Bryn Cethin Bach Caravan Park LL53 7UL ☎ (01758) 712719 OS map 123/304290 1m NW of
  Abersoch off A499 (Pwllheli) on Lon Garmon road Open Mar-Oct 74 pitches (53 static)–no tents,
  families only Level grass and hard standings 🗑♥⌀⊕⊕⊕🚏🏠 fishing

Seaview Camping Caravan Park, Sarn Bach LL53 7ET ☎ (01758) 712062 OS map 123/305266
  1½m SSW of Abersoch off Marchros road via Sarn Bach Open Mar-Oct 66 pitches 4½ acres
  level/sloping grass, sheltered 🗑♥⌀Ø↙♥ (Mastercard/Visa)

Tyn-y-Mur Camping and Touring Park, Lon Garmon LL53 7UL ☎ (01758) 712328 OS map
  123/300290 ½m W of Abersoch on Llangian road Open Mar-Oct 92 pitches 3 acres, level,
  gentle slope 🗑♥⌀⊕Ø⊕↙

Warren Touring Park LL53 7AA ☎ (01758) 712043 OS map 123/318303 2m N of Abersoch on
  A499 (Pwllheli) Open May-Oct–families only 90 pitches 4 acres, level/gentle slope 🗑⊕Ø⊕⊕✿
  (Mastercard/Visa)

See also Llanbedrog

AMLWCH, Anglesey   Map C2
EC Wed MD Fri SEE harbour, Church of our Lady, cliffs
✘ Trecastell, Bull Bay ☎ (01407) 830651

Point Lynas Caravan Park, Llaneilian LL67 9LT ☎ (01407) 831130 OS map 114/476930 2m E of
  Amlwch off A5025 (Pentraeth) at Twrcelyn Garage on Point Lynas road Open Mar-Oct 50 pitches
  Level grass, part sheltered 🗑♥⌀⊕ adj beach

Tyn-Rhos Farm, Penysarn LL69 9YR ☎ (01407) 830574 OS map 114/462902 2m SE of Amlwch
  on A5025 (Menai Bridge) at Penysarn Open Easter-Sept 32 pitches 2 acres level grass, part
  sheltered ♀⋏🗑⌀⊕♥🚏 golf, swimming, fishing £10.00-£15.00

See also Moelfre

For more up-to-date information, and for links to camping websites, visit our site at:
www.butford.co.uk/camping

BALA, Gwynedd **Map E4**
EC Wed MD Thurs *Attractive market town at head of Bala lake and popular walking centre* SEE
Bala lake, Gorsedd circle
🛈 Penllyn, Pensarn Rd ☏(01678) 521021
✗ Plas Yn Dre Restaurant, 23 Stryd Fawr ☏(01678) 521256
✗ Bryntirion Inn, Llandderfel ☏(01678) 530205

Bryn Gwyn Farm, Llanuwchllyn LL23 7SU ☏(01678) 540687 OS map 124/865308 5m SW of Bala
off A494 (Dolgellau) Open Easter-Oct 40 pitches 🅿🅰∅🚻(£50) 🏠 fishing

Bryn Melyn Farm, Llandderfel LL23 7RA ☏(01678) 520212 OS map 125/996363 4m E of Bala on
B4401 (Corwen) Open Apr-Oct—must book peak periods 139 pitches 🛒🗑∅🅰🚻 farm produce,
fishing, rough shoot

Crynierth Caravan Park (Camping Club), Cefn-ddwysarn LL23 7IN ☏(01678) 520324 OS map
125/962391 3m NE of Bala off A494 (Ruthin) Open Mar 20-Oct 30 50 pitches Level grass,
sheltered 🗑🅰∅🅰∅🔧♿

Glanllyn Lakeside Caravan Camping Park LL23 7ST ☏(01678) 540227 *Prop: ET & MW Pugh*
OS map 125/892324 3m SW of Bala off A494 (Dolgellau) by lake Open Mar 15-Oct 15 134
pitches Level grass, sheltered 🛒🗑🅰∅🅰♿ boat launching facs, fishing, canoeing £10.00-
£14.00 (Mastercard/Visa/Switch) *info@glanllyn.com www.glanllyn.com*

Penybont Touring and Camping Park, Llangynog Road LL23 7PH ☏(01678) 520549 OS map
125/932350 ½m SE of Bala on B4391 (Llangynog) Open Apr-Oct—must book peak periods
95 pitches Level/sloping grass and hard standing, sheltered 🛒🗑🗑🅰∅🅰🔧♿ £10.50-£14.00
(Mastercard/Visa/Maestro) *penybont@balalake.fsnet.co.uk www.penybont.bala.co.uk*

Pen-y-Garth Caravan Camping Park LL23 7ES ☏(01678) 520485 Fax (01678) 520401 OS map
125/940349 1m NE of Bala off B4391 (Lake Vyrnwy) Open Mar-Oct—must book peak periods
117 pitches (54 static) 20 acres level grass and hard standings, sheltered 🛒🗑🗑🅰∅🅰∅🔧🏕
table tennis, games room £7.95-£10.50* (most cards) *stay@penygarth.com www.penygarth.com*

Ty Isaf Caravan Park, Llangynog Road LL23 7PP ☏(01678) 520574 OS map 125/957355 2m E
of Bala on B4391 (Llangynog) Open Apr-Oct 30 pitches Level grass, part sheltered
🗑🗑🅰🅰🚻🏕

Tyn Cornel Camping Caravan Park, Frongoch LL23 7NU ☏(01678) 520759 OS map 125/895400
4m NW of Bala on A4212 (Porthmadog) by river Open Mar-Oct 37 pitches 2 acres level grass
🛒🗑🅰∅ *No showers*

Ty Tandderwen LL23 7EP ☏(01678) 520273 *Prop: RL Davies* OS map 125/951363 2½m SE of
Bala off B4391 (Llangynog) Open Easter-Oct 125 pitches (60 static) Level grass, sheltered
🗑🗑🅰🅰∅🔧♿ bathing, fishing £8.00-£12.00* inc hot water *www.tytandderwen.co.uk*

BANGOR, Gwynedd **Map D3**
EC Wed MD Fri SEE cathedral, University of Wales, museum, Menai Bridge, Penrhyn Castle 1m E
🛈 Town Hall, Deiniol Rd ☏(01248) 352786
✗ Union Hotel, Garth Rd ☏(01248) 362462

Tros-y-Waen Holiday Farm, Pentir LL57 4EF ☏(01248) 364448 OS map 114/115/570661 3½m S
of Bangor off A4087 (Caernarfon) and B4547 (Llanberis) Open all year 20 pitches 🛒🗑🅰🔧

BARMOUTH, Gwynedd **Map D5**
EC Wed MD Thurs *Popular seaside resort on N shore of Mawddach estuary* SEE Guild of St
George cottages, Fairbourne railway S, Llanaber church 2m NW, Bontddu gold mines 2m NE
🛈 Old Library ☏(01341) 280787 ✗ Tal-y-Don Hotel, High St ☏(01341) 280508

Hendre Mynach Touring Caravan and Camping Park LL42 1YR ☏(01341) 280262 *Prop: AR
Williams* OS map 124/609167 ½m N of Barmouth on A496 (Harlech) Open Mar-Jan—must book
peak periods (caravans) 200 pitches Level grass and hard standings, sheltered
🛒✗⊶🔧🗑🗑🅰🅰♿ £9.00-£23.00 (Mastercard/Visa/Maestro) *mynach@lineone.net
www.hendremynach.co.uk*
See also Llanbedr and Fairbourne

BEAUMARIS, Anglesey **Map D3**
EC Wed SEE castle ruins, 14c church, old gaol and courthouse
✗ Old Bulls Head, Castle St ☏(01248) 810329

Kingsbridge Caravan Park, Llanfaes LL58 8LR ☏(01248) 490636 OS map 115/607786 2m N of
Beaumaris off B5109 (Llangoed) on Llanfaes road Open Mar-Oct 77 pitches (29 static) Level
grass, sheltered 🛒🗑🅰🅰∅🅰🔧🏕

Hendre Mynach
Touring Caravan & Camping Park
Barmouth, Gwynedd, Wales, LL42 1YR
tel: 01341 280 262, fax: 01341 280 586

BEDDGELERT, Gwynedd   **Map D4**
EC Wed SEE priory church, Gelert's grave, Sygun copper mine, Aberglaslyn pass S, Gwynant valley
NE, Gwynant and Dinas lakes NE
✘ Royal Goat ☎ (01766) 890224

Beddgellert Camp Site LL55 4UU ☎ (01766) 890288 *Prop: Forest Holidays* OS map 116/578491
1¼m N of Beddgelert on A4085 (Caernarfon) Open all year 280 pitches Level grass and hard
standing ▒▤▨◪◐∅✆✌& common room £7.20-£12.20 (Mastercard/Visa)
www.forestholidays.co.uk

BENLLECH, Anglesey   **Map D3**
EC Thurs SEE Roman village
✘ Rhostrefor, Amlwch Rd ☎ (01248) 852347

Ad Astra Caravan Site, Brynteg LL78 7JH ☎ (01248) 853283 *Prop: Brian Iddon* OS map
114/490820 2m W of Benllech off B5108 (Brynteg) on B5110 (Llangefni) Open Mar-Oct
70 pitches (38 static) Level grass, sheltered ▤▨◪✆▱◪ £10.00-£15.00
brian@brynteg53.fsnet.co.uk www.adastracaravanpark.co.uk

Bodafon Caravan and Camping Site LL74 8RU ☎ (01248) 852417 *Prop: RG Roberts* OS map
114/516836 ½m N of Benllech on left of A5025 (Amlwch) Open Mar-Oct 50 pitches 5 acres
level/sloping grass and hard standing, sheltered ▨◪◐∅▦▱▩◪ £8.00-£20.00
robert@bodafonpark.fsnet.co.uk www.mysite.freeserve.com/bodafonpark

Bwlch Holiday Park, Bwlch Farm, Tyngongl LL74 8RF ☎ (01248) 852914 OS map 114/510820
½m SW of Benllech off B5108 (Llangefni) Open Mar-Oct 66 pitches (52 static) Grass and hard
standings ▤▨◪∅✌▦❀ games room

Garnedd Touring Park, Brynteg LL78 8QA ☎ (01248) 853240 OS map 114/495818 1½m SW of
Benllech off B5108 (Llangefni) Open Mar-Oct–must book peak periods 20 pitches–couples
preferred, children by arrangement Level/sloping grass, part sheltered ▤▨◐◪▦▱▩ battery
charging

Glan Gors Caravan Park, Brynteg LL78 8QA ☎ (01248) 852334 OS map 114/499819 1m W of
Benllech near junction of B5108 (Brynteg) and B5110 (Moelfre-Llangefni) Open Mar-Oct
195 pitches Level grass, sheltered ▒⚐▤◪◲(heated) ❀

Home Farm Caravan Park, Marianglas LL73 8PH ☎ (01248) 410614 OS map 114/496847 2m NW
of Benllech off A5025 (Amlwch) at Llanallgo Open Apr-Oct 133 pitches (72 static) Level grass
and hard standing, sheltered ▨▨◪◐∅◪✆& indoor play area, fully serviced pitches, tennis
court £10.50-£22.50* (Mastercard/Visa/Solo) *enq@homefarm-anglesey.co.uk www.homefarm-
anglesey.co.uk*

Nant Newydd Caravan Park, Brynteg LL78 7JH ☎ (01248) 852842/852266 OS map 114/484814
3m SW of Benllech off B5108 (Brynteg) on B5110 (Llangefni) Open Mar-Oct–must book peak
periods 113 pitches (83 static) 4 acres grass and hard standings, sloping/level, sheltered
▒⚐▤▨◪◐∅◲◪✌▦▱◪ Satellite TV

Plas Uchaf Caravan Camping Park, Benllech Bay LL74 8NU ☎ (01407) 763012 *Prop: Evans
Partnership* OS map 114/509835 ½m NW of Benllech on Marianglas road Open Mar-Oct
115 pitches (25 static) 10 acres level grass and hard standing, sheltered ▨◪◐∅✆✌◪▦▱◪
playhouse £8.00-£12.00

Rhos Farm, Pentraeth LL75 8DZ ☎ (01248) 450214 OS map 114/519794 2½m S of Benllech on
A5025 (Menai Bridge) Open Mar-Oct 120 pitches (66 static) 15 acres, level grass, sheltered
▒▤▨◪✌▱ (all cards)

St David's Park, Red Wharf Bay LL75 8RJ ☎ (01248) 852341 OS map 114/531819 1½m S of
Benllech off A5025 (Menai Bridge) Open Apr-Sept–must book 100 pitches Level/sloping grass,
sheltered ▒✘⚐⚐⚐⚐⚐⚐⚐⚐◐∅◪❀ lic club, own beach (Mastercard/Visa/Switch/Delta)

Ty Newydd Caravan Park, Llanbedrgoch LL76 8TZ ☎ (01248) 450677 OS map 114/115/507812
2m S of Benllech off A5025 (Menai Bridge) on Llanbedrgoch road Open Mar-Oct 100 pitches
(60 static) 9 acres level grass and hard standings, sheltered ▒✘⚐⚐⚐▤▨◪◐∅◪▱(heated)
◪✌▱▦▱& health centre (Mastercard/Visa)

See also Moelfre

BETHESDA, Gwynedd   **Map D4**
✘ Ty Uchaf 2½m NW at Tal-y-bont ☎ (01248) 352219

Ogwen Bank Caravan Park, Ogwen Bank LL57 3LQ ☎ (01248) 600486 OS map 115/627661 ½m
S of Bethesda on A5 (Betws y Coed) Open Mar-Oct 176 pitches (100 static)–touring pitches with
all mains services–no tents Gravel, level, terraced ▒✘⚐⚐▤▨◪∅▱▦(£75) ▱& lic club,
pony trekking, hill walks

SITE DIRECTIONS
The distance and direction of a campsite is given from the centre of the town under which it appears.

Cwm Cadnant Valley

Llanberis Road, Caernarfon, Gwynedd, LL55 2DF

Telephone: +44 (0)1286 673196 Fax: +44 (0)1286 675941

BETWS Y COED, Conwy   Map D4
EC Thurs SEE old church, Conwy Falls, Swallow Falls, Pont-y-Pair bridge, Railway Museum,
Dolwyddelan Castle 5m SW
i Royal Oak Stables ☎ (01690) 710426
✗ Royal Oak ☎ (01690) 710363

Cwmlanerch Farm LL24 0BG ☎ (01690) 710285/710363 OS map 115/800580 1m N of Betws-y-
   Coed on right of B5106 (Conwy) Open Mar-Oct 49 pitches (30 static) 3 acres, level, sheltered,
   grass and hard standings 🗑🔌⊕∅🔌↩🚐

Hendre Farm LL24 0BN OS map 115/784566 ½m W of Betws y Coed on left of A5 (Bangor)
   Open Apr-Oct 56 pitches 2 acres level grass 🗑∅❀

Riverside Caravan and Camping Ground LL24 0AL ☎ (01690) 710310 OS map 115/797564 In
   Betws y Coed off A5 adj golf course Open Mar-Oct 120 pitches (75 static) 7 acres level grass,
   sheltered 🗑🔌⊕∅🔌↩ farm produce, forest walks

BETWS GARMON–see Waunfawr

BRYNCRUG–see Tywyn

BRYNSIENCYN–see Menai Bridge

BRYNTEG–see Benllech

CAERNARFON, Gwynedd   Map C4
EC Thurs MD Sat *Town at SW end of Menai Strait dominated by great medieval fortress* SEE
Castle, town walls, Roman fort, Hafodty gardens
i Oriel Pendeitsh, Castle St ☎ (01286) 672232
✗ The Mill Cafe, Seiont Nurseries, Rhosbodrual ☎ (01286) 676549

Cwm Cadnant Valley Caravan Camping Park, Llanberis Road LL55 2DF ☎ (01286) 673196 *Prop:*
   DE & JP Bird OS map 114/491628 ½m E of Caernarfon on A4086 (Llanberis) Open Mar
   14-Oct–must book peak periods 70 pitches 5 acres level grass and hard standings, sheltered
   🗑🔌∅⊘❀↩🔌 £8.50-£16.00 (Mastercard/Visa/Switch/Delta) *butford@cwmcadnant.co.uk*
   www.cwmcadnant.co.uk

Glan Gwna Holiday Park, Caeathro LL55 2SG ☎ (01286) 673456/676402 OS map 114/502622
   1m SE of Caernarfon on A4085 (Beddgelert) Open Apr-Oct 100 pitches Level grass ✗🔌🖥 lic
   club, fishing (most cards)

Menai Caravan Park, Coed Helen LL53 7AA ☎ (01286) 672852 OS map 114/115/475625 1m W
   of Caernarfon off A487 (Porthmadog) Open Mar-Oct 50 pitches 🍴🗑🖥(heated) 🔌❀ children's
   room, lic club

Rhyd-y-Galen Caravan Park, Bethel Road LL55 3PS ☎ (01248) 670110 OS map 115/508644 2m
   NE of Caernarfon on right of B4366 (Bethel) Open Easter-Oct 35 pitches 3 acres grass, mainly
   sloping 🔌⊕↩

Riverside Camping, Caer Glyddyn, Pontrug LL55 2BB ☎ (01286) 678781 *Prop: Brenda Hummel*
   OS map 114/505627 2m E of Caernarfon on A4086 (Llanberis) Open Easter-Oct 60 pitches
   4½ acres hard standing and level grass, sheltered ✗↩🗑🔌⊕↩& £10.00-£18.00 inc awning
   brenda@riversidecamping.co.uk www.riversidecamping.co.uk

For other sites near Caernarfon see Dinas Dinlle, Llanrug, Llanwnda and Waunfawr

CERRIG-Y-DRUDION, Conwy   Map E4
✗ Plas Coch 10m S at Bala ☎ (01678) 520309

Glan Ceirw Caravan Site, Tynant, Corwen LL21 0RF ☎ (01490) 420346 Fax (01490) 420346 OS
   map 116/963462 1½m S of Cerrig-y-Drudion off A5 (Corwen) Open Mar-Oct 38 pitches
   (29 static) Hard standings, level 🍴🗑🖥🔌∅⊕↩🔌🖥 jacuzzi £6.00-£18.00*
   glanceirwcaravanpark@tinyworld.co.uk www.co.uk/glanceirw

Saracen's Head Hotel LL21 9SY ☎ (01490) 420684 OS map 116/950490 ¼m NW of Cerrig-y-
   Drudion on A5 (Betws-y-Coed) Open all year 21 pitches Level grass and hard standings ✗🍷🔌

CHIRK, Wrexham   **Map F4**
SEE castle
✘ Gales 5m NW at Llangollen ☎ (01978) 860089
Pontbell Caravan Park, Glyn Ceiriog LL20 7AB ☎ (01691) 718320 OS map 126/203378 6m W of
Chirk on B4500 (Llanarmon) Open Apr-Sept 12 pitches 1 acre level grass, sheltered ⊘ ✿ ♨ ⌂
fishing

CLYNNOG FAWR, Gwynedd   **Map C4**
✘ Caeau Capel 8m SW at Nefyn ☎ (01758) 720240
Aberafon Camping, Gyrn Goch LL54 5PN ☎ (01286) 660295 *Prop: Hugh & Clare Bird-Jones* OS
map 123/400485 1m S of Clynnog Fawr on A499 (Pwllheli) Open Mar-Oct 65 pitches 10 acres,
part level grass, sheltered ⬛ 🗓 ♨ ⊘ ✿ ⊘ ⌂ ♨ ⌂ private beach, pool room £9.00
hugh@maelor.demon.co.uk www.maelor.demon.co.uk/aberafon.html
Llyn-y-Gele Farm, Pontllyfni LL54 5EL ☎ (01286) 660283 OS map 115/432522 2m NE of Clynnog
Fawr on left of A499 (Caernarfon) by garage in Pontllyfni Open Easter-Oct 54 pitches (48 static)
4 acres, level grass ⬛ ♨ ⊘ ✿ £7.00-£10.00*

Help us make CAMPING CARAVANNING
BRITAIN better known to site operators – and
thereby more informative – by showing them
your copy when booking in.

Aberafon Camping, Clynnog Fawr

COLWYN BAY, Conwy   **Map E3**
EC Wed *Seaside resort with 3m long promenade overlooking Colwyn Bay with original nucleus a
short way inland* SEE Welsh Mountain Zoo, Puppet Theatre, Bodnant gardens 5m SW
🅸 Station Sq ☎ (01492) 530478
✘ The Semaphore Lodge, Ffordd Y Llan, Llysfaen ☎ (01492) 516774
Bron-y-Wendon Touring Caravan Park, Wern Road, Llanddulas LL22 8HG ☎ (01492) 512903
(24 hrs) *Prop: S & LJ Dent* OS map 116/785903 3m E of Colwyn Bay off A55 (Chester) at
Llanddulas–signposted Open all year 130 pitches–no tents 8 acres grass and hard standings,
level/sloping 🗓 ♨ ⊘ ✿ ⊘ ⊕ ⌂ ⚹ games room, internet access (hotspot), tourist info, heated
shower blocks £14.00-£18.00 (Mastercard/Visa) *bron-y-wendon@northwales-holidays.co.uk
www.northwales-holidays.co.uk*
Dinarth Hall, Rhos on Sea LL28 4PX ☎ (01492) 548203 OS map 116/825805 2m NW of Colwyn
Bay off A55 (Bangor) on B5115 (Llandudno)–entr opp college Open Mar-Oct 40 pitches Level
grass ⬛ 🗓 ♨ ⊘ ✿ ⊘ ⊕ ⚹
Westwood Caravan Park, Llysfaen LL29 8SW ☎ (01492) 517410 OS map 116/895775 ½m E of
Colwyn Bay off A547 (Llanddulas) on Highlands road Open Apr-Oct 88 pitches 🗓 ♨ ⊘ ✿

CONWY, Conwy   **Map D3**
EC Wed MD Tues, Sat SEE Castle, St Mary's church, Elizabethan mansion of Plas Mawr,
suspension bridge
🅸 Visitor Centre, the Castle ☎ (01492) 592248
✘ The Old Bull Inn, Llanbedr-y-Cennin ☎ (01492) 660508
Conwy Touring Park, Gyffin LL32 8UX ☎ (01492) 592856 OS map 115/775758 1¼m S of Conwy
on B5106 (Betws y Coed) Open Apr-Sept–must book Jul-Aug 400 pitches Level grass and hard
standing, sheltered 🗓 ♨ ⊘ ✿ ⊕ ⚹ ♨ £4.00-£14.42* (Mastercard/Visa/Delta)
sales@conwytouringpark.com www.conwytouringpark.com
Tyn Terfyn Touring Park, Tal-y-Bont LL32 8YX ☎ (01492) 660525 *Prop: B & G Turner* OS map
115/768695 5m S of Conwy on B5106 (Betws-y-Coed) Open Mar 14-Oct 30 15 pitches 2 acres
level grass and hard standings, sheltered 🗓 ♨ ⊘ ✿ ⊕ ⌂ £7.50

COMMENTS
We would be pleased to hear your comments about the sites featured in this guide or your
suggestions for future editions. Comments and suggestions may be emailed to ccb@butford.co.uk.
Alternatively, write to The Editor, CCB, Butford Technical Publishing Ltd at the address given at the
front of the book.

CORWEN, Denbighshire **Map F4**

✗Hand 11m E at Llangollen ☎(01978) 860303

Llaw Bettws Farm Caravan Park LL21 0HD ☎(01490) 460224 OS map 125/018425 3m W of Corwen off A494 (Ruthin-Bala) at Glan-yr-Afon Open Mar-Oct 105 pitches (68 static) Level/sloping grass, sheltered 🏪🗑🐕🖼️⊕∅❸⤴🎣🚽🗲🏪 fishing

Maerdy Mawr Caravan Park, Gwyddelwern LL21 9SD ☎(01490) 412187 OS map 116/070474 2½m N of Corwen off A5 (Bangor) on A494 (Ruthin) beyond Gwyddelwern Open Mar-Oct 30 pitches 🖼️🐕❀

Llawr Betws LL21 0HD ☎(01490) 460224 OS map 125/018425 3½m W of Corwen off A5 on A494 (Bala) road Open Mar 25-Oct 100 pitches (68 static) 🗑🐕⊕∅❸⤴🚽 fishing £6.00-£8.00 (£2 awning, £1.50 hook-up) david@llawrbetws.go-plus.net

See also Llandrillo

CRICCIETH, Gwynedd **Map C4**

EC Wed *Modest resort in sheltered position on Tremadoc Bay with sandy beaches on either hand* SEE Lloyd George Museum, view of Cardigan Bay from summit of headland, Llanystumdwy castle ruins 1½m W

✗Lion Hotel, Y Maes ☎(01766) 522460 Open 12-8.30

Cae Canol Farm, Caernarfon Road LL52 0NB ☎(01766) 522351 *Prop: Mrs EW Roberts* OS map 123/485402 1½m NW of Criccieth on B4411 (Caernarfon) Open Mar-Oct 20 pitches Level grass, sheltered 🖼️🐕⊕🏠 trout fishing, dog walk £5.50-£10.50

Eisteddfa Camp Site, Pentrefelin LL52 0PT ☎(01766) 522696 *Prop: Mr & Mrs Leech* OS map 124/520394 1m NE of Criccieth on A497 (Porthmadog) Open Mar-Oct 140 pitches Level/sloping grass and hard standing, sheltered 🏪🗑🖼️🐕⊕∅❸⤴🚽🗲🏪♿ £8.80-£14.80 eisteddfa@criccieth.co.uk www.eisteddfapark.co.uk

Gell Farm LL52 0PN ☎(01766) 522781 OS map 123/497398 1m NW of Criccieth on right of B4411 (Caernarfon) Open Apr-Oct 58 pitches (50 static) 5 acres, level grass, sheltered 🗑🐕🖼️🚽

Llwyn-Bugeilydd Farm LL52 0PN *Quiet family site with fine views* ☎(01766) 522235 OS map 123/498396 1m N of Criccieth on right of B4411 (Caernarfon)–signposted Open Apr-Oct 45 pitches 6 acres, level grass 🏪🖼️🐕⊕

Maes Meillion, Llwyn Mafon Isaf LL52 0RE ☎(01766) 522642 OS map 124/520417 3½m N of Criccieth on A487 (Porthmadog-Caernarfon) Open Apr-Oct 20 pitches 🖼️

Muriau Bach Touring Park, Rhoslan LL52 0NP ☎(01766) 530642 OS map 123/482420 3m N of Criccieth on B4411 (Caernarfon) Open Mar-Oct 20 pitches Level grass, sheltered 🖼️🐕⤴🗲

Ocean Heights Caravan Park, Pen-y-Bryn, Chwilog LL53 6NQ ☎(01766) 522519 OS map 123/435380 4m W of Criccieth off A497 (Pwllheli) Open Mar-Oct 94 pitches (74 static) Grass, level, sheltered 🗑🖼️🐕(£60) 🗲 farm produce, sep pitches

Tyddyn Cethin Farm LL52 0NF ☎(01766) 522115 OS map 123/492404 1½m N of Criccieth on B4411 (Caernarfon) by river Dwyfor Open Mar-Oct 80 pitches (40 static) 8 acres level grass 🏪🖼️🐕🖼️ £6.00-£8.00* trumper@henstabl147freeserve.co.uk

Tyddyn Morthwyl LL52 0NF ☎(01766) 522115 OS map 123/485402 1½m N of Criccieth on B4411 (Caernarfon) Open Mar 14-Oct 30 37 pitches (22 static) Level grass, sheltered 🖼️⊕∅❸🗲 £6.00

DENBIGH, Denbighshire **Map E3**

EC Thurs SEE castle ruins, St Hilary's Tower, old Bull Inn, old town walls ✗Bull, Hall Sq ☎(01745) 812582

Caer Mynydd Caravan Park, Pentre Saron LL16 4TL ☎(01745) 550302 OS map 116/028607 4½m SW of Denbigh off B4501 (Cerrigydrudion) Open Mar-Oct 29 pitches Level grass and hard standing, sheltered 🗑🖼️🐕⊕❸⤴🖼️📺❀🗲♿ games room

Station House Caravan Park, Bodfari LL16 4DA ☎(01745) 710372 *Prop: RS Hastings* OS map 116/094700 3½m N of Denbigh off A541 (Mold) on B5429 (Tremeirchion) Open Apr-Oct 26 pitches Level grass 🖼️🐕⊕⤴🖼️ games room £8.50-£9.50

Tyn-yr-Eignen Touring Caravan and Camping Park, Mold Road LL16 4BH ☎(01745) 813211 OS map 116/070568 ½m SE of Denbigh on A525 (Ruthin) Open Mar-Oct 45 pitches 🐕⊕

DINAS DINLLE, Gwynedd **Map C4**

SEE Iron Age fort ✗Stables 3m NE at Llanwnda ☎(01286) 830711

Dinlle Caravan Park LL54 5TW ☎(01286) 830324 Fax (01286) 831526 OS map 115/438568 ½m N of Dinas Dinlle off road to Morfa Dinlle Open Mar-Oct–booking advisable peak periods 388 pitches (138 static) 🏪🍴🔌🗑🐕⊕∅❸📺❸⤴🖼️(£35), 🗲♿ family room, boating, club, fishing £7.00-£15.50* (all major cards) enq@thorneyleisure.co.uk www.thorneyleisure.co.uk

Morfa Lodge Caravan Park LL54 5TP ☎(01286) 830205 Fax (01286) 831329 OS map 115/443587 1½m N of Dinas Dinlle on Foryd Bay road Open Mar-Oct 370 pitches (150 static) Level grass and hard standings 🏪🍴🔌🗑🐕⊕∅🗄️❸⤴🖼️🖼️🗲♿ children's room, clubhouse

DINAS MAWDDWY, Gwynedd   **Map E5**
EC Thurs
✘ Red Lion (off A470) ☎(01650) 531247
Tynypwll Camping SY20 9JF ☎(01650) 531326 OS map 124/862149 ¼m NE of Dinas Mawddwy on Llanymawddwy road Open all year 60 pitches (50 static) Grass, level, sheltered ⌁ fishing, climbing, walks

DOLGELLAU, Gwynedd   **Map D5**
EC Wed MD Fri SEE Precipice Walk NW, ruins of Cymmer Abbey 1m N, Torrent Walk NE, Coed-y-Brenin forest 2m N via A470, road S to Cader Idris
🛈 Ty Meirion, Eldon Sq ☎(01341) 422888
✘ Royal Ship, Queens Sq ☎(01341) 422209
Cwmrhwyddfor Caravan & Camping Site, Talyllyn, Tywyn LL36 9AJ ☎(01654) 761286/761380
   Prop: TD Nutting OS map 124/737120 3½m S of Dolgellau off A470 (Mallwyd) on A487 (Machynlleth) Open all year 25 pitches Level/sloping grass and hard standing ▣❸ pub nearby, dogs allowed
Dolgamedd Caravan Camping Park, Bont Newydd, Brithdir LL40 2DG ☎(01341) 422624 Fax (01341) 422624 OS map 124/773202 3m NE of Dolgellau on B4416 (Brithdir) by river Open Apr-Oct 65 pitches Level grass and hard standing, sheltered ▣❸✤ fishing
Llwyn yr Helm Farm, Brithdir LL40 2SA ☎(01341) 450254 OS map 124/778192 3m NE of Dolgellau off B4416 (loop linking A470 and A494) Open Easter-Oct 25 pitches 3 acres level grass and hard standing, sheltered ▣▣⌀❸❺▣⌁🏠✤ self catering accom avail £8.00
Tan-y-fron Camping Park, Arran Road LL40 2AA ☎(01341) 422638 OS map 124/735176 ½m E of Dolgellau on A470 (Mallwyd) Open Mar-Oct 63 pitches Level grass and hard standings, sheltered ▣▣⌀❸⌀❤▣▣🏠✤
Vanner Abbey Farm, Llanelltyd LL40 2HE ☎(01341) 422854 Prop: P J Rowlands & Co OS map 124/725194 1½m NW of Dolgellau off A470 (Barmouth) Open Apr-Oct 15–no adv booking for tents 50 pitches ▣⌀❸✤ fishing £8.00 adv booking for elec hook-up enquiries@vanner.co.uk www.vanner.co.uk

DULAS–see Moelfre

DYFFRYN ARDUDWY, Gwynedd   **Map D5**
Modest resort close to wide sandy beaches of Barmouth Bay
✘ Ael-y-Bryn on A496 ☎(01341) 247701
Benar Beach Camping and Touring Park, Talybont LL43 2AR ☎(01341) 247571 OS map 124/574227 1m W of Duffryn Ardudwy off A496 (Barmouth) at Llanddwywe, by beach Open Mar-Oct 230 pitches Level grass, sheltered ▣❸⌀ satellite and TV hook up
Dyffryn Seaside Estate LL44 2HD ☎(01341) 247622 OS map 124/573232 1m W of Dyffryn Ardudwy via Station road, by beach Open Easter-Oct 548 pitches (248 static) ▤✘⚓▣⌀▣ ❤🏠 lic club, sauna, jacuzzi, bowling green, private beach
Islawrfford Caravan Park, Tal-y-Bont LL43 2BQ ☎(01341) 247269 OS map 124/590212 ½m S of Dyffryn Ardudwy on right of A496 (Barmouth) Open Easter-Oct 366 pitches (216 static) Level grass ▤✘�▣▣❸⌀▣(heated) ❤⌁
Murmur-yr-Afon Touring Caravan Camping Park LL44 2BE ☎(01341) 247353 Prop: M & N Mills OS map 124/588234 In Dyffryn Ardudwy near service station Open Mar-Oct 67 pitches Level grass and hard standings ▤▣▣▣❸⌀❸❤♿ £8.50-£18.25 murmuryrafon@btinternet.com www.murmuryrafon.co.uk
Parc Isaf, Cors-y-Gedol Drive LL44 2RJ ☎(01341) 247447 Prop: Mrs J Edwards OS map 124/595226 ½m S of Dyffryn Ardudwy off A496 (Barmouth) on right of Cors-y-Gedol road Open Easter-Oct 30 pitches 3½ acres part level grass, sheltered ▣⌀❸⌁ farm produce £5.00-£10.00* parcisaf.wales@virgin.net
See also Barmouth and Llanbedr

KEY TO SYMBOLS

▤	shop	⌀	gas supplies	▣	winter storage for caravans
✘	restaurant	❸	chemical disposal point	℗	parking obligatory
⛉	bar	⌀	payphone	✤	no dogs
⚓	takeaway food	▣	swimming pool	⌁	caravan hire
⚒	off licence	❸	games area	🏠	bungalow hire
▣	laundrette	❤	children's playground	♿	facilities for disabled
▣	mains electric hook-ups	▣	TV	✤	shaded

DYSERTH, Denbighshire   **Map E3**
✖ New Inn, Waterfall Rd ☎ (01745) 570482

Penisar Mynydd Caravan Site, Caerwys Road, Rhualt LL17 0TY ☎ (01745) 582227 OS map
116/094769 2m SE of Dyserth–signposted on A55 expressway (Conway-Chester) Open Apr-
Oct–no tents 30 pitches 2 acres grass and hard standing, sheltered 🗑🔌🚿⊗∅🔀🚻♿
seasonal pitches avail. £8.00 -£12.00

FAIRBOURNE, Gwynedd   **Map D5**
EC Sat *Little-known resort on S shore of Mawddach estuary facing Barmouth on N* SEE beach,
railway to Penrhyn Point (ferry to Barmouth)
✖ Y Sosban Fach, 6 Lower Ala Rd, Pwllheli ☎ (01758) 613781 Open summer Mon-Sun 10-5,
winter Mon-Sat 10-4

Garthyfog Camp Site, Arthog LL39 1AX ☎ (01341) 250338 OS map 124/638143 2m NE of
Fairbourne on A493 (Dolgellau) Open all year 30 pitches Level/sloping grass and hard standings,
sheltered 🚜 farm produce, walks £2.50-£10.00 www.garthyfog.co.uk

Graig-wen Camping, Arthog LL39 1BQ ☎ (01341) 250482/250900 OS map 124/656158 3m NE of
Fairbourne on right of A493 (Dolgellau) Open Mar-Oct 210 pitches 42 acres partly level grass
and hard standings 🚿⊗∅🚜 B&B

See also Barmouth

HARLECH, Gwynedd   **Map D5**
SEE castle, pottery
🅸 Llys y Graig, Harlech ☎ (01766) 780658 ✖ Rum Hole Tavern, Ffordd Newydd ☎ (01766) 780477

Barcdy Touring Park, Talsarnau LL47 6YG *Quiet park near sea and mountains* ☎ (01766) 770736
Prop: Anwen L Roberts OS map 124/622371 4m NNE of Harlech on A496 (Maentwrog)
Open Easter-Sep 80 pitches (30 static) Grass, part level, part sheltered 🗑🔌🚿⊗∅⊗☂🚜
freezer pack service £14.00-£16.50 inc elect (all cards exc Amex) anwen@barcoly.co.uk
www.barcoly.co.uk

Cae Cethin, Llanfair LL46 2SA ☎ (01766) 780247 OS map 124/578287 1m S of Harlech off A496
(Barmouth) near slate caverns Open Easter-Nov 40 pitches 2½ acres terraced, grass and hard
standing farm produce

Min-y-Don Ideal Caravan Park LL46 2UG ☎ (01766) 780286 OS map 124/575317 ½m N of
Harlech off A496 (Talsarnau) Open Easter-Sept 250 pitches 🚿⊗🚜

Woodlands Caravan Park LL46 2UE ☎ (01766) 780419 OS map 124/582313 In Harlech,
entrance adj castle car park–signposted Open Mar-Oct 37 pitches–no tents 4 acres level grass
and hard standings, sheltered 🗑🔌🚿⊗☎ £14.00-£16.00 inc elect
www.woodlandscp.fsnet.co.uk

HAWARDEN, Flintshire   **Map F3**
✖ The Plough Inn, Aston Rd, Queensferry ☎ (01244) 811132

Greenacres Farm Park, Mancot, Deeside CH5 2AZ ☎ (01244) 531147 *Prop: JA Johnson* OS map
117/318672 1m N of Hawarden off A550 (Queensferry) Open Easter-Sept 45 pitches 3½ acres,
level grass 🛒✖ (café) 🔌⊗🔀♿ farm animals centre, animal petting area, fair rides, bouncy
castle, pony and tractor rides £10.00-23.00 greenacresfarm@btconnect.com
www.greenacresfarmpark.co.uk

HOLYHEAD, Anglesey   **Map B3**
EC Tues MD Fri, Sat *Terminus of ferries from Ireland. Main town of Holy Island linked to Anglesey
by causeway and bridge.* SEE harbour, Holyhead mountains, South Stack Lighthouse
🅸 Stena Line, Terminal 1 ☎ (01407) 762622 ✖ Beach 2m S at Trearddur Bay ☎ (01407) 860332

Bagnol Caravan Park, Trearddur Bay LL65 2AZ ☎ (01407) 860223 OS map 114/260780 3m S of
Holyhead off B4545 (Four Mile Bridge) at Bagnol Open Mar-Oct 200 pitches (150 static)–must
book (caravans) 28 acres, level grass 🗑🔌🚿⊗∅⊗🚜 beach access

Cliff Hotel Holiday Centre, Trearddur Bay LL65 2UR ☎ (01407) 860634 OS map 114/260777 2m
SE of Holyhead on B4545 (Trearddur Bay) Open Easter-Oct 15 250 pitches (100 static)
🛒✖🛎🗑🔌🚿⊗

Gwynfair Caravan Site, Ravenspoint Road, Trearddur Bay LL65 7AX ☎ (01407) 860289 OS map
114/256777 1½m S of Holyhead off B4545 (Trearddur Bay) Open Mar-Oct 100 pitches 12 acres
level grass ✖🗑🔌🚿⊗∅🔀🚻🚜

Valley of the Rocks Caravan and Camping Park, Porthdafarch Road, Trearddur Bay LL65 2LD
☎ (01407) 765787 OS map 114/236807 1½m S of Holyhead off B4545 (Trearddur Bay)
Open Mar 14-Oct 25 95 pitches Grass, level, sheltered 🛒🔌🗑🚿∅🚜 lic club

For other sites near Holyhead see Rhosneigr and Valley

Help us make CAMPING CARAVANNING BRITAIN better known to site operators – and thereby
more informative – by showing them your copy when booking in.

LLANBEDR, Gwynedd   **Map C5**
SEE Cwm Bychan lake and Roman steps, Shell Island, Harlech Castle 3m N
✘ Plas Cafe 3m N at Harlech ☎ (01766) 780204
Hendy Touring Caravan Park, Hendy LL45 2LT ☎ (01341) 247263 OS map 124/587258 ½m S of
   Llanbedr on left of A496 (Barmouth) Open May-Sept 20 pitches–no tents Level grass ▣❷❸
See also Dyffryn Ardudwy

LLANBEDROG, Gwynedd   **Map C5**
Village on E shore of Lleyn peninsula sheltered by promontory SEE views of St Tudwals island
✘ Ship Inn, Pig St ☎ (01758) 740270
Bolmynydd Touring Camping Park, Refail LL53 7NP ☎ (01758) 740511 OS map 123/324313 1m
   S of Llanbedrog off A499 (Abersoch) Open Easter-Sept 48 pitches 2 acres gently sloping grass,
   sheltered ▨(mobile) ▣❷❷❸❷❸❹
Crugan Caravan Park LL53 7NL ☎ (01758) 712045 OS map 123/335324 ½m N of Llanbedrog on
   left of A499 (Pwllheli) Open Mar-Oct–no tents or motor caravans 120 pitches (100 static) ▣❸❹
   beach access
Refail Touring Camping Park, Refail LL53 7NP ☎ (01758) 740511 Fax (01758) 740510 OS map
   123/327319 In Llanbedrog near junct of A499 and B4413 (Aberdaron) Open Easter-Sept
   33 pitches 3 acres level/sloping grass and hard standing, sheltered ▣❷❷❸❷❸❹❹ shop
   calls £9.50-£11.00* *refail.llanbedrog@ukonline.co.uk*

LLANBEDRGOCH–see Benllech

LLANBERIS, Gwynedd   **Map D4**
SEE Snowdon (rack railway to summit), Dolbadarn Castle, lake Padarn, Bryn Bras castle 3m NW
✘ Lake View Hotel at Tan-Y-Pant ☎ (01286) 870422
Snowdon View Caravan-Camping Park, Brynrefail LL55 3PD ☎ (01286) 870349 OS map
   114/562633 1m NW of Llanberis off A4086 (Caernarfon) on B4547 (Brynrefail) Open Mar-Oct
   436 pitches (174 static) ❷❷▣☐(indoor heated) ❹❹

LLANDRILLO, Denbighshire   **Map E5**
✘ Tyddyn Llan ☎ (01490) 440264
Hendwr Caravan Park LL21 0SN ☎ (01490) 440210 *Prop: J & B Hughes* OS map 125/035386
   1½m N of Llandrillo off B4401 (Corwen) near river Dee–signposted Open Apr-Oct 150 pitches
   (90 static) 4 acres level grass sheltered, some hard standings ❷▣❷❷❸❷❸❹❹❸ farm
   produce £14.00-£16.00 *www.hendwrcaravanpark.freeserve.co.uk*

LLANDUDNO, Conwy   **Map D3**
EC Wed SEE Rapallo House Museum, Haulfre Gardens, Happy Valley and Great Ormes Head NW
(by road or cabin lift)
ℹ Chapel St ☎ (01492) 876413
✘ St Tudno, North Par ☎ (01492) 574411
Penrhyn Hall Farm Caravan Park, Penrhyn Bay LL30 3EE ☎ (01492) 549207 OS map
   116/820815 2m E of Llandudno off B5115 (Colwyn Bay) Open Mar-Nov 161 pitches (151 static)
   7½ acres level/sloping grass and hard standings ▣❷❷❸❷❸❹

LLANDDULAS–see Colwyn Bay

FOLLOW THE COUNTRY CODE

Guard against all risk of fire. Fasten all gates.
Keep dogs under proper control. Keep to the
paths across farmland. Avoid damaging
fences, hedges and walls. Leave no litter.
Safeguard water supplies. Protect wildlife,
plants and trees. Go carefully on country
roads and be prepared for slow-moving
vehicles like tractors. Respect the life of the
countryside.

LLANGEFNI, Anglesey ✗ Tafarn Y Gors, Pentre Berw, Gaerwen ☎(01248) 422155 **Map C3**

Mornest Caravan Park, Pentre Berw, Gaerwen LL60 6HU ☎(01248) 421725 OS map 114/475720 2m S of Llangefni on A5 (Menai Bridge-Holyhead) near junct 7 of A55–signposted Open Mar-Nov 60 pitches (20 static) Level grass, sheltered ✗⌕🗓🔌🚿⊕✚⊡🅿 £10.00-£16.00

Trergof Caravan Park, Mona, Gwalchmai LL62 5EH ☎(01407) 720315 OS map 115/413744 2m SW of Llangefni off A5 (Menai Bridge-Holyhead) Open Mar-Oct 48 pitches 7 acres, level grass, sheltered ⓩ🔌🔗⊕

LLANGOLLEN, Denbighshire **Map F4**
EC Thurs *Small market town on S bank of river Dee best known as home of international music festival* SEE canal (by boat), Plas Newydd (home of `Ladies of Llangollen'), Dinas Bran Castle, Vale of Llangollen, Int. Eisteddfod (Jul)
🄸 Y Chapel, Castle St ☎(01978) 860828
✗ Hand, Bridge St ☎(01978) 860303

Ty Ucha Caravan Park, Maesmawr Road LL20 7PP ☎(01978) 860677 *Prop: K Prydderch* OS map 117/126/235425 1m E of Llangollen off A5 (Shrewsbury) Open Easter-Oct 40 pitches–no tents 4 acres level grass 🔌🔗⊕ £9.00

LLANRUG, Gwynedd **Map C4**
✗ Newborough Arms, Bontnewydd ☎(01286) 673126

Brynteg Holiday Park LL55 4RF ☎(01286) 871374 OS map 115/544625 1m SE of Llanrug off A4086 (Llanberis) near Bryn Bras Castle Open Mar-Nov 455 pitches (286 static) 35 acres, part sloping grass and hard standing ⓩ✗⌕❄🗓🔌🔗⊕∅🖥(indoor heated) ⊕⤵⊡🔗⚹ club, fishing, boating

Challoner Camping Caravan Park, Erw Hywel LL55 2AJ *Secluded park with views of Snowdon* ☎(01286) 672985 OS map 114/525635 ½m W of Llanrug on right of A4086 (Caernarfon) Open Easter-Oct 35 pitches 2 acres level grass, sheltered ⓩ🔌🔗⊕🔗

Plas Gwyn Caravan Park LL55 2AQ ☎(01286) 672619 *Prop: Hampton family* OS map 115/525635 ½m W of Llanrug on left of A4086 (Caernarfon) Open Mar-Oct 37 pitches 3½ acres, grass, level and sloping, hard standing, sheltered ⓩ🗓🔌🔗⊕∅🔌🔗 B&B £6.00-£15.00 (most cards) info@plasgwyn.co.uk www.plasgwyn.co.uk

Twll Clawdd Camping Caravan Park LL55 2AZ ☎(01286) 672838 OS map 115/530635 ½m W of Llanrug on A4086 (Caernarfon-Llanberis) Open Mar-Oct 40 pitches Level/sloping grass, sheltered 🗓🔌🔗⊕∅

Tyn-y-Coed Farm LL55 2AQ ☎(01286) 673565 OS map 115/523630 ½m W of Llanrug on left of A4086 (Caernarfon) Open Easter-Sept 80 pitches must book peak periods 🗓🔗🔌

LLANRWST, Conwy **Map D4**
EC Thurs MD Tues SEE parish church, Gwydir Park, Gwydir Castle, and gardens, Bodnant gardens 6m N on A470
✗ Meadowsweet ☎(01492) 642111

Bodnant Caravan Park, Nebo Road LL26 0SD ☎(01492) 640248 OS map 116/807608 ½m S of Llanrwst on B5427 (Nebo) Open Mar-Oct 54 pitches Grass, level, part sheltered 🔌🔗⊕∅❸🔗(2) £9.00-£14.50 (Mastercard/Visa) ermin@bodnant-caravan-park.co.uk www.bodnant-caravan-park.co.uk

Glyn Farm Caravans, Trefriw LL27 0RZ ☎(01492) 640442 OS map 115781632 1½m NNW of Llanrwst off B5106 (Conwy) Open Mar-Oct 28 pitches Level grass and hard standings, sheltered 🗓🔌🔗🔗

Maenan Abbey Caravan Park LL26 0VL ☎(01492) 640630 OS map 115/790658 3m N of Llanrwst on A470 (Llandudno) Open Mar-Oct 105 pitches (72 static) 3 acres level grass sheltered 🗓🔌🔗∅🔌(£60) 🔗

Plas Meirion Caravan Park, Gower Road, Trefriw LL27 0RZ ☎(01492) 640247 OS map 115/783631 1½m NW of Llanrwst on B5106 (Conwy) Open Mar-Oct 31 pitches (26 static) 2 acres level grass, sheltered 🗓🔌⊕❖🔗 mountain bike hire

LLANWNDA, Gwynedd **Map C4**
SEE Caernarfon Bay W
✗ The Harp Inn, Llandwrog ☎(01286) 831071 Open 12-2/6.30-8.30 (exc Mon)

Tyn Rhos Farm LL54 5UH ☎(01286) 830362 *Prop: WC & MJ Evans* OS map 115/455581 2m W of Llanwnda off Saron-Llanfaglan road Open Mar-Oct 20 pitches 2½ acres, level grass, sheltered 🔌⊕ farm shop £10.00-£12.00

White Tower Caravan Park, Llandwrog LL54 5UH ☎(01286) 830649 *Prop: Lee Warp* OS map 115/458582 2m W of Llanwnda on Saron-Llandwrog road Open Mar-Nov 106 pitches (54 static) 7 acres level grass and hard standings ⌕🗓🔌🔗⊕∅🖥⊕⤵⊡🔌🔗♿ fishing, lic club £10.00-£16.00 (all cards) whitetower@supanet.com www.whitetower.supanet.com

LLANDWROG–see Llanwnda

LLIGWY BAY–see Moelfre

LLWYNGWRIL, Gwynedd   **Map D6**
✗ Greenfield 4m S at Tywyn ✆ (01654) 710354

Borthwen Farm LL37 2JT ✆ (01341) 250322 OS map 124/588099 ½m W of Llwyngwril via level
crossing and road to station Open Mar-Oct 100 pitches (80 static) 8 acres level grass 🐕🕭
access to stony beach

MENAI BRIDGE, Anglesey   **Map C3**
EC Wed MD Mon *Gateway to Anglesey, `The Mother of Wales', where Telford's 1000ft long
suspension bridge crosses the Straits* SEE Telford suspension bridge, St Tysilio church
✗ Ty Gwyn Hotel, 8 Holyhead Rd, Llanfairpwll ✆ (01248) 715599 Open Mon-Sat 12-2/6-9,
Sun all day

Fron Caravan and Camping, Llanfairpwll, Brynsiencyn LL61 6TX *Wales Tourist Board 5 Star*
✆ (01248) 430310 *Prop: George, Dith & Mark Geldard* OS map 114/472668 6m SW of Menai
Bridge off A55 (Holyhead) on right of A4080 (Newborough) Open Apr-Sept 70 pitches 5 acres
level grass and hard standings, sheltered 🛁🗋🐕🕭⊕Ø⊡🕭⌇🕭 £13.50
mail@froncaravanpark.co.uk www.froncaravanpark.co.uk

Plas Coch Caravan Park, Llanedwen LL61 6EJ ✆ (01248) 714346 OS map 114/512683 3m SW
of Menai Bridge off A5 (Holyhead) on left of A4080 (Brynciencyn) Open Mar-Oct 300 pitches
(200 static) 200 acres, level grass, sheltered ♀🕭Ø🕭⊡ slipway

MOELFRE, Anglesey   **Map C3**
✗ Pilot Boat Inn, Dulas ✆ (01248) 410205 Open 12-Sep

Capel Elen Caravan Park, Lligwy Beach LL70 9PQ ✆ (01248) 410670 *Prop: John & Linda Howl*
OS map 114/484874 3m N of Moelfre off A5025 (Amlwch) at Brynrefail on Lligwy Beach road
Open Mar-Oct 75 pitches (45 static)–no tents 7 acres, gentle slope/level grass and hard
standings 🗋🐕🕭⊕Ø🏠 £15.00-£17.50 *john@capelelen.co.uk www.capelelen.co.uk*

Melin Rhos Farm, Lligwy Bay, Dulas LL70 9HQ ✆ (01248) 410213/410345 OS map 114/493864
½m S of Moelfre off A5025 (Benllech) Open Easter-Oct 80 pitches 6 acres level grass and hard
standings, sheltered 🐕⊕Ø🐕⌇

Tyddyn Isaf Caravan Park, Lligwy Bay LL70 9PQ ✆ (01248) 410203 OS map 114/480849 ½m W
of Moelfre off A5025 (Amlwch) Open Mar-Oct 80 pitches (50 static) Grass and hard standing,
sheltered 🛁✗♀⊶⏢🗋🐕Ø🕭⌇⊡🕭(£5/wk) 🚌 lic club, private path to beach

Tyn Rhos, Lligwy LL72 8NL ✆ (01248) 852417 *Prop: RG & SV Roberts* OS map 114/509865 2m
W of Moelfre on Lligwy road Open Mar-Oct 140 pitches (72 static) 16 acres, sloping
🗋🐕🕭⊕Ø🕭🕭🚌🕭🏠⌇ £8.00-£20.00 (Mastercard/Visa) *robert@bodafonpark.fsnet.co.uk*
www.bodafonpark.fsnet.co.uk

MOLD, Flintshire   **Map F3**
EC Thurs MD Wed, Sat *Busy market town in Alyn valley* SEE Theatr Clwyd, most advanced arts
complex in Wales, parish church, Daniel Owen centre art gallery and museum
🗓 Museum & Art Gallery, Earl Rd ✆ (01352) 759331
✗ The Antelope Hotel, Denbigh Rd, Rhydymwyn ✆ (01352) 741247

Fron Farm, Hendre CH7 5QW ✆ (01352) 741217 *Prop: DH & C Roberts* OS map 116/193678 4m
NW of Mold on A541 (Denbigh) Open Apr-Oct 50 pitches Level/sloping grass 🐕🕭⊕Ø⌇🕭
£8.00-£10.00 *dylanceriroberts@btconnect.com www.fronfarmcaravanpark.co.uk*

MORFA BYCHAN–see Porthmadog

NEFYN, Gwynedd   **Map C4**
SEE St Mary's church (now maritime museum)
✗ Lion Hotel, Tudweiliog, Pwllheli ☎ (01758) 770244 Open 12-2/6-9

Hirdre Fawr Farm, Edern LL53 8YY ☎ (01758) 720278 *Prop: AP Williams* OS map 123/249381
   3m SW of Nefyn on right of B4417 (Tudweiliog) Open May-Oct 20 pitches 3 acres level grass,
   sheltered ◻️𝄖⊕ fridge & freezer facilities £8.00-£12.00 *ann@hirdre-fawr.fsnet.co.uk*

NEWBOROUGH, Anglesey   **Map C3**
SEE Newborough Warren, Llanddwyn island
✗ Bay 6m NW at Rhosneigr ☎ (01407) 810332

Awelfryn Caravan Park LL61 6SG ☎ (01248) 440230 OS map 114/425656 ¼m SW of
   Newborough off A4080 (Llanfairpwll) Open Easter-Sept 52 pitches 2 acres level grass 🅿️𝄖⊕

PENMAENMAWR, Conwy   **Map D3**
EC Wed ✗ Bunkers, Conwy Old Rd ☎ (01492) 62565 Open 10-Sep

Tyddyn Du Touring Park, Conwy Old Road LL34 6RE ☎ (01492) 622300 *Prop: P Watson-Jones*
   OS map 115/729770 1m E of Penmaenmawr off A55 (Conwy) near golf course Open Mar 22-Oct
   1–adults only 100 pitches Level grass, hard standings, sheltered ◻️🅿️𝄖⊕⊘& £14.00-£16.00
   (most cards) *www.tyddyndutouringpark.co.uk*

Woodlands Camping Park, Pendyffryn Hall LL34 6UF ☎ (01492) 623219 OS map 115/741776 1m
   NE of Penmaenmawr off A55 (Conwy) Open Mar-Oct–no adv booking, families and couples only
   120 pitches Level grass and hard standings, sheltered 🍴🔥◻️🅿️𝄖⊘◻️🅿️❖ lic club, woodland
   walks

PENRHYNDEUDRAETH, Gwynedd   **Map D4**
EC Thurs SEE Portmeirion 2m S, nature reserve 2m NE, Ffestiniog railway
✗ Royal Sportsman 2m W at Porthmadog ☎ (01766) 512015

Blaencefn Caravan Park LL48 6NA ☎ (01766) 770889 OS map 124/620398 1m NE of
   Penrhyndeudraeth on left of A487 (Maentwrog) Open Easter-Oct 25 pitches 3 acres level grass
   No showers

Bwlchbryn Caravan Park LL48 6RY ☎ (01766) 771474 OS map 124/613395 ½m W of
   Penrhyndeudraeth off A487 (Porthmadog) Open Mar-Oct 49 pitches (42 static) ◻️𝄖🛒

PENTRAETH–see Benllech

PONTLLYFNI–see Clynnog Fawr

PONTRUG–see Caernarfon

PORTHMADOG, Gwynedd   **Map D4**
EC Wed MD Fri *Victorian town with extensive sandy beaches and safe port and harbour* SEE
Ffestiniog railway, Black Rock Sands, maritime museum
ℹ️ High St ☎ (01766) 512981 ✗ Royal Sportsman, High St ☎ (01766) 512015

Black Rock Camping Site, Morfa Bychan LL49 9LD ☎ (01766) 513919 OS map 124/531373 3m
   SW of Porthmadog at Black Rock Sands Open Mar-Oct 140 pitches Level grass ◻️🅿️𝄖⊕↩️
   www.bhhpa.org.uk

Cardigan View Park, Morfa Bychan LL49 9YA ☎ (01766) 512032 OS map 124/542372 3m W of
   Porthmadog at Black Rock Sands Open Easter-Oct 224 pitches (192 static) Grass and hard
   standings, level ◻️🅿️⊕⊘◻️(indoor) ⊕🛒

Garreg Goch Caravan Park, Morfa Bychan LL49 9YD ☎ (01766) 512210 OS map 124/543372 2m
   SW of Porthmadog off Morfa Bychan road Open Mar-Oct 85 pitches (61 static) Level grass and
   hard standings 🛒🅿️𝄖⊕⊘↩️◻️🛒

Greenacres Holiday Park, Black Rock Sands, Morfa Bychan LL49 9YB ☎ (01766) 512781 OS
   map 124/546372 2m SW of Porthmadog on Morfa Bychan road Open Mar-Oct 852 pitches
   (800 static) Level grass and hard standings 🛒🍴🔥◻️𝄖⊕⊘◻️↩️❖ clubhouse, bowling
   (most cards)

Gwyndy Caravan Park, Black Rock Sands, Morfa Bychan LL49 9YB ☎ (01766) 512047 OS map
   124/543371 2m SW of Porthmadog off Beach road at Morfa Bychan Open Mar 8-Oct 31
   60 pitches (44 static) Level hard standing sheltered 🛒◻️🅿️𝄖⊕⊘🅿️🛒🏠 super pitches
   £15.00-£16.50 *martin.gwyndycp@btinternet.com*

Tyddyn-Adi Camping, Morfa Bychan LL49 9YW ☎ (01766) 512933 OS map 124/540377 3m SW
   of Porthmadog off road to Black Rock Sands via Morfa Bychan Open Mar-Oct 200 pitches
   28 acres, level grass, sheltered 🛒◻️🅿️𝄖⊕↩️◻️ mini golf, games room

Tyddyn Llwyn Caravan Camping Park, Black Rock Rd LL49 9UR ☎ (01766) 512205 OS map
   124/561384 ½m SW of Porthmadog on right of Morfa Bychan road–signposted Open Mar-Oct
   206 pitches (53 static) Level/sloping grass and hard standings 🛒✗🍴◻️🅿️𝄖⊕⊘↩️◻️ games
   room

PRESTATYN, Denbighshire   **Map E3**
EC Thurs MD Tues, Fri *Popular resort with 3 beaches, once N terminus of Offa's Dyke* SEE Offa's Dyke Path
✗ Cross Foxes, Meliden Rd ☎ (01745) 854984

Nant Mill Farm LL19 9LY ☎ (01745) 852360 *Prop: K & BL Rowley* OS map 116/074831 ½m E of Prestatyn on A548 (Flint) Open Easter-Oct 150 pitches 5 acres level/sloping grass, sheltered 🔲🔳🔘🔲🔲🔲🔲🔲 £11.00-£16.00 *nantmilltouring@aol.com www.zeropointfive.co.uk/nant_mill*

Presthaven Sands Holiday Park, Shore Road, Gronant LL19 9TT ☎ (01745) 856471 OS map 116/095835 2m E of Prestatyn on A548 (Flint) Open March-Nov–no tents 1,200 pitches (1,100 static) 🔲✗🔲🔲🔲🔲🔲🔲 (out & indoor, heated) 🔲🔲🔲 hairdressing, sauna, solarium, disco, amusements, lic and family clubs, entertainment (all cards) *www.havenholidays.com*

Talacre Beach Caravan Park, Talacre CH8 9RD ☎ (01745) 852612/889616 OS map 116/182840 4m E of Prestatyn off A548 (Chester) Open Mar-Jan 620 pitches (600 static) Grass and hard standing 🔲✗🔲🔲🔲🔲🔲 (heated indoor) 🔲🔲 lic club, barbecue, bowling green, tennis

Tan y Don Caravan Park, Victoria Road LL19 7UT ☎ (01745) 853749/852563 OS map 116/055830 1m W of Prestatyn on A548 (Rhyl) Open Mar-Jan–must book peak periods 72 pitches (65 static) Level grass and hard standings 🔲🔲🔲🔲🔲🔲🔲🔲🔲 (Mastercard/Visa)

PWLLHELI, Gwynedd   **Map C4**
EC Thurs MD Wed SEE Gimblet Rock
🔲 Myn y Don, Station Sq ☎ (01758) 613000 ✗ The Seahaven, West End Pier ☎ (01758) 612572

Abererch Sands Holiday Centre, Abererch LL53 6PJ ☎ (01758) 612327 Fax (01758) 701556 OS map 123/403358 2m NE of Pwllheli off A497 (Criccieth) on Abererch Halt road Open Mar-Oct 155 pitches (85 static) Level grass 🔲🔲🔲🔲🔲🔲🔲 (heated) 🔲🔲 (most cards) *enquiries@abererch-sands.co.uk www.abererch-sands.co.uk*

Gimblet Rock Caravan Park, South Beach LL53 5AY ☎ (01758) 712043 OS map 123/383346 ½m S of Pwllheli on South Beach road Open Mar-Oct 140 pitches (115 static) 🔲🔲🔲🔲🔲🔲🔲🔲

Hendra Caravan Park, Efailnewydd LL53 8TN ☎ (01758) 712793 OS map 123/350359 2½m W of Pwllheli off A497 (Nefyn) on B4415 (Aberdaron) Open Mar-Oct 150 pitches (120 static) Hard standings 🔲🔲🔲

See also Llanbedrog

RHOSNEIGR, Anglesey   **Map C3**
EC Wed
✗ Minstrel Lodge, Station Rd ☎ (01407) 810970

Bodfan Farm LL64 5XA ☎ (01407) 810563 OS map 114/342736 ½m N of Rhosneigr on A4080 (Llanfaelog) near school Open Apr-Sept 60 pitches Level/sloping grass 🔲🔲🔲 freezer pack service, fishing, swimming, horse riding

Plas Caravan Park, Llanfaelog LL63 5TU ☎ (01407) 810234 OS map 114/331738 1m NE of Rhosneigr off A4080 near station Open Mar 15-Oct 31 72 pitches (55 static) 6 acres level grass and hard standings 🔲🔲🔲🔲 (most cards)

Shoreside, Tyn Morfa Farm LL64 5QX ☎ (01407) 810279 *Prop: AJ Carnall* OS map 114/324737 ½m NE of Rhosneigr off A4080 (Llanfaelog) opp golf club Open Easter-Oct 110 pitches 20 acres, level/gentle slope 🔲🔲🔲🔲🔲 (indoor) 🔲 pony trekking £5.00-£15.00 inc hot water *shoreside@amserve.net www.shoresidecamping.co.uk*

RHYL, Denbighshire   **Map E3**
EC Thurs MD Wed, Sat SEE Royal Floral Hall, Marine Lake Leisure Park, children's village
🔲 Town Hall, Wellington Rd ☎ (01745) 355068
✗ White Horse, Bedford St ☎ (01745) 334927

Edwards Leisure Parks, Gaingc Rd, Towyn LL22 9HY ☎ (01745) 342322 OS map 116/976797 2m SW of Rhyl on A547 (Abergele) Open Mar 21-Oct 2–no tents, no adv booking 432 pitches (400 static) 17 acres hard standings, level 🔲🔲🔲🔲🔲🔲🔲

Marine Holiday Park, Cefndy Road LL18 2HG ☎ (01745) 345194 OS map 116/003802 1m SW of Rhyl off A525 (Rhuddlan) near Marine Lake Open Apr-Oct 491 pitches (466 static) 🔲✗🔲🔲🔲 🔲🔲🔲 (indoor heated) 🔲🔲

Sunnyvale Holiday Park (Camping Club), Foryd LL18 5AS ☎ (01745) 339401 OS map 116/992807 1m W of Rhyl on right of A548 (Abergele) at rear of Ferry Hotel Open Apr 1-Sept 28 120 pitches 5 acres, level grass 🔲🔲

See also Dyserth and Rhuddlan

Capel Elen Caravan Park
Lligwy Bay, Dulas, Isle of Anglesey, LL70 9PQ
Tel/Fax: 01248 410670

See listing under Moelfre

RUABON, Wrexham   **Map F4**
SEE monuments in church, Wat's Dyke, Ruabon Mountain
✗ Wynnstay Arms ✆ (01978) 822187

James Caravan Park LL14 6DW ✆ (01978) 820148 *Prop: Mr John Bailey* OS map 117/302434
   ½m S of Ruabon on A539 (Llangollen) near junct with A483 Open all year 40 pitches, some hard
   standings 8 acres, part level 🅿🅰⊕⅄ £10.00 *ray@carastay.demon.co.uk*

RUTHIN, Denbighshire   **Map F4**
EC Thurs MD Tues, Thurs, Fri *Historic town and one most picturesque in Wales on ridge above*
Vale of Clwyd SEE St Peter's church (panelled roof), castle (now hotel)
🅸 Craft Centre, Park Rd ✆ (01824) 703992
✗ Castle and Myddleton Arms, St Peter's Sq ✆ (01824) 707215

Parc Farm Caravan Park, Llanarmon Yn Ial CH7 4QW ✆ (01824) 780666/780700 OS map
   116/198556 6½m E of Ruthin off A494 (Mold) on B5430 (Wrecsam) Open Apt-Oct 220 pitches
   (200 static) Level/sloping grass, sheltered 🅿🅱🅰⊕⅄🔲🅿 clubhouse

Three Pigeons Inn, Craigfechan LL15 2EU ✆ (01824) 703178 OS map 116/147545 3m SE of
   Ruthin off A494 (Mold) on B5429 (Craigfechan) Open Mar-Oct 14 pitches ✗⅄⊕⅄❀

ST ASAPH, Denbighshire   **Map E3**
EC Thurs SEE Rhuddlan castle NW, Denbigh castle S ✗ Red Lion ✆ (01745) 582716

Eryl Hall, Lower Denbigh Road LL17 0EW ✆ (01745) 582255 OS map 116/035729 1m S of St
   Asaph on right of B5381 Open Mar 21-Oct 7—no tents 301 pitches (240 static) Level grass and
   hard standings 🅿🅱🅰⊕⅄🅾⊗⅄❀

TALYBONT—see Dyffryn Ardudwy

TOWYN—see Abergele and Rhyl

TREARDDUR BAY—see Holyhead

TREFRIW—see Llanrwst

TYWYN, Gwynedd   **Map D6**
EC Wed *Seaside resort overlooking Cardigan Bay, with 6km of beach* SEE church, railway
museum, Tallylyn narrow gauge railway
🅸 High St ✆ (01654) 710070 ✗ Corbett Arms, Corbett Sq ✆ (01654) 710264

Pall Mall Farm LL36 9RU ✆ (01654) 710384 OS map 135/595013 ½m NE of Tywyn on A493
   (Dolgellau) Open Easter-Sept 135 pitches Level grass 🅿🅰

Pant y Neuadd Caravan Park, Aberdovey Road LL36 9HW ✆ (01654) 711393 OS map
   124/597003 ½m SE of Tywyn on A493 (Aberdovey) Open Mar-Oct—no tents 86 pitches (70
   static) Level grass, sheltered 🅱🅿🅰⊕⅄✔🔲🏠

Tynllwyn Caravan Camping Park, Bryncrug LL36 9RD ✆ (01654) 710370 OS map 135/615023
   2m N of Tywyn off A493 (Dolgellau) on B4405 (Abergynolwyn) via Bryncrug 7 acres, level grass
   Open Apr-Oct 104 pitches (56 static) 7 acres, level grass 🅱🅿🅰⊕⅄✔

Waenfach Caravan Park, Llanegryn LL36 9SB ✆ (01654) 710375 OS map 135/591050 3m N of
   Tywyn on A493 (Dolgellau) Open Apr-Oct 60 pitches (40 static) Level/sloping grass, sheltered
   🅱🅿🅰⊕⅄

Woodlands Holiday Park, Bryncrug LL36 9UH ✆ (01654) 710471 OS map 135/618035 4m NE of
   Tywyn off A493 (Dolgellau) on B4405 (Abergynolwyn) Open Apr-Oct—must book peak periods, no
   tents 142 pitches (122 static) Hard standings 🅱✗⅄🅱🅿🅰⊕⅄🔲(outdoor heated) ⊕✔🔲🔳

Ynysmaengwyn Park LL36 9RY ✆ (01654) 710684 *Prop: Tywyn Town Council* OS map
   135/601021 1m NE of Tywyn on left of A493 (Dolgellau) in grounds of former manor house
   Open Apr-Oct 195 pitches (115 static) 8 acres, mainly level grass 🅱🅱🅿🅰⊕✔ fishing,
   adventure park, secure bicycle lock-up £10.00-£17.00 *rita@ynysy.co.uk www.ynysy.co.uk*

VALLEY, Anglesey   **Map C3**
✗ Beach 4m W at Trearddur Bay ✆ (01407) 860332

Penrhyn Bay Touring Park, Llanfwrog LL65 4YG ✆ (01407) 730496 OS map 114/284847 5m N of
   Valley off A5025 (Amlwch) Open Easter-Oct 150 pitches (90 static) Grass, level, open
   🅱⊁🅱🅿🅰🅾🔲(indoor heated) ⊕✔🅿🔳

Pen-y-Bont Farm, Four Mile Bridge LL65 3EY ✆ (01407) 740481 OS map 114/282787 1m SW of
   Valley on B4545 (Trearddur Bay) Open Whit-Oct 30 pitches 3½ acres level grass *No showers*
   £5.00-£6.00

Sandy Beach Touring Caravan Park, Llanfwrog LL65 4YH ✆ (01407) 730302 OS map
   114/286848 4m N of Valley off A5025 (Amlwch) Open Mar-Oct 124 pitches (84 static)
   Level/sloping grass, sheltered 🅱✗🔲🅱🅿🅰⊕⅄✔🅿🔳

Silver Bay Caravan Park, Pentre Gwyddel, Rhoscolyn LL65 2RZ ✆ (01407) 860374 OS map
   114/287753 3m S of Valley off B4545 (Trearddur Bay) Open Easter-Jan—must book peak periods
   176 pitches (160 static) Sloping grass, sheltered 🅱🅱🅰🅾✔❀🔳 lic club, private beach

Plassey Touring Caravan and Leisure Park, Wrecsam

WAUNFAWR, Ceredigion   Map C4
Village 3m SE of Caernarfon

✗ Snowdonia Park Brew Pub, Snowdonia Park ✆ (01286) 650218 Open 11-8.30

Bedw Arian Camping, Cynefin, Betws Garmon LL54 7YR *Peaceful adults-only site, ideal for walkers and bird-watching* ✆ (01286) 650707 *Prop: Paul & Anita Rhys* OS map 115/545567 2m SE Waunfawr on right of A4085 (Caernarfon-Beddgelert) Open Mar-Oct 13 pitches–adults only part sloping grass, sheltered ▯✪▣ fishing, garden site, Snowdon path 1½ miles £8.00-£10.00 bedwariancamping@hotmail.com www.wishsong.co.uk/camping

Bryn Gloch Caravan Camping Park, Betws Garmon LL54 7YY ✆ (01286) 650216 *Prop: E Jones* OS map 115/535575 1m SE of Waunfawr on right of A4085 (Beddgelert) Open all year 180 pitches 12 acres level grass and hard standings, sheltered ▯▯▯▯▯▯▯▯▯▯▯▯▯ fishing, mini-golf, mother and baby room £14.00-£16.00 (most cards) eurig@bryngloch.co.uk www.bryngloch.co.uk

Tyn-yr-Onnen Farm LL55 4AX ✆ (01286) 650281 Fax (01286) 650043 OS map 115/535590 ½m W of Waunfawr centre on A4085–signposted Open Whitsun-Oct 50 pitches 3½ acres grass, gentle slope, sheltered ▯▯▯▯▯▯▯▯▯▯▯ hill walks, fishing £6.00-£10.00* (Delta/Mastercard/Switch/Visa) tom.griffith1@btopenworld.com www.tyn-yr-onnen.co.uk

WRECSAM (Wrexham)   Map F4
EC Wed MD Mon *Most important industrial town in Wales on N bank of river Clywedog* SEE St Giles church, Erddig mansion 1m S, Industiral Heritage Centre at Bersham 2m SW
🛈 Lambpit St ✆ (01978) 292015
✗ Cross Lanes 3m SE on A525 ✆ (01978) 780555

Cae Adar Farm, Bwlchgwyn LL11 5UE ✆ (01978) 757385 OS map 117/268529 4m NW of Wrecsam off A525 (Ruthin) Open May-Oct 12 pitches 2 acres, level grass, sheltered ▯▯▯

Plassey Touring Caravan and Leisure Park, Eyton LL13 0SP ✆ (01978) 780277 Fax (01978) 780019 *Prop: John Brookshaw* OS map 117/351450 2m S of Wrecsam off A483 (Oswestry) on B5426 (Bangor-on-Dee)–signposted Open Mar-Nov 120 pitches Level grass and hard standing, sheltered ▯▯▯▯▯▯▯▯▯▯▯(heated indoor May-S ▯▯▯▯▯▯▯(1) ▯ 9 hole golf, pitch and putt, table tennis, badminton, sauna, craft workshops £11.00-£19.50 inc elect (Mastercard/Visa) enquiries@theplassey.co.uk www.theplassey.co.uk

The Racecourse, Bangor on Dee LL13 0DA ✆ (01978) 781009 OS map 117/385448 4m SE of Wrecsam off A525 (Whitchurch) Open Mar 22-Nov 1 120 pitches 5 acres, level/sloping grass and hard standing, part sheltered ▯▯▯▯▯ (NB Campers may have to move on race days but they are given free entry to races if they do so) (Mastercard/Visa)

Help us make CAMPING CARAVANNING BRITAIN better known to site operators – and thereby more informative – by showing them your copy when booking in.

Covering two-thirds of the principality, Central and South Wales is made up of a great variety of unspoiled scenery.

Along the border with England is a moorland plateau drained by the beautiful Lake Vyrnwy and trout-rich rivers flowing through deep valleys, the most attractive of which is the Dovey. The area is crossed in an east-west direction by only two roads but many routes for walkers. In the centre is a district of hills and high moors dotted with isolated lime-washed farmhouses, cloaked on the east near New Radnor by a shady forest and occupied by four towns, none industrial: Presteigne, the once fashionable spas of Llandrindod and Bulith Wells and Rhayader, gateway to the scenic Elan Valley and its series of reservoirs. Offa's Dyke Path passes near Knighton and Kington on a line which links the Severn and the Dee. In the south is the wild Brecon Beacons National Park encircling the Black Mountains, with the Usk and its tributaries cutting through its wooded gorges. The south-eastern ramparts of Wales, the Black Mountains march east to the Wye, south to Crickhowell and northeast as far as Talgarth. Hay on Wye, half in England, is one gateway to the park, Abergavenny another.

An uninteresting coastline on the Severn Estuary is backed by lofty hills mined by coal in the northwest and a pastoral landscape near the English border in the east – at its most inviting in the Wye Valley above Chepstow. A waymarked scenic drive through the Ebbw Forest starts at Cwmcarn near Newport.

West is mountainous coalmining country in the north, pastoral and picturesque in the south. Popular seaside resorts like Porthcawl and Penarth alternate with industrial towns like Barry and Bridgend. West of Swansea is the wholly unspoiled Gower Peninsula ending

in limestone cliffs.

The extreme west of Wales is noted for the sandy beaches of Cardigan, Aberporth and New Quay and the high cliffs between Aberystwyth and Aberaeron backed by bare moorland dotted with Iron Age hill forts, rough uplands and steepsided valleys. Local fishermen still use coracles of ancient design on the main waterway, the Teifi. A narrow-gauge railway operates between Aberystwyth and Devil's Bridge, a popular beauty spot.

The remote and thinly populated southwest corner of Wales has a romantic coastline of wild cliffs and windswept headlands, a mountainous north and a fertile and sunlit south. The Pembrokeshire Coast Path starts at St Dogmaels near Cardigan and follows the bay and inlets round to Amroth near Saundersfoot.

Campsites are well distributed along the south and west coasts, with the greatest concentrations around Saundersfoot, Laugharne, St David's and Pembroke in the south and Aberporth, Aberystwyth and Fishguard in the west. Inland campsites are most numerous around Narberth in the south, though there are two or more at each of the main centres in Powys. Coastal campsites are usually the best equipped.

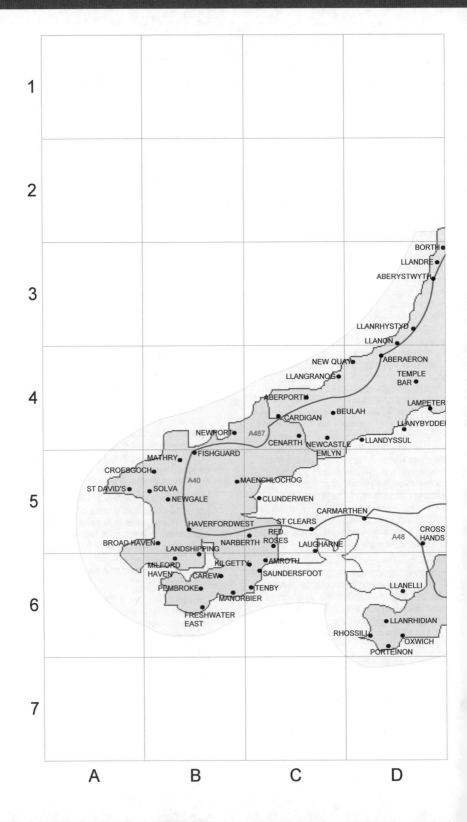

BORTH
LLANDRE
ABERYSTWYTH
LLANRHYSTYD
LLANON
NEW QUAY
ABERAERON
LLANGRANOG
TEMPLE BAR
ABERPORTH
LAMPETER
CARDIGAN
BEULAH
NEWPORT
A487
LLANYBYDDER
CENARTH
NEWCASTLE
LLANDYSSUL
MATHRY
FISHGUARD
EMLYN
CROESGOCH
A40
MAENCHLOCHOG
ST DAVID'S
SOLVA
NEWGALE
CLUNDERWEN
CARMARTHEN
HAVERFORDWEST
ST CLEARS
CROSS HANDS
RED ROSES
A48
BROAD HAVEN
NARBERTH
LAUGHARNE
LANDSHIPPING
MILFORD HAVEN
KILGETTY
AMROTH
CAREW
SAUNDERSFOOT
LLANELLI
PEMBROKE
TENBY
MANORBIER
LLANRHIDIAN
FRESHWATER EAST
RHOSSILI
OXWICH
PORTEINON

1
2
3
4
5
6
7

A   B   C   D

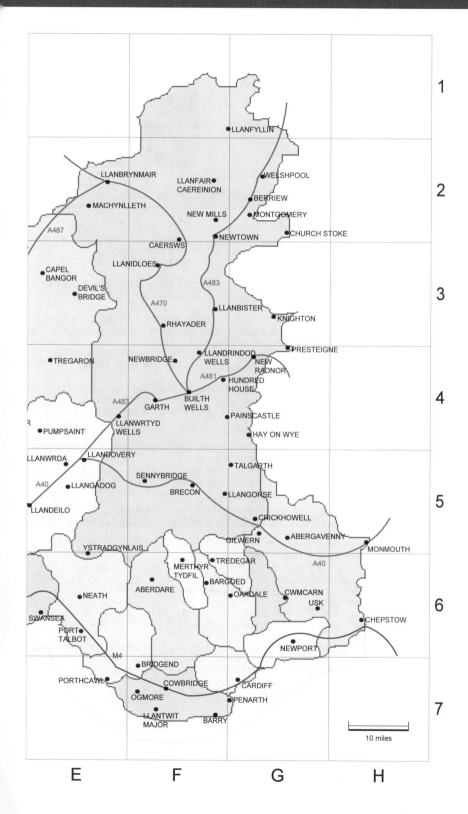

1

2

3

4

5

6

7

LLANFYLLIN

LLANBRYNMAIR
LLANFAIR
CAEREINION
WELSHPOOL
BERRIEW
MACHYNLLETH
NEW MILLS
MONTGOMERY
A487
NEWTOWN
CHURCH STOKE
CAERSWS
CAPEL
BANGOR
LLANIDLOES
A483
DEVIL'S
BRIDGE
A470
LLANBISTER
RHAYADER
KNIGHTON
TREGARON
NEWBRIDGE
LLANDRINDOD
WELLS
PRESTEIGNE
NEW
RADNOR
A481
HUNDRED
HOUSE
A483
GARTH
BUILTH
WELLS
PAINSCASTLE
PUMPSAINT
LLANWRTYD
WELLS
HAY ON WYE
LLANWRDA
LLANDOVERY
TALGARTH
A40
LLANGADOG
SENNYBRIDGE
LLANDEILO
BRECON
LLANGORSE
CRICKHOWELL
GILWERN
ABERGAVENNY
YSTRADGYNLAIS
MONMOUTH
TREDEGAR
A40
MERTHYR
TYDFIL
BARGOED
NEATH
ABERDARE
OAKDALE
CWMCARN
USK
SWANSEA
CHEPSTOW
PORT
TALBOT
NEWPORT
M4
BRIDGEND
PORTHCAWL
COWBRIDGE
CARDIFF
OGMORE
PENARTH
LLANTWIT
MAJOR
BARRY

10 miles

E F G H

Wernddu Golf Club
Old Ross Road
Abergavenny
Monmouthshire
NP7 8NG

Tel: 01873 856223
Fax: 01873 852177
Email:
info@wernddu-golf-club.co.uk

ABERAERON, Ceredigion   Map D4
EC Thurs *Early 19c harbour town at mouth of river Aeron* SEE Georgian houses and harbour
🏨The Quay ✆(01545) 570602
✖Feathers Royal ✆(01545) 570214

Aeron Coast Caravan Park, North Rd SA46 0JF ✆(01545) 570349 OS map 146/470634 In
   Aberaeron on A487 (Aberystwyth) Open Mar-Oct 200 pitches (150 static) Level grass
   🔌♀🔋🛢🌀⊕∅▭⊕↵🗆⅊ tennis £10.50-£14.00 (Mastercard/Visa/Switch/Delta)
   aeroncoastcaravanpark@aberaeron

Brynarion Caravan Park, Cross Inn SY23 5NA ✆(01974) 272231 OS map 146/540646 5m ENE
   of Aberaeron off A487 (Aberystwyth) on B4577 (Cross Inn) Open Mar-Oct 40 pitches (30 static)
   🔌🛢🌀♀⅊ Grass, level, sheltered

Hafod Brynog Caravan Park, Ystrad Aeron, Felinfach SA48 8AE ✆(01570) 470084 OS map
   146/524565 6m W of Aberaeron on A482 (Lampeter) Open Apr-Oct 60 pitches (30 static)
   Level/sloping grass, sheltered 🛢🔋🌀⊕∅↵🖌 £7.00-£10.00

Llanina Touring Park, Llanarth SA47 0NP ✆(01545) 580947 OS map 146/421574 4m SW of
   Aberaeron on A487 (Aberystwth-Cardigan) by Llanina garage Open Apr-Oct 45 pitches
   🔌♀🔋🌀⊕ £6.50 (min)*

Wide Horizons Caravan and Chalet Park SA46 0ET ✆(01545) 570043 OS map 135/440615 ¾m
   S of Aberaeron on right of A487 (Cardigan) by sea Open Mar-Oct 100 pitches (90 static) Grass
   and hard standings, sloping ♀🛢🔋🌀⊕∅⊕↵🗆⅊🍴 games room *www.widehorizons.com*

ABERCRAF–see Ystragynlais

ABERDARE, Rhondda   Map F6
✖Glandover Arms, Gadlys Rd (B4275) ✆(01685) 872923

Dare Valley Country Park, Rhondda-Cynon-Taff CF44 7RG ✆(01685) 874672 OS map
   170/985026 ¼m SW of Aberdare off A4233 (Maerdy)–signposted Open Jan 2-Dec 23 35 pitches
   Level grass and hard standings ✖🔋⊕ serviced pitches

ABERGAVENNY, Monmouthshire   Map G5
EC Thurs MD Tues, Fri SEE Castle Museum, St Mary's church, Sugar loaf mountain 4m NW, White
Castle 5½m E via Llantilio Crosseny, Llanfihangel Court 5m
🏨Swan Meadow, Monmouth Rd ✆(01873) 857588
✖Malthouse, Newmarket Close ✆(01873) 877842

Pyscodlyn Farm, Brecon Road NP7 7ER ✆(01873) 853271 *Prop: Mary Davies* OS map
   161/266155 2m W of Abergavenny on A40 (Crickhowell) Open Apr-Oct 60 pitches Grass, level,
   part sheltered 🛢🔋🌀⊕⅊ £8.00-£12.00 *pyscodlyn.farm@virgin.net*
   www.pyscodlyncaravanpark.com

The Rising Sun, Pandy NP7 8DL ✆(01873) 890254 OS map 161/332213 5½m N of Abergavenny
   on A465 (Hereford) Open all year 20 pitches Grass, part sheltered ✖♀🔋🌀🛢∅⊕↵ dairy
   produce (Mastercard/Visa)

Wern-ddu Farm, Old Ross Rd NP7 8NG ✆(01873) 856223 *Prop: Messrs Watkins* OS map
   161/322156 1½m NE of Abergavenny off A465 (Hereford) on right of B4521 (Skenfrith)
   Open Mar-Oct 20 pitches Level grass, sheltered ♀🔋⊕∅🌀⊕ golf range and golf course
   £7.00-£10.00 (Mastercard/Visa) *www.wernddu-golf-club.co.uk*

For other sites near Abergavenny see Crickhowell and Gilwern

For more up-to-date information, and for links to camping websites, visit our site at:
www.butford.co.uk/camping

SITE DIRECTIONS
The distance and direction of a campsite is given from the centre of the town under which it appears.

ABERPORTH, Ceredigion   **Map C4**
EC Wed SEE natural harbour, Tresaith beach 2m E ✗ Morlan Hotel ℰ (01239) 810611

Brynawelon Touring Caravan Camping Park, Sarnau SA44 6RE ℰ (01239) 654584 *Prop: Mr & Mrs Cowton* OS map 145/322508 4m E of Aberporth off B4333 (Newcastle Emlyn) and A487 (Aberaeron) opposite Sarnau chapel Open Apr-Oct 40 pitches, hardstanding and fully serviced Grass, level, open 🗑🔌🚿⊕😊↙⌂🛒📶 games room £10.00-£16.50 *info@brynaweloncp.co.uk www.brynaweloncp.co.uk*

Caerfelin Caravan Park SA43 2BY ℰ (01239) 810540 OS map 145/257511 ¼m SW of Aberporth centre off B4333 (Cardigan) Open Mar-Oct 105 pitches (91 static) Grass, sheltered 🗑🔌🚿⊘😊🛒📶 short walk to beach

Helyg Fach Farm SA43 2EB ℰ (01239) 810317 OS map 145/269513 ½m E of Aberporth off B4333 (Newcastle Emlyn) Open Easter-Oct 290 pitches (200 static) 8 acres, level 🛒🍴🍷🗑🔌🚿 lic clubs

Llety Caravan Park, Tresaith SA43 2ED ℰ (01239) 810354 OS map 145/273515 1m E of Aberporth in Tresaith near beach Open Mar-Oct 150 pitches 12 acres level/sloping grass 🗑🔌🚿⊕🛒

Manorafon Caravan Park, Penbryn, Sarnau SA44 6QH ℰ (01239) 810564 Fax (01239) 810564 OS map 145/300520 2½m E of Aberporth off B4333 (Newcastle Emlyn) and A487 (Aberaeron) near Penbryn beach Open Easter-Oct 30 pitches Grass, part level, sheltered 🔌🚿⊕⊘📶

Pilbach Caravan and Camping Park, Bettws Evan, Rhydlewis SA44 5RT ℰ (01239) 851434 OS map 145/308477 4m SE of Aberporth off B4333 (Newcastle Emlyn) Open Mar-Oct–must book peak periods 135 pitches (70 static) Grass, part sloping, sheltered 🛒🍷↙🗑🔌🚿⊕⊘🖵(outdoor, heated) ⊕↙🛒📶 bar snacks, clubhouse, games room (Mastercard/Visa)

Talywerydd Caravan Park, Penbryn, Sarnau SA44 6QY ℰ (01239) 810322 OS map 145/298508 4m NE of Aberporth off A487 (Cardigan-Aberaeron) Open Feb-Oct 40 pitches 4 acres, grass and hard standing, part sloping 🛒✗(lic) ↙🗑🔌🚿⊕⊘🖵⊕↙⌂ 9 hole pitch and putt (Mastercard/Visa)

Treddafydd Farm, Sarnau SA44 6PZ ℰ (01239) 654551 OS map 145/305512 4½m NE of Aberporth off B4333/A487 (Aberaeron) and Penbryn beach road on left at Sarnau church Open Apr-Oct 40 pitches Grass, sloping, part sheltered 🗑🔌🚿📶 dry ice

See also Llangranog

ABERYSTWYTH, Ceredigion   **Map D3**
EC Wed MD Mon *Seaside resort, university town and admin centre for Cardigan Bay coast* SEE Nat lib of Wales, Vale of Rheidol narrow gauge railway to Devil's Bridge
ℹ Terrace Rd ℰ (01970) 612125 ✗ Castle, South Rd ℰ (01970) 612188

Aberystwyth Holiday Village, Penparcau Road SY23 1TH *Nearest site to town centre* ℰ (01970) 624211 OS map 135/586810 ¼m S of Aberystwyth on A487 (Aberaeron) Open Mar-Oct–no adv booking 302 pitches (150 static) 30 acres level grass and hard standings, sheltered 🛒✗🗑🔌🚿⊕⊘🖵(indoor) ↙⌂🛒📶 snack bar, lic club, fishing

Bryncarnedd Dairy Farm SY23 3DG ℰ (01970) 615271 OS map 135/603892 1m N of Aberystwyth on B4572 (Clarach Bay) Open all year 100 pitches Grass, level, part sheltered 🛒 dairy produce

Glan-y-Mor Leisure Park, Clarach North Beach SY23 3DT ℰ (01970) 828900 OS map 135/585841 2½m N of Aberystwyth off A487 (Machynlleth) Open Mar-Nov 235 pitches (160 static) 24 acres level grass 🛒✗🍷↙🏹🗑🔌🚿⊕⊘🖵⊕↙🛒🎣 ten-pin bowling (Mastercard/Visa/Switch)

Midfield Caravan Park, Southgate SY23 4DX *Peaceful park with fine views of surrounding area* ℰ (01970) 612542 OS map 135/596796 1½m ESE of Aberystwyth on A4120 (Devil's Bridge) Open Easter-Oct 132 pitches (57 static) Grass, part level, part sheltered 🔌🚿⊕⊘↙

Morfa Bychan Holiday Park, Llanfarian SY23 4QQ ℰ (01970) 617254 OS map 135/565771 4m S of Aberystwyth off A487 (Aberaeron) by beach Open Mar-Jan 264 pitches (214 static) Grass, sloping, open 🛒🍷🗑🔌🚿⊕⊘🖵(heated) ⊕↙⌂🛒 club (Mastercard/Visa/Switch)

Ocean View Caravan Park, North Beach, Clarach Bay SY23 3DT *Small family-run site on land overlooking the sea* ℰ (01970) 828425 Fax (01970) 820215 OS map 135/591842 2½m N of Aberystwyth off A487 (Machynlleth) on B4572 (Clarach) near beach Open Mar-Oct 74 pitches (50 static) Grass and hard standings, level 🛒🗑🔌🚿⊕⊘🖵🛒📶🏨 £10.50-£13.50* *alan@grover10.freeserve.co.uk www.oceanviewholidays.com*

Rheidol Caravan Park, Felin Rhiw Arthen, Capel Bangor SY23 4EL ℰ (01970) 880863 OS map 135/650802 4m E of Aberystwyth off A44 (Rhayader) at Capel Bangor near S bank of river Rheidol Open Mar-Oct 33 pitches Level/sloping grass and hard standings, sheltered 🗑🔌⊘↙📶 horse riding, narrow gauge railway

For other sites near Aberystwyth see Borth and Llandre

AMROTH, Pembs   Map C6
Modest seaside resort fronted by sandy beaches
✘ Malin House 2m W at Saundersfoot ☎ (01834) 812344

Meadow House Holiday Parc SA67 8NS ☎ (01834) 812438 OS map 158/150065 ¾m W of
   Amroth centre on Saundersfoot road Open Whitsun-Sept–no adv bkg (families only, no m/cycles)
   220 pitches (150 static) Level grass, sheltered 🎫🎫🎫🎫🎫(indoor) 🎫 leisure centre
   (Mastercard/Visa)

Village Touring and Caravan Park, Summerhill SA67 8NS ☎ (01834) 811051 OS map 158/155075
   1m NW of Amroth centre at Summerhill Open Mar-Oct 42 pitches (22 static) Level/gently sloping
   grass 🎫🎫🎫🎫(Spring BH, Jul-Aug) 🎫

See also Kilgetty

ANGLE–see Pembroke

BARGOED, Caerphilly   Map F6
✘ Tregenna 5m NW at Merthyr Tydfyl ☎ (01685) 723627

Parc Cwm Darran, Cwm Llwydrew Farm, Deri CF81 9NR ☎ (01443) 875557 OS map 171/113037
   3m NW of Bargoed off A469 (Rhymney) Open Apr 1-Sep 30 30 pitches–booking advisable
   3 acres part level, grass in country park 🎫🎫🎫🎫🎫 3 lakes, waymarked walks, adventure
   playground, cycle track, BMX track and picnic sites, fishing £5.00-£10.00*

BARRY, Vale of Glamorgan   Map F7
EC Wed *Harbour town from which coal used to be exported, now lively resort and shopping centre*
SEE castle ruins, zoo, Porthkerry country park, Dyffryn House
🎫 Barry Island (The Triangle, Paget Rd) ☎ (01446) 747171
✘ Mount Sorrel, Porthkerry Rd ☎ (01446) 740069

Fontygary Park, Rhoose CF6 9ZT ☎ (01446) 710386 OS map 170/051660 5m W of Barry off
   B4265 (St Athan) Open Mar-Oct–no tents 484 pitches (430 static) Level grass and hard
   standings 🎫🎫🎫🎫🎫🎫🎫🎫🎫(heated) tennis, fishing, fitness suite, games room

Vale Touring Caravan Park, Port Road West CF62 3BT ☎ (01446) 719311 OS map 170/079679
   1½m W of Barry on A4226 (Cardiff Airport) Open Apr-Dec 33 pitches, level grass £8.50-£9.50
   🎫🎫🎫🎫🎫🎫

BERRIEW, Powys   Map G2
✘ Royal Oak 5m NE at Welshpool ☎ (01938) 572217

Maes yr Afon Caravan Park, Berriew SY21 8QB ☎ (01686) 640587 OS map 136/161022 2m
   WNW of Berriew on B4390 (New Mills) near river Rhiw Open mid Mar-late Oct 96 pitches (76
   static) Grass, level, sheltered 🎫🎫🎫🎫🎫🎫🎫🎫 fishing

BORTH, Ceredigion   Map D3
Holiday village on Cardigan coast
🎫 Cambrian Terrace ☎ (01970) 871174
✘ Friendship, High St ☎ (01970) 871213

Cambrian Coast Caravan Park, Ynslas SY24 5JU *Seaside park with top-grade facilities* ☎ (01970)
   871233 OS map 135/620933 1m N of Borth on left of B4353 (Tre'r-ddol) near level crossing
   Open Mar-Oct 175 pitches (125 static) 12 acres level grass 🎫🎫🎫🎫🎫🎫🎫🎫🎫🎫(indoor)
   🎫🎫🎫🎫 lic club, access to blue flag beach (Mastercard/Visa/Switch/Euro)

Glanlerry Camping and Caravan Park SY24 5LU ☎ (01970) 871413 *Prop: RP Richards* OS map
   135/617886 ½m SE of Borth on B4353 (Llandre) Open Apr-Oct 100 pitches Grass, level,
   sheltered 🎫🎫🎫🎫🎫🎫🎫 £10.00-£14.00 (all major cards) www.glanlerrycaravanpark.co.uk

Mill House Caravan Park, Dolybont SY24 5LX ☎ (01970) 871481 OS map 135/623880 1m SE of
   Borth off B4353 (Llandre) on Dol-y-Bont road Open Easter-Sept 40 pitches (15 static) Grass,
   level, sheltered 🎫🎫🎫🎫 fishing

Ty Craig Holiday Park, Llancynfelyn SY20 8PU ☎ (01970) 832339 OS map 135/643922 4m NE of
   Borth on B4353 (Machynlleth) Open Mar-Oct 75 pitches (30 static) Grass, level, part open
   🎫🎫🎫🎫🎫🎫🎫🎫🎫🎫

Ty Mawr Caravan Camping Park, Ynyslas SY24 5LB *Quiet secluded park close to sea* ☎ (01970)
   871327 *Prop: PG & CC Beech* OS map 135/630927 3m NE of Borth on right of B4353
   (Machynlleth) Open Easter-Sept 72 pitches (51 static) Level grass, sheltered
   🎫🎫🎫🎫🎫🎫🎫🎫 £9.00-£12.00

COMMENTS
We would be pleased to hear your comments about the sites featured in this guide or your
suggestions for future editions. Comments and suggestions may be emailed to ccb@butford.co.uk.
Alternatively, write to The Editor, CCB, Butford Technical Publishing Ltd at the address given at the
front of the book.

Redlands Touring Caravan & Camping Park, Broad Haven

> ## STEEP HILLS
>
> Steep hills between Little and Broad Heaven make the route impassable for towed caravans.

BRECON, Powys   Map F5
EC Wed MD Tues, Fri *Cathedral town on ridge above confluence of 3 rivers and popular touring centre for Brecon Beacons national park* SEE Cathedral, castle ruins, county museum, Welsh Borderers regimental museum (Zulu wars), whisky distillery
🅘Cattle market Car Park ☎(01874) 622485
✗The Barn at Brynch, Brynch ☎(01874) 623480 Open 12-2.30/6-9.30 (closed Mon Nov-Mar)

Bishops Meadow Caravan Park, Hay Road LD3 9SW ☎(01874) 610000 Fax (01874) 614922 OS map 160/056300 1m NE of Brecon on B4602-A470 (Hay on Wye) Open Mar-Oct 80 pitches Grass, level, sheltered, some hard standings 🛒✗🅡🗑🛒🗷🕀🗷🖾🔌🛒🖾 (all cards) enquiries@bishops-meadow.co.uk

Brynich Caravan Park LD3 7SH *Family park in Brecon foothills* ☎(01874) 623325 *Prop: CR, AM & M Jones & C Maggs* OS map 160/069278 1m E of Brecon on A470 (Builth Wells) near junction with A40 (Abergavenny) Open Mar 28-Oct 28 130 pitches Grass and hard standings, level, open 🛒✗🏹🅡🗑🛒🗷🕀🗷🕀🔌🛒🖾🖾 baby room, indoor play barn £13.00-£18.00 (Mastercard/Visa/Delta/Switch) holidays@brynich.co.uk www.brynich.co.uk

Pencelli Castle Caravan Camping Park LD3 7LX *Immaculate site in Brecon Beacons* ☎(01874) 665451 Fax (01874) 665452 OS map 161/095250 3m SE of Brecon off A40 (Abergavenny) on B4558 (Talybont) Open all year 80 pitches 10 acres level grass and hard standings, sheltered 🛒🅡🗑🛒🗷🕀🗷🕀🔌🛒🖾🖾 £6.00-£14.00* (most cards) pencelli.castle@virgin.net www.pencelli-castle.co.uk

Royal Oak Inn, Pencelli LD3 7LX ☎(01874) 86621 OS map 161/094250 3m SE of Brecon off A40 (Abergavenny) on B4558 (Talybont) Open all year 30 pitches ¾ acre mainly level, hard standings ✗♀ fishing, boating, canoeing
See also Llangorse

BROAD HAVEN, Pembs   Map B5
EC Wed
✗The Castle, Grove Place, Little Haven ☎(01437) 781445 Open 12-2/6-9

Broad Haven Caravan Park SA62 3JD ☎(01437) 781277 OS map 157/864141 ½m N of Broad Haven on B4341 (Haverfordwest)–approach from east Open Mar-Oct 210 pitches (175 static) Grass, level, sheltered 🛒🏹🅡🗑🛒🗷🕀🗷🔌🖾

Cove Holiday Park, Howelston, Little Haven SA62 3UU ☎(01437) 781818 OS map 157/850120 2m S of Broad Haven off Talbenny road–approach from south Open Apr-Sept 100 pitches (60 static) Grass, part sloping 🗑🛒🗷🕀🗷🖾 freezer pack service (Mastercard/Visa)

Creampots Caravan and Camping Park SA62 3TU ☎(01437) 781776 OS map 157/882131 1½m E of Broad Haven off B4341 (Haverfordwest) at Broadway–signposted Milford Haven–2nd park 600 yds Open Apr-Oct 72 pitches Level grass and hard standing, part sheltered 🅡🗑🛒🗷🕀🗷🖾🖾 £9.00-£12.00* (all major cards) www.creampots.co.uk

Hasguard Cross Caravan Park, Hasguard Cross SA62 3SL ☎(01437) 781443 Fax (01437) 781443 OS map 157/850107 2m S of Broad Haven on B4327 (Dale)–approach from east Open all year–must book 60 pitches (35 static) Grass, level, sheltered 🛒✗♀🅡🗑🛒🗷🕀🗷🖾🖾 bar meals £15.00-£18.00 enquiries@hasguardcross.co.uk www.hasguardcross.co.uk

Redlands Touring Caravan & Camping Park, Little Haven SA62 3SJ ☎(01437) 781300 *Prop: Trevor & Jenny Flight* OS map 157/853109 1½ mile from Little Haven on B4327 (Dale)–approach from east Open Mar-Dec–booking advisable peak periods 60 pitches Grass and hard standings, tent field level 🛒🅡🗑🛒🗷🕀🗷🕀 deep freezers £10.00-£14.00 info@redlandscamping.co.uk www.redlandstouring.co.uk

South Cockett Touring Park, Broadway, Little Haven SA62 3TU ☎(01437) 781296 Fax (01437) 781296 OS map 157/878134 2m E of Broad Haven off B4341 (Haverfordwest) at Broadway Open Easter-Oct 73 pitches 6 acres level grass, part sheltered 🛒🅡🗑🛒🗷🕀🗷🕀🛒🖾🏠 £7.00-£10.50* wjames01@farming.co.uk www.southcockett.co.uk

GLANLERRY Caravan Park

Mr & Mrs R P Richards
Glanlerry Caravan Park
Borth
Ceredigion
SY24 5LU
Tel: 01970 871413

See listing under Borth

BRONLLYS–see Talgarth

BUILTH WELLS, Powys   Map F4
EC Wed MD Mon SEE Wyeside arts complex, Telford's iron bridge, riverside park, Wye Valley walk
🄸 Groe Car Park ✆(01982) 553307
✗ Caer Beris Manor ½m W off A483S ✆(01982) 552601

Llewellyn Leisure Park, Cilmery LD2 3NU ✆(01982) 552838 OS map 147/010515 2m W of Builth Wells on A483 (Llandovery) adj inn Open all year 56 pitches Level/sloping grass and hard standing 🛉🚻🅿️⊕↩🚿 snooker, wet weather functions room, B&B (Mastercard/Visa)

Prince Llewellyn Inn, Cilmery LD2 3NU ✆(01982) 552694 OS map 147/002515 2m W of Builth Wells on A483 (Llanwrtyd Wells) Open all year 18 pitches ✗🍴↩⊘↩ fishing

See also Hundred House

BURRY PORT–see Llanelli

CAPEL BANGOR–see Aberystwyth

CARDIFF, Cardiff   Map G7
EC Wed SEE national museum, Llandaff cathedral, St Fagan's castle (folk museum)
🄸 The Old Library ✆(02920) 227281
✗ Lincoln, Cathedral Rd ✆(01222) 395558

Pontcanna Caravan Park, Pontcanna Fields, Sophia Close, Llandaff CF1 9JL *Landscaped site near city centre* ✆(01222) 398362 OS map 171/171773 1m NW of Cardiff centre on right of A4119 (Llantrisant) near river Taff Open all year 43 pitches–no tents 2 acres level, hard standings 🛉🗲🚻⊘🚻

CARDIGAN, Ceredigion   Map C4
EC Wed MD Mon, Sat SEE Mwnt viewpoint 6m N, castle and wildlife park at Cilgerran 4m SE
🄸 Theatr Mwldan, Bath House Rd ✆(01239) 613230
✗ Boncath Inn, Boncath ✆(01239) 841241

Blaenwaun Farm, Mwnt SA43 1QF ✆(01239) 612165 OS map 145/204513 4m N of Cardigan off A487 (Aberaeron) at Penparc on Traeth-y-Mwnt road Open Easter-Sept 80 pitches 10 acres, level/gentle slope 🛉🗲🚻⊘⊘↩ fishing

Brongwyn Mawr Farm, Penparc SA43 1SA ✆(01239) 613644 *Prop: Anna Giles* OS map 145/209487 2½m NE of Cardigan off A487 (Aberystwyth) at Penparc on Ferwig/Mwnt road Open Apr-Oct 20 pitches 2 acres, level grass, sheltered 🗲🚻⊕⊘🖵(heated, indoor) ⊕↩🅿🏠 sauna, steam room and gym £8.50-£11.00* (Mastercard/Visa/Delta/Switch) *enquiries@cardiganholidays.co.uk www.cardiganholidays.co.uk*

Penralltllyn Farm, Cilgerran SA43 2PR ✆(01239) 682350 *Prop: CH & EM James* OS map 145/215413 4m SE of Cardigan off A484 (Newcastle Emlyn) at Llechryd on Boncath road Open Mar-Oct 20 pitches 1 acre, mainly level grass 🗲 £5.00-£7.00* inc hook-up

CAREW, Pembs   Map B6
SEE castle, high cross, tidal mill, museum, Cleddau valley
✘ Milton Manor 1m SW at Milton ✆ (01646) 651398

Hazelbrook Caravan Park, Sageston SA70 8SY ✆ (01646) 651351 *Prop: AP Sole* OS map
158/058033 ½m E of Carew centre on right of B4318 (Tenby) via Sageston Open Mar 1-Jan 9
120 pitches (50 static) 7½ acres level grass, hard standing ▣♪▣▣∅⊛∅↵ £8.00-£10.00
(Mastercard/Visa)

Milton Bridge Caravan Park, Milton SA70 8PH ✆ (01646) 651204 OS map 157/040032 1m SW of
Carew off A477 (Pembroke Dock) at Milton Brewery Inn Open Mar-Oct 38 pitches (23 static)
▣▣∅⊛∅⊙Ⓢ £10.00-£15.00

CARMARTHEN, Carmarthenshire   Map D5
EC Thurs MD Mon, Tues, Wed, F SEE St Peter's church, county museum, Roman amphitheatre,
Kidwelly castle 8m S
▣ Lammas St ✆ (01267) 231557
✘ Boars Head, Lammas St ✆ (01267) 222789

Sunrise Bay Caravan Park, Llanstephan SA33 5LP ✆ (01267) 241394 OS map 159/352106 9m
SSW of Carmarthen off B4312 (Llanstephan) Open Apr-Oct 60 pitches (52 static) Hard
standings, level grass, sheltered ✘▾↵▣▣∅⊛∅Ⓢ(heated) ⊛↵▢🏠& tennis, sailing,
fishing (most cards)

CENARTH, Ceredigion   Map C4
SEE falls, coracle fishing, museum, Teifi valley
✘ Three Horseshoes ✆ (01239) 710119

Cenarth Falls Holiday Park SA38 9JS ✆ (01239) 710345 *Prop: DH & YM Davies* OS map
145/265421 ¼m W of Cenarth on right of A484 (Cardigan) Open Mar-Jan–booking advisable
119 pitches (89 static) Hard standings, sheltered ✘▾▣▣∅⊛∅Ⓢ(indoor) ↵▢🏠& games
room, sauna, fitness suite £13.00-£23.00 (Mastercard/Visa) enquiries@cenarth-holipark.co.uk
www.cfhp.co.uk

CHURCH STOKE, Powys   Map G2
Village at junction of A489 (Newton-Craven Arms) and A490
✘ Dragon 3m NW at Montgomery ✆ (01686) 668359

Bacheldre Watermill SY15 6TE ✆ (01588) 620489 Fax (01557) 840105 OS map 137/243928 2m
SW of Church Stoke on A489 at Bacheldre–signposted Open all year 25 pitches 2 acres mainly
level grass, some hard standings, sheltered, in grounds of working watermill ▣▣⊛∅🏠 flat
rental £8.00 (min) info@bacheldremill.co.uk www.bacheldremill.co.uk

Daisy Bank Caravan Park SY15 6EB ✆ (01588) 620471 OS map 137/303929 2m SE of Church
Stoke on A489 (Craven Arms) Open all year–adults only 40 pitches Level/sloping grass and hard
standings, sheltered ▣∅⊛↵▣& serviced pitches, TV aerial hook-up, dog walk, putting green

Mellington Hall Caravan Park SY15 6HX ✆ (01588) 620853 OS map 137/259920 2m SW of
Church Stoke off A489 (Newtown) and B4385 (Bishops Castle)–best approach Open all year
180 pitches (136 static) Grass, level, sheltered ▣✘▾↵▣▣∅⊛∅▢🍴 £5.00-£18.00*
info@mellingtonhallcaravanpark.co.uk www.mellingtonhallcaravanpark.co.uk

CLUNDERWEN, Carmarthenshire   Map C5
✘ Plas Hyfryd 3m S at Narberth ✆ (01384) 860653

Derwenlas Caravan Park SA66 7SU ✆ (01437) 563504 OS map 158/122204 1m N of Clunderwen
on left of A478 (Cardigan) Open Mar-Oct 28 pitches Level grass, sheltered ▣▣∅⊛∅⊛↵
£5.00-£10.00

Llandyssilio Caravan and Camping Site, Llandyssilio SA66 7TT ✆ (01437) 563408 OS map
158/128233 ½m N of Clunderwen on left of A478 (Cardigan) Open Mar-Oct 58 pitches Level
grass, sheltered ▣∅🍴(£20) 🚐

CRICKHOWELL, Powys   Map G5
EC Wed MD Thurs *Country town in picturesque setting between Brecon Beacons and Black
Mountains* SEE church, old bridge, castle ruins, Vale of Usk
✘ The Dragon Hotel, High Street ✆ (01873) 810362 Open Mon-Sun 12-2/6.30-9 (closed Sun eve)

Bluebell Inn Caravan Park, Glangrwyne NP8 1EH ✆ (01873) 810247 OS map 161/240162 2m SE
of Crickhowell on A40 (Abergavenny) at rear of inn Open Apr-Oct 10 pitches Level grass
✘▾∅⊛∅ No showers, fishing (Mastercard/Visa/Switch)

Cwmdu Camping and Caravan Site, Cwmdu NP8 1RU ✆ (01874) 730441 OS map 161/176242
4m NW of Crickhowell on A479 (Talgarth) Open Mar-Oct 100 pitches Grass, level/sloping,
sheltered ▣♪▣∅⊛∅🍴

Riverside Caravan Park, New Road NP8 1AY ✆ (01873) 810397 *Prop: Ruth Price* OS map
161/215186 ¼m W of Crickhowell off A4077 (Gilwern) and A40 (Brecon) Open Mar-Oct–no
children under 18 yrs 65 pitches (20 static) Hard standings and grass, level, sheltered ▣∅⊛
£9.00-£18.00

CROESGOCH, Pembs   Map B5
Village short way inland of rocky Pembrokeshire coast SEE Baptist chapel, Porthgain harbour 2m NW, Abereiddi Bay 2m W, Pembrokeshire coast path
✗ Old Cross 3m W at St David's ☎ (01437) 720387

Prendergast Caravan and Camping Park, Cartlett Lodge, Trefin SA62 5AL ☎ (01348) 831368 OS map 157/842324 2m NE of Croesgoch off A487 (Fishguard) in Trefin village Open Apr-Sept 37 pitches Level/sloping grass, sheltered 🚻🅿️♿🐕🔌

Torbant Caravan Park SA62 5JN ☎ (01348) 831261 OS map 157/843308 1m NE of Croesgoch on right of A487 (Fishguard) Open Easter-Oct 7—must book peak periods 131 pitches (91 static) 🛇🅿️⌀⌗🐕🔌♿🏪

CROSS HANDS, E Ayrs   Map D5
✗ Cobblers, 3m NE at Llandybie ☎ (01269) 850540

Black Lion Caravan Camping Park, Black Lion Road, Gorslas SA14 6RU ☎ (01269) 845365 Fax (01269) 831882 OS map 159/575133 1m N of Cross Hands at Gorslas on Llandeilo road, near W terminus of M4 Open Apr-Oct 46 pitches 12 acres grass and hard standings 🏪✗🛒🛇🅿️⌀♿☕🔌♿🏪 £6.00-£20.00* inc elect baz@gorslas.com www.caravansite.com

Marlais Caravan Park, Carmel SA14 7UF ☎ (01269) 842093 OS map 159/585168 4m N of Cross Hands on A476 (Llandeilo) Open Mar-Oct 60 pitches 🏪✗🛒🛇🅿️⌀♿☕🔌♿🏪 fishing

CROSS INN (Dyfed)–see New Quay

CROSS INN (Powys)–see Llandovery

CWMCARN, Caerphilly   Map G6
SEE Cwmcarn Forest Drive, Caerleon Roman Fort 8m SE; Caerphilly Castle 10m SW
✗ Michael's 3m S at Risca ☎ (01633) 614300

Cwmcarn Forest Drive Campsite, Nantcarn Road NP11 7FA ☎ (01495) 272001 OS map 171/229937 1m E of Cwmcarn on forest drive Open all year 37 pitches 3 acres, part sloping, grass and hard standings 🛇🅿️♿🔌 mountain bike trail, forest drive with picnic BBQ spots £6.00-£10.00 (Mastercard/Visa) cwmcarn-vc@caerphilly.gov.uk/visiting www.caerphilly.gov.uk

DEVIL'S BRIDGE, Ceredigion   Map E3
SEE railway to Aberystwyth, nature trails
✗ Hafod Arms ☎ (01970) 890232

Erwbarfe Farm SY23 3JR ☎ (01970) 890665 OS map 135/748784 1m N of Devil's Bridge on A4120 (Ponterwyd) Open Mar-Oct 75 pitches (50 static) Grass, level, sheltered 🛇🅿️⌀♿🔌 (£40) 🏪 (all cards)

Woodlands Caravan Park SY23 3JW ☎ (01970) 890233 OS map 135/746773 ½m NE of Devil's Bridge on A4120 (Ponterwyd) Open Mar-Oct 122 pitches (100 static) Grass and hard standings, level, part sheltered 🏪✗🛒🔌🛇🅿️⌀♿⌀🔌♿🅿️⛺ fishing, bike shelter £8.50-£9.50 (Visa/Mastercard/Solo/Maestro) touring@woodlandsdevilsbridge.co.uk www.woodlandsdevilsbridge.co.uk

DINGESTOW–see Monmouth

FISHGUARD, Pembs   Map B5
EC Wed MD Thurs SEE Strumble Head lighthouse and cliffs 4m N
ℹ️ Hamilton St ☎ (01348) 873484
✗ Cartref, High St ☎ (01348) 872430

Fishguard Bay Caravan and Camping Park, Garn Gelli SA65 9ET ☎ (01348) 811415 *Prop: CN Harries* OS map 157/991388 3m E of Fishguard off A487 (Cardigan) Open Mar 1-Jan 10 100 pitches (50 static) Grass, level, part sheltered 🏪🥾🛇🅿️⌀♿⌀🔌♿🅿️🏪 pool table, games room £11.00-£14.00 (most cards) neil@fishguardbay.com www.fishguardbay.com

Gwaun Vale Caravan Park, Llanychaer SA65 9TA ☎ (01348) 874698 *Prop: E & M Harries* OS map 157/973357 1m SE of Fishguard on B4313 (Gwaun Vale) Open Mar-mid Jan 30 pitches 3 acres, terraced, grass, hard standings 🏪🛇🅿️⌀♿🔌♿🅿️ £10.00-£11.50* margaret.harries@talk21.com

FRESHWATER EAST, Isle of Wight   Map B6
SEE crescent beach, ruined Lamphey palace, Hodgeston church NE, Swanlake Bay E
✗ Freshwater Inn ☎ (01646) 672329

Upper Portclew Farm SA71 5LA ☎ (01646) 672112 OS map 158/013988 ½m W of Freshwater East off B4584 (Lamphey) Open May 1-Sept 10 40 pitches Level grass 🛇🅿️♿

❖ DOGS
Dogs are usually allowed but must be kept on a lead. Sometimes they have to be paid for.

GARTH, Powys   **Map F4**

✕ The New Inn, Newbridge-on-Wye ✆ (01591) 620572 Open all day

Irfon River Caravan Camping Park, Upper Chapel Road LD4 4BH ✆ (01591) 620310 OS map 147/959495 ¼m SE of Garth on B4519 (Upper Chapel) by river Open Easter-Oct 70 pitches (45 static) Grass and hard standings, part level, part open ▨🏕🛁⊕Ø🚻🔌 fly fishing £10.00

Riverside Caravan Park, Llangammarch Wells LD4 4BY ✆ (01591) 620629 OS map 147/935471 2m SW of Garth off A483 (Llanwrtyd Wells) Open Easter-Oct 30 pitches Grass and hard standings, level, part open 🅿▨🏕🛁⊕⌄🚻🔌 fishing

GILWERN, Monmouthshire   **Map G5**

SEE Brecon and Abergavenny canal, Heads of Valleys road

✕ Somerset Arms 4m SE at Abergavenny ✆ (01873) 852158

Aberbaiden Caravan Camping Park, The Lodge NP7 0EF ✆ (01873) 830157 OS map 161/259146 ½m E of Gilwern off A465 (Abergavenny) near junct with A4077 (Crickhowell) Open Apr-Oct 60 pitches 6 acres, grass and hard standings, part sloping, sheltered Ø⊕⌄ *No showers*

HAVERFORDWEST, Pembs   **Map B5**

EC Thurs MD Tues SEE Castle remains, county museum, St Mary's church (13c), priory ruins

ℹ Old Bridge ✆ (01437) 763110 ✕ Mariners, Mariners Sq ✆ (01437) 713353

Pelcomb Cross Farm, Pelcomb Cross SA62 6AB ✆ (01437) 710431 OS map 157/919179 3m NW of Haverfordwest on right of A487 (St David's) near Pelcomb Cross Inn Open Mar-Dec 30 pitches 2 acres grass mainly level secluded Ø⊕⌄

The Rising Sun Inn, Pelcomb Bridge, St David's Road SA62 6EA ✆ (01437) 765171 OS map 158/933171 1½m NW of Haverfordwest on A487 (St David's) Open Mar-Oct 30 pitches Grass, part level, part open 🅿▨🏕⊕Ø🚻🏠 bar meals, B&B

Scamford Caravan Park, Keeston SA62 6HN ✆ (01437) 710304 OS map 158/912198 4m NW of Haverfordwest off A487 (St David's) Open Apr-Oct 30 pitches (25 static) Grass, level, open ▨🏕🛁⊕ØⓈ⌄🚻 £8.50-£10.50 (most cards)

HAY ON WYE, Powys   **Map G4**

EC Tues MD Mon, Thurs *Historic border stronghold famous as the `town of books'* SEE bookshops, river Wye, Hay Bluff (4m S), 2220 ft cliff in Black Mountains

✕ Lions Corner House, Lion St ✆ (01497) 820175

Fforest Cwm Farm, Clyro HR3 5SG ✆ (01497) 820649 OS map 161/201438 1½m NW of Hay on Wye off B4351 (Clyro) and Paincastle road Open Mar 15-Oct 20 pitches Grass, sloping, sheltered Ø⊕Ø🚻🔌

Harbour Farm, Newchurch HR5 3QW ✆ (01544) 370248 OS map 148/188518 6m NNW of Hay on Wye off B4594 (Painscastle-Newchurch) on Glascwm road Open Easter-Oct 30 pitches 🔌 farm produce

Holly Bush Inn HR3 5PS ✆ (01544) 370371 OS map 161/195404 2m SW of Hay on Wye on B4350 (Brecon) by river Open Apr 12-Oct 31 22 pitches Grass, level, sheltered ✕🅿🏕⌄ slipway, bar meals

Radnors End HR3 5RS ✆ (01497) 820780 *Prop: Mrs Zena Davies* OS map 148/224431 ½m NW of Hay on Wye off B4351 (Clyro) by river Wye Open Mar-Oct 15 pitches 1 acre level grass, sheltered ▨🏕⊕Ø⌄ £9.00-£10.00 *radnorsend@hotmail.com www.radnorsend.hotmail.com*

HUNDRED HOUSE, Powys   **Map F4**

✕ Hundred House Inn on A481 ✆ (01982) 570231

Fforest Fields Camping Caravan Park LD1 5RT ✆ (01982) 570406 Fax (01982) 570444 OS map 147/098535 Near Hundred House on A481 Open Easter-Nov 60 pitches (all with mains elect) 7 acres level grass and hard standing 🅿▨🏕🛁Ø⊕⌄ £9.50 (min)* *office@fforestfields.co.uk www.fforestfields.co.uk*

KILGETTY, Pembs   **Map C6**
EC Wed MD Fri *Inland village N of Saundersfoot* SEE Carew Castle 6m SW
▣ Kingsmoor Common ☎ (01834) 814161
✗ Begelly Arms Hotel, New Rd, Begelly ☎ (01834) 813285

Croft Caravan Park, Reynalton SA68 0PE ☎ (01834) 860315 OS map 158/090089 2m MW of
Kilgetty off A477 (Pembroke) at Reynalton Open Easter-Nov 145 pitches (90 static) Grass, level,
part open ▨✗⚲⏦▢◨◪◉◯⌣▥ lic club £6.50-£21.00 (Mastercard/Visa)
enquiries@croftholidaypark.com www.croftholidaypark.com

Cross Park, Broadmoor SA68 0RS ☎ (01834) 811244 OS map 158/098060 2m SW of Kilgetty at
junction of A477 (Pembroke) and B4586 Open Apr-Oct 135 pitches (85 static) Sloping grass and
hard standings, sheltered ▨✗⚲⏦⚲◨◪◉◯◳◉⌣▢▥🏠 baths (Mastercard/Visa)

Heathfield Court Caravan Park, Pleasant Valley, Stepaside SA69 9BT ☎ (01834) 812310 OS map
158/142074 1m E of Kilgetty on Stepaside road Open Mar-Oct 150 pitches Grass, level
▨⚲◪◉▥🏠

Little Kings Park, Amroth, Ludchurch SA67 8PG ☎ (01834) 831330 *Prop: Mr & Mrs D Jones* OS
map 158/146092 2m NE of Kilgetty off A477 (St Clears) on Ludchurch road Open Easter–
Sept–must book 75 pitches Grass and hard standing, level, sheltered ▨✗⚲⏦◨◪◉
◪▥(heated indoor) ◉⌣▢▥🏠♿ £13.00-£20.00 (Mastercard/Visa/Switch/Maestro)
www.littlekings.co.uk

Masterland Farm Touring Caravan and Tent Park, Broadmoor SA68 0RH ☎ (01834) 813298 Fax
(01834) 814408 OS map 158/123071 ½m W of Kilgetty on Pembroke road at Cross Inn Open
Jul-Aug & bank holidays 38 pitches Level grass and hard standings, sheltered ▨✗⚲⏦◨◪◪
◉◪◯⌣▢▥🏠 baby room, games room £8.00-£16.00* *bonsermasterland@aol.com*
www.ukparks.co.uk/masterland

Ryelands Caravan Park, Ryelands Lane SA68 0VY ☎ (01834) 812369 *Prop: D Jenkins* OS map
158/125085 1m N of Kilgetty on right of Trewern road Open Easter-Oct 45 pitches 4 acres
level/sloping grass sheltered ◪◪◉⌣ £7.00-£10.00

Stone Pitt Caravan Park, Begelly SA68 0XE ☎ (01834) 811086 *Prop: Mr & Mrs P Morris* OS map
158/116077 1m NW of Kilgetty on left of A478 (Narberth-Tenby) Open Mar-Jan 55 pitches
Level/sloping grass and hard standing, sheltered ▢◪◪◉◪◯⌣▥🏠♿ £8.00-£14.00
(Mastercard/Maestro/Solo/Visa) *info@stonepitt.co.uk www.stonepitt.co.uk*

Windberry Top Farm, Begelly SA68 0XA ☎ (01834) 812394 OS map 158/115089 1m NW of
Kilgetty on A478 (Narberth) Open Whit-Sept 10 pitches ◪◪◉⌣

LAMPETER, Ceredigion   **Map D4**
EC Wed MD Alternate Tues SEE St David's college
✗ Black Lion Royal, High St ☎ (01570) 422172

Moorlands Caravan Park, Llangybi SA48 8NN ☎ (01570) 493543 OS map 146/598543 5m N of
Lampeter off A485 (Tregaron) at Llangybi Open Apr-Oct 102 pitches (48 static) 4½ acres level
grass and hard standings, sheltered ▨⚲▢◪◪◉◯◪⌣▥ lic club

Red Lion Caravan Park, Pencarreg SA40 9QG ☎ (01570) 480018 OS map 146/535451 3½m SW
of Lampeter on A485 (Llanybydder) Open Mar-Oct 20 pitches Grass, part sloping, sheltered
▨▢◪◪◉◪▥ (inc showers)

LANDSHIPPING, Pembs   **Map B6**
SEE river Cleddau
✗ Stanley Arms ☎ (01834) 891227

New Park Caravan Site SA67 8BG ☎ (01834) 891284 *Prop: Eric & Christine Jones* OS map
158/025112 1m E of Landshipping on Templeton road Open Spring Holiday-Sept 45 pitches
Grass, part sloping, hard standings ▢◪◪◉◪◯ £15.00

Quay House SA67 8BE ☎ (01834) 651262 OS map 158/010110 ½m S of Landshipping centre on
Landshipping Quay road Open Easter-Sept 10 pitches 1½ acres mainly level grass

LAUGHARNE, Carmarthenshire   **Map C5**
SEE grave and boathouse of Dylan Thomas, Pendine Sands 4m W
✗ Forge Motel 4m N at St Clears ☎ (01994) 230300

Ants Hill Caravan and Camping Park SA33 4QN ☎ (01994) 427293 OS map 159/300119 ¼m N
of Laugharne off A4066 (St Clears)–signposted Open Easter-Oct–must book peak periods–
120 pitches (60 static) Grass, level, part open ▨⚲⏦▢◪◪◉◪▥ (outdoor heated)
◉⌣◪❀ (Jul-Aug) ▥ first aid

LITTLE HAVEN–see Broad Haven

LLANARTH–see New Quay

LLANBISTER, Powys   Map F3
✗ Park Motel 7m S at Cross Gates ✆(01597) 851201
Brynithon Caravan Site, Llandrindod Road LD1 6TR ✆(01597) 840231 OS map 136/103743 ½m
  N of Llanbister on A483 (Newtown) Open Mar-Oct 25 pitches Hard standings, grass, level,
  sheltered ⌂⊛⌗⌂ rambling, fishing

LLANBRYNMAIR, Powys   Map E2
✗ Wynnstay Arms on A470 ✆(01650) 521431
Cringoed Caravan Camping Park SY19 7DR *Welcoming site in fine walking country* ✆(01650)
  521237 OS map 135/886012 2m S of Llanbrynmair off B4518 (Llanidloes) Open Mar-Jan
  70 pitches (30 static) 5 acres level grass and hard standings ⌂⌗⌂⊛⌀⊛⌀⌂⌗⌐⌂
  £8.00-£12.00

LLANDEUSANT–see Llandovery

LLANDOVERY, Carmarthenshire   Map E5
EC Thurs MD Fri SEE castle ruins, parish church, Usk reservoir 5m SE
▨ Heritage Centre ✆(01550) 720693
✗ White Hart, Stone St ✆(01550) 720152
Black Mountain Caravan and Camping Park, Llandeusant SA19 9YG ✆(01550) 740217 *Prop:
  David Rainsley & Sharon Brooker* OS map 160/772259 5m S of Llandovery via Myddfai–access
  by narrow mountain roads Open all year 34 pitches 5 acres level grass and hard standings
  ✗⌗⌂⌂⌂⌀⌂⌐⌂⌂ £8.00-£10.00 (Mastercard/Visa)
  davidandsharon@blackmountainholidays.co.uk www.blackmountainholidays.co.uk
Erwlon Caravan and Camping Park SA20 0RD ✆(01550) 720332 OS map 146/779344 ½m E of
  Llandovery on A40 (Brecon) Open all year 40 pitches 8 acres level grass and hard standings,
  sheltered ⌂⌗⌂⊛⌀⌂⌗⌂(£1.50/wk) ⌂⌂⌂ pony trekking, fishing £8.00-£10.00*

LLANDRE, Ceredigion   Map D3
✗ Felin Gyffin Watermill 1m S at Bow Street ✆(01970) 828852
Riverside Caravan Park SY24 5BY ✆(01970) 820070 OS map 135/631878 ¾m NNE of Llandre
  on Glanfraid road Open Mar-Oct 100 pitches (76 static) Grass, level, sheltered–some hard
  standings ⌂⌂⌗⌂⌂⊛⌀⌂⌗⌂⌂⌂⌂ fishing, dog walk

LLANDRINDOD WELLS, Powys   Map F4
EC Wed MD Fri SEE Spa, Castell Collen (Roman fort) 1m N, Elan Valley NW
▨ Old Town Hall, Memorial Gdns ✆(01597) 822600
✗ The Laughing Dog, Howey ✆(01597) 822406 Open 12-2/7-9
Dalmore Caravan Park, Howey LD1 5RG ✆(01597) 822483 *Prop: B Thorpe* OS map 147/034582
  2m S of Llandrindod Wells off A483 (Builth Wells) Open Mar-Oct–adults only 41 pitches
  (21 static) 2 acres grass and hard standings, part sheltered ⌗⌂⊛⌀⌂⌂⌂ £7.00-£10.00
Park Camping and Caravan Site, Cross Gates LD1 6RF ✆(01597) 851201 OS map 147/085650
  3m NE of Llandrindod Wells off A483 (Welshpool) on A44 (Rhayader) by Park Motel Open Mar-
  Oct 35 pitches Grass, level, sheltered ⌂✗⌂⌂⌗⌂⌂⌀⌂⌂⌐⌂⌂ games room
See also Hundred House

LLANELLI, Carmarthenshire   Map D6
EC Tues MD Thurs, Sat *Home of Welsh rugby, once prosperous harbour town* SEE Parc Howard
  museum (tinplate industry), Pembrey country park 7m W
✗ Diplomat 1m NE on A476 ✆(01554) 756156
Shoreline Leisure Home Park, Burry Port SA16 0HD ✆(01554) 832657 OS map 159/440005 4m
  W of Llanelli off A484 (Carmarthen) at Burry Port near sea–signposted Open Mar-Nov–must book,
  no tents 250 pitches (210 static) Level grass and hard standing ⌂✗⌗⌂⌂⌂⊛⌂⌂⌂⌂⌂
See also Cross Hands

LLANFAIR CAEREINION, Powys   Map F2
✗ Goat, High St (off A458) ✆(01938) 810428
Riverbend Caravan Park, Llangadfan SY21 0PP ✆(01938) 820356 OS map 125/013106 6½m W
  of Llanfair Caereinion off A458 (Mallwyd) Open Apr-Sept 140 pitches (88 static) 7½ acres level
  grass ⌂⌀⊛⌀⊛⌂⌂ fishing, putting green

LLANFYLLIN, Powys   Map F1
✘ New Inn Hotel, Llangynog ☎(01691) 860229
✘ Station Grill, Llansantffraid ☎(01691) 828478

Henstent Caravan Park, Llangynog SY10 0EP ☎(01691) 860479 *Prop: Mr & Mrs Morris* OS map
125/060260 6½m NW of Llanfyllin on B4391 (Llangynog) by River Tanat Open Mar-Oct
65 pitches (40 static) 4½ acres gently sloping grass 🗑🗑🗑🗑🗑 fishing £10.00-£13.00 inc
elect *henstent@mac.com www.homepage.mac.com/henstent*

Vyrnwy Caravan Park, Llansantffraid SY22 6SY ☎(01691) 828217 OS map 126/218203 5m E of
Llanfyllin off A490 (Welshpool) and B4393 (Four Crosses) Open Apr-Oct 220 pitches (180 static)
Grass, level, hard standing, part open 🗑🗑🗑🗑 £10.00

LLANGADOG, Carmarthenshire   Map E5
SEE Carn Goch Iron Age fort
✘ Cawdor Arms 6m SW at Llandeilo ☎(01558) 823500

Abermarlais Caravan Park SA19 9NG ☎(01550) 777868 OS map 146/160/695298 2m NW of
Llangadog on left of A40/A482 (Llandovery) Open Feb-Nov 88 pitches Grass and hard
standings, sheltered 🗑🗑🗑🗑🗑🗑🗑 £8.50-£9.00 (most cards)

Pont Aber Inn, Gwynfe SA19 9TA ☎(01550) 740202 OS map 160/238226 3m S of Llangadog on
left of A4069 (Brynamman) by river Open all year 30 pitches 1 acre mainly level grass, some
hard standings, sheltered 🗑🗑🗑🗑🗑🗑🗑🗑 fishing

LLANGAMMARCH WELLS–see Garth

LLANGORSE, Powys   Map F5
SEE Lake
✘ Red Lion ☎(01874) 845238

Lakeside Caravan Camping Park LD3 7TR ☎(01874) 658226 Fax (01874) 658430 OS map
161/135275 ½m SW of Llangorse off Llanfihangel road near Llangorse Lake Open Apr-Oct
122 pitches (82 static) Grass, level, sheltered 🗑🗑🗑🗑🗑🗑🗑🗑🗑🗑🗑🗑🗑🗑🗑🗑 clubhouse,
boat hire/launching, fishing, bike hire, pony trekking £7.50-£9.50* (Mastercard/Visa/Switch/Delta)
holidays@lakeside.zx3.net www.lakeside-holidays.net

Llynfi Holiday Park LD3 7TR ☎(01874) 658283 Fax (01874) 658575 OS map 161/125278 ½m
NW of Llangorse off Llanfihangel road Open Apr-Oct 188 pitches (108 static) Level grass,
sheltered 🗑🗑🗑🗑🗑🗑🗑🗑(heated) 🗑🗑🗑🗑 lic club, slipway

See also Brecon

LLANGRANOG, Ceredigion   Map C4
EC Wed SEE cliffs, Ynys Lochtyn headland (NT)
✘ Y Gegin Fach ☎(01239) 654642

Arthen Caravan Park, Glyn Arthen SA44 6PP ☎(01239) 851333 OS map 145/325485 4½m S of
Llangranog off B4334 (Rhydlewis) Open Mar-Oct 32 pitches 4 acres level grass, sheltered
🗑🗑🗑🗑🗑🗑🗑

Greenfields Caravan and Camping Park, Plwmp SA44 6HF ☎(01239) 654333 OS map
145/355523 3m SE of Llangranog on B4321 (Pentregat) at junction with A487 (Aberaeron-
Cardigan) Open Mar-Jan 200 pitches (150 static) 33 acres level/gentle slope, grass, sheltered
🗑🗑🗑🗑🗑🗑🗑🗑🗑🗑🗑🗑🗑🗑🗑🗑🗑 lic club, lake fishing, tennis, bowling green, golf
(Mastercard/Visa)

Maes Glas Caravan Park, Penbryn SA44 6QE ☎(01239) 654268 *Prop: Tim & Sally Hill* OS map
145/302520 1m SW of Llangranog on coast above beach at Penbryn Open Mar-Oct 43 pitches
Level grass, sheltered 🗑🗑🗑🗑🗑🗑🗑🗑 £7.50-£9.50 (Mastercard/Visa)
enquiries@maesglascaravanpark.co.uk www.maesglascaravanpark.co.uk

See also Aberporth

LLANGYNOG–see Llanfyllin

LLANIDLOES, Powys   Map F3
SEE market hall, museum, Llyn Clywedog lake
🗺 54 Longbridge St ☎(01686) 412605
✘ Red Lion, Great Oak St ☎(01686) 412270

Dol-Llys Farm SY18 6JA ☎(01686) 412694 OS map 136/962857 1m NE of Llanidloes off B4569
(Caersws) on Oakley Park road Open Easter-Oct 20 pitches Level grass 🗑🗑🗑🗑🗑 shooting,
fishing, campers' kitchen for walkers/cyclists £10.00

LLANON, Ceredigion   Map D3
SEE Llansantffraid village NW, Llanrhystyd church 2m N
✘ Bikerehyd Farm at Pennant ☎(01974) 202365

Woodlands Caravan Park SY23 5LX ☎(01974) 202342 Fax (01974) 202342 OS map 135/511668
On W edge of Llanon Open Apr-Oct 100 pitches (60 static) Grass, level, sheltered–some hard
standings 🗑🗑🗑🗑🗑🗑 £10.00-£12.00*

Tel: 01974 202 253

Mørfa Farm *Caravan Park* *by the sea*

LLANRHIDIAN, Gower **Map D6**
✕ Welcome to Town (off B4295) ✆ (01792) 390015
Llanrhidian Holiday Park SA3 1EU ✆ (01792) 391083 OS map 159/509933 1½m NE of
Llanrhidian on B4295 (Crofty) Open Mar 1-Jan 10 390 pitches (240 static) Grass, level, sheltered
⬛♀⬛⬛⬛⬤∅◻⬤⬆⬜⬛⬧ clubhouse

LLANRHYSTYD, Ceredigion **Map D3**
✕ Black Lion 6m SW at Aberaeron ✆ (01545) 570576
Morfa Farm Caravan-Camping Park SY23 5BU ✆ (01974) 202253 OS map 135/524692 ½m S of
Llanrhystyd off A487 (Aberaeron) Open Apr-Oct 170 pitches (150 static) level grass slipway,
⬛⬛⬛⬛⬤⬤∅⬆⬛ tennis, snooker £8.00-£10.00* *morfa@morfa.net www.morfa.net*
Pengarreg Caravan Park, Pengarreg SY23 5DJ ✆ (01974) 202247 OS map 135/533701 ½m SW
of Llanrhystyd off A487 (Aberaeron) Open Apr-Oct–must book 150 pitches ⬛⬤ club fishing
Penrhos Golf and Country Club SY23 5AY ✆ (01974) 202999 OS map 135/540698 ¼m E of
Llanrhystd centre off A487 (Aberystwyth) Open Apr-Oct 150 pitches (135 static) ⬛⬆⬛⬤
fishing, 18 hole golf course and leisure centre

LLANSANTFFRAID–see Llanfyllin

LLANTEG–see Red Roses

LLANTWIT MAJOR, Vale of Glamorgan **Map F7**
✕ Victoria Inn, Sigingstone, Cowbridge ✆ (01446) 773943
Acorn Camping and Caravanning, Rosedew Farm CF61 1RB ✆ (01446) 794024 Fax (01446)
794024 OS map 170/975675 ½m S of Llantwit Major off B4265 (Barry) Open Feb-Dec–bkg
advisable 105 pitches Grass, level ⬛⬆⬛⬛⬛⬤⬤∅⬆⬛⬧ barbecue hire £8.00-£9.00
(most cards) *info@acorncamping.co.uk www.acroncamping.co.uk*
Llandow Touring Caravan Park, Llandow CF7 7PB ✆ (01446) 794527 and 792462 *Prop: A & S
Evans* OS map 170/956713 2m N of Llantwit Major off B4270 (Cowbridge) Open Feb-Nov
100 pitches 5½ acres level grass and hard standing, sheltered ⬛⬛⬛⬛⬤⬤∅⬆⬛
£10.00-£14.00 (Mastercard/Visa) *enq@llandow.com www.llandowcaravanpark.com*

LLANWRDA, Carmarthenshire **Map E5**
SEE Tywi and Dulais valleys, gold mines at Pumpsaint 6m NW
✕ Bridgend Inn on A482 ✆ (01558) 650249
Penlan Wen Caravan Park, Ciao SA19 8RR *Farm site near Pumpsaint gold mines* ✆ (01558)
650667 OS map 146/705340 2m NW of Llanwrda on right of A482 (Lampeter) by river Cothy
Open Mar-Oct 20 pitches 3 acres level grass ⬤

LLANYBYDDER, Carmarthenshire **Map D4**
✕ Cross Hands ✆ (01570) 480224
Rhydcymerau Caravan Park, Rhydcymerau SA19 7PS ✆ (01558) 685527 OS map 146/579389
5m SE of Llanybydder on B4337 (Llansawel) Open Apr-Oct 30 pitches Level grass, sheltered
✕♀⬆⬛⬛⬤⬤⬛⬛ lake fishing

LONGSTONE–see Kilgetty

LUDCHURCH–see Narberth

LYDSTEP BEACH–see Manorbier

Help us make CAMPING CARAVANNING BRITAIN better known to site operators – and thereby
more informative – by showing them your copy when booking in.

MACHYNLLETH, Powys   **Map E2**
EC Thurs MD Wed *Ancient town in lower Dyfi valley with spacious main street* SEE Owain Glyndwr
Institute
🄸 Canoflan Owain Glyndwr ☏ (01654) 702401
✗ Skinners Arms, Main St (A487) ☏ (01654) 702354

Dyffryn Dyfi Caravan Park, Brynmelyn, Llanwrin SY20 8QJ ☏ (01650) 511252 OS map
124/808053 5m N of Machynlleth off A487 (Dolgellau) and B4404 (Cemmaes Road) Open Mar
27-Oct 31 60 pitches 4 acres grass, level 🄰 🄴

MAENCHLOCHOG, Pembs   **Map C5**
Remote village on S slopes of Preselly Hills, laced with rivers and footpaths. SEE Taf valley E
✗ Wolfscastle 10m W at Wolf's Castle ☏ (01437) 532225

Rosebush Caravan-Camping Park, Rhoslwyn, Rosebush SA66 7QT ☏ (01437) 532206 *Prop:
Gareth Williams* OS map 145/074293 1½m NW of Maenchlochog on B4313 (Fishguard)
Open Apr 1-Oct 14–adults only 80 pitches (15 static) Grass and hard standing, level, sheltered
🄰 🄴 £6.50-£9.50

Trefach Caravan Park, Mynachlog-ddu SA66 7RU ☏ (01994) 419225 OS map 145/148290 4m NE
of Maenchlochog off A478 (Cardigan-Tenby) near Glandy Cross Inn Open Easter-Oct 70 pitches
(50 static) Grass, part sloping, level, sheltered ✗🄿🄳🄰🄰🄰🄰🄳 (heated) 🄴🄴🄳🄴 lic club
(all cards)

Manorbier Country Park

Manorbier Country Park, Station Road, Manorbier, Tenby, Pembrokeshire SA70 7SN.

Tel. 08704 606 607   E-Mail enquiries@countrypark.co.uk

MANORBIER, Pembs   **Map B6**
*Village in centre of rugged headland built around ruins of impressive moated Norman Castle
overlooking lovely bay, with a sandy beach on either hand. Other fine beaches are at nearby Lydstep
and Jameston.* SEE castle, church, King's Quoit burial chamber
✗ Lydstep Tavern, Hillside, Lydstep ☏ (01834) 871521

Buttyland Touring Caravan and Tent Park SA70 7SN ☏ (01834) 871278 OS map 158/068990
1m N of Manorbier centre on road to station Open Mar-Sept–booking advisable peak periods
50 pitches 10 acres level grass 🄴🄿🄳🄰🄴🄰🄴

Manorbier Bay Caravanserai SA70 7SR ☏ (01834) 871235 OS map 158/065989 1m N of
Manorbier on A4139 (Tenby-Pembroke) Open Mar-Oct 84 pitches (65 static) Grass, level, open
🄴🄿🄰🄴🄴

Manorbier Country Park, Station Road SA70 7SN ☏ (01834) 871534 OS map 158/068993 1m N
of Manorbier centre on road to station Open Apr-Oct 151 pitches (101 static) Hard standings and
grass, level, sheltered 🄴✗🄿🄳🄴🄰🄰🄳 (heated) 🄴🄴🄿🄴 (mid Jun-Aug) 🄴🄳 tennis court, lic
country club £15.50-£22.50 (Mastercard/Visa) *enquiries@countrypark.co.uk
www.countrypark.co.uk*

Park Farm Caravans SA70 7SU *Quiet site, own footpath to beach* ☏ (01834) 871273 OS map
158/063981 ½m NW of Manorbier off Pembroke road Open Easter-Oct 142 pitches (70 static)
25 acres level grass and hard standings, sheltered 🄴🄿🄳🄰🄴🄰

Tudor Glen Caravan Park, Jameston SA70 7SS ☏ (01834) 871417 OS map 158/060990 1½m
NW of Manorbier on A4139 (Tenby-Pembroke) Open Mar-Oct 56 pitches (20 static) Grass
sloping, hard standings, sheltered 🄴🄿🄳🄰🄴🄰🄳 (outdoor) 🄴🄴🄴🄴🄳 £10.00-£25.00
info@tudorglencaravanpark.com www.tudorglencaravanpark.com

Whitewell Camping Park, Lydstep Beach SA70 7RY ☏ (01834) 871569 *Prop: Brian & Diane Kelly*
OS map 158/095988 2m E of Manorbier on Tenby road at Whitewell near beach Open Apr-Oct
150 pitches (50 static) Level grass 🄴✗🄿🄴🄴🄴🄴🄳 £12.00-£17.00

SITE DIRECTIONS
The distance and direction of a campsite is given from the centre of the town under which it appears.

MERTHYR TYDFIL, Merthyr Tydfil — Map F6
EC Thurs MD Tues, Sat SEE Cyfartha castle (museum)
🛈 Glebeland St ✆ (01685) 379884
✗ Baverstock Hotel, Heads of Valley Rd ✆ (01685) 386221

Grawen Farm, Cwm Taff, Cefn Coed CF48 2HS ✆ (01685) 723740 *Prop: Ms Freda Pugh* OS map 160/016112 2m NW of Merthyr Tydfil on left of A470 (Brecon) Open Apr-Oct 50 pitches 3½ acres level grass and hard standings, sheltered 🔳🔌🚿⊕↩🚐 forest walks, fishing, farm produce £9.00-£13.00

Rhydycar Sports and Leisure Centre, Rhydycar CF48 1UP ✆ (01685) 71491 OS map 160/050055 ½m S of Merthyr Tydfil off A470 (Brecon-Cardiff) Open May-Oct—no adv booking (max stay 3 nights) ✗♀ bowls, squash, sauna (facs avail only at centre from 7.30am to 11.30pm—otherwise no charge)

MILFORD HAVEN, Pembs — Map B6
EC Thurs MD Fri *Late 18c town above one of world's finest natural harbours thronged most days by supertankers delivering crude oil to nearby refineries* SEE Dale and Marloes peninsulas SW guarding N side of harbour, with small villages and sandy beaches
🛈 Charles St ✆ (01646) 690866
✗ Lord Nelson, Hamilton Terrace ✆ (01646) 695341

Sandy Haven Caravan Camping Park, Herbrandston SA73 3ST *Unspoilt site in beautiful location*
✆ (01646) 698844 OS map 157/856074 2½m W of Milford Haven by beach Open Easter-Sept 25 pitches Level/sloping grass, sheltered 🛒🔌⊕ boats accepted £11.00 (min)
www.sandyhavencampingpark.co.uk

MILTON—see Carew

MITCHEL TROY—see Monmouth

MONMOUTH, Monmouthshire — Map H5
EC Thurs MD Mon, Sat *Market town on English border with rich history and centre still retaining its medieval street plan* SEE Monnow bridge (fortified gateway), museum with Nelson collection, Wye Valley, Skenfrith castle and church 6m NW
🛈 Shire Hall, Agincourt Sq ✆ (01600) 713899
✗ The Somerset Arms, Dingestow ✆ (01600) 740632 Open 12-3pm/6-9.30pm

Bridge Caravan and Camping Park, Dingestow NP25 4DY ✆ (01600) 740241 *Prop: SA Holmes*
OS map 161/458103 4m SW of Monmouth off A40-A449 (Newport) on Dingestow road Open Easter-Oct 123 pitches Grass and hard standings, level, sheltered 🛒↗🔳🔌🚿⊕∅🚐🚍♿
fishing £11.00-£13.00 *info@bridgecaravanpark.co.uk*

Glen Trothy Caravan and Camping Park, Mitchel Troy NP25 4BD ✆ (01600) 712295 OS map 162/495100 2m SW of Monmouth off new A40 (Raglan) and B4293 (Mitchel Troy) Open Mar-Oct—must book peak periods 140 pitches Grass, level, sheltered—some hard standings
✗♀🔳🔌🚿⊕∅♿🌳 river fishing

Monnow Bridge Caravan Camping Park, Drybridge Street NP5 3AB ✆ (01600) 714004 OS map 162/504124 ½m SW of Monmouth centre on right of B4233 (Abergavenny)—entrance at side of Three Horseshoes pub Open all year 33 pitches 1 acre level grass by river 🔌

MONTGOMERY, Powys — Map G2
Small Georgian town dominated by castle ruins. SEE castle, Montgomery canal, ruined Caersws fort 7m W, once hub of Roman road network in Wales
✗ Dragon ✆ (01686) 668359

Argae Hall Caravan Park, Garthmyl SY15 6RU ✆ (01686) 640216 *Prop: Phillip & Daphne Jones*
OS map 136/194982 2m W of Montgomery off B4385 (Garthmyl) by river Severn Open all year (closed some periods winter)—no tents 144 pitches (114 static) Grass, level, sheltered—some hard standings ✗♀🔳🔌🚿⊕∅🚍↩ pub/club meals £10.00 *djones@telco4u.net*

See also Church Stoke

KEY TO SYMBOLS

🛒	shop	⊘	gas supplies	🚐	winter storage for caravans
✗	restaurant	⊕	chemical disposal point	🅿	parking obligatory
♀	bar	∅	payphone	⊗	no dogs
↩	takeaway food	🏊	swimming pool	🚍	caravan hire
↗	off licence	⊙	games area	🏠	bungalow hire
🔳	laundrette	↩	children's playground	♿	facilities for disabled
🔌	mains electric hook-ups	🖵	TV	🌳	shaded

NARBERTH, Pembs   Map C5

EC Wed SEE St Andrew's Castle 3m NW
✘ Plas Hydryd, Moorfield Rd ✆ (01834) 860653

Allensbank Holiday Park, Providence Hill SA67 8RF ✆ (01834) 860243 OS map 158/113134 1m S of Narberth off A478 (Tenby) on Cold Blow road Open Whitsun-Oct 15 39 pitches (18 static) Grass, level ▯▯▯▯▯▯▯▯▯▯▯▯ games room

Dingle Farm Caravan Park, Jesse Road SA67 7DP ✆ (01834) 860482 OS map 158/113149 ½m N of Narberth centre on A478 (Cardigan) Open Easter-Sept 60 pitches (30 static) Grass, level, sheltered ▯▯▯▯▯▯▯ lic club

Noble Court Caravan Park, Redstone Road SA67 7ES ✆ (01834) 861191 OS map 158/110155 ½m N of Narberth on B4313 (Fishguard) Open Mar-Nov 152 pitches (60 static) Grass and hard standings, level sheltered ✘▯▯▯▯▯▯▯▯▯▯▯▯▯▯& lic club, coarse fishing (Mastercard/Visa)

Redford Caravan Park, Princes Gate SA67 8TD ✆ (01834) 860251 OS map 158/135132 2m SE of Narberth on B4314 (Princes Gate) Open Apr 19-Oct 15 125 pitches (75 static) ▯▯▯▯▯▯▯ ▯▯▯▯▯ lic club, farm produce

Woodland Vale Caravan Park, Ludchurch SA67 8JE *Site with pitches attractively set between areas of water* ✆ (01834) 831319 OS map 158/140110 3½m SE of Narberth off A477 in Ludchurch Open Mar 1-Dec 1 110 pitches (80 static)—no tents Level grass, sheltered ▯✘▯▯▯▯▯▯▯▯▯▯▯▯▯▯ lic club, fishing

Wood Office Caravan Park, Templeton SA67 8RR ✆ (01834) 860565 OS map 158/120128 2m SE of Narberth off A478 (Tenby) Open Mar-Oct 45 pitches Grass, level, open ▯▯▯▯▯▯▯▯▯

For other sites near Narberth see Clunderwen and Kilgetty

NEATH, Neath   Map E6

EC Thurs MD Wed
✘ Castle Hotel, The Parade ✆ (01639) 641119

Gelli Farm Caravan and Camping Park, Crynant SA10 8PP ✆ (01639) 750209 OS map 160/795066 6m N of Neath off A465 (Hirwaun) on Severn Sisters road beyond Crynant Open all year 30 pitches ✘▯

NEWBRIDGE ON WYE, Powys   Map F4

SEE church, river Wye
✘ New Inn ✆ (01597) 860211

Disserth Park, Howey LD1 6NL ✆ (01597) 860277 OS map 147/035583 1½m E of Newbridge on Wye off B4358 (Llandrindod Wells) near Disserth church Open Mar-Oct 54 pitches (21 static) Grass, level, sheltered ✘▯▯▯▯▯▯▯▯▯(£2/wk)▯ fishing

NEWCASTLE EMLYN, Carmarthenshire   Map C4

EC Wed MD Fri SEE castle ruins, Teifi Falls, Cenarth Falls 2m W
✘ Pensarnau Arms, Pentrecagal ✆ (01559) 371370 Open 12-2/6-9
✘ The Bunch of Grapes ✆ (01239) 711185 Open 12-2/6.30-8.30

Afon Teifi Caravan Camping Park, Pentre Cagel SA38 9HT *Well-run site in secluded valley* ✆ (01559) 370532 *Prop: Mrs S Bishop* OS map 145/338403 2m E of Newcastle Emlyn on A484 (Carmarthen) Open Apr-Oct 110 pitches Grass and hard standings, level ▯▯▯▯▯▯▯▯& fishing on site £13.00 *afon.teifi@btinternet* *www.afonteifi.com*

Dolbryn Farm Campsite, Capel Iwan Road SA38 9LP ✆ (01239) 710683 *Prop: D & B Spencer* OS map 145/296384 2m S of Newcastle Emlyn on Capel Iwan road Mar-Oct 60 pitches Grass, part sloping, sheltered ▯▯▯▯▯▯▯▯▯&▯ £8.50-£10.00 *dolbryn@btinternet.com* *www.ukgeocities.com/dolbryn*

Moelfryn Caravan Camping Park, Pant-y-Bwlch SA38 9JG ✆ (01559) 371231 *Prop: Ike & Rose* OS map 145/321370 2½m S of Newcastle Emlyn off B4333 (Cynwyl Elfed) Open all year 25 pitches 2 acres, level grass and hard standing, part sheltered ▯▯▯▯▯▯▯ £6.00-£13.00 *moelfryn@tinyonline.co.uk www.moelfryncaravanpark.co.uk*

Pilbach Holiday Park, Bettws Ifan, Rhydlewis SA44 5RT ✆ (01239) 851434 Fax (01239) 851969 OS map 145/306476 2m S of Newcastle Emlyn off B433 (Camarthen) Open Mar-Oct 135 pitches (70 static) 15 acres, grass and hard standing, sheltered ▯✘▯▯▯▯▯▯▯(outdoor heated) ▯▯▯ games room, clubhouse, live entertainment, bike and skateboard track £8.00-£20.00* (most cards) *info@pilbach.com www.pilbach.com*

See also Cenarth

FACTS CAN CHANGE

We do our best to check the accuracy of the entries in this guide but changes can and do occur after publication. So if you plan to stay at a site some distance from home it makes sense to ring the manager or owner before setting off.

NEWGALE, Pembs   **Map B5**

✘ Ship Inn, 15 Main St, Solva ✆ (01437) 721247

Brandy Brook Caravan and Camping Site, Roch SA62 5PT ✆ (01348) 840272 OS map 157/884239 3m NE of Newgale off A487 (Haverfordwest) via Roch Open Easter-Sept 110 pitches (36 static) Level grass, sheltered ◐ ✿

Newgale Beach Holiday Park SA62 6BD ✆ (01437) 710675 and 710812 OS map 157/835212 1½m S of Newgale off A487 (Haverfordwest) on coast road adj beach Open Mar-Oct 90 pitches (45 static) Grass, level, part sheltered ▙ ✘ ⊶ 🛢 🗑 ◐ ✿ ∅ ☯ ⟆ ♥ (£30) 🚏 surfing

Park Hall Caravan Park, Maerdy Farm, Penycwm SA62 6LS ✆ (01437) 721282/721606 *Prop: ER & HM Harries* OS map 157/841244 2m N of Newgale off A487 (St David's) on 14 Signals Regiment road Open Mar-Oct 120 pitches (12 static) Grass and hard standings, level, open 🗑 🗑 ✿ ♥ fishing (5 acre lake) £10.00-£12.00

NEW MILLS, Powys   **Map F2**

✘ Bear 8m S at Newtown ✆ (01686) 626964

Llwyn Celyn Caravan Park, Adfa SY16 3DG ✆ (01938) 810720 OS map 136/055006 3m W of New Mills off B4389 on road beyond Adfa Open Fri prior to Good Friday-Oct 74 pitches (58 static) Grass, level, sheltered ⊶🛢🗑◐✿∅☯⟆♥⚓

Gwernydd Caravan Park, Gwernydd SY16 3NW ✆ (01686) 650236 OS map 136/087019 1m NW of New Mills off B4389 (Llanfair Caereinion) Open Mar-Oct 125 pitches (120 static) Grass and hard standings, level, sheltered ▙♈🛢🗑🗑◐∅⟆♥🚏

NEWPORT, Pembs   **Map B4**

EC Wed SEE church, castle, hill fort, Pentre Ifan chambered tomb 2m SE

✘ Llwyngwair Arms, East St ✆ (01239) 820267

Morawelon, Parrog SA42 0RW ✆ (01239) 820565 OS map 145/050396 ½m NW of Newport at Parrog beach Open Easter-Oct 85 pitches 6 acres, grass, level/gentle slope ▙✘⚚🗑🗑◐✿∅ sailing, boat club, pony trekking £8.40-£16.00 (Mastercard/Visa)

Tredegar House & Park Caravan Club Site, Coedkernew NP10 8TW ✆ (01633) 815600 OS map 171/285858 2m SW of Newport on A48 (Cardiff) at junction with A4072 (Bassaleg) near junction 28 of M4—signposted Open Mar 26-Dec 13 82 pitches Grass and hard standings, sheltered ✘♈🛢🗑◐✿∅☯⟆♿ £14.60-£20.60* inc showers (Mastercard/Visa/Switch/Delta) *www.caravanclub.co.uk*

NEWPORT–see Cardiff

NEW QUAY, Ceredigion   **Map D4**

Small coastal town with history of smuggling on headland sheltering a sandy bay on either hand, with cliffs on S providing a breeding ground for sea birds. The town is said to have been the model for Dylan Thomas' Under Milk Wood

🄸 Church St ✆ (01545) 560865

✘ Black Lion, Glanmor Terr ✆ (01545) 560209

Llwynon Farm, Cei Bach SA45 9SL ✆ (01545) 580218 OS map 146/409596 2m E of New Quay off B4342 (Llanarth) Open Jul 16-Aug 13 100 pitches Grass, sloping, part open ✿ 🚏

Pencnwc Holiday Park, Cross Inn SA44 6NL ✆ (01545) 560479 OS map 145/383566 2m S of New Quay on A486 (Synod Inn) Open Mar-Oct 225 pitches (175 static) Level grass and hard standings ▙♈⊶🛢🗑🗑◐✿∅🖃♿ clubhouse, games room

Wern Mill, Gilfachreda SA45 9SP ✆ (01545) 580699 OS map 146/412588 2m SE of New Quay on B4342 (Llanarth) Open Easter-Oct 50 pitches Level grass, sheltered 🗑🗑◐✿♿ £4.50-£8.00*

NEW RADNOR, Powys   Map G4
EC Wed
✗ The Harp Inn, Old Radnor ☎ (01544) 350655

Walton Court, Walton LD8 2PY ☎ (01544) 350259 *Prop: Glyn & Jean Price* OS map 48/255598
   2½m ESE of New Radnor on A44 (Kington) Open all year 55 pitches Grass, level, sheltered
   🔲🔲🔲⊕🔲🔲 £6.00 (tent) (£7.50 with hook-up)

See also Hundred House

NEWTOWN, Powys   Map F2
EC Thurs MD Tues SEE Robert Owen and textile museums
🔳 The Park, Back Lane ☎ (01686) 625580
✗ Bear, Broad St ☎ (01686) 626964

Smithy Caravan Park, Abermule SY15 6ND ☎ (01584) 711280 OS map 157/865033 9m N of
   Newtown on A483 (Welshpool) Open Mar-Nov 95 pitches (60 static) Level grass and hard
   standings, sheltered 🔲🔲🔲⊕🔲⊕⊕🔲🔲 fishing

OAKDALE, Caerphilly   Map G6
✗ The Travellers Rest, Pen-y-Fan Caravan & Leisure, Manmoel Rd ☎ (01495) 226636

Penyfan Caravan and Leisure Park, Manmoel Road NP2 0HY *3-star Wales Tourist Board*
   ☎ (01495) 226636 *Prop: Graham Davies* OS map 171/190011 1½m N of Oakdale off B4251
   (Crumlin) on Manmoel road via Croespenmaen Open all year 75 pitches–booking advisable 4
   acres grass and hard standing, level ✗🔲🔲🔲🔲⊕🔲🔲🔲 lic club, snacks £9.00-£13.00 (most
   cards) *info@penyfancaravanpark.co.uk www.penyfancaravanpark.co.uk*

OXWICH, Gower   Map D6
SEE nature reserve, Oxwich Burrows 1m E, Oxwich Point 1m SE
✗ Fairyhill 3m N at Reynoldston ☎ (01792) 390139

Greenways Holiday Park SA3 1LY ☎ (01792) 390220 OS map 159/497860 ¼m S of Oxwich on
   Oxwich Green Open Apr-Oct 430 pitches (100 static) 🔲✗🔲🔲🔲🔲🔲🔲⊕🔲🔲🔲

Oxwich Camping Park SA3 1LS ☎ (01792) 390777 OS map 159/498865 ¼m SW of Oxwich in
   village Open Apr-Sept 180 pitches, no caravans Level/sloping grass and hard standings,
   sheltered 🔲✗🔲🔲🔲🔲⊕🔲🔲 (heated) 🔲🔲 club

See also Llanrhidian, Port Eynon and Rhossili

PAINSCASTLE, Powys   Map F4
SEE castle mound, village green, Llanbedr hill
✗ Harp 4m S at Glasbury ☎ (01497) 847373

Rhosgoch Holiday Park, Rhosgoch LD2 3JB ☎ (01497) 851253 OS map 148/189467 2m NE of
   Painscastle on B4594 (Gladestry) Open Mar-Oct 25 pitches–must book peak periods–no tents
   Grass, level, sheltered 🔲🔲⊕🔲 (£2/wk) 🔲 (exc small breeds) 🔲 pony trekking, golf, tourist
   information

PANDY–see Abergavenny

PEMBROKE, Pembs   Map B6
EC Wed SEE castle, Monkton Priory, Lamphey Palace ruins 2m SE
🔳 The Commons Rd ☎ (01646) 622388
✗ Coach House, Main St ☎ (01646) 684602

Castle Farm Camping Site, Angle SA71 5AR ☎ (01646) 641220 *Prop: GB Rees & Sons* OS map
   157/865033 9m W of Pembroke on B4320 (Angle) Open Easter-Oct 25 pitches Grass, part
   level, part open 🔲🔲⊕🔲🔲🔲 shops/pubs in the village £6.00-£10.00

Windmill Hill Caravan Park, Windmill Hill Farm SA71 5BT ☎ (01646) 682392 OS map 158/979002
   ½m S of Pembroke on B4319 (Bosherton) Open Mar-Oct 30 pitches 3 acres level grass
   🔲🔲⊕🔲 milk

For other sites near Pembroke see also Carew and Manorbier

PENARTH, Vale of Glamorgan   Map G7
EC Wed SEE Turner House art gallery, Penarth Head
🔳 The Esplanade, Penarth Pier ☎ 0202 070 8849
✗ Glendale, Plymouth Rd ☎ (01222) 706701

Lavernock Point Holiday Estate, Fort Road CF6 2XQ ☎ (01222) 707310 OS map 171/182682
   2m S of Penarth off B4267 (Sully) on road to Lavernock Point Open Apr-Oct 200 pitches
   Level/sloping grass 🔲🔲🔲🔲🔲⊕🔲🔲🔲

SHOWERS
Except where marked, all sites in this guide have flush lavatories and showers. Symbols for these
amenities have therefore been omitted from site entries.

PORTEINON (PORT EYNON), Gower   **Map D6**
✗ Barrows 6m E at Mumbles ✆(01792) 361443

Bank Farm, Horton SA3 1LL ✆(01792) 390228 *Prop: Mr Richards* OS map 159/472860 ¼m ENE of Porteinon at Horton Open Mar-Nov 230 pitches (100 static) 🅿🍴⚡♿🅿🚿⊙🎣♨⊘◻⊙🔌🏠
£11.00-£25.00 (most cards) *bankfarmleisure@aol.com www.bankfarmleisure.co.uk*

Carreglwyd Camping SA3 1NN ✆(01792) 390795 Fax (01792) 390796 OS map 159/850466 On S edge of Porteinon off A4118 near beach Open March-Dec 280 pitches (80 static) Level/sloping grass, sheltered 🅿⚡🚿⊙♨⚡♿ £14.00 (min)* (all cards)

Gower Farm Museum and Caravan Park, Llandewi SA3 1AU ✆(01792) 391195 OS map 159/462895 2m N of Porteinon off A4118 (South Gower) Open Apr-Oct 100 pitches 15 acres level/sloping grass ⚡🚿♨⊙🔌♨♿

Hillend Camping Park, Llangennith SA3 1JD ✆(01792) 386204 *Prop: G Howells* OS map 159/418909 6½m NW of Porteinon on B4295 Open Apr-Oct 250 pitches–no touring caravans, no adv booking Grass level/sloping 🅿✗⚡🎣⚡🚿♨⊙⊘🔌♨♿🍴

Newpark Holiday Park SA3 1NP ✆(01792) 390292 OS map 159/465858 ¼m S of Porteinon centre Open Easter-Oct 172 pitches Level grass and hard standings, sheltered 🅿⚡🎣⚡🚿♨⊙⊘⊙🔌♨🏠

Three Cliffs Bay Caravan and Camping Site, North Hills Farm, Penmaen SA3 2HB ✆(01792) 371218 OS map 159/534886 5m E of Porteinon off A4118 (Swansea) Open Easter-Oct 95 pitches Grass, part sloping/level, sheltered 🅿⚡🚿♨⚡⊙

PORTHCAWL, Bridgend   **Map E7**
EC Wed *Family resort once small fishing village, with sandy beaches and large amusement park*
SEE Porthcawl Point, St John's church at Newton 1m E, Merthyr Mawr Warren 2m E
ℹ Old Police Station, John St ✆(01656) 786639/782211
✗ Rose and Crown at Heol-Y-Capel ✆(01656) 784850

Brodawel Camping Park, Moor Lane, Nottage CF36 3EJ ✆(01656) 783231 OS map 170/816790 1m NW of Porthcawl off A4229 (Nottage) Open Apr-Oct 100 pitches Grass, level, part sheltered 🅿🎣⚡🚿♨⊙⊘⊙🔌♨♿

Happy Valley Caravan Park CF32 0NG ✆(01656) 782144 OS map 170/852780 2m E of Porthcawl on A4106 (Bridgend) Open Apr-Sept 450 pitches (350 static) Grass and hard standings, sheltered 🅿🍴⚡⚡🚿♨⊙⊘🔌♨🔌 lic club (Mastercard/Visa)

Kenfig Pool Caravan Park, Ton Kenfig CF30 9PT ✆(01656) 740079 OS map 170/800814 3m NW of Porthcawl off B4283 (Port Talbot) Open Mar-Nov–no tents 78 pitches (75 static) 3½ acres sloping grass and hard standings ⚡🚿♨♨⊙🔌

PORT TALBOT, Neath   **Map E6**
EC Wed MD Tues, Sat
✗ Aberavan Beach ✆(01639) 884949

Afan Argoed Countryside Centre, Afan Forest Park, Cynonville SA13 3HG ✆(01639) 850564 OS map 170/812952 6m NE of Port Talbot on A4107 (Cymmer)–latest time of arrival 1800 unless advance notice given Open Apr-Oct 10 pitches 1 acre grass and hard standing 🅿✗♿ bike hire, fishing, *No showers* (Visa)

PRESTEIGNE, Powys   **Map G4**
EC Thurs
ℹ Old Market Hall, Broad St ✆(01544) 260650
✗ Radnorshire Arms, High St ✆(01544) 267406

Rockbridge Mobile Home and Holiday Park LD8 2NF ✆(01547) 560300 Fax (01547) 560300 OS map 137/295654 1m W of Presteigne on B4356 (Llangunllo) near river Open Easter-Oct 55 pitches (21 static) Grass, level, sheltered 🅿⚡🚿♨(25) 🚐♿ £8.00-£14.00*
dustinrockbridge@hotmail.com

See listing under St David's

Maesbach Caravan and Camping Park, Pumpsaint

PUMPSAINT, Carmarthenshire   **Map E4**

✗ Drovers Arms, Ffarmers, Llanwrda ☎ (01558) 650157 Open Mon-Fri 5-9.30, Sat-Sun 12-9.30

Maesbach Caravan and Camping Park, Horseshoe Village, Ffarmers, Llanwrda SA19 8EX ☎ (01558) 650650 *Prop: Kath & Graham Stoddart* OS map 146/657451 Turn R off A482 (Llanwrda-Lampeter) 1½m NW of Pumsaint, in 1½m at Ffarmers, turn R opposite Drovers Arms, ¾m on L Open Mar 1-Oct 31 40 pitches (20 static) 5 acres grass level/gently sloping, hard standing ▣◨◪❀◔◨▣▫ rallies welcome, shop/bar/restaurant nearby £9.00-£12.00 *graham.stoddart@which.net*

RED ROSES, Carmarthenshire   **Map C5**
Village at crossroads inland of Pendine
✗ Waungron Farm 4m N at Whitland ☎ (01994) 240682

Old Vicarage Caravan Park SA34 0PG ☎ (01834) 831637 OS map 158/204117 In Red Roses at junct of A477 and B4314 Open Mar-Jan 40 pitches (24 static) Grass, level ✗♀↳▣◪◨❀▱◕▨▫ lic club

Pantglas Farm, Tavernspite SA34 0NS ☎ (01834) 831618 Fax (01834) 831193 OS map 158/175120 1½m NW of Red Roses off B4314 (Templeton) at Tavernspite Open Easter-Oct 75 pitches 7 acres level/gently sloping grass and hard standings, sheltered ▙♀▣◨◪❀∅◕◡◨& £6.00-£12.50* *neil.brook@btinternet.com www.pantglasfarm.com*

Rose Park Farm, Llanteg SA67 8QJ ☎ (01834) 831203 OS map 158/164098 2m SW of Red Roses on right of A477 (Pembroke) Open Whitsun-Oct 20 pitches—must book 3½ acres grass, part level, secluded ◨◪◡◡◨▫▩

South Caravan Holiday Park, Tavernspite SA34 0NL ☎ (01834) 831586/831451/831651 OS map 158/180127 2m NW of Red Roses on B4314-B4328 (Narbeth) opp Alpha inn Open Mar-Oct 180 pitches (115 static) 10 acres level grass ♀↳▣◨❀∅▱(indoor) ❀◡ bar meals

RHAYADER, Powys   **Map F3**
EC Thurs MD Wed SEE Elan Valley reservoirs SW
ℹ Visitor Centre, North St ☎ (01597) 810591
✗ Triangle Inn, Cwmdauddwr ☎ (01597) 810537 Open 12-2/6.30-8.30 (closed Mon lunch)
✗ Lamb & Flag Inn, North St ☎ (01597) 810819 Open 12-2/6-9

Gigrin Red Kite Caravan Site, South Street LD6 5BL ☎ (01597) 810243 *Prop: EP & LM Powell* OS map 147/980678 ½m S of Rhayader off A470 (Builth Wells) Open all year exc Xmas/New Year 15 pitches 2 acres level grass sheltered ◨◪❀▩ nature trail, red kite centre £7.00-£9.50 inc elect *accom@gigrin.co.uk www.gigrin.co.uk*

Wyeside Caravan Camping Park LD6 5LB ☎ (01597) 810183 *Prop: Keith Brumwell* OS map 147/968686 ¼m N of Rhayader on left of A470 (Llangurig) beside river Wye Open Feb-Nov 190 pitches (40 static) Level grass and hard standing ▣◨◪❀∅▱& pony trekking, fishing, bowls, putting, tennis £11.00 (most cards) *info@wyesidecamping.co.uk* *www.wyesidecamping.co.uk*

RHOSSILLI, Gower   **Map D6**
SEE Rhossili Bay
✗ Worms Head Hotel ☎ (01792) 390512

Pitton Cross Caravan and Camping Park SA3 1PH ☎ (01792) 390593 Fax (01792) 391010 *Prop: ER & EL Button* OS map 159/434878 1¼m E of Rhossilli on B4247 (Pilton Green) Open Feb-Oct 100 pitches 6 acres level grass and hard standings, sheltered ▙▣◨◪❀∅◕◡◨& close to coast path & Gower Way £10.00-£18.00 (Mastercard/Visa/Maestro) *admin@pittoncross.co.uk* *www.pittoncross.co.uk*

Pantglas Farm Caravan Park
Tavernspite, Whitland, Pembrokeshire SA34 0NS
pantglasfarm@btinternet.com

Marloes National Trust Beach Pembrokeshire

RHYDLEWIS–see Beulah

ST CLEARS, Carmarthenshire   **Map C5**
EC Wed MD Tues SEE 12c church, Castle House
✘ Black Lion ✆ (01994) 230700

Afon Lodge Caravan Park SA33 4LG ✆ (01994) 230647 OS map 158/274197 2m N of St Clears off Llanboidy road Open Mar-Dec 70 pitches (35 static) 5 acres part level grass and hard standings, woodland setting ▮✗♀▰▯�▰●▰▰▰▰▰ TV hook-up

ST DAVID'S, Pembs   **Map A5**
SEE cathedral, Bishop's Palace ruins
✘ Glan-y-Mor Inn, Caerfai Rd ✆ (01437) 721788 Open Apr-Sep 12.30-2.30/6.30-9

Caerfai Bay Caravan and Tent Park SA62 6QT ✆ (01437) 720274 *Prop: D Panton* OS map 157/758244 ¾m S of St David's off road to Caerfai Bay adj coast path Open Mar-Nov 140 pitches (33 static) 10 acres level/sloping grass ▮▰▰●▰▰▰ beach £8.50-£14.50 (Mastercard/Visa/Delta/Maestro) *info@caerfaibay.co.uk www.caerfaibay.co.uk*

Glan-y-Mor Tent Park, Caerfai Bay Road SA62 6QT ✆ (01437) 721788 *Prop: Nick & Helen Sime* OS map 157/247756 ½m SE of St David's on Caerfai Bay road Open Apr-Sept–no trailer caravans 55 pitches ✗♀▰▯ £10.00-£15.00 (most cards) *info@glan-y-mor.co.uk www.glan-y-mor.co.uk*

Hendre Eynon Caravan Camping Park SA62 6DB ✆ (01437) 720474 *Prop: Mr & Mrs Ian Jamieson* OS map 157/773280 2m NNE of St David's off B4583 (Whitesands) on Llanrian road Open Apr-Oct 74 pitches Grass level, part sheltered ▮▰▰●▰▰▰▰▰ farm produce, first aid, 5 shower rooms £6.00-£10.00 *www.ukparks.co.uk/hendreeynon*

Porthclais Farm, Porthclais Road SA62 6RR ✆ (01437) 720256 *Prop: RG Morgan* OS map 157/744243 1m SW of St David's off Porthclais road Open Mar-Oct 200 pitches 4 acres level grass ▰●▰ farm produce £11.00 *rgporthclais@yahoo.co.uk*

See also Croesgoch, Newgale and Solva

Moreton Farm Leisure Park, Saundersfoot

✘ RESTAURANTS

The restaurants recommended in this guide are of three kinds – pubs, independent restaurants and those forming part of hotels and motels. They all serve lunch and dinner – at a reasonable price – say under £10 a head. We shall be glad to have your comments on any you use this season and if you think they are not up to standard, please let us have your suggestions for alternatives.

WYESIDE
Rhayader ~ Powys
LD6 5LB
Tel: 01597 810183
CARAVAN AND CAMPING PARK

See listing under Rhayader

ST FLORENCE–see Carew

SAUNDERSFOOT, Pembs   **Map C6**
EC Wed SEE harbour, Wiseman's Bridge 1m N, Monkstone Point 1m SE
✗ Wood Ridge Inn, Wooden ✆ (01834) 812259 Open 11-Nov

Moreton Farm Leisure Park, Moreton SA69 9EA ✆ (01834) 812016 *Prop: Nixon Ltd* OS map
158/118049 1½m W of Saundersfoot on A478 (Narberth-Tenby) opp chapel Open Mar 1-Nov 1
80 pitches (12 static) 12 acres level/sloping grass and hard standings, sheltered
🛒 🖥 🗑 🍴 ⊕ ∅ ↵ ❀ 🏠 ♿ £11.00-£15.00 *moretonfarm@btconnect.com www.moretonfarm.co.uk*

Trevayne Caravan and Camping Park, Monkstone Bay SA69 9DL ✆ (01834) 813402 OS map
135/140030 2m S of Saundersfoot off B4316 (Tenby) on road to Monkstone Point Open Easter-
Oct 280 pitches (90 static) Grass, part sloping 🔌 🍴 farm produce, near beach
See also Amroth and Kilgetty

SOLVA, Pembs   **Map B5**
✗ Harbour House ✆ (01437) 721267

Mount Farm SA62 6XL ✆ (01437) 721301 OS map 157/828248 2m E of Solva on A487
(Haverfordwest) Open Apr-Oct 45 pitches Level grass, sheltered (20 static) 🛒 🖥 🗑

Nine Wells Caravan Camping Park, Nine Wells SA62 6UH ✆ (01437) 721809 *Prop: Nigel Bowie*
OS map 157/787248 ½m W of Solva on A487 (St David's) Open Easter-mid Oct 60 pitches
Grass, level/sloping, part sheltered 🔌 ⊕ 🔌 £8.00-£12.00

STEPASIDE–see Kilgetty

SWANSEA, Swansea   **Map E6**
EC Thurs MD Sat SEE museum, Clyne castle gardens, civic centre
📖 Plymouth St ✆ (01792) 468321
✗ Annie's, St Helen's Rd ✆ (01792) 655603

Riverside Caravan Park, Ynysforgan Farm, Morriston SA6 6QL ✆ (01792) 775587 Fax (01792)
775587 OS map 159/679991 3m N of Swansea on right of A4067 (Pontardawe) near junct 45 of
M4, by river Tawe Open all year 120 pitches 7 acres, level grass and hard standings, sheltered
🛒 ♀ 🖥 🔌 🗑 ⊕ ∅ 🏊 ⊕ 🖥 🔌 🚻 ♿ jacuzzi, lic club, fishing (most cards)

TALGARTH, Powys   **Map G5**
✗ Three Cocks 2m N at Three Cocks ✆ (01497) 847215

Anchorage Caravan Park, Bronllys LD3 0LD ✆ (01874) 711246 OS map 161/142350 1m NW of
Talgarth off A479 (Bronllys) on A438 (Brecon) Open all year 193 pitches (77 static) Grass, part
sloping, sheltered, some hard standings 🛒 🖥 🔌 🗑 ⊕ ∅ ↵ 🖥 🔌 ♿ Post office, baby bathroom,
hairdresser £10.00 *www.anchoragecp.co.uk*

Riverside International Caravan Camping Park LD3 0HL ✆ (01874) 711320 Fax (01874) 712064
OS map 161/148347 1m NW of Talgarth on A479 (Bronllys) Open Easter-Oct 84 pitches Grass
and hard standings, level, sheltered 🛒 ✗ ♀ ↵ ↗ 🖥 🔌 🗑 ⊕ ∅ 🏊 (indoor) ⊕ ↵ 🖥 🔌 ❀ 🏠 ♿ lic
snack bar, fishing, sauna, jacuzzi, solarium, gym £10.00-£13.50* (Mastercard/Visa/Delta/Switch)
riversideinternational@bronllys1.freeserve.co.uk www.riversideinternational.co.uk

TAVERNSPITE–see Red Roses

KEY TO SYMBOLS

🛒	shop	🗑	gas supplies	🔌	winter storage for caravans
✗	restaurant	⊕	chemical disposal point	🅿	parking obligatory
♀	bar	∅	payphone	❀	no dogs
↵	takeaway food	🏊	swimming pool	🔌	caravan hire
↗	off licence	⊕	games area	🏠	bungalow hire
🖥	laundrette	↵	children's playground	♿	facilities for disabled
🔌	mains electric hook-ups	🖥	TV	🌳	shaded

TENBY, Pembs   **Map C6**
EC Wed SEE castle ruins, old town walls, Tudor Merchant's House, Caldy Island and monastery (men only)
⊞ The Croft ☎(01834) 842404
✗ Sandyhill Guesthouse Coffee Shop, Tenby Road, Saundersfoot ☎(01834) 813165 Open Apr-Oct 9-5

Kiln Park Holiday Centre, Marsh Road, Kiln Park SA70 7RB ☎(01834) 844121 Fax (01834) 845159 OS map 158/126005 1m SW of Tenby on A4139 (Pembroke) Open Mar-Oct–must book (maximum stay 2 wks) 780 pitches (550 static) Level grass and hard standings ⚡✗⚏⤸⤳⚐ ⚏⌀⊕∅☐⊕⤳⤸(Jun 21-Aug) lic club, petrol, amusements (most cards) gary.turner@bourneleisuregroup.co.uk

Lodge Farm, New Hedges SA70 8TN ☎(01834) 842468 *Prop: K Keedey* OS map 158/130029 1¾m N of Tenby on A478 (Narberth) Open Mar-Sept 105 pitches (40 static) Grass, level, open ⚡✗⤳⚐⚏⊕⤳⚏⌀ games room £10.00-£22.00

Moysland Farm, Narberth Rd SA69 9DS ☎(01834) 812455 *Prop: V Rawson & M Humphries* OS map 158/127032 2m N of Tenby on A478 (Cardigan) near New Hedges roundabout Open Whitsun-Sept–must book 14 pitches 3 acres level grass, sheltered ⚏⊕ £12.00-£21.00*

Rowston Holiday Park, New Hedges SA70 8TL ☎(01834) 842178 OS map 158/132028 1½m N of Tenby off A478 (Narberth) Open Apr-Oct 230 pitches (120 static) Grass and hard standings, part sloping, part open ⚡✗⤳⚏⌀⊕∅⤳⚛(Jul-Aug) ⊡⚷ beach near

Rumbleway Caravan and Tent Park, New Hedges SA70 8TR ☎(01834) 845155 OS map 158/127028 1m N of Tenby off A478 (Cardigan)–signposted Open Apr-Oct 240 pitches (130 static) 25 acres level/sloping grass and hard standings, sheltered ⚡⚏⤸⤳⚏⚏⌀⊕∅⊘☐⤳⤸☐⚛⊡⚷

Well Park, New Hedges SA70 8TL ☎(01834) 842179 OS map 158/129027 1½m N of Tenby on A478 (Narberth) Open Mar-Oct 122 pitches (42 static) Grass and hard standings, part level, part open ⚏⤳⤳⚏⚏⌀⊕∅⊘⤳⤳⊡⚏⚷ games room, super pitches with TV hook-ups £10.00-£20.00 enquiries@wellparkcaravans.co.uk www.wellparkcaravans.co.uk

Windmills Camping Park, Brynhir Lane SA70 8TJ ☎(01834) 842200 OS map 158/125020 ½m NW of Tenby on A478 (Begelly) Open Easter-Sept 45 pitches–booking advisable Grass, level ⚏⊕ www.camping-tenby.co.uk

Wood Park Caravans, New Hedges SA70 8TL ☎(01834) 843414 *Prop: EM & JE Hodgkinson* OS map 158/131130 1½m N of Tenby off A478 (New Hedges bypass) Open Easter-Sept–must book 150 pitches (90 static) Grass, level/sloping and hard standings, sheltered ⚏⤳⚏⚏⌀⊕∅⊘⤳ ⚛(Jul-Aug) ⊡ games room £8.00-£20.00 info@woodpark.co.uk www.woodpark.co.uk

See also Carew and Manorbier

TREDEGAR, Blaenau Gwent   **Map F6**
SEE memorial to Aneurin Bevan on A4047 1m NE, Sirhowy valley S, Bedwellte church 2m S
✗ Tregenna 6m W at Merthyr Tydfil ☎(01685) 723627

Parc Bryn Bach, Merthyr Road NP2 3AY ☎(01495) 711816 OS map 161/125102 1½m NW of Tredegar off A465 (Abergavenny-Merthyr Tydfil) Open Jan 2-Dec 24 30 pitches Level grass and hard standing in 600 acre country park with water sports, hang gliding and fishing ✗⤳⚏⚏⊕∅⤳⚷ hostel

TREGARON, Ceredigion   **Map E4**
Remote hill town and popular trekking centre in Teifi valley
▨ The Square ✆ (01974) 298144
✘ Talbot, The Square ✆ (01974) 298208

Hendrewen Caravan Park, Pencarw, Llangeitho SY25 6QU ✆ (01974) 298410 OS map
146/642950 3m W of Tregaron off A485 (Lampeter) on B4342 (Llangeitho) Open Mar-Oct 35
pitches (35 static) 4½ acres grass level/gentle slope ▙✘⚊☷⌀

TRESAITH–see Aberporth

USK, Monmouthshire   **Map G6**
EC Wed SEE old inns, Usk Valley
✘ Three Salmons, Bridge Street ✆ (01291) 672133

Bridge Inn, Chainbridge NP5 1PP ✆ (01873) 880243 *Prop: Dale Powell & Sherrie Vaughan* OS
map 161/346054 3m N of Usk on B4598 (Abergavenny) by river Usk Open Mar-Oct 15 pitches
1½ acres mainly level grass ✘⚊☺ fishing (£5) £8.00-£12.00 (most cards)

WELSHPOOL, Powys   **Map G2**
EC Thurs MD Mon SEE Powis Castle, Powys Museum, old inns, narrow gauge railway to Llanfair
Caereinion 8m W
▨ Flash Leisure Centre ✆ (01938) 552043
✘ Royal Oak, The Cross ✆ (01938) 552217

Bank Farm Caravan Park, Middletown SY21 8EJ ✆ (01938) 570526 *Prop: David & Gill Corfield*
OS map 126/294122 5½m E of Welshpool on A458 (Shrewsbury) Open Mar-Oct 56 pitches
(34 static) Grass, part sloping, part sheltered ⚊☷⌀⊕∅☺☺⚊☷⌫ first aid, coarse fishing,
jacuzzi, snooker £10.00-£12.00 gill@bankfarmcaravans.fsnet.co.uk www.bankfarmcaravans.com

Severn Caravan Park, Kilkewydd Farm, Forden SY21 8RT ✆ (01938) 580238 OS map 126/233025
3m S of Welshpool on A490 (Church Stoke) Open Apr-Oct 156 pitches (86 static) Grass and
hardstanding level, sheltered ⚊☷☺☺☷ games room

YSTRADGYNLAIS, Powys   **Map E6**
EC Thurs MD Fri SEE Craig-y-nos country park and Dan-yr-Ogof caves 6m NE
✘ Copper Beech 2m NE at Abercraf (Heol Tawe off A4067) ✆ (01639) 730269

National Show Caves Centre Caravan-Tenting Park, Abercraf SA9 1GJ ✆ (01639)
730284/730693 OS map 160/840160 4m NE of Ystradgynlais on A4067 (Sennybridge) Open
Easter-Oct–no adv booking 60 pitches Grass, sloping, sheltered ✘☷⌀ fishing, trekking, dry
ski slope

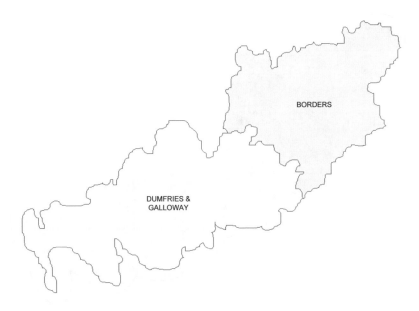

BORDERS

DUMFRIES &
GALLOWAY

Just across the border with England, several counties join up as Dumfries & Galloway and Borders, a region in which few northbound travellers ever stop, yet one with superb coastal scenery, a mild climate and uncrowded roads.

The Cheviots roll away to the west from Castle Bar, a popular gateway to the region. These and the heather-clad hills beyond provide extensive areas for gentle hill walking. On the east is a narrow and rugged coast inset with the fine sands of Coldingham Bay and the picturesque fishing ports of St Abbs and Eyemouth, famous for sea angling. In the centre of the country is Melrose, heart of Walter Scott country, for which Galashiels is a popular centre, Hawick, one of the largest Border textile towns and Jedburgh, with its museum housing the death mask of Mary Queen of Scots. Above the vast depression of the Devil's Beeftub near Moffat is the source of the Tweed, one of the most scenic of the country's many rivers and one of the most rewarding to fish. Further north it provides a beautiful setting for Peebles and nearby Niedpath Castle.

Dumfries and Galloway forming the western half of the region has a coastline that extends some 200 miles between the smithies of Gretna, where runaway couples used to get married, and Stranraer on the northwest. The lovely Solway coast in the south is indented with deep river estuaries at the head of which

lie picturesque Newton Stewart, its houses lining both banks of the Cree, Dumfries with its memories of Bonnie Prince Charlie and the colourful market town of Kirkcudbright, dominated by the sixteenth-century MacLellan Castle.

North of Newton Stewart is the vast and hilly Glen Trool Forest Park centred on the 2764ft high Merrick Peak and mirrored in the tiny Loch Glen Trool. Criss-crossed by nature trails, the forest abounds in deer, red squirrel and less common species of birds, including the occasional golden eagle. An accessible yet rewarding vantage point is Robert the Bruce's victory stone.

To the southwest the sandy stretches of Wigtown and Luce Bay are a haven for sailing and sea angling and catches may sometimes even include a porbeagle shark. Whithorn, Sandhead and Portpatrick are good centres in this area, and the sub-tropical gardens at Logan are well worth visiting. Panoramic views follow one another on the cliff top run from Stranraer through Ballantrae to popular Girvan in the north. Inland, owing perhaps to the milder climate, towns and villages seem more cheerful and colourful than in other parts of Scotland.

Campsites are not too plentiful in the region and those that exist tend to be near the larger towns. In the main they are more plentiful on the coast but less frequent inland, especially in the west.

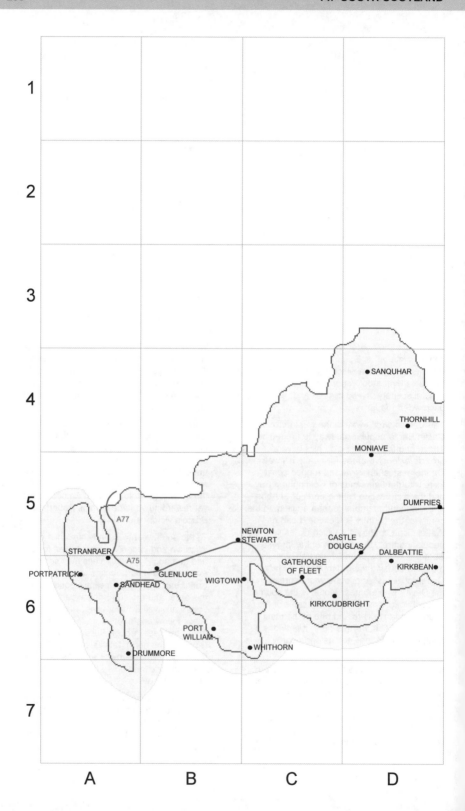

COCKBURNSPATH

A1 EYEMOUTH

WEST LINTON

DUNS

LAUDER GREENLAW

COLDSTREAM

PEEBLES

GALASHIELS

KELSO

SELKIRK A68

JEDBURGH

HAWICK

ETTRICK A7

MOFFAT

BEATTOCK

A74(M)

LANGHOLM

LOCKERBIE
ECCLEFECHAN

A75

GRETNA

ANNAN

1
2
3
4
5
6
7

E F G H

10 miles

ANNAN, Dumfries & Galloway   **Map E5**
EC Wed MD Fri, Sat SEE Moat House, old church
✗ Blue Bell Inn, High St ✆ (01461) 202385

Galabank Park, North Street DG12 6AQ *Well maintained site near centre* ✆ (01556) 503806 Fax
(01556) 503806 OS map 85/194673 ½m N of Annan on B722 (Waterbeck) beside River Annan
Open April-Sept–no adv booking 30 pitches Grass, level, sheltered ▢❀

Queensberry Bay Caravan Park, Powfoot DG12 5PU ♿ (01461) 700205 OS map 85/138653
3½m W of Annan off B724 (Dumfries) on Powfoot road by Solway Firth Open Apr-Oct 172 pitches
(70 static) Hard standing and grass, level, open ▦⚲▢▢⬭❀∅ fishing

BEATTOCK, Dumfries & Galloway   **Map E4**
EC Wed
✗ Beattock House ✆ (01683) 300403

Beattock House Hotel Caravan Park DG10 9QB *Pleasant wooded site in grounds of country
house adj main road* ✆ (01683) 300403 OS map 78/079027 ¼m N of Beattock centre near hotel
Open Apr-Oct 15 pitches Grass, some hard standings, level, sheltered ▢∅⤳🛉🔥 lic bar

Craigielands Caravan Park DG10 9RB ✆ (01683) 300591 *Prop: Darren Fowler & Mark Seton* OS
map 78/079019 ¼m S of Beattock centre beyond railway bridge Open all year 125 pitches
(75 static) Level/sloping grass and hard standings ✗⚲▢▢∅❀❂⤳🔥🛉🏪& fishing, boating
£10.00 (Mastercard/Visa/Delta) admin@craigielandsleisure.com www.craigielands.co.uk

BONCHESTER BRIDGE–see Hawick

CASTLE DOUGLAS, Dumfries & Galloway   **Map D5**
EC Thurs MD Tues SEE ruined Threave Castle 1m W, Threave Estate gardens 1m SW, Carlingwork
Loch with bird sanctuary
▣ Markethill Car Park ✆ (01556) 502611
✗ Douglas Arms, King St ✆ (01556) 502231

Loch Ken Holiday Park, Parton DG7 3NE ✆ (01644) 470282 Fax (01644) 470297 OS map
84/685705 7m NW of Castle Douglas on A713 (Ayr) by Loch Ken Open Mar-Oct 85 pitches
(35 static) Grass, part level, sheltered ▦⚲▢▢∅❀❂▢❀⤳🔥🛉& fishing, canoe, dinghy and
cycle hire, windsurfing, sailing (launching facs) office@lochkenholidaypark.freeserve.co.uk
www.lochkenholidaypark.freeserve.co.uk

Lochside Park DG7 1EZ ✆ (01556) 502949/503806 Fax (01556) 503806 OS map 84/765618 ½m
S of Castle Douglas off A75 (Gatehouse of Fleet) by Carlingwark Loch Open Easter-Oct–no adv
booking 161 pitches Grass and hard standings, level ▦▢▢❀∅⤳& boating, fishing, putting
www.dumgal.gov.uk/lochside.htm

COCKBURNSPATH, Borders   **Map H2**
✗ Harvesters 13m NW at East Linton ✆ (01620) 860395

Chesterfield Caravan Park, The Neuk TD13 5YH ✆ (01368) 830459 Fax (01368) 830394 OS map
67/770695 1m SW of Cockburnspath off A1 (Berwick) on Abbey St Bathans road Open Apr-Oct
75 pitches (40 static) Level grass ▢▢∅❀∅⤳🔥🛉

Pease Bay Caravan Site, Pease Bay TD13 5YP ✆ (01368) 830206 OS map 67/794707 1½m SE
of Cockburnspath off A1 (Berwick on Tweed) Open Apr-Oct 321 pitches (307 static)–no tents
Level grass, sheltered, hard standings ▦✗▢⤳⚲▢▢∅❀❂∅⤳🛉

COLDINGHAM–see Eyemouth

CROCKETFORD–see Dumfries

DALBEATTIE, Dumfries & Galloway **Map D6**
EC Thurs
✗ Douglas Arms 7m W at Castle Douglas ☎(01556) 502231

Barlochan Caravan Park, Palnackie DG7 1PF ☎(01556) 600256–bkgs (01557) 870267 Fax (01557) 870319 *Prop: TC Gillespie* OS map 84/819571 2½m S of Dalbeattie on A711 (Kirkcudbright) Open Apr-Oct 60 pitches (40 static) Level grass and hard standing, sheltered ⛺🅿️🄱🄱🄰🄾Ø🄲🄾⊙✓◻🄿🄲🄰⚓& fishing £9.75-£14.00 (most cards) info@barlochan.co.uk www.gillespie-leisure.co.uk

Beeswing Caravan Park, Drumjohn Moor, Kirkgunzeon DG2 8JL ☎(01387) 760242 OS map 84/885684 6m NE of Dalbeattie on A711 (Dumfries) Open Mar-Oct 60 pitches 🄱🄰🄱🄰⊛🄾🄲& donkey rides, fishing

Castle Point Caravan Site, Rockcliffe DG5 4QL ☎(01556) 630248 OS map 84/855532 6m S of Dalbeattie off A710 (Coast road to Dumfries) on Rockcliffe road, by sea Open Easter-mid Oct 55 pitches 5 acres, level grass ⛺🅿️🄱🄰🄱🄰⊛🄲🄰& £11.30-£14.00* kce22@dial.pipex.com

Islecroft Caravan Site, Mill Street DG6 4HE ☎(01556) 610012 OS map 84/835614 ¼m E of Dalbeattie centre off A711 (Dumfries) by Colliston Park Open Easter-Sept 74 pitches–no adv booking Grass, level 🄱🄰⊛Ø✓

Kippford Holiday Park, Kippford DG5 4LF ☎(01556) 620636 Fax (01556) 620607 OS map 84/843564 3m S of Dalbeattie on A710 (Solway coast road) Open all year 196 pitches (60 static) Grass, part level, separately screened pitches, terraced, sheltered, some hard standings ⛺🅿️🄱🄰🄱🄰⊛Ø✓🄲🄰⚓ pony trekking, fishing, sea trips, golf, cycle hire £9.00-£17.00* (Mastercard/Visa/Switch/Delta) info@kipfordholidaypark.co.uk www.kipfordholidaypark.co.uk

Mossband Caravan Park, Kirkgunzeon DG2 8JP *Small friendly park, family run* ☎(01387) 760208 Fax (01387) 760628 OS map 84/872665 3½m NE of Dalbeattie on left of A711 (Dumfries) Open Mar-Oct 36 pitches Level grass and hard standings ⛺🅿️🄱🄰🄱🄰⊛✓ tennis, pool room £6.50-£8.50*

Sandyhills Bay Leisure Park, Sandyhills DG5 4NY ☎(01387) 780257 Fax (01387) 870319 OS map 84/891549 6m SE of Dalbeattie on right of A710 (Dumfries) beyond golf course Open Apr-Oct 94 pitches (34 static) Level grass, sheltered ⛺🅿️🄱🄰🄱🄰🄱🄰⊛Ø🄲⊙✓🄲🄰 golf, beach £9.00-£13.00* (Switch/Visa) info@sandyhills-bay.co.uk www.gillespie-leisure.co.uk

DRUMMORE, Dumfries & Galloway **Map A6**
EC Wed SEE church, ruined chapel, Mull of Galloway 2m S
✗ Queens, Mill St ☎(01776) 840300

Clashwannon Caravan Site DG9 9QE ☎(01776) 840632/840374 OS map 82/132374 ½m N of Drummore on A716 (Stranraer) Open Apr-Sept 20 pitches ½ acre level/sloping grass ⛺🅿️✗🄰🄲🄱🄰🄱🄰Ø🄲🄰

DUMFRIES, Dumfries & Galloway **Map D5**
EC Thurs MD Wed SEE Burns house and mausoleum, burgh museum, Globe Inn, Caerlaverock Castle and Wildfowl centre
🄲 Whitesands ☎(01387) 853862
✗ The Grapes, Springholm, Castle Douglas ☎(01556) 650566

Barnsoul Farm and Wildlife Area, Shawhead DG2 9SQ *One of Galloway's most scenic sites, well-known wildlife area–David Bellamy Gold Award Prop: AJ Wight & Co. Ltd* (01387) 730249 6m W of Dumfries off A75 (Castle Douglas) into Shawhead–signposted Open Mar-Nov 50 pitches (30 static) Level/sloping grass and hard standings, sheltered 🄱🄰🄱🄰Ø⊛Ø🄲⊛🄲🄰 campers £10.00-£15.00 barnsouldg@aol.com www.barnsoulfarm.co.uk

Courthill Caravan Park, Auldgirth DG2 0RR ☎(01387) 740336 OS map 78/926837 6m NW of Dumfries on A76 (Kilmarnock) Open all year–no adv booking 33 pitches Grass, level, open ✗🄲🄱🄰Ø⊛🄲

Craigsview Caravan Site, 296 Annan Road DG1 3LN ☎(01387) 753812 OS map 84/005762 1½m E of Dumfries on A780/A75 (Annan) 1½ acres, level Open Easter-Oct 20 pitches ⛺Ø

Galloway Arms, Crocketford DG2 8RA *Site with top facilities of adj hotel* ☎(01556) 690248 OS map 84/832729 9m W of Dumfries on A75 (Newton Stewart) in Crocketford adj hotel Open Apr-Oct 30 pitches Level grass, hard standings, sheltered ⛺✗🄲🄰🄱🄰Ø🄱🄰🄱🄰⊛Ø🄲⊙✓🄲🄰🄲&

Mouswald Caravan Park, Mouswald DG1 4JS ☎(01387) 830226 OS map 84/060740 4½m ESE of Dumfries off A75 (Annan) Open Mar-Oct 50 pitches Grass, level, sheltered, hard standings 🄲🄱🄰🄱🄰Ø⊛Ø🄲🄰

Newfield Caravan Park, Annan Road DG1 3SE ☎(01387) 740228 OS map 84/009759 2½m E of Dumfries on A75 (Annan) Open all year 40 pitches 2½ acres, level ⛺🄱🄰Ø dairy produce, fishing

Park of Brandedleys, Crocketford DG2 8RG ☎0845 4561760 OS map 84/830725 9m W of Dumfries on A75 (Castle Douglas) Open all year 107 pitches (30 static) Grass, part level, hard standing, open ⛺✗🄲🄰🄱🄰Ø🄱🄰🄱🄰Ø⊛Ø🄲🄾⊙✓◻🄲(35)🄲🄰⚓& tennis, sauna £9.00-£15.00 (Mastercard/Visa/Switch)

ECCLEFECHAN, Dumfries & Galloway   Map E5
EC Thurs SEE Carlyle's birthplace
✗ The Courtyard 3m SE at Eaglesfield ✆ (01461) 500215

Cressfield Caravan Park DG11 3DR ✆ (01576) 300702 Fax As Tel OS map 85/196744 ¼m S of Ecclefechan centre on B7076 near junct 19 of A74(M)–signposted Open all year 153 pitches (54 static) Level grass, hard standing ⬛🔲🔵⊕∅⊖↩⛽ dog exercise area, golf nets, putting green, boules, giant chess and draughts, hotel adj

Hoddom Castle Caravan Park, Hoddom Bridge DG11 1BE ✆ (01576) 300251 Fax (01576) 300757 OS map 85/155730 3m SW of Ecclefechan on right of B725 (Dalton) at Hoddom Bridge Open Apr-Oct 250 pitches (44 static) 28 acres, part sloping, part hard standings, sheltered ⛽✗⬛↩⚲🔲🔵⊕∅⊖↩⬛⛽⚹ golf, fishing, tennis, nature trails, guided walks £6.50-£12.00* (Mastercard/Visa/Switch) hoddomcastle@aol.com www.hoddomcastle.co.uk

ETTRICK, Borders   Map F4
✗ Etrrickshaws Lodge 10m NE at Ettrick Bridge ✆ (01750) 52229

Angecroft Caravan Park TD7 5HY ✆ (01750) 62251 OS map 79/277135 ½m S of Ettrick on B709 (Eskdalemuir) Open all year 49 pitches (41 static) Level grass and hard standing, sheltered ⛽⬛🔲🔵⊕∅⛽⬛🏠

Honey Cottage Caravan Park, Hope House TD7 5HU ✆ (01750) 62246 Prop: CA & S Woof OS map 76/295165 2m N of Ettrick on B709 (Selkirk) near junction with B711 (Hawick) Open all year 80 pitches (40 static) 7 acres, level grass, part open some hard standings ⛽↩⬛🔲🔵⊕∅⊖↩⬛⛽ fishing £8.00 www.honeycottagecaravanpark.co.uk

EYEMOUTH, Borders   Map G2
EC Wed SEE harbour, museum, memorial garden, Coldingham Priory 4m NW
🅘 Auld Kirk ✆ (01890) 750678
✗ Contented Sole at harbour ✆ (01890) 750268

Coldingham Caravan Park, Coldingham TD14 5NT ✆ (01890) 750316 OS map 67/896662 4m NW of Eyemouth on A1107 (Cockburnspath) Open Mar-mid Nov 180 pitches (150 static) Hard standings ⚲🔵⬛🏠

Eyemouth Holiday Park, Fort Road TD14 5ER ✆ (01890) 751050 Fax (01890) 751462 OS map 67/941648 ½m N of Eyemouth on A1107 (Burnmouth) Open Mar-Nov 290 pitches (270 static) Level grass and hard standings ⛽✗⚲↩⚲🔲🔵⊕∅⊖↩⚹⬛⛽ children's room, barbecue area, boat storage, private beach (Mastercard/Visa/Switch)

Highview Caravan Park, Coldingham TD14 5TX ✆ (01890) 771221 OS map 67/843663 6m WNW of Eyemouth on A1107 (Cockburnspath) Open Mar 31-Oct 31 286 pitches (150 static) grass and hard standing, level ⛽⚲🔲🔵⊕∅↩⬛ chip shop

Scoutscroft Caravan and Camping Park, Coldingham TD14 5NB ✆ (018907) 71338 Fax (018907) 71746 Prop: The Hamilton Family OS map 67/907662 2½m NW of Eyemouth off A1107 (Dunbar) on B6438 (Coldingham) Open Mar-Nov–no tents 180 pitches (120 static) Grass, level, hard standings, sheltered ✗⚲↩⬛🔵⊕∅⊖↩⛽(50) ⚹⬛🏠 diving centre £16.00-£22.00 (Mastercard/Visa/Switch) holidays@scoutscroft.co.uk www.scoutscroft.co.uk

GALASHIELS, Borders
Map F2

EC Wed SEE Mercat Cross, Old Gala House, Sir Walter Scott's home at Abbotsford 2m SE, Melrose Abbey 4m E

🛈 St John's St ☎ (01896) 755551 ✗ Abbotsford Arms, Stirling St ☎ (01896) 822517

Gibson Park, Melrose TD6 9RY ☎ (01896) 822969 OS map 73/544341 4m SE of Galasheils on right of A6091 (St Boswells) in Melrose Open all year 60 pitches 3 acres, level grass and hard standings 🛢🕹🖉⤴🚐 £16.10-£21.50 (Mastercard/Visa/Delta/Switch) www.caravanclub.co.uk

GATEHOUSE OF FLEET, Dumfries & Galloway
Map C6

EC Thurs SEE ruined Cardoness castle, Anwoth churchyard

🛈 Car Park, Castle Douglas ☎ (01557) 814212

✗ The Masonic Arms, 10 Ann St ☎ (01557) 814335 Open 12-2/6-9 (closed Mon & Tue Nov-Mar)

Anwoth Caravan Park, Garden Street DG7 2JU ☎ (01557) 814333 Fax (01557) 814333 OS map 83/595562 ¼m S of Gatehouse of Fleet off A75 (Newton Stewart) Open March-Oct 66 pitches Grass, level, sheltered 🏋🛢🕹🖉 £15.00-£20.00* (Mastercard/Visa/Delta/Switch) enquiries@auchenlarie.co.uk www.ukparks.co.uk/anworth

Auchenlarie Holiday Farm DG7 2EX ☎ (01557) 840251 Fax (01557) 840333 OS map 83/536522 5m SW of Gatehouse of Fleet on A75 (Newton Stewart) Open Easter-Oct 447 pitches (160 static) 35 acres level grass part sheltered 🏋✗🍴⤴🏹🛢🖉🕹🌐🕹⤴🖊 crazy golf £15.00-£25.00* (most cards) enquiries@auchenlarie.co.uk www.auchenlarie.co.uk

Mossyard Caravan Site, Mossyard DG7 2ET ☎ (01557) 840226 Prop: McConchie Partnership OS map 83/548519 4½m SW of Gatehouse of Fleet on A75 (Newton Stewart) Open Easter-Oct–must book peak periods 55 pitches 6½ acres, level/gentle slope 🛢🖉🕹🚐🏠⛸ beach location £8.00-£13.00 enquiry@mossyard.co.uk www.mossyard.co.uk

GLENLUCE, Dumfries & Galloway
Map B6

✗ George 10m W at Stranraer ☎ (01776) 872487

Cock Inn Caravan Park, Auchenmalg DG8 0JT ☎ (01581) 500227 OS map 82/236518 5m SE of Glenluce on left of A747 (Port William) Open Mar-Oct–must book peak periods 120 pitches (70 static) Level/sloping grass and hard standings 🏋✗🍴⤴🛢🖉🕹🌐🕹⤴🍴🚐⛸ first aid, sauna

Glenluce Caravan and Camping Park DG8 0QR ☎ (01581) 300412 Prop: Robert & Richard Rankin OS map 82/197574 ½m W of Glenluce off A75 (Stranraer) Open Mar-Oct–must book peak periods 45 pitches (29 static) Grass, level, sheltered, hard standings ✗🛢🖉🕹⊡(indoor, heated) ⤴🍴🚐⛸ meals £12.00-£17.00 dogs £2.00 per day (most cards) enquiries@glenlucecaravans.co.uk www.glenlucecaravans.co.uk

Whitecairn Farm Caravan Park DG8 0NZ ☎ (01581) 300267 Prop: Robert & Irene Rankin & Sons OS map 82/205598 1½m N of Glenluce on Penninghame Forest road Open Apr-Oct 50 pitches (40 static) Grass, level, open 🛢🕹🖉🕹🖉⤴🅿🚐 1½m to bar/restaurant and shops £12.00-£17.00 dogs £2.00 per day (Mastercard/Visa) enquiries@whitecairncaravans.co.uk www.whitecairncaravans.co.uk

GREENLAW, Borders   **Map G2**
✗Purves Hall 4m SE on A697 ☎(01890) 840558

Greenlaw Caravan Park, Bank Street TD10 6XX ☎(01361) 810341 OS map 74/709461 ¼m N of
Greenlaw on A6105 (Duns) by river Open Easter-Oct 115 pitches (90 static) 11 acres, level grass
🖩⌀ sep pitches, fishing

GRETNA, Dumfries & Galloway   **Map F5**
EC Wed SEE marriage smithy and museum at Gretna Green
🄳Blacksmith's shop ☎(01461) 337834
✗Solway Lodge Hotel, 97-99 Annan Rd ☎(01461) 338266

Braids Caravan Park, Annan Road DG16 5DQ ☎(01461) 337409 *Prop: John & Isabel Scott* OS
map 85/318674 In Gretna on B721 (Annan) Open all year–advisable book peak periods
94 pitches 5 acres part grass, part hard standings, sheltered 🖩🖩⌀✿⌀🚿 £8.00-£12.00 (most
cards + surcharge) enquiries@thebraidscaravanpark.co.uk www.thebraidscaravanpark.co.uk

King Robert the Bruce's Cave Caravan-Camping Park, Kirkpatrick Fleming DG11 3AT ☎(01461)
800285 OS map 85/267703 3m NW of Gretna off A74 (Lockerbie) Open Apr-Oct 80 pitches
Grass and hard standings, part sloping, sheltered 🖩🖩⌀🖩🚻(1) ☂ fishing £10.00

HAWICK, Borders   **Map F4**
EC Tues SEE parish church, Goldielands Peel Tower, Wilton Lodge Park, museum
🄳Drumlanrig's Tower ☎(01450) 372547
✗Kirklands, West Stewart Pl ☎(01450) 372263

Riverside Caravan Park, Hornshole Bridge TD9 8SY ☎(01450) 373785 *Prop: Border Caravans
Ltd* OS map 79/537169 2m NE of Hawick on left of A698 (Kelso) by river Teviot Open Mar-Oct
104 pitches (60 static) 8 acres hard standings and grass, level/gentle slope
🖩⌀✿⌀❀⌁🖵🖩🚿 fishing, 9-hole golf course £10.00-£15.00

JEDBURGH, Borders   **Map G3**
EC Thurs *Border town set in beautiful landscape* SEE abbey, Queen Mary's House, Jedburgh
Castle (jail museum)
🄳Murray's Green ☎(01835) 863435
✗Buccleuch & Queensberry Hotel, 112 Drumlanrig St, Thornhill ☎(01848) 330215

Jedwater Caravan Park TD8 6PJ ☎(01835) 869595 Fax (01835) 869595 OS map 80/667160 3m
S of Jedburgh on A68 (Carter Bar) Open Easter-Oct 135 pitches (60 static) Grass, level, open,
hard standings 🖩⌀🖩🖩⌀✿⌀❀⌁🖵🖩(20) ☂ footballl pitch, giant trampolines
jedwater@clara.co.uk www.jedwater.co.uk

Lilliardsedge Park, Ancrum TD8 6TZ ☎(01835) 830271 *Prop: Portzim Ltd* OS map 74/620267
5m N of Jedburgh on A68 (St Boswells) Open Apr-Sept 140 pitches (90 static) 🖩🖩➰🖩🖩⌀⌁
bar meals, campers' kitchen, fishing, 9-hole golf course £12.50-£17.00 (Mastercard/Visa/Amex)

KELSO, Borders   **Map G3**
EC Wed *Attractive town on bend of river Tweed* SEE abbey ruins, bridge, Floors Castle
🄳Town House, The Square ☎(01573) 223464
✗Cross Keys, The Square ☎(01573) 223303

Kirkfield Caravan Park, Town Yetholm TD5 8RU ☎(01573) 223346 OS map 74/821281 7m SE of
Kelso off B6352 (Yetholm) Open Apr-Oct 31 pitches–no tents Level/sloping grass and hard
standing, sheltered 🖩⌀✿

Springwood Caravan Park, Springwood Estate TD5 8LS ☎(01573) 224596 Fax (01573) 224033
OS map 74/720333 1m SW of Kelso on left of A699 (St Boswells) Open Easter-Oct 15 250
pitches (210 static) 30 acres level/sloping grass and hard standing, sheltered 🖩🖩🖩(16 amp)
⌀✿⌀❀⌁🖩🖩 £16.00 (min)* (most cards) tourers@springwood.biz www.springwood.biz

KIPPFORD–see Dalbeattie

KIRKBEAN, Dumfries & Galloway **Map D6**
✗ Abbey Arms 5m N at New Abbey ☎ (01387) 880277

Lighthouse Leisure, Southerness DG2 8AZ ☎ (01387) 880277 *Prop: Catherine Robertson* OS map 84/550970 3m S of Kirkbean on A710 (Sandyhills) Open Mar-Oct 200 pitches (180 static) 8 acres level grass ▮✗▮▮▮▮▮▮▮▮▮▮▮ Lighthouse open in summer £12.00-£14.00 (most cards) lighthouseleis@aol.com www.lighthouseleisure.co.uk

Southerness Holiday Village DG2 8AZ ☎ (01387) 880256 Fax (01387) 880429 OS map 84/976544 2m S of Kirkbean off A710 on road to Southerness Point Open Mar-Oct 600 pitches (400 static) Grass, level ▮✗▮▮▮▮▮▮▮▮▮(heated) ▮▮▮▮(25) ▮▮ lic club/bar, campers' kitchen private beach £9.00-£15.00* (most cards) enquiries@parkdeanholidays.co.uk www.parkdeanholidays.co.uk

KIRKCUDBRIGHT, Dumfries & Galloway **Map C6**
EC Thurs SEE Mercat Cross, museum, tolbooth, Broughton House, harbour
▮ Harbour Sq ☎ (01557) 330494
✗ Selkirk Arms, High St ☎ (01557) 330402

Brighouse Bay Holiday Park, Borgue DG6 4TS ☎ (01557) 870267 *Prop: TC Gillespie* OS map 83/626451 6m SW of Kirkcudbright off B727 (Borgue) on Brighouse Bay road Open all year 300 pitches (143 static) 24 acres, part sloping, part hard standings ▮✗▮▮▮▮▮▮▮▮ ▮▮(indoor) ▮▮▮▮(120) ▮▮▮ fishing, slipway, pony trekking, 18-hole golf par 72, jacuzzi, steam room, quad bikes, 10-pin bowling, driving range, nature trails £11.90-£16.75 (Mastercard/Visa/Switch/Maestro) info@brighouse-bay.co.uk www.gillespie-leisure.co.uk

Seaward Caravan Park, Dhoon Bay DG6 4TJ ☎ (01557) 331079 (bookings 01557 870267) Fax (01557) 870319 OS map 83/664494 2½m SW of Kirkcudbright on right of B727 (Borgue) Open Mar-Oct 50 pitches (30 static) Some hard standings, level grass, sheltered ▮▮▮▮▮▮▮▮▮▮▮▮(20) ▮▮ serviced pitches, mini golf, games room, 9 hole golf course, sea angling £9.50-£13.50* aa@seaward-park.co.uk www.gillespie-leisure.co.uk

Silvercraigs Caravan-Camping Park, Silvercraigs Road DG6 4BT ☎ (01557) 330123 OS map 83/685510 ¼m S of Kirkcudbright off A711 (Dundrennan) Open Easter-Oct–no adv booking 50 pitches Grass, part sloping, open ▮▮▮▮▮▮▮

LANGHOLM, Dumfries & Galloway **Map F5**
EC Wed SEE remains of castle, Common Riding last Fri Jul, Gilnockie Tower 4m S
✗ Eskdale, Market place ☎ (01387) 380357

Whitshiels Caravan Park DG13 0HG ☎ (01387) 380494 OS map 79/365854 ¼m N of Langholm on left of A7 (Hawick) adj café Open all year 10 pitches ½ acre grass and hard standings, sheltered ✗▮▮▮▮▮▮▮

LAUDER, Borders **Map F2**
EC Thurs SEE church, Thirlestane Castle (plasterwork ceilings). Border County Museum
✗ Black Bull, Market Pl ☎ (01578) 722208

Thirlestane Castle Caravan and Camping Park TD2 6RU ☎ (01578) 718884 Mobile (07976) 231032 *Prop: G Maitland-Carew* OS map 74/538473 ¼m SE of Lauder off A697 (Coldstream) and A68 Open Easter-Oct 1 60 pitches Grass, part sloping, part open ▮▮▮▮▮ £12.00 thirlestanepark@btconnect.com www.thirlestanepark.co.uk

LOCHMABEN–see Lockerbie

LOCKERBIE, Dumfries & Galloway **Map E5**
EC Tues MD Tues, Thurs, Fri *Pretty market town of red sandstone* SEE lamb sales market on Lamb Hill, Lochmaben Castle 3m W
✗ Blue Bell ☎ (01576) 302309

Halleaths Caravan Park, Lochmaben DG11 1NA ☎ (01387) 810630 *Prop: G Hoey* OS map 78/098818 3m W of Lockerbie off A709 (Dumfries) Open Mar-Nov 70 pitches Grass, level, sheltered ▮▮▮▮▮▮▮▮▮▮▮ family facs £7.00-£12.00 halleathscaravanpark@btopenworld.com caravan-sitefinder.co.uk/sites/2436

Kirk Loch Brae Municipal Caravan Site, Kirk Loch Brae, Lochmaben DG12 6AQ ☎ (01556) 503806 OS map 78/081826 4m W of Lockerbie on A709 (Dumfries) Open Apr-Oct–no adv booking 30 pitches Grass and tarmac, level ▮▮▮▮▮ golf, boating, fishing

MELROSE–see Galashiels

MONIAVE, Dumfries & Galloway **Map D5**
EC Thurs SEE fort, burial place of Annie Laurie
✗ Woodlea ☎ (01848) 200209

Woodlea Hotel Caravan Park DG3 4EN ☎ (01848) 200209 OS map 78/776895 1½m SW of Moniave on A702 (New Galloway) in grounds of hotel Open Easter-Oct 10 marked pitches 1 acre, mainly sloping, hard standings ✗▮▮▮▮▮▮▮(indoor) ▮▮▮ tennis, games room, croquet, bowls, badminton, cycle hire, sauna, putting green (all cards)

For more up-to-date information, and for links to camping websites, visit our site at:
www.butford.co.uk/camping

NEWTON STEWART, Dumfries & Galloway   **Map B5**
EC Wed MD Thurs SEE church, museum, Galloway Forest Park
🛈 Dashwood Sq ☎ (01671) 402431
✖ Brambles Bistro & Coffee Shop, 43 Main St, Glenluce ☎ (01581) 300494

Caldons Campsite, Glentrool DG8 6AJ ☎ (01671) 820218 OS map 77/400790 13m N of Newton
Stewart off A714 (Girvan) at Bargrennan via Glentrool (Forestry Commission) Open Apr-Oct–no
adv booking 160 pitches Grass, level, sheltered 🛒🖥🔌🗑⊕∅🕒🍴🎮(20) ♿

Castle Cary Holiday Park, Creetown DG8 7DQ ☎ (01671) 820264 Fax (01671) 820670 OS map
83/477576 7m S of Newton Stewart on left of A75 (Castle Douglas) Open all year 95 pitches–no
adv booking Grass and hard standing, level, sheltered 🛒✖♀⌐➤🖥🔌🗑⊕∅🗔(indoor and
outdoor) ⊕↩☐🍴(30) 🚐♿ paddling pools, solarium, slipway, donkey park, nature trails, games
room, coarse fishing loch, crazy golf £10.80-£13.50* (most cards)
enquiries@castlecarypark.19.co.uk www.castlecary-caravans.com

Creebridge Caravan Park, Minnigaff DG8 6AJ ☎ (01671) 402324/402432 Fax (01671) 402324 OS
map 83/415657 ¼m E of Newton Stewart off A75 (Gatehouse of Fleet) Open Mar-Nov 86 pitches
(42 static) Grass and hard standing, sheltered 🛒🖥🔌🗑⊕∅🕒🚐 £8.00-£10.00*
johnsharples@btopenworld.co.uk www.creebridgecaravanpark.com

Creetown Caravan Park, Creetown DG8 7HU ☎ (01671) 820377 *Prop: J & B McNeill* OS map
83/475585 6m SE of Newton Stewart off A75 (Castle Douglas) Open Apr-Oct 66 pitches
(50 static) 🖥🔌🗑⊕∅🗔↩☐🍴🚐 indoor hot tub £12.00 (all cards)
creetowncaravan@btconnect.com www.creetowncaravans.co.uk

Glentrool Holiday Park, Bargrennan DG8 6RN ☎ (01671) 840280 *Prop: M & CA Moore* OS map
76/77/353772 8m NW of Newton Stewart off A714 (Girvan) at Bargrennan on Glentrool road
Open Mar-Oct 42 pitches (24 static) grass and hard standings, sheltered
🛒🖥🔌🗑⊕∅↩🍴🚐♿ £8.50-£9.50 enquiries@glentroolholidaypark.co.uk
www.glentroolholidaypark.co.uk

Talnotry Campsite (Forest Enterprise) DG8 6AJ ☎ (01671) 402420 OS map 77/491715 6m NE
of Newton Stewart on right of A712 (New Galloway) Open Apr-Sept 60 pitches 15 acres, part
sloping, hard standing and grass, sheltered ⊕∅↩♿ fishing, forest trails (Mastercard/Visa)

Three Lochs Caravan Park, Balminnoch, Kirkcowan DG8 0EP ☎ (01671) 830304 OS map
82/272654 9m W of Newton Stewart off A75 (Glenluce) Open Easter-1st Sat in Oct 145 pitches
(100 static) Level grass and hard standing 🛒🖥🔌⊕🗔(heated) ↩☐🍴🚐 children's playroom,
snooker, sailing, pitch and putt, fishing £11.00-£12.00* info@3lochs.co.uk www.3lochs.co.uk

PEEBLES, Borders   **Map F3**
EC Wed MD Fri SEE parish church, Neidpath Castle
🛈 Chambers Institute, High St ☎ (01721) 720138
✖ Cross Keys Hotel, 24 Northgate ☎ (01721) 724222

Crossburn Caravan Park, Edinburgh Road EH45 8ED ☎ (01721) 720501 Fax (01721) 720501 OS
map 73/250416 ½m N of Peebles on left of A703 (Edinburgh) Open Apr-Oct–must book
130 pitches (80 static) Level grass and hard standing, sheltered 🛒🖥🔌🗑⊕∅🕒↩🍴🚐♿
fishing, mountain bike hire, putting green £12.00-£13.00* (Mastercard/Visa/Switch/Delta)
enquiries@crossburncaravans.co.uk www.crossburnscaravans.com

Rosetta Touring Caravan-Camping Park, Rosetta Road EH45 8PG ☎ (01721) 720770 *Prop: The
Clay Family* OS map 73/244414 ½m W of Peebles off A72 (Biggar) adj golf course Open Apr-Oct
200 pitches (60 static) Grass and hard standings, level/sloping sheltered
🛒♀🖥🔌🗑⊕∅🕒↩☐🚐 bowling green £13.00

Tweedside Caravan Site, Montgomery Street, Innerleithen EH44 6JS ☎ (01896) 831271 OS map
73/330564 6m SE of Peebles on A72 (Innerleithen) Open Apr-Oct–no adv booking 80 pitches
Hard standings 🛒➤🖥🔌🗑⊕∅🕒↩🍴🎮🚐♿

KEY TO SYMBOLS

🛒	shop	🔌	gas supplies	🚐	winter storage for caravans
✖	restaurant	⊕	chemical disposal point	🅿	parking obligatory
♀	bar	∅	payphone	⊗	no dogs
⌐	takeaway food	🗔	swimming pool	🚐	caravan hire
➤	off licence	🕒	games area	🏠	bungalow hire
🖥	laundrette	↩	children's playground	♿	facilities for disabled
🔌	mains electric hook-ups	☐	TV	☀	shaded

PORTPATRICK, Dumfries & Galloway   **Map A6**
EC Thurs SEE Dunskey castle, parish church
✗Harbour House ✆(01776) 810456

Castle Bay Caravan Park DG9 9AA ✆(01776) 810462 OS map 82/008536 ½m SE of Portpatrick off A77 (Stranraer) Open Mar-Oct 125 pitches (106 static) 22 acres, level grass and hard standing, sheltered ▓▐▤▨◉∅◉↩▭▰▱

Galloway Point Holiday Park, Portree Farm DG9 9AA ✆(01776) 810561 OS map 82/008538 ½m SE of Portpatrick off A77 (Stranraer) Open Mar-Oct 200 pitches (80 static) 16 acres, grass and hard standings, part level, sheltered ✗♀↩≯▐▤▨◉∅◉↩▰(£50) ▱ £8.00-£16.00
www.gallowaypointholidaypark.co.uk

Sunnymeade Caravan Park DG9 8LN ✆(01776) 810293 OS map 82/005540 ½m SE of Portpatrick off A77 (Stranraer) Open Easter-Oct 90 pitches (50 static) 8 acres, level/gentle slope, grass and hard standings ▐▰▨◉▱ fishing

PORT WILLIAM, Dumfries & Galloway   **Map B6**
EC Wed
✗Monreith Arms, The Square ✆(01988) 700232

Knock School Caravan Park, Monreith DG8 8NJ ✆(01988) 700414/700409 *Prop: Mrs P Heywood* OS map 83/368405 3m SE of Port William on A747 (Isle of Whithorn) near sea Open Easter-Sept—must book peak periods 15 pitches Grass, part sloping, hard standing, sheltered ▓▰ golf, sea fishing £9.00* *pauline@knockschool.com www.knockschool.com*

Monreith Sands Holiday Park, Monreith DG8 9LJ ✆(01988) 700218 OS map 82/365415 3m SE of Port William on A747 (Isle of Whithorn) in village of Monreith Open Mar-Oct 60 pitches (45 static) Level grass, sheltered ▐▨ near beach

West Barr Farm Caravan Park DG8 9QS ✆(01988) 700367 OS map 82/316462 2m NW of Port William on A747 (Glenluce) Open Mar-Oct 30 pitches ▐▰▨◉

SANDHEAD, Dumfries & Galloway   **Map A6**
✗North West Castle 8m N at Stranraer ✆(01776) 834413

Sandhead Caravan Park DG9 9JN ✆(01776) 830296 OS map 82/102508 ¼m NE of Sandhead on right of A716 (Glenluce) Open Apr-Oct 130 pitches (70 static) 10 acres, mainly level grass, sheltered ▓♀≯▐▰▨∅⚿ by sea

Sands of Luce Caravan Park DG9 9JN ✆(01776) 830456 Fax (01776) 830477 OS map 82/103510 1m N of Sandhead on A716 (Stranraer) Open Mar-Oct 90 pitches (40 static) Grass, part level, part open ▓▐▰▨◉∅↩▰(25) ▱⚿ games room, freezer pack service, private beach, boat launching ramp £12.00 (min)* (Visa/Switch) *info@sandsofluceholidaypark.co.uk www.sandsofluceholidaypark.co.uk*

SANQUHAR, Dumfries & Galloway   **Map D4**
EC Thurs SEE Tolbooth Museum, castle ruins, Riding of Marches Ceremony (Aug)
✗Nithsdale, High St ✆(01659) 550506

Castle View Caravan Park, Townfoot DG4 6AX ✆(01659) 50291 OS map 78/788094 At S end of Sanquhar on A76 (Dumfries) at Esso petrol station Open Mar-Oct 30 pitches Grass, level, some hard standings ▓▨ £10.00 (all cards)

SELKIRK, Borders   **Map F3**
EC Thurs SEE town hall, Flodden memorial, Bowhill House
▨Halliwell's House ✆(01750) 20054
✗Cross Keys Inn, Market Place ✆(01750) 21283

Victoria Park, Buccleuch Road TD7 5DN ✆(01750) 20897 Fax (01750) 20897 OS map 73/465288 ¼m W of Selkirk off A708 (Moffat) by Ettrick Water Open Apr-Oct 60 pitches Level grass and hard standing ▐▰▨◉∅▭◉↩ gym (Visa/Switch)

SOUTHERNESS–see Kirkbean

STRANRAER, Dumfries & Galloway   **Map A6**
EC Wed SEE Peel Tower, Lochinch, Kennedy Gardens 3m E, Logan Botanic Garden 10m S
🖈28 Harbour St ☎(01776) 702595
✗George, George St ☎(01776) 702487

Aird Donald Caravan Park, London Road DG9 8RN ☎(01776) 702025 OS map 82/074605 ¼m E
of Stranraer off A75 (Newton Stewart) Open all year 75 pitches grass and hard standings
🗎🖴🗘⊗🗘↵ £10.00-£11.50 e-mail email@airddonald.co.uk www.aird-donald.co.uk

Cairnryan Caravan and Chalet Park, Cairnryan DG9 8QX ☎(01581) 200231 OS map 82/075674
5m N of Stranraer on A77 (Girvan) by Loch Ryan Open Apr-Oct–must book peak periods
110 pitches (85 static) Hard standings, level, sheltered 🖪🛒🗘🗎🖴🗏🗘🖴(50) 🚻 billiards
(all cards)

Drumlochart Caravan Park, Lochnaw DG9 0RN ☎(01776) 870232 OS map 82/998634 4½m NW
of Stranraer on B7043 (Lochnaw) Open Mar-Oct 120 pitches (90 static)–no tents 22 acres level
grass and hard standings, sheltered 🖪🗎🖴🗎🗘🖴🗏(heated) 🗘↵🚻🕾 lic club, pony trekking,
coarse fishing (Mastercard/Visa/Delta/Switch)

Ryan Bay Caravan Park, Cairnryan Road DG9 8QP ☎(01776) 889458 OS map 82/084628 1½m
NE of Stranraer on A77 (Girvan) by Loch Ryan Open Mar-Oct 200 pitches (170 static) Grass,
level 🖪🛒🗎🖴↵🖴(50) 🚻 (all cards)

Wig Bay Holiday Park, Loch Ryan DG9 0PS ☎(01776) 853233 OS map 82/034664 4¼ NNW of
Stranraer on A718 (Kirkcolm) by Loch Ryan Open Mar-Oct 120 pitches (96 static) Level grass
and hard standings, sheltered 🛒🗎🖴🗎🗘⊗🗎🗏↵🗗🖴 dance hall

THORNHILL, Dumfries & Galloway   **Map D4**
EC Thurs SEE 18c cross, Drumlanrig Castle
✗George, Drumlanrig St ☎(01848) 330326

Penpont Caravan Camping Park, Penpont DG3 4BH ☎(01848) 330470 *Prop: Nick & Nesta van
der Wielen* OS map 78/850949 2m W of Thornhill on left of A702 (Moniaive) Open Apr-Oct
40 pitches (14 static) Grass, level, open 🗎🖴🗘⊗🖴🖴 £8.00-£10.00
penpont.caravan.park@ukgateway.net www.penpontcaravanandcamping.co.uk

TOWN YETHOLM–see Kelso

WHITHORN, Dumfries & Galloway   **Map C6**
EC Wed SEE priory church, museum
✗Steam Packet 3m SE at Isle of Whithorn ☎(01988) 500334

Burrowhead Holiday Village, Isle of Whithorn DG8 8JB ☎(01988) 500252 OS map 83/450345
3m SE of Whithorn off A750 (Isle of Whithorn) on Burrowhead road Open Apr-Oct 300 pitches
(200 static) Grass and hard standings, part level, part open 🖪✗🛒↗🗎🖴🗘⊗🗎🗘↵🗗🖴(25)
🖴(2) 🕾 tennis, football, mini golf, solarium, bubble spa, sauna (Mastercard/Visa)

Castlewigg Caravan Camping Park DG8 8DP ☎(01988) 500616 Fax (01988) 500616 OS map
83/435450 2m N of Whithorn on A746 (Wigtown) Open all year 35 pitches Hard standing and
grass, level, sheltered ✗🛒🗎🖴⊗🗎🗘🖴🖴 fishing

Dominating the sunny southern shore of the Firth of Forth is the dramatically sited grey-stone city of Edinburgh, an eastern landmark in the busy industrial belt that stretches across Scotland to Glasgow and beyond. The main resort on the coast is Dunbar, backed by the Lammermuir Hills. The northern shore of the Forth estuary is more accessible, the fine sands running east from Aberdour all the way to St Andrews, with its golf courses and bottle dungeons. To the north is charming Loch Leven, a famous trout water ringed by the Lomond Hills.

In adjoining Tayside, the main resort on the coast north of the Tay estuary is Dundee, linked to the southern shore by two long bridges. Backing it and the more pleasant smaller resorts to the north is fertile farmland crossed by the Vale of Strathmore, with its views of the Grampian peaks. Pitlochry, north of Perth on the A9 to Inverness, is an enjoyable place to stay. In western Tayside are the Trossachs, a richly wooded gorge linking Lochs Achray and Katrine, with high mountains and forests on the north and rolling farmland on the south.

In the centre is Rob Roy country, in which the principal town is Stirling, dominated by its cliff-top castle above the Forth. And west of the densely populated industrial belt around Glasgow in mainland Strathclyde is the scenic holiday estuary of the Firth of Clyde. The best known resorts are Ayr, with miles of sands, Ardrossan, linked by ferry with the Isle of

Arran, Dunoon, on the Cowal Peninsula, Gourock, from which there are cruises on the Firth, Largs, in a superb setting and with fine views of the islands, and Wemyss Bay, where ferries sail to Rothesay on the Isle of Bute.

North of Dumbarton, where the Clyde ceases to be industrial, is Loch Lomond, dotted with islands and with a length of twenty-four miles the largest stretch of inland water in Britain. Quiet places to stay around the loch are Aberfoyle, Ardgarten and Arrochar. North and west of the Firth of Clyde are the deep sea lochs, long peninsulas and romantic islands of westernmost Strathclyde, with their breathtaking scenery. In the upper half of the deeply indented coast is Oban, the hub of ferry services to the islands – Mull to the north, Jura and Islay to the west. The mainland capital is Inverary, and the head of Loch Fyne. West of the town is the Pass of Glencoe, scene of the infamous massacre in the seventeenth century, and to the south, on the tip of the peninsula is Southend, ringed by prehistoric barrows and hill forts.

Campsites tend to be large and numerous on the east coast, small and infrequent on the west. Many of those within reach of the industrial belt or on popular through routes like the A9 tend to fill up early in season. Main concentrations are at the better-known places, like Stirling, Ayr, Pitlochry, Blairgowrie, Dunoon, Maybole and Oban. Many of the campsites on the west can only be reached by narrow single-track roads.

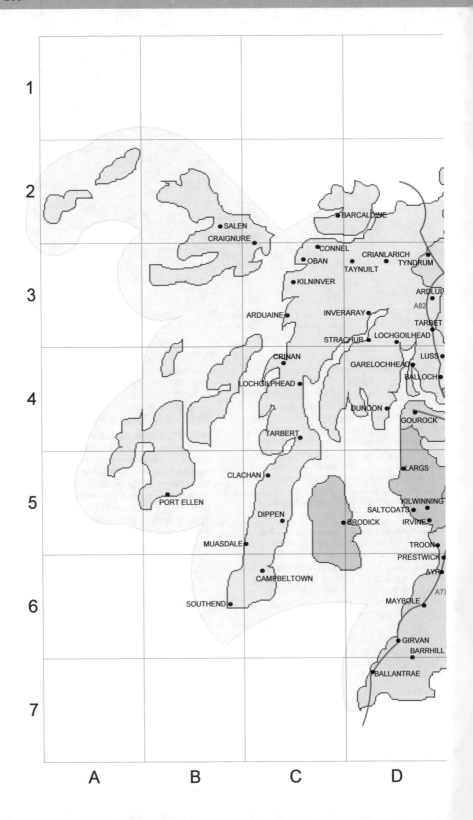

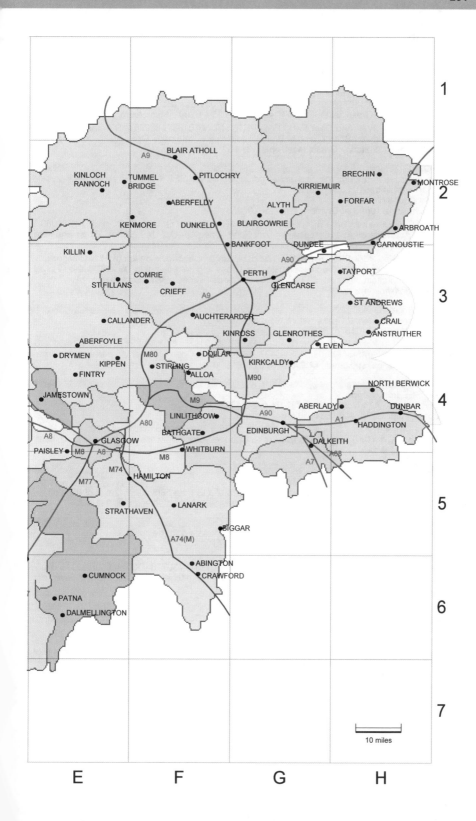

ABERFELDY, Perth & Kinross   **Map F2**
EC Wed *Vacation resort beautifully set on river Tay between Pitlochry and Loch Tay* SEE Black
Watch monument, Gen. Wade's Bridge (18c), Birks nature trail, Loch Tay 6m SW
🅸 The Square ☏(01887) 820276
✗ Weem 1m NW at Weem ☏(01887) 820381

Aberfeldy Caravan Camping Park, Dunkeld Road PH15 2AF ☏(01738) 475211 Fax (01738)
   475210 Aberfeldy (01887) 820662 ¼m E of Aberfeldy on A827 (Ballinluig) Open Apr-Oct 132
   pitches (40 static) Grass, level ▣🅟⊕∅⌁🅟& £9.35-£13.00* (Mastercard/Visa)

Glengoulandie Caravan and Deer Park, Foss PH16 5NL ☏(01887) 830261 OS map 51/768526
   9m NW of Aberfeldy on B846 (Tummel Bridge) adjoining wildlife park Open Apr 1-Oct 10–no adv
   bkg 40 pitches (32 static) Grass, level, open ⚑∂∅

ABERFOYLE, Stirling   **Map E3**
Village well placed for touring the Trossachs and Loch Lomond SEE Trossachs N, Queen Elizabeth
Forest Park (forest trails), Loch Katrine
🅸 Main St ☏(01877) 382352
✗ Buchanan Arms 10m S at Drymen ☏(01360) 870588

Cobleland Caravan and Camp Site, Gartmore FK8 3RR ☏(01877) 382392 OS map 57/531988
   2½m S of Aberfoyle off A81 (Glasgow) by river Forth Open Apr-Oct 140 pitches Grass and hard
   standing, level, sheltered ⚑▣🅟∂⊕∅⌁& fishing, forest walks (Mastercard/Visa/Switch)

Trossachs Holiday Park FK8 3SA (01877) 382614 3m S of Aberfoyle on left of A81 (Glasgow)
   Open Apr-Oct 99 pitches 40 acres, part sloping Grass and hard standing ⚑⚲▣🅟⊕∅⊕
   ⌁▯⚑▭ mountain bike hire £10.00-£18.00 (all cards) info@trossachsholidays.co.uk
   www.trossachsholidays.co.uk

ABERLADY, East Lothian   **Map H4**
SEE parish church, Mercat Cross, nature reserve
✗ Kilspindle House ☏(01875) 870682

Aberlady Caravan Park, Haddington Road EH32 08Z ☏(01875) 870666 Fax (01875) 870666 OS
   map 66/476783 ½m S of Aberlady on A6137 (Haddington) Open Mar-Oct 15 pitches Level grass
   and hard standings, sheltered 🅟∂⚑🏠 £8.00-£14.00*

ABINGTON, S Lanarkshire   **Map F6**
EC Wed SEE Iron Age fort
🅸 Welcome Break, A74 Northbound ☏(01864) 502436
✗ Abington, Carlisle Rd ☏(01864) 502467

Crossburn Caravan Park, Douglas ML11 0QA ☏(01555) 851029 OS map 72/835305 10m NW of
   Abington off M74 (Glasgow) on A70 (Douglas) Open all year 30 pitches 2 acres, terraced, hard
   standings ▣∂⊕⚑

ALLOA, Clackmannanshire   **Map F4**
✗ Royal 8m W at Bridge of Allan ☏(01786) 832284

Diverswell Farm, Fishcross FK10 3HL ☏(01259) 62802 OS map 58/892958 2m N of Alloa off
   A908 (Tillicoultry) Open Apr-Oct 60 pitches 20 acres level hard standings ▣🅟∂⊕&

ANSTRUTHER, Fife   **Map H3**
EC Wed SEE Scottish Fisheries Museums, Chalmers House, Forth (by boat)
🅸 Scottish Fisheries Museum, St Ayles ☏(01333) 311073
✗ Craw's Nest, Baukwell Rd ☏(01333) 310691

St Monans Caravan Park, The Common KY10 2DN ☏(01333) 730778 OS map 59/530018 2m
   SW of Anstruther on A917 (Crail) Open Mar 21-Oct 31 128 pitches (110 static) Grass, level, hard
   standings, sheltered ▣🅟⊕∅⊕⌁

ARBROATH, Angus   **Map H2**
EC Wed SEE Vigeans museum, abbey church ruins, Signal Tower Museum
🅸 Market Place ☏(01241) 872609
✗ Glencoe 8m SW at Carnoustie ☏(01241) 53273

Red Lion Caravan Park, Dundee Road DD11 2PT ☏(01241) 72038 OS map 54/615393 1m S of
   Arbroath off A92 (Dundee) near West Links Open Mar-Oct 320 pitches (280 static) Level grass
   ⚑✗⚲⚲⚲▣🅟∂⊕∅⌁▭& TV hook-ups (all cards)

Seaton Estate Caravan Park, Seaton House DD11 5SE ☏(01241) 874762 OS map 54/660426
   ½m N of Arbroath off A92 (Aberdeen) Open Mar-Oct 150 pitches (75 static) 60 acres level grass
   ⚑✗⚲▣🅟∂⊕⌁▯

ARDLUI, Argyll & Bute — Map D3
SEE Rob Roy's Cave, Pulpit Rock
✗ Ardlui ☎ (01301) 704243

Ardlui Caravan Park G83 7EB ☎ (01301) 704243 OS map 56/315155 ¼m N of Ardlui on right of A82 (Fort William) on north shore of Loch Lomond Open Mar-Oct 96 pitches (84 static) Grass and hard standings, level 🛒 ✗ ♀ ⇥ 🗟 🔌 🖉 ⊕ ∅ ⤳ 📺 🖤 ⌫ boating (moorings), water skiing, fishing

ARDUAINE, Argyll & Bute — Map C3
✗ Culfail 5m NE at Kilmelford ☎ (01852) 200274

Arduaine Caravan Camping Park PA34 4XQ ☎ (01852) 200331 OS map 55/802102 ¼m S of Arduaine on right of A816 (Lochgilphead) near Arduaine Gardens Open Mar-Oct 40 pitches Level/sloping grass and hard standings, sheltered 🔌 ⊕ boating (jetty adj), fishing, moorings, dinghy launch

ARROCHAR–see Tarbet

AUCHINLECK–see Cumnock

AUCHTERARDER, Perth & Kinross — Map F3
Small town bypassed by A9 with main St almost 2m long SEE Heritage Centre, Innerpeffray Library, founded 1691, 6m N
🛈 90 High St ☎ (01764) 663450
✗ Coll Earn House, High St ☎ (01764) 663553

Auchterarder Caravan Park PH3 1ET *Friendly park at gateway to Highlands* ☎ (01764) 663119 OS map 58/964137 ½m NE of Auchterarder at junct of A824 (Aberuthven) and B8062 (Dunning) Open Jan-Dec 23 pitches 5 acres level grass and hard standings, sheltered 🗟 🔌 🖉 ⊕ ∅ 🎮 🔌 🏠 private fishing, barbeques £8.00-£10.00

AYR, S Ayrshire — Map D6
EC Wed MD Mon, Tues *Popular tourist and commercial centre on west coast with many associations with Robert Burns, whose home town it was* SEE Burns' cottage, Tam O'Shanter inn museum, Auld Kirk, Auld Brig (bridge), Alloway church 3m S
🛈 22 Sandgate ☎ (01292) 288688
✗ Balgarth 3m S at Alloway ☎ (01292) 242441

Ayr Racecourse, Whitletts Road KA8 0JE OS map 70/352225 1m E of Ayr off A77 (Glasgow) Open Easter May 22-Sept 11–no adv booking 150 pitches Some hard standings 🗟 🎮 snacks

Craigie Gardens Caravan Club, Craigie Road KA8 0SS ☎ (01292) 264909 OS map 70/355214 ½m E of Ayr off A719 (Galston) Open May 26- Oct 25–no tents 90 pitches 🗟 🔌 🖉 ⊕ 🛒 ♿ £15.50.00-£20.60* (Mastercard/Visa/Switch/Delta) www.caravanclub.co.uk

Crofthead Caravan Park KA6 6EN ☎ (01292) 263516 OS map 70/369205 2m E of Ayr off A70 (Holmston) Open Mar-Oct–no adv booking 156 pitches (60 static) Level/sloping grass and hard standings, sheltered 🛒 ✈ 🗟 🔌 🖉 ⊕ ∅ ⤳ 📺 🔌

Heads of Ayr Caravan Park, Danure Road KA7 4LD ☎ (01292) 442269 *Prop: D & V Semple* OS map 70/254158 5m SW of Ayr off A719 (Girvan) Open Apr-Sept 161 pitches (125 static) Grass, level, sheltered 🛒 ♀ 🗟 🔌 🖉 ⊕ ∅ ⤳ 🔌 (20) ⌫ meals, dancing £10.00-£16.00 (most cards) semple@headsofayr.wanadoo.co.uk www.caravanparksayrshire.com

Middlemuir Caravan Park, Tarbolton KA5 5NR ☎ (01292) 541647 OS map 70/437257 6m NE of Ayr off B743 (Mauchline) Open all year 115 pitches (63 static) 19 acres, part sloping grass and hard standing, sheltered 🗟 🔌 🖉 ⊕ ∅ ⤳ 📺 🔌 ⌫

Sundrum Castle Holiday Park, Coylton KA6 6HX ☎ (01292) 570057 Fax (01292) 570065 OS map 70/404206 4m E of Ayr on A70 (Cumnock) near Coylton Open Mar-Oct 283 pitches (103 static) 11 acres, level grass and hard standings 🛒 ✗ ♀ ⇥ ✈ 🗟 🔌 🖉 ⊕ ∅ 🖻 (indoor) 🎮 ⤳ 📺 🅿 ♿ ⌫ lic club/bar, entertainment, cabaret suite, tennis, basket ball, putting green £8.00-£23.00* (most cards) enquiries@parkdeanholidays.co.uk www.parkdeanholidays.co.uk

---

KEY TO SYMBOLS

🛒	shop	🖉	gas supplies	🔌	winter storage for caravans
✗	restaurant	⊕	chemical disposal point	🅿	parking obligatory
♀	bar	∅	payphone	♿	no dogs
⇥	takeaway food	🖻	swimming pool	⌫	caravan hire
✈	off licence	🎮	games area	🏠	bungalow hire
🗟	laundrette	⤳	children's playground	♿	facilities for disabled
🔌	mains electric hook-ups	📺	TV	🌳	shaded

SITE DIRECTIONS
The distance and direction of a campsite is given from the centre of the town under which it appears.

BALLANTRAE, S Ayrshire   Map D7
✘Royal Hotel ✆(01465) 831555

Laggan House Leisure Park KA26 0LL ✆(01465) 831229 OS map 76/117835 3m SE of
  Ballantrae off A77 (Stranraer) on Heronsford road Open Mar-Oct 120 pitches (95 static) Level
  grass and hard standing, sheltered ⚏◻⊟⊘✤∅◻⊕⌿◻◪◻⌂ sauna (all major cards)

BALLOCH, W Dunbartonshire   Map D4
SEE Loch Lomond (boat trips), Cameron Estate gardens, wildlife park
ℹBalloch Rd ✆(01389) 753533
✘Lomond Castle 2m N at Arden ✆(01389) 785681

Lomond Woods Holiday Park, Tullichewan, Balloch G83 8QP ✆(01389) 755000 Fax (01389)
  755563 OS map 56/382816 ½m E of Balloch centre at junction of A82 and A811 on S shore of
  Loch Lomond–signposted Open all year–booking advisable peak periods 200 pitches (40 static)
  Hard standings and grass, part sloping, sheltered ⚏◻⊟⊘✤∅⌿◻◪(50) ◪⌂⛐ leisure suite
  with sauna, jacuzzi, games room, table tennis, pool table, mountain bike hire £13.00-£18.00*
  (Mastercard/Visa/Switch/Delta) lomondwoods@holiday-parks.co.uk www.holiday-parks.co.uk

BALMAHA–see Drymen

BARRHILL, S Ayrshire   Map D7
✘King's Arms 12m W at Girvan ✆(01465) 823322

Queensland Holiday Park KA26 0PZ ✆(01465) 821364 Prop: David & Jo Russell OS map
  76/216836 1m N of Barrhill on A714 (Girvan) Open Mar-Oct 48 pitches 8 acres grass, level,
  sheltered ⚏◻⊟⊘✤∅⌿◪◻◪⌂⛐ £8.50-£11.50 info@queenslandholidaypark.co.uk
  www.queenslandholidaypark.co.uk

BIGGAR, S Lanarkshire   Map F5
EC Wed MD Sat SEE Boghall Castle ruins, 16c church, Gladstone Court Museum
ℹHigh St ✆(01899) 21066
✘Toftcombs ✆(01899) 20142

Biggar Park ML12 6JS ✆(01899) 20319 OS map 72/049380 ½m E of Biggar off A702 (West
  Linton) on B7016 (Broughton) Open Apr-Oct 60 pitches (40 static) Grass, level, open ⚏⊘◪
  tennis, golf, boating

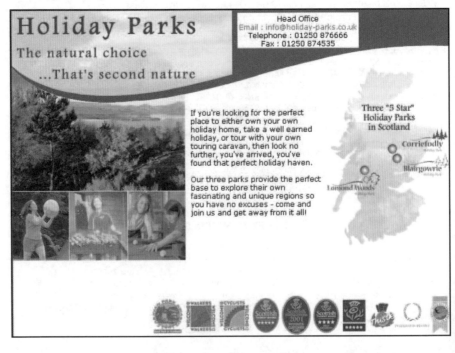

Queensland Holiday Park

Relax and Enjoy the Beauty of Ayrshire

Queensland Holiday Park
Barhill
Girvan, Ayrshire
KA26 0PZ
Scotland

info@queenslandholidaypark.co.uk

BLAIR ATHOLL, Perth & Kinross   Map F2
EC Thurs SEE Blair Castle, Garry Falls, Killiecrankie Pass
✗ Atholl Arms ☎ (01796) 481205

Blair Castle Caravan Park PH18 5SR ☎ (01796) 481263 Fax (01796) 481587 OS map 43/872655
  In Blair Atholl off A9 (Perth-Inverness) in Blair Castle grounds Open Mar-Nov—must book peak
  periods 283 pitches (108 static) Grass and hard standings, level, open 🏕️🅱️🚿🅰️🅿️🅾️🅾️🅾️↩️
  🅿️🚇♿ pony trekking, fishing, serviced pitches £10.00-£13.00* (Mastercard/Visa/Switch/Delta)
  mail@blaircastlecaravanpark.co.uk www.blaircastlecaravanpark.co.uk

BLAIRGOWRIE, Perth & Kinross   Map G2
EC Thurs SEE Ardblair Castle, Craighall Mansion, Fish Pass, Beech Hedge of Meikleour
ℹ️ Wellmeadow ☎ (01250) 872960
✗ Angus, Wellmeadow ☎ (01250) 872838

Ballintuim Caravan Park, Bridge of Cally PH10 7NH ☎ (01250) 886276 OS map 53/103548 9m N
  of Blairgowrie centre off A93 (Braemar) on A924 (Pitlochry) in grounds of hotel Open all year
  100 pitches (74 static) Grass and hard standings, sloping 🅱️🚿🅰️🅾️↩️🚇

Beech Hedge Caravan Park, Cargill PH2 6DU ☎ (01250) 883249 OS map 53/163373 5m S of
  Blairgowrie on A93 (Perth) Open Apr-Oct 20 pitches Grass and hard standing 🅱️🚿🅰️🅾️🚇🚇🏠
  golf, fishing

Blairgowrie Holiday Park PH10 7AL ☎ (01250) 876666 Fax (01250) 874535 OS map 53/181461
  ½m N of Blairgowrie centre off A93 (Braemar) Open all year 150 pitches (120 static) Grass,
  level, hard standings, sheltered 🅱️🚿🅰️🅾️🅾️🅾️↩️🚇(30) 🚇🏠 putting green £13.00-£15.00*
  inc elect (Mastercard/Visa/Switch) blairgowrie@holiday-parks.co.uk www.holiday-parks.co.uk

Corriefodly Holiday Park, Bridge of Cally PH10 7JG ☎ (01250) 886236 Fax (01250) 874535 OS
  map 53/133514 6m N of Blairgowrie near junction of A924 (Pitlochry) and A93 (Braemar)
  Open all year 150 pitches (80 static) Grass, sloping, hard standings, sheltered
  🍴🅱️🚿🅰️🅾️🅾️↩️🅿️🚇🚇♿ bar, games room, fishing £13.00-£15.00* inc elect (all cards)
  corriefodly@holiday-parks.co.uk www.holiday-parks.co.uk

Nether Craig Caravan Park, Alyth PH11 8HN ☎ (01575) 560204 OS map 53/265527 6m E of
  Blairgowrie off A926 (Kirriemuir) on B954 (Bridge of Craigisla) 40 pitches
  Level grass and hard standings, part sheltered 🏕️🅱️🚿🅰️🅾️🅾️🅾️↩️🅿️♿
  (Mastercard/Visa/Switch/Solo)

BRECHIN, Angus   Map H2
EC Wed SEE cathedral, Round Tower, Maison Dieu chapel ruins, Edzell castle 5m N
ℹ️ Brechin Castle Centre ☎ (01356) 623050
✗ Balbirnie Mill, Montrose Rd ☎ (01356) 624482

Glenesk Caravan Site, Glenesk by Edzell DD9 7YP ☎ (01356) 647565/648523 OS map 45/602717
  7m N of Brechin off A94 (Laurencekirk) and B966 (Fettercairn) beyond Edzell Open Apr-Oct
  45 pitches 8 acres, level, sheltered 🏕️🅱️🚿🅰️🅾️🅾️↩️🅿️🚇 Hard standings and grass

East Mill Caravan Park, East Mill Road DD9 7AL ☎ (01356) 628810 OS map 54/605594 ¼m SE
  of Brechin off A933 (Arbroath) and A935 (Montrose) near Brechin bridge Open Apr-Sept 100
  pitches (40 static) Level grass, sheltered 🏕️✗🅱️🚿🅰️🅾️ Hard standings and grass

---

❄ DOGS
Dogs are usually allowed but must be kept on a lead. Sometimes they have to be paid for.

BRODICK, Isle of Arran   Map C5
EC Wed MD Thurs
🏛 The Pier ✆(01770) 302401
✘ Glencoy Farm ✆(01770) 302351
Middleton Camping Caravan Park, Lamlash KA27 8NN ✆(01770) 600251 OS map 69/025303
4m S of Brodick off A841 (Whiting Bay) Open Apr-Sept 72 pitches Grass and hard standings,
level, sheltered 🖃🏕🚿∅🌳

CALLANDER, Stirling   Map E3
EC Wed SEE Trossachs, Bracklin Falls, Loch Vennacher, Ben Ledi (2,875ft)
🏛 Visitor Centre, Ancaster Sq ✆(01877) 330342
✘ The Crown Hotel, 29 Main Street, Thornhill ✆(01786) 850217 Open 12-Sep
Gart Caravan Park, Stirling Road FK17 8HW ✆(01877) 330002 Fax (01877) 330002 OS map
57/645070 ½m SE of Callander on A84 (Doune) Open Apr 1-Oct 15 200 pitches (70 static)–no
tents Grass, level, sheltered 🖃🏕🚿⊕∅↵♿ £16.00* (most cards) enquiries@gart-caravan-
park.co.uk www.gart-caravan-park.co.uk
Keltie Bridge Caravan Park, Cambusmore Estate FK17 8LQ ✆(01877) 330606 OS map
57/649069 1m SE of Callander on A84 (Doune) Open Apr-Oct 80 pitches (30 static) 12 acres
level grass 🖃🏕🚿⊕∅♿
Mains Farm, Thornhill FK8 3QR ✆(01786) 850605 Prop: John Steedman OS map 57/660000 6m
S of Callander on B822 (Kippen) Open Apr-Oct 45 pitches 3½ acres grass, gentle slope
🛒🖃🏕🚿⊕☉↵♨🍴📷♿ £8.00 gsteedman@lineone.net

CAMPBELTOWN, Argyll & Bute   Map C6
EC Wed MD Mon SEE Celtic cross, Davaar island, lighthouse
🏛 Mackinnon House, The Pier ✆(01586) 552056
✘ White Hart Hotel, Main St ✆(01586) 552440
Peninver Sands Caravan Park, Craigview, Peninver PA28 6QP ✆(01586) 552262 Prop: E
MacCallum OS map 68/755245 4½m N of Campbeltown on B842 (Dippen) Open Apr-Oct–no
adv booking 50 pitches (40 static) 3 acres level grass, sheltered 🖃🏕🚿⊕∅↵♨🍴
info@peninver-sands.com www.peninver-sands.com

CARNOUSTIE, Angus   Map H2
EC Tues SEE Buddon Ness, Waterwheel Mill
🏛 The Library, High St ✆(01241) 852258
✘ Glencoe, Links Par ✆(01241) 53273
Woodlands Caravan Park, Newton Road DD7 6GR ✆(01241) 854430 OS map 54/558350 ¼m N
of Carnoustie centre off A92 (Dundee-Arbroath) Open Apr-Oct 120 pitches Level grass, sheltered
🖃🏕🚿⊕∅↵♿

CARRADALE–see Dippen

CLACHAN, Argyll & Bute   Map C5
✘ Old School (lunch only) 8m NE at Whitehouse ✆(01880) 740215
Kirkland Caravan Park PA29 6XL ✆(01880) 740200 OS map 62/767562 ¼m S of Clachan centre
on A83 (Campbeltown) Open Apr-Nov 30 pitches (21 static) 3 acres, hard standings 🌳⊕🍴
fishing, pony rides, B&B

COMRIE, Fife   Map F3
EC Wed SEE Museum of Scottish Tartans
✘ Earnbank House Hotel, Drummond St ✆(01764) 670239
Loch Earn Caravan Park, South Shore Road, St Fillans PH6 2NL ✆(01764) 685270 OS map
51/670235 5m W of Comrie off A85 (Lochearnhead) Open Apr-mid Oct 270 pitches (240 static)
Level grass, sheltered 🛒✘♀⚓⌇🖃🏕🚿⊕∅↵ (Mastercard/Visa)
Riverside Caravan Park, Station Road PH6 2EA ✆(01764) 670555 and 670207 OS map
52/58/780223 ½m E of Comrie on A85 (Crieff) Open Apr-Oct 155 pitches (125 static) Grass,
level and hard standing 🖃🏕🚿∅⊕↵♨🍴 putting and bowling green (inc showers)
Twenty Shilling Wood Caravan Park PH6 2JY ✆(01764) 670411 OS map 52/762222 ½m W of
Comrie on A85 (Lochearnhead) Open Easter-Oct–must book–no tents (gates locked 10pm-8am)
90 pitches 10 acres, hard standings, woodland 🖃🏕🚿⊕∅∅↵□🍴 £14.50
(Mastercard/Visa/Delta/Maestro) alowe20@aol.com www.ukparks.co.uk/twentyshilling
West Lodge PH6 2LS ✆(01764) 670354 Prop: PS, EL & PP Gill OS map 52/784225 1m E of
Comrie on A85 (Crieff) Open Apr-Oct–booking advisable in season 60 pitches 3 acres level
grass, sheltered 🛒🖃🏕🚿⊕∅♨🍴♿ £13.00-£16.00 www.westlodge.bravehost.com

---

Help us make CAMPING CARAVANNING BRITAIN better known to site operators – and thereby
more informative – by showing them your copy when booking in.

CONNEL, Argyll & Bute **Map C3**
EC Wed SEE falls, bridge, Dunstaffnage Castle 3m SW, Ardchatten Priory 6m E
✗ Lochnell Arms Hotel, North Connel ☏ (01631) 710408 Open 12-2.30/6-9

North Ledaig Caravan Site PA37 1RT ☏ (01631) 710291 *Prop: The North Ledaig Co Ltd* OS map
49/908369 1m N of Connel on left of A828 (Fort William) Open Easter-Oct 260 pitches Hard
standings ⚑⚐◨⊟◕❁∅⌣⌖ baby room £10.60-£17.60 inc elect (debit cards)

CRAIGNURE, Isle of Mull **Map B2**
EC Wed
🄸 The Pierhead ☏ (01680) 812377
✗ Isle of Mull ☏ (01680) 812351

Shieling Holidays PA65 6AY *Visit Scotland 5 stars* ☏ (01680) 812496 *Prop: David Gracie* OS
map 49/724369 ½m S of Craignure off A849 (Bunessan) by sea Open Apr-Oct 42 pitches Grass
and hard standing, part level, sheltered ◨⊟◕❁∅⊕⌣⌖⌂⌖ beach £13.00-£14.50
(Mastercard/Visa/Switch/Solo/Electron/Maestro) *www.shielingholidays.co.uk* (e-mail enquiry facs)

CRAIL, Fife **Map H3**
EC Wed SEE Mercat cross, Balcombie castle ruins, Crail museum and heritage centre
🄸 Museum Marketgate ☏ (01333) 450869
✗ Croma, Nethergate St ☏ (01333) 450239

Ashburn House, St Andrews Road KY10 3UL ☏ (01333) 450314 OS map 59/613080 ¼m N of
Crail centre on A917 (St Andrews) in grounds of country house Open Mar-Oct 62 pitches (52
static) 3 acres level grass and hard standings, sheltered ◨⊟❁∅⊕∅ serviced pitches

Sauchope Links Caravan Park KY10 3XJ ☏ (01333) 450460 OS map 59/626083 1m NE of Crail
off Balcomie road Open Mar-Oct 150 pitches (100 static) Level grass and hard standings
⚑◨⊟❁∅⊕∅⊟(heated) ⊕⌣⌖ (Mastercard/Visa)

CRIANLARICH, Stirling **Map D3**
✗ Benmore Lodge ☏ (01838) 300210

Glendochart Caravan Park, Glendochart FK20 8QT ☏ (01567) 820637 OS map 51/479279 5m E
of Crianlarich on right of A85 (Lochearnhead) past junct with A827 (Killin) Open Mar-Oct 45
pitches 15 acres level grass and hard standings ✗⊟❁∅⊕⌣⌖

CRIEFF, Perth & Kinross **Map F3**
EC Wed SEE glass works, pottery, Drummond castle gardens 2m SW, Glenturret Distillery (tours)
🄸 Town Hall, High St ☏ (01764) 652578
✗ George, King St ☏ (01764) 652089

Braidhaugh Caravan Park, South Bridgend PH7 4HP ☏ (01764) 652951 OS map 58/855210 ¼m
SW of Crieff off A82 (Dunblane) Open Jan-Dec 95 pitches–no tents, must book peak periods
Grass and hard standings, level ⚑✗◨⊟❁∅⊕⊕⌣⌖⌂⌖

Crieff Holiday Village, Turret Bank PH7 4JN ☏ (01764) 653513 OS map 58/858226 ½m W of
Crieff off A85 (Comrie) Open all year 106 pitches (45 static) 3 acres, terraced
⚑⚐◨⊟❁∅⊕∅⊕⌣⌖⌂⊕(85) ⌖⌂ Grass and hard standings, level, sheltered

CRINAN, Argyll & Bute **Map C4**
EC Sat SEE Donald Hill, Crinan canal
✗ Crinan Hotel ☏ (01546) 870261

Leachive Caravan Park, Leachive Farm, Tayvallich PA31 8PL ☏ (01546) 870206 OS map
55/745875 7m S of Crinan on B8025 (Tayvallich) Open Apr-Sept 52 pitches (37 static) 5 acres,
level grass and hard standings, sheltered ⚑✗⚐⚐◨⊟❁∅⊕⌖ £10.00 *fiona@leachive.co.uk*

CULZEAN–see Maybole

CUMNOCK, E Ayrs **Map E6**
EC Wed MD Fri SEE Baird Institute, home of Keir Hardie
✗ Royal, Glaishock St ☏ (01290) 420822

Glenafton Park, Glenafton, New Cumnock KA18 4PR ☏ (01290) 332251/332228 OS map
71/617103 6m S of Cumnock off B741 (Dalmellington) Open all year 50 pitches (30 static)
Level grass and hard standing, sheltered ⚑✗⚐⌣⌖◨∅❁⊕⊕⌣⌖⌂⊕ (most cards)

DALKEITH, Midlothian **Map G4**
EC Tues MD Mon SEE St Nicholas church, King's Park, Dalkeith Palace, Newbattle Abbey
✗ Eskbank Motel, Dalhousie Road ☏ (0131) 663 3234

Fordel Camping Caravan Park, Lauder Road EH22 2PH ☏ (0131) 663 3046/(0131) 660 3921 OS
map 66/360668 1½m S of Dalkeith on left of A68 (Edinburgh-Newcastle) by Esso petrol station
Open Mar-Sept 45 pitches–no adv booking Grass and hard standing, sheltered
⚑✗⚐⌣⌖⚐◨⊟❁∅⊕⊕⌣⌖⌖ (Mastercard/Visa)

DIPPEN, Argyll & Bute   Map C5
✗Carradale 2m E at Carradale ☎(01583) 431223

Carradale Bay Caravan Park, Carradale PA28 6QG ☎(01583) 431665 *Prop: Mr & Mrs Burgess*
  OS map 68/805374 1m E of Dippen on B879 (Carradale) Open Apr-Oct 60 pitches Grass on
  sand dunes, level, sheltered ▣🔌🚿🚻🚽🚾🏪 fishing (sea and river), canoeing £10.00-£14.00
  (all cards) *info@carradalebay.com www.carradalebay.com*

DOLLAR, Clackmannanshire   Map F4
EC Thurs SEE Castle Campbell ruins
✗Castle Campbell, Bridge St ☎(01259) 781519

Glendevon Caravan Park, Glendevon FK14 7JY ☎(01259) 781569 OS map 58/981052 6m NE of
  Dollar off A91 (Cupar) on A823 (Crieff) Open Apr-Oct 164 pitches (130 static) Level grass
  ⛽✗♀🚿🚽 snack bar, disco dances, amusements, boating, fishing, shooting, quad bikes, gold
  panning, pony trekking (Jul-Aug) (Mastercard/Visa)

Riverside Caravan Park FK14 7LX ☎(01259) 742896 OS map 58/926970 ½m S of Dollar on
  B913 by river Devon Open Apr-Sept 60 pitches (22 static) 7 acres level grass, sheltered
  🚿🚽🚾🏪 fishing *info@riversidecaravanpark.co.uk www.riversidecaravanpark.co.uk*

DRYMEN, Stirling   Map E4
EC Wed SEE Loch Lomond, Potts of Gartness salmon leap
ℹLibrary, The Square ☎(01360) 660068
✗Buchanan Arms ☎(01360) 870588

Cashel Caravan Camping Park, Balmaha G63 0AW ☎(01360) 870234 OS map 56/396939 7m
  NW of Drymen on Balmaha-Rowardennan road along E shore of Loch Lomond in Queen Elizabeth
  Forest Park Open Apr-Sept–adv booking min 7 nights 200 pitches Grass, part level, part open
  ⛽▣🚿🚽🚾🏪⚓♿ fishing, boating

DUNBAR, East Lothian   Map H4
EC Wed *Popular coast resort noted for its elegant main street (High St), with safe bathing from
beaches of Bellhaven on W and White Sands on E. At Barns Ness, adj White Sands, are fossil-rich
limestone cliffs.* SEE castle ruins, parish church
ℹTown House, High St ☎(01368) 863353
✗Bayswell, Bayswell Park ☎(01368) 862225

Battleblent Hotel Caravan Park, West Barns EH42 1TS ☎(01368) 862234 OS map 67/660782
  1m W of Dunbar on A1087 (West Barns) Open Apr-Oct, 10 marked pitches 1 acre level grass,
  sheltered ✗♀🚿🚽🚾 (all cards)

Thurston Manor Holiday Park, Thurston, Innerwick EH42 1SA ☎(01368) 840643 Fax (01368)
  840261 OS map 67/710730 2m SE of Dunbar off A1 (Berwick on Tweed) on Elmscleugh road
  Open Mar-Jan 500 pitches (400 static) Level grass and hard standing, sheltered
  ⛽✗♀🚌🏕▣🚿🚽🚾🏪⚓♿ £10.00-£14.00* (Mastercard/Visa/Delta/Switch)
  mail@thurstonmanor.co.uk www.thurstonmanor.co.uk

THURSTON MANOR
A site better by far
Booking Hotline 01368 840643

DUNDEE   Map G3
EC Wed MD Tues SEE St Andrew's church, Camperdown park, cathedrals, Tay road bridge
ℹCastle St ☎(01382) 527527
✗Invercastle, Perth Rd ☎(01382) 569231

Inchmartine Caravan Park, Inchture PH14 9QQ ☎(01828) 686251 OS map 59/265278 8m W of
  Dundee on A85 (Perth) Open Apr-Sept 45 pitches Grass, part open 🚿

Riverview Caravan Park, Monifieth DD5 4NN ☎(01382) 535471 Fax (01382) 535475 OS map
  54/501323 6m E of Dundee off A930 (Carnoustie) on Marine Drive by sea Open Apr-Oct
  90 pitches Level grass and hard standing ⛽▣🚿🚽🚾♿⚓♿ £13.00-£15.00* (all cards)
  riverviewcaravan@btinternet.com www.ukparks.co.uk/riverview

---

SHOWERS
Except where marked, all sites in this guide have flush lavatories and showers. Symbols for these
amenities have therefore been omitted from site entries.

DUNKELD, Perth & Kinross **Map F2**
EC Thurs SEE cathedral, regimental museum, waterfalls
The Cross ☎(01350) 727688
✗Atholl Arms, Bridge St ☎(01350) 727219

Erigmore House Holiday Park, Birnam PH8 9XX ☎(01350) 727236 OS map 53/038417 1m SE of Dunkeld off A9 (Perth) Open Mar-Nov 243 pitches (185 static)–no tents Grass, level, part open ⚏✗⚏⚏⚏⚏⚏⚏⚏⚏(indoor heated)⚏⚏⚏(25) ⚏⚏⚏ pony trekking, river swimming, fishing

Inver Mill Farm Caravan Park, Inver Mill PH8 0JR ☎(01350) 727477 *Prop: Mr & Mrs Bryden* OS map 52/015422 ½m W of Dunkeld on A822 (Inver)–signposted Open Apr-Oct–no adv booking 65 pitches Level grass ⚏⚏⚏⚏⚏⚏⚏⚏ swimming, fishing, bike hire, tennis £11.00-£12.00 invermill@talk21.com www.visitdunkeld.com/pershire-caravan-park.htm

DUNOON, Argyll & Bute **Map D4**
EC Wed SEE Argyll national park, Kilman arboretum 6m N, Younger botanical gardens 7m NW, Cowal Highland gathering (Aug)
Alexandra Parade ☎(01369) 703785
✗Coylet Inn 5m N at Loch Eck ☎(01369) 840322

Cot House, Kilmun PA23 8QS ☎(01369) 840351 OS map 56/154831 3m N of Dunoon on A815 (Strachur) near junction with A880 Open Easter-Oct 40 pitches (20 static) 2½ acres level grass and hard standing ⚏✗⚏⚏⚏⚏⚏⚏ fishing, boating

Gairletter Caravan Park, Blairmore PA23 8TP ☎(01369) 840208 OS map 56/195823 10m N of Dunoon on A880 (Ardentinny) on W shore of Loch Long Open Apr-Oct–must book peak periods 40 pitches Hard standings and grass, level ⚏⚏⚏⚏⚏⚏⚏⚏⚏⚏⚏⚏

Glenfinart Park, Ardentinny PA23 8TS ☎(01369) 810256 OS map 56/184884 13m NE of Dunoon off A885/A815 (Strachur) on A880 (Ardentinny) Open Apr-Oct 40 pitches Grass, level, sheltered ⚏⚏⚏⚏⚏

Invereck Countryside Holiday Park, Sandbank PA23 8QS ☎(01369) 705544 OS map 56/148830 4½m N of Dunoon on left of A815 (Strachur) at head of Holy Loch Open Apr-Oct 30 pitches Grass and hard standing, level, sheltered ⚏⚏⚏⚏⚏⚏(20) ⚏⚏ fishing invereckholidaypark@aol.com www.caravancampingsites.co.uk

Stratheck Country Park, Inverchapel, Loch Eck PA23 8SG ☎(01369) 840472 Fax (01369) 840504 OS map 56/143865 7m NW of Dunoon on left of A815 (Strachur) by ferry Open Mar-Jan–must book peak periods 150 pitches (80 static) Hard standings and grass, level, sheltered ⚏⚏⚏⚏⚏⚏⚏⚏⚏⚏⚏⚏⚏⚏⚏ fishing, country club, animal corner £8.00-£18.00* enquiries@stratheck.com www.stratheck.com

EDINBURGH **Map G4**
SEE castle, palace of Holyrood House, National Museum, Royal Scottish Museum, Royal Botanic garden, Tattoo (Aug-Sept)
Information Centre, Princes St ☎(01314) 733800
✗Alp Horn, Rose St ☎(0131) 225 4787

Drum Mohr Caravan Park, Levenhall, Musselburgh EH21 8JS ☎(0131) 665 6867 Fax (0131) 653 6859 *Prop: W Melville* OS map 66/371735 7m E of Edinburgh between B1361 (North Berwick) and B1348 (Prestonpans) Open Mar-Oct 120 pitches Grass, level, sheltered–some hard standings ⚏⚏⚏⚏⚏⚏⚏⚏⚏⚏⚏ £13.00-£16.00 (Mastercard/Visa) bookings@drummohr.org www.drummohr.org

Linwater Caravan Park, West Clifton, by East Calder EH53 0HT ☎(0131) 333 3326 Fax (0131) 333 1952 *Prop: Jean Guinan* OS map 65/104696 7m W of Edinburgh off A8 (Newbridge) on B7030 (Linwater) Open Apr-Oct 60 pitches Level grass ⚏⚏⚏⚏⚏ sandpit, dog walk £9.00-£14.00 (Mastercard/Visa/Switch) linwater@supanet.com www.linwater.co.uk

Mortonhall Caravan Park, Mortonhall Gate, Frogston Road East EH16 6TJ ☎(0131) 664 1533 *Prop: Andrea & Stuart Hutson* OS map 66/262683 4m S of Edinburgh off city bypass at Lothianburn or Straiton junction–signposted Open Mar-Jan 250 pitches Grass and some hard standings, part sloping ⚏✗⚏⚏⚏⚏⚏⚏⚏⚏⚏⚏⚏⚏⚏ serviced pitches £12.00-£23.00 (Mastercard/Visa) mortonhall@meadowhead.co.uk www.meadowhead.co.uk

Pentland Park Caravan Site, New Pentland, Loanhead EH20 9PA ☎(0131) 440 0697 OS map 66/264657 3m S of Edinburgh on right of A701 (Penicuik) Open Apr-Oct 242 pitches (180 static) ⚏⚏⚏⚏⚏

Seton Sands Holiday Centre, Longniddry EH32 0PL ☎(01875) 811425 OS map 63/425758 10m E of Edinburgh off A1 (Dunbar) on B1348 (Port Seton) Open Mar 15-Oct 31 720 pitches Level grass ⚏⚏⚏⚏⚏⚏ club room with entertainment, amusements

Slatebarns Caravan Park, Slatebarns Farm, Roslin EH25 9PU ☎(0131) 440 2192 *Prop: R & M Crawford* OS map 66/275635 6m S of Edinburgh off A701 (Peebles) in Roslin Open Easter-Oct 30 pitches–no tents Level grass and hard standing, sheltered ⚏⚏⚏⚏⚏⚏ £13.50-£17.00 www.slatebarns.co.uk

See also Aberlady and Dalkeith

FINTRY, Stirling   Map E4
✗ Cross Keys 8m N at Kippen ☎(01786) 870293

Balgair Castle Caravan Park, Overglinns G63 0LP ☎(01360) 860283 Fax (01360) 860300 OS
map 57/603886 1½m N of Fintry off Kippen road Open Mar-Oct 148 pitches (85 static) 38 acres
level grass 🅱✗🅿🔌🅰🅱🅰🅰⊕∅🖵(outdoor) ⊕🔌🏕🅱🚿 bar meals, putting green, fishing,
games room

FORFAR, Angus   Map H2
EC Thurs SEE church, parks, castle and Angus Folk museum at Glamis 5m SW
ℹ️40 East High St ☎(01307) 467876
✗ Royal, Castle St ☎(01307) 462691

Lochside Caravan Park, Lochside DD8 1BT ☎(01307) 464201 OS map 54/450505 ½m NW of
Forfar off A94 (Brechin) Open Apr-Oct 74 pitches Grass, level, open 🅱🅱∅🔌 leisure centre
adjacent

GARELOCHHEAD, Argyll & Bute   Map D4
✗ Rosslea Hall 8m S at Helensburgh ☎(01436) 820684

Rosneath Castle Caravan Park, Rosneath G84 0QS ☎(01436) 831208 OS map 56/269821 7m S
of Garelochhead off B833 (Kilreaggan) Open Apr-Oct 500 pitches (450 static) 🅱✗(lic) 🅱🅰🔌
boating, sea angling

GIRVAN, S Ayrshire   Map D6
EC Wed SEE Turnberry championship golf courses 5m N
ℹ️Bridge St ☎(01465) 714950
✗ King's Arms, Dalrymple St ☎(01465) 893322

Balkenna Tearooms Caravan Site, Girvan Rd, Turnberry KA26 9LN OS map 76/202044 4m N of
Girvan on A77 (Ayr) Open all year 15 pitches 1 acre level grass ✗🅱🅰 (Mastercard/Visa)

Benane Shore Holiday Park, Lendalfoot KA26 0JG ☎(01465) 891233 OS map 76/110884 8½m S
of Girvan on A77 (Ayr-Stranraer) Open Mar-Oct 140 pitches (60 static) Level grass
🅱🅱🅰🏕🚿 private beach, boating

Carleton Caravan Park, Carleton Lodge, Lendalfoot KA26 0JF ☎(01465) 891120 OS map
76/129901 7m S of Girvan off A77 (Stranraer) Open Mar-Oct–must book 60 pitches Grass,
level, part open 🏕(20) 🚿

Jeancroft Holiday Park, Dipple KA26 9JW ☎(01655) 31288 OS map 76/208043 3½m N of Girvan
off A77 (Maybole) Open Mar-Oct 226 pitches (200 static) 11½ acres mainly level grass sheltered
🅱🅱🅰🔌🏕🚿

See also Barrhill

GLAMIS–see Kirriemuir

FACTS CAN CHANGE
We do our best to check the accuracy of the entries in this guide but changes can and do occur
after publication. So if you plan to stay at a site some distance from home it makes sense to ring
the manager or owner before setting off.

GLASGOW Map E4
Largest city in Scotland made so partly by trade in tobacco and cloth in 18c and then by shipbuilding on the Clyde SEE cathedrals, Kelvingrove Park, Old Glasgow museum, Transport museum, botanic gardens, Kelvin Hall,
🛈 11 George Sq ☎(0141) 204 4400
✗ Babbity Bowster, Blackfriars St ☎(0141) 552 5055

Craigendmuir Park, Campsie View, Stepps F33 6AF ☎(0141) 779 2973 OS map 64/660697 3m NE of Glasgow off A80 (Stirling) at Stepps Open all year 40 pitches (24 static) Level grass and hard standing Tea room (Mastercard/Visa)

Strathclyde Country Park, 366 Hamilton Road, Motherwell ML1 3ED ☎(01698) 266155 Fax (01698) 252925 OS map 64/720584 10m SE of Glasgow near Junction 5 of M74 off A725 (Bellshill) Open Easter-Oct 15—max stay 14 nights 100 pitches 20 acres level grass and hard standing 🛒✗♿🚿🅿🚽🚻♨🛁🅿🚰 sailing, boating, funfair, road train
strathclydepark@northlan.gov.uk

GLENDARUEL–see Strachur

GLENCARSE, Perth & Kinross Map G3
EC Wed, Sat
✗ Newton House ☎(01738) 860250

St Madoes Caravan Park, Pitfour PH2 7LZ ☎(01738) 860244 OS map 58/203206 ½m E of Glencarse off B958 (Errol) in grounds of Pitfour Castle Open all year–no tents 20 pitches Hard standings 🚿🚽♨🚰

GOUROCK, Inver Map D4
EC Wed *Popular resort and centre for boat trips around coast and ferry port for Dunoon* SEE coast on drive S to Ardrossan
🛈 Pierhead ☎(01475) 639467 ✗ Spinnaker, Albert Rd ☎(01475) 633107

Cloch Caravan Holiday Park, The Cloch PA19 1BA ☎(01475) 632675 OS map 63/204760 3m SW of Gourock on A770 coast road beyond ferry terminal opp lighthouse Open Apr-Nov–no tents 250 pitches (243 static) 18 acres hard standings and sloping gravel 🛒✗♿🚿🚽🅿🚽🚻♨🛁 games room (Mastercard/Visa)

HADDINGTON, East Lothian Map H4
EC Thurs
✗ Bayswell 5m E at Dunbar ☎(01368) 862225

The Monks' Muir EH41 3SB ☎(01620) 860340 Fax (01620) 861770 OS map 66/559760 3m E of Haddington on A1 (East Linton)–signposted Open all year 43 pitches Grass, part level, sheltered 🛒✗♿🅿🚿🚽🚽♨🛁🚰🚰🅿🚰 barbecue area, golf package (Mastercard/Visa)

INVERARAY, Argyll & Bute Map D3
EC Wed SEE Castle, bell tower, Crarae gardens 9m SW
🛈 Front St ☎(01499) 302063
✗ Fernpoint near pier ☎(01499) 302170

Argyll Caravan Park PA32 8XT ☎(01499) 302285 OS map 56/075054 2½m S of Inveraray on A83 (Campbeltown) Open Apr-Oct 300 pitches (200 static) Grass and hard standings, level, sheltered 🛒✗♿🅿🚿🚽🚽♨🛁🅿🚰🚰♿ squash court, fishing

IRVINE, N Ayrshire Map D5
EC Wed
✗ Hospitality Inn 1m E on A71 ☎(01294) 874272

Cunningham Head Estate Camping Park KA3 2PE ☎(01294) 850238 OS map 70/368416 3½m NE of Irvine on B769 (Stewarton) Open Apr-Sept–no adv booking 115 pitches (50 static) Grass, level, sheltered 🚿🚽♨🛁🚽(25) 🚰

KENMORE, Perth & Kinross Map F2
EC Wed *Model village set round a green at E end of Loch Tay* SEE church, 18c bridge, Loch Tay
✗ Kenmore, Village Sq ☎(01887) 830205

Kenmore Caravan and Camping Park PH15 2HN ☎(01887) 830226 Fax (01887) 829059 OS map 51/52/774457 In Kenmore near bridge on right bank of river Tay Open Apr-Oct 180 pitches (90 static) Hard standings and grass, level, sheltered 🛒✗♿🅿🚿🚽🚽♨🛁🚰🚰(30) 🚰🏠♿ super pitches, par 70 golf course £12.00-£16.00* (Mastercard/Visa)
info@taymouth.co.uk www.taymouth.co.uk

CHECK BEFORE ENTERING
There's usually no objection to your walking onto a site to see if you might like it but always ask permission first. Remember that the person in charge is responsible for safeguarding the property of those staying there.

KILLIN, Stirling   Map E3
Community at head of Loch Tay, one of most beautiful in Scotland SEE Finlarig castle ruins, healing stones in old mill, Dochart Falls, Loch Tay, MacNab clan chiefs burial ground, Ben Lawers (3,984ft)
🄸 Main St ✆ (01567) 820254
✗ Bridge of Lochay ✆ (01567) 820272

Cruachan Touring Park FK21 8TY ✆ (01567) 820302 *Prop: M & JP Campbell* OS map 51/613358 3m NE of Killin on A827 (Aberfeldy) Open Apr-Oct 80 pitches Grass and hard standing, part level, part open 🅱✗⌂🖩🅿🅰⊕∅🛇🚿🚐🏠 fishing, forest walks £8.00* (Mastercard/Visa) *www.cruachanfarm.co.uk*

Glen Dochart Caravan Park, Luib by Crianlarich FK20 8QT ✆ (01567) 820637 OS map 51/477279 6m W of Killin on right of A85 (Crianlarich) Open Mar-Oct 90 pitches (30 static) Grass and hard standings, level, part open 🅱⚲🖩🅿🅰⊕🚿🚐(20) 🚐

High Creagan Caravan Park FK21 8TX ✆ (01567) 820449 *Prop: A Kennedy* OS map 58/594352 2½m E of Killin on left of A827 (Aberfeldy) Open Apr-Oct 40 pitches Grass and hard standings, level, sheltered 🖩🅿🅰⊕🚐 £10.00-£12.00

KILNINVER, Argyll & Bute   Map C3
✗ Rowan Tree 9m N at Oban ✆ (01631) 562954

Glen Gallain Caravan Park PA34 4UU ✆ (01852) 316200 OS map 55/834195 2m S of Kilninver off A816 (Loch-gilphead) at Scammadale signpost Open Apr-Oct 65 pitches Grass and hard standings, part sloping, part open 🅱🅿🅰⊕🚿

KINLOCH RANNOCH, Perth & Kinross   Map E2
EC Wed
✗ Loch Rannoch ✆ (01882) 632201

Kilvrecht Caravan Camping Park (Forestry Comm.), Lochend PH16 5QA ✆ (01882) 632335 OS map 42/617566 3m W of Kinloch Rannoch on Carrie road along S shore of Loch Rannoch Open Apr-Oct–no adv booking 60 pitches Grass, level, sheltered ⊕🚻 *No showers*, cold water only, fishing boat hire

KINROSS, Perth & Kinross   Map G3
EC Thurs SEE Loch Leven and Castle
🄸 Kinross Service Area, M90 Junct 6 ✆ (01577) 863680
✗ Green ✆ (01577) 863467

Gairney Bridge Caravan Park KY13 7JZ ✆ (01577) 862336 OS map 58/130985 3m S of Kinross on B996 (Cowdenbeath) near Junct 5 of M90 Open Jun-Sept 25 pitches Grass, level, open 🅱🅿🅰⊕

Gallowhill Caravan Camping Park, Gallowhill Farm KY13 0RD ✆ (01577) 862364 OS map 58/106037 1m NW of Kinross on Gallowhill road Open Mar-Nov 50 pitches 5 acres level grass and hard standings 🖩🅿🅰⊕🚿🏵

Turfhills Tourist Centre (Granada) KY13 7NQ ✆ (01577) 863123 OS map 58/106027 ½m W of Kinross centre on A977 (Alloa) near Junction 6 of M90 Open all year 60 pitches–no adv booking Hard standings 🅱✗🖩🅰🚿

KINTYRE PENINSULA–see Campbeltown, Clachan, Dippen, Muasdale, Southend and Tarbert

KIRKCALDY, Fife   Map G4
EC Wed SEE Sailor's Walk, Ravenscraig Castle, Falkland Palace 10m NW
🄸 Whytes Causeway ✆ (01592) 267775
✗ Parkway, Abbotshall Rd ✆ (01592) 262143

Dunnikier Caravan Park, Dunnikier Way KY1 3ND ✆ (01592) 267563 OS map 59/282940 1m N of Kirkcaldy off A910/B981 (Glenrothes) Open Mar-Jan 60 marked pitches Level grass and hard standings 🅱🖩🅿🅰⊕∅🚐🅿♿

Pettycur Bay Holiday Park, Kinghorn KY3 9YE ✆ (01592) 890321 and 890913 OS map 66/260864 3m SW of Kirkcaldy on A92 (Inverkeithing) Open Mar-Oct–no adv booking 583 pitches (533 static) Grass, level, sheltered–some hard standings 🅱✗🍴⌂🖩🅿🅰∅⊕🚿🗔🚐(50) 🚐

KIRRIEMUIR, Angus   Map G2
SEE JM Barrie's birthplace and Barrie Pavilion
🄸 Cumberland Close ✆ (01575) 574097 ✗ Royal 6m SE at Forfar ✆ (01307) 462691

Drumshademuir Caravan Park, Glamis, Roundyhill by Forfar DD8 1QT ✆ (01575) 573284 OS map 54/382508 2m S of Kirriemuir on A928 (Dundee) Open all year 110 pitches (33 static) Hard standings, grass, part sloping, sheltered 🅱✗🍴⌂🖩🅿🅰⊕∅🗔🚿🚐(55) ♿ bar food, putting £8.00-£12.75 (most cards) *info@drumshademuir.com www.drumshademuir.com*

The distance and direction of a campsite is given from the centre of the town under which it appears.

Beecraigs Country Park

The Park Centre, Beecraigs Country Park Near Linlithgow, West Lothian EH49 6PL
Tel: 01506 844516/844517/844518 e-mail: **mail@beecraigs.com**

LANARK, S Lanarkshire   **Map F5**
EC Thurs SEE parish church, New Lanark, Craignethan castle ruins 4m NW
🖫 Horsemarket, Ladycare Rd ✆ (01555) 661661
✖ La Vigna (Italian), Wellgate St ✆ (01555) 664320

Newhouse Caravan Camping Park, Ravenstruther ML11 8NP ✆ (01555) 870228 OS map
72/927457 3m NE of Lanark on left of A70 (Edinburgh) past junction with A743 adj golf course
Open Mar-Oct 45 pitches Grass and hard standings, level, sheltered 🖫 🗄 🔌 ⊕ ∅ ⊕ ⤳ 🗴 🚏 ⅋
loch fishing

LARGS, N Ayrshire   **Map D5**
EC Wed SEE Skelmorlic Aisle
🖫 Promenade ✆ (01475) 673765
✖ Glen Eldon, Barr Cres ✆ (01475) 673381

LEVEN, Fife   **Map G3**
EC Thurs
✖ Old Manor 2m E at Lundin Links ✆ (01333) 320368

Letham Feus Caravan Park, Letham Feus KY8 5NT ✆ (01333) 351900 OS map 59/374049 3m N
of Leven on A916 (Cupar) Open Apr-Sept 151 pitches (125 static) Grass, sloping, sheltered
🖫 🗄 🔌 ⊕ ∅ ⊕ ⊕ ⤳ 🗴

Shell Bay Caravan Park, Elie KY9 1HB ✆ (01333) 330283 Fax (01333) 330008 OS map
59/465000 7m E of Leven off A917 (Elie) on single track road near beach Open Mar-Oct 440
pitches (320 static) Grass, level 🖫 ✖ 🍴 ⤳ ⼈ 🗄 🔌 ∅ ⊘ ⊕ ⤳ 🗴 🚏 ⅋ £10.00-£18.00*
(Mastercard/Visa/Switch)

Woodland Gardens Caravan and Camping Park, Blindwell Road, Lundin Links KY8 5QG
✆ (01333) 360319 OS map 59/418038 3m E of Leven off A915 (St Andrews) at eastern end of
Lundin Links Open Apr-Oct 25 pitches Grass, level, sheltered 🖫 🔌 ⊕ ⊘ 🗴 🚏 🚏 £10.00-
£15.00* woodlandgardens@lineone.net www.woodland-gardens.co.uk

---

LINLITHGOW, W Lothian   **Map F4**
SEE site, Linlithgow Palace, old town, St Michael's church
🖫 Burgh Halls, The Cross ✆ (01506) 844600
✖ Four Marys, High Street ✆ (01506) 844535

Beecraigs Caravan and Camping Park, Beecraigs Country Park EH49 6PL Modern site with
serviced landscaped bays ✆ (01506) 844516 Fax (01506) 846256 OS map 65/005746 2m S of
Linlithgow off Bathgate road–signposted Open all year 36 pitches Level grass and hard
standings, sheltered ✖ 🗄 🔌 ∅ ⊘ ⤳ 🗴 ⅋ country walks (Mastercard/Visa/Switch/Solo/Delta)
mail@beecraigs.com www.beecraigs.com

Loch House Caravan Camping Park, Loch House Farm EH49 7RG ✆ (01506) 842144 OS map
65/993777 ½m N of Linlithgow on left of A706 (Bo'ness) beyond motorway bridge Open all year
10 pitches Level/sloping grass 🗄 🔌 ∅ ⊕ 🗴

LOCHGILPHEAD, Argyll & Bute   **Map C4**
EC Tues SEE church
🖫 Lochnell St ✆ (01546) 602344
✖ Stag, Argyll St ✆ (01546) 602496

Lochgilphead Caravan Site, Bank Park PA31 8NX ✆ (01546) 602003 Fax (01546) 603699 OS
map 55/859881 ¼m S of Lochgilphead at junction of A83 (Ardrishaig) and A816 beside Loch Gilp
Open Apr-Oct 70 pitches (35 static) Grass and hard standings, level, part open 🖫 🗄 🔌 ∅ ⊘ ⊕
⤳ 🗴 (30) 🚏 £10.00 (min)* (Mastercard/Visa/Switch) info@lochgilheadcaravanpark.co.uk
www.lochgilheadcaravanpark.co.uk

SINGLE TRACK ROADS

On single track roads you need to drive further ahead than usual and pull into a passing place whenever you see another vehicle coming, though many drivers will flash their headlights to tell those towing caravans to come on. Keep an eye on your rear-view mirror and if a queue of vehicles builds up behind you pull into a passing place to allow them to overtake.

Oban Divers' Caravan Park, Oban

LOCH LOMOND–see Ardlui, Balloch, Drymen, Luss and Tarbet

MAIDENS–see Maybole

MAYBOLE, S Ayrshire   **Map D6**
SEE Culzean Castle and country park 4m W
✗ Malin Court, 10m SW on A77 ☏ (01655) 760457

Ardlochan House, Culzean KA19 8JZ ☏ (01655) 760208 OS map 70/221090 6m W of Maybole off B7023-A719 (Turnberry) on Ardlochan road adj country park Open Easter-Oct 60 pitches (50 static) 4 acres level grass and hard standings ⊘ ⊛

Culzean Bay Holiday Park, by Croy Shore KA19 8JS ☏ (01292) 500444 OS map 76/248125 4m W of Maybole on B7023/A719 (Dunure) at Croy Shore Open Mar-Oct 130 pitches (100 static) Hard standings and grass, level, sheltered ⊑◻▢⊕⊘⊕↵⊕(20) ⊡ games room

Old Mill Caravan Site, Maidens KA19 8LA ☏ (01655) 760254 OS map 76/223087 6m W of Maybole off A719 (Maidens) near beach Open Apr-Sept 26 pitches ✗◻▢⊘⊘⊜

Sandy Beach Caravan Park, Maidens KA26 9NS ☏ (01655) 331456 OS map 76/2100083 6m SW of Maybole on A719 (Girvan) Open Apr-Oct 45 pitches (40 static) Grass, level ⊑◻▢⊘⊕⊘&

MEMUS–see Kirriemuir

MONTROSE, Angus   **Map H2**
EC Wed SEE museum, Melville gardens
▣ Bridge St ☏ (01674) 672000
✗ Park, John St ☏ (01674) 673415

East Bowstrips Caravan Park, St Cyrus DD10 0DE *Quiet coastal park with excellent facilities* ☏ (01674) 850328 *Prop: PM & G Tully* OS map 45/741653 6m N of Montrose on A92 (Stonehaven)–signposted Open Apr-Oct 60 pitches 4 acres grass and hard standings, part sheltered ⊑◻▢⊘⊘⊕⊘& £11.00-£12.00* inc elect *tully@bowstrips.freeserve.co.uk* *www.ukparks.co.uk/eastbowstrips*

South Links Caravan Park, South Links DD10 8EJ ☏ (01674) 672105 OS map 54/720575 ½m N of Montrose off A92 (Stonehaven) Open Apr-Oct 15 170 pitches ◻▢⊕⊘↵&

MOTHERWELL–see Glasgow

MUASDALE, Argyll & Bute   **Map C5**
✗ Putechan Lodge 4½m S on A83 at Bellochantuy ☏ (01583) 421207

Muasdale Holiday Park PA29 6XD ☏ (01583) 421207 OS map 68/678399 ¼m S of Muasdale off A83 (Campbeltown) on seafront Open Apr-Sept 30 pitches (10 static) Grass, part level, part sheltered ⊑✗(tea room) ◻▢⊘⊕◻⊡ games room

Point Sands Caravan Park, Tayinloan PA29 6XG ☏ (01583) 441263 OS map 62/696485 4½m N of Muasdale off A83 (Tarbert) Open Apr-Oct 150 pitches (70 static) Level grass ⊑⊁◻▢⊘⊕⊘⊕↵⊕(£50) ⊡& beach access (Visa)

NORTH BERWICK, East Lothian   **Map H4**
EC Thurs SEE Tantallon Castle 3m E
▣ 18 Quality St ☏ (01620) 892197
✗ Point Garry, West Bay Rd ☏ (01620) 892380

Tantallon Caravan Park, Lime Grove EH39 5NJ ☏ (01620) 893348 Fax (01620) 895623 OS map 67/566850 1m E of North Berwick on A198 (Dunbar) near golf course Open Mar-Oct 200 pitches (60 static) 14 acres level grass ⊑⊁◻▢⊘⊕⊘⊕↵◻⊡& boating, fishing, golf, games room £10.00-£19.00* (Mastercard/Visa/Switch) *tantallon@meadowhead.co.uk www.meadowhead.co.uk*

OBAN, Argyll & Bute Map C3
EC Thurs SEE cathedral, museum, Highland gathering (end Aug)
🅸 Boswell House, Argyll Sq ☏ (01631) 563122
✘ Rowan Tree, George St ☏ (01631) 562954

Ganavan Sands Caravan Park, Ganavan PA34 5TU ☏ (01631) 562179 OS map 49/862325 2m N
of Oban on coast road to Ganavan, by sea Open Easter-Oct 80 pitches Grass and hard
standings, sheltered 🚻💶🖥🚿🛒⊕🅿🛁☂🚰

Oban Caravan and Camping Park, Gallanach Road PA34 4QH ☏ (01631) 562425 Fax (01631)
566624 OS map 49/831273 3m S of Oban on Gallanach road Open Apr-Oct 150 pitches
Level grass and hard standing 🚻💶🖥🚿🛒⊘⊕🚰🛒🏠 £10.00-£12.50 (all cards)
info@obancaravanpark.com www.obancaravanpark.co.uk

Oban Divers' Caravan Park, Glenshellach Rd PA34 4QJ ☏ (01631) 562755 *Prop: Mr & Mrs D Tye*
OS map 49/841277 1½m SW of Oban off coast road Open Mar 29-Oct 31 45 pitches Grass and
hard standings, part sloping, sheltered 🚻🖥🚿🛒⊕🚰⊗🛁ᚷ £10.00-£14.00
info@obandivers.co.uk www.obandivers.co.uk

PATNA–see Maybole

PERTH, Perth & Kinross Map G3
EC Wed MD Fri SEE St Ninian's Cathedral, Black Watch museum, leisure pool, Greyfriars
churchyard, Scone Palace 2m N
🅸 Caithness Glass ☏ (01738) 638481
✘ Coach House, North Port ☏ (01738) 627950

Scone Racecourse, Scone PH2 6BE ☏ (01738) 635232 OS map 58/108274 2m N of Perth off
A93 (Braemar) at Old Scone Open Apr-mid Oct–adv booking min 5 nights 150 pitches
🚻🖥🚿🛒⊕ᚷ fishing £7.00

✘ RESTAURANTS

The restaurants recommended in this guide
are of three kinds – pubs, independent
restaurants and those forming part of hotels
and motels. They all serve lunch and dinner –
at a reasonable price – say under £10 a head.
We shall be glad to have your comments on
any you use this season and if you think they
are not up to standard, please let us have
your suggestions for alternatives.

Scone Racecourse, Perth

PITLOCHRY, Perth & Kinross Map F2
EC Thurs (winter) *See Loch Faskally Dam (fish ladder and observation chamber), Highland games
(Sept), whisky distilleries, Blair castle and Blair Atholl 7m NW, Queen's View 6m NW*
🅸 22 Atholl Rd ☏ (01796) 472215
✘ Birchwood, East Moulin Rd ☏ (01796) 472477

Faskally Home Farm PH16 5LA ☏ (01796) 472007 Fax (01796) 473896 OS map 43/922598 2m N
of Pitlochry off A9 (Inverness) on B8019 (old A9) Open Mar 15-Oct 31 315 pitches (80 static)
Level/sloping grass, sheltered 🚻✘💶🖥🚿🛒⊘🛀(indoor heated)🚰ᚷ fishing,steam room, spa &
sauna £10.50-£14.40* (most cards) ehay@easynet.co.uk www.faskally.co.uk

Milton of Fonab Caravan Park PH16 5NA ☏ (01796) 472882 *Prop: M Stewart* OS map 52/944573
½m S of Pitlochry off A9 (Perth) opp Bells distillery Open Apr 6-Oct–families only, no motor cycles
150 pitches Level grass, sheltered 🚻🖥🚿🛒⊕⊘🚰🛒 free trout fishing, mountain bike hire
£13.00-£15.00 info@fonab.co.uk www.fonab.co.uk

PITTENWEEM–see Anstruther

PRESTWICK, S Ayrshire Map D6
EC Wed SEE Cuthbert's church
✘ St Nicholas, Ayr Rd ☏ (01292) 79568

Prestwick Holiday Park KA9 1UH ☏ (01292) 479261 OS map 70/343278 1m N of Prestwick off
A79 (Prestwick airport) on coast road–signposted Open Mar-Oct 186 pitches (155 static) Grass,
level 🚻💶🖥🚿🛒⊘⊘⊕🚰🅿(35) 🛒

Milton of Fonab Caravan Site	Telephone: 01796 472882
Pitlochry, Perthshire	Fax: 01796 474363
Scotland PH16 5NA	E-Mail: info@fonab.co.uk

ST ANDREWS, Fife   **Map H3**
EC Thurs SEE cathedral, chapter house and museum, botanic gardens, West Port, Dutch village in Craigtown Park
🛈70 Market St ℓ (01334) 472021 ✗ Grange Inn, Grange Rd ℓ (01334) 472670

Cairns Mill Caravan Park, Largo Road KY16 8NN ℓ (01334) 473604 OS map 59/498148 1m S of St Andrews on A915 (Largo) Open Apr-Oct 265 pitches (170 static) Grass and hard standings, level, open 🛒♥🗄🔌🅿🔥🅿🚿(heated) ⊕❤🔌🅿(50) 🚽🏃 games room, coffee bar £13.00-£15.00 (Mastercard/Visa/Switch) cairnsmill@aol.com www.ukparks.co.uk/cairnsmill

Clayton Caravan Park KY16 9YE ℓ (01334) 870242 OS map 59/430183 5m W of St Andrews on A91 (Cupar) Open Apr-Oct 265 pitches (195 static) Level/sloping grass and hard standings, sheltered 🛒✗♀🚶🔌🅿🔌🅿⊕❤🔌🅿🚽🏃 (Mastercard/Visa)

Craigtoun Meadows Holiday Park, Mount Melville KY16 8PQ ℓ (01334) 475959 Fax (01334) 476424 OS map 59/483153 1½m WSW of St Andrews off B939 (Pitscottie) on Craigtoun road Open Mar-Oct 244 pitches (146 static) 🛒✗♀🔌🅿⊕❤🏃 tennis, gymnasium, cycle hire £15.50-£22.00 (Delta/Switch/Mastercard/Visa) craigtoun@aol.com www.craigtounmeadows.co.uk

ST CYRUS–see Montrose

ST FILLANS, Perth & Kinross   **Map E3**
EC Wed Sailing and mountaineering centre at E end of Loch Earn. SEE museum of Scottish tartans (Easter-Sept) 5m E at Comrie
✗ Drummond Arms ℓ (01764) 685212

Loch Earn Caravan Park, South Shore Road PH6 9NL ℓ (01764) 685270 OS map 51/680238 1m W of St Fillans on South Lochearn road by private beach Open Apr-Oct 270 pitches 20 acres level grass, sheltered 🅿🔌⊕ (Mastercard/Visa/Switch)

ST MADOES–see Glencarse

SCOTLANDWELL–see Glenrothes

SOUTHEND, Argyll & Bute   **Map B6**
✗ Muneroy Licensed Tearoom & Stores ℓ (01586) 830221

Machribeg Caravan Site PA28 6RW ℓ (01586) 830249 Prop: James Barbour OS map 68/686085 ½m SW of Southend on road to Keil Point Open Easter-Sept 140 pitches (60 static) 8 acres, grass, level, open 🅿⊕🅿🚽 boating, fishing, golf £6.00

STIRLING, Stirling   **Map F4**
EC Wed MD Thurs SEE castle, Chapel Royal museum and art gallery, Darnley's house, Abbey Craig with Wallace monument 2m NE, Bannockburn memorial, Doune castle 6m NW
🛈 Royal Burgh Visitor Centre ℓ (01786) 479901
✗ Golden Lion, King Street ℓ (01786) 475351

Auchenbowie Caravan Site, Auchenbowie FK7 8HE ℓ (01324) 823999 Fax 01324 822950 OS map 57/795880 3m S of Stirling off A872 (Glasgow) south of Junction 9 of M80/M9 Open Apr-Oct—no adv booking 60 pitches Grass, part level, sheltered, some hard standings 🛒(mobile) 🅿🔌⊕❤🔌🅿(35) 🚽 £9.00-£10.00* (Mastercard/Visa/Switch)

Witches Craig Caravan-Camping Park, Blairlogie FK9 5PX ℓ (01786) 474947 Prop: A & V Stephen OS map 57/822968 3m NE of Stirling on left of A91 (Stirling-St.Andrews Road) Open Apr-Oct 60 pitches Grass and hard standings, level, sheltered 🅿🔌🅿⊕❤🔌🅿🚽🏃 £11.00-£15.00 info@witchescraig.co.uk www.witchescraig.co.uk

For more up-to-date information, visit our site at: **www.butford.co.uk/camping**

STRACHUR, Argyll & Bute   **Map D3**
✗ Creggans Inn ☏ (01369) 820279

Glendaruel Caravan Park, Glendaruel PA22 3AB *Award-winning park in woodland garden*
☏ (01369) 820267 Fax (01369) 820367 OS map 55/999868 10½m SW of Strachur on A886
(Colintraive) Open Apr-Oct 65 pitches (30 static) Grass and hard standings, level, sheltered–
3 acres within 22 acre country park 🔌 ⚓ 🗑 🔌 ∅ ⊘ ⌀ ⊕ ⤳ 🔌 ▭ fishing (salmon and sea trout),
barbecue, under cover campers' kitchen (OAP discount) (Mastercard/Visa/Switch)
mail@glendaruelcaravanpark.co.uk www.glendaruelcaravanpark.co.uk

Strathlachlan Caravan Park, Strathlachlan PA27 8BU ☏ (01369) 860300 OS map 55/005955 6m
S of Strachur off A886 (Tighnabruaich) on single track B8000 (Kilfinan) beside Loch Fyne
Open Apr-Oct 104 pitches (96 static)–no tents Hard standings, level 🔌 🗑 🔌 ∅ ⌀ ∅ 🔌

TARBERT, Argyll & Bute   **Map C4**
EC Wed
ℹ Harbour St ☏ (01880) 820429
✗ West Loch Hotel ☏ (01880) 840283

Point Sands Caravan Park, Tayinloan PA29 6XG *Quality site amid wonderful scenery* ☏ (01583)
441263 OS map 62/698484 8m S of Tarbert on A83 (Campbeltown) Open Apr-Nov 135 pitches
(60 static) 15 acres level grass 🔌 🗑 🔌 ∅ ⊕ ⤳ 🔌 ▭ (Mastercard/Visa)

Port Ban Holiday Park, Kilberry PA29 6YD ☏ (01880) 770224 OS map 62/707655 15m W of
Tarbert off A83 (Lochgilphead) on single track B8024 (Kilberry) Open Apr-Oct 92 pitches
(62 static) Grass, part level, part sheltered 🔌 ✗ ⤳ 🗑 🔌 ∅ ⊕ ⊘ ⊕ ⤳ 🔌 ▭ tennis, putting, crazy
golf, boat hire, sailing, fishing £10.00-£12.00* (Mastercard/Visa) *portban@aol.com*
www.portban.com

See also Clachan

TARBET, Highland   **Map D3**
SEE Rest and Be Thankful Hill at Arrochar 2mW, Ben Arthur (2,891ft) NW
ℹ Main St ☏ (01301) 702260
✗ Ardlui 8m N at Ardlui ☏ (01301) 704243

Ardgartan Campsite (Forestry Commission), Arrochar G83 7AL ☏ (season) 0131 314 6100 (out
season) OS map 56/275030 4m W of Tarbet on left of A83 (Inveraray) in Argyll Forest Park on
west shore of Loch Long Open Apr-Oct 200 pitches Hard standings and grass, level, open
🔌 🗑 🔌 ∅ ⊕ ⊘ ⤳ 🔌 (50) ⚿ pony trekking, rock climbing, boating, sea fishing

Loch Lomond Holiday Park, Inveruglas G83 7DW ☏ (01301) 704224 Fax (01301) 704206 OS
map 56/320091 3m N of Tarbet on A82 (Fort William) beside Loch Lomond Open Mar-Oct and
Dec-Jan 90 pitches (64 static) 1 acre level grass and hard standings
🔌 🗑 🔌 ∅ ⊕ ⊘ ⊕ ⤳ 🔌 ⌂ 🛒 ⚿ all-weather pitches, fishing, beach, boating £13.00-£18.00*
(Mastercard/Visa/Delta/Switch) *enquiries@lochmond-caravans.co.uk www.lochmond-*
caravans.co.uk

TAYINLOAN–see Tarbert

TAYNUILT, Argyll & Bute   **Map D3**
EC Wed SEE Nelson monument, Cruachan power station, old blast furnace, Loch Etive N, Brander
Pass E
✗ Brander Lodge ☏ (01866) 822243

Crunachy Caravan Camping Park, Bridge of Awe PA35 1HT ☏ (01866) 822612 OS map
50/032296 2m SE of Taynuilt on right of A85 (Dalmally-Oban) near Bridge of Awe Open Mar-Oct
100 pitches 9 acres level grass and hard standings, sheltered 🔌 ✗ (tea room)
⤳ 🗑 🔌 ∅ ⊕ ⊘ ⤳ 🔌 ▭ ⚿ games room (most cards)

TAYPORT, Fife   **Map H3**
✗ Sandford Hill 6m W at Wormit ☏ (01382) 541802

Tayport Links Caravan Park DD6 9ES ☏ (01382) 552334 OS map 59/463285 ¼m E of Tayport off
B945 (Leuchars) on sea front Open Apr-Oct 100 pitches (70 static) Grass and hard standings,
level, sheltered 🗑 🔌 ∅ ⊕ ∅ ▢ (heated) 🛒

TROON, S Ayrshire   **Map D5**
EC Wed SEE Lady Isle bird sanctuary
✗ Ardneil Hotel, 51 St Meddans St ☏ (01292) 311611 Open Mon-Sun 12-9

St Meddans Caravan Site KA10 6NS ☏ (01292) 312957 *Prop: Ronnie Heron* OS map 70/332312
¼m E of Troon off A759 (Loans) Open Mar-Oct 25 pitches (18 static) Level grass sheltered
🔌 ∅ ⊕ £10.00-£11.50

Help us make CAMPING CARAVANNING BRITAIN better known to site operators – and thereby
more informative – by showing them your copy when booking in.

TUMMEL BRIDGE, Perth & Kinross   Map E2
✕ Loch Rannoch 6m W at Kinloch Rannoch ☎ (01882) 632201
Tummel Valley Holiday Park PH16 5SA ☎ (01882) 634221 Fax (01882) 634302 OS map
  52/764592 ¼m E of Tummel Bridge on left of B8019 (Pitlochry) Open Mar-Oct 160 pitches (110
  static)
  50 acres, part sloping, part hard standings 🛒 ✕ ♀ ⊸ ♪ 🗑 🗐 🖉 ✿ ∅ 🖾 (indoor) 🄿 🚂 🏠 ♿
  solarium, entertainment (Jun-Aug), bike hire £8.00-£23.00* (all major cards)
  enquiries@parkdeanholidays.co.uk www.parkdeanholidays.co.uk

TURNBERRY–see Girvan

TYNDRUM, Stirling   Map D3
🄸 Main St ☎ (01838) 400246
✕ Ardlui 13m S at Ardlui ☎ (01301) 704243
Pine Trees Caravan Park FK20 8RY ☎ (01838) 400243 OS map 50/327301 ¼m S of Tyndrum off
  A82 (Tarbert) on road to lower station Open Jan-Oct 42 pitches Grass, level 🛒 🖉 ✿ 🖃 (50) 🚂

WHITBURN, W Lothian   Map F4
✕ Dreadnought 4m NE at Bathgate ☎ (01506) 630791
Mosshall Farm Caravan Park, Blackburn EH47 7DB ☎ (01501) 762318 OS map 65/975647 1m E
  of Whitburn on A705 (Blackburn Road) Open all year 25 pitches Level grass and hard standings,
  sheltered 🗐 ✿ £7.50-£8.50

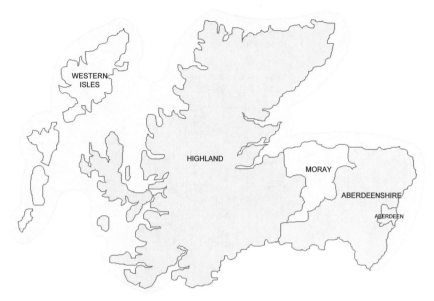

North Scotland contains what is probably the most beautiful scenery to be found anywhere in Britain.

The coastline is most spectacular on the north and west, where giant arms of rock reach out towards the islands. Between them are deep lochs, linked from east to west by countless rivers and streams feeding innumerable lakes surrounded by wooded glens and majestic peaks. The most dominant inland feature in the country is the great rift which extends diagonally from Inverness to Fort William, in which the Caledonian Canal provides a continuous waterway from the North Sea to the Atlantic.

The best known centre in the south is Aviemore on the ski slopes of the Cairngorms. At nearby Kingussie is the Highland Wildlife Park where bison, beaver, lynx and even rarer osprey can be seen in a natural setting. Southwest lies Ben Nevis, at 4406ft Britain's highest mountain, and farther west still Loch Morar, our deepest lake.

On the west coast is Skye, linked between Fort William and Mallaig by the famous Road to the Isles. Ferries to the island run from Glenelg and Kyle of Lochalsh as well as from Mallaig. Portree and Broadford are handy bases for exploring the island. From Uig, in northern Skye, boats leave for the Outer Hebrides. Facing Skye between the Kyle of Lochalsh and Ullapool is a wild and magnificently remote region of mountain peaks and forests, for which Applecross, Torridon, Gairloch and Kinlochewe are obvious centres. Further north is Lochinver, most famous of all the west coast fishing villages.

The northern coast has its own rugged grandeur and fine beaches at Balnakiel Bay, reached from Durness. Here too are the cliffs of Clo Mor, at 900ft Britain's highest, and the waterfall near Kylesku which plummets 660ft. The towns of Golspie, Dornoch, Helmsdale and Brora are each lively holiday centres with good beaches and facilities. Inland lie extensive nature reserves and national forest parks with awe-inspiring lochs and towering bens. Further south the Firths of Dornoch, Cromarty and Beauly flank not only high peaks but lush and fertile farmland and valleys brilliant with displays of wild flowers through the season.

The bold right angle of the Grampian coastline has many charming seaside villages and towns on its northern edge, while on the eastern edge after Peterhead fifteen miles of sands and dunes roll on towards the granite fishing port and resort of Aberdeen. West of Aberdeen is the pretty Dee Valley, with the royal hunting lodge of Balmoral and Braemar, home of the Highland Games. The Grampian is the main centre of whisky, too, and distilleries can be visited near Dufftown, Elgin and Keith.

Campsites on the west and north Highland are sparse. The eastern Highland is slightly better served, but the campsites all tend to be along the coast. The few inland often have primitive facilities and are very crowded in season. Sites in the east are more regularly spaced, but are too few to cope with the high demand in season.

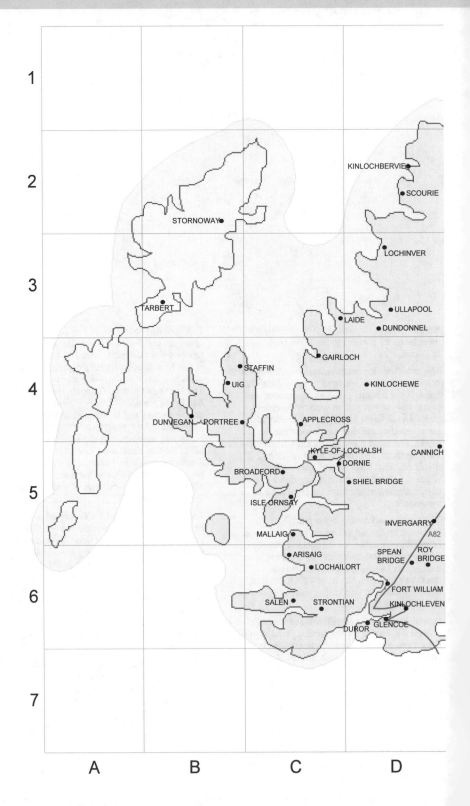

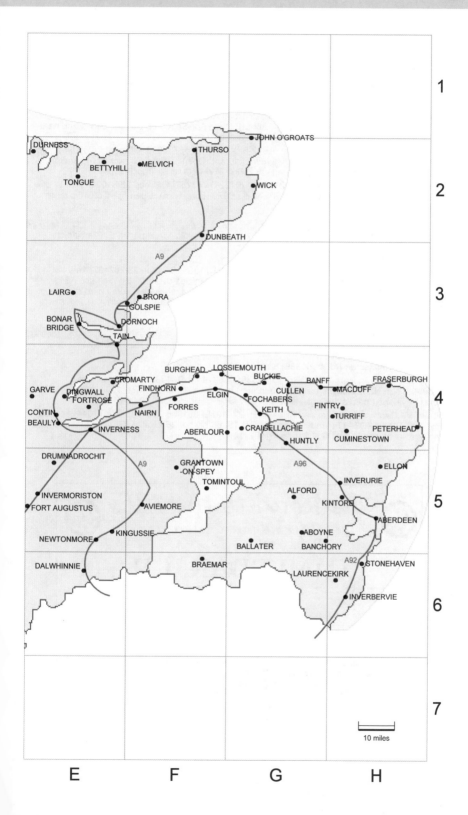

ABERDEEN   Map H5
EC Wed MD Fri SEE cathedral regional museum, fish market, Girdleness lighthouse
▮ St Nicholas House, Broad St ✆ (01224) 632727
✖ Music Cellar, Union St ✆ (01224) 580092

Craighill Farm, Bridge of Dee AB1 5XJ ✆ (01224) 781973 OS map 38/923027 ¾m S of Aberdeen
   on A90 (Stonehaven) Open Apr-Oct–no adv booking 20 pitches Grass, sloping, hard standings,
   sheltered 🔊🖉⊕🔊🖭

Hazelhead Caravan Park and Campsite, Groats Road AB1 8BL ✆ (01224) 321268 OS map
   38/894057 3½m W of Aberdeen off A944 (Alford) Open Apr-Sept 165 pitches Grass and hard
   standings, level, sheltered 🅿🔊🖉⊕🖉🔊 (Mastercard/Visa)

Lower Deeside Caravan Park, Maryculter AB12 5FX ✆ (01224) 733860 OS map 38/860955 6m
   SW of Aberdeen off A93 (Banchory) adj hotel/restaurant Open all year 75 pitches (45 static)
   Level grass and hard standings, sheltered 🅿🔊🖉⊕🖉🔊🗆🖭 (most cards)

Skene Caravan Park, Mains of Keir AB32 6YA ✆ (01224) 743282 OS map 38/810082 7m W of
   Aberdeen off A944 (Alford) at Kirkton of Skene on B979 (Blackburn) Open Apr-Oct 10 pitches
   🔊🖉⊕🔊🖭

ABERLOUR, Moray   Map F4
EC Wed SEE waterfalls on Aberlour Burn, Huntly Castle (heraldic carvings) 1m E, Glenfiddich
distillery 4m SE
✖ Dowans ✆ (01340) 871488

Aberlour Gardens Caravan Park AB38 9LD ✆ (01340) 871586 OS map 28/282437 1m N of
   Aberlour off A95 (Keith)–signposted on unclassed road–vehicles over 10ft 6in high use A941
   (Dufftown) Open Mar-Oct 104 pitches (30 static) Grass, level, sheltered, some hard standings
   🅿🏷🔊🖉⊕🔊🔊🗆🖭🔊 milk, motorhome service point (Mastercard/Visa)

See also Craigellachie

ABOYNE, Aberdeens   Map G5
EC Thurs SEE winter sports centre, St Thomas's church, Aboyne games (Sept), Glentaner deer
forest, Craigievar Castle 7m NE
✖ Birse Lodge, Charleston Rd ✆ (01339) 882243

Aboyne Loch Caravan Park AB34 5BR ✆ (01339) 886244 Fax (01339) 811669 OS map
   44/539995 ½m NE of Aboyne on A93 (Aberdeen) near loch Open Apr-Oct 128 pitches (48 static)
   8 acres, level, part hard standings 🅿🔊🖉⊕🔊🔊🖭 fishing £9.00-£12.00*

Drummie Hill Caravan Park, Tarland AB34 4UP ✆ (01339) 881388 OS map 37/477044 5m NW of
   Aboyne off B9094-A974 (Tarland) Open Apr-Oct 15 98 pitches (67 static) Grass and some hard
   standings, level, open 🅿🔊🖉⊕🖉🔊🔊(40)🖭

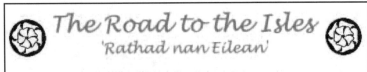

ALFORD, Aberdeens   Map G5
SEE Haughton House 1m N
ℹ Railway Museum, Station Yard ☏ (01975) 562052
✘ Grant Arms 12m E at Monymusk ☏ (01467) 651226

Haughton House Country Park AB33 8NA ☏ (01975) 562107 OS map 37/583168 1m N of Alford on Montgarrie road Open Apr–Sept–no adv booking 175 pitches (40 static) Grass and hard standings, level, sheltered ⚏🚿♿⛽⊕∅☯⛏🚽⛺ putting green, guided walks, narrow gauge railway

ALVES–see Burghead

APPLECROSS, Highland   Map C4
SEE Applecross forest
✘ Potting Shed Café & Restaurant ☏ (01520) 744440 Open Tue-Sat 10-8, Sun-Mon 10-5

Applecross Campsite, Strathcarron IV54 8ND ☏ (01520) 744268 OS map 24/715446 ¼m E of Applecross on Kishorn road–only poss approach for caravans from N via Kenmore Open Apr-Oct 60 pitches Level grass, sheltered ⚏✘(lic) 🚿♿∅⊕⛺ wet weather area, tea room £8.00

ARISAIG, Highland   Map C6
SEE site, Sound of Arisaig, Silver Sands of Morar 6m N, islands (boat trips)
✘ Old Library Lodge ☏ (01687) 450651

Camusdarach Camping Site PH39 4NT ☏ (01687) 450221 Prop: A Simpson OS map 40/663915 4m N of Arisaig on B8008 (Mallaig) Open Mar 15-Oct 15–booking advisable Jul-Aug 42 pitches Grass, part level 🚿♿∅⊕∅♿ adj sandy beach £10.00-£12.00 inc showers (Mastercard/Visa) camdarach@aol.com www.camusdarach.com

Gorten Sands Caravan Site, Gorten Farm PH39 4NS ☏ (01687) 450283 OS map 40/640879 1m W of Arisaig off A830 (Mallaig) on Back of Keppoch road across cattle grid Open Easter-Sept 45 pitches Grass and hard standings, level, part sheltered ⚏🚿♿∅⊕∅ adj seashore £9.50-£12.50*

Portnadoran Camping and Caravan Site PH39 4NT ☏ (01687) 450267 Fax (01687) 450267 OS map 40/652889 2m N of Arisaig off A830 (Mallaig) Open Apr-Oct 40 pitches Grass, level ⚏🚿♿⊕∅☯⛺ adj sandy beach at-macdonald@portnadoran.freeserve.co.uk

Skyeview Caravan Park PH38 4NJ ☏ (01687) 450209 OS map 40/654880 1m N of Arisaig off A830 (Mallaig) Open Apr-Oct 20 pitches 2 acres, level/gentle slope, grass, sheltered 🚿∅⊕

AVIEMORE, Highland   Map F5
EC Wed Britain's premier skiing centre SEE Cairngorms centre, curling centre, reindeer herd, Ben Macdhui (4,296ft), Wildlife park, osprey sanctuary, Strathspey rlwy to Boat of Garten (5m), Craigellachie Rock (rallying point for the Clan Grant)
ℹ Grampian Rd ☏ (01479) 810363
✘ La Taverna Pizzeria, High Range, Grampian Rd ☏ (01479) 810683/810637 Open 12-Oct

Campground of Scotland, Boat of Garten PH24 3BN ☏ (01479) 831652 Fax (01479) 831652 OS map 36/939191 6m NE of Aviemore off A9 (Inverness) and A95 (Grantown on Spey) in Boat of Garten Open all year 97 pitches (60 static) Grass and hard standings, level, part open ⛺🚿∅⊕☯⛺ sep pitches £7.50-£17.50

Dalraddy Caravan Park PH22 1QB ☏ (01479) 810330 Prop: JDA Williamson OS map 36/857083 3m S of Aviemore on right of B9152 (Kingussie) Open all year–must book 149 pitches (104 static) Level/sloping grass and hard standing, sheltered ⚏⚲🚿♿∅⊕∅☯🍴⛺🏠 fishing £4.50-£20.00 (Mastercard/Visa/Delta/Solo) dhp@alvie-estate.co.uk www.alvie-estate.co.uk

Glenmore Forest Park Campsite PH22 1QU ☏ (01479) 861271 OS map 36/975097 7m E of Aviemore on B970 (Coylumbridge) by Loch Morlich Open all year–booking advisable 220 pitches Grass and hard standings, level, part open ⚏✘🚿♿∅⊕∅☯🚽♿ forest trails

High Range Touring Park, Grampian Road PH22 1PT ☏ (01479) 810636 OS map 35/36/894120 ½m S of Aviemore centre on B9152 (Kincraig) near junction with B970 Open Dec-Oct 68 pitches Hard standing and grass, level, sheltered ✘⚲⛺🚿⊕⊕☯🍴🏠♿ £13.00-£15.00 (Mastercard/Visa) info@highrange.co.uk www.highrange.co.uk

Rothiemurchus Camp and Caravan Park, Coylumbridge PH22 1QH ☏ (01479) 812800 OS map 36/915106 1½m E of Aviemore off A951 in Coylumbridge Open all year 89 pitches (50 static) Level/sloping grass and hard standings, sheltered ⚏⚲🚿♿∅⊕∅🍴⛺🏠 TV hook-up (Mastercard/Visa/Switch)

Speyside Caravan Park PH22 1PX ☏ (01479) 810236 OS map 35/985115 ¼m S of Aviemore off B970 (Coylumbridge) beside River Spey Open all year 154 pitches (105 static) 10 acres, level grass and hard standings ⚲🚿♿∅⛺ serviced pitches, cycle hire, fishing

For more up-to-date information, and for links to camping websites, visit our site at:
www.butford.co.uk/camping

BALLACHULISH–see Glencoe

BALLATER, Aberdeens   Map G5
EC Thurs SEE Falls of Muick, Loch Kinord 4m NE, Highland games (Aug)
🅸 Station Sq ☏(01339) 755306
✘ Darroch Learg, Braemar Rd ☏(01339) 755443
Ballater Caravan Site AB3 5QR ☏(01339) 755727 OS map 37/370955 ¼m SW of Ballater off A93
   (Braemar) near bridge over river Dee Open Easter-Oct–Jun-Aug maximum stay 14 nights
   159 pitches (93 static) Grass and hard standing, level 🖿◪⊕∅☻⏏🕮

BALMACARA–see Kyle of Lochalsh

BANCHORY, Aberdeens   Map G5
EC Thurs SEE Bridge of Feugh, Crathes castle 2m E, Deeside Heather Centre 7m E
🅸 Bridge St ☏(01330) 822000
✘ Burnett Arms, Main St ☏(01330) 824944
Banchory Lodge Caravan Park, Dee Street AB3 3HY ☏(01330) 822246 OS map 38/698954 ¼m
   SE of Banchory off A493 (Aberdeen) Open Apr-mid Oct–no adv booking Grass, level, sheltered
   🖿☻🕮(20) 🕮
Campfield Caravan Park AB31 4DN ☏(01339) 820250 OS map 38/652004 5m NW of Banchory
   on A980 (Bridge of Alford) Open Apr-Sept 45 pitches (30 static) Grass, level, sheltered
   🛒☻🕮(30) 🕮 petrol
Feughside Caravan Park, Strachan AB31 6NT ☏(01330) 850669 Prop: Graham Hay OS map
   38/643924 5m SW of Banchory off B976 (Aboyne) behind Feughside inn Open Apr-mid Oct
   72 pitches (52 static) Grass, level, sheltered ✘♨⏏🖿🕮◪⊕∅🕮(30) ♿☂ £10.00-£14.00
   contact-us@feughsidecaravanpark.co.uk www.feughsidevaravanpark.co.uk
Silver Ladies Caravan Park, Strachan AB31 3NL ☏(01330) 822800 OS map 38/692936 1m S of
   Banchory on left of B974 (Strachan) Open Apr-Oct 103 pitches (88 static) 7 acres level grass
   and hard standing 🛒⏏🖿🕮◪⊕∅☻⏏🕮

BANFF, Aberdeens   Map G4
EC Wed SEE site, Mercat cross, museum, miniature railway from harbour, Duff House 1m S
🅸 Collie Lodge ☏(01261) 812419
✘ Banff Springs, Golden Knowes Rd ☏(01261) 812881
Links Camping Park AB4 2JD ☏(01261) 812228 OS map 29/675642 1m W of Banff off A98
   (Portsoy) on B9139 (Whitehills) by sea Open Apr-Sept 145 pitches (85 static) Grass, level
   🛒⏏🖿🕮◪⏏🕮

BEAULY, Highland   Map E4
EC Thurs SEE Priory, Highland Craftpoint
✘ The Priory Hotel, The Square ☏(01463) 782309
Lovat Bridge Caravan and Camping Park IV4 7AY ☏(01463) 782374 Prop: Allan Lymburn OS
   map 26/517450 1½m S of Beauly on A862 (Inverness) by River Beauly Open Apr-Oct 40 pitches
   11½ acres, level grass and hard standings ✘♨🖿🕮◪∅☻⏏🔲🕮 bar meals, milk, fishing
   £10.00-£12.00 allanlymburn@beauly782.fsnet.co.uk

SINGLE TRACK ROADS

On single track roads you need to drive further ahead than usual and pull into a passing place whenever you see another vehicle coming, though many drivers will flash their headlights to tell those towing caravans to come on. Keep an eye on your rear-view mirror and if a queue of vehicles builds up behind you pull into a passing place to allow them to overtake.

Cannich Caravan Park, Cannich

BETTYHILL, Highland   Map E2
ℹ Clachan ✆ (01641) 52342 (summer)
✘ Bettyhill ✆ (01641) 521352

Craigdhu Camping KW14 7SP ✆ (01641) 521273 OS map 10/709620 ½m E of Bettyhill centre on A836 (Thuro) Open Easter-Oct 90 pitches 5 acres, level/gentle slope, grass, sheltered ▣

BRORA, Highland   Map F3
EC Wed SEE woollen mills
✘ Links ✆ (01408) 621225

Crakaig Caravan Park, Loth Beach KW8 6HP ✆ (01408) 621260 OS map 17/960095 5m NE of Brora off A9 (Helmsdale) at Crakaig near beach Open May-Sept 36 pitches 7 acres gentle slope, sheltered

Riverside Croft Caravan Site, Stonehouse, Doll KW9 6NJ ✆ (01408) 621819 OS map 17/885032 1½m SW of Brora off A9 (Golspie) at Doll Open May-Sept 18 pitches Grass, part level, part sheltered ▣ ⊕ ↵ ⌂

BUCKIE–see Cullen

BURGHEAD, Moray   Map F4
Fishing town on Burghead Bay SEE Burghead Well, Burghead Bulls (7-8c Pictish stones)
✘ Torfness ✆ (01343) 835663

Burghead Caravan Park, West Beach IV30 2UN Burghead (01343) 835799 ¼m W of Burghead centre on west beach Open Apr-Sept 135 pitches (58 static) Grass, level, part open, hard standings ▣▣◿⊕⊘↵▣▣⌂⚿ adj sandy beach

North Alves Caravan Park, Alves IV30 3XD ✆ (01343) 850223 OS map 28/122623 3m S of Burghead on A96 (Elgin-Forres) Open Apr-Oct 90 pitches (30 static) Level grass ▣▣▣◿⊕▣⌂

Red Craig Hotel Caravan Camping Park IV30 5XX ✆ (01343) 835663 OS map 28/124689 ½m E of Burghead centre off B9012 (Hopeman) Open Apr-Oct 38 pitches 4½ acres sloping/level grass ✘▣↵↗▣▣◿⊕⊘▣▣ weekend entertainment (Mastercard/Visa/Delta)

Station Caravan Park, West Beach, Hopeman IV30 5RU ✆ (01343) 830880 *Prop: David & Angie Steer* OS map 28/145696 2m NE of Burghead off B9040 (Lossiemouth) Open Apr-Oct 100 marked pitches (60 static) Level grass, sheltered ▣▣◿⊕⊕↵▣⌂ private beach £8.50-£12.50* *stationcaravanpark@talk21.com www.stationcaravanpark.co.uk*

CANNICH, Highland   Map D5
SEE Glen Cannich W, Glen Affric SW, Plodda Falls, Corrimony chambered cairn 3m E, Loch Ness Monster exhibition 12m E at Drumnadrochit
✘ Glen Affric ✆ (01456) 476214

Cannich Caravan Park IV4 7LN ✆ (01456) 415364 *Prop: F & MG Jones* OS map 26/341314 ¼m N of Cannich centre on A831 (Balblair) Open Mar-Oct 43 pitches (15 static) Level grass and hard standings ▣▣◿⊕⊕↵▢▣⌂⚿ mountain bike hire £9.00 (all cards) *enquiries@highlandcamping.co.uk www.highlandcamping.co.uk*

CONTIN, Highland   Map E4
Village noted for its pleasant walks inc nearby Torrachilty forest trail SEE fish lift at Torrachilty dam, spa of Strathpeffer 2m NE
✘ National Hotel 7m NE at Dingwall ✆ (01349) 862166

Riverside Caravan Park IV14 9ES ✆ (01997) 421351 *Prop: L Finnie* OS map 26/457559 In Contin on A835 (Inverness-Ullapool) at junct with Strathpeffer road Open all year 30 pitches Grass, sloping ▣✘↵▣◿⊕⊘▣ (£50/6mths) ⌂⚿ hot water, post office, fishing £10.00 *lrfinnie@hotmail.com www.riversidecontin.co.uk*

CROMARTY, Highland   Map E4
SEE church, Hugh Miller's cottage
✘ Royal, Marine Terrace ☎ (01381) 600217

Ferry Inn, Balblair IV7 8LG ☎ (01381) 610250 OS map 21/703668 7m W of Cromarty on B9163 (Conon Bridge) in Balblair Open Apr-Sept 7 pitches–booking advisable ⚲ boating, fishing

Shore Mill IV11 8XU ☎ (01381) 610216 OS map 21/750657 2½m SW of Cromarty on B9163 (Conon Bridge) near beach Open Apr-Sept 15 pitches Grass, part level ▦(20) 🚐

CULLEN, Moray   Map G4
EC Wed SEE Auld Kirk (carved panels)
✘ Seafield Arms, Seafield Street ☎ (01542) 840791

Links Caravan Park, Portsoy AB4 2SS ☎ (01261) 842695 OS map 29/592662 5½m E of Cullen off A98 (Banff) Open Apr-Sept 75 pitches 2½ acres, part level, grass ▦🌢⊕∅⚘🚐

Cullen Bay Caravan Park AB54 4TW ☎ (01542) 840766 OS map 29/516676 ¼m W of Cullen off A98 (Fochabers) Open Easter-Sept 100 pitches (60 statics) 4½ acres on cliff-top, level grass and hard standing ▦🌢⊕∅🚐

Sandend Caravan Camping Park, Portsoy AB45 2UD ☎ (01261) 842660 OS map 29/555663 3m E of Cullen off A98 (Banff) adj sandy beach Open Apr-Oct, 72 marked pitches (25 static) Level grass 🏪✘⚲⚘▦🌢⊕▦(£40) 🚐♿ £11.00-£14.00 *sandendholidays@aol.com*

CUMINESTOWN, Aberdeens   Map H4
✘ Towie 4m SW on A947 at Auchterless ☎ (01888) 511201

East Balthangie Farm AB53 5XY ☎ (01888) 544261 Fax (01888) 544921 OS map 29/841516 2m E of Cuminestown off B9027 (New Byth) Open Mar-Oct 12 pitches 7 acres level/sloping grass, sheltered ▦🌢🌢⊕∅🚐 dog walk

DAVIOT–see Inverness

DINGWALL, Highland   Map E4
EC Thurs SEE museum, Highland games (Jul)
✘ Royal, High St ☎ (01349) 862130

Black Rock Caravan Park, Evanton IV16 9UN ☎ (01349) 830917 OS map 21/606665 5m NE of Dingwall off A9 (Tain) by River Glass Open Apr-Oct 107 pitches Level grass, sheltered ▦🌢🌢⊕∅⊗⚘🚐🚐 tennis, fishing, forest walks (Mastercard/Visa/Delta/Eurocard)

DORNIE, Highland   Map C5
SEE Eilean Donan Castle
✘ Castle Inn ☎ (01599) 555205

Ardelve Caravan Site, Dornie Bridge IV40 8DY ☎ (01599) 555231 *Prop: M MacRae* OS map 33/877268 ¼m W of Dornie on A87 (Kyle of Lochalsh) near Dornie Bridge by Loch Alsh Open May-Sep–no adv booking 21 pitches Level/sloping grass and hard standing, sheltered 🌢⚘🚐 £8.00

DORNOCH, Highland   Map E3
EC Thurs SEE cathedral, Skelbo Castle ruins, sandy beaches
▯ The Square ☎ (01862) 810400
✘ Dornoch Castle, Castle St ☎ (01862) 810216

Dornoch Links Caravan and Camping Site, The Links IV25 3LX ☎ (01862) 810423 OS map 21/800895 ¼m E of Dornoch centre, entrance via River Street Open Apr-Oct 200 pitches (80 static) Grass, level, pitches in bays on sand dunes 🏪▦🌢🌢⊕∅⚘▯🚐♿ putting green (Mastercard/Visa)

Pitgrudy Farm, Poles Road IV25 3HY ☎ (01862) 810001 OS map 21/795911 1m N of Dornoch on B9168 (Golspie) Open May-Sept–no tents, no single sex groups, no motor cycles 40 pitches Grass, sloping, part sheltered 🏪▦🌢🌢⊕∅⚘🚐(no charge) 🚐

Seaview Farm Caravan Park, Hilton IV25 3PW ☎ (01862) 810294 OS map 21/807916 1½m NE of Dornoch on Embo road Open May-Sept–must book 20 pitches Level grass, sheltered 🌢⊕ hot water *No showers*

DRUMNADROCHIT, Highland   Map E5
EC Thurs SEE Urquhart Castle ruins, Corrimony Stone Circle, Cobb Memorial, Loch Ness, Loch Ness Monster Exhibition
✘ Polmaily House (dinner only) 2m W on A831 ☎ (01456) 450343

Highland Riding Centre, Borlum Farm IV3 6XN ☎ (01456) 450220 OS map 26/513293 1m S of Drumnadrochit off A82 (Fort William) Open May-Oct–no adv booking 25 pitches Hard standing, grass sloping open, gravel level, sheltered ▦🌢⊕∅🏠 riding, fishing, boat trips on Loch Ness (Mastercard/Visa)

DUNDONNELL, Highland   **Map D3**
Small resort at head of Little Loch Ryan
✘ The Broombeg Bar & Highlander Restaurant, The Dundonnell Hotel, Little Loch Broom by Garve
☎ (01854) 633204 Open 8-9/11-2.30/6-9.30pm (coffee & sandwiches all day)
Badrallach Bothy and Campsite, Croft 9, Badrallach IV23 2QP ☎ (01854) 633281 *Prop: Mick & Ali
Stott* OS map 19/065915 3m N of Dundonnell off A832 (Poolewe) by loch shore Open all year
15 pitches 2½ acres level grass 🚐🚫🚽🏠♿ B&B, games room, boat and bike hire
£10.00-£12.00 *michael.stott2@virgin.net www.badrallach.com*

CHARGES

Charges quoted are the minimum and
maximum for two people with car and caravan
or tent. They are given only as a guide and
should be checked with the owner of any site
at which you plan to stay.
Charges markded * are the prices for last
year. Otherwise, the prices are those quoted
for the current season.
Remember to ask whether hot water or use of
the pool (if any) is extra and make sure that
VAT is included.

Badrallach Bothy and Campsite, Dundonnell

DUNVEGAN, Isle of Skye   **Map B4**
✘ Harlosh 3m S on A863 ☎ (01470) 521367
Dunvegan Caravan Park IV55 8WF ☎ (01470) 521206 OS map 23/257477 ½m NE of Dunvegan
on A850 (Portree) Open Apr-Sept 33 pitches–peak booking advisable 2 acres, level grass and
hardstandings 🔲✦

DURNESS, Highland   **Map E1**
SEE Smoo Cave 1m E, Balnakeil Craft Village 1m W
ℹ️ Sango ☎ (01971) 511259
✘ Kinlochbervie 20m SW at Kinlochbervie ☎ (01971) 511275
Sango Sands Caravan Camping Park IV27 4PP ☎ (01971) 511262 *Prop: FRM Keith* OS map
9/407677 ¼m S of Durness on A838 (Lairg) overlooking Sango Bay Open Easter-mid Oct–no adv
booking 84 pitches Grass and hard standings, level, part sheltered 🐾✘🍴↩🔲🚐🚿✦ campers'
kitchen £9.50 *keith.durness@btinternet.com*

DUROR, Highland   **Map D6**
SEE Loch Linnhe W
✘ Stewart ☎ (01631) 740268
Achindarroch Farm PA38 4BS ☎ (01631) 740277 OS map 49/992550 In village on A828 (Oban-
Glencoe) Open Apr-Oct 25 pitches 3 acres level grass and hard standings 🐾🔲🚐✦

ELGIN, Moray   **Map F4**
EC Wed SEE site, cathedral (chapter house), museum, Braco's Banking House
ℹ️ 17 High St ☎ (01343) 542666
✘ Park House, South St ☎ (01343) 547695
Riverside Caravan Park, West Road IV30 8UN ☎ (01343) 542813 OS map 28/190625 ½m W of
Elgin on A96 (Forres) by River Lossie Open Apr-Oct 82 pitches Grass, level, part open, some
hard standings 🐾⚲🔲🚿🚐

ELLON, Aberdeens   **Map H5**
EC Wed MD Mon *Market town on river Ythan* SEE castle ruins, old bridge, toll house, Haddon
House 5m NW, Pitmeddan Gardens 4m SW
✘ New Inn, Market St ☎ (01358) 720425
Ythan Hotel, Newburgh AB41 6BP ☎ (01358) 789257 OS map 38/988248 6m SE of Ellon off A975
(Foveran-Cruden Bay) Open Apr-Oct 50 pitches (20 static)–no adv booking 3 acres, mainly level,
hard standings 🚿✦

EVANTON–see Dingwall

FINDHORN, Moray   Map F4
Once a port, now a beach resort SEE Culbin Sands and Forest
✖ Crown and Anchor ☎ (01309) 690243

Findhorn Bay Caravan Park IV36 3TY ☎ (01309) 690203 Fax (01309) 690933 OS map 27/048637
1m S of Findhorn off B9011 (Forres) Open Apr-Oct 150 pitches (50 static) 6 acres, level, grass
and hard standings ⚫ ✖ (café) ⊿⚫⚫⚫⚫⚫⚫⚫⚫

Findhorn Sands Caravan Park IV36 3YZ ☎ (01309) 690324 Fax (01309) 690325 OS map
27/040645 ¼m N of Findhorn off B9011 Open Apr-Oct–no adv booking 200 pitches (150 static)
Level grass ⚫⚫⚫⚫

FOCHABERS, Moray   Map G4
EC Wed SEE parish church, Tugnet Ice House (fisheries museum), folk museum
✖ Mill 4m NE on A98 at Tynet ☎ (01542) 850233

Burnside Caravan Site IV32 7PF ☎ (01343) 820511/820362 Fax (01343) 821291 OS map
28/350580 ½m S of Fochabers on right of A96 (Aberdeen) Open Apr-Oct 110 pitches (50 static)
Grass, level, sheltered ⚫⚫⚫⚫⚫ (heated) ⚫⚫⚫⚫⚫ £10.00-£14.00* (most cards)

Spey Bay Caravan Park, Spey Bay IV32 7PJ ☎ (01343) 820424 OS map 28/356650 4m N of
Fochabers on right of B9104 (Spey Bay) Open Apr-Sept 35 pitches–no adv booking Level grass
✖⚫⚫⚫⚫⚫⚫⚫⚫⚫⚫ meals, golf, putting, driving range, tennis

FORRES, Moray   Map F4
EC Wed SEE Falconer museum, Witches' Stone, Sueno's Stone NE, Nelson Tower (view)
🅸 Falconer Museum ☎ (01309) 672938
✖ Park, Victoria Rd ☎ (01309) 672328

Riverview Leisure, Mundole Court IV36 0SZ ☎ (01309) 673932 OS map 27/015600 1m W of
Forres off A96 (Nairn) Open Apr-Nov 72 pitches (12 static) 50 acres level grass, sheltered
⚫✖⚫⚫⚫⚫⚫⚫⚫

FORT AUGUSTUS, Highland   Map E5
EC Wed *See abbey, Gen Wade's road over Corrieyarrick Pass, Inchnacardoch Forest, Loch Ness,
Caledonian Canal*
🅸 Car Park ☎ (01320) 366367
✖ Neuk Restaurant, Canalside ☎ (01320) 366208

Fort Augustus Camping, Market Hill PH32 4DS ☎ (01320) 366618 *Prop: B Clark* OS map
34/373084 ½m S of Fort Augustus centre on right of A82 (Fort William) adj golf course Open mid
April-Sept 50 pitches 4 acres grass, part sheltered ⚫⚫⚫⚫⚫⚫⚫ camp kitchen £10.00*
info@campinglochness.co.uk www.campinglochness.co.uk

FORT WILLIAM, Highland   Map D6
EC Wed (winter) SEE Ben Nevis (4,418ft), West Highland Museum
🅸 Cameron Centre, Cameron Sq ☎ (01397) 703781
✖ Glen Nevis Restaurant, Glen Nevis ☎ (01397) 705459 Open summer 12-9.30, winter 5-9.30

Glen Nevis Caravan and Camping Park, Glen Nevis PH33 6SX ☎ (01397) 702191 OS map
41/125723 2½m N of Fort William off A82 (Inverness) on right of Glen Nevis road Open Mar 31-
Oct 31 380 pitches Grass and hard standings, part level, part open ⚫✖⚫⚫(season)
⊿⚫⚫⚫⚫⚫⚫⚫⚫ £7.40-£9.80 *holidays@glen-nevis.co.uk www.glen-nevis.co.uk*

Linnhe Lochside Holidays, Corpach PH33 7NL ☎ (01397) 772376 Fax (01397) 772007 OS map
41/073771 5m NW of Fort William on left of A830 (Mallaig) Open Easter-Oct 31 190 pitches
(100 static) Hard standings, terraced ⚫⊿⚫⚫⚫⚫⚫⚫⚫⚫⚫⚫ slipway, sailing, free fishing,
barbecue area, private beach, toddler's play room £10.50-£16.50* (all cards exc Amex)
holidays@linnhe.demon.co.uk

Lochy Caravan Park, Camaghael PH33 7NF ☎ (01397) 703446 OS map 41/125764 2m N of Fort
William off A830 (Mallaig) on Camaghael road Open all year–no adv booking 150 pitches
⚫✖⚫⚫⚫⚫

FRASERBURGH, Aberdeens   Map H4
EC Wed SEE Wine Tower (16c), lighthouse
🅸 Saltoun Sq ☎ (01346) 518315
✖ Alexander, High St ☎ (01346) 328249

Esplanade Municipal Caravan Site, Harbour Road AB4 1US ☎ (01346) 510041 OS map
30/001663 ¼m S of Fraserburgh off A92 (Aberdeen) adj beach Open Apr-Sept 50 pitches
⚫⚫⚫⚫⚫⚫⚫

Kessock Road Camping AB4 4AE ☎ (01346) 510042 OS map 30/999661 ¼m S of Fraserburgh
off A92 (Aberdeen) Open Apr-Sept 120 pitches (50 static) ⚫⚫⚫⚫⚫⚫

Rosehearty Caravan Camping Park, Shore Street, Rosehearty AB4 4JQ ☎ (01346) 861314 OS
map 30/934676 5m W of Fraserburgh off A98 (Banff) on Rosehearty road Open Apr-Oct 40
pitches 1½ acres level on seafront ⚫⚫⚫⚫⚫⚫⚫⚫

✗ RESTAURANTS

The restaurants recommended in this guide are of three kinds – pubs, independent restaurants and those forming part of hotels and motels. They all serve lunch and dinner – at a reasonable price – say under £10 a head. We shall be glad to have your comments on any you use this season and if you think they are not up to standard, please let us have your suggestions for alternatives.

Glencoe Camping and Caravanning Club Site, Glencoe

GAIRLOCH, Highland   **Map C4**
EC Wed *Fishing village, vacation resort and excellent touring centre for Wester Ross* SEE Heritage museum, Loch Maree, Red Point (view), Victoria Falls, Inverewe gardens 5m NE
🅘 Achtercairn ✆ (01445) 712130
✗ Mustn't Grumble Cafe Bar, Melvaig ✆ (01445) 771212

Auchtercairn Farm Caravan Rest IV21 2BN ✆ (01445) 712248 OS map 19/804770 ¼m N of Gairloch at junction of A832 (Poolewe) and B8021 (Melvaig) Open May-Sept 60 pitches 🅿 ✗ *No showers*

Gairloch Caravan Camping Park, Strath IV21 2BX ✆ (01445) 712373 OS map 19/798774 ½m NW of Gairloch off B8021 (Melvaig) at rear of Millcroft Hotel Open Easter-Oct 80 pitches 6 acres, level grass 🅿🗑🚻♿∅🚿🚮🏪🏠 fishing and boating near £8.00-£11.00* (Mastercard/Visa) *info@gairlochcaravanpark.com www.gairlochcaravanpark.com*

Sands Holiday Centre IV21 2DL ✆ (01445) 712152 OS map 19/760785 3m NW of Gairloch on left of B8021 (Melvaig) Open Apr-Sept 250 pitches 50 acres level/sloping grass 🅿⛱🗑🚻♿
∅🚿🏪🏠♿ fishing, sandy beach adj £10.00-£15.50 (Mastercard/Visa/Amex)
litsands@aol.com www.sandsholidaycentre.co.uk

GLENCOE, Highland   **Map D7**
Scene of one of grimmest episodes in clan history when Campbells in league with authorities massacred MacDonalds. The glen – traversed by A82 – is best approached from S to get full impact of 3 Sisters peaks. SEE MacDonald memorial, Signal Rock
✗ Clachaig Inn behind NT centre ✆ (01855) 811252

Glencoe Camping and Caravanning Club Site, Ballachulish PA49 4LA ✆ (01855) 811397/811278 *Prop: The Camping and Caravanning Club* OS map 41/112576 1m E of Glencoe on left of A82 (Tyndrum) Open Apr-Oct 120 pitches Grass, part level, open 🅿🗑🚻♿∅♿ fishing, forest trails £14.70-£19.20 (Mastercard/Visa/Switch/Delta) *www.campingandcaravanningclub.co.uk*

Invercoe Caravan Park PA49 4HP ✆ (01855) 811210 Fax (01855) 811210 OS map 41/099591 ½m N of Glencoe on B863 (Kinlochleven) near Glencoe crossroads by Loch Leven Open all year 60 pitches Grass and hard standings, level, open 🅿🗑🚻♿🚻♿∅🚮🏪♿ fishing £14.00-£16.00* (Mastercard/Visa) *invercoe@sdl.co.uk www.invercoe.co.uk*

Red Squirrel Camping Site PA49 4HX ✆ (01855) 811256 OS map 41/120574 1½m SE of Glencoe off A82 (Glasgow) Open all year 200 pitches Grass and hard standings, level, part sheltered ♿∅🅿🏠 camp fires, swimming, fishing

---

GRANTOWN ON SPEY, Highland   **Map F5**
EC Thurs *Most elegant of Spey Valley resorts, founded 1776. Well placed for tours to E coast as well as to the Great Glen and Inverness. The malt whisky trail passes near.*
🅘 54 High St ✆ (01479) 872773
✗ Rosehall, The Square ✆ (01479) 872721

Grantown on Spey Caravan Park, Seafield Avenue PH26 3JQ ✆ (01479) 872474 Fax (01479) 873696 OS map 36/028283 ½m N of Grantown in Seafield Avenue Open Apr-Oct 154 pitches (50 static) Grass and hard standings, level/sloping, sheltered 🅿🗑🚻♿∅🚻♿∅🚮(15)🏪♿ sep pitches £10.00-£16.00* (most cards) *team@caravanscotland.com www.caravanscotland.com*

HALLADALE–see Melvich

HOPEMAN–see Burghead

HUNTLY, Aberdeens   **Map G4**
Holiday resort and market town centred on two main streets and an attractive square. SEE palatial castle ruins, museum, Leith Hall 8m S
🛈 The Square ✆ (01466) 792255.
✗ Castle ✆ (01466) 792696

Huntly Castle Caravan Park AB54 4UJ *Centrally located and well equipped park ideal for touring castle and whisky trails* ✆ (01466) 794999 OS map 29/525405 ½m NW of Huntly near A96 (Keith) Open Mar 23-Oct 28 146 pitches 15 acres level grass and hard standings 🖵🛒🔌⊕∅↩️ 🚌⛟ fully serviced pitches, indoor sports hall (Mastercard/Visa)

INVERBERVIE, Aberdeens   **Map H6**
✗ St Leonards 10m NE at Stonehaven ✆ (01569) 762044

Burgh Haugh Caravan Site DD10 0SP ✆ (01561) 361182 OS map 45/830720 ½m S of Inverbervie off coast road Open Apr 5-Oct 31 75 pitches Grass, level, sheltered 🖵🛒🔌⊕∅↩️ putting green, tennis

Lauriston Camping and Caravan Site, St Cyrus DD10 0DJ ✆ (01674) 850316 OS map 45/736646 7m SW of Inverbervie off A92 (Montrose) Open Apr-Sept 80 pitches (60 static) 7 acres level grass, sheltered 🛒↗🖵🛒∅◯⊕↩️🚽

Waird's Park, Johnshaven DD10 0HD ✆ (01561) 362616/362280/362395 OS map 45/800672 5m SW of Inverbervie off A92 (Montrose) Open Apr-mid Oct 70 pitches (50 static) Level grass and hard standings 🛒🖵🛒⊕∅↩️🛒⛟ first aid, putting, bowling, tennis

INVERGARRY, Highland   **Map D5**
Village where Road to Isles begins and ends at Kyle of Lochalsh SEE Well of Seven Heads monument, Loch Garry, Caledonian Canal
✗ Glengarry Castle ✆ (01809) 501254

Faichem Park, Ardgarry Farm, Faichem PH35 4HG ✆ (01809) 501226 Fax (01809) 501307 OS map 34/287015 1m W of Invergarry off A87 (Kyle of Lochalsh) on Faichem road Open Mar-Oct 30 pitches Grass and hard standings, level and sloping, part open 🛒∅⊕∅🚌🏠 forest trails

Faichemard Farm PH35 4HG ✆ (01809) 501314 OS map 34/287018 2m W of Invergarry off A87 (Kyle of Lochalsh) on Faichem road–signposted Open Apr-Oct 40 pitches 10 acres level grass and hard standings, sheltered 🖵🛒⊕∅🏠 Sep pitches with picnic table, hill walking, fishing £5.00-£6.50* *dgrant@fsbdial.co.uk www.visitscotland.com*

INVERMORISTON, Highland   **Map E5**
EC Thurs SEE hydro-electric works, Glen Moriston, Loch Ness
✗ Glenmoriston Arms ✆ (01320) 351206

Loch Ness Caravan and Camping Park, Easter Port Clair IV3 6YE ✆ (01320) 351207 *Prop: Bob, Liz & Robbie Girvan* OS map 34/425151 1½m SSW of Invermoriston on A82 (Fort Augustus) beside Loch Ness Open Mar 15-Oct 15–adv booking min 3 nights 75 pitches Hard standings and grass ♀↩️🖵🛒∅⊕∅◯⊕↩️🚽🚌 slipway, fishing £14.00-£16.00
bob@girvan7904.freeserve.co.uk www.lochnesscaravanandcampingpark.co.uk

INVERNESS, Highland   **Map E4**
EC Wed MD Mon, Tues SEE cathedral, castle, museum, Northern Meeting Piping Competition (Sept) Tonnahurich Cemetery (view), Culloden battlefield (visitor centre) 6m E, chapel and regimental museum of Queen's Own Highlanders at Fort Grange 12m NE
🛈 Castle Wynd ✆ (01463) 234353
✗ Brookes, Castle St ✆ (01463) 225662

Auchnahillin Caravan Camping Park, Daviot East IV2 5XQ ✆ (01463) 772286 *Prop: Donald & Anita Gibson* OS map 27/740386 8m SE of Inverness off A9 (Aviemore) on B9154 (Moy) Open Mar-Oct 100 pitches Grass, level 🛒🖵🛒∅⊕∅◯⊕↩️🚌(25) 🚽 £8.00-£14.00 (Mastercard/Visa/Amex/Maestro) *info@auchnahillin.co.uk www.auchnahillin.co.uk*

Balachladaich Farm, Dores IV1 2XP ✆ (01463) 751204 OS map 26/583329 9m SW of Inverness on B862 (Dores) at northern end of Loch Ness Open Apr-Oct 45 pitches *No showers,* boat hire, fishing

Bunchrew Caravan Park IV3 6TD ✆ (01463) 237802 OS map 26/615600 3m W of Inverness on A862 (Beauly) Open Mar 15-Oct 15 125 pitches Grass, level, sheltered
🛒↗🖵🛒∅⊕∅◯⊕↩️🚽

Coulmore Bay Caravan Park, North Kessock IV1 1XB ✆ (01463) 731313 OS map 26/619482 3m N of Inverness off A9 (Cononbridge) by sea Open May-Sept 112 pitches 🛒✗♀🛒∅∅ boating, canoeing, sailing

Torvean Caravan Park, Glenurquhart Road IV3 6JL ✆ (01463) 220582/233051 OS map 26/655483 1m SW of Inverness on A82 (Drumnadrochit) Open Apr-Oct–must book Jul-Aug–no tents, no single sex gro 50 pitches 2 acres hard standings 🛒🖵🛒∅∅↩️🚽

The distance and direction of a campsite is given from the centre of the town under which it appears.

JOHN O'GROATS, Highland   Map G1
SEE Duncansby Head cliffs and lighthouse, Canishay church (tomb of Jan de Groot), Orkneys (by day trip), Castle of Mey 6m W
🄸 County Rd ✆ (01955) 611373
✘ Seaview Hotel ✆ (01955) 611220 Open 12-2.30/5.30-8.30
John O'Groats Caravan Park KW1 4YR ✆ (01955) 611329 *Prop: W & CJ Steven* OS map 12/382735 At northernmost point of A99 beside Last House in Scotland on seafront Open Apr-Sep 90 pitches Level grass and hard standings 🅱 ✘ 🄸 🄳 🄳 ⊕ ∅ ⅙ petrol, day trips to Orkney £9.00-£10.00 *info@johnogroatscampsite.co.uk www.johnogroatscampsite.co.uk*
Stroma View, Huna KW1 4YL ✆ (01955) 611313 OS map 7/362731 2m W of John O'Groats on A836 (Thurso) Open Mar-Oct 30 pitches Grass and hard standings, level, sheltered 🄳 🄳 🄳 ⊕ ↩ ⊡ farm produce

JOHNSHAVEN–see Inverbervie

KEITH, Mcray   Map G4
EC Wed SEE Strathisla distillery, 17c bridge
✘ Royal, Church Rd ✆ (01542) 882528
Keith Caravan Site, Dunnyduff Road AB5 3JG ✆ (01542) 882078 OS map 28/434498 ¼m S of Keith on A96 (Huntly) Open Apr-Sept 50 pitches Grass, level, open 🅱 ✘ 🄸 🄳 ⊡ fishing

KINGUSSIE, Highland   Map E5
EC Wed SEE Highland Folk Museum, china studios, Highland Wildlife Park 3m NE
🄸 King St ✆ (01540) 661297
✘ Wood`n'Spoon, High St ✆ (01540) 661251
Kingussie Golf Club, Gynack Road PH21 1LR ✆ (01540) 661374 OS map 35/755015 ½m N of Kingussie centre off A9 (Aviemore) Open Apr-Sept–no tents 60 pitches Grass, level, open

KINLOCHBERVIE, Highland   Map D2
✘ Kinlochbervie ✆ (01971) 521281
Oldshoremore Caravan Site, Oldshoremore IV27 4RS OS map 9/211586 2m NW of Kinlochbervie on Oldshore road Open Apr-Sept–no adv bkg 15 pitches Part grass, part level, hard standings, sheltered 🄳 🄳 ⊡ 🏠

KINLOCHLEVEN, Highland   Map D6
EC Wed
✘ Tail Race ✆ (01855) 831777
Caolasnacon Farm PA40 4RS ✆ (01855) 831279 OS map 41/139607 3m SW of Kinlochleven on B863 (Glencoe) Open Apr-Oct 70 pitches Grass, level 🄳 🄳 🄳 ⊕ ∅ ⊡ boat and fishing tackle hire

KINTORE, Aberdeens   Map H5
SEE Roman camp
✘ Kintore Arms, The Square (adj A96) ✆ (01467) 632216
Hillhead Caravan Park AB51 0YX ✆ (01467) 632809 OS map 38/777163 ½m SW of Kintore off A96 (Aberdeen) and B994 (Kemnay) Open Jan-Dec 29 pitches 1½ acres level grass and hard standing, sheltered 🅱 ✘ 🄸 🄳 🄳 ⊕ ∅ ⊕ ↩ ⊡ ⅙ fishing £8.25-£13.05 (Mastercard/Visa) *enquiries@hillheadcaravan.co.uk www.hillheadcaravan.co.uk*

Situated just one mile West off the A96 Aberdeen - Inverness trunk road at Kintore, the park is just 13 miles from Aberdeen, in the centre of 'castle country' and on Scotland's Castle Trail in the Gordon District.

Hillhead Caravan Park

KYLE OF LOCHALSH, Highland   **Map C5**
EC Thurs SEE harbour, Balmacara House 3m E, Eilean Donan Castle 9m E
🅿Car Park ✆(01599) 534276
✗Kyle, Main St ✆(01599) 814204
Reraig Caravan Site, Balmacara IV40 8DH ✆(01599) 566215 OS map 33/816272 3m E of Kyle of
Lochalsh on A87 (Dornie) at rear of Balmacara Hotel Open May-Sept–no adv booking by
phone–no awnings or large 45 pitches Grass, part level, part open, some hard standings 🔌⊕
£9.80* (Mastercard/Visa) warden@reraig.com www.reraig.com

LAIDE, Highland   **Map C3**
SEE Inverewe Gardens 8m S
✗Old Smiddy Guest House ✆(01445) 731696 Open Mar-Oct tearoom 1-5, dinner 8pm
Gruinard Bay Caravan and Camping Park IV22 2ND ✆(01445) 731225 OS map 19/903919 ¼m
E of Laide on A832 (Dingwall) Open Apr-Oct 55 pitches 3½ acres, level grass 🔋🛢🔌⌀⊕🚻
£10.00 (Mastercard/Visa/Maestro) gruinard@ecosse.net www.highlandbreaks.com

LAIRG, Highland   **Map E3**
EC Wed SEE Falls of Shin, prehistoric hut circles
🅿Sutherland ✆(01549) 402160
✗Sutherland Arms, Main Rd ✆(01549) 402291
Dunroamin Caravan Camping Park, Main Street IV27 4AR ✆(01549) 402447 Prop: Mr & Mrs L
Hudson OS map 16/583066 At E edge of Lairg centre on A839 (Dornoch) at rear of Crofters
Restaurant Open Apr-Oct 50 pitches Grass and hard standing, level, part sheltered
✗⌐🛢🔌⌀⊕⌀🚻🚻 £6.50-£11.00 (Mastercard/Visa) enquiries@lairgcaravanpark.co.uk
www.lairgcaravanpark.co.uk
Woodend Caravan Site, Achnairn IV27 4DN ✆(01549) 402248 Fax (01549) 402248 OS map
16/558127 4m NW of Lairg off A836 (Altnaharra) and A838 (Durness) Open Apr-Sept 55 pitches
Grass, part sloping, open 🔋🛢🔌⌀⊕⌀⌣🚻 campers' kitchen £8.00 (min)*

LAURENCEKIRK, Aberdeens   **Map H6**
✗Panmure Arms Hotel, 52 High St, Edzell ✆(01356) 648950
Brownmuir Caravan Park, Fordoun AB30 1SJ ✆(01561) 320786 Fax (01561) 320786 Prop: M
Bowers OS map 45/740772 4m N of Laurencekirk off A90 (Stonehaven) and Fordoun road
Open Apr-Oct 60 pitches (51 static) Level grass, sheltered 🛢🔌⌀⊕⌀⌣🚻🚻⌖🅰 £7.00-
£10.50 brownmuircaravanpark@talk21.com www.brownmuircaravanpark.co.uk
Dovecot Caravan Park, Northwaterbridge AB30 1QL ✆(01674) 840630 OS map 45/646666 6m
SW of Laurencekirk off A90 (Forfar) on Edzell Woods road Open Apr-Oct 75 pitches (45 static)
Level grass, sheltered 🔋🛢🔌⌀⊕⌀🟢⌣🚻🚻⌖ £9.50-£10.50 info@dovecotcaravanpark.com
www.dovecotcaravanpark.com

TONY & ANN DAVIS
Gruinard Bay Caravan Park
Laide, Wester Ross, IV22 2ND
Tel/Fax: +44 (0)1445 731225

SHOWERS

Except where marked, all sites in this guide have flush lavatories and showers. Symbols for these amenities have therefore been omitted from site entries.

LOSSIEMOUTH, Moray   **Map F4**
EC Thurs
✗ Stotfield, Stotfield Road ✆ (01343) 812011

Silver Sands Leisure Park IV31 6SP ✆ (01343) 813262 Fax (01343) 815205 OS map 28/205712
2m W of Lossiemouth on right of B9040 (Burghead) Open Easter-Oct 350 pitches (200 static)
Level grass and hard standings 🛒♀⇌↗🔲🔌⊕∅⊕↩☂ amusements, cycle hire
(Mastercard/Visa/Delta/Switch) holidays@silversands.freeserve.co.uk www.travel.to/silversands

LOTH–see Brora

MACDUFF, Aberdeens   **Map H4**
EC Wed SEE open air pool at Tarlair, Gardenstown harbour 5m E
✗ Fife Arms, Shore Street ✆ (01261) 832408

Myrus Holiday Park AB4 3QP ✆ (01261) 812845 Prop: AJ Ritchie OS map 29/710633 1m SE of
Macduff on A947 (Turriff) near junction with B9026 Open Apr-mid Oct 60 pitches Level grass,
sheltered 🛒🔲🔌⊕🔌☂よ♖ adj golf driving range & coffee shop £13.00-£16.00
myrusholidaypark@btinternet.com

Wester Bonnyton Farm Camping and Caravan Park AB45 3EP ✆ (01261) 832470 Fax (01261)
832470 OS map 29/740636 2m E of Macduff on right of B9031 (Fraserburgh) Open Easter-Oct
45 pitches Level/sloping grass and hard standing 🛒🔲🔌∅⊕∅⊕↩🖵☂☂🏠よ
taylor@westerbonnyton.freeserve.co.uk

MELVICH, Highland   **Map F2**
Resort noted for its views across Halladale estuary to Orkneys
✗ Melvich ✆ (01641) 561032

Halladale Inn Caravan Par, k KW14 7YJ ✆ (01641) 531282 OS map 10/391640 In Melvich near
Halladale estuary Open Apr-Oct 14 pitches Level grass and hard standings 🛒✗♀🔲🔌∅⊕
∅⊕🖵🏠 (Mastercard/Visa/Delta)

MINTLAW–see Peterhead

NAIRN, Highland   **Map E5**
EC Wed SEE Cawdor Castle 5m SW, Fort George 10m W, Highland games (Aug)
⬛ King St ✆ (01667) 452753
✗ Windsor, Albert St ✆ (01667) 453108

Delnies Wood Camping Club IV12 5NX ✆ (01667) 455281 OS map 27/841555 3m W of Nairn on
A96 (Inverness) Open Easter-Oct 90 pitches Grass and hard core, level, sheltered
🛒🔲🔌∅⊕∅⊕↩ (Mastercard/Visa)

Loch Loy Holiday Park, East Beach IV12 4PH ✆ (01667) 453764 OS map 27/893572 ¼m NE of
Nairn on A96 (Forres) in Harbour Street near beach Open Mar-Nov 390 pitches (290 static)
Grass, level, open 🛒✗♀⇌↗🔲🔌∅⊕∅🖂⊕↩🖵☂(25) ⊛🖵🏠よ

Spindrift Caravan and Camping Park, Little Kildrummie IV12 5QU ✆ (01667) 453992 OS map
27/873537 2m SW of Nairn off B9090 (Cawdor) on Little Kildrummie road Open Apr-Oct
40 pitches 3 acres level/terraced grass 🔲🔌∅⊕∅ fishing permits

NEWTONMORE, Highland   **Map E5**
EC Wed
✗ Weigh Inn, Main Street ✆ (01540) 673203

Invernahavon Caravan Site, Glentruim PH20 1BE ✆ (01540) 673534 Fax (01540) 673219 OS
map 35/688950 3m S of Newtonmore off A9 (Perth) on Glentruim road Open Easter-Oct 100
pitches 12½ acres level grass 🛒🔲🔌∅⊕∅⊕↩🖵🏠よ

KEY TO SYMBOLS

🛒	shop	⌀	gas supplies	🔌	winter storage for caravans
✗	restaurant	⊕	chemical disposal point	🅟	parking obligatory
♀	bar	∅	payphone	⊛	no dogs
⇌	takeaway food	🖂	swimming pool	🖵	caravan hire
↗	off licence	⊕	games area	🏠	bungalow hire
🔲	laundrette	↩	children's playground	よ	facilities for disabled
🔌	mains electric hook-ups	🖵	TV	♖	shaded

PETERHEAD, Aberdeens　　　　　　　　　　　　　　　　　　　　　　　**Map H4**
EC Wed SEE 12c church, museum, harbour, Ravenscraig Castle, Collieston visitor centre (nature reserves) 10m SW
✘ Waterside Inn 2m NW on A952 ✆(01779) 471121

Aden Country Park, Aden Estate, Mintlaw AB42 5FQ ✆(01771) 623460/622857 OS map 30/985483 9m W of Peterhead on A950 (Banff) at Mintlaw station Open Apr-Oct 60 pitches Grass, level, sheltered/woodland setting 🔥🗗🔌⊗∅⊕⤴🖫占 dog exercise area

POOLEWE–see Gairloch

PORTREE, Isle of Skye　　　　　　　　　　　　　　　　　　　　　　　**Map B4**
EC Wed
🏱 Bayfield House ✆(01478) 612137
✘ King's Haven, Bosville Terr ✆(01478) 582290

Loch Greshornish Caravan Camping Park, Arnisort by Edinbane IV51 9PS ✆(01478) 582230 OS map 23/349531 10m NW of Portree on right of A850 (Dunvegan) Open Apr-Oct 130 pitches Grass and hard standings, part sloping, open 🔥⚲🗗🔌⊗∅ bike and canoe hire £8.00-£10.50* info@skycamp.com www.skycamp.com

Torvaig Caravan and Camping Site IV51 8BT ✆(01478) 611849 Prop: J Maclean OS map 23/481452 1m N of Portree on A855 (Staffin) Open Apr-Oct 90 pitches Level/sloping grass and hard standings, sheltered 🗗🔌⊗∅ £7.00-£8.00

ROSEHEARTY–see Fraserburgh

ROY BRIDGE, Highland　　　　　　　　　　　　　　　　　　　　　　　**Map D6**
SEE Glen Roy N, commando memorial 1m NW
✘ Spean Bridge 3m W at Spean Bridge ✆(01397) 712250

Bunroy Caravan Park PH31 4AG 4-star STB ✆(01397) 712332 Prop: Andy & Gail Markham OS map 34/274807 ¼m S of Roy Bridge off A86 (Newtonmore) beside River Spean Open Mar-Sept–adv booking accepted 25 pitches Grass, level and hard standing, sheltered 🗗∅⚬⊗🔥🏠 4 star STB £8.00-£13.00 (Mastercard/Visa/Debit) info@bunroycamping.co.uk www.bunroycamping.co.uk

Glenspean Holiday Park PH31 4AW ✆(01397) 712432 OS map 41/274807 In centre of village by Roy Bridge hotel Open all year 70 pitches 9½ acres part level, grass and hard standings 🔥∅

Inverroy Camping Caravan Site PH31 4AQ ✆(01397) 712275 OS map 34/257813 ½m W of Roy Bridge on A86 (Spean Bridge) Open all year 35 pitches Level grass and hard standing, sheltered 🗗🔥⊗🔥⤢

Kinchellie Croft Motel PH31 4AW ✆(01397) 712265 OS map 34/290806 ¼m E of Roy Bridge on A86 (Aviemore) Open Apr-Sept–no advance booking 20 pitches

SALEN　　　　　　　　　　　　　　　　　　　　　　　**Map C6**
EC Wed
✘ Kilcamb Lodge 4m E at Strontian ✆(01967) 402257

Resipole Farm Campsite, Loch Sunart, Acharacle PH36 4HX ✆(01967) 431235 Fax (01967) 431777 OS map 40/723640 2m E of Salen on left of A861 (Ardgour) Open Apr-Oct 60 pitches Grass and hard standings, level, part open ✘🍴🗗🔥∅⊗∅⤢🏠占 fishing, 9-hole golf, slipway £9.00-£10.50* (Mastercard/Visa/Switch/Delta) info@resipole.co.uk www.resipole.co.uk

SCOURIE, Highland　　　　　　　　　　　　　　　　　　　　　　　**Map D2**
SEE Handa Island bird sanctuary (boat trips)
✘ Anchorage ✆(01971) 502060

Scourie Caravan and Camping Park, Harbour Road IV27 4TG ✆(01971) 502060 OS map 9/155447 ½m S of Scourie at junction of A894 (Laxford Bridge) and Harbour Road Open Apr-Sept –no adv bkg except by phone prior to arrival 90 pitches Grass and hard standing, level, open 占

SHIEL BRIDGE, Highland　　　　　　　　　　　　　　　　　　　　　　　**Map D5**
✘ Kintail Lodge ✆(01599) 511275

Shiel Bridge Caravan Camping Park, Glenshiel IV40 8HW ✆(01599) 511221 OS map 33/940185 ¼m S of Shiel Bridge on A87 (Invergarry) Open May-Sept 75 pitches Level grass and hard standings 🔥✘🔥∅ (Mastercard/Visa)

Morvich Farm, Inverinate IV40 8HQ ✆(01599) 511354 OS map 33/964210 3m N of Shiel Bridge off A87 (Kyle of Lochalsh) beside River Croe Open March 26-Oct 25 75 pitches 🗗🔥∅⊗⤢ Fishing £15.50-£20.60* (Delta/Mastercard/Switch/Visa) www.caravanclub.co.uk

ISLE OF SKYE–see Broadford, Dunvegan, Portree, Staffin and Uig

---

For more up-to-date information, and for links to camping websites, visit our site at:
www.butford.co.uk/camping

SPEAN BRIDGE, Highland　　　　　　　　　　　　　　　　　　**Map D6**
EC Thurs
🄸 Woolen Mill Car Park　☎ (01397) 712576
✘ Spean Bridge　☎ (01397) 712250

Gairlochy Holiday Park PH34 4EQ　☎ (01397) 712711 Fax (01397) 712712　OS map 34/188835
　1m NW of Spean Bridge off A82 (Inverness) on B8004 (Gairlochy)　Open Apr-Oct　20 pitches
　Grass and hard standings, level, sheltered　🗆⊕𝟎⤳▱🖲(50)　🚽(6)　🏠

Stronaba Farm, Stronaba PH34 4DX　☎ (01397) 712259　*Prop: I MacDonald*　OS map 34/208845
　2½m N of Spean Bridge on A82 (Fort Augustus)　Open Apr-Sept　25 pitches　Grass, part sloping,
　sheltered, some hard standings　🖲⊕▱　golf & activity centre nearby　£7.00

STAFFIN, Isle of Skye　　　　　　　　　　　　　　　　　　**Map B4**
✘ King's Haven 17m S at Portree　☎ (01478) 612290

Staffin Caravan and Camping Park, Staffin IV51 9JX　☎ (01470) 562213　OS map 23/493672　1m
　S of Staffin on A855 (Portree)　Open Apr-mid Oct　50 pitches　Grass, level, sheltered, hard
　standings　🖲𝟎⊕𝟎▱🏠♿　£8.50　*staffin@namacleod.freeserve.co.uk*
　www.staffincampsite.co.uk

STONEHAVEN, Aberdeens　　　　　　　　　　　　　　　　　　**Map H6**
EC Wed　SEE 16c tolbooth, old town, Muchalls castle 5m N, Dunnottar castle 1m S, Catterline
fishing village 7m S
🄸 Allardice Sq　☎ (01569) 762806
✘ St Leonards, Bath St　☎ (01569) 762044

Queen Elizabeth Caravan Park, Queen Elizabeth Park AB3 2GF　☎ (01569) 764041　OS map
　45/875860　¼m N of Stonehaven on A92 (Aberdeen)　Open Apr-Oct　110 pitches (76 static)
　Hard standings, sheltered

STORNOWAY, Isle of Lewis, Western Isles　　　　　　　　　　**Map B2**
EC Wed
🄸 26 Cromwell St　☎ (01851) 703088
✘ Royal, Cromwell St　☎ (01851) 702109

Broad Bay Caravan Site, Coll Beach PA86 0HT　☎ (01851) 702053　OS map 8/464385　5m N of
　Stornoway on B895 (North Tolsta)　Open Apr-Oct　20 pitches　Grass (sand dune area)　⛟𝟎🖲(30)
　🚽 beach

STRATHPEFFER–see Dingwall

STRONTIAN, Highland　　　　　　　　　　　　　　　　　　**Map C6**
EC Wed　*Ferry to Fort William via Corran*
🄸 Argyll　☎ (01967) 402131
✘ Kilcamb Lodge　☎ (01967) 402257

Glenview Caravan Camping Park PH36 4JD　☎ (01967) 402123　OS map 40/816613　¼m E of
　Strontian off A861 (Corran)　Open Mar-Jan　41 pitches　Grass and hard standings, sheltered
　⛟⤳🗆🖲𝟎⊕🚽　pets corner

TAIN, Highland　　　　　　　　　　　　　　　　　　　　　**Map E3**
EC Thurs　SEE museum, distillery (Glen Morangie)
✘ Mansfield, Scotsburn Rd　☎ (01862) 892052

Meikle Ferry Caravan Park, Meikle Ferry IV19 1JX　☎ (01862) 892292　OS map 21/762842　2m NW
　of Tain off A9 (Bonar Bridge) by new Dornoch Firth bridge　Open all year　40 pitches　Grass, level,
　hard standings, part open　✘🍴🗆🖲𝟎⊕🕑⤳🖲🚽

TARBERT, Isle of Harris, Western Isles   **Map B3**
SEE quayside
🛈 Pier Rd ☎(01859) 502011
✖ Harris ☎(01859) 502154

Minch View Caravan Site, 10 Drinishadder HS3 3DX ☎(01859) 511207 OS map 14/177940 4½m
SE of Tarbert off A859 (Leverburgh) Open all year 26 pitches Level grass and hard standing,
sheltered 🚻🚮⊕∅🚐 free fishing

THURSO, Highland   **Map F2**
EC Thurs SEE ruined bishops palace (13c), St Peter's church, botanic collection of Robert Dick,
Dunnet Bay and Dunnet Head 8m E
🛈 Car Park, Riverside ☎(01847) 892371
✖ Pentland, Princes St ☎(01847) 893202

Dunvegan Euro Camping and Caravan Site, Reay KW14 7RQ ☎(01847) 811405 OS map
11/960647 11m W of Thurso on A836 (Tongue) Open Apr-Oct 15 pitches Grass, part level,
sheltered 🛒⚲🚮∅⤴

Scrabster Road Caravan and Camping Site KW14 7JY ☎(01847) 805503 OS map 11/12/112686
¼m W of Thurso off A882 (Scrabster) Open May-Sept 114 pitches Level/sloping grass and hard
standings ✖⤵🚻🚮⊕∅⊕⤴◻🚐♿ Grass, level, open

TONGUE, Highland   **Map E2**
SEE causeway across Kyle of Tongue (view), Ben Loyal (2,250ft), Loch Loyal 8m S
✖ Tongue ☎(01847) 611206

Bayview Caravan Site, 215 Talmine by Lairg IV27 4YS ☎(01847) 601225 OS map 10/586627 4m
N of Tongue off A838 (Durness) on Melness road Open Apr-Oct 15 pitches Hard standings,
sheltered

Kincraig Caravan and Camp Park IV27 4XF ☎(01847) 611218 OS map 10/593569 ¼m S of
Tongue centre off A836 (Lairg) Open Apr 1-Oct 8–no adv bkg 15 pitches 🚮⊛

TURRIFF–see Cuminestown

UIG, Isle of Skye   **Map B4**
SEE Skye Croft Museum, Hebrides (by organised boat trip).
✖ Uig ☎(01470) 542205

Uig Bay Camping IV51 9XU ☎(01470) 542714 OS map 23/381637 ¼m W of Uig on A87 (Staffin)
near ferry terminal Open all year 60 pitches 2½ acres, level, hard standings and grass
🛒🚻🚮𝄞⊕∅🚐♿ boating, fishing, cycle hire £8.00-£9.00 (most cards)
lisa.madigan@btopenworld.com www.uig-camping-skye.co.uk

ULLAPOOL, Highland   **Map D3**
EC Tues SEE waterfront, Summer Isles (boat-trips), Loch Broom, Corrieshalloch Gorge and Falls of
Measach (12m S), Inverpolly nature reserve (info centre at Knockham) 10m N
🛈 Argyle ☎(01854) 612135
✖ Ceilidh Place, West Argyle St ☎(01854) 612103

Ardmair Point Caravan Site IV26 2TN ☎(01854) 612054 Fax (01854) 612757 OS map 19/108984
3½m N of Ullapool off A835 (Elphin) Open Easter-Sept 45 pitches Grass, level, hard standings
🛒✖𝄞🚻🚮𝄞⊕∅⤴🚐🏠♿ boating by sea £10.00 (Mastercard/Visa/Switch/Euros)
sales@ardmair.com www.ardmair.com

Broomfield Holiday Park, Shore St IV26 2SX ☎(01854) 612020 Prop: SM Ross OS map
19/123939 In Ullapool near Ullapool Point Open Easter-Sept–no adv booking 140 pitches
11 acres level grass 🚻🚮⊕⤴♿ £10.00-£13.00 (most cards) s.ross@broomfieldhp.com
www.broomfieldhp.com

Index to Sites

Index to Towns